London and the Restoration, 1659–1683

Articulate and restless London citizens were at the heart of political and religious confrontation in England from the Interregnum through the great crisis of church and state that marked the last years of Charles II's reign. The same Reformed Protestant citizens who took the lead in toppling the Rump in 1659–60 took the lead in demanding a new Protestant settlement after 1678. In the interval, their demands for liberty of conscience challenged the Anglican order, while their arguments about consensual government in the city challenged loyalist political assumptions. Dissenting and Anglican identities developed in specific locales within the city, rooting the Whig and Tory parties of 1679–83 in neighborhoods with different traditions and cultures. *London and the Restoration* integrates the history of the kingdom with that of its premier locality in the era of Dryden and Locke, analyzing the ideas and the movements that unsettled the Restoration regime.

GARY S. DE KREY is Professor of History at St Olaf College in Northfield, Minnesota. His previous publications include *A Fractured Society: The Politics of London in the First Age of Party, 1688–1715* (1985).

Cambridge Studies in Early Modern British History

Series editors

ANTHONY FLETCHER
Emeritus Professor of English Social History, University of London

JOHN GUY
Fellow, Clare College, Cambridge

JOHN MORRILL
Professor of British and Irish History, University of Cambridge, and
Vice-Master of Selwyn College

This is a series of monographs and studies covering many aspects of the history of the British Isles between the late fifteenth century and the early eighteenth century. It includes the work of established scholars and pioneering work by a new generation of scholars. It includes both reviews and revisions of major topics and books which open up new historical terrain or which reveal startling new perspectives on familiar subjects. All the volumes set detailed research into our broader perspectives and the books are intended for the use of students as well as of their teachers.

For a list of titles in the series, see end of book.

LONDON AND THE RESTORATION, 1659–1683

GARY S. DE KREY
St Olaf College

CAMBRIDGE
UNIVERSITY PRESS

CAMBRIDGE UNIVERSITY PRESS
Cambridge, New York, Melbourne, Madrid, Cape Town, Singapore, São Paulo

Cambridge University Press
The Edinburgh Building, Cambridge CB2 2RU, UK

www.cambridge.org
Information on this title: www.cambridge.org/9780521840712

First published 2005

Printed in the United Kingdom at the University Press, Cambridge

A catalog record for this book is available from the British Library.

Library of Congress Cataloging in Publication Data
De Krey, Gary Stuart.
London and the Restoration, 1659–1683 / Gary De Krey.
p.   cm. – (Cambridge studies in early modern British history)
Includes bibliographical references and index.
ISBN 0 521 84071 6
1. London (England) – History – 17th century.   2. Great Britain – History – Restoration,
1660–1688.   I. Title.   II. Series.
DA681.D344   2004
942.106–dc22   2004045707

ISBN-13   978-0-521-84071-2 hardback
ISBN-10   0-521-84071-6 hardback

For my parents

CONTENTS

FIGURES

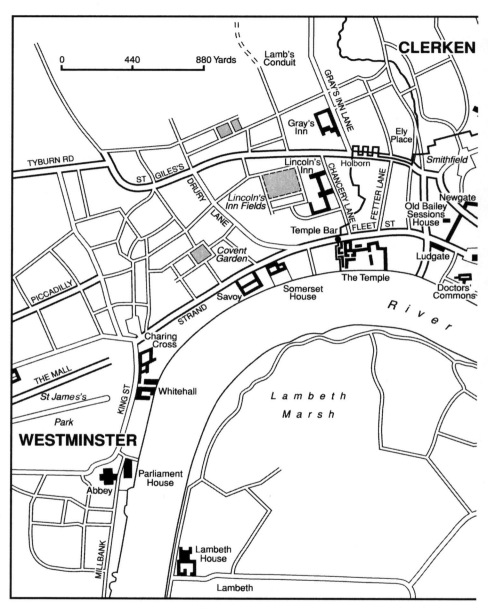

London in the late seventeenth century

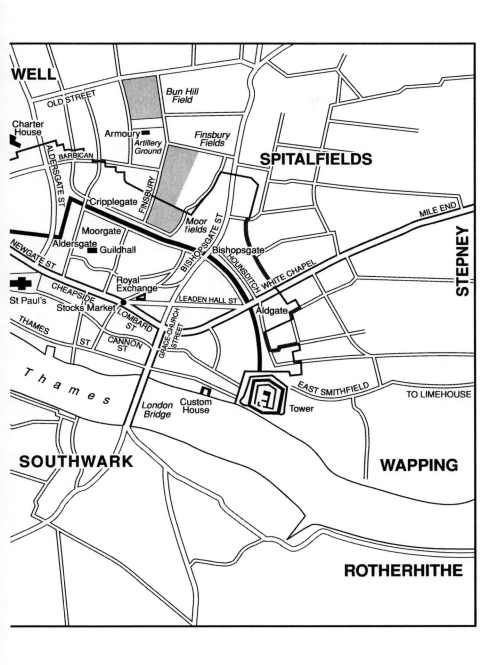

TABLES

PREFACE

When I started this study I intended to produce a short second book that I thought could be quickly researched and written. That was almost twenty years ago. The Restoration then seemed to be a fairly straightforward and relatively neglected field of English history. But since the early 1980s the period has attracted many creative and intellectually ambitious historians, while the old field of Tudor and Stuart English history has been transformed by a variety of revisionist approaches to Early Modern Britain.

London and the Restoration is my response to the new historical writing about the Restoration and to the transformation of the broader historical field. It could not have been written without engaging, both personally and professionally, with many other scholars at every stage of their professional work and with a few no longer living. I have disagreed about important questions with some of them, but I can think of no one with whom I have disagreed from whom I have not also learned a great deal. If I acknowledge only a few scholars, colleagues, and friends by name here, I hope that others will find my engagement with their work reflected in what follows. Henry Horwitz and Lois Schwoerer each took an interest in my work at an early stage; and they have, in their different ways, contributed to my understanding of the Restoration. They have provided countless recommendations and evaluations of my scholarship over the years, and I am deeply grateful to each of them. Tim Harris, Mark Knights, and Mark Goldie have shared some of their ongoing work with me over the years and have responded helpfully to my own. John Morrill was encouraging about this project as it began to take shape. Robert Bucholz and Newton Key have been good friends in the Midwest Conference on British Studies and supportive professional colleagues. I also want to thank Arthur Smith, who shared the results of his own research on the topic with me, and Tim Whipple, whose student work for me is reflected in some of the figures and interpretations in Chapter 6.

After I began this book, I changed jobs and locations, though not in directions that I could have predicted. I am happy to acknowledge the support I have received at St Olaf College from deans and colleagues involved in providing institutional grants, released time, and sabbaticals. The work could not have been completed without this assistance. I thank my long-time St Olaf friends Bob Nichols, Doug Schuurman, Jack Schwandt, and Pamela Schwandt for their active interest in my work and for their company and conversation. My departmental colleagues have responded generously to colloquium presentations over the years, while my colleague in the St Olaf Archives, Jeff Sauve, has indirectly contributed to the completion of the book by supporting other projects and work so professionally. The St Olaf librarians, especially those at the inter-library loan and circulation desks, have extended multiple courtesies to me. Sarah Entenmann was a wonderful help with the index.

I was fortunate to hold several fellowships and grants that permitted me to take the time and to undertake the research required for this study. It has been supported financially by the Guggenheim Foundation, the National Endowment for the Humanities, the American Philosophical Society, and the Folger and Newberry Libraries. The staffs of the Folger and Newberry were most helpful, as were the staffs of all the record offices and archives listed in the bibliography, especially those at the Corporation of London Records Office.

Finally, and most importantly, I want to acknowledge the love and care of those who have lived with this book as long as I have, my wife Catherine and my son William. Thankfully, other matters have been at the center of our relationships, and we have grown together as a family in spite of the book's long gestation. The work is dedicated to my parents, Lester and June, from whom I acquired the patience necessary to complete it and my interests in books and learning.

ABBREVIATIONS

Add. MS	Additional Manuscripts, British Library
AHR	*American Historical Review*
BDBR	Greaves, R. L. and R. Zaller. *Biographical Dictionary of British Radicals in the Seventeenth Century*, 3 vols. (Brighton, 1982–4).
BIHR	*Bulletin of the Institute of Historical Research*
BL	British Library
Bodl. Lib.	Bodleian Library
Bulstrode Newsletters	Newsletters of Richard Bulstrode, 1667–89, at the Harry Ransom Humanities Research Center, University of Texas, Austin
CJ	*Journals of the House of Commons*
CalCSP	*Calendar of Clarendon State Papers preserved in the Bodleian Library*, ed. F. J. Routledge *et al.*, 5 vols. (Oxford, 1872–1932).
MS Carte	Carte Manuscripts, Bodleian Library
MS Clarendon	Clarendon Papers, 1659–63, Bodleian Library
Clarke Papers	*The Clarke Papers. Selections from the Papers of William Clarke*, 4 vols. (1891–1901).
CLRO	Corporation of London Records Office
CLSP	*State Papers collected by Edward, Earl of Clarendon*, 3 vols. (Oxford, 1767–86).
CSPD	*Calendar of State Papers, Domestic*
CSPVen	*Calendar of State Papers, Venetian*
CTB	*Calendar of Treasury Books*
DNB	*Dictionary of National Biography*
DWL	Dr Williams's Library
EcHR	*Economic History Review*
EHR	*English Historical Review*
Evelyn, *Diary*	*The Diary of John Evelyn*, ed. E. S. De Beer, 6 vols. (Oxford, 1955).

GHL	Guildhall Library
GLRO	Greater London Record Office
Grey, *Debates*	Grey, Anchitell. *Debates of the House of Commons from the year 1667 to the year 1694*, 10 vols. (1763).
Hatton Correspondence	*The Correspondence of the Hatton Family*, ed. E. M. Thompson (1878).
HJ	*Historical Journal*
HMC	Historical Manuscripts Commission
HT	*History Today*
JBS	*Journal of British Studies*
JMH	*Journal of Modern History*
Journal	Journal of the Court of Common Council
JEcH	*Journal of Ecclesiastical History*
LC	Library of Congress
Luttrell	Narcissus Luttrell, *A Brief Historical Relation of State Affairs*, 6 vols. (Oxford, 1857).
Morrice	Roger Morrice, Ent'ring Book, Doctor Williams's Library
Newdigate	Newdigate Newsletters, Folger Shakespeare Library
OPH	*Parliamentary or Constitutional History of England*, 24 vols. (1760–3). [Old Parliamentary History]
Oxford DNB	*Oxford Dictionary of National Biography*
Pepys, *Diary*	*The Diary of Samuel Pepys*, ed. R. Latham and W. Matthews, 11 vols. (Berkeley and Los Angeles, 1970–83).
POAS	*Poems on Affairs of State; Augustan Satirical Verse, 1660–1714*, ed. G. deF. Lord [*et al.*], 7 vols. (New Haven, 1963–75).
PRO	Public Record Office
PP	*Past and Present*
Repertory	Repertory of the Court of Aldermen
Savile Correspondence	*Letters to and from Henry Savile, Esq.* (1959).
Somers Tracts	*A collection of scarce and valuable tracts . . . of the Late Lord Somers*, ed. Sir W. Scott, 13 vols. (1809–15).
SP	State Papers, Public Record Office
ST	*A Complete Collection of State Trials*, ed. T. B. Howell and T. J. Howell, 34 vols. (1811–28).
State Tracts	*State Tracts in two Parts: the first being a Collection of several Treatises relating to the Government*, 2 vols. (1689, 1692).
TCHS	*Transactions of the Congregational Historical Society*

I

Crisis, 1659–1660

Introduction to Parts I and II: London and the nation

When Charles II processed through the city of London on 29 May 1660, upon his return to England, the occasion marked more than a personal triumph for a king who had suffered a decade of political frustration after the execution of his father and the abolition of monarchy. Charles's return to the kingdom after years of exile and hardship was also a political and emotional catharsis for a city that had contributed more than any other locality to the collapse of Stuart monarchy in the 1640s. Charles's route was crowded and lined by the civic militia and by thousands of citizens drawn up in their guilds. The streets were hung with tapestries, pennants, banners, and spring flowers; and wine was said to be flowing in every conduit and fountain. The king's appearance was greeted by "such shouting as the oldest man alive never heard"; and this celebratory din was increased by the ringing of church bells and by the many trumpets and drums in the royal procession.[1] Charles required four hours to pass through the city and Westminster to Whitehall, and popular rejoicing continued for another three days and nights.[2]

The new king was well aware of the ironies of this frenzied London reception. Surely this could not have been the same city in which, less than a generation earlier, puritan crowds had competed with the parliamentary leadership in driving "reformation and liberty" at the expense of episcopacy and monarchy. The civic magistrates, liverymen, militia bands, and apprentices who greeted Charles II included many who had supported the Protectorate of Oliver Cromwell in 1653–8 and others who had backed the Commonwealth of 1649–53. Yet here they were, and mingled with them

---

[1] *The Diurnal of Thomas Rugg 1659–61*, ed. W. L. Sachse (1961), 89–90.
[2] Additional accounts of the king's procession through London include: *CSPVen 1659–61*, p. 155; *The Diary of Bulstrode Whitelocke*, ed. R. Spalding (Oxford, 1990), pp. 588–9; *The Diary of John Evelyn*, ed. E. S. De Beer, 6 vols. (Oxford, 1955), III, 246; HMC *Fifth Report*, pp. 167, 184. Also see, Sir Richard Baker, *A Chronicle of the Kings of England* (1665), p. 777; Thomas Gumble, *The Life of General Monck* (1671), 388–92, reprinted in OPH, XXII, 321–3.

were many others who had opposed the political course of Charles I in the 1630s but had found parliament's course, by 1642, even more unacceptable.

Such distinctions were less in evidence in London on 29 May 1660 than the almost universal hope for a healing of the nation's divisions. Charles's arrival in the capital, eagerly awaited for several weeks, marked the end of one of the most astonishing years London and its citizens had ever experienced. In September 1658, Richard Cromwell had quietly succeeded as Lord Protector upon the death of his father. The Venetian ambassador, who expected no end of trouble upon Oliver's death, had been astonished by the ease with which the city and the country accepted Richard.[3] But in April 1659, the leadership of the New Model Army had overthrown Richard and his parliament, which had been elected, as before 1640, by the counties and enfranchised boroughs. The generals and officers were supported in this action by republican intellectuals and politicians, by the gathered churches, and by many of the Baptist and Independent clergy, including, most notably, Dr John Owen. The 1659 coup put an end to the transformation, initiated by Oliver, of the English republic into a polity more similar to the country's "ancient constitution." Suddenly, revolution and "the good old cause" replaced Cromwellian efforts at "restoration" and settlement. Within days, the army recalled the Rump, the remnant of the Long Parliament that had sat in 1649–53, to govern from Westminster. The republic was back in business.

Under the most favorable circumstances, the army's action would have proven divisive; but the circumstances were not at all favorable. The country had been at war with Spain since 1655, and the war had accomplished little other than the disruption of the city's trade and the expansion of the government's debt. Money was scarce; food prices were high; prices for cloth and other export goods had fallen; and shipping losses to privateers were extensive. The political uncertainty of 1659 thus coincided with an economic depression that would have made the collection of taxes difficult for any regime. Neither the unrepresentative nature of the parliament at Westminster after April 1659 nor its installation through naked military force counted in its favor.[4]

The result was another grand crisis of church and state in which the nation confronted again some of the issues that had provoked civil war in 1642 and revolution in 1649. The status of parliament was again in doubt, as was the security of the Protestant church establishment. The city quarreled with the new government. Many common councilmen and aldermen perceived it

---

[3] *CSPVen 1657–9*, p. 248.

[4] W. R. Scott, *The Constitution and Finance of English, Scottish and Irish Joint-Stock Companies to 1720* (Cambridge, 1912), pp. 260–2; M. Ashley, *Financial and Commercial Policy under the Cromwellian Protectorate* (1962), pp. 44–5, 143–6, 174–8.

as a nothing more than an illegitimate clique of aging politicians who had usurped the place of the genuine national parliament elected under Richard. For its part, the Rump showed little regard either for the city's conventional rights and liberties or for the civic charter that guaranteed them. But as inadequate as it was, the Rump was at least the semblance of a parliament. After a second coup in October 1659, in which the army dumped the Rump, the city and the nation experienced a thinly disguised form of military rule. Opposition to this development seemed inexorably to be leading once again to civil war.

Outside London, in late autumn 1659, a movement developed on behalf of freely electing a new parliament. County gentry and borough leaders who aided this movement looked to the city to take the lead in stopping the army. Supporters of the displaced Rump, on the other hand, claimed that it alone could resettle the nation. Within London, the army confronted anxious magistrates and common councilmen as well as restless apprentices. In 1659, as in the early 1640s, the apprentices ardently supported civic liberties and parliamentary government. In the meantime, the enigmatic commander of the Scottish forces, General George Monck, began his slow progress to the south. By the end of the year, the Rump had re-established itself against the army; but the Corporation of London had proceeded to open rebellion, refusing to pay taxes, encouraging other boroughs to follow its lead, and preparing to defend itself, by arms if necessary, against all threats to its autonomy.

The crisis of 1659–60 was, then, a crisis about parliamentary government. It was also a crisis about Protestantism. Having freed the national church of diocesan episcopacy, Reformed Protestants had eventually embraced Cromwell's regime and his church order, with some misgivings on the part of Presbyterians, as safeguarding public Protestant ministry from the proliferating sects.[5] But in 1659 the army was again acting with those who demanded complete liberty of conscience outside the church and who wished to see the parochial establishment stripped of such resources as tithes. The sects – especially the Quakers – seemed again to be overrunning the land. Both the army's enemies in the city and General Monck in Scotland were as disturbed by this revival of militant sectarianism as they were by the army's making and unmaking of parliaments. On occasion, panic about the "sectaries" became distinctly reminiscent of the fears of popish massacres that had accompanied the breakdown of 1640–42, and one historian has likened

[5] In this study, "Reformed Protestantism" refers to Presbyterians, Independents, and other Protestants whose theology and ecclesiology were informed by the European Reformed or Calvinist tradition. "Anglican" refers to those English Protestants who strongly preferred diocesan episcopal governance for the national church and who were generally less influenced by the continental Reformed heritage.

the fear of the sects in 1659 to the *Grande Peur* of 1789.[6] Moreover, in the minds of some Reformed Protestants, the threats from popery and sectarianism were related.[7] Ironically, just as the desire for parliamentary government drove some of Charles I's old enemies toward his son, so the fear of sectarianism put many Reformed Protestants on common ground with those who had never truly abandoned the episcopal office and the old Anglican order.

THE CORPORATION OF LONDON IN THE CIVIL WAR AND INTERREGNUM

In London, the crisis of 1659–60 was deeply rooted in the city's civil and religious experiences since 1640. Adjacent to the seat of national government at Westminster, London and its citizens occupied a unique position in England's affairs. With a population that exceeded 375,000, London was the nation's metropolis, and it dwarfed all English provincial towns in size. Perhaps 135,000 of its residents lived within the city proper, the area that made up the Corporation of London, the focus of this study.[8]

But the centrality of London to English affairs was more than a matter of its large population. Its active merchants, who probably numbered about 800–1,000 by mid-century, were at the forefront of English overseas trade and investment. Their commerce made the city a national entrepôt, and the success of their trade was a critical matter in increasing customs revenues as well. The East India Company, the great national joint stock, was a London stock: its governing committee was largely made up of London men. Although the English universities were located elsewhere, London was nevertheless an intellectual capital, the center of national publication and print distribution and a Mecca for clergy in pursuit of well-endowed pulpits. The seasonal influx of the nobility and the gentry, who were attracted by the Court and by parliamentary and legal sessions, also made London the center of national fashion, of the theatre, and of the arts. Finally, and most importantly, London had a greater capacity for producing and exporting disorder than any other locality: its assertive and highly literate citizens and apprentices were well informed about issues of church and state and eager to make their voices heard.[9]

The political institutions of the Corporation of London were those of a participatory guild society in which magistrates enjoyed significant prerogatives as representatives of the crown. Guildhall and Whitehall traditionally

[6] B. Reay, *Quakers and English Revolution* (1985), p. 100.
[7] Richard Baxter, *A Holy Commonwealth*, ed. W. Lamont (Cambridge, 1994), pp. xvii–xix.
[8] The remainder made up the populations of the incorporated boroughs of Westminster and Southwark and of the urban parishes of the counties of Middlesex and Surrey.
[9] For London's centrality, see esp., *The Making of the Metropolis: London 1500–1700*, ed. A. L. Beier and R. Finlay (1986) and *London and the Civil War*, ed. S. Porter (1996).

operated as paired forces for order in the heavily intertwined microcosm and macrocosm that they governed. Yet, after 1640, magisterial authority declined as aroused citizens and their elected representatives assumed greater voice in civic affairs. In the early 1640s, parliamentary puritans contested for power in the city with a governing Anglican loyalist elite and gained the initiative in civic affairs by 1642–3.[10] The political and religious skirmishes that began in London in the early 1640s would continue into the early Hanoverian era as civic divisions about the ideal religious and political settlement of the nation persisted. The institutions of the Corporation, which will be introduced here, especially lent themselves to disagreement and unsettlement.

The city's 234 common councilmen were chosen in its twenty-six wards (Figure 6.2) at the annual wardmotes on 21 December. These assemblies were open to the resident householders of each ward whose freedom of the Corporation and one of its guilds entitled them to practice their regulated trades. The urban population included some 20,000 such resident freemen. The court of common council functioned as the city's legislature and constituted the largest elected assembly in England, other than the House of Commons. Summoned ordinarily by the lord mayor for only five or six annual meetings of a few hours' duration, the common councilmen could become both factious and independent; and they certainly did so after 1640. The 1640s witnessed much institutional tension between the common councilmen and the twenty-six magistrates who met one or twice a week as the court of aldermen.[11]

The aldermen attended to a host of administrative duties and decisions and were also responsible to the regime for the city's good order. Several were justices of the peace; and each of them presided over the affairs of their wards, including the annual wardmotes. Six of them were generally commanders of the London trained bands, and most of the others were included in the London lieutenancy commission. Members of common council *ex officio*, they voted separately, and a few of them sat on all common council committees. Their consent was required for the adoption of civic by-laws. The aldermen were chosen for life in a complicated electoral formula.[12] Their long-term tenure and the high wealth requirement for office (£10,000) strongly inclined them toward order and authority.

[10] V. Pearl, *London and the Outbreak of the Puritan Revolution* (Oxford, 1961).
[11] *Ibid.*, 53–8; I. W. Archer, *The Pursuit of Stability: Social Relations in Elizabethan London* (Cambridge, 1991), pp. 30–2; K. Lindley, *Popular Politics and Religion in Civil War London* (Aldershot, 1997), pp. 180–97.
[12] In the event of an aldermanic vacancy, ward householders submitted four names (two commoners and two senior aldermen) to the full court of aldermen. The court then permitted one of its senior members to transfer to the ward, elevated one of the commoners to their ranks, or rejected the entire submission and requested a new one.

The aldermen generally succeeded to the office of lord mayor according to their seniority, functioned as the city's chief magistrate for a year, and thereafter enriched the aldermanic bench with their mayoral experience. The office of lord mayor was both an honor and a burden, since the government expected the lord mayor to act on its behalf. The lord mayor regularly met with the principal officers of the realm, including (before 1640) both the Privy Council and the monarch himself, in order to ensure the security of the urban area. Indeed, the lord mayor ranked next to privy councilors in the hierarchy of the state. He presided at the court of aldermen and the court of common council. As the principal officer of justice in the Corporation, he also kept his own judicial court and presided over others.[13]

Contemporary explanations of London's governing structures, both before 1648–9 and after 1660, often referred to the relationship of the lord mayor, aldermen, and common councilmen as analogous to that of the king, lords, and commons. But the analogy was misleading, for it ignored an important electoral assembly, important officers of the Corporation, and the charter that incorporated the city and prescribed these institutional relationships and procedures. The overlooked assembly was the court of common hall, which was open to those freemen who had obtained the livery of their guild companies through their business success or long-term service. These 5,000–6,000 liverymen not only dominated the affairs of their companies but also possessed the franchise for the election of London's four members of the House of Commons. They also assembled twice yearly for the elections of the two Sheriffs of London and Middlesex on 24 June and the lord mayor on 29 September.

These common hall elections combined electoral right and magisterial prerogative in a confusing manner, however. The lord mayor claimed a right to "elect" one of the two sheriffs prior to 24 June, leaving the liverymen free to choose only one sheriff and to confirm the mayor's selection of the other. Moreover, junior aldermen expected the liverymen to elect them to the shrievalty soon after joining the court of aldermen, and they expected to be chosen lord mayor by the common hall in the order of their seniority. Indeed, the liverymen were expected to forward the names of two junior aldermen to the court of aldermen on 29 September, leaving the ultimate choice of a new lord mayor to the aldermen themselves.[14]

---

[13] Pearl, *London*, pp. 62–4.

[14] The number of liverymen grew throughout the seventeenth century. Pearl and Lindley accept a contemporary estimate of 4,000 liverymen in 1641. By the 1680s, the liverymen numbered about 6,500; and by 1700, their numbers exceeded 8,000. The liverymen also elected the chamberlain, the Corporation's chief financial officer on 24 June. But the incumbent chamberlain could expect to be continued in office from year to year, as long as his conduct was acceptable. Pearl, *London*, pp. 50–3, 65–6; Lindley, *Popular Politics*, p. 169; G. S. De Krey, *A Fractured Society: The Politics of London in the First Age of Party, 1688–1715* (Oxford, 1985), p. 41n.

The inherent conflict between electoral choice and magisterial expectations in these elections was not always realized. Nevertheless, both the large numbers of people present in common hall and the frequent importation of external issues into civic elections could produce rowdiness and defiance of the lord mayor and aldermen, who ordinarily guided the actions of the liverymen. When such disorder occurred, it was also a matter of concern to the regime, which had its own interest in the election of the city's principal officers. Just as much as the sheriffs the crown appointed for counties throughout the realm, for instance, the Sheriffs of London and Middlesex were essential intermediaries between central and local government. And the government generally perceived any departure from the customary succession to the mayoralty as a violation of the hierarchical principles that safeguarded political and social order. After 1640, disagreements about the choice of civic magistrates did frequently occur in common hall. Moreover, as parliament and Charles I confronted each other, first at Westminster, and then in the field, common hall assumed more deliberative functions like considering petitions and hearing appeals from both Charles and the MPs.[15]

Finally, nothing was more important to the citizens of London than the charter in which their "rights and privileges" were anchored. Few of them had read the charter or would have known where to locate it. It had a history, but few even of the London magistrates could have traced that history with any precision. There had, in fact, been many charters of London over the centuries, as the crown, parliament, and civic spokesmen had negotiated the jurisdiction of the city government and its relationship to the regime, most recently in 1638–40. But "the charter" had achieved mythic significance as the repository of the electoral and commercial rights of the citizens. Frequent rhetorical references to it summoned up collective memories of the long recognition, by kings and parliaments alike, of the city's self-governing corporate status.[16]

London citizens were zealous in defense of their local self-government through all the institutions mentioned here. Moreover, the issues of the 1640s further stimulated the active participation of the London freemen in both local and national affairs. Cautious London magistrates who identified with the crown in the early 1640s, as well as those who were hostile to the New Model Army in the late 1640s, ran afoul of widespread fears that the exercise of popular rights was in jeopardy.[17] When the army reconstituted the state in 1648–9, purging parliament and eliminating monarchy and the House of Lords, the Corporation of London experienced its own internal

---

[15] Pearl, *London*, pp. 120–5; Lindley, *Popular Politics*, pp. 169–80.
[16] Pearl, *London*, pp. 22–3, 27–8, 49, 80–8; Archer, *Pursuit*, pp. 22, 26, 38.
[17] I. Gentles, "The Struggle for London in the Second Civil War," *HJ* 26 (1983), 277–305; I. Gentles, *The New Model Army in England, Ireland and Scotland, 1645–1653* (Oxford, 1992), pp. 177–80, 190–7.

anti-magisterial revolution, one that was intended to recover and to secure the liberties of London freemen.

Both the national and urban revolutions of 1649 are best considered in light of the simultaneous fragmentation of parliamentary puritanism. Liberty for conscience was the principal issue that splintered the movement for reformation of the national church in the 1640s and that would sustain English Protestant division for two generations thereafter. Liberty for conscience was a major contributor to the separation of "Independents" from "Presbyterians" in the Westminster Assembly of Divines in 1644–5; and it was an issue that handicapped the new parliamentary church establishment from the beginning. Presbyterian supporters of the Solemn League and Covenant generally saw reformation as a collective obligation to God that required the maintenance of a national church, with uniformity in parish practices, modeled upon the best Reformed Protestant churches abroad. But London Independent clerics like John Owen, Joseph Caryl, and Philip Nye disagreed. They maintained instead that reformation required the acceptance of diversity within a loose national church, as individuals and local congregations exercised a liberty of conscience – bounded by obedience to God and to the magistrate – in determining their Christian practice.

The Independent understanding of the rights of conscience was not as expansive as that of separatists like Roger Williams and John Milton or of the Leveller movement. Independents left the Christian magistrate with important powers in protecting and promoting orthodox teaching. Nevertheless, the Independents had opened the door to wider claims for conscience by articulating arguments that separatists would employ to defend complete freedom from a national church order.[18] By the late 1640s, the cause of reformation, which had once been the rallying cry of parliamentary puritanism, had been splintered by conflicting Protestant agendas. Presbyterians insisted that the church and the state retained a coercive responsibility to persuade believers about which doctrines and practices were acceptable to God, while Independents and growing numbers of separatists insisted that the gospel alone should guide the individual Christian conscience.

---

[18] For Independent language about conscience and coercion, see *The Ancient Bounds, or Liberty of Conscience, tenderly Stated, modestly Asserted, and mildly Vindicated* (1645); Joseph Caryl, *Englands Plus Ultra, both of hoped Mercies, and of Required Duties* (1646); [William Bridge, Jeremiah Burroughes, Thomas Goodwin, Philip Nye, and Sidrach Simpson], *An Apologeticall Narration* (1644); John Owen, *A Sermon Preached to the Honourable House of Commons . . . with a Discourse about Toleration* (1649). For the separatist position, see Roger Williams, *The Bloody Tenent of Persecution* (1644); John Milton, *Treatise of Civil Power in Ecclesiastical Causes* (1659); M. Tolmie, *The Triumph of the Saints: The Separate Churches of London 1616–1649* (Cambridge, 1977). This brief treatment differs strongly from that presented by A. Zakai, "Religious Toleration and its Enemies: The Independent Divines and the Issue of Toleration during the English Civil War," *Albion* 21 (1989), 1–33.

The revolution carried out by the New Model Army in 1648–9 proved to be a revolution in which the advocates of conscience freed themselves not only from the old order in the state but also from the new order in the church. Most MPs who had supported a uniform Protestant church order were purged from parliament by the army. The revolution encouraged the growth of old and new sects alike by releasing Independents and separatists from the constraints that maintained conformity; and it left the clerical advocates of the newly reformed church establishment deeply distressed about the country's religious future.

In the city, the army's friends initiated a popular restructuring of the institutions of government. New qualifications for office-holding led to an unprecedented turnover on common council for 1648–9. Several Presbyterian aldermen bound by the Solemn League and Covenant to the preservation of monarchy were discharged from civic office, just as Presbyterian MPs had been removed from parliament. An obliging parliamentary Rump also provided for the emancipation of common council, which met over thirty times in 1649, free from mayoral and magisterial restraint. A statute of 28 February 1649 required a meeting of common council upon the request of any ten members, provided for the election of a common council chairman in the case the lord mayor declined to preside, eliminated the aldermanic veto over by-laws, and ensured that common council could be dissolved only by its own consent.[19] Magisterial authority in the city had been compromised in ways that would be remembered long after 1660.

This civic revolution had commercial and social implications as well. A body of prominent Presbyterian merchants, who had successfully challenged the city's Anglican elite earlier in the 1640s, and who were firmly anchored in such trading concerns as the East India Company and the Levant Company, was pushed aside. A body of colonial and interloping merchants assumed civic leadership: they were "new men" who had chaffed against the monopolies of such companies and who now hoped for freer trade. Largely Independent or separatist, they were the Rump's natural civic allies, the supporters of its 1651 Navigation Act and of the commercial war it began against the Dutch in 1652. Their republicanism was as piecemeal as that of the Rump, which fashioned a commonwealth out of bits and pieces of the old order. But just as the Rump fell short in the eyes of some of the sects and of the Levellers, so the new civic regime fell short in the eyes of

---

[19] Journal 40, fols. 312–313; *Acts and Ordinances of the Interregnum*, ed. C. H. Firth and R. S. Rait (1911), III, cxi–cxii; M. James, *Social Problems and Policy during the Puritan Revolution 1649–1660* (1930, 1966), pp. 223–40; J. E. Farnell, "The Politics of the City of London (1649–1657)," Unpublished Ph.D. thesis, University of Chicago, 1963, chs. 4–5; R. Brenner, *Merchants and Revolution: Commercial Change, Political Conflict, and London's Overseas Traders, 1550–1653* (Princeton, 1993), pp. 543–8.

those who believed it needed to be refounded on the basis of popular consent. Leveller spokesmen like John Lilburne and John Wildman argued that the city's chief magistrates ought to be elected in a more popular manner and questioned whether the Corporation's governing procedures were yet sufficiently consensual.[20] Their arguments would be revived in the reign of Charles II.

Yet the real problem for the civic regime that cooperated with the Rump was that its enthusiastic supporters remained but a godly faction of the civic population, just as the Commonwealth itself was the regime of a minority of the political nation. London may have been the principal seat of the sects, but it was also the heart of puritan England: by 1649 it rivaled Amsterdam as a capital of European Reformed Protestantism, despite the fragmentation of parliamentary puritanism. The city's more than 100 parochial pulpits were largely occupied by articulate supporters of a national Reformed Protestant ministry, and even the Independents among them had never perceived gathered churches and parochial churches as mutually exclusive. When the Rump's godly successor, the Nominated Parliament, considered proposals in 1653 further to encourage religious liberty, it persuaded many London supporters of reformed parochial ministry that sectarianism was now as great a threat to reformation as the pre-1642 "popish" bishops had ever been. Having already divided Reformed Protestants, conscience now threatened to undermine parochial ministry, or so the advocates of Protestant parish order feared.

This religious tension, experienced throughout the nation, was as important as the unrepresentative nature of the regime in prompting Oliver Cromwell's 1653 redirection of the republican experiment in government. He enjoyed considerable success in achieving a religious settlement that both secured parochial ministry in a broadly defined national church and provided a *de facto* toleration for separating Protestants. The local clerical associations that he sponsored further assisted Presbyterians and Independents in re-experiencing their common Protestantism with some clergy who really preferred bishops and with others who had gathered separate churches.[21]

---

[20] John Lilburne, *Londons Liberty in Chains Discovered* (1646); John Lilburne, *The Charters of London: or the second Part of Londons Liberty* (1646); *London's Liberties; or a Learned Argument of Law & Reason* (1651); Brenner, *Merchants*, esp. chs. 9–12; J. E. Farnell, "The Usurpation of Honest London Householders: Barebone's Parliament," *EHR* 82 (1967), 24–46; J. E. Farnell, "The Navigation Act of 1651, the First Dutch War, and the London Merchant Community," *EcHR*, 2nd Ser. 16 (1963–4), 439–54; B. Manning, *1649: The Crisis of the English Revolution* (1992), pp. 41–3.

[21] B. Worden, "Toleration and the Cromwellian Protectorate," in W. J. Sheils, ed., *Persecution and Toleration: Studies in Church History*, 21 (Oxford, 1984), 199–233; J. C. Davis, "Cromwell's Religion," in J. Morrill, ed., *Oliver Cromwell and the English Revolution* (1990), pp. 181–208; A. Woolrych, "Introduction," *Complete Prose Works of John Milton*, 8 vols. (New Haven, 1953–82), VII, 30–3; Baxter, *Holy Commonwealth*, pp. xx–xxi.

As Protestant accommodation proceeded in Oliver's church, cooperation among men of different perspectives also became more characteristic of county and borough government. In the city of London, leadership was tacitly reopened to men of once proscribed sentiments. Discharged Presbyterian alderman Major-General Richard Browne, for instance, who had once commanded the city's trained bands against Charles I, was elected City MP for Cromwell's 1656 parliament, after five years of imprisonment. Presbyterian mercer Theophilus Biddulph sat on common council during the Protectorate, became a director of the East India Company, and joined Browne in the parliament elected in 1656. Most spectacularly, merchant John Robinson, whose discreet Anglicanism obscured his status as a nephew of Archbishop William Laud, became master of the Clothworkers' Company, director of the Levant Company, an alderman, and Sheriff of London and Middlesex.[22] In Cromwell's London, the "new men" who had seized power in 1649 were rejoined by many of those whom they had dislodged. Men who advocated liberty of conscience found themselves sharing power, somewhat uncomfortably, with the advocates of parochial conformity.

Whether Oliver's settlement of the nation, the church, the localities, and the city might have been perfected, had he lived longer, is a fascinating question that cannot be answered. The collapse of the Protectorate was far from inevitable, even in 1658. Richard Cromwell succeeded to his father's place without his father's skills, experience, and charisma. But many Reformed Protestants who had supported Oliver's remodeling of the regime and his protection of the church greeted him with enthusiasm. Richard's parliament was filled with such men, including all four London MPs.

But Richard's army was filled with the godly, and the godly feared both that political liberty was imperiled by a revival of the old regime in Protectoral guise and that conscience was imperiled by conformity to the parish order. When the army leaders and the sects deposed Richard in April 1659, they were also responding to his parliament's affirmation of the church agenda of the Westminster Assembly and to its encouragement of local magistrates in curbing outspoken sectarians.[23] The result of the army's coup was not a successful re-establishment of the Commonwealth, however, but rather a reopening of the all the wounds that Oliver had sought to heal.

In London, the issues of the crisis were conscience and consent, or rather conscience against consent. Liberty for conscience was the issue that provided the restored Rump and the New Model Army with their core of sectarian supporters in the city and that also persuaded most other Protestants that

---

[22] B. D. Henning, *The House of Commons 1660–1690*, 3 vols. (1983), I, 650–1, 732, and III, 340–2; J. R. Woodhead, *The Rulers of London 1660–85* (1965), pp. 30–1, 39–40, 139–40.
[23] R. Hutton, *The Restoration: A Political and Religious History of England and Wales, 1658–1667* (Oxford, 1985), pp. 32–5; Woolrych, *Milton*, VII, 63.

the revived republic was a threat to parochial ministry.[24] But the unrepresentative nature of the regime – its foundation upon military force rather than upon any form of consent – produced the hostility of a majority of London citizens to it. Since the alteration of civic government in 1649 had opened the political processes of the Corporation to even greater participation, London became a volatile and critical political battleground in the crisis of 1659–60, just as it had been in the early 1640s.

CHARLES II, THE CITY OF LONDON, AND THE RESTORATION

The reaction in London and elsewhere against the army's coup of 1659 was, then, a reaction against the prospect of unsettlement by those who had welcomed Oliver's settling work. None of the regimes that followed each other in rapid succession in 1659–60 – the army and the Rump, the army without the Rump, and the Rump without the army – proved capable of devising formulae for the resettlement of the nation. Yet even as the nation fell into unsettlement, the restoration of Charles Stuart was far from certain.

In London, the opposition to the army and the Rump was not initially driven by the cavalier Anglican royalists who triumphed after 1660. Instead, the movement for settlement was dominated by Reformed Protestants, and especially by the Presbyterians, who feared losing parliamentary government and the national church order to republicans and sectarians again, as they had in 1649. London's contribution to the crisis of 1659–60 cannot be understood without recognizing the primacy of the city's Reformed Protestant political and clerical leaders. Indeed, neither can the restoration of monarchy be understood apart from the Reformed Protestant dominance of London, for, as Lord Macaulay noted long ago, "without the help of the City," Charles II "could scarcely have been restored."[25]

As the movement for a parliamentary resettlement of the nation gathered support throughout the realm, it did also bring about much cooperation between Reformed Protestants and Anglican royalists. In many counties, the Anglican royalist element dominated; and Charles's government in exile did all it could to further the movement. But the political circumstances of 1659–60 were far more fluid than much of the historiography of the Restoration assumes, as citizens and politicians groped with many possible scenarios into

---

[24] Fears that the restored Rump would elevate liberty for conscience above settled ministry were greatly exaggerated. *CJ*, VII, 662, 683, 694, 700, 732; CLRO Journal 45, fols. 204–205; *The Humble Petition of the Lord Maior, Aldermen, and Common-Council of the City of London* (1659), pp. 2–3; Reay, *Quakers*, p. 85; Woolrych, *Milton*, VII, 73–6; Hutton, *Restoration*, pp. 47–9.

[25] Lord Macaulay [T. B. Macaulay], *The History of England from the Accession of James the Second*, 6 vols., ed. C. H. Firth (1913–15), I, 344.

early 1660. Only after the February 1660 confrontation between General Monck and the city, on the one hand, and the twice-restored Rump, on the other, did the restoration of monarchy generally seem to provide the best guarantee of settlement to the reassembled Long Parliament and the nation. Referring to those who chose monarchy, at this point, as royalists artificially conflates unswerving Anglican loyalists with Presbyterians who embraced the king with the same mixed feelings they had previously directed toward Oliver.

The case for a Stuart restoration was also aided by the fear of sectarianism that panicked both Reformed and Anglican Protestants in 1659–60. The assurances Charles made about the church were as instrumental as his assurances about parliament in recovering his throne. He offered both to support a strong church establishment and to extend liberty of conscience to those who could not conform to it. Reformed Protestants perceived Charles as pledging a far different church order than the unreformed episcopal establishment that parliament had rejected in 1640–42. To them, Charles seemed to offer a broad, non-compulsory Protestant establishment in which episcopal and Reformed clergy could accommodate their differences, a formula not unlike the Cromwellian pattern.[26]

The restoration of Charles II nevertheless proved, within short order, to be deeply disappointing for Reformed Protestants, as well as for separatists. Presbyterians were outmaneuvred in parliament by county gentry who had never been enthusiastic about synodical church polity as a replacement for or supplement to episcopacy. Reformed Protestants were outmaneuvred in the church by old and newly appointed bishops determined to secure their institutional places by refashioning the church's identity around their own order. After some hesitation, Charles threw in his lot with this revanchist episcopal movement. Clergy who dissented from the new Anglican order erected in 1660–62 were driven from the church and laity unhappy with episcopacy were eventually proscribed from office-holding in the state and its localities. Exclusion replaced comprehension in the church; coercion replaced toleration in the state. But could exclusion and coercion – policies once fashioned by republicans but now adopted by cavaliers – settle either church or state?

Historians have generally treated the coercive Anglican regime as being solidly established after 1660, as "puritanism" declined. But, as we have come to learn, "Anglicanism" was largely a post-1660 creation rather than some inevitable expression of recovering national identity.[27] In London and

---

[26] "Declaration of Breda, 1660" and "Worcester House Declaration, 1660," in *English Historical Documents*, 12 vols. (Oxford, 1955–77), VIII, *1660–1714* (1953), ed. A. Browning, pp. 57–8, 365–70.

[27] J. Spurr, *The Restoration Church of England, 1646–1689* (New Haven, 1991).

in many other boroughs, as well as in some counties, Reformed Protestantism was deeply rooted in local religious culture. As the cavalier parliamentary majority turned to coercion, Presbyterians in London and the country joined Independents and sectarians, their former adversaries, in developing rationales for religious dissent based upon liberty for conscience. Indeed, Restoration Presbyterians retraced Cromwell's footsteps, envisioning a broad church settlement in which comprehension and conscience were reconciled. Their demands for church settlement on these grounds, the grounds that Charles himself had seemed to offer in 1660, intruded upon the state in 1669–72 and contributed to another grand crisis of state in 1679–82.

In fact, the narrow church settlement of 1660–62 was a source of unsettlement rather than settlement. Intended to produce stability, it instead perpetuated instability.[28] The religious divisions of the 1640s and 1650s were not resolved in 1660–62 but rather sharpened through persecution. Cavalier anxieties after 1662 about the church settlement were not exaggerated, for Reformed Protestants and sectarians were determined to replace uniformity and coercion with comprehension and toleration.

No locality gave the upholders of the restored episcopal order more difficulty than the Corporation of London. Indeed, just as the city played critical roles in the collapse of Stuart monarchy in the 1640s and in the restoration of Stuart monarchy in 1660, so it would, throughout Charles's reign, provide an arena for opposition as important as parliament. When the nation confronted a crisis again, in 1679–82, that crisis began as much in London as at Westminster. Employing language about conscience to demand a new church settlement, London's Protestant dissenters had also, by that time, revived pre-1660 civic language about consent. They used that language to recover their former dominance in the Corporation from the Anglican urban elite that had attempted to proscribe them from civic affairs. Charles could not resettle the regime after 1679 without dealing with London as well as with parliament: the crisis ended not with his out-flanking of the parliamentary opposition in 1681 but rather with his regaining of control over the city of London in 1682–3.

London's importance during the "exclusion" parliaments of 1679–81 has been the subject of previous historical analysis. But other parts of the story of London's restless citizenry and the Restoration have never been well integrated into the historiography of Stuart England. The importance of London in the crisis that brought Charles II to power has never been fully considered, for instance; and the crises of 1659–60 and 1679–82 have rarely been considered together. Yet the confusing urban events of 1659–60 are critical

---

[28] For this point, also see J. Scott, *England's Troubles: Seventeenth-Century English Political Instability in European Context* (Cambridge, 2000), pp. 420–2.

in understanding both why Charles was restored and why his government encountered, after 1679, many of the same pressures that had exploded the regime of his father in 1640–42. Restored in the midst of a frenzy of anti-sectarianism, the Stuart crown was nearly swamped two decades later by a wave of anti-Catholicism that swept both the city and the realm.

Anti-sectarianism and anti-popery operated as twin phobias of the English Protestant mind in the decades after 1649. They were complementary and contradictory expressions of widespread fears about the fragility of the nation's Protestant parochial order. They each had the capacity to unsettle the nation; and they were each rooted in religious divisions especially apparent in London, where Anglicans, Reformed Protestants, and sectarians were all highly visible and numerous. The Commonwealth of 1659–60 ran afoul of the anti-sectarianism that Reformed and Anglican Protestants then shared. But Anglican loyalists achieved their triumph in church and state after 1660 by employing the same anti-sectarianism against Reformed Protestants, repeatedly pointing to the dissent of Presbyterians and Independents as the principal obstacle to Protestant unity.

However, the preference of Restoration Anglicans for coercion over the accommodation of Protestant differences also ensured the revival, after 1660, of early Stuart "puritan" fears that popery lurked behind diocesan episcopacy. By the 1670s, London Reformed Protestants and their parliamentary allies were demanding an end to the "popish" practices of the bishops as well as a new church settlement with allowance for conscience. The crisis of 1679–82 proved to be one in which Reformed and Anglican Protestants were moved by rival fears about the security of the Protestant order. In London, conscience and consent became the watchwords of anti-Catholic Whig critics of a "popish" church establishment. But the Anglican Tory guardians of that establishment feared that a renewed sectarian threat to the unity and governance of the church lay behind the anti-popery of their opponents. These competing phobias about popery and fanaticism emphasized the endurance of Protestant divisions that coercion had been designed to efface in 1661–2. They also sustained parties and prevented agreement, either in parliament or in London, about the constitutional and religious issues of the crisis.

The first three chapters of this study – Parts I and II – explain the role of the Corporation of London and of its citizens in the making and unmaking of the Restoration settlement between 1659 and 1679. Chapter 1, which examines London in the crisis of 1659–60, shows how the city's Reformed Protestants, especially its Presbyterians, came to see Charles's restoration as the solution to the problem of settlement. Chapter 2 demonstrates how the unexpected and coercive Anglican religious settlement of 1660–62 actually unsettled the Corporation in the 1660s and created a dissenting community that championed Protestant conscience against Anglican coercion. Chapter 3 examines how a new civic opposition devoted to consent as well as to conscience emerged from this dissenting community and allied with the parliamentary Country. Parts III and IV, which will be separately introduced, examine London in the crisis of 1679–82, consider the emergence of parties, and reconstruct London plotting against Charles II in 1682–3.

1

London and the origins of the Restoration, 1659–1660

THE ALIENATION OF THE CITY

The disposal of Richard Cromwell and his parliament by the leaders of the New Model Army in April 1659 was the most significant turning-point in the English Revolution since 1649. As Protector, Richard had been supported in parliament and in the localities by broad and somewhat ambiguous coalitions of pragmatists, Presbyterians, and "royalists." He had been the hope of all those who saw in the Cromwellian church and in the last Protectorate parliament the best prospects for stable government and an enduring parochial establishment. But now the entire post-1653 Cromwellian endeavor to achieve political and religious reconciliation had been destroyed. The nation's affairs had fallen again into the hands of those who had purged the Long Parliament in 1648, who had abrogated the Solemn League and Covenant, who had killed the last king, and who had ever since (in the minds of their critics) threatened national ministry.[1]

The hostility of most London citizens and their leaders to the revived republican regime would prevent a successful resettlement of the nation and instead contribute to a rapidly enlarging national crisis. The Commonwealth's inability to control its capital was at the heart of its failure. The opposition movement that developed in the Corporation of London and that inspired opposition elsewhere sprang from an unexpected and ambiguous convergence of two broad groups dedicated to the pre-1649 constitution in church and state, Reformed Protestants and Anglican loyalists. The movement's complex character – its union of spokesmen of rather different sentiments behind loosely defined historical institutions – was both its strength and its weakness. The developing crisis afforded Reformed Protestants and Anglicans little time to consider the differences that had led them to civil war in the 1640s, and their inability to resolve those differences would contribute to instability and unsettlement for another generation. But what was apparent

---

[1] Baxter, *Holy Commonwealth*, pp. ix–x; B. S. Capp, *The Fifth Monarchy Men* (Totowa, NJ, 1972), pp. 124–5.

19

to them in April 1659 was only that they again confronted their foes of 1648–9.

Acting under army, sectarian, and republican pressure, Generals Charles Fleetwood and John Desborough – who were Richard's relatives by marriage – moved quickly after the destruction of the Protectorate to revive the constitutional forms of the Commonwealth. Those members of the Long Parliament who had served the republic as MPs in 1649–53 were summoned to Westminster. Forty-two MPs (of seventy-eight eligible) replaced Richard's freely elected parliament of 549. But as this Rump of the Long Parliament assembled at Westminster, so did several members who had been removed by the army in 1649, including such leading Presbyterians as City MP Richard Browne, Cheshire magnate Sir George Booth, William Prynne, and Sir William Waller. Their efforts to reclaim the seats for which they had once been chosen were frustrated by armed guards. Instead, the restored Rump was eventually joined by a Council of State that included the army's principal commanders and leading MPs like Sir Arthur Hesilrige, Edmund Ludlow, Thomas Scot, Algernon Sidney, Sir Henry Vane, and Bulstrode Whitelocke.[2]

The "radical political independents" who had gained power in the Corporation of London under the former republican regime, and who had been alarmed by the return to civic life of leading Presbyterians and Anglicans under Oliver, rejoiced at the downfall of the Protectorate. In the days following the April coup, they sought to regain the political initiative in the city. Lord Mayor John Ireton, another Cromwellian in-law, assumed leadership of civic sectarians and commonwealthmen, turning most frequently for advice to Alderman Robert Tichborne, a regicide.[3] But 1659 was not to see a successful repetition of the city's revolution of 1648–9. Far from finding the Corporation a political anchor, as it had a decade earlier, the Rump instead confronted a city full of opponents. Exaggerating somewhat, one royalist claimed that the citizens were "universally enraged" by the army's actions. The French ambassador reported that Presbyterians were "entirely opposed" and that the parochial clergy feared the government had now fallen into the hands "of the Anabaptists and other Sectaries."[4]

[2] MS Clarendon 60, fol. 465; *Clarke Papers*, IV, 4–6, 7–8, 21; *The Nicholas Papers: Correspondence of Sir Edward Nicholas Secretary of State*, 4 vols. (1886–1920), IV, 134; *The Memoirs of Edmund Ludlow*, ed. C. H. Firth, 2 vols. (Oxford, 1894), II, 84; *CSPVen 1659–61*, pp. 14–20; G. Davies, *The Restoration of Charles II, 1658–1660* (San Marino, Cal., 1955), ch. 6; Woolrych, *Milton*, VII, 66–73; Hutton, *Restoration*, pp. 42–5, 47.

[3] *Clarke Papers*, III, 213–14, Ludlow, *Memoirs*, II, 73, 84; Brenner, *Merchants*, pp. 533–50, 574; Farnell, "The Usurpation of Honest London Householders"; A. Woolrych, *Commonwealth to Protectorate* (Oxford, 1982), pp. 126, 218, 421; *BDBR*, I, 57–8; II, 134–5; III, 239–40.

[4] MS Clarendon 60, fol. 465; M. F. Guizot, *History of Richard Cromwell and the Restoration of Charles II*, 2 vols. (1856), I, 373.

The restored Rump itself was a divided body of politicians who were surprised by their sudden return to the political center-stage and edgy about their relationship to the army. Some MPs, like Speaker William Lenthall and Bulstrode Whitelocke, were chastened by the decade of constitutional and religious confusion that had opened in 1649. But moderate and pragmatic MPs shared power with committed commonwealthmen like Hesilrige, Scot, and Sidney and with sectarian spokesmen like Vane and Ludlow, all determined to undo Oliver's apostasy from republican forms.[5]

The MPs immediately turned to the critical matter of placing local militias in the hands of those of proven loyalty to commonwealth principles. But as they did so, they received contradictory signals from London. Sectarian citizens, who saluted them as "our legal Trustees," requested that the militias of London and the counties be settled in reliable hands, that all those ejected from public places for the sake of conscience be restored, and that a committee be created to consider how best to establish "a good and equall Commonwealth."[6] These welcome words were followed, however, by a far more officious and restrained response from the Corporation. When Lord Mayor Ireton summoned common council to address the Rump at the end of May, only a bare quorum of common councilmen attended; and the motion for an address was carried by a single vote. When the committee charged with preparing the address reported, however, so many common councilmen hostile to the new regime appeared that Ireton was forced to delay a vote. The text finally presented to parliament called for the preservation of public ministry, with allowance for liberty of conscience, and for a permanent settlement of the government. The Corporation asserted its customary right of presenting names to parliament for consideration as militia commissioners. And when parliament requested a loan from the Corporation, on the security of the assessments it had already voted, most aldermen and common councilmen responded with indifference.[7]

The apprehensions of many London Reformed Protestants about the Rump did not ease in the following weeks. Supporters of magistracy and ministry were relieved when the Rump abandoned its consideration of sectarian demands for the elimination of tithes, but they had already been frightened by the revival of parliamentary attention to the issue. The notable increase of

[5] *CSPVen 1659–61*, pp. 29–30; *CJ*, VII, 646.
[6] *The Humble Petition of Many Inhabitants in and about the City of London* (1659); *CJ*, VII, 647, 649–50.
[7] Journal 41, fols. 204–5; MS Clarendon 60, fol. 564. *The Humble Petition of the Lord Maior, Aldermen, and Common-Council of the City of London* (1659); *CJ*, VII, 671; Guizot, *History*, I, 408; Woolrych, *Milton*, p. 97n.; *Nicholas Papers*, IV, 163; Guizot, *History*, I, 420, 432; Ludlow, *Memoirs*, II, 96; G. V. Chivers, "The City of London and the State, 1658–1664," Unpublished Ph.D. thesis, Manchester University, 1961, p. 215; Davies, p. 104.

sectarian, republican, and leveling publications was also alarming to those who preferred the Cromwellian church settlement and the customary electoral liberties observed in the selection of Richard's parliament. As it had been in its first sitting, the Rump was also slow to consider the issue of its own replacement in a new parliamentary election. And when the Rump's appointments to local militia commissions were released, the fears of many of the "natural leaders" of society were confirmed.[8]

The militia commission approved by the Rump for London and Westminster, for instance, was a roll call of names abhorred by civic Presbyterians: Praise-God Barebone, Baptist merchant William Kiffin, and leading Quaker William Mead, to name but a few.[9] Adding insult to injury, the Rump's London militia act obliged the city to raise six regiments of horse and foot at the expense of the householders. Indeed, it contemplated turning the whole body of citizens capable of bearing arms into a mass force for employment outside the city whenever and wherever parliament deemed necessary. In conformity with the acts for the remaining county and urban militias, the London act also retained for parliament the authority of naming the regimental officers as well as the militia commissioners. In these respects, the Rump showed remarkable insensitivity to the city's customary rights and privileges. On 16 July, the Corporation presented a petition objecting to these features as contrary to the London charters and contrary to all previous parliamentary treatment of the London militia.[10] The Rump's reassurances that it would "be very tender of the Privileges" of the Corporation failed to persuade those citizens who believed that the Commonwealth regime of 1649–53 had trampled upon customary rights and liberties in its disregard for the "ancient constitution."[11]

The militia issue was further inflamed by the growing realization that these forces might be called into immediate action. Political unhappiness with the army and the Rump had given royalists their greatest opportunity for a rising on behalf of Charles Stuart. As the government reacted to signs of royalist planning, its counter-preparations in July created an atmosphere fraught with tension. Many in the city and elsewhere were already unhappy with the Rump's assessments; but in early August, parliament adopted an

---

[8] Davies, *Restoration*, pp. 120–1, 136; Woolrych, *Milton*, VII, 73–6, 96–101; Hutton, *Restoration*, pp. 47–9, 51–2.

[9] *CJ*, VII, 707; *Acts and Ordinances of the Interregnum*, II, 1293–5; HMC *Leyborne-Popham*, pp. 166–7; Guizot, *History*, I, 432; *Nicholas Papers*, IV, 168; *CSPVen 1657–9*, p. 44; Woolrych, *Milton*, pp. 97–8; Hutton, *Restoration*, pp. 51–2; Brenner, *Merchants*, pp. 530–1; Tolmie, *Triumph*, pp. 67, 187, 236n.; Elliot, "Elections," pp. 160, 166; Farnell, "City of London," pp. 356, 372, 378; *BDBR*, I, 37–8; II, 155–6, 234–5, 251–2, 273–4; III, 116–18, 281.

[10] Journal 41, fol. 206.

[11] *CJ*, VII, 721–2; *CSPVen 1659–61*, pp. 47–8; Guizot, *History*, I, 437; Woolrych, *Milton*, p. 100.

extraordinary London rate to be collected by the militia commissioners for the defrayment of their expenses. "This citty is sicke of its new militia," wrote one royalist observer, whose views reflected the popular fear that "vast sommes of mony by . . . violent meanes must be levyed." The political combination of heavy taxation in the midst of economic depression, of an unelected parliament enlarging an already unpopular military establishment, and of widespread fears about public ministry was simply too much for many citizens.[12]

A "royalist" insurrection began on 1 August. It involved skirmishes in several counties and the seizure of Chester by Sir George Booth, who had been among those turned away from his seat at Westminster. Although this effort collapsed within a few weeks, the Rump and the army had to contend simultaneously with a national military crisis and with a capital in which disenchantment had turned to active disaffection. As plans for the rising matured, civic Presbyterians developed their own device for undermining the Rump in the form of a petition calling for the readmission to parliament of those members secluded in 1649. But unlike Booth, the city Presbyterians were, for the most part, not yet ready for insurrection. When Alderman Richard Browne, their titular head and another spokesmen for the secluded MPs, was called before the Council of State after the commencement of the rising, he disappeared rather than organize the sympathetic urban disturbances that cavaliers had expected.[13]

The regime's military precautions in London peaked on 9 August, and then again ten days later, when it uncovered designs for risings of the apprentices. By the first date, declarations of purpose printed in Booth's name were posted throughout the city and the country. At both junctures, the government required the public reading of its own answering declarations, which condemned Booth and his associates as traitors. But when the Rump's initial declaration against Booth was read in some city churches, a hostile source reported "such laughing, hawking & spitting, yt they could hardly read through." The city was clearly kept quiet by the force of the Rump's arms rather than by the force of its words, and the London militia was quickly augmented by volunteer regiments raised from gathered churches supportive of the republic.[14]

[12] *CJ*, VII, 705, 708, 728, 730, 732, 745, 747–8; *CSPD 1659–60*, pp. 49, 54, 57–8, 88; *Nicholas Papers*, IV, 165, 172; *CSPVen 1659–61*, pp. 48, 50, 52; Guizot, *History*, I, 432, 435, 442; Davies, *Restoration*, pp. 131, 133.

[13] MS Clarendon 60, fols. 243–244; *Nicholas Papers*, IV, 75–6, 98, 171; Guizot, *History*, I, 427, 431, 432; *The Letter Book of John Viscount Mordaunt, 1658–60* (1945), p. 6; Woolrych, *Milton*, VII, 98–101.

[14] MS Clarendon 63, fols. 138, 141–142, 193, 204, 243; MS Clarendon 64, fols. 91, 95; *CJ*, VII, 753; *CSPVen 1659–61*, pp. 53, 56, 62; *CSPD 1659–60*, pp. 49, 54, 88, 90, 93, 113; *Clarke Papers*, IV, 29, 42, 44–5; *Nicholas Papers*, IV, 178; Guizot, *History*, I, 445, 448–9, 453, 457–8, 463; Rugg, *Diurnal*, p. 5; *Diary of Sir Archibald Johnston of Wariston*, 3 vols.

If few London citizens were prepared to resist the Rump in August 1659, many citizens nevertheless voiced their support for a free parliament – instead of the Rump – as the only path to settlement. Despite the military bustle about them in early August, and despite the charges of treason in the rhetorical air, London Presbyterians pursued their petition and apparently redirected it toward Booth's objective of a new, freely elected parliament. When Lord Mayor Ireton refused to summon a common council to consider a petition, those who desired one sought to convene common council without mayoral summons in accordance with the Rump's own 1649 London statute. Ireton responded by alerting the Council of State; and when some citizens appeared at Guildhall, they found their way blocked by soldiers. Council chair Bulstrode Whitelocke claimed in justification that rebels intended to fire the city.[15]

How should the urban movement for a free parliament be understood in the light of these origins? Stuart loyalists were, in the winter of 1659–60, to exploit the movement for a free parliament on behalf of the king. But reading too much articulate royalism into the rhetorical birth of the 1659 demand for a free parliament strains the evidence. In London, the demand initially gave political voice again to all those citizens and civic worthies who had fought the king in the 1640s only to find themselves pushed aside in 1648 by unacceptable people, by unacceptable ideas, and by unacceptable innovations. The views of those who promoted the August London petition for a free parliament were probably similar to those of the declaration to London's citizens published in Booth's name at the time of the abortive common council meeting. Defining freely elected parliaments as "the *English* mans *main Birthright*," this manifesto contrasted parliamentary government with the nation's principal experiences under the revived Commonwealth:

> Oppression, Injustice, and Tyranny raigneth … Arbitrary and illegal imprisonments, Pattents, Monopolies, Excise, and other payments brought upon us, and continued Contrary to *Magna Charta*, and the Petition of Right; no form or face of Government of *English Constitution* amongst us; the name and Authority of the People in Parliament usurped and abused. …

Conflating the history of 1648–53 with the issues of 1659, this declaration also included promises about reform of the law and about the annual election

(Edinburgh, 1911–40), III, 134; D. Underdown, *Royalist Conspiracy in England, 1649–1660* (Hamden, Conn., 1971), pp. 279–80.

15 MS Clarendon 63, fols. 193, 243; MS Clarendon 64, fol. 101; *The Humble Address of the Lord Maior, Aldermen and Common-Council of the City … the 9th of August* (1659), p. 6; Guizot, *History*, I, 450; *CSPVen 1659–61*, p. 57; HMC *Seventh Report*, p. 483; *Clarke Papers*, IV, 40; *Warriston Diary*, III, 129–30; Bulstrode Whitelocke, *Memorials of the English affairs from the Beginning of the Reign of Charles the First* (Oxford, 1853), p. 683; *Whitelocke Diary*, p. 526; Brenner, *Merchants*, p. 545; R. R. Sharpe, *London and the Kingdom*, 3 vols. (1894–5), II, 304–5.

of magistrates that were of concern to some Londoners. And like the other declarations issued in Booth's name, this appeal failed to make any mention of the king.[16]

In time, many civic Presbyterians would realize that the collapse of the protectoral alternative to kingship left a restored Stuart monarchy, perhaps with limitations, as the best constitutional alternative to the oligarchy of the Rump and army. Some leading citizens probably recognized this already in the summer of 1659. The civic program for a free parliament was, nevertheless, quite different from and much broader than the uncomplicated cavalier demand for restoring the king and punishing his enemies. The Presbyterians were the constitutional heirs of the parliamentary agenda of the 1640s; and they also saw themselves as rhetorical guardians of the pre-civil war language about the ancient constitution, a complex body of political discourse susceptible to both libertarian and conservative applications. In an unrepresentative regime installed by the army, London Presbyterians found a contradiction to their ideal even more blatant than that posed by Charles I; and in their opposition to the "tyranny of the Rump," they expressed the same passion for parliament that had moved them in the 1640s. Their case "that the present Parliament cannot exercise any legitimate authority because the greater number of its members have been expelled from it," was not a smoke screen for monarchy. It was an appeal to the regime and to "the whole People, for the prevention of a New War" through political "accommodation" within a new and freely elected parliament. Moreover, this appeal was expressed in language that had great potential for support among ordinary people who were beginning to blame the economic woes of depressed trade, underemployment, and burdensome taxes upon the Rump.[17]

If, in London, the demand for a free parliament was truly more about parliament than about the king, it was also a case for the ancient constitution against the republican schemes for senates and new parliamentary frameworks that had flooded the press. As republican theorists like James Harrington attacked the restored Rump for substituting the empty "form" of a commonwealth for its reality, London Presbyterians were only further convinced that the regime could not stand. For them, the real choice was between political accommodation in a free parliament or political disintegration under the army and the Rump.[18]

[16] *An Express from the Knights and Gentlemen now engaged with Sir George Booth; To the City and Citizens of London* (1659); Davies, *Restoration*, pp. 136–7; Woolrych, *Milton*, VII, 108–9. Also see [Booth, Sir George], *The Declaration of the Lords, Gentlemen, Citizens, Freeholders* [1659] and in Baker, *Chronicle*, p. 706.

[17] MS Clarendon 63, fol. 193; *Express from ... Booth*; Guizot, *History*, I, 450.

[18] *A Proposition in order to the Proposing of a Commonwealth or Democracie* [1659]; James Harrington, *A Discourse Shewing, that the Spirit of Parliaments, with a Council in the Intervals, is not to be trusted for a Settlement* (1659); Παναρμονια. *Or, the Agreement of the People* (1659); Woolrych, *Milton*, VII, 101–7.

Finally, the demand for a free parliament was promoted by those who feared for the future of Protestant settlement under a regime closely linked to the sects. Supporters of public ministry had been shocked and frightened by the reassertions in sectarian and republican literature of the cases for an unrestrained toleration and for an elimination of tithes. When the London supporters of a free parliament assured the gathered churches, in August 1659, that they were *"against all Coercive Power in matters of Religion,"* they meant, therefore, no more than what they said.[19] They opposed the use of compulsion by the magistrate on behalf of Protestant uniformity, a "healing" position still to be embraced by many Presbyterian clerics, and here intended primarily to reassure Independents. But a reassurance in these terms was not inconsistent with the maintenance of a Protestant establishment by the magistrate. Neither was it inconsistent with the magistrate's "negative" or "restrictive" power to preserve such an order against egregious doctrinal error, popery, atheism, and immoral behavior. These were, according to all Presbyterians, the likely consequences of the sectarian agenda of full toleration.

Not surprisingly, therefore, Sir George Booth's Chester rising was actively supported by some "illustrious Presbyterian ministers" of London, like Zachary Crofton of St Botolph Aldgate. The Venetian ambassador observed that many Presbyterian clergy read Booth's declaration in their pulpits, "urging that if the present parliament is not cast down the Gospel is lost." The idea of promoting a petition for a free parliament in the London common council may also have originated with the Presbyterian clergy. Moreover, in the wake of the collapsed rising, city Presbyterian clerics like Edmund Calamy and Lazarus Seaman met with some London Independent divines (Joseph Caryl, Philip Nye, and John Owen) and with some Baptist preachers to promote a Reformed Protestant front "for ordinances" and public ministry "against Quakers." Their objective was not to encourage a movement on behalf of the king but rather to promote religious accommodation within the Protestant establishment, just as the London petition was intended to promote political accommodation within a freely elected parliament.[20]

Despite the regime's survival of this first test of its strength, neither the tensions between pragmatic and dogmatic MPs (allied to the army) nor the tensions between the Rump and the Corporation had been eased. As the regime

[19] *Express from . . . Booth.*
[20] MS Clarendon 64, fols. 63–64; *CSPVen 1659–61*, p. 57; Guizot, *History*, I, 448, 450; *Warriston Diary*, pp. 129–30, 134–5; *Nicholas Papers*, IV, 177; *Calendar of the Correspondence of Richard Baxter*, ed. N. H. Keeble and G. F. Nuttall, 2 vols. (Oxford, 1991), I, 399, 403, 408–9, 413–14; G. J. Abernathy, Jr., *The English Presbyterians and the Stuart Restoration, 1648–1663* (Philadelphia, 1965), pp. 31–2.

celebrated its victory over the rebels, the Rump once again offended many citizens by exhibiting its indifference to electoral and civic rights. On 2 September, apparently fearing the election of a hostile lord mayor at the approaching Michaelmas common hall, the Rump resolved that John Ireton be continued in his mayoralty for another year.[21]

This order was easily construed in the city as a violation of the electoral rights of the city's liverymen. The Venetian ambassador noted that Ireton's partiality for the Rump had destroyed his credit in the city, leaving him "universally detested," and that the Rump's decision provoked so much hostile comment that the MPs were again "apprehensive of some disturbance." Common council finally met on 21 September, in the absence of Ireton; and it immediately approved a petition to the Rump, drafted by a large committee representing different persuasions, which defended the city's right to choose its own lord mayor. Because the charters specifically provided that no lord mayor should hold office for more than one year, the Rump's order was protested as a dangerous "entrenching upon" civic rights and privileges that had been confirmed by many parliaments.[22]

When the sheriffs and aldermen appeared at Westminster on 24 September to present the petition, they were put off for several days, an action that further inflamed city tempers. One royalist broadside encouraged Londoners to defy their "senseless Mayor" as well as "State Projectors . . . taxes, Redcoats, and Collectors." But in the end, the Rump backed down. Continuing disagreements between the House and army officers, as well as among MPs of different perspectives, made peace with the Corporation imperative. Pragmatic MPs like Speaker William Lenthall, whose brother Thomas Lenthall was on the London committee that drafted the petition against Ireton, persuaded the House to reverse their order about the mayoralty. A relatively inconspicuous alderman, Thomas Alleyn, was chosen as lord mayor for 1659–60. By this time much damage had already been done, however. The events that preceded Alleyn's election had accentuated the whole range of issues that had unnerved many citizens since the return of the Rump.[23]

---

[21] *CJ*, VII, 773; *CSPVen 1659–61*, pp. 57, 62, 70–1; Davies, *Restoration*, pp. 144–6, 149; Woolrych, *Milton*, VII, 111, Hutton, *Restoration*, pp. 60–1.

[22] CLRO Common Council Papers (1659); Journal 41, fols. 207–208; Repertory 66, fol. 311; *To the Supreme Authority of the Nation . . . The humble Petition of the Common-Council of the City of London* (1659); *CSPVen 1659–61*, p. 71.

[23] MS Clarendon 65, fols. 31, 51; *CJ*, VII, 785, 787–8; Journal 41, fol. 207; Guizot, *History*, I, 484, 490; *CSPVen 1659–61*, p. 72; Whitelocke, *Memorials*, p. 685; *Whitelocke Diary*, p. 532; Ludlow, *Memoirs*, II, 121; *The New Litany* (1659); Elliot, "Elections," p. 166; Hutton, *Restoration*, p. 61.

THE REVIVAL OF THE PARLIAMENTARY CAUSE

Within a few months of Booth's rising, the demand for a parliament had generated an urban movement that was reminiscent of the parliamentary movement that dominated London in the early 1640s. This revival of the parliamentary cause would eventually swamp both the Rump and its civic friends. The leaders of London's revolution of 1648–9 were driven from power in December by civic electors who purged them from common council. A Presbyterian-dominated Corporation confronted the Rump head-on by the end of 1659. But that it did so was, in fact, surprising: the army had dumped the Rump in October; and had the city not vigorously opposed this last strike against any semblance of parliamentary government, the Rump would not have been in power in December 1659 at all. How had this ironic situation come about?

After the fiasco of the London mayoral election, the Rump tried to mend its civic fences only to run afoul of the more extreme republican and sectarian elements in the army. As pragmatist and republican MPs divided over such issues as taxation, toleration, and a more permanent constitutional settlement, republican officers, led by Col John Lambert, gathered for political meetings. Suspicious of army plotting, Sir Arthur Hesilrige and his supporters in parliament moved to cashier Lambert and several other officers. They also adopted a bill that condemned any assessment of taxes, especially for the purpose of paying the soldiers, without parliamentary authorization. Lambert and his associates, supported by Generals Fleetwood and Desborough, responded on 13 October by preventing parliament from continuing its session. Leading MPs sent to the London magistrates and militia commissioners, whom they themselves had appointed, for assistance against the army; but neither appeal elicited a response. After a fortnight of confusion, civil government passed to a Committee of Safety dominated by the army's principal commanders, including Fleetwood, Desborough, and Lambert.[24]

If the Rump lacked a broad following among London citizens, the army could count upon even less active urban support. Recognizing its vulnerability in London, the army leadership approved the inclusion on the Committee of Safety of London Aldermen Ireton and Tichborne and of Henry Brandreth, another leading civic Independent with revolutionary credentials. But the appointments to the Committee of some prominent citizens and of some moderate MPs like Bulstrode Whitelocke could scarcely obscure the fact that the Committee of Safety ruled by the sword. Civic murmuring against it commenced immediately. Presbyterians were now convinced more

---

[24] Journal 41, fol. 209; MS Clarendon 65, fols. 166, 169, 222, 225; *CJ*, VII, 790, 792–3, 795; *CSPD 1659–60*, p. 233; Guizot, *History*, I, 490–1, 498; Rugg, *Diurnal*, pp. 7–8; Mordaunt, *Letter-book*, p. 60; *Warriston Diary*, pp. 138–9; Whitelocke, *Memorials*, p. 686; Davies, *Restoration*, pp. 144–53; Woolrych, *Milton*, VII, 112–17; Hutton, *Restoration*, pp. 64–6.

than ever that legitimate government was imperiled by brute force at the service of stark enthusiasm. In Scotland, General George Monck not only declared his opposition to the English army's action but also signaled his intention to reverse it, by military force if necessary, on behalf of the Rump. In early November, Lambert led a force into the north of England to counter any move by Monck.[25]

This division of the army against itself greatly enhanced the role the Corporation of London would play in determining the outcome of the developing crisis. London citizens responded to the standoff between the Committee of Safety and General Monck in three different ways. The army leaders were able to count upon the support of those London sectarians who had been unhappy with the Rump's failure to abandon tithes and a restraining power in religion. But other citizens who had supported or accepted the revival of the Commonwealth preferred a quick end to the crisis through a recall of the Rump, as did those citizens who perceived civil confusion as the worst of all possible evils. A third position was espoused by the many Londoners who had hoped for a free parliament at the time of Booth's rising: they continued to prefer a free parliament – or the restoration of the full Long Parliament – to the Committee of Safety or to a recall of the Rump. These supporters of a free parliament would weave powerful motifs about popular liberties, civic rights, and Protestant ministry into their case against the Committee.

Nevertheless, the division of urban citizens about these three options – government by the Committee, government by the Rump, or government by a free parliament – was not yet rigidly or exclusively defined. The political circumstances of London and of the nation from October through December 1659 were remarkably fluid. Some citizens moved back and forth between the parliamentary options of the Rump or of a freely elected successor. The demand for a free parliament was also the only position, of these three, that was open to those who hoped for a return of monarchy, whether limited by the terms of 1648 or not. But the demand for a free parliament was scarcely the preserve of those already committed to a return of the king. It was far more the cry of all those who preferred an open-ended resolution of the constitutional dilemma by representatives elected throughout the nation. And those who supported the army did not do so out of any desire to eliminate parliaments but rather out of their disappointment with a particular parliament. Indeed, as the Committee proved incapable of devising an acceptable formula for electing a parliamentary successor to the Rump, some citizens who had supported the October coup came to prefer a recall of the expelled MPs as the only parliament capable of sustaining the republic against royalism.

---

[25] Repertory 66, fol. 330; *Mercurius Politicus* 593 (3–10 Nov. 1659); Ludlow, *Memoirs*, II, 131; Guizot, *History*, II, 272–3, 277, 282; *Clarke Papers*, IV, 64–6; Woolrych, *Milton*, VII, 118–20, 131–2; Hutton, *Restoration*, pp. 66–7, 71–2.

As Lambert departed for the north with the majority of the London regiments, the Committee of Safety sought to engage the Corporation's military leaders against Monck. They encouraged the London militia commissioners to write a public letter to the general protesting his design. Advocates of unlimited liberty for conscience on the commission, already aroused by reports of Monck's efforts to dislodge sectarian officers in his Scottish army, were happy to oblige. The letter proposed on 3 November by the "armies party" on the London militia commission chastised the general for provoking civil war and demanded the rehabilitation of all "godly" officers. It also suggested that an accommodation between the English army and the expelled parliament could be obtained through their own good offices as mediators.

When the full London militia commission voted on this provocative letter, it was carried by a single vote among the sixty persons in attendance. Those who voted for the letter against Monck included several militant sectarians and outspoken reformers who had been active at the time of the city's 1649 revolution. The minority of commissioners who opposed the letter included the lord mayor, the five aldermen present, the brother of the Rump Speaker, and "all other persons of quality." The Committee of Safety responded by replacing many of the hostile commissioners with individuals more to their liking, but their remodeling of the militia commission was perceived as another challenge to the city's customary control of its militia.[26]

In the wake of these unhappy events, when the Committee of Safety moved to have its authority publicly proclaimed in the city, it instead stimulated common council consideration of a petition for a parliament. In order to prevent such a show of opposition, Committee members Fleetwood, Desborough, and Whitelocke remonstrated with common council on 8 November. Preying upon the citizens' aversion to warfare and to civil commotion, they charged that Monck sought to foment disunity and a rising in London, as Booth had, for the benefit of the "common Enemy." But they were clearly thrown on the defensive, denying that the ruling junta was hostile to public ministry or that they were "Enemies to Parliaments." Their request for a loan from the Corporation was ignored: the goldsmiths had already ceased business on rumors that the army was about to plunder the city to make up their arrears. When the Committee spokesmen tried to leave Guildhall, they were forced back by crowds crying for a free parliament.

As the common councilmen deliberated their response to these visitors, they were approached by worthies of another inclination altogether: Sir

---

[26] *A Narrative of the Proceedings of the Committee of the Militia of London* [1659]; *Clarke Papers*, IV, 91–4, 101–3; *Mercurius Politicus* 593 (3–10 Nov. 1659); Mordaunt, *Letter-book*, 96; Guizot, *History*, II, 283, 285, Whitelocke, *Memorials*, p. 688; HMC *Leyborne-Popham*, p. 125; *Baxter Correspondence*, I, 417; Elliot, "Elections," p. 157; Woolrych, *Milton*, VII, 143–4.

Anthony Ashley Cooper, Josias Berners (a London member of the deposed Council of State), and like-minded associates attended to encourage a Corporation petition for a recall of the Rump. In debate, a majority of the council were said to oppose the army. But when Major Thomas Chamberlain, a Presbyterian activist of the 1640s, seized upon the militia issue to suggest that the citizens "shutt up theire shops and all...take up armes for their own preservation," he frightened the more sober into a wait-and-see attitude. To the relief of the cautious lord mayor, and to the disappointment of Cooper and his friends, the fresh news that Monck had sent commissioners to treat with the Committee of Safety for an accommodation forestalled any civic petition at this juncture.[27]

A week later, the Committee of Safety concluded a deal with Monck's commissioners about the summoning of a new parliament. But the formula for determining qualifications of those eligible for election dissatisfied the general, who repudiated the arrangement.[28] The proposal also failed to satisfy many in London. Its announcement coincided with two hostile printed remonstrances, the first of which sought to redirect the swelling public sentiment for a free parliament toward a recall of the Rump. A second *Remonstrance* reflected the increasingly outspoken views of many apprentices and other "young men" of the city to whom it was attributed. The apprentices had good reason to be outspoken. The stagnation of the country's commerce and the seasonal complications of the approaching winter were especially frustrating to those trying to set up their own trades, struggling to maintain new trades, or contemplating the completion of their service. They forthrightly defended the rights and liberties they claimed as new citizens or citizens-in-waiting. Anchoring the liberty and "Birth-right" of subjects in the much-violated "Laws of this Land," the apprentices' *Remonstrance* demanded a return, without further specification, to the constitution that existed before the mishaps of the twelve previous years.[29]

---

[27] MS Clarendon 66, fols. 233, 235–236, 253; *Three Speeches made to the Right Honorable the Lord Maior* (1659); *OPH*, XXII, 10–17 (reprint of *Three Speeches*); *CSPVen 1659–61*, p. 92; Whitelocke, *Memorials*, p. 688; *Warriston Diary*, p. 152; Guizot, *History*, II, 283, 285, 287–8. Elliot, "Elections," p. 166; Woodhead, *Rulers*, p. 44; Davies, *Restoration*, p. 159; Woolrych, *Milton*, VII, 143–4; K. H. D. Haley, *The First Earl of Shaftesbury* (Oxford, 1968), pp. 116–23. My account differs from that in Hutton, *Restoration*, p. 77.

[28] *Clarke Papers*, IV, 81–3; Baker, *Chronicle*, pp. 726–9; Woolrych, *Milton*, VII, 136, 139–40, 142.

[29] *Remonstrance and Protestation of the Well-affected People of the Cities of London and Westminster, and Other the Cities and Places within the Commonwealth* (1659); *The Remonstrance of the Apprentices in and about London* [1659]; *CSPD 1659–60*, p. 265; Rugg, *Diurnal*, pp. 9, 11–12; Gumble, *Life*, p. 142; Haley, *First Earl*, p. 121; T. Harris, *London Crowds in the Reign of Charles II: Propaganda and Politics from the Restoration until the Exclusion Crisis* (Cambridge, 1987), pp. 42–3. The apprentice *Remonstrance* needs to be treated with some care as a possible royalist contrivance.

These and other signs of disaffection to the regime in London and the counties did not prevent the Committee of Safety from attempting the collection of assessments. But claiming, correctly, that parliament had just condemned the levying of taxes in its absence, London citizens refused to pay in such numbers that the collectors required escorts of soldiers. Leaders of the expelled Rump also sought to organize a nationwide taxpayers' strike to thwart the army leadership, but Londoners apparently needed no such encouragement.

Common council met again on 23 November to receive a letter written to the Corporation ten days earlier by General Monck. The letter showed the extent to which Monck regarded the city as central to his design: one member of the Committee heard that the letter was intended "to sturre them up to ryse in airmes." Referring to the junta's collection of taxes without parliamentary authorization and its threat to the city's charter, Monck called upon the Corporation to "use your utmost Endeavours in the South," while "their Army is waiting upon me in the North." The general also sought to gain the support of those who preferred a free parliament by declaring, ambiguously, that his intention was "to restore the Parliament to its former Freedom." Common council debate about the letter was so furious that Lord Mayor Alleyn adjourned the meeting; but this action only produced demands that the civic electorate be summoned in common hall to reply themselves to the general.[30] Unable to agree upon a response to Monck, the Corporation did agree to a day of humiliation to be observed in all the city churches on 2 December. The Committee of Safety could take little reassurance from these city prayers, however. According to a royalist observer, many London clergy took the occasion to reflect upon the Committee's legitimacy, claiming that the foundations of national government had been destroyed.[31]

As petitions were raised in prayer on 2 December, other petitions were being gathered by the apprentices and "Bachelors." For a week or more, crowds had gathered at a house in Cannon Street to place their names on a "monster" petition to the Corporation. It called for a new parliamentary election or for a recall of the entire Long Parliament, secluded members as well as those who sat in the Rump. More restrained than the

[30] MS Clarendon 67, fols. 35, 42, 48, 83; *CLSP*, III, 624–5; *A Letter of November 12. from General Monck* (1659), pp. 3–4; *OPH*, XXII, 46–8 (reprint of *Letter of November 12*); Baker, *Chronicle*, p. 731; *Clarke Papers*, IV, 126, 134–7, 141, 301; *CSPVen 1659–61*, pp. 94–5; Guizot, *History*, II, 284, 290, 293, 296; Mordaunt, *Letter-book*, p. 118; *Mercurius Politicus* 595 (17–24 Nov. 1659) [deliberately misleading]; *Warriston Diary*, p. 154; HMC *Leyborne-Popham*, pp. 166–8; Gumble, *Life*, pp. 158–9; Woolrych, *Milton*, VII, 137, 144; Hutton, *Restoration*, p. 78.

[31] Journal 41, fol. 211; MS Clarendon 67, fols. 110–111, 113–114, 115–116; *CLSP*, III, 619–21; *CalCSP*, IV, 660; *At a Common-Councel holden at the Guildhall . . . 23 day of November 1659* [1659]; Mordaunt, *Letter-book*, p. 136.

previous *Remonstrance* attributed to the apprentices, the petition nonetheless warned city leaders that their failure to endorse its ends would be "a palpable breach of trust." Who initiated the petition is unclear. Diarist Thomas Rugg thought the apprentices had the assistance of "better heade peces," whom the French ambassador identified as "some Presbyterian ministers, Royalists, and old Parliamentarians." The petition alarmed the Committee of Safety, which issued a proclamation forbidding the further gathering of signatures. However, the right of petitioning had been one of the liberties most strenuously asserted in the 1640s; and perhaps for this reason, the lord mayor declined to have the Committee's proclamation read in the city without first consulting common council. On the morning of 5 December common council convened in Guildhall; the apprentices and young men congregated in the streets on behalf of the petition; and the Committee of Safety ordered horse and foot into the city to accompany the reading of their proclamation.[32]

Street battles between rock-throwing apprentices intent upon pursuing the petition and the 2,000 troops eventually sent into the city continued throughout the day. The apprentices did not retire from the field until the lord mayor personally assured them that he would persuade the military grandees to withdraw their troops. Shops remained shut throughout the disturbances: the long-feared plunder of the city by the army seemed about to occur, providing many citizens with vicarious participation in the violence out-of-doors. The affair provided the young men of London both with new martyrs, in the persons of those who were killed, and with a new shibboleth for the horrors of military rule in the person of regicide John Hewson, the regimental commander and Committee of Safety member who ordered the firing.[33]

Like other memorable urban political "massacres," the melee of 5 December proved to be a watershed in the relationship between London citizens and the increasingly unsteady regime. The consequences were far more significant than the small number of casualties might indicate. The army's firing upon youthful crowds defending civic rights further stripped the republican

[32] MS Clarendon 67, fol. 119; Repertory 67, fol. 21; *To the Right Honourable, our right worthy and grave Senatours . . . The most humble Petition and Address of divers Young Men* [1659]; *By the Committee of Safety. A Proclamation* (1659); Rugg, *Diurnal*, pp. 9 [misplaced chronologically], 10, 13; Guizot, *History*, II, 299; Mordaunt, *Letter-book*, p. 124; *Warriston Diary*, p. 154; Whitelocke, *Memorials*, p. 690.

[33] Sources differ about the number of casualties, which are variously reported as between two and seven. MS Carte 73, fol. 329; MS Clarendon 67, fols. 181, 222–223, 224; *Mercurius Politicus* 597 (1–8 Dec. 1659); *The Out-Cry of the London Prentices* (1659); *CLSP*, III, 626; *Clarke Papers*, IV, 165, 166, 168; *CSP Ven 1659–61*, p. 101; *CSPD 1659–60*, p. 268; Guizot, *History*, II, 300–1; Rugg, *Diurnal*, p. 14; Ludlow, *Memoirs*, II, 177; Baker, *Chronicle*, p. 734; Harris, *London Crowds*, pp. 43–4; Davies, *Restoration*, pp. 181–2; Woolrych, *Milton*, VII, 145–6; *BDBR*, II, 82–3.

regime of its public credibility and drove some citizens and apprentices into more defiant postures. The Corporation of London responded to the bloodshed and to popular pressures with a show of independence that left the Committee of Safety as exposed in London as it was in the north. By the time the Rump was restored for the second time, three weeks later, the Corporation had already come under the leadership of those who would never accept it as the equivalent of a freely elected parliament. The affair cost the Commonwealth the loyalty of its capital, and the loss proved to be one the republic could not overcome.

The tumults of 5 December propelled common council into an unqualified defiance of military rule. It met another ten times in the month of December, initiating a pattern of more than weekly meetings that would continue for several months; and it appointed its own civic committee of safety. This body was charged with preserving the city's peace and with resuming authority over the London militia. The city committee's membership included two of the Presbyterian City MPs in Richard's parliament, the outspoken Thomas Chamberlain, and Anglican Alderman John Robinson. It also included several common councilmen who had publicly supported Monck's demand for the reinstatement of the Rump or the apprentice petition for a free parliament. Not since common council had chosen an unprecedented committee of safety in January 1642, in defense of parliament against Charles I, had the Corporation acted so provocatively.[34]

The appointment of the city committee of safety also reflected a growing belief that the Corporation should act on its own authority; and in the absence of a parliament, no longer "recognize any superior authority." Accordingly, when the ruling Committee of Safety commanded the lord mayor, the court of aldermen, and the sheriffs to appear before it to answer for the security of the city, the aldermen replied that the security of the city precluded their appearance before the Committee. Instead, they sent a delegation to the Committee at Wallingford House, "who spake plaine English to them," while another body of citizens appeared at Whitehall to press Fleetwood for a recall of the Rump. In the meantime, many apprentices were apparently entering into an engagement for a free parliament and the defense of common council.[35]

[34] Journal 41, fol. 212; Repertory 67, fol. 21; Rugg, *Diurnal*, p. 16; *CSPD 1659–60*, pp. 280–1; Pearl, *London*, pp. 139–40; Brenner, *Merchants*, pp. 368–71.
[35] Repertory 67, fols. 21–22; MS Clarendon 67, fol. 215; Guizot, *History*, II, 304; *To the General Council of Officers. The Representation of divers Citizens of London* (1659); *The Engagement and Remonstrance of the City of London* [1659]; *A Free Parliament Proposed by the City to the Nation* [1660]; *The Free-Mens Petition: to the Right Honourable, the Lord Mayor, Aldermen, and Commonalty of the City of London* [1659]; *Warriston Diary*, p. 155; *Clarke Papers*, IV, 168; Ludlow, *Memoirs*, II, 177; Woolrych, *Milton*, VII, 146.

The political atmosphere in London remained highly volatile for the remainder of the month. Every show of force in the streets by the soldiers garrisoned at St Paul's and Gresham College was accompanied by further rock throwing by the apprentices and the seamen, who were idled by the season and by the decline of trade. Rumors spread that the army had moved in heavy guns and firebombs in order to attack the city, if they could not win it over. These reports encouraged the Corporation to ready its own militia for all eventualities. "The citizens are arming and providing themselves," wrote one news writer, who also observed that shops remained shut in anticipation of further street confrontations.[36]

Any precipitous action by the Corporation was prevented, however, by the citizens' disunity about the best means for achieving a settlement. Most were unhappy with army rule, but leading citizens continued to articulate their different preferences for a new parliament, for the Rump as a parliament, or for the full Long Parliament. Confusion and misunderstanding therefore marked Corporation counsels for another two weeks. On 9 December, common council cautiously declined to receive a petition for a free parliament from substantial inhabitants because it ignored the existence of the army regime and referred to the current lord mayor as the "Chief Magistrate of England." In the meantime, a recall of the Rump seemed distinctly more possible after several MPs gained control of Portsmouth and began the conversion of its garrison into a parliamentary army. But Sir Anthony Ashley Cooper's plot to seize control of the Tower of London on behalf of the Rump was foiled.[37]

In response to such expressions of opposition in London and elsewhere, the military leadership attempted to answer demands for a parliament by calling one. The General Council of Officers and the ruling Committee of Safety agreed upon the election of a new parliament, with restrictive

---

[36] Repertory 67, fol. 23; MS Clarendon 67, fols. 185–186, 200–201, 209 a–b, 246; *CLSP*, III, 626, 630–1; *CSPVen 1659–61*, pp. 102, 103; *Engagement and Remonstrance*; *To the Right Honourable our Worthy and Grave Senators.... The further humble Petition and Remonstrance of the Free-men and Prentices* (1659); *Warriston Diary*, pp. 155, 157; *Clarke Papers*, IV, 186–7; Mordaunt, *Letter-book*, p. 138; *Nicholas Papers*, IV, 190–1; Guizot, *History*, II, 302–3, 305; Pearl, *London*, pp. 141–3.

[37] Journal 41, fol. 212; MS Clarendon 67, fol. 186; *Mercurius Politicus* 597 (1–8 Dec. 1659); *Publick Intelligencer* 207 (12–19 Dec. 1659); *A Letter to Sir Thomas Alyn* (1659); *To the Right Honourable, the Lord Mayor, Aldermen, ... of London ... the Humble Petition and Address of the Sea-men, and Water-men* [1659]; *The Further humble Petition*; *Warriston Diary*, p. 156; Rugg, *Diurnal*, p. 14; *Clarke Papers*, IV, 187, 188; *Nicholas Papers*, IV, 191; Whitelocke, *Memorials*, p. 691; Whitelocke, *Diary*, p. 549; Ludlow, *Memoirs*, II, 169; Guizot, *History*, II, 302, 304–5; W. D. Christie, *A Life of Anthony Ashley Cooper, First Earl of Shaftesbury. 1621–1683*, 2 vols. (1871), I, Appendix v., lxxiv–lxxvii; Hutton, *Restoration*, p. 78; Woolrych, *Milton*, VII, 146; Haley, *Shaftesbury*, pp. 120–1; Underdown, *Royalist Conspiracy*, pp. 293–4.

qualifications for membership, to meet on 24 January. Fleetwood communicated the news about this parliament to the city on 13 December, even before its public announcement. This political initiative came too late, however, to deter the defection from the Committee of Vice-Admiral John Lawson and the fleet. Like Monck before him, Lawson declared on behalf of the Rump, immediately wrote to the Corporation of London for its support, and moved the fleet into the Thames to challenge the governing clique.[38]

When common council met on 14 December, disagreement about what kind of parliament was acceptable softened the Corporation's previous hard line. "Wary Presbyterians" and other long-time office holders like Lord Mayor Sir Thomas Alleyn were apparently prepared to accept the offer of any parliament from the Committee as preferable to army domination. They were said to fear for the security of their property, some of it former church lands, at the hands of the parliamentary crowd or of Charles Stuart, should a free parliament lead to his restoration, a possibility some were now beginning to consider. When the petition of 9 December was again presented on the 14th, hesitant magistrates therefore again persuaded common council, over many objections, to return the petition to its sponsors.[39]

Representing a retreat from the civic brinkmanship of the previous week, the apparent compliance of the lord mayor and aldermen in the Committee of Safety's parliamentary agenda produced not the hoped-for pacification of the capital but rather additional frustration. Citizens and apprentices committed to a free parliament rejected the electoral formula offered by the Committee of Safety as more likely to confirm the army's position than to respect the rights and preferences of the electorate: a carefully contrived parliament was not the parliament of the "ancient constitution." Rumors spread that Lord Mayor Alleyn had provided Fleetwood and the governing Committee with intelligence about discussions in the city's own committee of safety. Redcoats returned by Alleyn's invitation to guard posts at the city gates; and the apprentices responded by pelting the coach of this civic "traitour," just as they had previously pelted the soldiers who now protected him. They threatened to take "our Swords in our Hands" against both "Force and Treason; having one Enemy within our Walls, and Another in our councils." Royalist

[38] Journal 41, fol. 213; *Clarke Papers*, IV, 186; Rugg, *Diurnal*, pp. 17, 19; Ludlow, *Memoirs*, II, 177–8; Woolrych, *Milton*, VII, 147–50; Hutton, *Restoration*, p. 80.

[39] Journal 41, fol. 213; MS Clarendon 67, fol. 209 a–b, 220–221, 246–247, 250–251; *CLSP*, III, 628, 631; *At a Common Councel holden in the Guild-hall London . . . 14th of December, 1659* [1659]; *Mercurius Politicus* 598 (8–15 Dec. 1659) [misleading]; *Nicholas Papers*, IV, 191; Mordaunt, *Letter-book*, p. 141; *Clarke Papers*, IV, 187; *Warriston Diary*, p. 158; Guizot, *History*, II, 307–8, 311.

agents, who had previously hoped that the Corporation would challenge the regime for them, now turned their attention to inciting an apprentice insurrection.[40]

The army's constitutional formula had clearly failed to satisfy the popular demand in London for a parliament. And on 20–21 December, the Corporation moved, again with some confusion, toward positions that would contribute directly to the collapse of the army and eventually to the collapse of the Commonwealth. On the 20th, common council declared for a "free parliament." Deceptively clear, the city's declaration for a free parliament was not, however, intended to tie the Corporation, exclusively, to the position advanced by the apprentices and other parliamentary advocates. Instead, the Corporation's declaration is best interpreted as an open-ended employment of popular rhetoric in order to advance peace among the different positions being articulated in London and the nation. According to the French ambassador, the "diversity of opinions resulted in the company agreeing to general terms." The declaration for a "free parliament" distanced the city from Monck, Lawson, and others who advocated the Rump. It distanced the city from the efforts of some Presbyterians to secure the return of the entire Long Parliament, a position now linked to speculation about restoring the king according to the terms offered Charles I in 1648. Finally, it distanced the city from the parliament offered by the army. However, since the ruling Committee was also distancing itself from its previous parliamentary formula, the city's loose declaration for a free parliament was also interpreted by ardent proponents of a new parliament as a submission to the army – or as leaving "the army at liberty to choose whichever [parliament] it should please."[41]

The annual selection of common councilmen by ward electors on the 21st made clear that the city's declaration for a free parliament on the 20th was insufficient in the eyes of many who desired a regime truly free of army interference. The common council elections for 1660 were a watershed event in the fall of the Committee of Safety and in the eventual fall of the republic. They demonstrated both the extent to which the London citizenry disliked the army and the extent to which they were disappointed by the muddled and

---

[40] Repertory 67, fol. 27; MS Clarendon 67, fols. 240–241, 249, 252, 262; Clarendon MS 68, fols. 10, 17, 18, 35, 40; *CLSP*, III, 638; *The Final Protest and Sense of the City* [1659]; *Englands Present Case Stated* [1659]; *Mercurius Politicus* 599 (15–22 Dec. 1659); *Nicholas Papers*, IV, 192; *Clarke Papers*, IV, 210–11; Rugg, *Diurnal*, pp. 17–18, 19–20; HMC *Seventh Report*, p. 483; Ludlow, *Memoirs*, II, 174–5; Guizot, *History*, II, 309–10; Whitelocke, *Memorials*, p. 691.

[41] Journal 41, fol. 213; *At a Common Councel holden in the Guildhall London, …the 20th of December, 1659* (1659); *The Resolve of the City* [1659]; *Mercurius Politicus* 599 (15–22 Dec. 1659); Guizot, *History*, II, 313–16; Rugg, *Diurnal*, p. 20; *Warriston Diary* p. 159; HMC *Seventh Report*, p. 461; Woolrych, *Milton*, VII, 152.

divided counsels that had prevailed in the city since October, and especially since 5 December.

Approximately one-third of the common councilmen chosen for 1660 had not served in the previous year. Many of the new members were prominent Presbyterians still committed to the Solemn League and Covenant.[42] Their election completed a process whereby Presbyterians regained the dominant civic voice they had lost in 1648–9. Among those common councilmen of 1659 not re-elected for 1660 were many who had been particularly active in 1649–52, in the flush years of civic revolution, and others who may be identified with religious separatism. The French ambassador believed that "all those Sectaries who lean towards the army were excluded."[43] The city was now largely in the hands of those who had once fought for king-in-parliament against the king only to lose both king and parliament to the army. They were joined by Stuart loyalists who had never accepted the 1640s' reformation of church and state. Whether the royalist rhetoric now gaining greater currency in political conversation and in the prints would strengthen or weaken this political alliance of old antagonists remained to be seen.

In any case, the new common council wasted no time in charting a bold and independent course for the city, a course that astonished and challenged all other parties to the nation's constitutional and military impasse. The temporizing and caution of Lord Mayor Alleyn and his aldermanic colleagues were abandoned as common council directly confronted an unpopular and discredited military regime. Meeting the day after their election, the common councilmen purged the city's committee of safety of those members with any republican ties, replacing them with leading Reformed Protestants like Sheriff William Love and with Anglican royalists like common councilman Richard Ford. On the following day, they adopted a report from the new committee declaring that "the Citty of London is at this tyme in Imminent & Extraordinary danger," and they tightened their control of the London militia. As common council set about appointing its own commanders for the trained bands, they also appointed commissioners to treat with Fleetwood, with the Rump leaders at Portsmouth, and with Vice-Admiral Lawson, for the sole purpose of "ye Conveneinge of a free parliament."[44]

As the Corporation acted, panic and indecision gripped the Committee of Safety, which now faced a choice between accepting the return of the parliament they had interrupted in October or acquiescing to the demand for

---

[42] *Admonition of the greatest Concernment* [1659]; *London's Out-Cry to her Sister-Cities* [1659]; Rugg, *Diurnal*, p. 20.

[43] *Warriston Diary*, p. 161; HMC *Seventh Report*, p. 461; Guizot, *History*, II, 317; Mordaunt, *Letter-book*, p. 146; Elliot, "Elections," esp. pp. 157–65, 171.

[44] Journal 41, fols. 214–215; MS Clarendon 68, fols. 11–12; Mordaunt, *Letter-book*, pp. 146, 151; *Mercurius Politicus* 600 (22–29 Dec. 1659); Rugg, *Diurnal*, p. 20; Guizot, *History*, II, 320; Henning, *House of Commons*, II, 344.

a free parliament. Regiments sent by the regime against Portsmouth had gone over to the Rump, and some regiments in London had also declared for it. The city's commissioners to Fleetwood, on the other hand, kept up their pressure for a free parliament, offering contributions toward the arrears of the army if the Committee would agree to one instead of restoring the Rump. The Committee responded by sending writs for a "free" parliamentary election to the Sheriffs of London and Middlesex on 21 December but then recalling them.[45]

In the end, Fleetwood and the Committee resigned their authority to the Rump rather than follow the city's lead. On 24 December, Speaker Lenthall and members of the deposed Council of State re-emerged to order a general muster of the London regiments for the following day. Without exception, the regiments acknowledged the Speaker's authority and that of the parliament he represented. Elsewhere in the country, many regiments were in the process of renouncing the Committee; and most of the soldiers with Lambert in the north decamped, returning to their previously assigned quarters. Lenthall and Sir Anthony Ashley Cooper visited the lord mayor and London sheriffs, informing them that the Rump would reconvene on the 26th; and the republican government retook possession of the Tower. Westminster, the army, and the Tower were again in the hands of those who had made the revolution of 1648–9 and purged the Long Parliament. London, on the other hand, was in the hands of those who had opposed revolution in 1648–9 and whose demand for a parliament could never be satisfied by what was left of the Rump. The reciprocal animosity between the returned Rump and an antagonistic city was at the center of a deepening crisis.[46]

THE REVOLT OF THE CITY

Now in its third sitting as the parliament of the English republic, the Rump quickly failed to persuade the advocates of parliamentary government that it represented a return to legitimacy. The few dozen MPs who reassembled at Westminster could not persuade a critical mass of active London citizens that they either constituted a free parliament or were sympathetic to the demand for one. They were no more successful in reassuring the many county and borough spokesmen who looked to the Corporation for political leadership, or – in the end – in reassuring the enigmatic commander of the Scottish forces, who had insisted upon the Rump's return as a re-establishment of parliamentary authority.

---

[45] MS Clarendon 67, fol. 344; MS Clarendon 68, fols. 16–18, 22, 26r; *CLSP*, III, 633–4, 647; HMC *Seventh Report*, p. 461; *Warriston Diary*, p. 161; *Clarke Papers*, IV, 215–16; Guizot, *History*, II, 317; Davies, *Restoration*, pp. 187–8; Woolrych, *Milton*, VII, 154; Hutton, *Restoration*, pp. 81–2.

[46] *Clarke Papers*, IV, 219–20; Rugg, *Diurnal* pp. 21–3; Guizot, *History*, II, 318–19, 321; Davies, *Restoration*, pp. 188–9; Woolrych, *Milton*, VII, 154–5.

The history of the Rump's last sitting has often been presented as the story of General Monck's progressive disillusionment with it, culminating in his insistence that the secluded members be readmitted in order to settle the nation with a Stuart restoration. But any historical construction that assumes that the Rump's discontented general was the prime mover in its demise, or in the rising fortunes of Charles Stuart, cannot adequately account for the sequence of events in the last two months of the republic. In fact, the Corporation of London remained the principal catalyst in the crisis after the Rump's return. The city rejected the MPs' legitimacy from the outset and immediately wrote Monck in support of the "Freedom of Parliaments." Although Lord Mayor Alleyn and some aldermen prevaricated, the common council did not at any point acknowledge the authority of the parliamentary fragment that sat at Westminster, treating with them only insofar as the MPs laid claim to the authority of the Long Parliament. This standoff between the Rump and the city quickly embroiled the nation, provoking a flood of "jeering" and "abusey bookes" and ballads that reflected and directed the sentiments of the reading public.[47]

The city's intransigence can largely be explained by the strengthening conviction that the liberties and rights of the Corporation and of its citizens were endangered by the succession of republican regimes that failed to represent electors in London and elsewhere. As the movement for a free parliament continued to develop, more and more attention was paid in the prints and the political discourse of the capital to the electoral rights of all those traditionally represented in parliament. The idea of a free parliament was also obviously endorsed and promoted by those who were actively committed to Charles Stuart, but many in the city were attracted to the cause of parliament on its own merits. The Corporation's new leadership demanded a free parliament as part of the country's ancient and accustomed constitution, largely without acknowledging the increasing possibility that the readmission of the secluded members or the election of a new parliament might also entail a return to Stuart monarchy.

In the meantime, General Monck commenced his January progress to Westminster, doing so without specific authorization from the Rump. At Westminster, however, MPs were more concerned about the immediate prospect of resistance from the city than about Monck; and they also remained uncertain about the loyalty of some country regiments. Common council had taken the defense of the city in hand by setting up posts and chains in the streets and by refurbishing the portcullises at the gates. Eyeing these measures on their first day of business, the MPs moved to secure the Tower of London, which was temporarily placed under the command of Sir

---

[47] Rugg, *Diurnal* pp. 23, 26.

Anthony Ashley Cooper. Common council responded by drafting a petition that demanded the readmission of the secluded members and that asserted the Corporation's right of settling the trained bands. The French ambassador learned that some citizens favored using the London militia "to put an end to the session of the present Parliament" if the Rump failed to readmit the secluded members. Another rumor suggested the secluded members might constitute themselves as the true representatives of the nation and meet as a parliament under the protection of the Corporation.

When the expelled MPs actually sought admission to the Rump, however, they were foiled by troops; and they were also without the support of the promised Corporation petition. Common council had dropped its inflammatory address, and the lord mayor and aldermen adopted a more conciliatory stance. When the Rump voted against the raising of militias by any without their orders, the citizens' bluff was called. The Speaker and other MPs visited the lord mayor and aldermen on 31 December, securing their agreement to take down their posts and chains and, according to a republican account, to "own this Parliament." Much as the common council leaders disliked the Rump, few of them were yet prepared to risk their property and the city's security in a direct confrontation. Nevertheless, common council proceeded in its reconstitution of the London militia.[48]

Passionate royalists were disappointed at the citizens' failure to take on the regime at this juncture. "The City are sneakers," Sir Edward Hyde (Charles's lord chancellor) was informed, having moderated their intransigence again, as in early December, and "now are obedient asses and willing to be ridden." But such stark thoughts were premature. As the Rump divided again between republican and pragmatic factions, and as speculation about Monck's intentions continued, the city remained essentially out of control. Neither the Rump's election of such prominent London merchants as Sheriff Love and Slingsby Bethel to the reconstituted Council of State, nor its decision to fill up its membership with new elections (rather than with the secluded members) reassured hostile citizens. Nor did the behavior of Sir Arthur Hesilrige, spokesmen for committed republican MPs. In a January parley between visiting MPs and city magistrates, he charged that the city's charter was forfeit

---

[48] Journal 41, fols. 216–218; *CJ*, VII, 796, 802; Clarendon MS 68, fols. 48–49, 53–54, 63–64, 85–86; *A True Copy of the Letter sent from the Lord Mayor, Aldermen and Common-Council . . . on the 29th of December, 1659. Directed to . . . George Monck*; C. D., *A Seasonable Letter of Advice delivered to the Lord Mayor of London* [1659]; *Publick Intelligencer* 209–210 (26 Dec. 1659–2 Jan. 1660, 2–9 Jan. 1660), 988, 992; *Mercurius Politicus* 601 (29 Dec. 1659–5 Jan. 1660), 995; Rugg, *Diurnal*, pp. 23, 25; *The Diary of Samuel Pepys*, ed. R. Latham and W. Matthews, 11 vols. (Berkeley and Los Angeles, 1970–83), I, 1, 3; Whitelocke, *Memorials*, p. 694; Gumble, *Life*, p. 200; *OPH*, XXII, 48–50; Guizot, *History*, II, 320–1, 323, 325; Davies, *Restoration*, pp. 256–7; Woolrych, *Milton*, VII, 157–8; Hutton, *Restoration*, p. 88; Haley, *Shaftesbury*, p. 123.

through its disloyalty to the regime. When apprentices mocked John Hewson and other enemies in snow sculptures, Hesilrige gathered some regiments at Somerset House on the 17th and marched with them through the Corporation, a provocative gesture met by "many hard words." As Monck proceeded southward, each side merely waited to secure the general's assistance in putting down the other.[49]

The city's confidence in Monck was somewhat shaken by an ambiguous letter he sent in early January. The general acknowledged the city's long-time leadership in securing "the Freedom of successive Parliaments" against "Tyranny and Arbitrary Government," but he was equally outspoken in acknowledging the "just and lawful Authority" of "this Parliament." After some deliberation, the Corporation sent three commissioners, all Presbyterians, to meet the general *en route* and to communicate with him. This decision displeased the MPs, who had already sent their own commissioners to greet the general. In the meantime, civic royalists, distrustful of "this clouded Soldier," charted their own course. Alderman John Robinson, together with his Presbyterian colleagues John Langham and Richard Browne, were apparently raising money for Lord Mordaunt in the hope of buying off some of the London regiments in favor of the king.[50]

General Monck suffered from no lack of advice during his progress to London and Westminster. A broad public repudiation of the Rump was in full swing, and the Corporation was widely perceived as being at the center of it. The general received several county petitions *en route* that called for a free parliament or for the readmission of the secluded members.[51] Some of these county addresses referred to the militant stance of the Corporation of London as an example for the remainder of the nation. The remonstrating "knights, gentlemen, and freeholders" of Gloucester, for instance, saw their refusal to accept the Rump's authority as a joining with the Corporation of London, as did a similar body of petitioners from Warwickshire. Presbyterians in Lincolnshire and Suffolk wrote to the Corporation in support of common council's declaration for a free parliament. And Charles's agents in the field

---

[49] MS Clarendon 68, fols. 104, 146; *CJ*, VII, 801; *CSP Ven 1659–61*, p. 112; *Mercurius Politicus* 603 (12–19 Jan. 1660), 1035; *Publick Intelligencer* 212 (16–23 Jan. 1660), 1026; Guizot, *History*, II, 330; Pepys, *Diary*, I, 9, 16, 28; Rugg, *Diurnal*, pp. 27, 29; Davies, *Restoration*, pp. 260, 272; Woodhead, *Rulers*, p. 74.

[50] MS Clarendon 68, fols. 146, 159, 173, 175; *CLSP*, III, 649–50; Journal 41, fol. 219; *Two Letters; the One, Sent by the Lord Mayor . . . to Gen. Monck* [1660], p. 5; *OPH*, XXII, 50–3; *CSP Ven 1659–60*, p. 112; Pepys, *Diary*, I, 16, 22; Mordaunt, *Letter-book*, p. 165; Guizot, *History*, II, 330, 332; Gumble, *Life*, p. 219; Woolrych, *Milton*, VII, 160.

[51] *A Declaration of the People of England for a Free-Parliament* [1660]; *A Free Parliament*; Rugg, *Diurnal*, pp. 27, 29, 31–2; Gumble, *Life*, p. 223; Ashley, *Monck*, p. 189; Hutton, *Restoration*, p. 89; D. Ogg, *England in the Reign of Charles II* (Oxford, 1934), p. 20; Haley, *Shaftesbury*, p. 126.

regarded London as "the master wheel, by whose motion the successive rotations of all the lesser must follow."[52]

In response to this outpouring of dissatisfaction, Monck again broke his cautious silence in the third week of January. From the Midlands, he publicly endorsed the authority of the Rump, as he had before, also decrying a return to monarchy on any terms. And he spoke and acted in a manner consistent with such statements after being joined by the parliamentary commissioners, Thomas Scot and Luke Robinson. When the commissioners sent by common council met with the general at Market Harborough, the city's bidding for the general's support against the republican MPs was starkly revealed: they pleaded the case of the secluded members and pointed out how "unreasonable" it was that the citizens "should be Govern'd by a Parliament, where they had not their Representatives."[53] Monck's refusal to break with the Rump at this point, despite the city's overtures, reassured and emboldened the MPs. They now pressed ahead with renewed assertions of their authority, declaring that the House would be filled up through new elections and adopting an assessment bill to fund the government, despite the nation's weariness with taxes.[54]

Just as much as Monck's approach to the capital, the Rump's resolve to tax brought the crisis to a head. Because the confusing events that followed led eventually to bringing in the king, the point needs to be stressed again that many citizens who defied the Rump were interested, in the first instance, in bringing in a parliament. That *"Parliaments are the Constitution Fundamental of the Nation"* was the chief premise of the Rump's London adversaries. Against the Rump's assertion of authority, its detractors turned all the familiar parliamentary rhetoric of the 1640s. According to one London address, those sitting at Westminster were nothing more than "Betrayers of the Peoples Rights, and Subverters of the Fundamental Laws of the English Nation." Maintained in their first sitting by the army, they were guilty of "failing in their Trust," of exercising an "Arbitrary Power and Will, contrary to all Civill and Religious bonds." Or, as Monck was informed at St Albans, by spokesmen who claimed "election" by the "apprentices and young men" of

---

[52] MS Clarendon 69, fols. 7–8; *Remonstrance of the Knights, Gentlemen, and Freeholders of the County of Gloucester* [1660]; *Mercurius Politicus* 605 (26 Jan.–2 Feb. 1660), 1064–7; *CLSP*, III, 654, 659–60; *CSPD 1659–60*, pp. 336, 340–1; Guizot, *History*, II, 333; Henning, *House of Commons*, III, 351; Woolrych, *Milton*, VII, 160–1; Hutton, *Restoration*, p. 88.

[53] MS Clarendon 69, fols. 9–10, 39; Baker, *Chronicle*, p. 742; Gumble, *Life*, p. 222; *OPH*, XXII, 68–71; Rugg, *Diurnal*, p. 31; Ashley, *Monck*, pp. 187–8; Woolrych, *Milton*, VII, 161–2; Hutton, *Restoration*, p. 90.

[54] *CJ*, VII, 818, 823; Guizot, *History*, II, 336–9; Rugg, *Diurnal*, p. 30; Pepys, *Diary*, I, 30, 33; *CSPVen 1659–61*, p. 113.

the city, the Rump's power was a denial of the birthright of every freeborn Englishman:

> our Civil Interest . . . consists in the Priviledges and Liberties to which we were born, and which are the undoubted Inheritance of all the free people of *England*, among which the grand and Essential Priviledge which discriminates free men from slaves, is the interest which every man hath in the legislative power of the Nation, by their Representatives assembled in Parliament: without which . . . we are truly no better than Vassals.[55]

However, those who demanded a restoration of free parliaments in this wintertime of the republic were far from repudiating the concerns that had prompted many of them (or their fathers and masters) to support parliament against the crown in the 1640s. Instead, the movement for a free parliament was taken up in "the defence of Religion, the Priviledges of Parliament, and Liberties of the Subject," or in the same "Cause for which we contended, in our adherency to the Parliament in the late War." Chief among the "liberties of the subject" for which the war had been fought was that of being taxed by no other means "than the Consent of the People in Parliament assembled," as the London common councilmen were reminded in one address. Just as Charles I's personal rule had collapsed amidst a national taxpayers' revolt, so now the credibility of a very different regime was similarly compromised by a perception that it presumed to tax without the consent of the duly chosen representatives of the electorate.[56]

The opposition to the Rump in London and elsewhere was, therefore, held together by the libertarian rhetoric of the 1640s; but different people employed that rhetoric for different purposes. The movement for a free parliament attracted many citizens attached to the claims of parliament, other citizens for whom the desirability of a return to monarchy was becoming an important sub-text, and still others for whom a Stuart restoration was now perhaps becoming the main text. Some excluded Presbyterian MPs, for instance, were reportedly agreed by late January upon "recalling the King . . . upon conditions which will not destroy the liberty of the people." Still, the royalist label is of limited utility in characterizing a parliamentary movement as diverse as that which engulfed the Rump. For most active

---

[55] *A Free Parliament; To the Right Honourable the Lord Maior, Aldermen, and Common Councel. . . . The Humble Petition and Remonstrance of Several Inhabitants and Citizens* [1660]; *To his Excellency the Lord General Monck. The Unanimous Representation of the Apprentices* [1660]; *Londons Diurnal* 1 (1–8 Feb. 1660), 2–3; *CSPD 1659–60*, pp. 340, 344; HMC *Leyborne-Popham*, p 144. My argument here follows that of Harris, *London Crowds*, pp. 36–7, 46–7.

[56] *To the . . . Lord Maior. . . . Petition and Remonstrance of Several Inhabitants and Citizens; Remonstrance of . . . Gloucester; To his Excellency the Lord General Monck; Remonstrance of the Noble-men, Knights, Gentlemen . . . of the late Eastern, Southern, and Western Associations* [1660]; *CSPD 1659–61*, p. 345.

London citizens, the principal object by February 1660 was simply to achieve a representative parliament as the "Bulwark" of "our Liberties."[57]

The conduct of George Monck in the three weeks following his arrival at Barnet, in Middlesex, should also be interpreted in light of this distinction between attachment to parliamentary government and attachment to the king. Royalist agents who distrusted the general would have been surprised by the conventional depiction of him as a wily royalist who acted according to a premeditated design.[58] Monck entered the maelstrom of Westminster and London politics with some firm guiding principles, but a commitment to Charles Stuart was not among them. He was instead committed to the maintenance of public magistracy and ministry and to the subordination or dispersal of forces in the capital not directly under his command. Most importantly, he was devoted to the settlement of the nation on the basis of parliamentary government, and his support for the Rump was dependent upon his perception of it as representing a recovery of parliamentary government from uppity officers and sectarians. Guided by these sentiments, Monck confronted a political tug-of-war between hostile MPs and citizens in which he was forced to intervene, now on one side, but ultimately on the other.

Civil order began to disintegrate in London immediately upon Monck's arrival in the capital, and developments elsewhere encouraged the belief that a broader collapse of authority was in the offing. The first ten days of February witnessed a mutiny of the English regiments already in London and a rising of several hundred city apprentices. Disturbances either broke out or threatened to break out in such regional centers as Bristol and Gloucester; and royalist agents redoubled their efforts to turn these events to the king's advantage. The London common council assumed the premier place in a gathering taxpayers' revolt; and the Rump responded by ordering a military occupation of the Corporation.[59]

The general responded to these events in a flexible manner, adjusting his actions the better to promote his principles, as changing circumstances suggested. Dubious about the reliability of the regiments in London, he requested that all but two of them be relocated elsewhere. The Rump agreed to Monck's suggestions, despite suspicions about the general from the more extreme MPs and outrage among soldiers who feared they would be dispersed without being paid. Mutiny among the foot regiments began at St James's Fields on 1 February; and it soon spread to Somerset House, which was occupied next day by soldiers who had thrown off their officers. By that time "all ye

---

[57] *A Free Parliament*; *Remonstrance of ... Gloucester*; Guizot, *History*, II, 331; Woolrych, *Milton*, VII, 161.

[58] For the conventional interpretation, see Ashley, *Monck*, esp. chs. 14–15.

[59] HMC *Fifth Report*, p. 181; *Warriston Diary*, pp. 174–5; HMC *Leyborne-Popham*, p. 148.

Towne was in a Tumult," with some thousands of troops out of control and with armed altercations in the Strand between mutineers and regiments of horse obedient to the parliamentary Council of State. Some of the mutineers may have cried out for the king, and some may have demanded Lambert back, but most of the shouting would appear to have been against the Rump and on behalf of a free parliament. As these scenes unfolded, large numbers of watermen were also to be found milling about Westminster, where they declared "for the City & Counties that have desired a free parliament."[60]

The mutiny was welcomed by disaffected apprentices who commenced a rising of their own on the night of 2 February. One observer reported that the apprentices wanted the "king and liberty," but the apprentices' disturbance coincided with a petition presented to Monck by some of their number for "Libertie, [and] Free Parliaments." Several hundred apprentices marched down Cheapside seeking to arouse the citizenry. But they were surprised and overwhelmed by a regiment of horse sent by the Council, which had been in communication with the lord mayor. Most of the apprentices escaped down the alleys and over the rooftops; but forty were captured and imprisoned to await trial on serious charges. The failure of the apprentices sobered most of the mutinous soldiers, who now agreed to depart the capital with assurances about their pay.[61]

When Monck entered London on 3 February, he must have been disturbed about these scenes of ordinary soldiers defying their officers, of mechanics massing at Whitehall, and of apprentices usurping the political roles of their masters. His entrance route – down Gray's Inn Lane to Holborn and Chancery Lane, and then to Whitehall through the Strand – was carefully chosen to distance himself from the politically impetuous householders of the Corporation. But Monck could not close his ears to popular expectations: the only shouts that greeted him in the streets were those for a free parliament. In response, when he appeared before the House on the 6th, he called for the broadest civil settlement possible as the only way to bring "the people" to "unite themselves with the present parliament." To lead the way, he declined to take the oath abjuring the Stuarts; and he recommended, contrary to the Rump's intention, that the parliament be filled up without the

---

[60] MS Clarendon 69, fols. 53–54, 55–57, 72; *CLSP*, III, 668; *CSPD 1659–60*, p. 357; *The Remonstrance of the Soldiery* [1660]; *Londons Diurnal* 1 (1–8 Feb. 1660), 5; Rugg, *Diurnal*, pp. 32–3, 34–5; Pepys, *Diary*, I, 36–8; *Warriston Diary*, p. 175; HMC *Fifth Report*, p. 181; HMC *Leyborne-Popham*, p. 144; Guizot, *History*, II, 342; *OPH*, XXII, 117–18; Ludlow, *Memoirs*, II, 214; Christie, *Life*, I, 205; Woolrych, *Milton*, VII, 164–5; Hutton, *Restoration*, pp. 90–1; Harris, *London Crowds*, pp. 47–8.

[61] MS Clarendon 69, fols. 81–82; *To his Excellency*; *Mercurius Politicus* 606 (2–9 Feb. 1660), 1073–4; *Publick Intelligencer* 214 (30 Jan.–6 Feb. 1660), 1067–8; *CSPD 1659–60*, pp. 344–5; *Londons Diurnal* 1 (1–8 Feb. 1660), 4–6; Rugg, *Diurnal*, pp. 34–5; Pepys, *Diary*, I, 39; Guizot, *History*, II, 342–3; Baker, *Chronicle*, p. 743; Woolrych, *Milton*, VII, 165–6.

imposition of restrictive oaths and qualifications.[62] The speech infuriated the more intransigent MPs who persuaded the House to ignore Monck's title of commander-in-chief and instead to treat with him only as one of several army commissioners-general. Despite this hostile gesture, Monck remained respectful of the sitting parliament.[63]

Within days, the Corporation of London tested both Monck and the Rump by denying the Rump's right to tax. Common council received addresses against the payment of taxes from Suffolk and Warwickshire on 8 February. Another address from "divers" London citizens argued that the Rump's impositions would leave them in "perpetual slavery" and that their "undoubted Birthright" was to be taxed only by a "*Full* and *Free Parliament*" made up of the "rightfull Representatives of the people." In response, common council apparently voted to refuse taxes until the city's four parliamentary seats were filled. Or, in the words of contemporaries, they again refused to "own the Parliament," in order to "defend the liberties of the whole nation and of the City."[64]

Propelled into action by the more extreme Hesilrige-Scot faction, the Council of State moved quickly to prevent this revolt of the city from spreading. It ordered the army commissioners to occupy the Corporation, to dismantle the city gates, to remove all posts and chains in the streets, and to arrest ten common councilmen and one alderman. The full Rump also voided the election of the current common council, began drafting an act for the election of a new common council with restrictive qualifications, and considered another act for the reconstitution of the London militia. And it received a carefully orchestrated petition in defense of these actions from Praise-God Barebone and other sectarian citizens.[65] The hostility between the Corporation and the Rump had finally brought the two governments into active

---

[62] *The Lord General Monck, his Speech delivered in Parliament* (1660); Pepys, *Diary*, I, 40; Rugg, *Diurnal*, p. 35; *CSPVen 1659–61*, pp. 116–17; Guizot, *History*, II, 343–4; Ludlow, *Memoirs*, II, 216; Gumble, *Life*, pp. 228, 230–3; Baker, *Chronicle*, 743; *OPH*, XXII, 89–90; Ashley, *Monck*, p. 195; Woolrych, *Milton*, VII, 167.

[63] HMC *Seventh Report*, pp. 462, 483; *CSPD 1659–60*, p. 347; Pepys, *Diary*, I, 45; Hutton, *Restoration*, p. 91.

[64] Journal 41, fol. 219. The account of this meeting in the Journal is incomplete. MS Clarendon 69, fols. 117, 126, 171; Guizot, *History*, II, 345. *To the Right Honourable the Lord Maior, Aldermen, and Commons of the City of London.... The Humble Petition of divers Well-Affected Householders and Freemen* [1660]; *Peace to the Nation* [1660]; *Wee the Knights, Gentlemen, Ministers, and Free-Holders of the County of Warwick* (1660); *A Letter agreed unto, and subscribed by, the Gentlemen, Ministers, Freeholders...of Suffolk. Presented to the Lord Mayor* (1660); *CJ*, VII, 834; *Acts and Ordinances of the Interregnum*, II, 1355ff.; *CSPVen 1659–61*, p. 116; *CLSP*, III, 674; HMC *Seventh Report*, pp. 462, 483; HMC *Leyborne-Popham*, p. 143; Rugg, *Diurnal*, p. 38; Pepys, *Diary*, I, 45, 47; Ludlow, *Memoirs*, II, 217; Baker, *Chronicle*, p. 746; Woolrych, *Milton*, VII, 161, 167–8.

[65] *The Petition of Mr. Praise-God Barebone, and several others, to the Parliament* (1660).

political warfare. Only one government could survive this contest, and the future of the nation's settlement depended upon the outcome.

Much evidence actually suggests that the city's defiance of the Rump was about to be imitated by opponents of the regime elsewhere, many of whom were already in communication with the city and with each other. The Council possessed intercepted letters that pointed to widespread support for a national tax strike, a political maneuvre that royalist agents were also actively promoting. Opposition was expected to the collection of assessments in the north; and a delegation from Yorkshire was shortly to make its way to the Corporation. More ominously, Suffolk was rumored to have promised the common council thousands of men; and the seamen of that county and of Norfolk were said to be ready for resistance. Apprentices in Bristol and Gloucester had taken their demand for a free parliament into the streets, and another mutiny occurred at Gravesend.[66]

The Rump's position at this juncture was as clear as that of the Corporation. But the position of George Monck, who carried out the orders directed to the army's commissioners, was not. Occupying the city with some 6,000 troops and horse, early on the morning of the 9th, and remaining until the afternoon of the 10th, Monck was confronted by much astonishment on the part of those who had thought him a friend to a free parliament. The general succeeded in arresting most of those named by the Rump, who included two of the commissioners sent to him by the Corporation in January. He deployed his soldiers at strategic points throughout the city and removed the posts and chains from the streets. Monck's carrying out of his orders was entirely consistent with his respect for parliamentary authority and with his concern about military resources – in this case, the London militia – in uncertain hands.[67]

---

[66] MS Clarendon 69, fols. 39, 93, 123 127; *A Letter and Declaration of the Nobility and Gentry of . . . York to . . . Monck* [1660]; *A Letter of the Apprentices of the City of Bristoll, to the Apprentices of the Honourable City of London* (1660); *CJ*, VII, 837–8; *Mercurius Politicus* 606–7 (2–9, 9–16 Feb. 1660), 1084, 1096–8, 1108; *The Publick Intelligencer* 215–16 (6–11, 13–20 Feb. 1660), 1085, 1088–9, 1097; *An Exact Accompt of the daily Proceedings in Parliament* 63 (3–10 Feb. 1660), 654–6; *Londons Diurnal* 1 (1–8 Feb. 1660), 4–6; *CSPD 1659–60*, pp. 356, 359, 570; *CSP Ven 1659–61*, pp. 116–17; Guizot, *History*, II, 343, 345; *OPH*, XXII, 91–7, 121; HMC *Leyborne-Popham*, pp. 142, 145, 148, 215; Pepys, *Diary*, I, 49; Rugg, *Diurnal*, pp. 37, 39, 40–2; Ludlow, *Memoirs*, II, 218–19; Baker, *Chronicle*, p. 747; W. C. Braithwaite, *The Beginnings of Quakerism*, 2nd ed. (Cambridge, 1955), p. 470; Davis, "Cromwell's Religion," pp. 278–9, 286; Woolrych, *Milton*, VII, 168–9; Haley, *Shaftesbury*, p. 127; Hutton, *Restoration*, pp. 91–2.

[67] MS Clarendon 69, fols. 95, 117, 124, *A Letter of his Excellencie the Lord General Monck, to the Speaker of the Parl.* (1660); *CSP Ven 1659–61*, p. 116; *OPH*, XXII, 109–10, 121; Guizot, *History*, II, 345–7; Rugg, *Diurnal*, p. 38; Gumble, *Life*, pp. 236–42; Pepys, *Diary*, I, 51; Christie, *Life*, I, 205–7; Ashley, *Monck*, pp. 197–8; Davis, "Cromwell's Religion," pp. 278–9; Woolrych, *Milton*, VII, 169, 171; Hutton, *Restoration*, p. 93. That Monck ever expressed support for a reduction of the city in the harsh words attributed to him by Edmund Ludlow is unlikely. Ludlow, *Memoirs*, II, 219–20.

But as he carried out his orders, General Monck may also have begun to realize that a policy of coercion was unlikely to bring the city to a genuine submission or to further his goal of settlement. Seeking to parley with city leaders, the general instead encountered their distrust and disappointment. John Jolliffe, a Presbyterian common councilman and leading Levant merchant, for instance, told him that the employment of force against the city would be no more effective now than it had been for the Committee of Safety in December. When Monck appeared at the court of aldermen, suggesting that he might be able to persuade parliament to moderate its punishment of the city, the aldermen refused to act without common council or even to express their own minds. As his soldiers stood around Guildhall, turning away common councilmen who sought to meet in defiance of the Rump, the general was told that "hee might plunder their houses but they would not pay one Farthing without a free Pa[rliamen]t." And "many" in the city "did...curse and sweare att him like divells." Rumors circulated that the government would impose a punitive fine of £600,000 upon the city and revoke its charter; but the general may well have wondered how either assessments or fines could be forced from such recalcitrant citizens.[68]

Retiring to Whitehall on the 10th, with much of his army but without parliamentary orders to leave the city, Monck "began to think over what he had done." Trusted officers and soldiers had already expressed their distaste for the humiliation of the city. Now their objections were seconded by Monck's wife, by sympathetic visitors like Sir Anthony Ashley Cooper, and by Monck's brother-in-law, Thomas Clarges, who pleaded the city's case for settlement and a free parliament. Clarges reportedly argued, with considerable effect, that if London "should be made a Village," then "all the Cities and Towns would be Alarm'd, believing...their Franchises and Priviledges would be quickly subverted." Suspicious of "fanatics," the general had also just implemented a policy in the city that was seemingly supported only by its sectarian inhabitants. Finally, the general's family and friends suggested that intransigent Rump MPs were abusing his respect for parliament in order to manipulate him. As if to confirm this suggestion, the Westminster politicians proceeded with a new bill to resettle the army leadership in commission, thereby depriving the general of the unified command he had just employed on their behalf.[69]

---

[68] Repertory 67, fol. 42; MS Clarendon 69, fols. 95, 126–127, 171; *CLSP*, III, 674–5; *Peace to the Nation* (1660); Gumble in *OPH*, XXII, 109, 112; HMC *Leyborne-Popham*, pp. 215–17; *CSPVen 1659–61*, p. 117; Rugg, *Diurnal*, p. 38; Pepys, *Diary*, I, 51; *Warriston Diary*, p. 176; Baker, *Chronicle*, p. 746; Gumble, *Life*, p. 243; Davis, "Cromwell's Religion," p. 270; Henning, *House of Commons*, II, 657; Elliot, "Elections," p. 173; Woodhead, *Rulers*, p. 99.

[69] MS Clarendon 69, fols. 123–124, 145, 171; *CLSP*, III, 692; Guizot, *History*, II, 348–9; *CJ*, VII, 840; HMC *Leyborne-Popham*, pp. 217–18; Rugg, *Diurnal*, pp. 38–40; Pepys, *Diary*, I,

The result of Monck's overnight considerations was a reversal of his position vis-à-vis parliament and the city that was apparent in two initiatives taken on 11 February. The first of these was a letter to parliament from Monck and his principal officers. They demanded that the Rump issue writs for filling up the House within one week. Once full, the House should conclude their sitting and give way to a freely elected parliament as soon as possible, but no later than May. The second initiative was a decision to move that part of his army in Westminster to Finsbury Fields in preparation for its reunion with those forces still in the city. This redeployment of his army within the Corporation was intended to join the principal army of the Commonwealth with the city friends of a parliamentary settlement and thereby to increase the pressure upon the Rump.[70]

The reconciliation that Monck now desired with the city was not easily accomplished, however. As news spread that the general was drawing up his forces again on the outskirts of the city, so did anxiety about his purposes. The citizens had just experienced a military occupation, and London's defenses were gone. The court of aldermen refused to consent to Monck's request for the quartering of troops among the citizens, even after reading his letter to the Rump. At length, Lord Mayor Alleyn invited the general to enter the city, without his troops, to parley over dinner; and it was only then that the ice began to break. Monck's discussion with the lord mayor was interrupted by the appearance of MPs Thomas Scot and Luke Robinson, acting as messengers for the Rump, which had read his letter with displeasure and demanded his return to Whitehall. But Monck refused to comply, rebuffing the messengers in the lord mayor's presence, and proceeding instead to an extraordinary meeting of common council at Guildhall, the very convening of which was a further act of defiance.[71]

By now, panic had given place to hope: throngs gathered around Guildhall to hear the news and to catch sight of the general. Within the hall, Monck informed the Corporation that he had been constrained by his commission to carry out orders he detested; but now that his former commission had expired with the Rump's new military arrangements, he was released to serve the cause of a free parliament. At length, several aldermen appeared outside to convey to the gathered assemblage that the "General and the City were

51; Baker, *Chronicle*, p. 747; OPH, XXII, 111–13; *CSPVen 1659–61*, p. 118; Christie, *Life*, I, 208; Woolrych, *Milton*, VII, 170; Haley, *Shaftesbury*, p. 128.

[70] *A Letter from the Lord General Monck and the Officers under his Command to the Parliament* (1660); OPH, XXII, 98–103, 123; Ludlow, *Memoirs*, II, 220; Davis, "Cromwell's Religion," pp. 281–2; Woolrych, *Milton*, VII, 170–1; Ashley, *Monck*, pp. 198–9; Hutton, *Restoration*, p. 93.

[71] Repertory 67, fol. 43; Guizot, *History*, II, 349; *CSPVen 1659–61*, p. 117; Pepys, *Diary*, I, 51–2; Baker, *Chronicle*, pp. 747–8; Gumble, *Life*, pp. 247–9; Davis, "Cromwell's Religion," p. 282.

of one mind, and resolved to adhere to each other for a free Parliament." The Corporation had captured the Rump's general. Exchequer clerk Samuel Pepys, who had joined the crowd outside Guildhall, reported that when Monck emerged he was greeted with "such a shout [as] I never heard in all my life." The city had agreed to receive the general's army; and the people released their hatred for the politicians at Westminster and their enthusiasm for a free parliament in nightlong revels.

The bonfires, the bell ringing, and the roasting of animal "rumps" on this occasion have been recounted ever since in studies of the Restoration, but what the people were actually celebrating remains open to interpretation. Royalists drank to the king's health "in some places," and the Venetian ambassador recorded that the king's name "came openly from all lips without any fear." Despite these royalist expressions, however, the night of "the roasting of the Rump" was primarily a celebration of the city's recovery from military occupation, of the anticipated collapse of the narrow clique who ruled from Westminster, and of the prospects for a free parliament. It was more a political catharsis for a citizenry who had been on edge since December than a celebration of a return to monarchy, and it had more to do with the immediate past than with any particular future beyond the assembling of a free parliament. That Charles Stuart's name was uttered in repudiation of the regicides at Westminster is not surprising, but royalists in the city were not yet confident that a free parliament spelled Charles II.[72]

Neither, apparently, were General Monck or the dominant figures in the Rump. What followed was ten days of political maneuvring in which the MPs sought to reclaim the general and his army for the republic, while the London opposition leaders sought to anchor their unexpected guest even more firmly to the parliamentary cause. The Council of State wrote to Monck several times, requesting his return to Whitehall for the sake of better communication. To these entreaties Monck remained largely indifferent, fearing reprisals if he should return, and claiming that the dispersal of arms among some citizens required him to remain in the city in order to protect parliament.[73] In the city, Monck came under considerable pressure from some secluded MPs

---

[72] MS Carte 213, fols. 592–593; MS Clarendon 69, fols. 183–185; *CLSP*, III, 692–3; *Peace to the Nation* [1660]; *The Petition of the Rump...to London* [1660]; *A Psalme sung by the People, before the Bone-fires* [1660]; *CSPD 1659–60*, p. 358; Guizot, *History*, II, 350; *CSPVen 1659–61*, p. 119; *OPH*, XXII, 114–16, 125; Pepys, *Diary*, I, 50, 52; Rugg, *Diurnal*, p. 39; *Warriston Diary*, p. 176; Ludlow, *Memoirs*, II, 222, 231; HMC *Leyborne-Popham*, pp. 219–20; HMC *Seventh Report*, p. 483; *Clarke Papers*, IV, 274–5; Gumble, *Life*, pp. 249–53; Baker, *Chronicle*, p. 748; Davis, "Cromwell's Religion," p. 282; Haley, *Shaftesbury*, p. 129; Woolrych, *Milton*, VII, 172; Hutton, *Restoration*, p. 93; Harris, *London Crowds*, pp. 49–50.

[73] *CSPD 1659–60*, pp. 364, 365, 367, 370; HMC *Seventh Report*, p. 483; Guizot, *History*, II, 351–2; Rugg, *Diurnal*, pp. 40–1; Pepys, *Diary*, I, 53, 54–5, 56.

and from advocates of a restoration of the Long Parliament, like Anglican Alderman John Robinson and Presbyterian cleric Edmund Calamy. In the meantime, pamphlets and petitions for a free parliament continued to pour from the London press.[74]

Responding to these influences, Monck arranged conferences between delegates from the Rump and representatives of the secluded members to see whether they could find any basis for accommodation. Although these meetings broke down, the Rump did provide for new elections with qualifications that neither required an oath against the Stuarts nor prevented the secluded members from standing, as Monck had requested. By the end of the week that began with the "roasting of the Rump," Monck seemed to have closed with the Rump again. Undaunted, the secluded members met on the 20th to plan another attempt to enter the House. The general was now confronted with a choice between filling up the parliament through elections or filling it up through the admission of the secluded members. His overnight decision for the secluded members, after consultations similar to those ten days earlier, was greatly pleasing to the city. The ensuing bonfires and bells on the evening of the 21st were a celebration of the city's acceptance of the restored Long Parliament as a full parliament that would soon give way to a free parliament. As on the 11th, the crowd cried in some places for "a free Parliament," in other places for the "king and [a] free Parliament," and in other places still, simply for the king.[75]

Taking up their seats and swamping the members of the Rump, the secluded MPs acted immediately to reverse the punishment meted out to the city, which had served as the principal redoubt of the parliamentary cause. The common councilmen were returned to authority. Those civic leaders arrested by order of the Rump were released, and the apprentices taken in the streets on the 2nd were returned to their masters. Alderman Browne, in hiding since Booth's rising, was restored to the House. Parliament also requested

[74] MS Clarendon 69, fols. 148, 152, 166, 170; *The Declaration of the County of Oxon to...Monck* (1660); *Letter and Declaration of the Nobility and Gentry of....York, to...Monck* [1660]; *Letter from divers of the Gentry of the County of Lincolne to...Monck* [1660]; [Fairfax, Thomas], *Declaration of...and the rest of the Lords,...at York* [1660]; *CSPD 1659–60*, pp. 358, 359, 360; *CSPVen 1659–61*, p. 119; *Clarke Papers*, IV, 261–4; HMC *Leyborne-Popham*, pp. 220–1; Rugg, *Diurnal*, p. 40; *Warriston Diary*, p. 177; Ludlow, *Memoirs*, II, 225; Guizot, *History*, II, 353–5; Baker, *Chronicle*, p. 749; Christie, *Life*, I, 210; Davis, "Cromwell's Religion," p. 284; Ashley, *Monck*, p. 200; Woolrych, *Milton*, VII, 173; Hutton, *Restoration*, p. 95.

[75] MS Carte 30, fol. 537; Repertory 67, fols. 45–47; MS Clarendon 69, fol. 176; [John Collins], *A Word in Season to all in Authority* (1660); *CSPD 1659–60*, p. 371; *CJ*, VII, 842–3, 845; HMC *Seventh Report*, p. 483; HMC *Leyborne-Popham*, pp. 154–5, 221–2; Guizot, *History*, II, 356–7, 359–60, 363; Rugg, *Diurnal*, pp. 43–4; Pepys, *Diary*, I, 57, 58, 60, 61–3; Ludlow, *Memoirs*, II, 228, 235; Gumble, *Life*, pp. 260–2; Christie, *Life*, II, 211–12; Davis, "Cromwell's Religion," pp. 285–6, 287–9; Ashley, *Monck*, pp. 201–2; Haley, *Shaftesbury*, pp. 129–31; Woolrych, *Milton*, VII, 173–4; Hutton, *Restoration*, pp. 95–6.

a loan from the Corporation, and the city responded with an offer of £60,000, the most it believed it could raise given the depression of its trade.

On its third day of business, the Long Parliament resolved that its successor would meet on 25 April, fulfilling the hopes of many in the city that a freely elected parliament would again sit at Westminster. In response, the Corporation proposed a day of thanksgiving on the 28th, a suggestion that was accepted with gratitude by the MPs and by the new Council of State chosen by the full parliament. Prominent London Presbyterian clerics Edmund Calamy and Thomas Manton preached at St Margaret Westminster, while the city chose Presbyterian Dr Edward Reynolds and Anglican Dr John Gauden to preach at St Paul's. The day of thanksgiving was preceded and followed by the feasting of General Monck by the city and by its major livery companies, all attended with further bonfires and bell ringing. Despite these repeated assertions of relief and thanksgiving, however, the constitutional situation remained uncertain. Many contemporaries expected a royalist settlement of the nation, and many historians have treated the Stuart restoration as inevitable from this point. However, as the Long Parliament proceeded with its own provisional settlement over the next three weeks, the restoration of the king remained but one of several options; and it was not an unambiguous one at that.[76]

Marking a repudiation of the 1649 revolution, the restoration of the Long Parliament placed government largely in the hands of men who had been the predominant "parliamentary" faction of the 1640s. Then they had warred against one king in the name of king-in-parliament. Whether these same men would be more successful in closing with the Stuart crown in 1660 than in 1648 was unclear. Many of them had made their peace with the Protectorate; and some had served in Richard Cromwell's parliament, which had been "free." In the Corporation of London, political expectations among Anglicans and Presbyterians diverged considerably in February 1660. A clique of Anglican royalists who had been active in the Corporation on behalf of the king for some time hoped that the restoration of the Long Parliament would lead to his restoration without conditions. Anglican royalists had successfully influenced the rhetoric of the civic movement for a free parliament, and the city's treating of Monck had been accompanied by some royalist expressions.[77] On the other hand, civic Presbyterians were as committed

[76] Journal 41, fol. 220; MS Clarendon 70, fols. 26, 28, 48; *CLSP*, III, 689; *CJ*, VII, 847–50; *OPH*, XXII, 137–40; *CSPD 1659–60*, pp. 375–6; HMC *Leyborne-Popham*, pp. 156; Rugg, *Diurnal*, pp. 44–8; Pepys, *Diary*, I, 64–5, 70–1; Guizot, *History*, II, 362–3; Ludlow, *Memoirs*, II, 239; Chivers, "City of London," pp. 215–16; Davis, "Cromwell's Religion," pp. 294–5, 297; Haley, *Shaftesbury*, p. 132; Woolrych, *Milton*, VII, 175; Hutton, *Restoration*, pp. 97, 100.

[77] MS Clarendon 69, fol. 142; MS Clarendon 70, fol. 48; *CLSP*, III, 679; HMC *Leyborne-Popham*, pp. 217, 220, 223.

to the ancient constitution of king-in-parliament as they were to the king himself. Like their parliamentary counterparts, civic Presbyterians who had opposed the "tyranny" of the Committee of Safety and that of the Rump in 1659–60 had opposed the "tyranny" of Charles I in the 1640s. Then, they had been "parliamentarians," or so historians have commonly labeled them. And again in 1660, civic Presbyterians are as properly labeled parliamentarians as they are labeled royalists.[78]

What kept these new allies from falling out again over their old quarrels was their common fear of the sectarian supporters of the republic. The Long Parliament returned to power amidst an escalating national panic about sectarianism and the security of the country's Protestant establishment. In Presbyterian minds, the war against Charles I had been fought as much to further reformation as it had been fought to defend the ancient constitution. But Presbyterians believed reformation and parish ministry were jeopardized by sectarian demands for complete liberty of conscience. Anglican royalists did not share the Presbyterian conception of reformation, but they did share Presbyterian fears about the security of parochial ministry. The royalist denouement of the crisis of 1659–60 needs, therefore, to be interpreted against the background of anti-sectarianism, which climaxed in the final weeks of the Commonwealth. Indeed, it was the widespread fear of the sects, more so than the widespread desire for a free parliament, that turned the strong possibility of a Stuart restoration into the inevitability of a Stuart restoration.

THE FEAR OF THE SECTS

The restoration of the Commonwealth in April 1659 was accompanied by a revival of pamphleteering and petitioning against the church establishment of the Protectorate that had frightened many "sober" Protestants as much as the removal of Richard's large and representative parliament. As James Harrington, John Milton, Henry Stubbe, Sir Henry Vane, and other commonwealthmen asserted new arguments for toleration, they actually persuaded Reformed Protestants and Anglicans that the republic threatened the nation's historic reformation as well as its "ancient constitution."[79] The

---

[78] *CJ*, VII, 849–50; *OPH*, XXII, 138; Henning, *House of Commons*, II, 352–3; Davis, "Cromwell's Religion," p. 294.

[79] See, for instance: James Harrington, *A Discourse* and *Aphorisms Political* (1659), also found in *The Political Works of James Harrington*, ed. J. G. A. Pocock (Cambridge, 1977), pp. 747–53, 761–79; *Ibid.*, "Introduction," pp. 100ff.; John Milton, *Considerations touching the Likeliest Means to Remove Hirelings* (1659); Henry Stubbe, *An Essay in defense of the Good Old Cause* (1659) and *A Light Shining out of Darkness* (1659); Sir Henry Vane, *A Needful Corrective or Ballance in Popular Government* (1659); Woolrych, *Milton*, VII, 77–95; J. R. Jacob, *Henry Stubbe, Radical Protestantism and the Early Enlightenment* (Cambridge, 1983), ch. 2; M. A. Judson, *The Political Thought of Sir Henry Vane the Younger* (Philadelphia, 1969).

movement for a free parliament was, therefore, accompanied from its beginning, in the summer of 1659, by a great fear about the future of the nation's
Protestant institutions.

Anxiety about the parochial order was nowhere more noticeable than in
London, where the sects flourished in their greatest numbers and variety, and
where the leading Presbyterian clergy became national spokesmen for the
defense of reformation. They complained loudly in their pulpits and in print
about the menace of the "Anabaptists," a generic label that covered all those
sectarians, both actual and imagined, who sought to strip the parochial clergy
of their state sponsorship. Presbyterian authors and speakers who employed
anti-sectarian rhetoric unwittingly created a specter more menacing than
they intended. As fear of the "Anabaptists" mounted, royalist agents and
propagandists seized upon fears about sectarianism to drive home the idea
that only Charles Stuart could preserve parliament and Protestantism from
the enthusiasts who ruled from Westminster. Public fear of the sects reached
its apex in late winter and spring 1660, when those who had supported the
parliamentary cause became convinced that the sects would again attempt
to overturn a broad national settlement, as they had a year earlier. But the
fear of the sects had been apparent in ever greater force at each juncture of
the crisis that began with the destruction of the Protectorate.

Anti-sectarianism had been as powerful, for instance, as hostility to the
army in shaping the city's response to the Committee of Safety. When leading members of the Committee addressed the Corporation on 8 November, they had been unable to weaken the perception that their regime was
dominated by "Anabaptists and overturners of magistracy, ministery, and
lawes and libertyes." It was against a mounting tide of anti-sectarianism
that the Corporation received General Monck's first letter to them, that of
12 November, in which he condemned "some Men ... [who] under pretence
of maintaining ... Liberty [of conscience], endeavour the overthrow of the
National Ministery." Monck's sentiments were echoed in the Corporation's
fast of 2 December, which was proclaimed in defense of the reformed "word
[,] worshippe & sabbaths Magistrates & ministers," and in implied criticism
of the army regime.[80]

What most aroused the religious fears of London Reformed Protestants
in late 1659 was the possession of arms by the sects. The London water-
men who petitioned in early December for a free parliament, for instance,
also demanded that sectarian militia commissioners be replaced by persons
"well-affected to ... Magistracy, Ministry, ... and Reformed Religion." The

---

[80] Journal 41, fol. 211; *An Alarum to the City and Souldiery* [1659]; *Three Speeches*; *Letter of November 12*; *Warriston Diary*, pp. 153, 155–7; *Clarke Papers*, IV, 121–4, 184–6; *Baxter Correspondence*, I, 416–17; *BDBR*, III, 283.

London apprentices who confronted troops in the streets on 5 December were persuaded that the army was hostile to "the Privileges of the Gospel" and the "sacred ordinances" of "Word and Sacraments." Popular speculation that the London separatist churches were gathering arms, as the Münster Anabaptists had done in the 1530s, climaxed on the fearful night of 12 December, when rumors and lights aroused the urban population against a supposedly impending "massacre" and "slaughter" by the "Anabaptists." Orders spread through the city and Westminster "for one man to watch in every house, with his arms in readiness." Not since the alarms of January 1642 had the citizens of London experienced so frightful a panic.[81]

The collapse of the Committee of Safety in late December 1659 and its replacement by the reassembled Rump failed entirely to ease these fears. In January 1660 leading London parochial clergy like Edmund Calamy, Thomas Jacombe, Thomas Manton, and Edward Reynolds issued a joint pastoral letter that condemned the "divers Sects of *Libertines* encreasing every day . . . under the various . . . names of *Quakers, Seekers, Ranters, Familists,* [and] *Behemists.*" These Reformed Protestant clergy accused the sects of *"the decrying and abasing of . . . Ministry as an useless thing"* and held them responsible for *"many horrid* and *hideous Errors."*[82] Fears about the security of Protestant ministry were also much in evidence in the petitioning campaign for a free parliament that was encouraged by the Corporation of London. Kentish petitioners, for instance, lamented "the apparent hazard of the Gospel, through the prodigious growth of blasphemies, heresies, and schism, all threatening universal ruin." The scare about religion gripped Reformed Protestant minds as firmly as the worries about parliament. In vain, the author of *Moderation* pleaded with "all publick Magistrates, Ministers, and Writers" to forbear from suggesting that "the crushing of *this Sect*, and the violent subduing *of that sort*" would cure the national ills.[83]

---

[81] MS Clarendon 67, fols. 209–209a, 246; *CLSP,* III, 631; *To the Right Honourable, our right worthy and grave Senatours; A Declaration of several of the People called Anabaptists, in and about the City of London* (1659); [William Prynne], *To the Right Honourable, the Lord Mayor, Aldermen, . . . of London . . . the Humble Petition and Address of the Seamen, and Water-men* (1659); *Nicholas Papers,* IV, 192; Pearl *London,* p. 142; B. Manning, *The English People and the English Revolution* (1976), pp. 97–8.

[82] *A True Copy of the Letter sent from the Lord Mayor;* [Edward Reynolds], *A Seasonable Exhortation of sundry Ministers in London to the People* (1660), esp. pp. 3, 6–7, 8–9, 12, 16–17; Baxter, *Holy Commonwealth,* pp. xvii–xviii, 18–47; *Baxter Correspondence,* I, 415.

[83] Almost lost in the panic about parochial ministry were the recommendations by Monck, Baxter, and some petitioners that "such Liberty be allowed to Tender Consciences as is agreeable to the Revealed Will of God in the holy Scriptures." *A Declaration of the Nobility, Gentry, Ministry . . . of Kent* [1660] in *CSPD 1659–60,* p. 340; *Remonstrance of the . . . late Eastern, Southern, and Western Associations* [1660]; *Wee the Knights, Gentlemen, Ministers . . . of Warwick;* S. T., *Moderation: Or Arguments and Motives tending thereunto* (1660), pp. A2, 2, 27; Baxter, *Holy Commonwealth,* p. 9.

General Monck's arrival in the capital brought these attacks upon the sects to an even higher pitch, and his anger at the Rump's alliance with sectarian petitioners was instrumental in his desertion of the Rump for the city.[84] Thereafter, concern about settled ministry underlay the *entente* between the general and leading London Presbyterian clergy like Calamy and Jacombe. Monck justified his presence in the city after 11 February by citing the "continuacion of armes in the hands of phanatique and disaffected persons." As the stand-off between Monck and the Rump continued, Monck's partisans spread rumors that irreconcilable MPs were secretly negotiating with Lambert "to put him at the head of an army of Anabaptists" to defeat the general, the Corporation, and all *"Sober Interests."* When Monck embraced the cause of the secluded members, the celebrations in the London streets were, therefore, as much about the preservation of Protestantism as about the return of the Long Parliament.[85]

But how could Protestant tradition and the state best be preserved? The brief session of the Long Parliament, from 21 February through 16 March 1660, was accompanied by the pronounced emergence of royalism as the predominant element in public thinking about the nation's need for settlement. The royalist sub-text in the movement for a free parliament now became the main text, and fear that sectarian adherents of the "good old cause" would manage still to undermine the cause of settlement was a decisive factor in driving many into the royalist camp. Presbyterians at Westminster and in the city, who struggled with their conflicting commitments to the king and to the accomplishments of the 1640s, were swamped and paralyzed, politically, by a popular monarchist tide that swept over their confusing qualifications and preconditions. The Presbyterian program for reformation, parliamentary security, and the king on terms was again overtaken by events.

Speculation nevertheless continued through the first weeks of the Long Parliament about whether its settlement would retain the republic, set up General Monck as a "Prince of Orange," bring back Richard, or bring in the king. Despite such uncertainty, parliament worked quickly toward a settlement founded on the parliamentary and Protestant accomplishments of the 1640s. The MPs confirmed the Westminster Confession as a rule of faith and appointed three London clerics – Calamy, Manton, and Reynolds – to superintend its publication. They ordered that the Solemn League and

---

[84] *The Lord General Monck, his Speech; Declaration of Many Thousand well-affected Persons* [1660]; *The Petition of Mr. Praise-God Barebone; CJ,* VII, 837–8; *OPH,* XXII, 111–12, 120; *An Exact Accompt,* 63 (3–10 Feb. 1659), pp. 654–6; Rugg, *Diurnal,* pp. 37, 39; Baker, *Chronicle,* p. 747; Reay, *Quakers and the English Revolution,* pp. 97–8; Hutton, *Restoration,* p. 71.

[85] *Peace to the Nation; Word in Season; To the Supreme Authority of the Nation: An Humble Petition on the behalf of . . . Quakers* (1660); *Clarke Papers,* IV, 263; *CSPVen 1659–61,* p. 119; HMC *Seventh Report,* p. 462; *OPH,* XXII, 112; Baker, *Chronicle,* p. 749.

Covenant be reprinted and read in the churches. They confirmed parish ministry, as organized in the puritan system of classes, but also provided for separatist worship. They placed the county militias firmly back in the hands of those who had been dislodged by the revolution of 1648–9, still excluding those who refused to acknowledge the justice of the war against Charles I. Monck himself assumed leadership of the London trained bands. Finally, the MPs provided for their own dissolution and the succession of a new parliament, to further advance settlement, in relatively free elections. Those who had been in arms against parliament in the 1640s were disqualified from standing, but those elected were not bound to preserve the Commonwealth.[86]

This provisional settlement was a puritan restoration of the parliamentary institutions and reformation ideals of the 1640s. As a program, it was unacceptable to sectarians and to republican officers in the New Model Army, many of them in and around London. The Long Parliament's readoption of the Solemn League and Covenant, in particular, implied a settlement with a king. The decision produced an agitated republican reaction, which in turn reignited the Protestant phobia about the sects. By late February rumors were circulating in the capital that General Desborough, lately a prime mover in the Committee of Safety, was massing republican troops to disturb parliament. Signs of army resistance were detected at Hull and elsewhere. A "common report" spread in the city "that all the Anabaptists were ready to rise and cut all the throats of them that weare not of theire judgment." Now meeting two or three times a week, the London militia commissioners demanded that the trained band officers previously appointed by the Rump surrender all arms, trophies, colors, and drums. The Council of State prepared an annotated list of the previous London militia leadership, detailing which commissioners and officers were "fanatics" and "pernicious sectaries." Baptist merchant William Kiffin, the "*Mufty* of all Hereticks and Sectaries," was among those sectarians seized one night on suspicion of stockpiling arms.

The actual appearance of Desborough and Lambert among disaffected officers congregating in Westminster in early March fed wild speculation. Reports spread from London about a plot of the "sectaries" and "Phanatiques"

[86] Journal 41, fol. 220–221; GHL MS 186/1 (Militia of London, Commissioners' Proceedings, copy, 1660), pp. i–ii, vi, xi; MS Clarendon 70, fols. 26, 48, 120; *CJ*, VII, 849–50, 855, 858, 862; *OPH*, XXII, 138–43; Pepys, *Diary*, I, 74–7; Rugg, *Diurnal*, pp. 44–6, 55, 63; *CSPVen 1659–61*, p. 126; Guizot, *History*, II, 351–2, 356, 360–1, 364–5, 368–73, 376, 381, 389; HMC *Seventh Report*, pp. 462, 483; *Nicholas Papers*, IV, 194, 196–7, 205; Ludlow, *Memoirs*, II, 236–7, 248; Gumble, *Life*, p. 270; R. S. Bosher, *The Making of the Restoration Settlement: The Influence of the Laudians 1649–1662* (1951), p. 102; Abernathy, *English Presbyterians*, pp. 40–1; Davies, *Royal African Company*, pp. 297–8, 304–5; Haley, *Shaftesbury*, p. 132; Woolrych, *Milton*, VII, 192, 194; Hutton, *Restoration*; pp. 100–5.

to "massacre...ye Generall and many of ye members of Parlement and Councell of State." The gentry in the western counties were reportedly "very much afrighted" that the "Quakers and Independents and Anabapti[s]ts" were about to plunder their estates. The London militia commissioners began to talk about raising auxiliary regiments of horse as republican and army disenchantment came to a head. Commonwealthmen like Sir Arthur Hesilrige reappeared in the House in numbers on 7 March as republican officers drew up and circulated a remonstrance against monarchy and other grievances. Such general meetings of officers had preceded other dramatic political disruptions; but this time, Monck succeeded in persuading most officers to accept a parliamentary road to settlement. Lambert found himself in the Tower, unable to provide the necessary security for his good behavior; and Hesilrige, required by the House to answer for his suspicious conduct, was mobbed by the apprentices.[87]

These alarms were a sobering factor for some civic Presbyterians. They had already been disappointed in their hope that the Long Parliament would provide for a new assembly of divines to preside over the renewed settlement of the church. Presbyterian leaders like Richard Baxter, Calamy, and MP William Prynne began to have second thoughts about a dissolution amidst so much uncertainty. Would not Presbyterian goals be better secured if the king were brought in by the sitting parliament rather than by another body? Some feared that the members of a new parliament would be more hostile to the accomplishments of the 1640s and less restrained in their acceptance of monarchy. Others feared that the provisional settlement of the Long Parliament might be destroyed, after a dissolution, by the renewed efforts of commonwealthmen, the army, and the sects. Calamy launched a city petition on behalf of retaining the Long Parliament for the time being, with the addition of the House of Lords. It was to have been brought forward in common council but fell victim to fears that it was a sectarian ruse to stave off a settlement according to the traditional constitution.[88]

---

[87] Journal 41, fol. 221; GHL MS 186/1, p. iv; MS Clarendon 70, fol. 48; MS Carte 30, fol. 537; *A Letter sent to the Right Honourable, the Lord Mayor...by Lieutenant Colonel Kiffin* [1660]; *A Serious Manifesto of the Anabaptist and Other Congregational Churches* (1660); *The Life and Approaching Death of William Kiffin* [1660], pp. 3, 5; *To the Right Honourable the High Court of Parliament,...the...Petition of Praise-God Barebone* (1660); *The Fanatique Powder-Plot* [1660]; Rugg, *Diurnal*, pp. 39, 49, 51–3, 55, 58; Pepys, *Diary*, I, 54, 65, 78–9, 81, 82, 84; Guizot, *History*, II, 367, 368–9, 373–4, 376, 379; *Nicholas Papers*, IV, 196–201, 203–5; *Clarke Papers*, IV, 265–6; Ludlow, *Memoirs*, II, 241, 246; Gumble, *Life*, pp. 266–7; OPH, XXII, 151–4, 174–6; HMC *Seventh Report*, pp. 462, 483; HMC *Leyborne-Popham*, pp. 163, 166–8, 170; Braithwaite, *Beginnings*, p. 471; Davies, *Royal African Company*, pp. 298–301; Woolrych, *Milton*, VII, 192–3; Hutton, *Restoration*, pp. 93, 98, 101–2.

[88] MS Clarendon 70, fols. 95, 121; Guizot, *History*, II, 377; *Nicholas Papers*, IV, 202; OPH, XXII, 176; Abernathy, *English Presbyterians*, pp. 40–4.

Presbyterian talk of terms and treaties with the king also served to place them on the wrong side of the divide, in the popular London mind, between those truly committed to settlement and those pursuing their own interests. The scare about the sects, the opposition of republican MPs and officers, and Presbyterian temporizing all accelerated the movement of popular opinion in London in the king's direction. By early March, royalist propaganda directed toward the urban audience had extended the demand for a free parliament into a broader demand for the king and the bishops, too. The parliamentary agenda of the 1640s was condemned in language as harsh as that hitherto reserved for the Rump, with one ballad arguing "though one *Rump* is gone, yet another sits still." Pepys commented on 6 March about "the affection of the people and City" for the king's restoration, reporting also that "Everybody now drink[s] the King's health without any fear, whereas before it was very private that a man dare do it." From about this time, Thomas Rugg remembered, "every body was in great hopes of a king." Common prayer was reportedly read in several city churches on the first Sunday of March. Monck's frequent appearances at city livery halls were accompanied by transparently royalist gestures.[89]

But as the MPs edged toward the precipice of a dissolution, many doubted that they would leap over the edge. The final days of the Long Parliament provoked more uncertainty, another renewal of 1640s-style agitation within the army, and a continuation of press warfare against the sects – much of it now contrived for royalist purposes. As before, Monck imposed discipline on the soldiers; and he was also instrumental in persuading some MPs that settlement really would be advanced through a dissolution. In the early hours of 16 March, the Long Parliament gave way to the Council of State, which presided over parliamentary elections.[90]

Both in London and in other constituencies, nerves and news remained focused upon the continuing expectation that sectaries and soldiers would act against the nation's settlement. Fearing a sectarian coup in the interval between parliaments, the Corporation petitioned the Council and General Monck to take up residence within the city. The London militia commissioners proceeded with the raising of a troop of 500 horse, and their search for arms in the hands of the disaffected was predictably fruitful. Anti-sectarian salvoes in the press kept fears of fanatics alive, and Aldermen Tichbourne

---

[89] MS Clarendon 70, fol. 141; Repertory 67, fol. 56; *The Rump serv'd in with a Grand Sallet* (1660); *Orthodox State-Queries* [1660]; Pepys, *Diary*, I, 77, 79; Guizot, *History*, II, 373, 378, *Nicholas Papers*, IV, 198, 199–200; Ludlow, *Memoirs*, II, 244; HMC *Seventh Report*, p. 483; Abernathy, *English Presbyterians*, pp. 41–3, 47–50; Haley, *Shaftesbury*, pp. 132–5; Woolrych, *Milton*, VII, 195–6; Hutton, *Restoration*, pp. 105–8.

[90] MS Clarendon 70, fol. 95; MS Clarendon 71, fols. 119–120; *CLSP*, III, 725; *CJ*, VII, 872, 880; Rugg, *Diurnal*, pp. 56, 60–1; Pepys, *Diary*, I, 86, 88, 89; Guizot, *History*, II, 380–3, 385; *CSPVen 1659–61*, p. 134; HMC *Seventh Report*, pp. 463–4, 483–4; Davies, *Royal African Company*, p. 300; Woolrych, *Milton*, VII, 193; Hutton, *Restoration*, pp. 103–4.

and Ireton were accused of being involved in the "barbarous Designs of the *Anabaptists*" against the city and the nation. A new London intelligencer appeared in scorn of "Anabaptists, Quakers, Adamites, Seekers...[and] Familists."[91] As London electors approached their choice of MPs, Anglicans sought to reassure their Presbyterian partners; but the Presbyterian interest itself appears now to have divided. Encouraged by the clergy, "the most popular Presbyterians" remained committed to a settlement that incorporated the accomplishments of the 1640s; and they continued publicly to argue the necessity of a "Treaty and accord" with the king. But other civic Presbyterians were "all of one judgement" with the Anglican royalists, having committed themselves to the royalist cause with less restraint.[92]

Both confusion and uncertainty were noticeable among civic Presbyterians at the common hall of 27 March. Between thirty and forty persons were apparently put up for the Corporation's four parliamentary seats; but Alderman Robinson, Major-General Browne, Recorder William Wilde, and Alderman William Vincent were chosen "without any dispute, which was never before known," according to Robinson. The four MPs were all strongly royalist, but three of them also had Presbyterian credentials. Throughout the country, in a parliamentary election that turned upon national issues, the republican cause was politically decimated, old Anglican royalists and their sons found enormous support (despite having been disqualified by the Long Parliament), and Presbyterian royalists also found many seats.[93]

That the new parliament would turn to the king was therefore clear. As this result became obvious, it produced further tensions between Anglicans and Presbyterians and prompted a military last stand on the part of some diehard republicans. Within days of the London election Alderman Robinson was warning the king against the "ill temper and extravagant discourses"

---

[91] Journal 41, fols. 223–224; GHL MS 186/1, pp. xviii, xxi, xxiii, xxvi; *A Brief Confession or Declaration of Faith; set forth by...Ana-Baptists* (1660), pp. 7, 10, 11; *The Apology of Robert Tichborne and John Ireton* [1660], pp. 6–7; *The Fanatique Powder-Plot*; *The Phanatick Intelligencer* 1 (21 March 1660); [Roger L'Estrange], *A Necessary and Seasonable Caution, concerning Elections* [1660]; Rugg, *Diurnal*, pp. 54–5, 61–3, 65–6; Pepys, *Diary*, I, 91; *CSPVen 1659–61*, pp. 134–35; *Clarke Papers*, IV, 266–7; Guizot, *History*, II, 386–7, 392, 393; HMC *Seventh Report*, pp. 463, 484; Woolrych, *Milton*, VII, 196; Hutton, *Restoration*, pp. 108–110.

[92] MS Clarendon 71, fols. 109, 112–113, 158; [William Prynne], *Seasonable and Healing Instructions, Humbly tendered* [1660]; *Alderman Bunce his Speech* (1660), pp. 3, 4, 5–6; *No King but the Old King's Son* (1660); Rugg, *Diurnal*, p. 65; Davies, *Royal African Company*, p. 320; Pearl, *London*, pp. 313–14.

[93] Nearby, Gilbert Gerard, son of a militant Presbyterian, and Sir Thomas Clarges, Monck's brother-in-law, claimed the Westminster seats. Anglican royalists and Presbyterians divided the Middlesex and Southwark seats, with the Southwark election clearly pitting royalists against sectarians. MS Clarendon 71, fols. 108–110, 112–113; *Nicholas Papers*, IV, 206; Henning, *House of Commons*, I, 31–2, 308, 311, 316, 415; II, 389, 393, 710; III, 644, 658, 720–1; Pearl, *London*, pp. 156, 321–3; Davies, *Royal African Company*, pp. 320–30; Abernathy, *English Presbyterians*, pp. 52–5; Hutton, *Restoration*, pp. 111–13.

of some Anglican supporters, who were hurting the royalist cause. Their intemperance had caused some Presbyterians, "a little to flag now, and fear the settlement of Episcopacy, and that your Majesty will slip in without conditions." A few weeks later, another Anglican writer worried that the king's "interest cools beyond expectation, thro' the indiscretion of his ranting party." In response, Anglican clerical agents in the city worked to "sweeten rigid presbyterians" with reassurances that "a lawful assembly of divines" would consider all disputed matters of church government and discipline. The Declaration of Breda of 4 April, which confirmed Charles's acceptance of a broad parliamentary settlement, also spoke to Presbyterian worries in its language about the composition of religious differences. One of the original copies was sent directly to the Corporation of London to reassure the dominant Presbyterian interest.[94]

The Declaration of Breda also offered religious liberty to those of "tender consciences," but it failed either to put at ease those most devoted to the "good old cause" or to assuage the fears of Reformed Protestants and Anglicans about them. The anti-sectarian fears of 1659–60 climaxed when John Lambert escaped from the Tower of London on 10 April. On the following night, the citizenry were again aroused from their beds by a rumor that "there would be a Massacre... and that there would rise 20,000 men and Lambert in the head of them." Lord Mayor Alleyn issued a precept to all householders "to provide themselves of Armes and Ammunition and to be in readiness for the defense of the City" against "Anabaptists, Quakers, and other Sectaries." About the same time the Council received spurious intelligence that General Desborough was conspiring with republicans Hesilrige and Vane and many London Independent churches to thwart the new parliament.[95]

The ease with which Lambert's rising was put down was a poor indicator of how much concern the rising provoked among London citizens and

[94] MS Clarendon 71, fols. 81–82, 109, 112–113, 158, 221, 230, 233; *CLSP*, III, 716, 723, 732; Matthew Griffith, *The Fear of God and the King* (1660); John Milton, *Brief Notes Upon a Late Sermon, Titl'd, The Fear of God* (1660); Rugg, *Diurnal*, p. 69; HMC *Seventh Report*, p. 484; *Nicholas Papers*, IV, 208; HMC *Leyborne-Popham*, p. 228; Guizot, *History*, II, 408; Browning, *Documents*, VIII, 57–8; Bosher, *Making*, pp. 108–11; Abernathy, *English Presbyterians*, pp. 43–7; Davies, *Royal African Company*, pp. 318, 340–1; Woolrych, *Milton*, VII, 201–4; Hutton, *Restoration*, pp. 108, 110–11. The city's Presbyterian clergy sent a delegation to Charles in May to secure his agreement to the meeting of a free synod or assembly of divines for the settlement of the church. Rugg, *Diurnal*, p. 81; *CJ*, VIII, 20; Bosher, *Making*, pp. 126–30; Abernathy, *English Presbyterians*, pp. 60–7.

[95] MS Clarendon 71, fol. 343; Repertory 67, fol. 59; GHL MS 186/1, pp. xxvii, xxxvii; MS Clarendon 71, fols. 81–82, 112–113, 234; *CLSP*, III, 714–16; *To the Right Honourable the Council of State. . . . The Humble Petition of many thousand Citizens and Freemen of London* [1660]; Guizot, *History*, II, 401, 404, 407; *CSPD 1659–60*, p. 409; Rugg, *Diurnal*, pp. 66, 69–70; Pepys, *Diary*, I, 101, 108–9; Ludlow, *Memoirs*, II, 251; Gumble, *Life*, pp. 278–9; Woolrych, *Milton*, VII, 197; Hutton, *Restoration*, pp. 109–10; R. L. Greaves, *Deliver Us from Evil: The Radical Underground in Britain, 1660–1663* (New York, 1986), p. 30.

observers. All the fears of the previous year seemed to find confirmation in Lambert's effort to seize the nation before the new parliament could perfect a national settlement. Quakers were reported to "have sold whole estates to assist Lambert's design"; and another story reported that 7,000 "Quakers and Anabaptists" had flocked to Lambert's standard in the Midlands. Pepys thought, "either the Fantiques must now be undone, or the Gentry and citizens throughout England and clergy must fall." The London militia commissioners placed the trained bands in an advanced state of readiness for Lambert's anticipated march toward the city. A general mustering of the trained bands and auxiliaries was appointed for Hyde Park on the Tuesday of Easter week, to coincide with a coordinated muster of the army regiments in and about London. A number of republican officers were apprehended, and Aldermen Ireton and Tichbourne were committed to the Tower.[96]

The principal effect of Lambert's rising on the city was that of confirming many citizens in the royalist posture they had adopted in defense of a parliamentary settlement and the security of Protestant ministry. Easter – still a forbidden holiday – was celebrated in London in 1660 with a resurrection of the accoutrements of kingship. Printed pictures of the king bedecked many houses; and the king's arms reappeared in some churches, on shop signs, and in livery halls. The Hyde Park rendezvous on 24 April coincided with the return to London of the defeated Lambert, and it preceded the opening of the Convention Parliament by a single day. Under these circumstances, the rendezvous became a celebration of the union of city and parliament for the anticipated restoration of monarchy. Enormous crowds gathered to celebrate the defeat of the "common enemy," a label reserved, until lately, for Charles Stuart. The jubilant atmosphere, in which many cried *"God save the King!,"* turned nasty when the hapless Lambert was forced to stand under the Tyburn gallows. The streets were filled with anti-sectarian, royalist crowds again on May Day night, when the Baptist meeting-house of William Kiffin was sacked, and again on the 8th, as Charles II was proclaimed king by the Convention. And when the new parliament requested a loan of £50,000 for Charles and his government, the Corporation voted to lend twice that amount.[97]

[96] MS Clarendon 71, fols. 343, 355; GHL MS 186/1, pp. xlv–lxi; HMC *Fifth Report*, pp. 167, 181, 199; HMC *Leyborne-Popham*, p. 228; *CSPD 1659–60*, p. 574; Pepys, *Diary*, I, 111; Rugg, *Diurnal*, pp. 70–4, 76; Guizot, *History*, II, 410, 411; Whitelocke, *Memorials*, p. 701; Whitelocke, *Diary*, p. 579; Greaves, *Deliver Us*, pp. 27–8; Hutton, *Restoration*, pp. 113–16.

[97] Journal 41, fols. 230–232; GHL 186/1, p. lxx; MS Clarendon 72, fols. 47, 149–150; MS Carte 214, fol. 99; *CalCSP*, IV, 678; *Declaration of the Nobility and Gentry that adhered to the Late King* (1660); *CSPD 1659–60*, p. 430; *CSPVen 1659–61*, p. 142; *OPH*, XXII, 247–8; Pepys, *Diary*, I, 106, 113, 122; Rugg, *Diurnal*, pp. 73, 76, 78–80; HMC *Fifth Report*, pp. 145, 167, 181, 204; HMC *Seventh Report*, p. 80; *CSPVen 1659–61*, pp. 143, 146; Guizot, *History*, II, 416, 422, 424, 426; Gumble, *Life*, p. 287; Hutton, *Restoration*, p. 125; Harris, *London Crowds*, p. 52.

CONCLUSION

The citizens of London had been highly visible, at every stage of the way, in the sequence of events that led from the collapse of the Commonwealth to the recall of Charles II. Their efforts had frequently surprised and overtaken the initiatives of the republican regime, of General Monck, and of the royalist court in exile. The Corporation of London had moved the nation toward a free parliament and had acted in defense of Protestant ministry. The force of urban public opinion had aroused other localities against the sects, the army, and the Rump. Charles II owed his throne, ironically, to a popular movement that had begun in the rebellious capital of his father. Indeed, he had benefited from many of the political devices and developments that had been employed against Charles I – popular petitioning, press agitation, demands for reformation, and the coordination of opposition in London and other boroughs and counties, to name but a few.

Usually treated as a coda to the Civil War and Interregnum, the crisis of 1659–60 was as much a prelude to the Restoration, for it announced many of the issues and problems of the reigns of Charles II and James II. Liberty of conscience had undermined the Rump in 1659–60. For the next thirty years, liberty of conscience would bedevil all efforts at settlement, including those that indulged conscience as well as those that coerced conscience. Fears about the security of the Protestant establishment were directed against the sects in 1659–60. Such fears retained their force thereafter, sometimes directed against Protestants who could not embrace the restored Anglican church order, sometimes directed against Roman Catholics, and sometimes directed against the Anglican clerical leadership itself. The demand for a free and representative parliament that was heard in 1659–60 was heard again and again in the ensuing decades – against the Earl of Danby in the 1670s, throughout the great crisis of 1679–82, and again in 1687–8. In 1659–60, both the volatility of opinion in London and the city's unrestrained press compromised a sequence of regimes. After 1660, London opinion and the London press retained their destabilizing force, despite the best efforts of successive ministries to contain them.

Perhaps most importantly for this study, the principal leaders of the Corporation of London in the crisis of 1659–60 were the heirs of the Reformed Protestant movement of the 1640s. And some of them – or their sons, near relations, business partners, and co-religionists – would play a similar role in the defense of Protestantism and parliamentary government in 1679–82. Moreover, in 1660, the city continued to speak with a distinctly Presbyterian voice as the Convention Parliament proceeded with the further settlement of the nation and as Charles II returned to his kingdom. In the opening days of the Convention, for instance, London aldermen and common councilmen published a *Declaration and Vindication . . . of the City* that was as much a Presbyterian apology as a royalist manifesto. It affirmed the "Just and fundamental government of hereditary and well-tempered Monarchy, according to the ancient Laws of the Nation." It placed the responsibility for the "subversion of that Antient and happy forme of Government of King, Lords, and Commons" upon sectarians and republicans. It vindicated those civic and parliamentary leaders who, in 1648–9, had, "according to their allegiance and Covenant," been "ingaged to procure and secure a Personal Treaty with the king." And if this *Declaration* endorsed the reformation of the state in the 1640s, the civic government also stood by the reformation of the church. The aldermen and common councilmen informed Charles that they expected to enjoy "the Exercise of the Protestant Religion, according to the scriptures, and the Example of the best Reformed Churches."[98]

Charles II, the Anglican royalist gentry of the counties, and all those clergy reverting to episcopal practices were already uneasy about this unabashed civic favor for the puritan ideals of the 1640s. Civic Presbyterians were loyal to a vision of a national Protestant order that had shattered the church in the 1640s. They were loyal to an understanding of the ancient constitution that had fractured the political nation and provoked counter-veiling royalist constructions of the same ideal.[99] For their part, Anglican royalists were already finding discursive motifs in the traumatic experiences of 1659–60 that were perfectly suited for defending an unequivocal return to the forms of settlement that had been uprooted in 1641–2. Just as the crises of 1641–2, 1648–9, and 1659–60 were being collapsed into a single frightening memory of unsettlement and disorder, so the anti-sectarian rhetoric of 1659–60 was beginning to be employed against all those – Reformed Protestants as well as sectarians – who dissented from Anglican royalist forms of settlement as enemies of settlement *per se*.

Finally, the crisis of 1659–60 provides another example of the remarkable ability of ordinary London citizens to play a major role in the determination of national affairs. Charles II began his reign as the king of the London crowd. Indeed, the crowds that fed the parliamentary movement of 1659–60 – a movement that became royalist – had the same objectives as the crowds that fed the parliamentary movement of the early 1640s – a movement that had become anti-royalist. The London mechanics, apprentices, shopkeepers,

---

[98] Journal 41, fols. 225–230; MS Clarendon 72, fol. 67; MS Carte 214, fol. 99; *Declaration and Vindication of the Lord Mayor, Aldermen and Commons of the City of London* (1660), esp. pp. 1–5, 19, 26; *OPH*, XXII, 271; Henning, *House of Commons*, I, 311 (where the *Declaration* is misdated), 650–1 and II, 353; Woodhead, *Rulers*, pp. 23, 113; Davies, *Royal African Company*, p. 344.

[99] G. Burgess, *The Politics of the Ancient Constitution: An Introduction to English Political Thought* (University Park, Penn., 1992), pp. 212–31.

and merchants who gradually turned to Charles in 1659–60 saw him as the guarantor of parliamentary government and public Protestant ministry. Their zeal for the rights, liberties, privileges, and customs of the commons of London had driven them in a royalist direction. But the experiences of 1659–60 had also confirmed many London citizens in their consensual and representative assumptions about both civic and parliamentary government. Just as Anglican loyalists would direct the anti-sectarian language of 1659–60 against those loyal to the reformation of the 1640s after 1660, so many London householders would redirect their fear of "arbitrary government" against any who sought to manage their freedom and autonomy. Charles II would find the welcoming householders of the city of London to be fickle friends indeed: the citizens of the English metropolis would remain one of the greatest obstacles to the kingdom's political and religious settlement.

II

Settlement and unsettlement,
1660–1679

2

The Restoration settlement and an unsettled city, 1660–1670

None of the issues confronted by king and kingdom in 1660 would prove more divisive than that of church settlement. The irenic spirit that brought Presbyterians and Anglicans together in the city of London and in many counties in 1659–60 was genuine, but it was also founded on the common fear of the sects. As the sects were subdued, Anglicans and Presbyterians discovered they feared each other as much as they feared the opponents of monarchical and parochial structures in church and state. Presbyterians hoped to preserve as much as possible of the reformation of the 1640s in the restored church; but Anglicans sought instead to return the church to its pre-1642 hierarchical orders, forms, and patterns. As Anglican royalists gained the upper hand in the country and in parliament, they imposed their church settlement on Reformed Protestants, on the city, and on the king himself. The result was a rigidly episcopal national church that was exclusivist in its personnel and uncompromising in its practice. Reformed Protestant parochial clergy were given the choice of conformity or expulsion. The restored church was also anchored on the magistrate's sword: new statutes forbade worship outside the established order, under various pains, and even regulated the place of residence of expelled clergy.

The Anglican royalist church agenda was, however, constructed upon two unrealistic expectations that reflected the pre-revolutionary world of the early Stuart ecclesia. To be successful, the Anglican settlement required that most Reformed Protestants accept a restored church full of practices that they had sought to eliminate. It also required the full support of a monarch who doubted the wisdom of religious coercion. Neither of these Anglican expectations was fulfilled in Restoration England, and the Corporation of London was a critical testing ground in the disappointment of each.

Instead of achieving political and religious uniformity in London, the Anglican royalist church agenda unsettled the city. Reformed Protestantism was rejuvenated, rather than reduced, in London in the late 1660s by the interlocking traumas of coercion, plague, fire, and war. Moreover, Presbyterian reservations about conscience and about separate worship weakened under constraint. After 1660, most Presbyterian clergy and laity accepted the Independents' case for liberty of conscience within and without a national church that they still hoped to reform. Reformed Protestants and sectarians in London also set aside their troubled political past to offer challenges to the Anglican policy of coercion. These challenges reinforced Charles's own doubts about a coercive settlement. By 1670, the Church of England was clearly failing in the Corporation of London, and it was challenged by the vigorous expression of Reformed Protestant and sectarian beliefs elsewhere as well. Anglican royalist political hegemony fractured after the fall of Edward Hyde, Earl of Clarendon; and although the ill-suited ministers of the Cabal disagreed about much, they eventually agreed about the need for toleration.[1] As in 1659–60, so in 1669–72, the Corporation of London played a critical role in checking coercion and in suggesting the need for reconsideration of the national religious settlement.

But in the summer and autumn of 1660 all this lay ahead. Then, still influenced by the cooperative spirit of the Cromwellian church, many London Presbyterian clergy and laity continued to work for Protestant accommodation and reformation. Responding to overtures from the king and from moderate Anglicans, Richard Baxter and Edward Reynolds, for instance, led many urban Presbyterian clergy in adapting their synodical preferences to the scheme for modified episcopacy formerly proposed by Irish Archbishop James Ussher. They also suggested alterations to the Book of Common Prayer and dispensations from the surplice, the sign of the cross in baptism, and kneeling at communion. Their work was rejected, however, by the more rigid London Presbyterian clergy, like Edmund Calamy and Zachary Crofton, who hoped to persuade Charles to continue the Long Parliament's religious settlement.[2] And Anglican MPs in the Convention became less interested in religious accommodation after the surviving bishops also rejected the Presbyterian proposals, and after Charles began to fill the episcopal bench with new appointees.

Charles also continued to press Anglicans to adopt an extensive package of proposals acceptable to Presbyterians, and he continued to advocate liberty

---

[1] J. Spurr, *England in the 1670s: 'This Masquerading Age'* (Oxford, 2000), pp. 13–15, 26, 28–9; J. P. Montaño, *Courting the Moderates: Ideology, Propaganda, and the Emergence of Party, 1660–1678* (Newark, Del., 2002), pp. 96, 107.

[2] Edward Stillingfleet, *Irenicum* (1661); [Zachary Crofton], *Berith Anti-Baal* (1661); Pepys, *Diary*, I, 220; HMC *Fifth Report*, p. 168; HMC *Le Fleming*, p. 26; Richard Baxter, *Reliquiae Baxterianae*, ed. Matthew Sylvester (1696), Lib. I, Part II, 218, 229, 232; Hutton, *Restoration*, pp. 143–4; Abernathy, *English Presbyterians*, pp. 66–8; Bosher, *Making*, pp. 117–22, 150–4; I. M. Green, *The Re-Establishment of the Church of England 1660–1663* (Oxford, 1978), pp. 14–15, 19, 84; Spurr, *Restoration Church*, pp. 31–2, 143–4.

of conscience for peaceable sectarians who could not accept comprehension in the national church. Presbyterian clergy were, nevertheless, mostly unwilling to accept leadership positions in the restored establishment, insisting they could do so only after episcopal structures and practices had been modified by statute. Presbyterian hopes collapsed in November 1660 when the House of Commons narrowly failed to proceed with a bill for Protestant accommodation.[3]

The immediate prospects for a broad religious settlement were perhaps not yet completely dead, but two London events of 1661 contributed to Charles's acceptance of the punitive Uniformity Act of 1662. The first of these was the London Fifth Monarchist rising (or Venner's rising) of January 1661. Insignificant in its support and numbers, this actual "Anabaptist" rising in the heart of the city revived the sectarian alarums of 1659–60. It also persuaded Anglican royalists to dig in their heels in the belief that puritan foot-dragging merely left church and state open to further republican or sectarian attack. Secondly, when London Reformed Protestants sought to turn the election of City MPs for the new parliament of 1661 into a plebiscite against an unequivocal Anglican restoration in the church, they confirmed Anglican fears that rebellion still lurked in the cause of reformation. The rejection of Anglican royalist candidates by the London electors (examined below) contributed to the success of Anglican candidates elsewhere. Both events maintained the fear of the sects, now directing it into an electoral reaction against upholders of Reformed Protestant principles that was encouraged by some Anglican clergy and gentry. In the face of mounting Anglican royalist intransigence, conversations between episcopal and Presbyterian clerical spokesmen collapsed in spring 1661.[4]

When the "Cavalier" Parliament met in May 1661, almost its first order of business was the condemnation of the Solemn League and Covenant, an action that signaled repudiation of the Cromwellian church and of the 1659–60 efforts to maintain it. Restored to the House of Lords in this parliament, the

[3] MS Clarendon 73, fols. 184–185; *To the Kings Majesty. The humble and grateful acknowledgement of many Ministers . . . in and about London* (1660); HMC *Fifth Report*, p. 168; Baxter, *Reliquiae*, Lib. I, Part II, 241–2, 276–84; Rugg, *Diurnal*, pp. 113–14, 121; Pepys, *Diary*, I, 204; *Baxter Correspondence*, II, 7–8, 10; Browning, *Documents*, VIII, 365–70; Bosher, *Making*, pp. 119n. 164–99; Abernathy, *English Presbyterians*, pp. 70–7, 78; I. M. Green, *Re-Establishment*, pp. 20, 29, 83–8; Hutton, *Restoration*, pp. 144–6; Paul Seaward, *The Cavalier Parliament and the Reconstruction of the Old Regime, 1661–1667* (Cambridge, 1988), p. 163; N. H. Keeble, *The Literary Culture of Nonconformity in later Seventeenth-Century England* (Leicester, 1987), p. 28.

[4] MS Clarendon 74, fol. 297; Rugg, *Diurnal*, pp. 138, 139–40; Pepys, *Diary*, II, 57; HMC *Fifth Report*, p. 170; *CSPVen 1659–61*, pp. 239, 272; HMC *Le Fleming*, pp. 116, 120; Bosher, *Making*, pp. 204–6, 219, 226–30; I. M. Green, *Re-Establishment*, pp. 182–3; Abernathy, *English Presbyterians*, pp. 80–1; Keeble, *Culture*, p. 29; Henning, *House of Commons*, I, 312; Hutton, *Restoration*, pp. 150–3, 174.

bishops were zealous promoters of the Uniformity Act that received reluctant royal support by May 1662, as the foundation of a new church settlement.[5] The act required the deprivation of all parish clergy who failed to conform to the entire Book of Common Prayer, to accept episcopal ordination, to repudiate the Covenant, or to renounce the legitimacy of political resistance under all circumstances. The new Uniformity Act was accompanied by a second statute against separatist worship, directed especially at Quakers, who refused to take the oaths of allegiance and supremacy that upheld civil government. And it was followed in 1664 by a Conventicle Act, triggered by further sectarian plotting, that was intended to prevent private worship outside the revived episcopal order. The Conventicle Act provided fines for Protestants caught worshipping outside the church, and it also make them liable to prosecution under the 1593 statute against conventicles. The 1665 Five Mile Act was intended to discourage contact between deprived clergy and their friends among the laity by physically removing them from the vicinities of their former churches. By then, modern Protestant nonconformity had originated in the common witness of many Reformed Protestants and sectarians against the strictures of a coercive Anglican settlement.

Reformed Protestant clergy were scarcely quiet as they experienced what was, for them and their followers, a disastrous sequence of events. The press of 1660–62 was awash with Reformed Protestant apologetics. Burgess's *Reasons shewing the Necessity of Reformation* (1660), Baxter's *Grand Debate between . . . the Bishops and the Presbyterian Divines* (1661), and Zachary Crofton's *Reformation not Separation* (1662) were but a few pieces in this flood. Baxter reminded Charles that the newly proscribed charter of national reformation had been the source of his deliverance: "the obligation of the *Covenant* upon the *consciences* of the Nation, was not the weakest Instrument of your *Return*." But this rearticulation of all the language that divided Reformed Protestants from Anglicans merely fed the Anglican reaction and assisted Anglican propagandists in assimilating the advocates of reformation into their sectarian *bête noire*. Baxter felt undermined in his dialogue with episcopal spokesmen by "common talk" in which Reformed clergy were portrayed "as the most Seditious People." His friend John Corbet insisted, as early as 1660, that Presbyterians "are no Fanaticks, although they begin to be . . . abused under that name."[6]

By 1663, Sir Roger L'Estrange was acting, under the new Licensing Act, as surveyor of the press and as chief Anglican watchdog against the

---

[5] Bosher, *Making*, pp. 221–3, Seaward, *Cavalier Parliament*, p. 164, Hutton, *Restoration*, p. 155.

[6] Richard Baxter, *Two Papers of Proposals concerning the Discipline and Ceremonies of the church of England* (1661), p. 12; Baxter, *Reliquiae*, Lib. I, Part II, 333, 373, 384; [J]ohn [C]orbet, *The Interest of England in the Matter of Religion* (1660), p. 24.

circulation of "heretical, schismatical [and] . . . seditious" discourse. As Reformed Protestant clergy were expelled from the church, Reformed Protestant language was proscribed and condemned in the press as a body of
"Arguments, Pretences, Wayes, and Instruments" that had produced rebellion. The Licensing Act was also directed against the "teeming freedom" of
discussion that had been especially characteristic of civil war and interregnum London.[7] But the effect of this uncompromising Anglican settlement
upon the capital of English puritanism did not at all correspond to Anglican
intention.

UNSETTLING THE CITY, 1660–1665

The Restoration Settlement failed to bring settlement to the Corporation
of London. Instead, it overturned the civic restoration that had occurred
in December 1659, when common council elections returned Presbyterians
to the dominant position they lost in the Corporation in 1648–9. The civic
regime that welcomed Charles II to his capital in May 1660 was a broad one,
for civic Presbyterians had regained their dominant voice without depriving
Independents and sectarians or Anglican royalists of theirs. The London
regime that welcomed the king was also one open to all men of commercial
talents: merchant princes of the Levant Company, investors in the East India
Company, and the entrepreneurial and interloping men who dominated the
colonial trades.

Within three years, however, the broadly representative civic regime that
had challenged the Rump and turned to Charles as a guarantor of parliament
and Protestant order was swept away by the Cavalier Parliament. Under the
terms of the Corporation Act of 1662, Reformed Protestant citizens who
could not embrace the new episcopal establishment were formally disabled
from holding civic offices and joined their former sectarian adversaries in
the political wilderness. In London, the Corporation Act created and artificially sustained an Anglican governing elite that insufficiently encompassed
the city's natural rulers and that also failed to represent a significant proportion of the city's population and electorate. Ironically, Anglican persecution
now restored a measure of unity to those who had opposed Charles I and
the bishops in 1640–42, even though Reformed Protestants and sectarians
continued to construe the need for reformation differently. The realignment
of most citizens into conformist and nonconformist camps also provided the

---

[7] Roger L'Estrange, *Interest Mistaken; or, the Holy Cheat* (1662); Roger L'Estrange, *Considerations and Proposals in Order to the Regulation of the Press* (1663), esp. unpaginated
dedicatory epistle to Charles II and p. 9; Browning, *Documents*, VIII, 67; Seaward, *Cavalier
Parliament*, pp. 158–60; Hutton, *Restoration*, pp. 156–7.

groundwork for the emergence of political parties in London in the crisis of 1679–82.

Finally, the city became unsettled after 1660 because the Restoration Settlement was experienced by citizens as anti-metropolitan in nature. The government of Charles II sought politically to subordinate the country's premier corporation and better to harvest its wealth for state purposes. Many articulate and enterprising citizens who demanded the protection of their trading interests were soon disillusioned with the cavalier triumph. They were suspicious about the government's fiscal claims, and they resented the cost, the control, and – eventually – the perceived Catholicism of the Court establishment.

The city and the country were on different political courses in the year between the Corporation's extravagant reception of the king in May 1660 and the opening of the 1661 parliament. While country Anglicans employed the anti-sectarian language of 1659–60 to prune many counties and boroughs of their Reformed Protestant and sectarian political growths, Presbyterians retained their visibility in the city. By August 1660, the Corporation of London was expressing dissatisfaction to the crown and the Convention about the same issues that had recently divided the city from the restored Commonwealth, namely taxes and religion. The ending of the war with Spain had not ended the depression of London trade, which made it difficult for London citizens to accept new fiscal burdens; and as Presbyterian laity saw their parochial clergy marginalized by episcopal leaders, they became anxious about the future of the church.

When the Convention confirmed Charles's collection of half the Cromwellian excise, as compensation for his loss of the Court of Wards, common council objected to this substitution of a tax on commerce for a landed revenue.[8] The government's August request for a loan from the Corporation on the security of a poll tax also met with indifference and hostility. Some citizens active during the Commonwealth were reluctant to lend because they feared the Act of Indemnity and Oblivion would not protect them. Others were reluctant to lend because they feared the act would protect too many to redress the wrongs of 1648–9; and still others were cautious because they had fears about the security of their titles to former church lands. Some leading common councilmen obstructed the loan on the grounds that "the King had not performed his promise in settling religion and the Church Government," and they considered petitioning for a settlement with Presbyterian features. Instead of agreeing to a loan, therefore, the Corporation created a grievance committee to consider religion, the poll tax, and the continuation

[8] Journal 41, fols. 239–240; *CSPVen 1659–61*, p. 170; Rugg, *Diurnal*, p. 98; HMC *Fifth Report*, p. 169; Seaward, *Cavalier Parliament*, p. 103.

of the excise. This action in turn irritated some MPs, leaving "the Parliament and City . . . all disjointed." In September, the grievance committee was replaced by a larger body for the promotion of the city's trade and "to consider of the grievances & remidyes therof & of the Charters & priviledges of the Citty."[9]

Those who pursued these courses were largely the same Reformed Protestant leaders who had rejected the Rump and the army. When one disgruntled cavalier complained that the Presbyterians "have the best offices in Court and City," he was right about the city. Presbyterians outnumbered Anglican royalists on the two Corporation committees of August and September 1660 by almost three to one. The reinstatement of several aldermen who had been dismissed by the Rump in 1649, in place of several Independents removed by the Act of Indemnity, did not alter this Presbyterian dominance, for some of the restored magistrates were icons of civic Presbyterianism. Indeed, Reformed Protestants on the aldermanic bench still outnumbered Anglican royalists by over two to one after this alteration.[10]

One of the leading Presbyterian aldermen, Sir Richard Browne, was chosen lord mayor for 1660–61 in September, and he was expected to be "troublesome to the clergy of the old stamp." Presbyterians also retained their dominance on Corporation committees after the selection of common councilmen for 1661, despite a notable decline in the number of common councilmen who can subsequently be identified with religious nonconformity (Table 2.1). The government acknowledged both the extent of civic concerns about trade and the leadership of Presbyterians in the Corporation in its appointment of a new Council for Trade in November 1660. Several of the Council's city members were Presbyterians; some were also members of the Corporation's committee for trade. Yet the government also worried that the Corporation was again "falling too much into the hands of a factious common council."[11]

If they were dominant in the Corporation, civic Presbyterians were, nevertheless, beginning to feel much less secure within the parochial establishment they had labored to maintain in 1659–60. Separatist worship had been restricted by a royal proclamation after Venner's rising. Harassment of Quakers, Baptists, and Independents who worshipped in defiance of the proclamation had begun soon thereafter. Some notable Presbyterian

---

[9] Common council agreed to a loan only in late October, and then the money came in but slowly. Journal 41, fols. 240–244; HMC *Fifth Report*, pp. 174, 200; *CSPVen 1659–61*, p. 187; Chivers, "City of London," pp. 194, 235–8; Hutton, *Restoration*, pp. 132–3, 138.

[10] Journal 41, fols. 240–244; CLRO Remembrancia, IX, 5; *CSPD 1660–1*, p. 255; Rugg, *Diurnal*, pp. 114–16; HMC *Fifth Report*, p. 174; A. B. Beaven, *The Aldermen of the City of London*, 2 vols. (1908–13), II, 90.

[11] SP 29 19/21, 19/24; Add. MS 40,712, fol. 8; Journal 41, fols. 244, 246; Rugg, *Diurnal*, p. 129; *CSPD 1660–1*, pp. 319, 461, 538; HMC *Fifth Report*, p. 200; Bosher, *Making*, pp. 220–1; Hutton, *Restoration*, p. 128.

Table 2.1[12] *Definite or probable dissenters on London common council, 1660–1666*

	Seats	1660	1661	1662	1663	1664	1665	1666
Inner City	113	53	27	28	14	16	14	15
Middle City	88	39	22	17	9	5	4	4
City Without	33	18	4	7	3	3	2	2
Total seats	234	110	53	52	26	24	20	21

MPs, like William Prynne and Lord Mayor Browne, endorsed the case for persecution of separatists. But the commencement of persecution disturbed other Presbyterian clergy and laity who had long accepted liberty of conscience, provided it did not come at the expense of a national Protestant establishment. Moreover, city Presbyterians soon found themselves confronting harassment within the church, as the new Bishop of London stepped up the supervision of his parochial clergy. Gilbert Sheldon made test cases in 1661 of prominent Presbyterian incumbents who refused to accept episcopal reordination or who had reservations about the prayer book and ceremonies. Such popular urban parish clergy as William Bates, Zachary Crofton, Thomas Jacombe, Thomas Manton, and Thomas Watson were soon disputing with the bishop. Others, like William Jenkin and Lazarus Seaman, were out-shouting the Independents in public sermons against diocesan episcopacy. In fact, both the harassment of separatists outside the church and the anxiety of Presbyterians within the church were creating a mounting puritan panic about the future of Protestant ministry and worship that took precedence over previous differences.[13]

The revival of puritan unity against the bishops and on behalf of the reformation of church and state was dramatically displayed in the city's election of new MPs for the 1661 parliament on 19 March. Reformed Protestant and separatist electors appeared *en masse* at Guildhall to ensure the choice of "honest" men and to shout against the "Lord Bishops." They hissed Anglican office-holders put up for MP; and they rejected cautious Presbyterians, like the lord mayor and the recorder (who sat for the city in the Convention), as insufficiently zealous in promoting the commercial and religious interests of the citizenry. The Presbyterians John Fowke, John Jones, and Sir William

[12] The inner city, middle city, and city without the walls are mapped below in Figure 6.1. For a fuller definition, see G. S. De Krey, *A Fractured Society* (Oxford, 1985), pp. 171–6. Identifications of dissenting common councilmen have been made with numerous sources, including Woodhead and Elliot.

[13] BL MS Egerton 2543, fol. 24; SP 29 32/97, 104, 108–9, 116, 125, 139, 144; *CSPD 1660–1*, pp. 537, 539–42; Rugg, *Diurnal*, pp. 140, 142, 154; HMC *Finch*, I, 101; Bosher, *Making*, pp. 205–8; Greaves, *Deliver Us*, pp. 56, 58–9.

Thompson and the Independent William Love, a member of the Council of State after the second restoration of the Rump, were elected. Reformed Protestants and sectarians clearly put aside their former differences in celebrating this common electoral triumph: "Heretofore wee have been many parties...yet honest sober men apeared this day as one man."

Anglican observers were alarmed about the electoral convergence of militant Presbyterians with Independents and Baptists in an "anti-episcopal party." Hyde attributed the result to republican orchestration, but the orchestration had actually come from anti-republican Presbyterians who had been comfortable with the Cromwellian church and who now saw it threatened by the bishops rather than by the sects. Zachary Crofton and other clerics were involved in a campaign to promote similar results in many constituencies through the writing of letters. Some sixty intercepted letters from London citizens encouraged the election of MPs elsewhere who would support "a well Grounded settlement," security for Protestant "religion in its power and purity," and the "establishment of our Civell rights upon a firme foundation." The authors claimed to "love the king in sincereity," but they had no patience for the "superstition" and "humane Inventions" now being imposed by the "rigour" of the bishops upon "Godly ministers" in the church. The city's Reformed Protestant electors were also backed by their leaders in the Corporation. When the government removed offending letters from the posts, common council reportedly talked about protesting such intrusiveness.[14]

The city's election of MPs in 1661 was an important turning-point in the direction of Corporation affairs as well as in the gathering Anglican reaction. Presbyterian militancy ended the political convergence of Reformed and Anglican Protestants that had produced the Restoration, and it also reflected a passing of the initiative in the city from Presbyterians to Anglicans. Stripped of many of their Westminster allies in the course of the parliamentary elections, civic Presbyterians were, in fact, very much on the defensive thereafter. Charles reportedly considered skipping the London procession scheduled to precede his coronation, in retaliation for the city election; but Anglicans took steps to assure the king of the citizens' loyalty. They promoted a loyal address from the trained bands. Sir Richard Ford mustered his regiment of auxiliaries

---

[14] SP 29 32/83, 85, 98, 103–4, 108, 116, 125–7, 133, 139–41; MS Clarendon 74, fols. 292, 297; *CSPD 1660–1*, pp. 536, 538–42, 546; *CSPD 1670*, p. 660; *CSPVen 1659–61*, pp. 272, 275; HMC *Finch*, I, 116, 120; HMC *Fifth Report*, pp. 170, 181–2; *The Loyal Subjects Lamentation for Londons Perverseness* (1661); *A Dialogue between the two Giants in Guildhall* (1661), pp. 4–8, 13; Pepys, *Diary*, II, 57, 58–9; Edmund Ludlow, *A Voyce from the Watchtower, Part Five, 1660–1662*, ed. A. B. Worden (1978), pp. 285–6; Bosher, *Making*, pp. 208–13; Henning, *House of Commons*, I, 312, 415; Hutton, *Restoration*, p. 152; Seaward, *Cavalier Parliament*, pp. 144–5; M. Ashley, *John Wildman: Plotter and Postmaster* (New Haven, Conn., 1947), pp. 180–1.

for exercises in the presence of the Duke of York and for a speech on behalf of "the legall rights of church and state." And on 22 April, the day of his coronation procession, Charles was reassured in the city by loyal speeches and by civic entertainments that celebrated "the power which Episcopacy hath over Presbytery." A few weeks later, when the Cavalier Parliament ordered the burning of the Solemn League and Covenant at strategic locations in London and Westminster, anti-puritan crowds pulled the Covenant out of those churches where it was still affixed.[15]

In the midst of these celebratory occasions, Lord Mayor Sir Richard Browne, who had been rejected as City MP by his own Presbyterian following, and who was well aware of the extent of the cavalier reaction, exchanged his Reformed Protestant past for an Anglican royalist future. On the first Sunday after the opening of Convocation, Browne attended worship at St Paul's, observed all the prayer book rituals and ordered others to do the same. A few weeks later, this new "dutiful son of the Church of England" provided the bishops with a lavish entertainment, informing them, according to an Anglican account, that "he had invited them on purpose to let the Presbyterians know that he disavowed them and their principles." Over the next year, Browne would join Alderman Sir John Robinson, the high Anglican Lieutenant of the Tower, as one of the "chief Captains" in the persecution of sectarians in the city and its environs.[16]

Browne's spectacular desertion was unnerving, but parliament's consideration of a bill to cleanse boroughs of those office-holders unwilling to accept the restored diocesan hierarchy was even more disturbing to Presbyterians. Indeed, the Corporation of London was a principal target of the Corporation bill. Two of its Reformed Protestant MPs had been conspicuous in the opening weeks of the session by their absence from the communion of members according to Anglican rite, and both the government and the Commons were aware of the hostility of many London Presbyterians to their plans for the church. The Corporation bill did not reach Charles until December. Its progress was delayed by the divergent priorities of Anglican MPs, who were interested primarily in restricting offices to conformists, and of the government, which hoped also to curb the independence of municipal regimes like that of London. The act empowered Charles to name commissioners to eject from borough offices all those who refused to disavow the legitimacy

---

[15] Rugg, *Diurnal*, pp. 159–60, 163–4, 169–73, 180; *Dialogue between the two Giants*, pp. 11–12; *The City's Remonstrance and Addresse to the King's most excellent Majesty* (1661), HMC *Fifth Report*, pp. 170, 175, 185; John Ogilby, *The Entertainment of His Most Excellent Majestie Charles II* (1662), facsimile ed. R. Knowles (Binghamton, NY, 1988), pp. 17–18; Bosher, *Making*, pp. 221–2.

[16] Add. MS 10,116, fols. 216, 223; *Behold a Cry!* (1662), p. 11; HMC *Le Fleming*, p. 28; Bosher, *Making*, p. 221; Hutton, *Restoration*, pp. 168, 170.

of resistance, who refused to repudiate the Covenant, or whose possession of office was otherwise deemed contrary to "public safety." Future office-holders were also required to demonstrate that they had taken the sacrament in the restored Church of England within the year prior to their selection.

The response to the Corporation Act of the still dominant Presbyterian element in London government was muted during the summer and winter parliamentary sessions of 1661. Because the status of the London charter was uncertain until the king confirmed it, the Corporation seemingly preferred to focus officially on its case for renewal of the charter. In July, for instance, the city formally petitioned the king for confirmation of the charter, some features of which were actually jeopardized by early drafts of the Corporation bill preferred by the government. But not all Presbyterians maintained their silence about a measure that restricted to Anglican conformists the same rights and liberties that the Rump and the army had once restricted to the sects. Writing on behalf of "some Citizens and Members of London, and other Cities," William Prynne blasted the bill's agenda as an "un-magistrating, dis-officing, [and] dis-franchising" of reliable and legally elected office-holders. Edmund Ludlow also remembered that London citizens were "much enraged" by proposals, in one draft of the bill, that would have deprived the city of the right of electing its own lord mayor.[17]

As the Corporation continued to press its case for renewal of the charter, Charles began to press, even before the adoption of the Corporation bill, for the removal of unacceptable civic office-holders, as a precondition for its confirmation. In December, as the choice of common councilmen approached, and as fears about sectarian plotting mounted again, Charles wrote to the Corporation to encourage the election of loyal conformists. He complained about the exertions of "turbulent spirits" who were "labouringe" in certain wards on behalf of individuals who were "known opposers of all regular gov[ern]ment both in Church and state." Should men of this nature be chosen, their elections would be annulled, Charles intimated. Although no elections were in fact undone in London, the new common council learned in February 1662 of the king's desire that they should obliterate from the city records all interregnum acts and decisions that reflected the "disloyalty of those times." And in May, commissioners appointed by the king, and acting under the authority of the Corporation

---

[17] Journal 41, fols. 248, 254; Add. MS 10,116, fol. 229; [William Prynne], *Summary Reasons, humbly tendered ... by some Citizens and members of London, and other Cities ... against the new intended Bill for ... Corporations* [1661]; HMC *Fifth Report*, p. 171; CSPD 1661–2, pp. 37–8; Browning, *Documents*, VIII, 375–6; Ludlow, *Voyce*, p. 290; Bosher, *Making*, p. 222; Chivers, "City of London," pp. 241–7; John Miller, "The Crown and the Borough Charters in the Reign of Charles II," *EHR* 100 (1985), 59–63; Seaward, *Cavalier Parliament*, pp. 152–5; Hutton, *Restoration*, pp. 158–61.

Act, discharged two aldermen, City MP William Love and Tempest Milner, both Reformed Protestants with offensive interregnum records. They were replaced by merchants William Turner, a puritan conformist, and Thomas Bludworth, who had lately prevailed as an episcopal parliamentary candidate at Southwark. Only then did the crown provide the Corporation with confirmation of its charter.[18]

The steady efforts of Charles's Anglican ministry and of the Anglican royalist majority in parliament to ensure the hegemony of episcopal men in the Corporation of London were successful in the end, and they had already led to the disappearance of most Independents and sectarians from civic affairs. Nevertheless, the city's Presbyterians were able to retain influence for another year. The apostate Presbyterian Lord Mayor Browne was succeeded in that office by the circumspect Dutch Reformed merchant, Sir John Frederick, who had Presbyterian support.[19] Despite the decline in Reformed Protestants on common council (Table 2.1), the principal Corporation committees for 1662 – including the committee charged with inspecting civil war and interregnum by-laws – also still included more individuals with Presbyterian pasts than with Anglican attachments.[20] With men like these still in positions of leadership, the Corporation also continued to assert its voice in ways unwelcome to the regime. It complained again, in 1662, about the state of the country's trade; and it raised concerns about a parliamentary militia bill that was similar to that adopted by the Rump in showing insufficient respect for the "rights and priviledges of this City."[21]

All this had changed by early 1663, when Anglican royalists in London achieved the political control the Corporation Act was intended to secure for them. The staunchly Anglican Sir John Robinson was chosen lord mayor for 1662–3; and when common council met for the first time after the December 1662 wardmotes, it was a much altered body. The noticeable decline in all common councilmen for 1663 who can be identified as dissenters (Table 2.1) suggests that many were unable to comply with the Corporation Act, even though only four common councilmen are known to have been "removed and discharged" by the commissioners. Many of the Reformed Protestant

---

18 Journal 41, fols. 255–256; Journal 45, fols. 142, 161, 183–184; Repertory 67, fol. 311; CLRO Remembrancia, IX, 14, 17–18; *CSPD 1661–2*, pp. 179, 287, 361; *CSPD 1663–4*, pp. 37, 94; *CSPVen 1661–4*, p. 64; Chivers, "City of London," p. 199, Sharpe, *London*, II, 395–6, 398; Miller, "Crown and the Borough Charters," p. 63; Henning, *House of Commons*, I, 670; Hutton, *Restoration*, p. 160.

19 For Frederick, see, O. P. Grell, "From Persecution to Integration," in *From Persecution to Toleration: The Glorious Revolution and Religion in England*, ed. O. P. Grell, J. I. Israel, and N. Tyacke (Oxford, 1991), p. 125; Henning, *House of Commons*, II, 363.

20 The London lieutenancy commission at the time of Frederick's mayoralty, on the other hand, was predominantly Anglican loyalist. SP 29/66/44; Journal 45, fols. 161, 191.

21 Journal 45, fol. 162; Repertory 68, fol. 47.

members of the city's major committees for the previous year – including such prominent civic Presbyterians as Sir Lawrence Bromfield, John Jekyll, and John Mascall – were not returned to the common council for 1663. Half the members of these committees for 1663 were newcomers, and none of them can be identified as a Reformed Protestant.[22]

By March 1663, elections to replace deceased and discharged aldermen, including Presbyterian City MP Sir William Thompson, who resigned from the bench, had also given Anglicans a working majority on the court of aldermen. Nevertheless, the Reformed Protestant presence in civic government had not been entirely eliminated, for some aldermen and common councilmen of Reformed Protestant background appear to have conformed to the extent now required by law. Such Reformed or dissenting aldermen as Sir John Frederick and Sir John Lawrence remained in office, as did Reformed Protestant common councilmen like Sir Thomas Chamberlain and Deputy Aldermen Thomas Lenthall and Jeremy Sambrooke.

Like other boroughs, the Corporation of London therefore experienced a dramatic purge of office-holders in 1662–3. Presbyterians who had been shut out of Corporation leadership by the Independents, the army, and the sects in 1648–9 had been shut out again by their onetime Anglican allies. And, just as was the case in 1648–9, this removal flew in the face of their continuing support from the London guild and ward electorates. Without the parliamentary constraint of the Corporation Act, electors would likely have continued many Presbyterians in office, just as they had in 1660–62. Presbyterian cleric Zachary Crofton, admittedly not an impartial observer, described the result as a "rude and disorderly Government" for the Corporation of London.[23] The act produced an Anglican civic regime that spoke for some citizens at the expense of others. Many Londoners now experienced an abridgment of the very rights and liberties they hoped the king would secure in 1659–60.

What, then, were the prospects of the Anglican royalist regime that was imposed upon London in 1662–3? From the very beginning, it labored under three handicaps, each of which will be considered here. First, some citizens perceived it as the instrument of a cavalier regime in the state that was insufficiently attentive to advancing the trade of the nation. Secondly, it promoted hierarchical social and political ideals that, in some respects, contradicted both the recent experiences and the aspirations of many London citizens.

---

[22] Journal 45, fols. 216, 270; Zachary Crofton, *Reformation not Separation*, p. 68. Anglican efforts to replace Reformed Protestants in civic offices were paralleled by Bishop Sheldon's effort to remove Reformed Protestants from London vestries: P. Seaward, "Gilbert Sheldon, the London Vestries, and the Defence of the Church," in *The Politics of Religion in Restoration England*, ed. T. Harris, P. Seaward, and M. Goldie (Oxford, 1990), pp. 49–73.

[23] Zachary Crofton, *Reformation not Separation*, p. 68.

And, thirdly, it was intimately associated with an episcopal leadership that preferred to coerce dissenting Protestants back into the church rather than to accommodate them through alterations of church government and worship.

Civic expressions of concern about the nation's trade in 1660–62 had little effect upon the crown or parliament. The Council of Trade appointed in 1660 quickly lapsed into obscurity, and government efforts to raise money in the city in 1662–3 had disappointing results. Unsettled by the expulsion of many Reformed Protestants from civic offices and civic pulpits, some citizens began to remember the Interregnum as a time of "quick trading," which contrasted favorably with an ensuing "shrinkage" of commerce. After losing his place in the church for nonconformity, Edmund Calamy noted that his former parishioners were now complaining obsessively "of Taxes, and decay of Trading." In 1663, London sectarian conspirators against the cavalier regime hoped to gain support through a promise to require the king to "take away excise, chimney-money, and all taxes whatever." Many citizens who had been upset by the stagnation of English trade during Oliver's Spanish war, and who had resented the taxes of the Rump, seem to have found little to appreciate in the commercial and fiscal policies of the restored monarchy. Only when Anglican royalist parliamentarians hit upon the strategy of another Dutch War in 1664–5 was the government able to proclaim its credentials as a champion of commerce. But even then, the war was more reflective of cavalier anti-republicanism than of real civic animus against the Dutch.[24]

The new Corporation governing elite was at a disadvantage in countering these perceptions of Anglican royalist disregard for trade because it was notably less well integrated with the commercial leadership of the city than the Presbyterians had been. In time, Anglican merchants and investors would become something of a Restoration joint-stock establishment; but in 1663–5, only three Anglican stock company directors, including Sir Thomas Bludworth, sat on the court of aldermen. This represented a significant loosening of the ties between the Corporation leadership and the city's principal commercial organizations, especially the Levant and East India Companies.

The Reformed Protestant aldermanic and common council leadership of 1660–62 had been quite different in character. It had included such sitting Levant and East India Company office-holders as Sir Anthony Bateman, Sir Theophilus Biddulph, Sir John Frederick, John Joliffe (Levant Treasurer), William Love (Levant Deputy Governor), John Mascall, Sir William

---

[24] Add. MS 10,117, fols. 43–46; Edmund Calamy, *Eli Trembling for Fear of the Ark* (1662), p. 28; *CSPVen 1661–64*, pp. 111, 185, 190–1, 205; *CSPD 1663–64*, pp. 64, 352; *The Mather Papers*, Collections of the Mass. Hist. Soc., 4th ser. 8 (Boston, Mass., 1868), pp. 182, 196; S. C. A. Pincus, *Protestantism and Patriotism: Ideologies and the Making of English Foreign Policy, 1650–1658* (Cambridge, 1996), p. 253 and chs. 15–16 generally; Henning, *House of Commons*, II, 760; Haley, *Shaftesbury*, p. 228; Chivers, "City of London," pp. 247–77.

Thompson, and Sir William Vincent (Levant Deputy Governor). Many of these Reformed Protestant merchants and investors, now withdrawn from leadership in the Corporation, remained active in the trading companies, for dissent was less an obstacle in the stocks than in city government. Moreover, dissent quickly emerged as a major element within the population of London merchants, leaving the Corporation government ill matched, on religious grounds, to the trading community as a whole. The situation was not improved by Archbishop Sheldon's suggestion that dissenting merchants be encouraged to withdraw from trade. Ironically, the Anglican royalist regime in the city suffered from one of same issues as its Commonwealth civic predecessor of 1649–53: it was too narrowly constituted to speak for many of the most enterprising people in London.[25]

Moreover, the Anglican regime in the Corporation spoke a distinctive and traditional social and political language that did not command universal respect, despite its association with the Court of Charles II. The Anglican aldermen eagerly responded, for instance, to the 1663 republication, by royal directive, of Richard Mocket's *God and the King*. Originally published in 1618, the work marshaled patriarchal analogies on behalf of divine right monarchy and condemned resistance to kings and disobedience to social superiors. The aldermen required the ward beadles to hawk the book from door to door so that masters might better instruct their households in the habits of deference and respect for authority. A similar concern for the re-establishment of social deference was evident in a 1663 mayoral precept condemning the "rudeness, affronts and insolent behaviour" of the "meaner sort of people," especially hackney coachmen, carmen, draymen, and colliers. Their "contempt of their Superiours," which had grown during the late "oppression," was to be restrained by the constables so that "Noblemen, Ladies, Gentlemen & persons of quality" might again travel and trade without molestation.

These Anglican ideals of order, hierarchy, and precedence were also applied to the workings of the Corporation itself. In May 1663, common council appointed another committee to inspect its journals and records in order to eliminate passages reflecting the "disloyal" behavior of the previous decades. The principal purpose of this inspection was to remove all traces of the 1648–9 emancipation of common council from mayoral and magisterial restraint. A few months later, the aldermen reasserted their precedence over the common councilmen, reaffirming their privileges of overseeing the

---

[25] SP 105/152 (Levant Company Court Minutes 1660–1671). In addition to Bludworth (Levant, East India Companies), Sir Richard Ford and Sir Richard Ryves were East India Company directors. Pincus, *Protestantism and Patriotism*, pp. 243n., 326–8; Henning, *House of Commons*, I, 650–1, 670–1; II, 344–6, 363–5, 657–8, 760–4; III, 555–6, 644; Woodhead, *Rulers*, pp. 30, 33, 42, 44, 57, 71, 73, 96, 99, 110, 113, 161–2, 168.

conduct of common council business and of separately approving common council acts. The crown encouraged this return to the pre-1648 patterns of civic order; and Charles's December 1662 letter about the choice of common councilmen was accompanied by what was to become an annual mayoral precept recommending the choice of "the more discreet and wealthy Inhabitants."[26]

This reassertion of hierarchical principle and of magisterial control within the Corporation unsettled Reformed Protestant and sectarian citizens. They had been moved, in the 1640s and 1650s, by somewhat different political ideas and language. Electoral choice and consent remained important to many who could not forgo their memories of a civic regime in which citizens had regularly acted and spoken in defense of their rights and liberties, even against the government and magistrates when necessary. Moreover, the Anglican royalist emphasis upon authority and obedience could also be misunderstood in ways that sapped confidence in the restored regimes in city and state. Pepys reported rumors, as early as February 1664, for instance, that some of the king's councilors had advised him that "his will is all" and that "neither privileges of Parliament nor City is anything." The statutory proscription of so many citizens from civic office fed perceptions that Anglican royalism was inherently prejudicial to the rights and liberties that Londoners had sought to preserve in 1659–60.[27]

Finally, the new Anglican civic regime was strongly associated with religious persecution, a strategy for achieving uniformity that Reformed Protestants rejected as a popish means for suppressing lively faith and Christian conscience. For Anglicans, persecution was an appropriate response to disobedience to authority in church and state. They welcomed the April 1663 additions of the Archbishop of Canterbury and the Bishop of London to the Privy Council as signs of a closer union between crown and miter against the enemies of order. But Reformed Protestants saw persecution as an episcopal tool that was intended to drive reformation principles from an ostensibly Protestant church. They found no contradiction in obeying the king, in matters of civil government, while preserving Protestant tradition against the punitive Anglican settlement of 1662–5. And, they could point to Charles himself on behalf of their position.

In August 1662, when Reformed Protestant clergy were ejected from their London pulpits, both civic and clerical Presbyterian leaders were hopeful of a royal indulgence for the benefit of those who could not fully conform. In December 1662, such an indulgence was actually offered through a royal declaration. Charles provided for the licensing of separate public "devotions"

---

[26] Journal 45, fols. 249, 258, 264, 313, 333 and Repertory 69, fols. 57, 208; [Richard Mocket], *God and the King* (1663); *CSPD 1663–64*, p. 66; G. J. Schochet, *Patriarchialism in Political Thought* (New York, 1975), pp. 88–90.

[27] Pepys, *Diary*, V, 60; Pincus, *Patriotism and Protestantism*, p. 233.

for nonconformists in the hope that the experience of religious liberty would eventually bring dissenters to "a full submission" to the church, but he merely announced this policy as desirable. Implementation of the indulgence was made dependent upon the agreement of parliament, in its next session, to a bill confirming the king's power to provide dispensations from the Act of Uniformity and from other penal legislation. When parliament met in February 1663, Charles sent for the leading London Presbyterian clergy to assure them that he intended to restore them to public ministry. He also met with the foremost Independent clergy in the city, who pleaded for liberty of conscience, while also professing that they and their followers were "heartilie for kinglie government," rather than "for a Republique."[28]

Coercion rather than indulgence was to prevail in parliament in 1663 and for the remainder of the decade, however. Charles's indulgence had also been extended to Roman Catholics, a provision that made Reformed Protestant leaders like Baxter uncomfortable; and the constitutional implications of statutory confirmation of a royal dispensing power were equally troublesome.[29] Moreover, sectarian plotting after 1660 provided Anglican opponents of indulgence with rhetorical grounds for rejecting concessions to conscience and for proceeding with persecution.

Sporadic but serious expressions of sectarian hostility to the coercive religious regime kept alive Anglican fears about a reversion to the instability from which the nation had been delivered. Scarcely any plot or suspected plot of the early Restoration was without a London dimension. When Anglican royalist ministers and MPs played the conspiratorial card at Westminster, they often did so, therefore, with an eye to the Corporation. When Clarendon disclosed intelligence about a major suspected plot in December 1661, for instance, allegations were extended to leading London Reformed Protestants, including current Aldermen and City MPs John Fowke and William Love.[30] City Reformed Protestant clergy like George Cokayne and Philip Nye fell under suspicion of plotting after the implementation of the Uniformity Act, as did leading Baptist merchant William Kiffin. In 1663, the involvement of a shadowy committee of London malcontents in the Northern Plot, rumors of a London rising, and the interception of libels

---

[28] MS Carte 47, fols. 359, 361, 365; Add. MS 4107 (Sloan), fols. 17–19; Add. MS 10, 117, fols. 58, 61; CLRO Waiting Book, II (5 Jan. 1663); Browning, *Documents*, VIII, 373; *CSPD 1663–4*, p. 10; *CSPVen 1661–4*, pp. 187, 229; Christie, *Life*, I, appendix vi, lxxviii–lxxxi; *Mather Papers*, pp. 207–9; Pepys, *Diary*, IV, 5–6; *POAS*, I, 289–97; Abernathy, *English Presbyterians*, pp. 84–8; Bosher, *Making*, pp. 259–62; Haley, *Shaftesbury*, pp. 163–4; Seaward, *Cavalier Parliament*, pp. 181–2; Hutton, *Restoration*, pp. 193–4.

[29] Baxter, *Reliquiae*, Lib. I, Part II, 430, 433; Pepys, *Diary*, IV, 44; Haley, *Shaftesbury*, pp. 164–6; Abernathy, *English Presbyterians*, pp. 88–90, D. R. Lacey, *Dissent and Parliamentary Politics in England, 1661–1689* (New Brunswick, NJ, 1969), pp. 52–4; Seaward, *Cavalier Parliament*, pp. 182–92; Hutton, *Restoration*, pp. 196–200.

[30] Add. MS 10,117, fol. 3; Greaves, *Deliver Us*, pp. 78–81; Hutton, *Restoration*, pp. 164–5.

calling for the king's assassination prompted an increase in the militia tax and a proposal for a powerful Major-General of London.[31]

Re-employment of the sectarian alarums of 1659–60 provided Anglican royalists with a useful ideological prop, then; and militant Anglican apologists in press and in pulpit as frequently directed their ire at Presbyterians as at other dissenters. "They embroiled us in war with their Solemn League and Covenant once before," thundered Roger L'Estrange in 1662, "and now they propose to do the same again."[32] Anglican magistrates followed the lead of Sir Richard Browne and Sir John Robinson in turning these words into action, especially after the passage of the Conventicle Act in May 1664. A mayoral precept of August 1664, requiring constables to prevent unlawful meetings, initiated a flood of presentations in the lord mayor's court. By November 1664, the aldermen had agreed upon a weekly rotation of responsibility for searching out and suppressing Sabbath meetings.[33]

These strident words and harsh acts were not, however, the signs of a confidant Anglican loyalist civic regime. To the contrary, they expressed the anxiety of Anglican royalists about the extent of dissent in the Corporation and about the narrow foundations of their own rule. Like the regimes of the Interregnum, London's ruling Anglican royalists of the 1660s sought to establish their control by employing fear and vilification of those excluded from full public life. But, given the numbers and conviction of the excluded, the result was unsettlement rather than settlement. Distrusted by many merchants, and distrusted by many citizens who preferred a less hierarchical interpretation of the civic constitution, the royalist magistrates of early Restoration London were also perceived by many as acting in episcopal interests rather than in those of king and kingdom. Charles's preference for a church order based upon accommodation rather than upon persecution kept alive the hopes of many Reformed Protestants for a return to something more similar to the broad Cromwellian church. And some suspected that, left to their persecuting policies, the bishops would soon "ruin themselfs" rather than those clergy they drove from the church.[34]

---

[31] HMC *Seventh Report*, p. 463; *CSPD 1663–4*, pp. 256–7, 281, 284, 289, 348, 352, 376, 382, 405, 412, 485; *CSPVen 1661–64*, p. 205; Bosher, *Making*, p. 266 & n.; A. Marshall, *Intelligence and Espionage in the Reign of Charles II, 1660–1685* (Cambridge, 1994), pp. 142–50, 158–9; Pincus, *Patriotism and Protestantism*, pp. 214–18, 223–26; Greaves, *Deliver Us*, pp. 112–29, 176–92; Hutton, *Restoration*, pp. 178–9, 204–7.

[32] Add. MS 10,117, fol. 67; Roger L'Estrange, *Interest Mistaken; or, the Holy Cheat* (1662), preface; *Master Edmund Calamies Leading Case* (1663), p. 15.

[33] Journal 45, fol. 400; CLRO Waiting Book, III, fols. 6ff.; Add. MS 10,117, fol. 114; *CSPD 1663–64*, pp. 603, 632, 678; *CSPD 1664–65*, pp. 64–5, 74, 82, 173, 183, 363; R. L. Greaves, *Enemies under his Feet; Radicals and Nonconformists in Britain, 1664–1677* (Stanford, 1990), pp. 131–3; Hutton, *Restoration*, pp. 209–10, 230, 263.

[34] Pepys, *Diary*, IV, 44.

ESTABLISHING DISSENTING IDENTITY

No single event of the early Restoration was more unsettling for London citizens than the expulsion of sixty-four Reformed Protestant clergy from the pulpits of London, Westminster, and Middlesex on 24 August 1662.[35] The diocese of London was the most heavily purged in the country. Intended to strengthen the national church by reserving its ministry for those who accepted the prayer book and episcopal authority, the act instead severely weakened public ministry in the city. Not until the early eighteenth century did the Anglican order recover the stature and visibility it lost in London by re-establishing itself upon the ruin of dozens of respected teachers.

Many of the displaced London clergy had acquired national reputations through their writing and preaching. William Bates, Edmund Calamy, Joseph Caryl, Thomas Gouge, Thomas Jacombe, Lazarus Seaman, and Thomas Watson were but some of the better known of them. After its own years in the wilderness, the Anglican order could initially fill few city pulpits with clergy of the equivalent stature. As a result, many of the city's most articulate Protestant lay people continued to identify with their former pastors, often in full or partial dissent from the church settlement, but sometimes in outward conformity.

Ironically, the Uniformity Act disabled the restored Church of England from being the restored church of London. Instead, the continuing but illicit ministries of the expelled clergy shaped a powerful dissenting identity that quickly and widely emerged in defense of Reformed Protestant teachings and traditions in the city. Indeed, the principal creation of the Uniformity Act in London was actually religious multiplicity: the proportion of the civic population that looked beyond the parochial order for spiritual guidance and ministry vastly increased after 1662. Nothing from the years of sectarian proliferation in the 1640s and 1650s could compare to the creation of a thriving and multiform nonconformist culture dominated by Reformed Protestant pastors and parishioners who had previously identified with their parish churches. Truly, the Church of England was itself as much a victim of the Uniformity Act in London as the clergy who were "church-outed" by it.

The Cavalier Parliament could not possibly have chosen a less auspicious day for the deprivation of nonconformist clergy than 24 August, the blackest day of the French Reformation, and a coincidence that colored dissenting interpretation of the event from the very beginning. Puritan crowds flocked to the London churches on St Bartholomew's Day to hear the final sermons

---

[35] A. G. Matthews, *Calamy Revised, being a revision of Edmund Calamy's account of the ministers and others ejected and Silenced, 1660–2* (Oxford, 1934 and 1988), p. xii; I. M. Green, *Re-Establishment*, p. 157; Greaves, *Deliver Us*, p. 103. Almost forty other greater London clergy had been ejected in 1660.

of those about to be deprived. The day passed with few disturbances, for Reformed Protestant leaders understood that their prospects for relief from Charles depended upon his perceptions about their loyalty. Still, Pepys noted in 1662 that "the City is much dissatisfied" with the loss of its clergy; and the diarist predicted that if the bishops failed to bring in good preachers in their places, "all will fly a-pieces." In fulfillment of his own fears, Pepys was soon lamenting the state of the church, especially in the city. "The present clergy will never heartily go down," he believed, noting in 1664 that the London churches were "very empty." New and inexperienced incumbents labored to establish their reputations in London; but one observer noted "they are hated and laughed at by everybody."[36]

The "invention of Anglicanism" clearly took time in the city of London, then; but the expelled clergy had no difficulty inventing urban nonconformity. Most of London's ejected clergy remained in the city or its environs. They were soon joined by others of similar stature who had been displaced elsewhere, like Richard Baxter, James Innes, John Owen, and Nathaniel Vincent. As a whole, the ejected pastors of London in the 1660s constituted the most distinguished collection of English Reformed clergy since the meeting of the Westminster Assembly in 1644–5. Creation of dissenting identity began with the widespread popular veneration of them as living successors to the Marian martyrs. Supposedly silenced, their words actually reverberated as evidence for many that the Reformation in England was now in a perilous state. The collected sermons of 24 August 1662 were illicitly published and widely circulated as the first "best seller" of the Restoration. Roger L'Estrange condemned the *Farewell Sermons* as "one of the most *Audacious*, and *Dangerous Libels*, that hath been made publique under any Government," and he was right.[37]

Despite their outward respect for the king and his government, London's Reformed Protestant clergy interpreted the church settlement as an unmitigated spiritual calamity and as a denial of the country's historic Reformation. Dissenting identity originated in London not in fussy, peripheral disputes about liturgy and ceremony but rather in the fundamental assumption that

---

[36] Add. MS 10,117, fols. 43, 45; Henry Newcome, *The Diary of the Rev. Henry Newcome* (Manchester, 1849), pp. 113–14; HMC *Seventh Report*, p. 484; *Mather Papers*, p. 201; "The Religious Condition of London in 1672 as reported to King and Court by an Impartial Outsider," ed. G. L. Turner, *TCHS* 3 (1907–8), 203–5 (partial transcript of BL MS Stowe 186, fols. 5ff.); Pepys, *Diary*, IV, 372 and V, 190; I. M. Green, *Re-Establishment*, pp. 165, 176.

[37] *A Complete Collection of Farewel Sermons* (1663), with quotation from unpaginated preface; L'Estrange, *Regulation of the Press*, A3; Seaward, "London Vestries," p. 51. Also, see the selected *Sermons of the Great Ejection* (1962). The government's anxiety about the quality and activities of the expelled London clergy can be examined in SP 9/26 (Joseph Williamson's Index or Spy Book, *c*. 1662–68), also transcribed as "Williamson's Spy Book," [ed. G. L. Turner], *TCHS* 5 (1911–12), 242–58, 301–19, 345–56.

the gospel was being driven out of the church in favor of the "Idol" of episcopal authority. Edmund Calamy preached in the heart of the city, at St Mary Aldermanbury, on 24 August 1662, that the land was on the verge of "a spiritual famine." He repeated the theme in his old pulpit during Charles's brief indulgence: "when the Gospel is in danger, the Ministers of the Gospel in danger, and the Ordinances in danger," then "the Ark of God" was also in danger of being lost, he suggested. John Collins, once a chaplain to George Monck, was now persuaded that "the Church of Christ is in the wilderness" as it was "in Queen *Maries* dayes." Calamy attributed this unexpected disaster to the "power ... of Antichrist, [and] of his seducing spirits." William Bates blamed the misfortunes of the church on the devil. Thomas Watson, deprived at St Stephen Walbrook, and Lazarus Seaman, ejected from Allhallows Bread Street, applied this language to the advocates of conformity. "The Devil hath his Ministers as well as Christ," said Watson, while Seaman distinguished between the "great Shepherd" to be followed and "inferiour shepherds" who could mislead. Independent John Goodwin condemned the new Anglican establishment as "*Egyptian* Sorcerers" and as "pleaders for *Baal.*"[38]

The first dissenting teachers also challenged both the authority and the Protestant credentials of the Anglican MPs responsible for adopting and enforcing the Uniformity Act. Calamy anticipated Milton's conceptualization of the conflict as one between oppressed Hebrews and the triumphant warlords of other gods: "Magistrates must not be as the Philistines," he wrote, implying that such was in fact the case: "they had the Ark, but ... they set it up in the house of Dagon." Similarly, Baptist doyen William Kiffin reportedly compared coercive magistrates to the "presidents and the princes" of Babylon, who had conspired against Daniel. Although the ejected clergy counseled that "the weapons of our warfare are not carnal, but spiritual," they also elevated the internal witness of conscience against the external authority of persecuting magistrates. Parochial Independent Joseph Caryl reminded his listeners at St Magnus the Martyr, on St Bartholomew's Day, "there is no such thundering Preacher in the World as Conscience is." And at Shadwell, Stepney, departing Independent Matthew Mead warned his flock that they should "*in all conditions, chuse suffering rather than sinning.*"[39]

[38] *Farewel Sermons*, preface, A3–4, Aa3, [Aa5–6], [Aa8], Bb3, L3, N4, Rr5–6, Sf[1], T2; Calamy, *Eli Trembling for Fear of the Ark*, pp. 24, 26, 31; *Sermons of the Ejection*, pp. 61–2, 65–6, 69, 71, 75, 138; John Goodwin, *Prelatique Preachers None of Christ's Teachers* (1663), pp. 8, 12, 24; Greaves, *Deliver Us*, p. 92.

[39] SP 29/42/36I; SP 29/43/57; *Farewel Sermons*, Aa[1], C4, N3, N7, [R8], Sf[1], Z4, [Z5]; Calamy, *Eli Trembling*, p. 31; *Sermons of the Ejection*, pp. 46–7, 58, 136, 143; M. D., *A Short Surveigh of the Grand Case of the Present Ministry* (1663), pp. 21, 25, 27; L'Estrange, *Regulation of the Press*, p. 23; John Milton, *Samson Agonistes* (1671).

Historians who have suggested a passive public acceptance of the Uniformity Act have largely missed the trauma experienced by Reformed Protestants in 1662.[40] If the Restoration was accompanied by little physical "terror," it was nevertheless accompanied by a devastating psychological blow to all those who had expected Charles to maintain a Reformed Protestant church rather than to preside over the destruction of one. Presbyterians were, at first, more cautious than Independents in substituting private teaching for public ministry, for they continued to hope for accommodation. Their initial desire was to return to the national church order they had sought to protect against separatists, not to organize separate Reformed churches. Nevertheless, in the 1660s, they shared expulsion with parochial Independents, and they shared persecution with the sects. And they also shared the defining dissenting conviction that reformation in England was imperiled by the same "popish" forces that had threatened it before 1640. Similarly, Presbyterian laity were more likely than their Independent counterparts to keep one finger in the prayer book, in order to reform it; but they also saw no inconsistency between supporting both their parish order and the pastors who had formerly presided over it.

If a common dissenting identity originated in the shared disasters of 1660–62, it matured quickly through the additional traumas that followed close upon that of St Bartholomew's Day. By the end of the decade, the episcopal order had not yet established itself in the city; but the deprived clergy had regained many of their former flocks. The great plague of 1665 provided an early ministerial test for Anglican pastors, but the excluded clergy met the test instead. As the epidemic spread, so did anger about the flight of parish clergy from the city. The places of established pastors who sought to "escape the *storm*" were taken by some of those they had replaced. As Bishop Gilbert Burnet reported, some of the ejected clergy "went into the empty pulpits, and preached . . . with very good success." Baxter remembered the experience as a decisive turning-point for Presbyterian teachers, who overcame their hesitation about public preaching and ministered to "the dying and distressed people."

In 1666, disaster followed disaster, both for the people and for the parochial clergy, when the Fire of London consumed two-thirds of the parish churches and the cathedral. The conflagration deprived the parish clergy of their physical assets in maintaining public ministry against their dissenting competitors. The excluded clergy had no need of parish edifices for their work, but the Anglican clergy had less rationale for theirs without the historic structures within which it had been centered. As conformist clergy struggled

<hr />

[40] Bosher, *Making*, pp. 265–7; Abernathy, *English Presbyterians*, p. 86.

to maintain their visibility, nonconformist preachers filled the parochial vacuum created by the fire, preaching in surviving warehouses, in guild halls, and even in hastily built meeting-houses. According to Baxter, in the wake of the plague and fire, the city's nonconformist clergy, "did keep their Meetings very openly, and prepared large Rooms, and some of them plain Chappels, with Pulpits, Seats, and Galleries for the reception of as many as could come. . . . So that many of the Citizens went to those Meetings called private, *more, than went to the publick Parish Churches.*" Similarly, Burnet wrote that "in that time conventicles abounded in all the parts of the city. It was thought hard to hinder men from worshipping God any way as they could, when there were no churches, nor ministers to look after them."[41]

This return of civic dissenting clergy to public ministry outside the parochial order did not escape the notice of Anglican royalist MPs. In 1665, the Cavalier Parliament adopted the Five Mile Act in response to dissenting ministry in London during the plague. But neither the damage to parochial ministry in the city nor the establishment of dissenting ministry could be undone by acts of parliament. The experiences of plague and fire were signature events for a generation of Londoners embarking upon their life's work or still in apprenticeship and service. Fear of sudden death, the loss of family members or friends, and temporary economic displacement provoked a spiritual crisis for many younger adults. When young and old alike found their needs met by nonconformist clergy, their dissenting identity was formed in almost unbreakable moulds. The urban dissenting pastors were already functioning as an alternate priestly tribe to that enjoined by law, laboring in the same vineyards and competing for the leadership of the same faithful.

Indications abound from the late 1660s that nonconformist worship in the urban area was both open and extensive and that wary magistrates hesitated to enforce the measures against it. Pepys observed in December 1667 that "the Nonconformists are mighty high and their meetings . . . connived at"; and a year later, he noted "the non-conformists do now preach openly in houses in many places." John Evelyn heard Anglican fears in 1668 that the Anabaptists were "swarming" again. Another observer noted sixteen conventicles in the single London ward of Cripplegate Without. Monitoring the spiritual mood of the citizens, MP Sir William Waller reported to his parliamentary colleagues that he had asked his city friends "why they did not [re-]build their Churches" quickly, only to discover that they preferred

---

[41] *A Pulpit to be Let* (1665), and in *POAS*, I, 298–301; Baxter, *Reliquiae*, Part III, 19 (my italics); Richard Baxter, *The Nonconformists Plea for Peace: or an Account of their Judgement* (1679), pp. 236–8; Gilbert Burnet, *Burnet's History of My Own Time*, ed. O. Airy, 2 vols. (Oxford, 1897–1900), I, 400, 489.

ministry outside those churches and were "afraid to be whipped into them." Reflecting a few years later upon the resilience and success of London non-conformity since the Fire, Undersecretary of State Sir Joseph Williamson thought "*fanatics have increased*, because the people wanted churches, and the [Anglican] City preachers are generally not well thought of." Another Anglican commentator agreed that the plague and fire had compounded the difficulties of the established clergy: "Those two dreadfull callamities seperated [*sic*] Ministers and people, not only in place, but Affection, and many of them are not yet returned to a good understanding one of Another."[42]

As dissenting ministry was established in defiance of law, and as dissenting identity emerged in defense of reformation, anti-episcopal language also again became a London commonplace. By the late 1660s, the restraint of the expelled clergy was giving way, in some instances, to rhetorical impatience, as dissenters gained in confidence and resolve. Pepys observed in December 1667, that spoken and written words against the bishops were "as bad...as ever in the year 1640." Steven Coven apparently preached in London in 1668 that the "good soldier of Jesus Christ" should, in contrast to St Peter, "strike not at Malchus Ear" but rather "at the High-Priests Head." Similarly, Joseph Wilson, an irreconcilable Presbyterian, pointed in 1668 to a classic text of sixteenth-century Calvinist iconoclasm in defense of reformation: "'Ye shall overthrow their altars, and break their pillars, and burn their groves with fire.'" (*Deuteronomy* 12:2–30) The apprentices' riots against bawdy houses in 1668 were accompanied by strongly anti-episcopal rhetoric, and the government became alarmed that the riots were a prelude to rebellion. A few years later, an Anglican observer of city affairs noted that the "great designe" of the Independents and Presbyterians had, for several years, been "to cast all the reproach of Ignorance, Lazyness, and immorality upon the conforming clergy, that they might take off the esteem of the people from them." Significantly, he added, they had "in great measure succeeded." By that time, the activism of dissenting clergy under constraint and the establishment of dissenting identity had also inspired a variety of challenges to the Anglican royalist regimes in the city and the state.[43]

[42] Add. MS 36,916 (Aston Papers, XVI), fols. 107, 137, 139; *CSPD 1671*, p. 581 (my italics); Grey, *Debates*, I, 160; Pepys, *Diary*, VIII, 584 and IX, 385; Evelyn, *Diary*, III, 513; "Religious Condition of London," p. 203.

[43] BL MS Stowe 186, fol. 20; "Religious Condition of London," pp. 200–1; Pepys, *Diary*, VIII, 585, and IX, 485; [Steven Coven], *The Militant Christian, or the Good Soldier of Jesus Christ* (1668), unpaginated opening poetry and pp. 38, 41, 60; [Joseph Wilson], *Nehushtan: or, a sober and peaceable Discourse* (1668), title page; N. Davis, *Society and Culture in Early Modern France* (Stanford, 1975), p. 152; T. Harris, "The Bawdy House Riots of 1668," *HJ* 29 (1986), 537–56; Greaves, *Deliver Us*, p. 88.

ESTABLISHING A DISSENTING PRESENCE IN
THE CORPORATION, 1665–1669

As a dissenting identity was asserted within London's religious culture, a strong dissenting presence was also established in the Corporation of London. By decade's end, leading sectarians and Reformed Protestant dissenters had regained visibility in civic affairs. The narrow Anglican regime that assumed power in the city in 1662–3 proved incapable of dealing successfully with the strains produced by plague, fire, and the Anglo-Dutch War of 1665–7. The war was a turning-point in the civic rehabilitation of nonconformist spokesmen, some of whom had also provided leadership in the Corporation of London before 1662. As a contrivance for crushing dissent in a great campaign against the sects and republicans at home and abroad, the war not only failed; but in its failure, it jeopardized the entire Anglican settlement of church and state.

The war proved a tonic to dissenting political energy in the city for a number of reasons. Before its lamentable conclusion, London citizens had experienced a major invasion scare in 1667 after the humiliation of the English fleet. By then, fears that the war would be injurious to English trade had been justified.[44] Many London citizens believed that the fire of 1666 had been a wartime popish device to destroy English trade; and many of them also came to see the Court of Charles II as a den of vice, political self-interest, and Catholic intrigue. Many in the city and some in parliament blamed the Anglican establishment for these intersecting martial, commercial, and moral failures; and by association, they questioned the Anglican policy of persecuting Protestant dissenters. Schemes for a more comprehensive church settlement were revived in 1667; and although such ideas were abandoned with the fall of the Earl of Clarendon, public discussion of the religious question had broken Anglican self-confidence and encouraged even greater dissenting assertiveness. Under the Cabal, which eventually advanced toleration against coercion, Anglican royalists found their control of the Corporation contested by those they had sought to exclude in 1662–3. This civic contest would continue, with occasional lulls, until the forfeiture of the London charter in 1683.

The war terminated a brief interlude of civic peace, under Anglican royalist auspices, that coincided with a recovery from the economic depression of the 1650s and early 1660s. A Corporation-sponsored public feast for the lord chamberlain and the Privy Council in December 1664 was a celebration of Anglican hegemony in city and state as well as of the crown's recent raising of

---

[44] Pincus, *Protestantism and Patriotism*, pp. 292–6, 318–30.

£200,000 in subscription loans from London citizens.[45] But Anglican royalist hegemony in London was severely tested in 1665–7. The declaration of war against the Dutch was initially greeted with enthusiasm in London, and the naval victory off Lowestoft in June 1665 was the occasion for spontaneous popular rejoicing in the city and Westminster. But joy turned to distraction as the plague drove the Court and many substantial citizens from the urban area within a few weeks.[46]

A year later, the mood of a city still mourning its plague victims had become quite sober. The entrance of France into the war, early in 1666, had been accompanied by a torrent of public Franco-phobia that would soon dwarf hostility toward Holland. English naval successes in July and August, duly celebrated in London, dispelled fears of a French invasion. But the disruption of the city's trade, both by war and by the plague, had reduced the Corporation's ability to raise money for the government at a time when money was badly needed. One privy councilor opposed the government's June 1666 request for another £100,000 from the Corporation for fear of an embarrassing refusal. Pepys learned from the Lombard street goldsmith-bankers that a loan would be denied by the city, "they being little pleased" either with news of French successes against English plantations or with "the King's affairs" more generally. Rumors about ministerial peculation, strategic mismanagement of the war, and royal philandering were by now widespread. When a city loan was in fact requested, it was granted; but it also proved to be the last financial assistance the city was able to provide before it was engulfed in the flames of September 1666.[47]

As the Corporation began to struggle with the rebuilding of the city, both civic and parliamentary opinion turned decidedly pessimistic and antagonistic to Clarendon's government. The spreading belief that the Fire of London had been a Catholic or a French design bred a panicky fear of popery, while the fire itself prompted Anglicans and dissenters to point to each other's sins as the source of divine wrath. In parliament, the Duke of Buckingham fanned a Country reaction against Clarendon that was fueled by suspicions about ministerial abuse and designs for French-style absolutism. Buckingham's parliamentary following included a "Presbyterian faction" and other critics of religious coercion. In the burned out city, defeatism triumphed. Merchants

---

[45] Reformed Protestant merchants and traders were notable among the 800 subscribers to the June loan. CLRO Card Index of Lenders to Certain Loans, 1660–64, comp. T. F. Reddaway, *et al.*; Journal 45, fols. 389, 423; Add. MS 10,117, fol. 124; Chivers, "City of London," pp. 266–77.

[46] Add. MS 10,117, fols. 140–141; John Evelyn, *Diary*, III, 410; Pincus, *Protestantism and Patriotism*, pp. 281–2.

[47] Journal 46, fol. 99; Add. MS 10,117, fols. 167, 169; Pepys, *Diary*, VI, 211, and VII, 152–3, 159, 171–2, 174, 225, 248; Evelyn, *Diary*, III, 439–40; *CSPVen 1664–66*, pp. 247, 266, 281; Pincus, *Protestantism and Patriotism*, pp. 285–8, 352, 356, 360–1.

who contemplated the alternatives of further war or a bad peace expected to be ruined by either. James Houblon, scion of a leading French Reformed trading family, informed Pepys that his commercial colleagues all "do give over trade and the nation for lost." Such sentiments were noticeable even among leading civic Anglicans: Edward Backwell and Alderman Sir Robert Vyner, the principal royalist goldsmith-bankers, for instance, were reluctant to make further advances of money. Given this mood, Country MPs found much support from London citizens and merchants in opposing a Court-sponsored excise proposal.[48]

Dejection turned to anger in the wake of the crippling of the English fleet at anchor in the Medway by the Dutch in June 1667. A naval disaster on the London doorstep and continuing fears about a French invasion sparked a massive panic. Charles and the Duke of York sought to embolden the London citizenry by personally assembling the trained bands for possible employment. The Corporation scraped together £10,000 for hastily thrown up defensive works along the river, but many citizens had already given up the contest. Some fled with their valuables and others beat upon closed goldsmiths' doors to recover their deposits. "Every body were flying, none [knew] why or whither," wrote John Evelyn, who sent his plate out of town. Others vented their wrath in the streets. "People do cry out... of their being bought and sold," Pepys recorded, and "that we are... governed by Papists and... are betrayed by people about the King and shall be delivered up to the French." Calls for a session of parliament were among the more restrained slogans of crowds that milled about Clarendon's mansion. Some in the Corporation were said to be promoting a petition for a session. The government responded by calling one for July, but it was terminated with the arrival of the peace that had been negotiated at Breda. Neither the news of the peace nor the proroguing of parliament until the fall improved tempers among many London merchants and citizens, however. "They look... upon it [the peace] as... made only to preserve the King... in his lusts... and to sacrifice trade and his kingdoms... to his own pleasures."[49]

---

[48] Frustration about the slow development of a coherent rebuilding program sustained this dark mood. In January 1667, common council was forced to disclaim a rumor that only those citizens who had disavowed the Solemn League and Covenant would be permitted to rebuild. Journal 46, fols. 135–137; Pepys, *Diary*, VII, 330–1, 371, and VIII, 113, 157–8; *POAS*, I, 114; Andrew Marvell, *Poems and Letters*, ed. H. M. Margoliouth, 3rd ed., 2 vols. (Oxford, 1971), II, 45, 53, 310; Seaward, *Cavalier Parliament*, pp. 272, 293, 299, 300–1; Pincus, *Protestantism and Patriotism*, pp. 347–51, 366–78, 393–7.

[49] Journal 46, fol. 163; Repertory 72, fols. 124ff.; *CSPD 1667*, p. 247; Pepys, *Diary*, VIII, 263–5, 268, 269–70, 283–4, 354–5, 362, 398–9; Evelyn, *Diary*, III, 484; *POAS*, I, 88–96; Marvell, *Poems and Letters*, II, 310; Sharpe, *London*, II, 436–7; Seaward, *Cavalier Parliament*, pp. 306–7; Pincus, *Protestantism and Patriotism*, pp. 392–3, 409–10, 417, 426.

The disasters of 1665–7 provoked much reflection about whether the 1660–65 settlement of church and state had either healed the nation's wounds or secured its institutions. The king's sacking of Clarendon and the earl's impeachment in the parliamentary session that opened in October 1667 were but the most dramatic signs of this general revisiting of the issues of settlement. Seeking to pre-empt the religious question, Clarendon had himself opened conversations with Presbyterian clergy and also with Independent John Owen. Before his fall at the end of August, a comprehension bill was being drafted by MPs allied with the embattled minister. And among Clarendon's critics, Buckingham's parliamentary coterie continued to include many friends of dissent, including Lord Ashley, for whom John Locke now prepared his first essay on toleration. In London, dissenting meetings flourished as magistrates hesitated to enforce the laws against them, while dissenting patriotism during the war had belied Anglican allegations about their republicanism and disloyalty. In view of these circumstances, moderate Anglican leaders like Bishop Edward Reynolds (the former London Presbyterian), Bishop Herbert Croft, and future bishop John Wilkins reopened dialogue about comprehension.[50]

Expectations for Protestant reunion on acceptable terms and for indulgence were thus quite high, at least among dissenters, when comprehension and toleration bills were prepared for the Commons by Buckingham's allies in early 1668. The king himself was known to be sympathetic. But these measures were rejected without a reading by a parliament composed of MPs elected in the midst of Anglican reaction, seven years earlier; and the Commons accompanied its rejection with a request to the king that the Act of Uniformity be strictly enforced. Had a new parliament been chosen, as some expected, to accompany the ministerial rearrangement that followed the fall of Clarendon, the result might well have been different. According to Pepys, the Commons had rejected a new religious formula that was "desired by much the greater part of the nation." But the effectiveness of religious coercion was nevertheless left in doubt. The Conventicle Act of 1664 was due to expire upon the next prorogation of a parliamentary session; and debate continued within and without the Commons over what should replace it.[51]

[50] Pepys, *Diary*, VIII, 265, 584; *CSPD 1667*, 179, 181, 182, 189, 199; Seaward, *Cavalier Parliament*, pp. 301, 318–19; Pincus, *Protestantism and Patriotism*, pp. 412ff.; Hutton, *Restoration*, pp. 265–6; Spurr, *Restoration Church*, p. 57; Richard Ashcraft, *Revolutionary Politics & Locke's Two Treatises of Government* (Princeton, 1986), pp. 94–101; N. E. Key, "Comprehension and the Breakdown of Consensus in Restoration Herefordshire," in T. Harris, *et al.*, eds., *The Politics of Religion*, pp. 196–98; J. Marshall, *John Locke: Resistance, Religion and Responsibility* (Cambridge, 1994), pp. 49–62; P. Toon, *God's Statesman: The Life and Work of John Owen* (Exeter, 1971), p. 134.

[51] Pepys, *Diary*, IX, 31, 60, 277–8, 398–9; Grey, *Debates*, I, 104–6, 146–7, 160–1, 174–5, 220–3, 227–8; Marvell, *Poems and Letters*, II, 67, 70, 76; Pincus, *Protestantism and Patriotism*,

In the city, London dissenters openly challenged the political domination of the Anglican elite, beginning in 1667. They contested for magisterial positions, secured several aldermanic places, and returned in significant numbers to the court of common council. An Anglican loyalist observer noted, in retrospect, that a deliberate effort was made at this time "to bring in such a party into the Court of Aldermen, favorers of Nonconformists, as might be an Overballance to the Loyall Church Party." These dissenting political endeavors were in part a delayed response to the proscription of so many of the city's natural leaders from office-holding in the Corporation. London dissenters were also emboldened in their challenge to the ruling Anglican civic elite by the example of Buckingham and his parliamentary friends, and the duke clearly encouraged them. Buckingham's city agent was Independent Henry Brandreth, once a Leveller sympathizer, a Commonwealth civic activist, and a member of the Committee of Safety in 1659. Buckingham's secretary was John Wildman, another former London Leveller with numerous connections to civic dissent.[52]

One indication of dissenting political determination in the city after 1667 is the number of times the court of aldermen needed to veto unacceptable wardmote returns for vacancies on the bench. Vetoes of aldermanic nominations had been little used since 1660; but the aldermen employed their veto on no fewer than eighteen occasions between 1667 and 1670, and then not again until 1680. Not all those rejected for service on the aldermanic bench were nonconformists, but nonconformity appears to have been the most frequent reason for rejection. The climactic vetoes of 1669–70 featured several nominees of particular importance and indicate that sectarians were as active as Reformed Protestants in contesting for civic positions. Buckingham's agent Brandreth was a rejected aldermanic nominee at this time, and Baptist merchant William Kiffin was twice vetoed. (Kiffin would shortly enter into business ventures with Lord Ashley, one of the most active ministerial friends of dissent.) Hamburg merchant Slingsby Bethel, a Commonwealth common councilman and republican member of Richard's parliament, who had also recently written with alarm about the rising power and commercial expansiveness of France, was another rejected nominee. So was Patience Ward, a substantial Reformed Protestant merchant whose outspoken criticism of

pp. 430–1; P. Seaward, *The Restoration* (New York, 1991), pp. 51–2; Harris, "Bawdy House Riots," pp. 545–7; J. Spurr, "The Church of England, Comprehension and the Toleration Act of 1689," *EHR* 104 (1989), 933–5; Greaves, *Enemies*, pp. 142–4; A. Swatland, *The House of Lords in the Reign of Charles II* (Cambridge, 1996), pp. 132–3.

52 BL Stowe MS 186, fol. 8; "The Character of the Lord Mayor of London, and the whole Court of Aldermen," *The Gentleman's Magazine* 39 (1769), 517; SP 29/207/74: *CSPD 1667*, p. 240; Pepys, *Diary*, VIII, 299; Ashley, *John Wildman*, pp. 205–9; Pincus, *Protestantism and Patriotism*, pp. 428–30.

the government's handling of trade had already once landed him in the Fleet prison.[53]

Despite these vetoes, so many dissenters were selected in the wards for aldermanic vacancies, that other nonconformists – nominees without such controversial pasts – were per force accepted as new magistrates by the sitting aldermen. John and Dannet Forth, brothers and government revenue farmers, became city magistrates in 1668–9, despite marriage connections to such prominent Commonwealth office-holders as Sir Henry Vane and Oliver St John. Lead merchant John Moore, sometime member of George Cokayne's gathered church, served as alderman in 1666–7 and again after 1671; and Patience Ward was accepted as alderman upon his second election. Some of these men could be construed as spokesmen for moderate, reconciling religious views or were perceived as such by their Anglican contemporaries. Moore reportedly had an interest among "sober, discreet people," and his support for Protestant accommodation would soon take him back into the Anglican fold. Ward was a partial conformist as well as an Independent. These new dissenting magistrates joined favorers of comprehension like Aldermen Sir John Frederick and Sir John Lawrence, who had reconciled their Reformed Protestant pedigrees with the requirements of the Corporation Act.[54]

The increasing visibility of dissenters in the politics of the aldermanic bench was accompanied by a strengthening of the dissenting common council presence. The decline in the number of nonconformists on common council that followed the Uniformity Act reached its nadir in 1665–6. (Table 2.1) By 1669, however, dissenting numbers on common council recovered as the ejected clergy returned to active ministry, and as the assertion of dissenting identity became increasingly unapologetic. (Table 2.2) The forty-one common councilmen of 1669 who can be identified as definite or probable dissenters compare favorably in number to those on common council in 1662, the last year in which Reformed Protestants had retained a strong civic voice. This return to local office by London dissenters both circumvented the statutory restriction of office to conformists and alarmed the government. Charles's ministers were aware that, in London, "many persons avoid . . . [the religious qualifications] by absenting themselves from the wardmote when

---

[53] Some of those vetoed are quite obscure, suggesting that some nominations may reflect the difficulty the Corporation had, in the first years after the fire, in recruiting office-holders of means. Beaven, *Aldermen*, II, 247–8; Slingsby Bethel, *The World's Mistake in Oliver Cromwell* (1668); *BDBR*, I, 61–2; II, 155–6; III, 289–91; Henning, *House of Commons*, III, 667–70; Haley, *Shaftesbury*, pp. 228, 232; G. S. De Krey, "Slingsby Bethel" and "Sir Patience Ward," *Oxford DNB*.

[54] BL Stowe MS 186, fols. 5–8; Henning, *House of Commons*, II, 349, 363–5, and III, 92–4, 668; Woodhead, *Rulers*, 71–2, 73, 106, 117, 170; Grell, "Persecution," p. 125.

Table 2.2[56] *Definite or probable dissenters on London common council, 1667–1672*

	Seats	1667	1668	1669	1670	1671	1672
Inner City	113	18	13	21	16	20	22
Middle City	88	7	9	15	11	15	13
City Without	33	4	2	5	5	5	3
Total Seats	234	29	24	41	32	40	38

chosen, and then coming to [common] council and taking the oaths, but not the sacrament; or by staying away from the council at first, till the thing is forgotten, and then coming in slyly."[55]

Several Reformed Protestants who had served on common council before 1663 were among those dissenters chosen for service after 1667. These included leading civic Presbyterians, like merchant John Mascall (prominent in the East India Company) and haberdasher John Jekyll, as well as Independent linen-drapers John Brett and James Hayes, who had been active in Corporation affairs during the Commonwealth. Other dissenting spokesmen were first chosen for common council after 1667. Some of these younger men were at the beginning of civic careers that would propel them into critical roles during the Restoration Crisis and the Glorious Revolution. Among these new men was Levant merchant Thomas Pilkington, Whig sheriff in 1681–2 and lord mayor in 1689–91, and draper Thomas Stamp, who succeeded Pilkington as lord mayor in 1691. A few men who had managed to continue their common council service throughout the years of Anglican hegemony filled out the dissenting ranks. This recovery of the Reformed Protestant presence in civic counsels also strengthened the integration of Corporation affairs with those of the different mercantile and investing interests that dominated city commerce: Mascal, Pilkington, and Ward, for instance, were all leading traders.[57]

By 1669–70, then, the Anglican royalist monopoly on office-holding in London had been decisively broken. The artificially narrow civic regime of the mid-1660s had been broadened to include major spokesmen for

[55] *CSPD 1668–69*, p. 616.   [56] See note 12 above.
[57] PRO PROB 11: 401 Dyke, qu. 155 (will of John Jekyll); DWL Congregational Library MS 52.a.38 "Register of all the Names of the Members of the Church of Christ...Bury Street in Duke's Place" (James Hayes); Henning, *House of Commons*, III, 245–7; Woodhead, *Rulers*, pp. 37, 87, 98, 107, 113, 130, 143, 155; Pincus, *Protestantism and Patriotism*, p. 293.

those Reformed Protestants who had rejected conformity, and sectarians had regained political visibility as well. Indeed, the assertiveness of London dissenters and the establishment of a dissenting presence in the Corporation of London were important breaches of the Restoration settlement that prompted Anglican royalist MPs to reaffirm the policy of coercion in 1670. But when Anglican MPs attempted to reimplement their policy of uniformity in church and state through a second Conventicle Act, the dissenting response was far different from that of 1662. London dissenting writers and citizens took the lead in contesting coercion, presenting Charles with a strong public showing on behalf of liberty for conscience.

ARGUING FOR LIBERTY OF CONSCIENCE

As London dissenters re-established their visibility in the Corporation of London, dissenting writers who shared their objections to the coercive Anglican settlement re-established visibility in the religious and political debate of the nation. Stimulated by the serious reconsideration of the church settlement in 1667–8, clerical authors like John Owen, John Humfrey, and Philip Nye and lay writers like Sir Charles Wolseley, Slingsby Bethel, and William Penn developed and published sophisticated rationales for liberty of conscience. The arguments of dissenting spokesmen who remained hopeful about inclusion in a broadened church establishment differed somewhat in application from those who preferred to practice religious liberty outside the parochial order, but these different dissenting cases for conscience nevertheless shared much common ground. Moreover, the development of the language of conscience by these authors represented some of the most sophisticated public writing of the Restoration. It was writing that put Anglican authorities on the defensive, for it substituted persecution for sectarianism as the major threat to English Protestantism. Indeed, the dissenting advocates of conscience not only recaptured the initiative, in print, from Anglican apologists for coercion; but they also put the issue of liberty for conscience at the center of parliamentary and local affairs for the remainder of Charles II's reign. The growing body of work on behalf of conscience was work that especially mattered in London, where civic dissenters were already pressing for reconsideration of the narrow church settlement of 1662–5, where the literature of conscience was printed, and where most of these authors resided or were well known.[58]

Dissenting development of the language of conscience also carried into the Restoration a critical body of thought that had originated in the civil war

---

[58] Also see G. S. De Krey, "Rethinking the Restoration: Dissenting Cases for Conscience, 1667–1672," *HJ* 38 (1995), 53–83; Ashcraft, *Revolutionary Politics*, pp. 39–74.

era. Historical inquiry into connections between the "revolutionary" ideas of the 1640s and the "radical" language of the late Stuart era needs to begin with discourse about conscience, which had a much broader circulation and a much broader following after 1660 than any form of republicanism.[59] Moreover, unlike republican ideas, which had divided Reformed Protestants against each other and against sectarians, the language of conscience succeeded in drawing together the disparate fragments of 1640s' puritanism. Under the duress of persecution, Presbyterians who had once smarted, when the language of conscience was directed against them by a John Lilburne or a Richard Overton, found themselves joined with Independents and sectarians as the heirs and re-formulators of such language. Discourse about conscience had especially flourished in London in the 1640s, as Protestant perspectives proliferated. In the Restoration, this discourse retained its currency in the city, as dissenters of all persuasions became a community for conscience. Early Restoration arguments for religious liberty are therefore the best guide to the political and religious thinking of the London dissenters who confronted the civic Anglican elite in 1669–70; and these ideas continued to shape opposition discourse in London during the Restoration Crisis, a decade later.

Like their civil war predecessors, Restoration proponents of conscience premised their arguments upon a fundamental distinction between the public and the personal spheres of life. The first of these spheres – the external, civil domain that includes public morality and religious order – was, for them, the proper arena of the prince's authority, the sphere of governance for which he is responsible to God. The second sphere, an internal sphere that centers upon the personal domain of faith, also extends into the visible expression of religious belief in conduct and worship, according to them. Reformed Protestant authors – Independents as well as Presbyterians – acknowledged that the monarchy exercised an ecclesiastical jurisdiction in the external sphere that was both "inherent" and confirmed in the English Reformation. Sectarian writers, on the other hand, saw the prince's responsibility for external religious order as a "collateral" one only, rather than as a responsibility exercised through an integral connection with particular church structures.[60] Reformed Protestant and sectarian authors agreed, however, that in the personal sphere, believers are directly

---

[59] Scott, *England's Troubles*, esp. pp. 342–64.

[60] John Owen, *Truth and Innocence Vindicated* (1669), in *The Works of John Owen*, 16 vols. (1852), XIII, 346, 381; J. Marshall, *John Locke*, pp. 42–5; Philip Nye, *The king's Authority in dispensing with ecclesiastical laws, asserted and Vindicated* (1687), p. 27. Completed before Nye's death in 1672, *The king's Authority* was apparently not published before 1687. [Sir Charles Wolseley], *Liberty of Conscience upon its true and proper Grounds asserted and Vindicated* (1668), p. 27.

responsible for their religious behavior to God – through the exercise of their consciences – rather than being responsible to the prince or to any lesser magistrate.

Distinguishing between these two spheres, Presbyterian Edward Bagshaw had written as early as 1661 that "Civil government is properly and adequately concerned only in Civil things;...religious matters belong only to him that is Inspector and Lord of the Conscience." Bagshaw's London Presbyterian colleague John Humfrey similarly maintained, drawing upon Hugo Grotius, that "the inward acts of mans *soul*...and *conscience* are not within his [the magistrate's] *cognizance*." London Independent Philip Nye wrote that the civil power "reacheth not the Inner-Man." Quaker William Penn differentiated between "*An External Order of Justice*" and a spiritual sphere "wholly independent of...secular Affairs." Sir Charles Wolseley, once a Cromwellian councilor of state, and by the late 1660s an intellectual protégé of Buckingham and Lord Ashley, wrote of "two Dominions," one ruled by "the Sword of Justice" and the other ruled by the "sword of the Spirit."[61]

In response, Anglican writers like Samuel Parker dismissed conscience as little more than fancy, as "weak, silly, and ignorant" and swayed by the passions toward "fond and absurd principles." But dissenting authors saw conscience as a critical human faculty which believers must employ to determine whether their personal behavior accords with divine expectation. "Conscience is an ability in the understanding of man, by a reflect[ive] act to judge of himself in all he does, as to his acceptance, or rejection with God," wrote Wolseley. As Wolseley implied, conscience is also a rational faculty: indeed, for dissenting authors, conscience is a critical faculty that distinguishes rational human beings from other creatures. John Humfrey argued that "every man must have a judgement or private discretion...in respect to his own actions: or else he acts as a *Bruite*." Or as Wolseley suggested, to deprive an individual of the exercise of conscience "is to unman him, and change him from a rational Creature." Moreover, just as God holds the prince accountable for the exercise of authority in the external sphere, so God holds the individual accountable for the exercise of conscience in the

---

[61] [Edward Bagshaw], *The Second Part of the Great Question* [1661], p. 12; J[ohn] H[umfrey], *The Authority of the Magistrate, about religion, Discussed* (1672), p. 43; Philip Nye, *The Lawfulness of the Oath of Supremacy, and power of the king in Ecclesiastical Affairs* (1683), pp. 20–1; William Penn, *The Great Case of Liberty of Conscience* (1670) in *The Political Writings of William Penn*, ed. A. R. Murphy (Indianapolis, Ind., 2002), pp. 86, 95; Wolseley, *Liberty of Conscience upon its true and proper Grounds*, p. 35. Nye's *Lawfulness of the Oath* appears to date from the 1660s, although the preface and postscript suggest that it did not reach final form until shortly before Nye's death.

internal sphere. Failure to exercise conscience in matters of faith is a failure to obey God.[62]

Dissenting discourse about conscience also employed the concepts of vicegerency, of natural law, and of an ancient constitution to maintain an inviolable boundary between the sphere of civil authority and the personal sphere governed by conscience. Humfrey wrote that, in matters of faith, "Gods Vicegerent within me, my Conscience" takes precedence over the "external Voice" of the magistrate. John Owen insisted that conscience rules as "God's great vicegerent" in matters "of its proper cognizance and duty." Wolseley suggested that God exercises his "solemn claim of Soveraignty" over the soul through conscience as His "vicegerent . . . and Vicar-general."[63]

These authors pointed to universal and English practice, as well, in grounding the right to employ conscience in nature and in history. Owen wrote that the exercise of conscience is a "right . . . which naturally belong[s] unto . . . men" and that to impose upon conscience is "contrary to the principles of the law of nature." Indeed, he suggested that liberty of conscience had generally been "provided for" in "the fundamental law of all civil societies." Suggesting that the state originates in "common consent" or a "joynt-coalition and agreement," Wolseley contended that no "publick power" was ever intended to have authority over the private domain of faith. Any attempt to "force and pen men up" in matters of faith is therefore "wholly unnatural."[64] Where Wolseley found coercion inconsistent with the consensual origins of any state, William Penn found it inconsistent with the fundamental laws of the English state. These he found in Saxon procedures, in Magna Charta, and in certain statutes of Edward III's reign. For him, this normative ancient constitution protected "*our undoubted Birthright of English Freedoms*," the chief of which was liberty for conscience.[65]

---

[62] [Samuel Parker], *A Discourse of Ecclesiastical Politie*, 3rd ed. (1671), p. 7; Wolseley, *Liberty of Conscience upon its true and proper Grounds*, pp. 5, 44; Humfrey, *Authority of the Magistrate*, p. 72.

[63] John Owen, *Indulgence and Toleration considered* (1667), in *Works*, XIII, 528; [John Humfrey], *A Case of Conscience* (1669), pp. 29–30; Sir Charles Wolseley, *The Reasonableness of Scripture-Belief* (1672), intro. R. W. McHenry, Jr. (Delmar, NY, 1973), p. 31.

[64] Owen, *Indulgence and Toleration*, p. 526; Owen, *Truth and Innocence vindicated*, p. 491; [John Owen], *A Peace-offering in an Apology* (1667), in *Works*, XIII, 558; Wolseley, *Liberty of Conscience upon its true and proper Grounds*, pp. 12–13; [Sir Charles Wolseley], *Liberty of Conscience, the Magistrates Interest* (1668), p. 6.

[65] Penn, *Great Case*, pp. 82, 99–100. Also see Penn's ideas as incorporated into [Thomas Rudyard], *The Peoples Antient and just Liberties asserted, in the Tryal of William Penn, and William Mead* (1670), pp. 32–48. The authorship of this tract has recently been assigned either to Rudyard alone or to Rudyard and Penn, but its appendix clearly presents Penn's thinking in 1670: *The Papers of William Penn*, V, ed. E. B. Bronner and D. Fraser (Philadelphia, 1986), p. 119.

These arguments completely undermined the premises and purposes of the church settlement of 1660–65. Dissenting writers turned coercion from the chief defense of faith and civil order, as Anglicans regarded it, into the chief threat to Protestant belief and its civic expression. "Religion . . . is the choice of men," argued John Owen: "Every man is to be fully persuaded [about the gospel] in his own mind," and where rational choice is constrained, neither faith nor its fruits can flourish. Moreover, coercion destroys responsible citizenship as well as Christian liberty, producing "a people nuzled in ignorance and superstition, [who] are more easily seduced . . . by those that have dominion over their Consciences." Uniformity was no religious desiderata for these writers. It was instead a contrivance neither demanded by God nor necessary for the state. For Wolseley, as for John Milton, diversity of religious opinion was a sign of spiritual and intellectual vitality: "As Knowledge encreaseth, it expatiates it self into a variety of Thoughts and Principles; and as it enlargeth all other Sciences, so Religion." Presbyterians, who had once feared the religious pluralism of the sects, were now beginning to embrace the Protestant diversity they had formerly reviled. At the beginning of the Restoration, John Corbet had written, somewhat cautiously, "uniformity in Religion is beautiful and amiable; but we ought to consider . . . what is attainable." But by 1668, John Humfrey was enthusiastically defending "diversity of Religion" as analogous to a well-kept garden in which "the variety of . . . flowers enrich and beautifie that plot of ground, where they [grow] sweetly together." Reformed Protestants and sectarians were thus uniting against assumptions about the best means for achieving Protestant security that had operated in the English church-state for over a century.[66]

These dissenting authors were also actually experiencing coercion that they believed violated their consciences, infringed their civil rights, and required them either to disobey God or to disobey the state. Reformed Protestant authors like John Owen and John Humfrey nevertheless counseled their followers to "quietly and peaceably . . . bear the troubles and inconveniences" of their dissent, while respecting the authority of the magistrate. But they publicly shuddered about the consequences for the state of the perpetuation of persecution. Owen noted that "magistrates who coerce conscience must irresistibly extinguish the community itself," and Humfrey worried that, should the estates of the realm deadlock over religious policy, "the Government [would be] dissolved, and the power returned . . . to the people."[67]

[66] Owen, *Indulgence and Toleration*, p. 532; [John Corbet], *A Discourse of the Religion of England* (1667), p. 20; J[ohn] C[orbet], *The Second Part of the Interest of England* (1660), p. 60; Wolseley, *Liberty of Conscience, the Magistrates Interest*, p. 8; [John Humfrey], *A Defence of the Proposition* (1668), pp. 20–1; John Milton, *Areopagitica* (1644).

[67] Owen, *Truth and Innocence vindicated*, p. 376; Owen, *Peace-offering*, p. 557; Humfrey, *Authority of the Magistrate*, pp. 29, 53; Humfrey, *Case of Conscience*, p. 5.

Other writers moved from theory to practice, from warnings about the dissolution of government to advocating resistance. An anonymous pamphleteer wrote that, when parliament adopts legislation, like the Anglican church settlement, that is destructive to ancient rights, including that of conscience, "the people are obliged ... to disobey the Laws they make, and to give obedience to *Magna Charta*." William Penn wrote that "*Temporary*" laws "should be broke" when they conflict with more "*Fundamental*" laws in which the right to conscience is embedded. An early Restoration Fifth Monarchist tract suggested that "If Governours break Covenant with the People, they break the bond of Relation, and the People are disengaged, on their part from Subjection."[68]

But the principal response to persecution on the part of dissenting writers was neither arguments for passive disobedience nor active espousal of the grounds for resistance. Instead, nonconformist authors and their followers sought to persuade Charles and the larger Protestant public that persecution was neither in the interest of the restored monarchy nor in the interest of the nation. Cases for conscience that drew upon the interest theory of Henri, Duc de Rohan, a French Reformed Protestant theorist of the early seventeenth century, carried particular weight in London, as fears about Catholic France began to replace older anxieties about the Protestant Dutch Republic.[69] Reformed Protestant authors offered interest arguments on behalf of both comprehension and liberty for conscience, while Sir Charles Wolseley saw liberty for a plurality of religious perspectives as the best means for securing the state.

Presbyterian John Corbet, a friend of Baxter who preached in London in the mid-1660s, had advanced interest arguments at the time of the Restoration. He suggested to Charles II that a successful church would need to be erected upon the "large Foundation" of a "comprehensive Interest" rather than upon the "partial interest" represented by Anglicanism. By 1666–7, he maintained again that only a broadening of the church settlement would recall the "Multitudes every where" who had abandoned their parish churches for religious assemblies more to their liking. Employing a metaphor with particular resonance in London, Corbet suggested that the national religious "joint Stock" of Protestantism had been divided in the settlement of 1660–65: it needed now to be reunited by enlarging "the Rule and Square of the Ecclesiastical State" until it encompassed most Protestants. John Humfrey made similar arguments in his case for comprehension as in the best interest

---

[68] *The Englishman, or a Letter from a Universal Friend* (1670), p. 10; Penn, *Great Case*, pp. 96–7; *The Saints Freedom from Tyranny Vindicated* (1667), p. 23.

[69] For the Duc de Rohan, see J. A. W. Gunn, *Politics and the Public Interest in the Seventeenth Century* (1969), pp. 36–8, and J. Scott, *Algernon Sidney and the English Republic, 1623–1677* (Cambridge, 1988), ch. 12.

of English Protestantism. Claiming that nonconformist Protestants "out-balance[d] those that do conform," he thought the "Interest of *England*" was best promoted by "tak[ing] in[to the church] the greatest part and strength of the Nation." Both these Restoration Presbyterians also reached to their sectarian fellow sufferers, seeing no incompatibility between comprehension of Reformed Protestants and religious liberty for those of more "*Rigid Principles.*"[70]

Such a dual policy of comprehension and liberty was also in the interest of the prince and the state. Corbet had warned Charles in 1660 that, were any partial interest given exclusive control of the church, that interest would "in time lift it[self] up above his own Imperial interest." Responding to fears about the disloyalty of nonconformists that were still being fanned by Anglicans, Humfrey pointed out in 1668 that "the Supreme Power... which gratifies... all [persuasions] in this Liberty of their Consciences" removes the grounds for "Insurrection." Moreover, religious coercion actually threatens the state, for it encourages persecuted factions to band together in a "common Interest against the Laws." The prince who practices toleration, on the other hand, wisely shows favor to subjects of different religious persuasions, leaving them "disbandied into their single Interests." Or, as Corbet wrote, by "ballancing... the opposite parties [,]... a Prince doth... appear... as a moderator and true Governour... of all interests."[71]

Wolseley was the most explicit, among dissenting authors, in applying this Polybian or Harringtonian concept of balance to religious diversity, while London merchant Slingsby Bethel most successfully applied arguments for conscience to the advancement of English trade. Like Corbet and Humfrey, Wolseley warned Charles II against permitting himself to be "confined" by any religious party; but unlike these authors, Wolseley rejected the ideal of Protestant unity through comprehension. Instead, given the irreversible existence of different religious interests, the king needed to display "an equal Political Aspect to all his Subjects." The unity and safety of the state required neither privileges for one religious persuasion nor comprehension of many, but rather that "divided Interests and Parties in Religion" should "be prudently managed to balance each other."[72]

Less theoretical, and more practical, Bethel put the interest case for conscience into the language of London traders. He had already questioned the

---

[70] Corbet, *The Second Part of the Interest of England*, pp. 13, 106; Corbet, *A Discourse of the Religion of England*, pp. 21, 24, 26–8, 32, 38; [John Corbet], *A Second Discourse of the Religion of England* (1668), pp. 3, 8; Humfrey, *Defense of the Proposition*, pp. 57–8, 99–100.

[71] Corbet, *Second Part of the Interest of England*, pp. 104, 129; Humfrey, *Defense of the Proposition*, pp. 83, 99–100, 103.

[72] Wolseley, *Liberty of Conscience, the Magistrates Interest*, pp. 3–5, 9–10, 17.

foreign policy of Oliver Cromwell, who had broken the "Balance of *Europe*" by attacking Spain, rather than guarding against the commercial and military rise of France. If Charles II was to do better than Oliver, in advancing the "public Interest of Christendom" against France, he needed both to recognize that the "principal interest of *England*" was trade and that "Imposing upon Conscience" was "a mischief unto Trade, transcending all others." According to Bethel, the coercion of Protestants in England both damaged the "reformed Interest" of Europe and discouraged the most "industrious sort of people." Instead of promoting the nation's commerce, persecution left trade "in too few hands, and to a kind of people that do but rarely mind it," while the Corporation Act barred from government many of the most "publick spirited Citizens and Townsmen."[73]

Even more so than other dissenting authors, Bethel articulated the aspirations for comprehension and liberty of conscience that moved his fellow nonconformist merchants and commercial dealers. More generally, the intellectual effect of this entire body of writing about conscience was to uncouple the nexus between coercive magistracy and Protestant ministry that had been fundamental in English Protestant thought since the Reformation. More locally, its immediate public impact was to provide a powerful rationale for London citizens who, in a variety of ways, challenged religious coercion and the Anglican church settlement in the Corporation in 1669–70.

CONTESTING COERCION, 1669–1670

The advancement of arguments for conscience in print, sermon, and oral discourse after 1667 had a powerful impact upon the Corporation of London and upon the Cavalier Parliament. In London, the language of conscience encouraged the political assertiveness of dissenting office-holders, but the parliamentary response took the form of a second Conventicle Act. Adopted in April 1670, it was intended to end uncertainty about the religious settlement that had developed since 1667. Responding both to the political emergence of dissent and to the renewed fear of Roman Catholicism, Anglican royalist MPs were determined to provide the established church with even greater security than before. The act provided for distraint of the property of those who were apprehended at conventicles, and it provided incentives to informers. It also provided harsh punishments for dissenting clergy who continued to preach. Most ominously, in the minds of some, the act substituted a single JP for a panel of jurors in the trials of conventiclers; and it

---

[73] Bethel, *The World's Mistake*, pp. 4, 11, 19; [Slingsby Bethel], *The Present Interest of England Stated* (1671), pp. 2, 13–14, 16–17, 30; De Krey, "Slingsby Bethel."

established penalties for magistrates and others who failed to carry out its provisions.

The new Conventicle Act failed entirely to settle the church. It was defied in the city by vigorous dissenting congregations, whose religious identity did not allow them to accept it, and whose actions stimulated dissenting determination elsewhere.[74] The urban contest about coercion in 1669–70 bears comparison with better-known seventeenth-century crises in which thousands of London citizens confronted a parliament or a regime. Like the crisis of 1659–60, for instance, the contest about coercion in 1669–70 was one in which the actions and words of London citizens aroused much support in other localities and did, in fact, undermine critical policies of the state. Londoners broke the back of coercion in 1669–70, just as they had been critical in breaking the army and the Rump in 1659–60. Acting and arguing in the streets and in their religious assemblies, the press, the law courts, and before the House of Commons and the king, they carried their challenge to the coercive religious settlement to the point of resistance, as far as their opponents were concerned.

This challenge to coercion began a year before parliamentary adoption of the new Conventicle Act. In 1669, London dissenters sought, for the first time, to employ their newfound political presence in the Corporation on behalf of religious liberty. Indeed, their audacity in the mayoral election of that year may have contributed to Anglican resolve at Westminster. Nonconformists had enjoyed "all manner of Liberty" in the city in 1668–9, during the mayoralty of Sir William Turner, a puritan conformist who had "espoused" their interest. But the presumptive lord mayor for 1669–70, the senior alderman beneath the chair, was Sir Samuel Sterling, a staunch churchman and advocate of coercion who had served on the regicide juries. Led by Alderman Sir John Lawrence, leading civic dissenters gathered in "frequent consultations" prior to the September common hall to discuss how to prevent Sterling's election. They hoped to secure a second election for Turner, and Presbyterian pastor Thomas Watson dedicated a spiritual treatise to him, suggesting that London, like Sparta, should not lose so valuable a governor after a single year. Some of Turner's dissenting supporters were confident that his re-election would lead to their regaining of the civic magistracy, and they claimed that London citizens were about to "see such an overturneing of the state of things as they never experienced in there lives." But in a tumultuous common hall, Turner's "party" was thwarted when

---

[74] Greaves, *Enemies*, pp. 154–66; T. Harris, *Politics under the Later Stuarts: Party Conflict in a Divided Society 1660–1715* (1993), p. 41; A. Fletcher, "The Enforcement of the Conventicle Acts 1664–1679," in *Persecution and Toleration*, ed. W. J. Sheils (Oxford, 1984), pp. 235–46; P. Gauci, *Politics and Society in Great Yarmouth 1660–1722* (Oxford, 1996), pp. 122–3.

Sterling was elected instead, thanks in part to the intervention of Anglican courtiers.[75]

Undismayed by this defeat and by a decline in their common council numbers for 1670 (Table 2.2), civic dissenters turned the shrieval election of 1670 into a referendum upon the recently adopted Conventicle Act. Baptist William Kiffin, whose name was a symbol of the anti-sectarian panic of 1659–60, was chosen Sheriff of London and Middlesex. Kiffin had met with the king in July 1669 on behalf of liberty for conscience, had been an active opponent of the Conventicle Act, and had sought the legal advice of Bulstrode Whitelocke in finding weaknesses in it. His election had the potential to disrupt implementation of the act in the city, for an unsympathetic sheriff could empanel like-minded jurors for conventicle trials – jurors like those who had twice acquitted John Lilburne, or like those who would subsequently acquit the Earl of Shaftesbury. To the relief of Anglican royalists, Kiffin declined his election; but dissenting efforts to block the Conventicle Act through city elections continued. Indeed, the sheriffs eventually chosen for 1670–71 were the nonconformists Patience Ward and Dannet Forth. And the election as bridgemaster of Methusalem Turner, a Commonwealth civic activist, was prevented only when Sterling dissolved a common hall bent upon choosing him.[76]

By 1670, the city's Anglican magistrates were deeply alarmed by the renewed visibility of such Commonwealth stalwarts as Kiffin, Slingsby Bethel, and Henry Brandreth, each of whom had also been associated with the revived republic of 1659–60. And, although the professed goal of London's leading dissenters was only relief for conscience, Anglicans feared that the "late troubles" were on the verge of breaking out again. They accused dissenting common councilmen of "setting up for defenders of the liberties of the city, fomenting popular notions, and alienating the affections of the unwary multitude." Fearing challenges to their dominance, they authorized another Corporation committee to prune civic records of all traces of the "disloyal" civic by-laws implemented after 1649. Renewed Anglican vigilance against conventicles and their teachers prompted the apprehension of such leading London Reformed clergy as Thomas Manton and Richard Baxter. The government was similarly concerned. An alteration of the London Lieutenancy Commission removed aldermen like John Forth, Sir John Frederick, Sir John

[75] BL Stowe MS 186, fols. 5, 8; SP 29/263/54I; *CSPD 1668–69*, pp. 419–20; *CSPD 1671–72*, p. 148; Thomas Watson, *Heaven taken by Storm* (1670), preface; [Sir Samuel Sterling], *An Answer to the Seditious and Scandalous Pamphlet* (1671), pp. 5–6; Baxter, *Reliquiae*, Part III, 48.

[76] Add. MS 36,916, fols. 186, 190; *CSPD 1663–64*, p. 405; *CSPD 1668–69*, p. 420; *CSPD 1670*, pp. 409, 420; Whitelocke, *Diary*, p. 754; *The Nature of a Common-Hall Briefly Stated* (1682), Farnell, "City of London," p. 392.

Lawrence, and Sir William Hooker, who had supported religious accommodation. But these signals failed to deter London householders from returning a significant number of dissenters to serve on the court of common council for 1671 (Table 2.2).[77]

As dissenting office-holders shattered Anglican hegemony in the Corporation, the Conventicle Act of 1670 was also tested in the London streets by thousands of urban nonconformists. One historian has described these angry scenes between massed conventiclers and the trained bands as a "battle of London." James Hayes, a member of Joseph Caryl's gathered church, and John Jekyll, a follower of Presbyterian Thomas Watson, assumed leadership of the cadres for conscience. Both common councilmen, Hayes and Jekyll attended the spring parliamentary debates about the Conventicle Act in a display of opposition to it. After searching for loopholes, they sought to dissuade Lord Mayor Sterling from enforcing the act. Sterling and Alderman Sir John Robinson, Lieutenant of the Tower, were, however, determined to crush London dissent; and the Duke of York encouraged them. Numerous London dissenting teachers and lay leaders, on the other hand, were ready to follow Hayes and Jekyll against the Anglican magistracy. Country dissenters and interregnum notables also flocked to the city to assist their London brethren, despite a new proclamation banning Oliverian soldiers and officers from the capital. Among these external "agitators" were Coronet George Joyce, who had secured Charles I for the Army in 1647, and William Boteler, one of Cromwell's Major Generals.[78]

Sabbath confrontations that pitted dissenting congregations against magistrates, constables, and the trained bands began in May 1670. The Corporation was instructed by the crown to take precautions similar to those adopted in 1661, at the time of Venner's rising. But decisive action against the 12,000 persons, "besides boys," reportedly attending numerous public assemblies in the spring and summer of 1670 proved difficult. Militia companies were often unable to press through the crowds to reach pulpits and preachers: according to one source "there were thousands in the streets, like a rebellion." Meetings that were dispersed in the morning regathered in the afternoon "in fuller assemblys." Attempts to turn dissenting premises over to Anglican incumbents whose churches had not yet been rebuilt were a failure. Congregations dispossessed of their meeting places simply relocated. The arrest

---

[77] Journal 47, fol. 26; Repertory 74, fol. 223; Add. MS 36,916, fols. 173, 178–179; SP 29/268/47; 29/275/18-18A; *CSPD 1668–69*, p. 616; *CSPD 1670*, pp. 96, 182; *CSPD 1671–2*, p. 148; Baxter, *Reliquiae*, Part III, 74. Like its predecessors, the committee appointed in 1670 to expunge the Corporation books failed to complete its work.

[78] Add. MS 36,916, fols. 178–179; SP 29/268/47; SP 29/275/18-18A; *CSPD 1670*, pp. 96, 182, 233–4, 235; Grey, *Debates*, I, 294–7; HMC *Le Fleming*, p. 71; Whitelocke, *Diary*, p. 759; *The Parliamentary Diary of Sir Edward Dering 1670–1673*, ed. B. D. Henning (New Haven, Conn., 1940), pp. 5–6; Greaves, *Enemies*, p. 159.

of hundreds of activists, including both Hayes and Jekyll and the Quaker spokesmen William Penn and William Mead, failed to daunt the spirit of others. "They are a stubborne people and seeme to be armed with patience and perseverance," commented one news writer. Equally disturbing to the government was the obvious sympathy of bystanders for those who defied magistrates and soldiers. Joseph Williamson, the under-secretary, learned that "there are strange looks and hints of dislike amongst spectators, some of whom say they love the Liturgy of the Church, but like not this way."[79]

Should this opposition to the Conventicle Act – opposition so much "like a rebellion" – be interpreted as actual "resistance"? The urban session records suggest that the authorized use of force met with much actual resistance.[80] When a woman told Sir John Robinson, who was suppressing her meeting, that she wished his "soul might burn in hell," for instance, she dispensed with more than the customary deference to authority.[81] A Cheapside stationer defending his meeting threatened that anyone who harmed the preacher "would be killed." Five conventiclers in Lothbury were indicted for "wounding" a soldier and others engaged in suppressing their meeting.[82] The Anglican rector appointed to read in the friends' meeting-house in Grace-church Street was "assaulted and bruised" by Quakers who sought to "pull off his Long robe," calling it "the Garment of the Beast" and calling him a "Popish Priest and Jesuit."[83] A Bishopsgate haberdasher reportedly exclaimed, "Wee never had good dayes since the King came in, nor ever shall whilst we have a King."[84] Soldiers were wounded in their work by the brickbats and stones that were in the air almost as frequently as these angry words. One alderman who headed a militia company reported "his soldiers arms were taken from them" by the crowd and that "they were in danger of their lives." Reflecting upon these episodes, Alderman Robinson concluded that the contest was about "whether the King & his lawes shall governe or them."[85]

[79] Add. MS 36,916, fols. 181–184; SP 29/275/104, 152, 173; 29/276/63, *CSPD 1670*, 209, 220–1, 234, 239–40, 314; Grey, *Debates*, I, 295–6, 305; Dering, *Diary*, p. 6; HMC *Le Fleming*, p. 71; W. C. Abbott, "English Conspiracy and Dissent, 1660–1714, II," *AHR* 14 (1909), 713–15.

[80] In general, see BL Middlesex County Records, Calendar of Sessions Books, 1664–1673; GLRO MJ/SR/1389–90, Sessions of the Peace and Oyer and Terminer Rolls, Middlesex, 1670; CLRO Waiting Book, VI (1670–71); CLRO 1670 Sessions in Sessions Minutes 33–35 (Sessions Files 201–212); *Middlesex County Records*, ed. J. C. Jaeffreson, 4 vols. (1887–1892), IV, 14–31; Greaves, *Enemies*, pp. 121–9, 154–60.

[81] BL Middlesex Sessions Book Calendar, p. 102: Book 271 (Aug. 1670), p. 41.

[82] CLRO Sessions File 201, Recognizance 75 (15 May 1670); Sessions File 203, Gaol Delivery (31 Aug. 1670).

[83] Greaves, *Enemies*, pp. 136–7; CLRO Waiting Book, VI, 23 (3 July 1670).

[84] CLRO Sessions File 202, Indictment 22 (25 June 1670); DWL Lyon Turner MS 89.32: Notes about London Sessions Rolls 1664–84 (Sessions Roll for Sept. 1670).

[85] CLRO Sessions File 203: Gaol Delivery, 31 Aug. 1670; Add. MS 36,916, fol. 188; SP 29/276/63; Grey, *Debates*, I, 294–8.

These extra-constitutional episodes of 1670, which followed so shortly after the apprentice rioting of 1668, demonstrated both the political resilience of urban dissent and widespread disenchantment with the Anglican establishment. For the first time since 1659–60, citizens in the streets and office-holders in the Corporation had cooperated in an effort to impede the implementation of decisions made by the national regime. Their actions also produced much litigation, as both dissenting leaders and followers were charged with riot and other offenses under a variety of acts. Undaunted, they carried their contest against coercion and their arguments for liberty of conscience into the king's courts and the House of Commons. As words took the place of blows and brickbats, they assaulted the rhetorical defenses of Anglican royalism in the forum of public opinion.

Civic dissenting leaders James Hayes and John Jekyll were arrested in June 1670. Charged with "inviting and stirring up his Majesty's subjects . . . to the disobedience of his laws," they were committed after refusing £5,000 bonds intended to prevent their further attendance at conventicles. Freed on a writ of habeas corpus, they sued the London magistrates for false imprisonment. The dispute quickly reached the Commons. Appearing before the House, Hayes and Jekyll defended meetings held in defiance of law and condemned the bonds as extravagant. Sympathetic MPs like Andrew Marvell agreed that Hayes and Jekyll would have "betrayed the liberties of *Englishmen*" by accepting "illegal" bonds that constrained men in their worship of God. These MPs also urged the House to condemn the London magistrates for their use of "illegal and arbitrary" power. Instead, the Commons voted that loyalist city aldermen had acted for "the preservation of the King, and peace of the Kingdom"; and they appointed a committee to strengthen the new Conventicle Act. Anglican MPs were outraged when Jekyll nevertheless persisted in his suit against his arresters, asserting that actions commended by the Commons were in fact "an injury and a wrong." Legal and constitutional questions ranging from the rights of subjects to the privileges of the Commons had thus been raised.[86]

In the meantime, the trial of the Quaker leaders Penn and Mead had gained public attention. Arrested for conspiring to "raise a tumult" at the Grace-church Street meeting, they were tried before a bench of ten London magistrates that included Lord Mayor Sterling and Alderman Robinson. Penn and his counsel, the Quaker Thomas Rudyard, who had also been indicted during the disturbances, succeeded in turning the trial into an arraignment of the Conventicle Act itself. In scenes reminiscent of the trials of

---

[86] CLRO Sessions File 202; *CSPD 1670*, pp. 254, 264, 275, 300, 312, 566; Marvell, *Poems and Letters*, II, 117–18, 317–18; Grey, *Debates*, I, 294–300, 303–10; Dering, *Diary*, pp. 4–7, 9–12.

John Lilburne, Penn maintained that liberty of conscience was part of "the undoubted Birth-right of every *English*-man" that could not be abridged by parliament or by the crown. According to him, the question of the case was whether the "the Rights and Priviledges of every *English man*" and the "Fundamental Laws of *England*" would be upheld against the "*Will* and *Power*" of arbitrary magistrates.[87]

The libertarian political premises from which dissenters developed their defense of conscience were made even more explicit in a trial transcript published with commentary by Penn and Rudyard. These arguments were also made widely known: the trial transcript was reprinted nine times in the last quarter of 1670. In response to the incarceration and fining of conventiclers, the Quaker leaders argued that "to take away the LIBERTY and PROPERTY of any (which are natural Rights)" is "breaking the Law of *nature*." Parliament also "errs" when it adopts laws that "cross" the fundamental liberties preserved in Magna Charta. The likely consequences of the policy of coercion were depicted in stark terms: "Where Liberty and Property are destroyed, there must always be a state of force and war, which ... will be esteemed intolerable by the *Invaded*, who will no longer remain subject." Or as Penn suggested in the *Great Case of Liberty of Conscience* (1670), such a denial of rights preserved in the "primitive institution" of a state was a "*clear overthrow of its own constitution*," reducing the people "*to their* statu quo prius, *or first principles*." A vocabulary for resistance was clearly being articulated that legitimated the resistance to coercion being offered in the London streets.[88]

Jury deliberations in the trial of Penn and Mead enlarged the issues of the case. Eight of the jurors originally found against the defendants, but the Quakers could count upon the sympathy and influence of Edward Bushell and three other dissenters empaneled by the dissenting sheriffs. The jury was sent back five times, after its original report, in order to achieve the desired consensus against the Quaker leaders. But the jurors instead found Penn merely guilty of "preaching to an assembly," at one point, and Mead not guilty at all – an untenable result for a conspiracy trial. Eventually the recalcitrant jurors were warned that the court would mark them, cart them, and shut them up until they agreed upon the appropriate verdict. The freedom of jurors to follow their consciences was thus added to the issue of

---

[87] CLRO Sessions Minutes 34, p. 29; Sessions File 202; Rudyard, *Peoples*, pp. 11, 31, 47–8; HMC *Leyborne-Popham*, p. 167. Most of the pamphlet is reprinted in *ST*, VI, 951–1000. For recent accounts of the trial, see T. A. Green, *Verdict According to Conscience* (Chicago, 1985), pp. 229–36; C. W. Horle; *The Quakers and the English Legal System, 1660–1688* (Philadelphia, 1988), pp. 116–17.

[88] Rudyard, *Peoples*, pp. 3, 47–48; Penn, *Great Case*, p. 100; *ST*, VI, 975, 990; Penn, *Papers*, V, 119–20.

freedom of conscience for religious worship. The presiding magistrates also fell under suspicion of popery. Penn and Rudyard claimed that the Recorder of London, serving as prosecutor, had exclaimed that "it will never be well with us, till some thing like unto the Spanish inquisition be in England."[89]

Bushell and his three dissenting colleagues were fined and imprisoned when the jury at length reported an acquittal. Pointing to a perceived disregard for juries in the Conventicle Act itself, Penn and Rudyard suggested that this "rape . . . on the consciences" of the jury was a "demonstration that juries are now but mere formality." The jurors remained in gaol for three months, "rather than to betray the Liberties of the Country," by gaining freedom by any means other than habeas corpus. They then successfully appealed their fines to the Court of Common Pleas, which agreed, in its decision in Bushell's Case, that the magistrates had violated the recent parliamentary declaration against the fining and imprisoning of juries. Interestingly, juror Edward Bushell, an Independent, was a patron of two of Oliver Cromwell's chaplains after the Restoration.[90] His case further dramatized how liberty of conscience had become the critical issue of the early Restoration and provoked additional legal and constitutional disputes.

CONCLUSION: UNSETTLING THE CHURCH

The London contest about coercion in 1669–70 showed the remarkable extent to which civic dissenters had rebounded politically from the disappointments of the early 1660s. Nonconformists of all persuasions reasserted their political interests in a display of tactical creativity and rhetorical ingenuity. Anglican loyalist hegemony in the city had proven short-lived indeed. The contest that London dissenters carried out against coercion in the Corporation, in the streets, and in the courts was also one that required a high level of communication and organization. The occasional use of the word "party" in the political language of the contest is one demonstration of the increasing sophistication of the dissenting response to persecution. Moreover, this challenge to coercion was effective: loyalist magistrates tired of efforts to

---

[89] Although the recorder's outburst seems improbable, even from a frustrated prosecutor, the story is repeated in other sources. Rudyard, *Peoples*, pp. 15–23, 58–9; *ST*, VI, 964–9, 982–3, 989–92; 999–1025; Add. MS 36,916, fols. 191, 233; Sterling, *Answer to the Pamphlet*, pp. 8–9; Browning, *Documents*, pp. 86–9; Horle, *Quakers*, pp. 116–17; T. A. Green, *Verdict*, ch. 6.

[90] One of these chaplains was the Cambridge Platonist Peter Sterry, who also enjoyed ties to Algernon Sidney. *CSPD 1682*, p. 610; *The Life of Richard Kidder, D. D.*, ed. A. E. Robinson (1924), pp. 40–1; F. Bate, *The Declaration of Indulgence 1672* (1908), p. xl; V. S. Pinto, *Peter Sterry, Platonist and Puritan, 1613–1672* (Cambridge, 1934), pp. 59–60; *BDBR*, III, 206–7. I am grateful to the Honourable Society of Lincoln's Inn for permission to consult the apparently unique copy of *The Case of Edward Bushel, John Hammond, Charles Milson and John Baily* [1671] in their library.

suppress conventicles; Anglican MPs were outraged; and government ministers were driven to "melancholy."[91] Charles II was again forced to confront the fundamental contradiction between his own religious agenda and that of the parliament elected in 1661.

The disruption of civic affairs by the contest against coercion was not another "unsettlement" of the Corporation, however. To the contrary, it represented the return to civic affairs, albeit in some unusual guises, of London citizens who had been artificially excluded in 1662. The unsettlement the contest marked was rather an unsettlement, in the capital, of the Church of England, a situation that had momentous implications for the broader church and the state alike. Reformed Protestants and sectarians in London had not only united in asserting liberty for conscience, they had also united in demanding a new church settlement that better accommodated Protestants of all persuasions. In the face of parliamentary adoption of a second Conventicle Act, influential dissenting authors had made a powerful public case that coercion was the principal threat to Protestant security in the nation. The Anglican order was also unsettled elsewhere, as nonconformists in different localities undermined the enforcement of the new act.[92] As Charles moved toward another external contest with the Dutch, therefore, the internal contest about coercion – a contest centered in London – required his ministers to reconsider the settlement of the church.

[91] *CSPD 1670*, pp. 233–4, 235.   [92] Spurr, *1670s*, p. 14.

3

Protestant dissent and the emergence of a civic opposition, 1670–1679

INTRODUCTION: UNSETTLING THE STATE IN THE ERA OF DANBY'S
ANGLICAN POLITY

The future of the church establishment remained the most critical domestic issue confronting the Restoration regime in the 1670s. If the Conventicle Act of 1670 and the rejection of coercion by London dissenters left the church unsettled, the inability of Charles's governments to achieve religious accommodation thereafter left the state vulnerable to unsettlement as well. Recognizing this vulnerability, the ministry of the Cabal sponsored a royal indulgence for dissenters in 1672 that provoked both a parliamentary reaction and a strong parliamentary effort to find new grounds for Protestant accommodation. But parliament left the work of Protestant accommodation unfinished in 1673. Some historians have assumed that the Anglican settlement was impregnable in 1672–3, but urban dissenters and their parliamentary friends remained determined to free conscience from its cavalier shackles.

Unfortunately for these advocates of conscience, however, the dominant ministerial agenda of the 1670s was not the search for accommodation but rather a strengthening of the confessional exclusivity of the Restoration state. After the Cabal dissolved in 1673, the political dynamics of the early 1660s reappeared. Thomas Osborne, who was soon made Earl of Danby, emerged as the king's principal minister. The new lord treasurer and his associates encouraged another Anglican reaction, claiming that the Protestant establishment was imperiled by papists and sectarians alike.[1] By the spring 1675 parliamentary session, the ministry was, however, more focused upon reviving the sectarian alarms of 1659–60 than upon any perceived Catholic threat. Danby and parliamentary churchmen had begun, by then, to re-establish the Anglican polity that had been challenged in the city in 1669–70 and

---

[1] Danby and some bishops apparently favored accommodation through limited concessions to Presbyterians as late as February 1674; but they executed an abrupt about-face thereafter. Swatland, *House of Lords*, pp. 183, 243.

116

reconsidered in parliament in 1673. Danby proposed new statutory oaths that would have established an even more thoroughly confessional state than that adopted in the first sessions of the Cavalier Parliament. This Court program aroused intense opposition in parliament from Country lords like Shaftesbury and Buckingham and from Country MPs like Andrew Marvell, who succeeded in blocking it.

Danby's initiatives were also little appreciated by the numerous dissenting office-holders in the Corporation of London. They were openly hostile to the ministry's attempts to re-create a political society based upon prescription, coercion, obedience, and the control of printed and spoken words. Moreover, by 1675, the animus against coercion, which had so impeded enforcement of the Conventicle Act, was embodied within a maturing civic dissenting community dedicated to maintaining English Reformed Protestant tradition. Distinctions among dissenting persuasions remained, of course; but Independents and Presbyterians were more united against the Anglican polity of Danby than they once had been in defense, against the Rump, of the Cromwellian church.

Dissenting citizens were, moreover, at the heart of a civic political opposition that had emerged by 1675 and that had converged with the parliamentary Country. This London opposition revived the civic quarrels of the 1640s – quarrels that had led, a generation earlier, to the emancipation of the electorate and common council from magisterial control. Arguments about electoral consent joined arguments about conscience as rhetorical flash-points in the city. Once again opposition common councilmen and Court-inclined aldermen advanced contradictory claims about the rights of citizens and the prerogatives of magistracy.

Historians have paid particular attention to the political happenings of 1675 ever since J. G. A. Pocock made his now classic claim for a revival of Harringtonian republicanism in the pamphlet literature of that year. Some recent analysis of connections between the parliamentary events of 1675 and the political crisis that began in 1679 has broadened the focus from Court and Country constitutional stances to a consideration of religious postures as well.[2] The history of civic opposition in London in the 1670s reinforces this emphasis upon religious issues. Like the Country, the civic opposition feared for the future of parliament, given the duration of the 1661 parliament; and they came to fear that military resources entrusted to the crown for protection against France might leave citizens unprotected

---

[2] J. G. A. Pocock, *The Machiavellian Moment: Florentine Political Thought and the Atlantic Republican Tradition* (Princeton, 1975), pp. 406ff.; Harris, *Later Stuarts*, ch. 3. Also see J. Miller, *After the Civil Wars: English Politics and Government in the Reign of Charles II* (Harlow, 2000), ch. 11; Spurr, *1670s*, ch. 2; Montaño, *Courting*, ch. 9.

against the crown itself.[3] But what the civic opposition came to fear most was that Danby's Anglican polity was a political cloak for the adoption of popish practices within the Protestant Church of England. The opposition's fear of popery may have driven its fear of arbitrary government, rather than the other way around.

Although Danby sought to rekindle popular fears about the sects, he was actually more successful in provoking fears about the bishops; and some Anglican apologists who had raised the specter of Catholicism in defense of the church establishment found themselves suspected of popery. The Country propaganda that was produced by Shaftesbury and Andrew Marvell, among others, pointed to episcopal pretensions as the chief threat to the Protestant order in church and state. Indeed, Country writers rearticulated arguments against the bishops that had ignited the kingdom in 1641–2 and that were nicely crafted to appeal to those Reformed Protestants who were excluded from the church establishment.[4] Ironically, what Danby accomplished in 1675 was not, then, a revival of the Anglican confessional state but rather a revival of arguments for a new Protestant settlement in which accommodation took precedence over episcopacy.

The Country case against the bishops competed with the Anglican case against dissent after 1675; but neither case ever obscured its opposite. Instead, when the revelations of the Popish Plot destabilized an already fragile settlement of church and state, Reformed and Anglican Protestants read the country's circumstances in quite different ways. For Anglicans, the unraveling of the Popish Plot demonstrated how republicans and dissenters were seeking to exploit the Catholic threat to undermine the settlement of church and state "by law established." But city dissenters and their parliamentary friends instead read the revelations of the Popish Plot as proof that Danby, the bishops, the Duke of York, and other leading Catholics were attempting to bring in popery and arbitrary government. Fears about dissenters drove Anglican loyalists to defend the church and state they had erected against the "sects," while fears about popery drove Reformed Protestants to demand a strengthening of church and state through a broader Protestant settlement.

The political divisions that brought the city and the nation to crisis again after 1679 clearly preceded and predated the explosive issue of the succession. The succession was an important issue in the crisis, and the exclusion of the king's Roman Catholic brother from the crown was the solution to that issue preferred by dissenters in the city, as well as by much of the parliamentary Country. But the Restoration Crisis of 1679–83 was broader than the

---

[3] L. G. Schwoerer, *"No Standing Armies!" The Antiarmy Ideology in Seventeenth-century England* (Baltimore, 1974), ch. 7.

[4] M. Goldie, "Danby, the Bishops and the Whigs," in Harris, *et al.*, eds., *The Politics of Religion*, pp. 75–105.

issue of the succession. What hung in the balance was the entire Restoration paradigm of a cavalier state, an exclusively episcopal church, and the political proscription of those unable to swear to their unqualified allegiance to each.

LONDON AND THE SEARCH FOR ACCOMMODATION, 1670–1673

The civic contest about coercion in 1669–70 had revealed the ability of London dissenters to unsettle the church. As Charles and his mixed ministry of Anglicans, Catholic sympathizers, and friends of dissent moved in the direction of another war against the Dutch, they worried about the ability of those same London dissenters to unsettle the state. The disillusionment of London merchants and traders with the previous war had contributed to its disappointing results. Charles eventually adopted another Declaration of Indulgence in 1672, on the eve of the new war, as a strategy for achieving a better religious settlement, one that would remove the grievances of dissenters without, he hoped, aggrieving Anglican loyalists. Both the willingness of dissenters to accept the king's indulgence and the hostility of Anglicans to it have been much misunderstood, however. Dissenters embraced the king's indulgence without embracing the king's understanding of his prerogative. And some Anglican MPs approached the ensuing parliamentary Test Act of 1673 not as a reaffirmation of coercion, but rather as a preservative for the Church within a broader Protestant settlement. But the adoption of the Test Act without an accompanying bill for a provisional and limited liberty of conscience left both church and state open to further unsettlement.

Much insight into ministerial thinking prior to the issuance of the Declaration of Indulgence can be gained from the memoranda of Sir Joseph Williamson, the under-secretary of state and the director of the government's extensive domestic intelligence efforts. What needs to be explained, of course, is not why crypto-Catholic or tolerationist ministers promoted the indulgence, but rather why it also attracted support from some Anglican royalists like Williamson. As Charles persisted after 1670 in his Francophile and anti-Dutch foreign course, Williamson became almost obsessed about the loyalty of the increasingly resilient urban dissenting population. The confrontation about coercion in London had been eased through a relaxation in enforcement of the 1670 Conventicle Act. But as Williamson tracked the urban activities of such "dangerous and disaffected persons" as Major John Gladman, the onetime army agitator, he worried much about how the "stout, sturdy, and dissatisfied" dissenting citizens would respond to Charles's stance in foreign affairs.[5]

---

[5] PRO SP 29/294/68; *CSPD 1671*, pp. 496, 562–3, 570; *CSPD 1671–72*, pp. 28, 63. Also see Greaves, *Enemies*, pp. 215–23; A. Marshall, *Intelligence and Espionage*, ch. 1.

Indeed, Williamson became convinced by reports from Colonel Thomas Blood and other city agents that the church settlement had failed in London, with potentially disastrous consequences for the nation.[6] By November 1671 the under-secretary was writing of the need for religious settlement as if none had ever been made: "We are very loose and running into madness, if not brought to some [church] settlement." And given that London was the "nursery" of dissent in the country, any new effort at religious accommodation needed to begin there. Williamson, Secretary of State Lord Arlington, and other ministers therefore attempted to lay the groundwork for an accommodation through Sir George Waterman, Lord Mayor of London for 1671–2. The lord mayor was instructed, after a conference with the king, to inform the leading city dissenting clergy that he would not proceed against private conventicles if public meetings, held in more flagrant violation of the law, were abandoned. But given that parliament was not sitting, and given that any such arrangement departed from the clear intent of the Conventicle Act, Waterman was to make this offer in his own name rather than in the name of the king or of the ministry. The dissenting clergy were also told that their failure to accept this compromise would trigger a full-scale resumption of persecution.[7]

An accommodation in London upon these terms – terms that avoided all the political and religious issues raised in the dissenting literature about conscience – proved stillborn from the outset, in part because the intransigence of many Presbyterian clergy now matched that of their Independent and sectarian counterparts. Williamson learned that the Presbyterian "dons" – a group of older, more "churchly" Reformed teachers, like William Bates, Thomas Jacombe, and Thomas Manton – did prefer the greater security of private meetings to the greater stir of public assemblies. Seeking to achieve comprehension through cooperation, these moderates were nevertheless unable to prevail over their younger Presbyterian cohorts. The latter – the militant "ducklings" – were described to Williamson as "leaders of the vulgars" with strong ties to "the middling people." The ducklings included clerical spokesmen like James Innes, his brothers-in-law Nathaniel and Thomas Vincent, and Samuel Annesley. Having resumed open and regular ministry in defiance of the policy of persecution, the ducklings were not prepared to compromise their public commitment to the gospel, even in the hope of gaining some form of comprehension for themselves. Williamson perceived the militancy of the ducklings as reflecting the spirit of the London Presbyterian laity: "Congregations now come to ride their teachers, and

---

[6] *CSPD 1671*, pp. 496, 560; A. Marshall, *Intelligence and Espionage*, ch. 6; A. Marshall "Colonel Thomas Blood and the Restoration Political Scene," *HJ* 32 (1989), 561–82.

[7] *CSPD 1671*, pp. 554, 561, 562, 581; Spurr, *1670s*, pp. 23, 26.

make them do what they will. . . . The people grow more fanatic; all the Presbyterians are growing to Independents, and so must the teachers."[8]

Indeed, these "fiercer" Presbyterians joined with other urban dissenters in an effort to set their own terms for religious accommodation. Duckling James Innes appeared before the king in November 1671 to demand a liberty for London's "great meeting-houses." This demand may well have had the support of the ministerial friends of dissent with whom Innes had already developed ties, namely Lord Ashley, the Duke of Buckingham, and Sir John Trevor (the junior secretary of state). In the city, Anglican Alderman Sir John Robinson's desire for another show of force threatened to revive the urban contest about coercion, but Lord Mayor Waterman, backed by Reformed Protestant magistrates, refused to return to active persecution. Charles himself wished to avoid a return to street confrontations, while leading Anglican office-holders like Williamson and Arlington now concluded that the interests of the king and kingdom were better served by religious compromise than by religious coercion.[9]

Two days prior to the declaration of war against the Dutch Republic in March 1672, a Declaration of Indulgence was issued under the king's prerogative. It reflected a variety of ministerial motives: Treasury Lord Sir Thomas Clifford and the Duke of York sought relief for Catholics; Buckingham and Ashley sought liberty for dissenters; Arlington and Williamson sought to preserve Anglican hegemony through accommodation with dissent. The under-secretary hoped for settlement under a "rule . . . as wide as may be" accompanied by "liberty to all Dissenters" outside the church "under certain incapacities." Despite its retention of civil penalties for dissent, this rather Cromwellian formula of comprehension and indulgence was structurally similar to the proposals of Presbyterians like John Humfrey. Williamson believed the formula could both "Gratify the Gentry" and pacify the nonconformists.[10]

But the wording of the actual Declaration was somewhat less ambitious. It affirmed the current "doctrine, discipline and government" of the Church of England without compromise, while permitting public dissenting worship, after royal licensure. It also suspended the penal laws under an affirmation

[8] *CSPD 1671*, pp. 496, 568–70; *CSPD 1671–72*, pp. 28–9; R. Thomas, "Comprehension and Indulgence," in *From Uniformity to Unity, 1662–1962*, ed. O. Chadwick and G. F. Nuttall (1962), pp. 204–9.

[9] BL Stowe MS 186, fol. 6; *CSPD 1671*, pp. 356–7, 385–6; 496–7; 553–4, 561, 562, 569; *CSPD 1671–72*, pp. 45; *CSPD 1660–85 Addenda*, pp. 341–2; Lacey, *Dissent*, p. 103; Greaves, *Enemies*, p. 159.

[10] *CSPD 1671*, p. 554; *CSPD 1671–2*, p. 45. Also see Hutton, *Charles the Second, King of England, Scotland, and Ireland* (Oxford, 1989), pp. 284–5; J. R. Jones, *Charles II: Royal Politician* (1987), pp. 96–8; John Miller, *Charles II* (1991), pp. 188–90; Bate, *Declaration*, pp. 74–5, 80–5.

of the king's "prerogative power to settle Church matters *as he will.*"[11] This suspension was to benefit Catholics as well as dissenters, although the former were permitted private worship only. In London, most dissenting teachers and congregations accepted the Declaration, with only the Quakers remaining aloof from toleration under royal auspices. Over 150 dissenting clergy and places of worship were licensed in the Corporation, Westminster, and Middlesex over the course of the year in which the indulgence was in effect. Many urban dissenters understood the indulgence in a quite expansive manner that entirely blurred the distinction between comprehension and indulgence. Philip Nye, for instance, argued that dissenters who worshipped under royal licensure were "fully comprehended." And John Humfrey suggested that authorized conventicles, "having the Authority of the Supream Head of the Church, equally with the Parish Churches ... are manifestly ... thereby parts of the Church National."[12]

London dissenters, especially those of Reformed Protestant antecedents, therefore saw the 1672 Declaration as the beginning of the broader church settlement they had hoped for in 1660 and demanded in 1669–70. But historians have long been troubled by dissenting enthusiasm for an indulgence that rested upon the prerogative, especially given the apparent inconsistency between this posture and the dissenting-Whig desire to overrule prerogative in critical matters in 1679–81.[13] Suggestions of inconsistency do not, however, well reflect the fluid political circumstances of the 1670s or the centrality of the issues of conscience and church settlement. And London dissenters did not, in any case, embrace sweeping claims for the royal prerogative as they escaped statutory coercion. Such dissenting apologists as Owen, Humfrey, Corbet, and Nye would have preferred a parliamentary indulgence to one that rested upon prerogative. Owen wrote that dissenters expected "no liberty but from his majesty's favour and authority, *with the concurrence of the parliament*"; and Corbet placed "our Help ... in ... our SOVEREIGN *and* his PARLIAMENT."[14]

---

[11] Browning, *Documents*, pp. 387–8; *CSPD 1671*, p. 563 (my italics); Bate, *Declaration*, pp. xxxvii–xl, lxxiii.

[12] [John Humfrey], *Defense of the Proposition*, p. 58; Nye, *The Lawfulness of the Oath of Supremacy*, p. 69; J[ohn] H[umfrey], *Authority of the Magistrate*, p. 24. Also see C. Condren, *George Lawson's 'Politica' and the English Revolution* (Cambridge, 1989), pp. 143–50.

[13] Scholars have similarly wrestled with explaining the support for the Declaration by future Whig leaders like Shaftesbury, a Cabal principal, and future Whig theorists like John Locke. For recent discussion of these related questions, see Harris, *Politics under the Later Stuarts*, pp. 64–5, 68–75; J. Marshall, *John Locke*, pp. 81–3; P. Seaward, *The Restoration* (New York, 1991), p. 53; Ashcraft, *Revolutionary Politics*, pp. 111–23; C. C. Weston and J. R. Greenberg, *Subjects and Sovereigns: The Grand Controversy over Legal Sovereignty in Stuart England* (Cambridge, 1981), p. 163.

[14] Owen, *Peace-offering*, p. 570 (my italics); Corbet, *Second Discourse*, p. 2.

However, these authors recognized that parliaments, no less than monarchs, might err in favoring laws, like the 1670 Conventicle Act, that intruded upon the internal sphere of faith and devotion governed by conscience. In these circumstances, according to them, the prince has a responsibility, to God and to the people, to intervene. Nye wrote, for instance, that there must be "a Power to review, judg, and dispense" with "Laws and Statutes in Ecclesiastical Affairs... [that] derogate from the Prerogative of Christ Jesus, or the Laws and Institutions of his Kingdom." This royal dispensing power was a part of the historic ecclesiastical responsibilities of the English monarch. But it was also a special case: the monarch's authority to dispense with laws that interfered with the exercise of conscience in the internal, spiritual sphere did not extend to the external, civil sphere. Were the magistrate to possess such an authority in the civil constitution, it would prove "destructive to the great Ends of a Common-Wealth," according to Nye and Humfrey.[15]

If dissenters accepted liberty of conscience under a royal indulgence without embracing an expansive understanding of the civil prerogative, some Anglicans objected to liberty of conscience by means of prerogative while now coming to accept the need for liberty of conscience by means of statute. Indeed, the Anglican cry against the king's Declaration in the parliamentary session of 1673 was actually more a reaction against the toleration of papists than it was a reaction to the indulgence of dissenters. The Declaration served as a trip-wire for a national explosion of cultural anti-Catholicism that had been building from the beginning of the ministry. The anti-Catholicism of 1673 reflected concerns about a foreign policy that victimized Protestant states, about the presence of Catholics in high places, about Ireland, and about the advisability of subjecting Protestant subjects to a papist policy of persecution. Anti-Catholicism was, moreover, an ideological force that cut against the division between churchmen and dissenters, enabling some Anglicans to forget again their fear of the sects in the common fear of Rome. By 1673, anxiety about Roman Catholicism convinced some leading conformist politicians that Protestant reconciliation offered a more secure future than Protestant recrimination.

As the House of Commons considered an act to require an Anglican sacramental test of all MPs, it also therefore, agreed, "with very few negatives," that "ease should be given to Protestants that would subscribe to the doctrinal articles" of the church. In part, this measure was promoted as a means of securing the king's relinquishment of his Declaration by placing the indulgence of dissenters upon a statutory basis. More significantly, however, the bill is evidence that a House that had reaffirmed the policy of persecution in

---

[15] Nye, *The King's Authority*, pp. 14, 30; Humfrey, *Authority of the Magistrate*, p. 15.

1670 now included many MPs prepared to break with that decision in the interests of religious accommodation. Arguing from "empirical" grounds, for instance, William Garway called for reconciliation to achieve the "pacification of *England*" in the midst of war. Edmund Waller argued, "the persecuted party ever gets uppermost," but the king's "liberty has kept Peace." Henry Powle asserted that the dissenters "teach nothing but the truth" and demanded to know "why we should deny these people liberty, that have it in all places but where the Inquisition is."[16]

The arguments and actions of dissenting writers and activists in London had thus clearly had an impact at Westminster as well as at Whitehall, but parliamentary consensus ended over the precise form of the ease to be granted. The relative merits of "uniting Protestant subjects" through comprehension and of indulging those of "tender conscience" were again debated. The Commons eventually agreed upon a bill that provided provisional relief for Presbyterians and Independents. Its continuation beyond the next session of parliament was made dependent upon dissenting behavior and upon parliamentary confirmation. It offered little to sectarians who could not subscribe to all the required doctrinal articles of the church. Full of limitations and qualifications, and far less generous than Charles's indulgence, the bill bespoke the contradictory impulses of Anglican MPs retreating from coercion. Their retreat was not completed, however. The bill to relieve dissenters became the object of intense maneuvring among Charles, different ministers, the Lords, and the bishops. The session ended before agreement had been reached, leaving dissenters without statutory ease. The demise of the bill was greeted with relief by Bishop George Morley, who argued that it represented a worse threat than the Declaration itself as "an establishment of schisme by a Law."[17]

The failure of parliament to adopt any formula for Protestant accommodation in 1673 was a watershed in the histories of Restoration Anglicanism and dissent. Leading London Anglican clergy like Edward Stillingfleet would look back to 1672–3 as critical in the preservation of the restored establishment; and leading London Presbyterian divines like Vincent Alsop would look back to the events of 1672–3 as a critical lost opportunity for Protestant union.[18] The same formula of comprehension and indulgence was debated in parliament again in 1680–81 and in 1689. But by 1680, the difficulties

---

[16] Dering, *Diary*, 114–23 (quote at 123), 133–5; Grey, *Debates*, II, 27, 32, 44, 47, 69, 132–3.

[17] Sir Richard Bulstrode, *The Bulstrode Papers* (1897), pp. 262–3; Bate, *Declaration*, pp. 126, 172; Haley, *Shaftesbury*, pp. 325–6 Hutton, *Charles II*, p. 306; Lacey, *Dissent*, pp. 66–70; Miller, *Charles II*, 203–5; Spurr, *1670s*, pp. 38–9; Spurr, "Comprehension and the Toleration Act," pp. 935–6; N. Tyacke, "The 'Rise of Puritanism' and the Legalizing of Dissent, 1571–1719," in Grell, *et al.*, eds., *From Persecution to Toleration*, pp. 32–4.

[18] Vincent Alsop, *The Mischief of Impositions* (1680), p. 5; J. Marshall, "The Ecclesiology of the Latitude-men 1660–1689: Stillingfleet, Tillotson and 'Hobbism'," *JEcH* 36 (1985), 407–27.

of the 1672–3 debate were enlarged by the further consolidation of separate Anglican and dissenting communities, languages, and identities. In London, schism had been established in fact, if not in law, by 1672: dissenting roots were sturdy; the language of conscience had established itself; and dissenting congregations and their clergy acted with self-confidence. Sectarians, Independents, and Presbyterians who had once been fractured by the events of the civil wars and Interregnum had already coalesced into a dissenting community with considerable political potential.

Who were the London dissenters who challenged coercion in 1669–70, whose demands contributed to the issuance of the 1672 Indulgence, and for whom the advocates of conscience spoke? Recognition of the importance of religious nonconformity in Restoration politics has always been blunted by the difficulty of knowing who the dissenters were. Two overlapping groups of London dissenters active at this time will be analyzed here in order to characterize the lay leadership of London nonconformity in its formative era.

The first group includes 155 London dissenters who sought to influence Charles's religious policy by lending to the crown in 1670. In the midst of the street engagements of that year, a financially burdened monarch approached the city magistrates for a loan of £60,000. Still recovering from plague, fire, and war, the Corporation was able to raise a scant £20,000. Seizing upon the opportunity presented by this shortfall, the London dissenters organized their own loan of the remaining £40,000. Unlike the Corporation leaders who crippled Charles I in 1640 by refusing to lend to him, these dissenting subscribers took the financial risk of investing in the monarchy of Charles II. Their loan was intended to drive a wedge between Charles and his persecuting parliament and to encourage him to abandon the Conventicle Act. The second group includes fifty-one additional nonconformists who served on common council in 1669–71. These citizens were prepared to accept office, despite their formal religious incapacity, in order to impede implementation of the Conventicle Act.

The 200 dissenters included in these two groups are not a cross-section of the dissenting population but rather an elite group of Reformed Protestants and sectarians who were actively committed to the achievement of liberty for conscience. They are, nevertheless, representative of all those for whom the dissenting advocates of conscience spoke and wrote. Indeed, they include many individuals who were personally acquainted with the chief dissenting authors and divines. Their careers and commitments also indicate how the cause of conscience was shaping an urban dissenting community. The names

Table 3.1[20] *Subscriptions to the 1670 dissenting loan to the crown*

Persuasion	Subscribers	Subscriptions
Presbyterians	55	£11,600
Independents	39	£ 7,900
Other Reformed Protestants	7	£ 950
Baptists	6	£ 4,800
Persuasion unknown	48	£14,420
Totals	155	£39,670

and selected biographical details of these 200 dissenters are recorded in Appendices I and II.[19]

Reformed Protestants dominated the 1670 loan to Charles II and the dissenting common council leadership of these years. Over two-thirds of the subscribers can be identified by persuasion. Of these, over 90 percent were Reformed Protestants. (Table 3.1) Similarly, twenty-five of thirty additional dissenting common councilmen of 1669–71 of known persuasion were Reformed Protestants. Quakers neither participated in the loan nor accepted election to common council. But the small number of Baptists in the subscription is more likely a reflection of the relative wealth of Baptist adherents than of any unwillingness on their part to join with other dissenters on behalf of conscience. The largest loan subscription was actually that of Baptist merchant and lay preacher William Kiffin, whose £3,600 subscription represented almost a tenth of the total and may have included contributions he gathered from his co-religionists.

Some of the heaviest subscribers to the loan were six Presbyterian and three Independent clergy whose contributions may also have come, in part,

---

[19] The names of those who subscribed to the £40,000 London dissenting loan to the crown of 1670 have been taken from CLRO MS 40/30. Some of the data in Appendix II has been derived from Woodhead, *Rulers*, who also provides many additional details. Major sources for the attributions of religious persuasion in the two appendices include wills; numerous dissenting congregational records, especially DWL Congregational Library MS 52.a.38, which is partially transcribed in T. G. Crippen, "Dr. Watts's Church-book," *TCHS* 1 (1901), 26–30; Farnell, "City of London," appendices; G. S. De Krey, "Trade, Religion, and Politics in London in the Reign of William III," Unpublished Ph.D. thesis, Princeton University, 1978, appendices; Brenner, *Merchants*; Elliot, "Elections to the Common Council"; T. Liu, *Puritan London: A Study of Religion and Society in the City Parishes* (Newark, Del., 1986). My discussion of language and community among Restoration London dissenters is indebted to R. Wuthnow, *Communities of Discourse: Ideology and Social Structure in the Reformation, the Enlightenment, and European Socialism* (Cambridge, Mass., 1989).

[20] The line in Table 3.1 for other Reformed Protestants includes three subscribers with connections to both Presbyterianism and Independency and two members each of London French Reformed and Dutch Reformed congregations. Of the 1669–71 dissenting common councilmen of known persuasion, fourteen were Presbyterians, eight were Independents, two had connections to each of these persuasions, and one was French Reformed.

from funds pooled within their churches. The most prominent Independent churches involved in the loan were those gathered by Joseph Caryl and John Owen, which merged in 1673, following Caryl's death. Owen himself subscribed £1,000 to the loan, while Caryl's and Owen's friends and followers included such leading subscribers or opponents of coercion as common councilmen James Hayes and John Brett, merchant William Pennoyer (prominent in the Commonwealth era), and Benjamin Shute.[21] Among the Presbyterian clerical subscribers, Thomas Jacombe may be singled out as one whose lay friends and followers were also notable contributors. Among Jacombe's lay associates were subscribers Robert Blaney (secretary to Lord Ashley in 1667–8) and John Jolliffe and Sir Stephen White, both leading merchants.[22]

Although many of these early Restoration loan subscribers and common councilmen can be connected to particular Presbyterian, Independent, or Baptist congregations, the convergence of Reformed Protestants and Baptists in a single dissenting community is equally apparent from study of their lives and careers. Never firm, the boundaries between civic Presbyterianism and Independency were becoming increasingly fluid by the second decade of the Restoration. The Presbyterian Barnardiston family, for instance, which was represented in the 1670 loan by merchant brothers Nathaniel and Palatia, had Independent roots and had also intermarried with the Independent Brett family. Similarly, Presbyterian linen-draper John Hulbert subscribed to the 1670 loan in the company of several lenders from Joseph Caryl's gathered church, which included members of his own family. Independent William Pennoyer was a friend of Presbyterian merchants John Jolliffe and Henry Ashurst Sr, and he was also intimate with Baptist leader William Kiffin. Alderman and loan subscriber Sir John Frederick, of Dutch Reformed beliefs, made his 1670 loan subscription jointly with Independent merchant George Perryer. Frederick also took Independent pastor Joseph Caryl's son as his apprentice, and his son-in-law and eventual executor was a leading city Baptist.[23]

---

[21] DWL Congregational Library MS 52.a.38. Robert Ferguson also served this church after 1674 and joined Owen as a principal dissenting advocate in the press: Toon, *God's Statesman*, p. 156; Ashcraft, *Revolutionary Politics*, p. 55. PRO PROB 11: 341 Pye, qu. 33 (Caryl); 367 North, qu. 123 (Shute); 391 Exton, qu. 80 (Hayes); Woodhead, *Rulers*, pp. 37, 87 (Brett, Hayes); *BDBR*, III, 28 (Pennoyer); Brenner, *Merchants*, pp. 137–8 (Brett, Pennoyer).

[22] Blaney and Jolliffe were both related to Jacombe by marriage, and Blaney served as his pastor's co-executor in 1687. PRO PROB 11: 358 Reeve, qu. 148 (White); 387 Foot, qu. 50 (Jacombe). *CSPD 1667*, pp. 17, 48 (Blaney); Pepys, *Diary*, IX, 152 (Blaney); Ashcraft, *Revolutionary Politics*, p. 114 (Blaney); Brenner, *Merchants*, p. 138 (Jolliffe); Henning, *House of Commons*, II, 657–8 (Jolliffe); Woodhead, *Rulers*, pp. 71–2 (Jolliffe).

[23] PRO PROB 11: 341 Pye, qu. 33 (Caryl); 355 Duke, qu. 25 (Pennoyer); 362 Bath, qu. 2 (Barnardiston); 380 Cann, qu. 56 (Frederick). DWL Congregational Library MS 52.a.38 (Hulbert family); Henning, *House of Commons*, II, 363–5 (Frederick); Brenner, *Merchants*, pp. 421, 425n. (Barnardistons); Grell, "Persecution," p. 125 (Frederick). Frederick's son-in-law and executor was Baptist merchant Francis Gosfright, for whom see *Baptist Quarterly* 20 (1963–4), 129–30.

Examples like these, which could easily be multiplied, point to the parallel difficulty that scholars have had in identifying some dissenting clergy as either Presbyterian or Independent. In fact, these categories were not mutually exclusive, and Presbyterian churches operating without classical Presbyterian structures were actually practicing Independent polity. Similarly, the distrust between commonwealthmen and supporters of the Cromwellian order – a distrust that had contributed so much to the collapse of the revived republic in 1659–60 – was also much less evident a decade later among London dissenting loan subscribers and common councilmen.

Former adversaries of the Long Parliament and critics of the Protectorate were quite noticeable among the civic dissenting leaders of 1669–71. William Kiffin and fellow Baptist subscriber Thomas Dafforne, for instance, had once been associated with John Lilburne, whose leveling agenda included an end to the coercion of Protestants. At least thirteen of these dissenting subscribers and common councilmen – including John Brett, James Hayes, and William Pennoyer – had once served the Rump or the New Model Army as London militia commissioners. Such subscribers as Brett, Hayes, John Ireton, and Maximilian Bard had also been highly visible during and after the city's constitutional revolution of 1649. Bard had been a commissioner for the High Court of Justice in 1649 and an army treasurer. Benjamin Shute and Thomas Waring were members of mercantile families that came to power in the Corporation in 1649.[24]

In 1669–71, these onetime republicans, Levellers, and commonwealthmen were, however, acting in concert with men of a different stripe altogether. Loan subscribers from the Presbyterian Ashurst and Jolliffe families had a record of hostility to the New Model Army, to the sects, and to republicanism. Subscriber Henry Ashurst Sr had authored an anti-Leveller manifesto in 1648. John Jolliffe had been instrumental in turning General Monck against the republican Council of State. Subscribers Benjamin Ducane, Stephen Hams, and Jeremy Sambrooke were among the Presbyterian common councilmen of 1659 who had dislodged the Rump's civic allies from Corporation government. But these men now acted with their former adversaries on behalf of liberty for conscience.[25]

---

[24] HMC *Leyborne-Popham*, pp. 166–8, *Narrative of the Proceedings of the Committee of the Militia*; *Acts and Ordinances of the Interregnum*, I, 956, and II, 365 (Bard); Brenner, *Merchants*, pp. 430–1, 520–1, 636 (Shute, Waring); *BDBR*, I, 209 (Dafforne); II, 134–5 (Ireton); III, 28 (Pennoyer); Tolmie, *Triumph*, pp. 36, 180 (Kiffin, Dafforne, Lilburne) and ch. 7; Greaves, *Deliver Us*, p. 98 (Dafforne); Brenner, *Merchants*, pp. 430, 549 (Bard).

[25] Humfrey, *Authority of the Magistrate*, p. 96; William Ashhurst, *Reasons against Agreement with a late printed Paper* (1648); HMC *Leyborne-Popham*, p. 216 (Jolliffe); Henning, *House of Commons*, I, 596 (Barnardiston), and II, 657–8 (Jolliffe); De Krey, *A Fractured Society*, pp. 89–90 (Ashurst); Elliot, "Elections"; Woodhead, *Rulers*, pp. 62, 83, 143 (Ducane, Hams, Sambrooke).

Table 3.2 *Occupations of dissenting lenders and common councilmen, 1669–1671*

Occupation	Presbyterian	Persuasion Independent	Other & unknown	Total
Overseas merchants	32	17	27	75
Domestic traders	12	9	5	26
Tradesmen		2	12	14
Urban professionals	5	4	3	12
Clergy	6	3		9
Industrial employers		1	7	8
Money-lenders	2	1	3	6
Urban gentry	1	1	1	3
Occupation unknown	11	9	32	52
Total	69	47	90	206

The social caliber of the leading London dissenters of the early Restoration contributed greatly to the effectiveness of their opposition to coercion. Over one-third of the civic subscribers of 1670 and additional dissenting common councilmen of 1669–71 are known to have come from households devoted to overseas trade. (Table 3.2) Others came from the ranks of domestic traders (grocers, drapers, haberdashers, factors), from the retail shopocracy, and from the ranks of urban professionals (physicians, lawyers, booksellers, and office-holders, for instance). Well might Anglican apologist Samuel Parker worry that "the Fanatick Party" and "the Trading part" of the nation were so much the same, that "the inriching of this sort of People" would only promote what he called "Seditious Practices."[26]

Merchants from all sectors of London's developing overseas trade were noticeable in London's contest about coercion. Leading Turkey merchants like Palatia Barnardiston, John Jolliffe, John Langley, Thomas Pilkington, Henry Spurstowe, and Charles Thorold (all Levant Company assistants in the 1660s) acted on behalf of conscience. So did leading colonial and interloping merchants like William Kiffin, John Lane, William Pennoyer, Samuel Powell, and Samuel Swynoke. A generation earlier the commercial rivalries of merchants from these two groups had contributed to the tensions in London between political Presbyterians and Independents.[27] But in London's contest about coercion, the common advancement of conscience assumed preference over these old disputes; and merchants of divergent interests could easily agree about the need to advance English trade against the

[26] Samuel Parker, *Discourse of Ecclesiastical Politie*, 3rd ed. (1671), pp. xxxix–xli.
[27] Brenner, *Merchants*, esp. ch. 7.

emerging threat from France. Some leading dissenting merchants had already reached or passed the apex of their commercial careers. Others, like Thomas Pilkington and Samuel Swynoke, were at the beginning of theirs; and the families of subscribers Henry Ashurst Sr, John Eyles, Charles Thorold, and Robert Western would continue to provide entrepreneurial and political leadership in future generations.[28]

Associated with these merchant households in the advancement of conscience were other men of means, office-holders, and representatives of the city's thriving "middling sort." Dissenting aldermen and brewers John and Dannet Forth, for instance, were among the largest loan subscribers. Major revenue farmers, they were principals in a syndicate that offered the crown £600,000 for the customs in 1670. Office-holders among the dissenting subscribers included William Forth, doctor of law and excise commissioner; John Casse, a Rolls Office clerk; Robert Blaney, paymaster to the prizes commissioners; and Captain Thomas Bromhall, who held the wardenship of Fleet prison. Subscribers Dr John Micklethwaite and Dr Edmond Trench were fellows of the Royal College of Physicians, and among the numerous domestic traders who opposed coercion were cloth factor Stephen Hams and Baptist chalk dealer Major Edward Brent.[29] Not all loan subscribers and common councilmen were among the city's wealthiest householders, of course; but many of them were, and less prosperous individuals were often tied to the more affluent through congregational or personal affinities.

The sense of common purpose that had developed within the dissenting community led by these individuals was fed by numerous patterns of association and commitment. Proximity of residence and common involvement in local affairs, apprenticeships and friendships, intermarriage and family networks, and support of particular London clergy and of Reformed churches abroad combined to create an intersecting and endogamous dissenting social milieu. The notable residential concentration of leading dissenters in the city's densely inhabited inner wards provided almost constant opportunities for communication about public and personal matters.[30] Some dissenters who had worked together for reformation in the affairs of small parishes

---

[28] Woodhead, *Rulers*, pp. 19, 66, 130, 159; De Krey, *A Fractured Society*, pp. 76, 89–90, 95, 143; Henning, *House of Commons*, I, 558–60; II, 285–6; III, 557–8, 692; G. S. De Krey, "Sir Henry Ashurst," and "Sir Thomas Pilkington," *Oxford DNB*.

[29] PRO PROB 11: 332 Penn, qu. 11 (Trench); 336 Duke, qu. 76 (W. Forth); 342 Pye, qu. 100 (Casse). PRO T70/100, fols. 8–22 (Forths); *CSPD 1670*, pp. 329, 333, 341, 346, 362, 444, 571 (Blaney, Forths); *CSPD 1660–85*, pp. 469–70 (Bromhall); *DNB*, XIII, 337–8 (Micklethwaite); Greaves, *Deliver Us*, p. 29; Woodhead, *Rulers*, pp. 36, 83.

[30] Residence has been determined for most of the 1670 loan subscribers and 1669–71 common councilmen. About half of those who were resident within the Corporation, at one time or another, had addresses within the twelve wards or parts of wards that made up the Inner City (83 of 169).

in the heart of the commercial city before 1660 clearly continued to do so thereafter.[31]

Younger dissenting leaders of 1669–71 had often absorbed the pre-1660 religious commitments of fathers, fathers-in-law, and uncles. Subscriber George Marwood, for instance, was the nephew of trade and toleration advocate Slingsby Bethel and the son-in-law of dissenting common councilman Samuel Swynoke. Apprenticeship within the dissenting community also seems to have been an important experience in the transmission of reforming sentiments from one generation to the next. Merchant subscribers John Jolliffe and Henry Spurstowe, for instance, had once been the apprentices of Matthew Craddock, first governor of the Massachusetts Bay Company, a puritan leader in the Long Parliament, and the onetime partner of subscriber William Pennoyer. Similarly, haberdasher Laurence Baskerville and linen-draper William Wavell joined haberdasher John Jekyll and linen-draper James Hayes, once their masters and now their partners, in challenging coercion in the city in 1669–71.[32]

The ties of kinship, friendship, and family association that were so apparent among leading London dissenters also connected them to prominent Reformed families in the country and in the House of Commons. Presbyterian subscribers John and William Jolliffe, John Lane, and Elizabeth Ashe, for instance, were connected by marriage to the parliamentary Foley family. James Hayes was the brother-in-law of Yorkshire MP Sir John Hotham Bt; and as a member of Joseph Caryl's church, Hayes personally connected civic opposition to coercion to Country politics in the Commons. Grocer Edward Underhill was the brother-in-law of William Love, dissenting MP for London. Common councilmen Edward Nelthorpe and Richard Thompson were kin of Country MP and poet Andrew Marvell.[33]

Among the shared commitments that tied these and other London dissenters together as a dissenting community was an interest in New England. Indeed, connections between Reformed Protestantism in early Restoration London and the colonies were as numerous as they had been in the early

---

[31] Loan subscribers John Langley and William Webb (both onetime aldermen), Captain Thomas Bromhall, and Sir Stephen White, for instance, were as visible in the public affairs of St Bartholomew Exchange during the early Restoration as they had been during the Interregnum. *The Vestry Minute Books of the Parish of St. Bartholomew Exchange in the City of London, 1567–1676*, ed. E. Freshfield (1890), pp. 85ff.

[32] PRO SP 29/417, Pt. 2 (Marwood); Brenner, *Merchants*, pp. 137–8 (Craddock); Pearl, *London*, pp. 185–7 (Craddock); Henning, *House of Commons*, II, 657 (Jolliffe); Woodhead, *Rulers*, pp. 25, 99, 155, 172 (Baskerville, Jolliffe, Spurstowe, Wavell).

[33] PRO PROB 11: 357 Reeve, qu. 57 (Thomas Foley Sr); 391 Exton, qu. 80 (Hayes-Hotham); 448 Lort, qu. 251 (Lane); 449 Pott, qu. 1 (Ashe). Lacey, *Dissent*, p. 397 (Ashe-Foley); Henning, *House of Commons*, II, 336–40 (Foleys), 584–7 (Hotham); Woodhead, *Rulers*, pp. 99, 105 (Jolliffes, Lane); L. N. Wall, "Marvell's Friends in the City," *Notes and Queries* 204 (1959), 204–7.

Stuart colonizing ventures. Nineteen of the dissenting leaders of 1669–71 had been or would become members of the New England Company during the Restoration, and many of them had personal ties to the colonies. Subscriber Thomas Bell Sr had once lived in Roxbury, Massachusetts. William Pennoyer had relatives in Stamford, Connecticut; and Harmon Sheafe's New England relatives were intermarried with leading Bay colony families. Because the taking of degrees at the English universities was now restricted to conformists, London dissenters saw Harvard College as a critical foundation for the education of Reformed Protestant clergy. Subscribers Andrew Dandy, Nathaniel Houlton, and William Pennoyer were among Harvard's chief late Stuart benefactors, as were the Ashursts; and subscriber Nicholas Gregson served as a Harvard trustee for the reception of English legacies.[34]

As important as New England was in the minds of these London dissenters, they also continued to look to the Reformed churches of Europe as models of reformation. Their insistence on observing Reformed practices in their congregations was not insular but rather an application of principles drawn from a Protestant world broader than Anglicanism. The presence within their community of numerous Protestants of recent continental ancestry sustained London dissenters in an expansive geographical understanding of reformation, as did their own commercial contacts with the continent. The marriage ties to leading civic dissenting families of important Dutch Reformed Protestants, like subscribers Sir John Frederick and Abraham Dolins, for instance, served as an antidote to Anglican-inspired hostility to the Dutch. Similarly, the marriages and friendships of merchants active in London's Threadneedle Street French church, like subscribers John Dubois and Robert Delima, reminded London dissenters of the perils and persecution of their co-religionists in France. With the fate of French Protestantism in mind, for instance, Nathaniel Barnadiston recorded gratitude in his will at being "borne under the light of the Gospel *here in England*," but he feared that light was being obscured, both in Europe and at home, by "the blind superstition and Idolatry of papists."[35]

The Reformed Protestant commitments of leading London dissenters reached into the Anglican order, as well. Presbyterians, in particular, hoped

---

[34] PRO PROB 11: 335 Duke, qu. 25 (Pennoyer); 339 Eure, qu. 56 (Bell); 343 Pye, qu. 122 (Dandy); 419 Box, qu. 54 (Houlton). W. Kellaway, *The New England Company 1649–1776* (1961), pp. 17–18 (Bell), 57–9, and see index, pp. 289–303, for a complete list of New England Company members; B. Bailyn, *The New England Merchants in the Seventeenth Century* (New York, 1964), pp. 80, 128 (Bell), 137 (Sheafe); S. E. Morison, *Harvard College in the Seventeenth Century*, 2 vols. (Cambridge, Mass., 1936), II, 383–4; *Transactions of the Colonial Society of Massachusetts*, 1917–19 (Boston, Mass., 1920), pp. 193, 200–3.

[35] PRO PROB 11: 358 Reeve, qu. 148 (White); 363 Bath, qu. 91 (Barnardiston: my italics); 378 Hare, qu. 169 (Dubois); 390 Exton, qu. 3 (Delima).

to achieve union again with the parish order they had left so recently. Indeed, some Presbyterians supported dissenting congregations without separating from their parish churches, and other leading London dissenters maintained connections with those of Reformed views within the church established by law. Presbyterian subscriber John Jolliffe, for instance, included among his friends and relations the wives of the Cambridge Platonists Ralph Cudworth and Benjamin Whichcote, the latter of whom was vicar of St Lawrence Jewry, near Guildhall. Presbyterian Sir Stephen White counted John Tillotson, Dean of Canterbury Cathedral, among his friends; and French Reformed merchant John Dubois asked the dean to preach his funeral sermon. Similarly, subscriber John Casse, Clerk of the Rolls, left legacies for dissenting clergy and for the latitudinarian Edward Stillingfleet, who preached at the Rolls Chapel.[36]

The London subscribers and common councilmen of 1669–71 were also part of a community devoted to advancing the discourse and traditions of English Reformed Protestantism. Leading dissenting clergy found both their most supportive audiences and much of their financial support from among these committed merchants, urban professionals, and shopkeepers. Moreover, their support of dissenting ministry reflected the broader commitment of these leading dissenters to propagating and defending Protestant ideas through the spoken and printed word. Subscriber John Dubois, for example, was a trustee for the Welsh educational venture launched by the London Presbyterian teacher, Thomas Gouge. Subscriber William Jolliffe and other civic dissenters were trustees for the Worcestershire educational foundation of dissenting MP Paul Foley. Dutch Reformed Protestant Abraham Dolins contributed to the endowment of the dissenting lecture at Salters' Hall.[37]

Like their puritan predecessors, these leading civic dissenters also valued the printing press and their personal libraries as tools for maintaining Reformed Protestantism. Several of them made careful dispositions of significant book collections in their wills, and the subscribers included both the dissenting bookseller John Starkey and an associate of the outspoken Baptist printer Francis Smith.[38] Persuasion, and not coercion, was the best

---

[36] Tillotson had once enjoyed the patronage of the Barnardiston family. PRO PROB 11: 342 Pye, qu. 100 (Casse); 358 Reeve, qu. 148 (White-Tillotson); 362 Bath, qu. 6 (Jolliffe-Cudworth-Whichcote); 378 Hare, qu. 169 (Dubois); *DNB*, XVIII, 1263 (Stillingfleet); XIX, 874 (Tillotson); XXI, 3 (Whichcote).

[37] PRO PROB 11: 357 Reeve, qu. 57 (Foley-Jolliffe); 378 Hare, qu. 169 (Dubois); 490 Eedes, qu. 210 (Dolins); Matthews, p. 230 (Gouge).

[38] Baptist subscriber Captain Thomas Bromhall, who was involved in printing an unlicensed book in the late 1660s, was subsequently suspected of setting up an illegal press with Francis Smith: *CSPD 1668–69*, p. 405 and *CSPD 1660–85 Addendum*, pp. 469–70. For the disposition of books, see PRO PROB 11: 336 Duke, qu. 76 (William Forth); 362 Bath, qu. 41 (William Staines); 377 Hare, qu. 124 (Thomas Cockett); 439 Pyne, qu. 174 (Thomas Strudwick).

means for maintaining Christianity, according to dissenting writers on behalf of conscience. Correspondingly, the primary civic supporters of conscience were committed to preaching, teaching, printing, and reading as the means of persuasion. Indeed, they led a community that was determined to persuade the regime that Protestant security was better achieved through the unrestricted advancement of Protestant ideas than through the advancement of one Protestant voice at the expense of others.

THE EMERGENCE OF A CIVIC OPPOSITION, 1672–1675

In 1670, the dissenting community of London demonstrated its effectiveness in disrupting the implementation of parliamentary policy. By 1675, the dissenting community of London had produced a civic opposition, which could, by acting in cooperation with Country MPs, disrupt parliament itself. This political transformation of London dissent occurred during the years of the regime's second disappointing war against the Dutch.

Even before the war was declared, the guiding political spirits of London dissent, men like Alderman Sir John Lawrence, had begun to revive the quarrels about authority in the Corporation that had disrupted civic politics in the 1640s. In early 1672, for instance, Lawrence persuaded Lord Mayor Sir George Waterman to summon a common council for the election of a new town clerk on the very day of the previous incumbent's decease. Loyalist aldermen like Sir John Robinson claimed that Lawrence was trying to undermine "the just perquisites" of the lord mayor in orchestrating a hasty and popular choice. For his part, Lawrence agreed that the issue was magisterial influence: he allegedly informed the common councilmen that "If you let slip this opportunity for two or three days, your privilege of election will be taken out of your hands." Robinson worked hard to get Lawrence in trouble with the crown, and Lawrence had to work just as hard to avoid a damaging royal rebuke.[39]

In view of such "villainous arts," Anglican loyalists took particular pleasure in retaining the position of chamberlain in 1672, upon the retirement of Sir Thomas Player, who had served since 1651. The office was claimed in common hall, against dissenting candidates, by Player's son and namesake, who was promoted by Robinson and who was also a friend of Under-Secretary Williamson. Already a member of common council, the younger Sir Thomas Player was Robinson's great hope for providing the Corporation with vigorous Anglican leadership in the future.[40] But the new chamberlain

---

[39] SP 29/302/243, 29/303/59, 29/303/59I; Repertory 77, fol. 145; *CSPD 1670–71*, pp. 40–1, 127, 148.

[40] Those put forward for the office included the leading civic Independents John Jekyll and Methusalem Turner. *CSPD 1671–2*, p. 40; *CSPD 1672–3*, p. 159.

gradually abandoned his loyalist friends for their opponents, falling back in the process, upon his political patrimony of parliamentary puritanism. Player would become an outspoken Whig critic of Charles II; and his political turnabout began almost immediately, amidst growing frustration in London about the city's recovery from the Fire. Player's movement toward the dissenting bloc among Corporation office-holders seems to have begun when the loyalist aldermen discouraged the communication to the crown, in early 1673, of civic concerns and grievances. Joining Player in his dissatisfaction was Alderman Sir Robert Clayton, another onetime friend of Robinson and Williamson.

Shortly before the adjournment of the first 1673 parliamentary session in March, common council received the report of a new grievance committee. Including Player and Clayton, the committee was dominated by dissenting magistrates like Lawrence and Patience Ward and by dissenting common councilmen like Thomas Pilkington and Richard Thompson. The committee complained about the decay of the city's trade since the Fire, the movement of business and population to the suburbs, the residence outside the Corporation of too many magistrates, and the failure of many guild members to take up the responsibilities of the freedom. Common council approved a petition to the crown that incorporated these complaints and that requested a reduction in the city assessments, in light of these grievances and the wartime disruption of trade. But the court of aldermen refused to endorse the petition. In the face of strains within the ministry and of a notable lack of victories against the Dutch, loyalist magistrates suggested that the petition would only advertise weaknesses to the enemy. Indeed, they claimed that the grievance committee and the petition were evidence of "seditious designes" and "mutinous proceedings" in the Corporation. Alderman Robinson blamed much of the affair on Player, who seemed to him to be aiming at "popularity" by allying himself with the opponents of religious coercion. The overriding issue for Player and Clayton, though, was probably the right of subjects to address the king.

Player suggested to Williamson that the rejection of the petition by the aldermen "was such a breach upon the Common Councell as hath not beene knowne." His rhetoric points to his newfound agreement with the position enunciated the previous year by Alderman Lawrence, namely, that loyalist aldermen were exercising magisterial prerogatives to the detriment of civic rights. Although the aldermen eventually agreed, in the autumn, to present a more narrowly focused draft of the petition to Charles, the king's apparent indifference to much of its substance further "discomposed the Cittie." By then, disillusionment about the alliance with Louis XIV, whose intentions were suspected by many citizens, was also feeding the desire for peace in the Corporation. And, still smarting from his rebuff at the hands of his onetime Anglican sponsors, Sir Thomas Player continued to develop into a city "statesman."[41]

These conflicts within the Corporation were clearly connected to the escalating political and religious tensions within the nation. The parliamentary Test Act had not eased the fears about popery and arbitrary government that had been so apparent in 1672–3. Instead, growing public awareness of the Roman Catholicism of the Duke of York – heir to the throne in the absence of any legitimate issue of Charles II – aroused new fears about the security of English Protestantism. Indeed, the unhappiness of leading London citizens with the king's French alliance reflected as much concern about the security of Protestantism, both at home and abroad, as it did about French threats to English trade. Both anti-Catholicism and Franco-phobia were critical components of the opposition mentality shared by some common councilmen and some MPs by 1675.

Among the most active anti-French merchants in London in the mid-1670s were Thomas Papillon, John Dubois, and Alderman Patience Ward, each of whom would join Player and Clayton as leaders of the civic opposition. Of French Protestant stock, Papillon and Dubois had good reason to wonder about the alliance of Charles II and Louis XIV against the Protestant Dutch Republic. Papillon was a friend of Robert Ferguson, the city Independent divine, who dedicated one of his early treatises to him. Papillon was also acquainted with Peter Du Moulin, the Huguenot advocate, whose astute *England's Appeal* (1673) made the fear of popery into the heart of a case against the war. Alderman Ward, for his part, was outspoken in his concerns about popery. In October 1673, as an outbreak of anti-Catholicism preceded another parliamentary session, Ward led three other city magistrates who refused to act as stewards for a feast of the Honourable Artillery Company to which the Duke of York had been invited. Parliament was quickly prorogued on this occasion, in part because of Commons' attacks upon York's marriage to a new Catholic bride; but public anti-Catholicism could not be silenced so easily. A day after the end of the session, 5 November was celebrated in the city and its environs with hundreds of bonfires and with a revived pope-burning procession.[42]

---

[41] Repertory 78, fol. 213; Journal 47, fols. 262–263, 264–265, 275; *Letters addressed from London to Sir Joseph Williamson*, ed. W. D. Christie, 2 vols. (1874), I, 113–14, and II, 16, 55; *CSPD 1673*, pp. 557, 569; *CSPD 1673–75*, pp. 2–3, 28, 154; Haley, *Shaftesbury*, p. 334; Henning, *House of Commons*, II, 85, and III, 250.

[42] Robert Ferguson, *The Interest of Reason in Religion* (1675); [Peter Du Moulin], *England's Appeal from the Private Cabal to the Great Council of the Nation* (1673); *CSPD 1673*, 594–5; *CSPVen 1673–5*, p. 174; *Williamson Letters*, II, 67, 71; *Correspondence of the Family of Hatton*, ed. E. M. Thompson, 2 vols. (1878), I, 119; K. H. D. Haley, *William of Orange and the English Opposition 1672–4* (Oxford, 1953), pp. 97–100; M. Priestley, "London Merchants and Opposition Politics in Charles II's Reign," *BIHR* 29 (1956),

In the midst of the brief parliamentary session of autumn 1673, Sir Thomas Player had also informed Sir Joseph Williamson about a great meeting of MPs, especially "country gentlemen," who were interested in "uniteing" in their hostility to Catholicism and to the French alliance. How the city's chamberlain, who was not a member of parliament, came to be so well informed about the actions and attitudes of MPs is unclear, but Player may already have been acting as a political liaison between the reviving parliamentary Country and the civic opposition. As Player anticipated, a Commons opposition emerged in the 1674 session; and MPs prepared bills for further guarantees against Catholicism, for disbanding the army, and for securing judicial tenure. Simultaneously, the Corporation showed further signs of the spread of political discontent.[43]

The dissatisfaction of many common councilmen with the civic magistracy now took the form of demands that common council meet more frequently and that civic electors have a free hand in the choice of sheriffs. At their first court for 1674, the common councilmen chose one committee to consider procedures in shrieval elections and another committee to respond to a motion for more frequent meetings. The second committee, which included Player and Clayton, was also top-heavy with leading Reformed Protestants. The king himself was said to have interpreted these maneuvres as "Republican drifts" intended to put the government of the Corporation upon a more popular foundation. And Lord Mayor Sir William Hooker certainly confronted opposition drifts when many liverymen objected to his exercise of a right to nominate one sheriff prior to the Midsummer's Day common hall.

These protests were directly related to the shrieval election of the previous year, when the Quaker William Mead, who was William Penn's co-defendant in 1670, had been chosen. Mead's election may initially have been orchestrated, like many shrieval elections of the previous decade, by loyalist magistrates searching for fines from those whose religious dissent formally disqualified them from office. But Mead had unexpectedly sealed a bond to serve and had also challenged enforcement of the Conventicle Act by inserting a clause in the bond that he would not act as sheriff "contrary to the commands of Christ." This maneuvre had earned the Quaker leader a sojourn in Newgate, after which the Anglican magistrates proceeded to secure the election of two of their number as sheriffs for 1673–4. But the episode had nevertheless drawn attention to how electoral choice had been compromised by mayoral nominations and aldermanic influence in recent

205–19; O. W. Furley, "The Pope-Burning Processions of the Late Seventeenth Century," *History* 44 (1959), 16–23; Harris, *Crowds*, p. 93; Montaño, *Courting*, pp. 176–8; Henning, *House of Commons*, III, 668.

[43] *Williamson Letters*, II, 55–6; Haley, *Shaftesbury*, p. 359; Spurr, *1670s* pp. 47–57.

years. When the liverymen balked at Lord Mayor Hooker's shrieval nominee in 1674, common hall was quickly adjourned so that the liverymen
might "be better informed" about mayoral privileges in shrieval elections.
But this action merely provoked dissatisfied common councilmen to proceed
with their bill about shrieval elections.[44]

Despite efforts at mediation, the matters in dispute between the court of
common council and the court of aldermen continued to broaden in scope.
In September 1674, common council approved a bill to establish a schedule
of penalties, concluding with disfranchisement, for aldermen who failed to
take up residence in the city. Many common councilmen regarded the bill
as adopted after its reading. But the aldermen responded to this initiative
by reasserting their right to veto all matters in common council, by insisting
that city bills be read first in their court, and by declaring that the two
required readings in common council could not occur at the same meeting.
When the bill about non-resident aldermen was brought up again at the
next common council, Recorder John Howell made a protest on behalf of
the court of aldermen, which amounted to a veto. "Several of the Commons
in the name of the whole did thereupon protest against the protest," and
another committee (again heavy with dissenters) was named to determine
the respective authority of aldermen and common councilmen in the making
of by-laws.[45]

As disputes in the city simmered through the summer and early autumn of
1674, Thomas Osborne, soon to become the Earl of Danby, also established
his commanding position among Charles's ministers. Doing so as the archi-
tect of a new Court and Anglican "party," Danby inadvertently promoted an
even more intimate connection between the parliamentary Country and the
bloc of dissenting and Reformed Protestant office-holders who had played
such an important role in civic politics since 1669–70. As Danby pushed
the Court and the church back together again at Westminster, London dissenters, who had once looked for assistance to friends within the ministry
and to the king himself, increasingly defined their politics by alliance with
the parliamentary Country. They could already look for Westminster leadership to the Earl of Shaftesbury, who had just transformed himself from
leading minister and courtier to Country statesman, and who was enlarging
his numerous civic connections. Some citizens may also have attended the

---

[44] Journal 48, fols. 20, 24, 72–74; Repertory 79, fols. 267–269, 274, 309; *CSPVen 1673–
75*, pp. 274–5; *Williamson Letters*, II, 16, 18, 156–7; Haley, *Shaftesbury*, p. 361. Hooker's
election as lord mayor had been the occasion for "some opposition" after his abandonment of ties with Reformed Protestant civic leaders. BL Stowe MS 186, fol. 6; *CSPD 1673*,
p. 569.
[45] Journal 48, fols. 72, 90–91, 122; Repertory 79, fols. 377, 405–408, 413; Repertory 80, fols.
16–17, 73; *CSPVen 1673–75*, pp. 337–8; Sharpe, *London*, II, 448–51.

first meetings, in 1674, of the Green Ribbon club, which was to become an important forum for bringing together the London and parliamentary oppositions.[46] Finally and rather suggestively, the constitutional ruckus in the Corporation in 1674 began in the midst of Westminster discussions about excluding from the succession any future heir to the throne who married a papist.

The assumption of the mayoralty in 1674–5 by goldsmith-banker Sir Robert Vyner, who became Danby's protégé, intensified this politicization of Corporation affairs. A staunch loyalist and churchman, Vyner had, in 1672, paid for and erected in the Stocks Market a much-discussed equestrian statue of Charles II triumphing over Oliver Cromwell. After the king and the Duke of York attended Vyner's mayoral installation, the aldermen reciprocated the favor by making them freemen of the city, in December 1674. Yet Oliver Cromwell rather than Charles II triumphed in the city, a few weeks later, in the wardmote returns of common councilmen. The number of dissenters chosen for the 1675 common council increased noticeably.[47]

Vyner's trouble-filled mayoralty would demonstrate that a coherent civic opposition had emerged around this nucleus of dissenting common councilmen.[48] By 1675, fears about Catholicism and about French military and commercial hegemony had coalesced with the dissenters' program for religious liberty to create a political movement capable of reaching well beyond the dissenting churches. Moreover, while the political contest in the Corporation remained a contest about conscience, it had also become a contest about consent. The London opposition had revived a variety of civic issues derived from the era of the civil wars and the Commonwealth. The right of English localities to petition for redress of grievances again became a London issue. So did the relative authority of the common councilmen and the aldermen, as did the accountability of the magistracy to London's extensive liveried electorate. Both the rights of the electorate and the rights of common councilmen in the selection of Corporation officers had been asserted against loyalist exercise of magisterial prerogatives. Indeed, as the events of 1675 would demonstrate, nothing was more likely to arouse the new civic

---

[46] J. R. Jones, "The Green Ribbon Club," *Durham University Journal* 49 (1956), 17; Harris, *Crowds*, p. 93; Montaño, *Courting*, ch. 10.

[47] Vyner's stepdaughter married Danby's son. *POAS*, I, 237–42, 266–9; Marvel, *Poems and Letters*, II, 150, 336, 338, 389; Montaño, *Courting*, pp. 194, 311–16; A. Browning, *Thomas Osborne Earl of Danby and Duke of Leeds, 1632–1712*, 3 vols. (Glasgow, 1944–51), I, 138–41.

[48] Nonconformists made up a majority of the common councilmen chosen for Corporation committees devoted to constitutional issues in 1672–4. This fact suggests that the total number of common councilmen identified with dissent was actually much greater than what can be demonstrated in Table 3.3.

Table 3.3 *Definite or probable dissenters on London common council,*
1673–1678

	Seats	1673	1674	1675	1676	1677	1678
Inner City	113	21	23	32	28	25	20
Middle City	88	11	12	17	20	20	14
City Without	33	2	2	4	5	3	4
Total Seats	234	34	37	53	53	48	38

opposition than ministerial or magisterial behavior that seemed to infringe upon electoral consent.

THE CIVIC OPPOSITION AND THE PARLIAMENTARY COUNTRY, 1675–1678

The two parliamentary sessions of 1675 saw a dramatic transformation of Restoration politics as the confrontation between the parliamentary Country and Danby's Court following climaxed. Many of the issues of this confrontation would continue to trouble the Restoration polity long afterwards. In the Corporation of London, conflict between the civic opposition and the Anglican loyalist magistracy erupted even before the April 1675 session. Indeed, it revealed that many London citizens and some Westminster statesmen shared anxious, if quite different, expectations about the approaching session.

Lord Mayor Sir Robert Vyner delayed the first meeting of the common council chosen in December 1674 until early March. He probably hoped thereby to defuse the tensions between the aldermen and the common councilmen that had become so noticeable. When Vyner finally summoned common council, his agenda for the meeting was limited to the naming of standing committees and to the administration of oaths. The latter concern was prompted by the increased number of dissenters among the common councilmen for 1675. Opposition common councilmen did not, however, intend to surrender the initiative within the Corporation to the lord mayor.

In a premeditated and carefully orchestrated effort, John Dubois, Sir Thomas Player, Edward Nelthorpe, Richard Thompson, and other common councilmen rose to speak against the court of aldermen's recent filling of a judicial vacancy in the sheriffs' courts. Claiming that the right of election to the office actually belonged to the common councilmen "by the charters and Magna Carta," these speakers suggested that the aldermanic action had "much invaded" the privileges of common council, which proceeded to its own election for the disputed position. When Vyner responded by dissolving common council and leaving Guildhall, Common Sergeant George Jeffreys, himself a disappointed suitor for the position in the sheriff's court, assumed the authority to put questions to common council, which continued to meet for some time.[49]

In reporting this affair to the government, Lord Mayor Vyner found historical justification for his intransigence in memories about the years before 1660. He suggested that the dispute over the minor office in question was not the main issue at all. Instead, according to him,

The designe of this faction is to take the Sole Power of Gouvernment into the hands of the Commons, [and] . . . to make the Lord Mayor and . . . Aldermen wholly insignificant . . . by taking away their power in the making of laws [and] . . . denying the management of the Court by the Chaire . . . contrary to all our Charters, rights, Lawes, usages, and Customes before the late Rebellion. These were the things contended for in those times, but never in so insolent a manner.[50]

Danby, Lord Keeper Sir Heneage Finch, and Joseph Williamson (now one of the secretaries of state) listened to Vyner and to a delegation of aldermen on the morning after the eruption in Guildhall, agreeing with the magistrates that the situation was of "infinite importance" to the nation. Writing to Secretary Henry Coventry, who was with the king at Newmarket, they urged the monarch's early return to Westminster to deal with a critical situation. Ministerial suspicions that the incident had been "designed to give a trouble in ye Parliament" suggest a probable additional reason for the forwardness of leading common councilmen. The Guildhall speakers may well have been acting in concert with some Country spokesmen who were planning "trouble" for the approaching session of parliament. Charles's ministers feared that only a prompt resolution of the London affair would prevent an unfortunate opening of the session in the midst of ongoing altercations in the city. Moreover, like the lord mayor, they were alarmed about the parallels between the situation at hand and the scenario of the city's 1649 revolution. Then, common council's defiance of a lord mayor had been the prelude to a successful elimination of the magisterial veto over actions of common council.[51]

The principal effect of a ministerial effort to mediate in the city was a cooling of tempers. In a Westminster arbitration session to which representatives of the aldermen and common council were invited, the issue of the aldermanic veto over common council decisions was avoided in the interests of

---

[49] Journal 48, fol. 138; Repertory 80, fols. 130–131; BL M/863/11, Coventry MS (Bath Papers), XVI, fols. 9–11; *CSPVen 1673–75*, p. 380; Marvell, *Poems and Letters*, II, 150; *The Case between the Ld. Mayor and Commons of London* (1682), p. 6; Sharpe, *London*, II, 451; Henning, *House of Commons*, III, 250; G. W. Keeton, *Lord Chancellor Jeffreys and the Stuart Cause* (1965), pp. 65–6.

[50] Sir R. Vyner to Henry Coventry, 18 March 1675, in BL Coventry MS, XVI, fols. 21–22.

[51] BL Coventry MS (Bath Papers), XVI, fol. 16; *CSPD 1675–76*, pp. 21, 31.

reconciliation. The common council spokesmen acknowledged the authority of the lord mayor as presiding officer in their court, but they remained unsettled about recent employments of mayoral and magisterial prerogatives. Only in January 1676, after the selections of a new lord mayor and of a new common council, was another election held for the disputed place in the sheriff's court.[52]

By that time, the politics of the city and the politics of the nation had been transformed by the parliamentary sessions of 1675, in which the Court and the Country confronted each other in an extended political deadlock. Although the Corporation of London was peripheral to the maneuvring in both houses at Westminster, the issues that had so aroused London dissenters and opposition common councilmen since the late 1660s were not. Fundamental to the Earl of Danby's new polity in church and state was a repudiation of the accommodation between Anglican and Reformed Protestants that had recently been attempted in parliament and demanded in the city. Both Danby's effort to resecure the Anglican confessional state and the reaction his efforts provoked are indications of the effectiveness of recent dissenting arguments about liberty for conscience.

Danby's preparations for the first 1675 session were extensive. At the lord treasurer's invitation, several bishops participated in political consultations with leading ministers. Bishop Morley became a privy councilor. The bishops encouraged enforcement of the acts against conventicles and the discharge of nonconformists from the county commissions of peace. This renewal of the policy of coercion was accompanied by discussions about some grand London monumental testimonies to the reunion of crown and miter. A new equestrian statue of Charles the Martyr was to have been placed at Charing Cross. The late king's remains were to have been reinterred in an imposing mausoleum. In the city, the rebuilding of St Paul's Cathedral was to have been accelerated. In all these ways, Danby hitched his government to the outspoken defense of episcopal authority and sacerdotalism that was becoming characteristic of the Anglican establishment. And like the recent London altercation, Danby's program also revived memories of an earlier time: Archbishop William Laud's promotion of ceremony in the church had been accompanied, in the 1630s, by a revival of episcopal authority in the state.[53]

---

[52] Journal 48, fols. 143, 147, 193; Repertory 80, fols. 130–131, 143–144, 152–153; *CSPD 1675–6*, pp. 26–7, 31–2, 471, 537; Sharpe, *London*, II, 451–4.

[53] *CSPD 1673–5*, pp. 548–9, 551, 578; *Bulstrode Papers*, I, 284; [Anthony Ashley Cooper, Earl of Shaftesbury], *Letter from a Person of Quality, to his Friend in the Country* (1675), pp. 7–8; *CSPVen 1673–5*, pp. 312, 330, 350; Marvell, *Poems and Letters*, II, 341–2; Browning, *Danby*, I, 146–9; Goldie, "Danby, the Bishops and the Whigs," pp. 81–3; Spurr, *Restoration Church*, pp. 67–70; R. A. Beddard, "Wren's Mausoleum for Charles I and the Cult of the Royal Martyr," *Architectural History* 27 (1984), 36–49.

These designs and decisions ensured that debate about the future of English Protestantism would be central to the parliamentary confrontation between Danby's Court and the Country opposition. The 1675 sessions produced unprecedented protests in the House of Lords, razor-thin margins in the House of Commons, regular evening proceedings, and angry breaches in parliamentary etiquette. The first session was memorable for a protracted debate, in the Lords, about an abortive test bill introduced by the ministry. The bill was designed to require all future members of both houses and all office-holders to swear an oath against the alteration of the government, either in church or in state. The clear intent of the oath was to purge politics of all those interested in a new church settlement that accommodated Reformed Protestants. Just as the Corporation Act of 1662 had been intended to create Anglican hegemony in the boroughs, so the test bill of 1675 was intended to restore Anglican hegemony in parliament and the government against any who had recently advocated a broader Protestant establishment. And just as fear of the "fanatics" had been effective in securing the Restoration church settlement, so the fear of the "sects" was revived by the ministry in the first 1675 session in order to resecure the Anglican confessional state.

In the House of Lords, the Earl of Shaftesbury condemned this policy as misguided. According to him, it would serve only to divide English Protestants further and to weaken the Protestant interest. In the House of Commons, Country advocates responded to Danby's initiative by attempting to impeach the lord treasurer and to relaunch the legislative program they had lost at the last prorogation.[54] Moreover, many Country MPs and lords preferred to find security for the church through the promotion of Protestant accommodation rather than through Danby's policy of Anglican exclusivity. Parliament's consideration of religion was accompanied by renewed appeals for accommodation from dissenters and from Reformed Protestants within the church. Pleading against coercion, John Humfrey, for instance, wrote about the need for confining "Bishop *Laud* ... to his Cathedral" and for expelling "Chancellor *Hide*" from "our Acts of Parliament." Shaftesbury argued that giving "*Liberty to dissenting Protestants*" was "*the best means to keep up the Ballance against* [the] *boundless Prerogative*" favored by churchmen. The Duke of Buckingham sought to introduce a bill for the

---

[54] The efforts of Country MPs were frustrated as much by Shaftesbury and by the House of Lords as by Danby. The former lord chancellor promoted constitutional quarrels between the Houses, hoping that addled sessions would force the king's agreement to the election of a new parliament in which the opposition might gain the upper hand. Shaftesbury, *Letter from a Person of Quality*, pp. 1, 5; Browning, *Danby*, I, 152–64; Lacey, *Dissent*, pp. 76–8; Swatland, *House of Lords*, pp. 213–16, 242–6; Marvell, *Poems and Letters*, II, 147; Haley, *Shaftesbury*, pp. 372–80; Spurr, *1670s*, pp. 63–9, 73–9; Montaño, *Courting*, pp. 261–4.

relief of dissenters in November 1675, only to be thwarted by the abrupt termination of the session.[55]

When Charles prorogued parliament for an unprecedented fifteen months at the conclusion of the autumn 1675 session, he deprived the Country of its chief forum. But the prorogation also gave the Country an additional issue that could be rehearsed in the public prints – the issue of consent, or put in parliamentary terms, the issue of representation. Given the fifteen-year interval since the last parliamentary election, and given the use of ministerial influence and the prerogative to manage and to terminate sessions, the Country began to argue that the Commons of the Cavalier Parliament no longer represented the electorate. "Is it agreeable with the nature of Representatives to be continued for so long a time," inquired one Country writer, who went on to argue that those who chose representatives ought "to be allowed frequent opportunity of changing the hands, in which they are obliged to put so great a Trust." Similarly, drawing upon his fifty years of parliamentary experience, Baron Holles claimed that a parliament of a "monstrous" fifteen years' duration could "never be the *Representative* of half the people," failing entirely to represent the "Major part" of the electorate, who had come of legal age since 1661.[56]

Arguments of this nature found much support among dissenting common councilmen in London, whose quarrels with Anglican magistrates mirrored the Country's quarrel with Danby's Anglican ministry. The long prorogation of November 1675 to February 1677 opened the way for a more intentional convergence of the civic and parliamentary oppositions. Deprived of their parliamentary venues, Shaftesbury and Buckingham, in particular, turned to the city as a substitute arena for challenging the ministry.

How successfully the London civic opposition could function as a surrogate for the Country opposition in parliament was apparent at the shrieval election of 24 June 1676. When a Cornhill linen-draper appealed to the Corporation to address the crown for a new parliament, common hall was quickly transformed from a local electoral assembly into a national forum

---

[55] [John Humfrey], *The Peaceable Design; being a Modest Account, of . . . the way of Accommodation in the matter of Religion* (1675), p. 63; [Anthony Ashley Cooper, Earl of Shaftesbury], *A Letter from a Parliament man to his Friend* (1675), pp. 3, 4; George Villiers, 2nd Duke of Buckingham, "The D. of Buckinghams Speech in the House of Lords, the 16th of November 1675," in [Anthony Ashley Cooper, Earl of Shaftesbury], *Two Speeches* (Amsterdam, 1675), p. 13; [Herbert Croft], *The Naked Truth* (1675); HMC *Ninth Report*, Part II, p. 68; Grey, *Debates*, III, 15–19, 174–5, 178–80, 186, 425; *CSPVen 1673–75*, pp. 363, 381, 390–1; Marvell, *Poems and Letters*, II, 146, 148, 157–8; R. Thomas, "Comprehension and Indulgence," pp. 215–21; Lacey, *Dissent*, pp. 79–81; Haley, *Shaftesbury*, pp. 380–5, 393–4, 403; Spurr, *Restoration Church*, pp. 70–1.

[56] [Anthony Ashley Cooper, Earl of Shaftesbury?], *Two Seasonable Discourses* (Oxford, 1675), pp. 2–3; Shaftesbury, *Letter from a Parliament man*, pp. 5–6; [Denzil, Baron Holles], *The Long Parliament Dissolved* (1676), pp. 4, 18; Haley, *Shaftesbury*, p. 403.

for the arraignment of the king's ministry. The speaker, Francis Jenks, was the son-in-law of the aged William Walwyn, the onetime Leveller theorist and advocate of liberty for conscience. Jenks was also a friend of John Wildman, another Leveller, who had once promoted the devolution of power in the city to the freemen.[57] Touching upon the widespread perception that Charles and successive ministers had, ever since the Fire, been insufficiently concerned about the city's trade, Jenks quickly aroused the crowd in Guildhall. He reviewed evidence about the growing threat of French commercial competition, and he complained that Lord Mayor Sir Joseph Sheldon had failed to summon a meeting of common council to consider a petition about trade that had been "subscribed by a great number of citizens." Jenks was also quick to point out the broader implications of the plight of London and the kingdom. The military and commercial hegemony sought by Louis XIV put both "his Majesty and the Protestant religion" in considerable danger.

Amidst encouraging cries from the audience, Jenks moved that common hall desire the lord mayor to summon a common council for the purpose of petitioning the king for a new parliament. According to Jenks, statutes of 4 and 36 Edward III required annual parliaments, and the Cavalier Parliament was technically dissolved because its long endurance violated law. Similar arguments were shortly to earn both Shaftesbury and Buckingham sojourns in the Tower; but the liverymen quickly endorsed Jenks's proposal. The result of his success in common hall was not, however, a mayoral summons of common council for the sake of petitioning but rather a royal summons that Jenks appear immediately before the king-in-council. Displaying the same verbal confidence in debate with his prince, Jenks outraged Charles by declining to answer questions about his connections to Country statesmen. He was consigned to the Gatehouse as a prisoner. Refusing to petition the crown for release, he remained in custody for three months, "molest[ing] all judicatures" with demands for his freedom by means of habeas corpus or a writ of mainprize. He thereby raised additional contentious issues and created arguments for the subsequent Habeas Corpus Amendment Act of 1679.[58]

The Jenks episode abounded with historical meanings and associations. Danby had sought to prevent any agreement between Reformed and

[57] *CSPD 1677–77*, p. 352; *London's Liberties*; Henning, *House of Commons*, I, 313.
[58] GL MS 3589, fols. 1–5; PRO Prob 11: 365 North, qu. 13; *An Account of the Proceedings at Guild-hall, London, at the tolke-moot* [sic] [1676]; *CSPD 1676–77*, pp. 180, 193–4, 253–6, ST, VI, 1189–1208; Marvell, *Poems and Letters*, II, 348; *Selections from the Correspondence of Arthur Capel Earl of Essex 1675–1677*, ed. C. E. Pike (1913), pp. 61ff.; Haley, *Shaftesbury*, pp. 409–10; G. S. De Krey, "London Radicals and Revolutionary Politics," in Harris, *et al.*, eds., *The Politics of Religion*, pp. 138–40, 157–8 n.26; Spurr, *1670s*, pp. 80–1; Woodhead, *Rulers*, p. 147. Jenks's 1676 speech was subsequently reprinted as *Mr. Francis Jenk's Speech in a Common Hall, the 24th of June 1679*.

Anglican Protestants by elevating anti-sectarianism above anti-popery. But Jenks's speech and another speech prepared by an unknown person for the same common hall audience demonstrated instead the extent to which civic electors of all persuasions could be aroused by anti-popery. "Not only our houses, trades, liberties and lives but our Protestant religion is in eminent [*sic*] danger," wrote Jenks's anonymous colleague, who boldly stated the dominant issue of the next decade: "What safety is there provided for the Protestant religion, if a Catholic shall possess the Crown?"[59]

These 1676 demands for Protestant security and for a new parliament announced themes that would reverberate throughout the city of London in the ensuing national crisis. But the Jenks affair also revived an understanding of civic government that had been proscribed since 1662. Jenks and his rhetorical associate spoke a language about civic rights that had obviously not been forgotten during the years of Anglican hegemony. They explicitly restated the consensual and participatory conception of the Corporation that had been implicit in the recent jurisdictional squabbling between some common councilmen and aldermen. According to them, common hall was the penultimate authority in the city. Political ownership of the city's ancient liberties and customs ultimately belonged to all the freemen, who had been confirmed in their possession of these rights by Magna Charta and dozens of statutes. Because all the freemen could not conveniently be assembled, however, the liverymen acted in their place and expressed the consent "of the whole body of the freemen" to the acts of the Corporation. Common hall was, therefore, the city's "greatest assembly, and court of greatest power," subordinate only to the freemen for whom the liverymen acted.

The implications of this assertion for the operation of the civic constitution were far-reaching. According to opposition spokesmen in 1676, common hall had "cognizance of any thing relating to the good of the City." Therefore, "the chief binding acts in our City government have always been made by the Common Hall, and the acts of the lord mayor, aldermen, and Common Council have been, and may be, nulled by the acts of the Common Hall." To make the authority of the lord mayor superior to that of common hall was to allow "the lesser authority of the City ... [to] confine the greater ... [and] to turn the government of the City topsy turvy." If common hall desired the lord mayor to summon a common council for the sake of petitioning the crown, the lord mayor was obliged to do so. The incarceration of a citizen for speaking his mind in common hall would, moreover, discourage any liveryman from exercising his undoubted right "to debate whatever he thinks for the service of the King and the good of the City." Should the arrest of Jenks go unchallenged, then "the wills of a few courtiers" would triumph

[59] GL MS 3589, fols. 6–7; *Account of the Proceedings at Guild-hall*; CSPD 1676–77, pp. 254–5.

over "the common liberty of Englishmen." For the civic opposition, the need for a new parliament was greater than ever after the ministerial silencing of Jenks. Without an immediate parliamentary response to the nation's ills, the liverymen were informed, they "must bid farewell to the happy security of... [their] lives, liberties and estates."[60]

Sir Robert Vyner's 1675 complaint that his opponents intended "to take the Sole Power of Gouvernment into the hands of the Commons," as in "the late Rebellion," had thus proven to be remarkably prescient. The understanding of the civic constitution articulated by Francis Jenks and others rested upon the precedents of the city's 1649 revolution, and Jenks's whole approach to the intertwined politics of the city and the nation audibly echoed that of the London Levellers. His promotion of petitioning, his emphasis upon the rights of individuals, his insistence upon popular authority in the Corporation, his veneration of "ancient liberties and customs," and his demand for frequent parliaments are – taken together – distinctly reminiscent of the objectives of John Lilburne.[61] Indeed, Jenks's self-conscious posturing in the Gatehouse was reminiscent of Lilburne in the Tower, and his personal and family relationships with John Wildman and William Walwyn point to his likely familiarity with the Leveller agenda.

What Jenks and his political allies had accomplished in the city in the summer of 1676 was a compelling rearticulation of the issues of consent and representation in language as dramatic and powerful as that contained in Country publications. Indeed, Jenks and his friends would succeed in combining consent and conscience in a potent rhetorical formula that would be utilized time and again in the city during the remainder of Charles II's reign. That Jenks and his associates displayed such strong indebtedness to the libertarian language of the civil war and Commonwealth years is, perhaps, not so surprising. Analysis of the leadership of the civic opposition in 1675–6 demonstrates that it had largely emerged from the discursive and social community in which dissenting identity had been fashioned since 1660. All but five of a group of about thirty civic opposition leaders of these years were nonconformists.[62] Several of these men – including Alderman John Forth and merchants John Dubois, George Perryer, Thomas Waring, and James Winstanley – had subscribed to the dissenting loan of 1670; and others had actively opposed coercion in the Corporation. Others still had been prominent in the city during the Commonwealth or had close relatives active then.

---

[60] GL MS 3589, fols. 6–7; *Account of the Proceedings at Guild-hall*, esp. pp. 11–12; *CSPD 1676–77*, pp. 194, 255–6.

[61] BL M/863/11, Coventry MS (Bath Papers), XVI, fols. 21–22; "The City Painter," Add. MS 34,362, fol. 13.

[62] Those analyzed for these statements include most aldermen and common councilmen who served on the Corporation committees that pursued an anti-magisterial agenda in 1673–6.

The Jenks episode was not, then, an isolated example of rhetorical creativity. It was rather a deliberate and strategic expression of political and religious language that had been circulating for some time within the London dissenting community. Just as writers about conscience had fashioned an alternate political language to the Anglican language of moderation and non-resistance, so civic activists like Jenks were prepared to adapt the libertarian language of the 1640s and the 1650s to the political circumstances of the 1670s. In doing so, they enlarged the body of discourse that provided many London dissenters with their working political vocabulary. Anglican loyalists in the city were, therefore, understandably dismayed to learn of plans to raise a public stock to maintain "honest men" like Francis Jenks in the city's aldermanic and shrieval offices.

For its part, the ministry remained concerned about the connections between Jenks and Country statesmen. They were informed on the eve of Jenks's common hall speech that, if the liverymen supported a petition for a new parliament, the news was to have been circulated "speedily into the countries." Shaftesbury was suspected of encouraging Jenks, but the Cornhill draper was in fact a city agent for Buckingham, to whom he had been introduced by Wildman. Both Jenks's arguments on behalf of a new parliament and the timing of his speech were part of a strategy developed by Buckingham for obtaining a new parliamentary election as soon as possible.[63]

If Shaftesbury was not behind Jenks's successful arousal of the common hall electorate, the earl had nevertheless also developed strong ties to the London opposition. Sir Robert Clayton, Sir Robert Peyton, and city merchants Sir Samuel Barnardiston and Thomas Papillon were observed at Shaftesbury's townhouse in the months preceding Jenks's common hall speech: Barnardiston, MP for Suffolk, had seconded the Commons' motion for Danby's impeachment in April 1675; and Papillon, MP for Dover, had gathered evidence on behalf of the impeachment. Secretary Williamson was also informed about a regular London meeting of opponents of the government that brought Shaftesbury together with Chamberlain Sir Thomas Player and Player's friends Edward Nelthorpe and Richard Thompson, both opposition common councilmen.[64] Bankers Nelthorpe and Thompson, partners,

---

[63] Jenks's ties to Buckingham were also evident at the opening of the next session, when he was seen with Buckingham and accompanied the duke on his surrender at the Tower. George Villiers, 2nd Duke of Buckingham, *A Speech made by the Duke of Buckingham, the First Day of the Session of the Parliament* (1677) reprinted in *State Tracts: Being a Collection of Several Treatises Relating to the Government* (1689), pp. 237–40; *CSPD 1676–77*, pp. 180, 564; Haley, *Shaftesbury*, p. 409; Henning, *House of Commons*, I, 313.

[64] Williamson visited Shaftesbury in February 1676 to inform him of Charles's desire that he leave London and stop meddling in public affairs between sessions of parliament. *CSPD 1675–76*, pp. 559–61, 562–3; Henning, *House of Commons*, I, 596, and III, 203, 233; Haley, *Shaftesbury*, pp. 404–6; Lacey, *Dissent*, p. 81.

and close relatives of Andrew Marvell, were pivotal figures in the emerging civic opposition. By 1675, both Player and Jenks had become directly involved in their bank, and Shaftesbury may have as well.[65]

Much evidence, therefore, points to effective and concerted political liaison, by 1676, between principal Country spokesmen in parliament and the civic opposition. Indeed, the connections between Buckingham and Shaftesbury and the civic opposition of the 1670s were already as structured as the early 1640s' connections between parliamentary leaders like John Pym and dissident London merchants and common councilmen. Prominent traders like Barnardiston and Papillon were deeply involved in both parliamentary and civic opposition circles. The financial resources of the civic opposition included not only the credit and the stock of financier Sir Robert Clayton but also that of the additional banking house of Nelthorpe and Thompson. The association between these moneyed men and the custodian of the London Chamber, Sir Thomas Player, is intriguing. So is the suggestion made by Country MPs in October 1675, that any money raised for the support of the navy be deposited, not in the Exchequer, but rather in the Chamber of London. Further developing their civic connections, both Buckingham and Shaftesbury moved their urban residences from Westminster to the city during the lengthy parliamentary prorogation. Rumors even circulated that Buckingham was interested in election to the aldermanic bench.[66]

In fact, the evidence about London opposition in 1675–6 suggests that, for this important, but sometimes exceptional locality, some structures of party were already in place. The mid-1670s London opposition was quite adept at appealing to and mobilizing public opinion through the spoken and printed word. Civic activists and Country leaders were quick to take their cause into the taverns, coffeehouses, and print shops of the capital. The spate of Country manifestoes of 1675–6, Francis Jenks's appeal to the electorate, and the latter's attempt at public petitioning showed that Country captains and civic tribunes were more than able to carry politics out of doors once again. So did the convergence of parliamentary and civic figures in the Green Ribbon club and the revival of pope-burnings. And for their part, the loyalist magistrates who had captured the Corporation in the 1660s were working closely with the ministry to advance Danby's confessional state.

Despite these developing roots of party, the 1675–6 alliance between Country leaders and the civic opposition made little headway against the ministry. The long prorogation of 1675–7 left the Country without unified leadership, coherent strategies, or a clear agenda. But in the Corporation,

---

[65] *CSPD 1675–76*, p. 562; Wall, "Marvell's Friends," pp. 204–7; Haley, *Shaftesbury*, p. 405.
[66] Grey, *Debates*, III, 354ff.; Add. MS 34,362, fol. 7; Evelyn, *Diary*, IV, 185; *Bulstrode Papers*, I, 320; Haley, *Shaftesbury*, pp. 409, 411; Henning, *House of Commons*, II, 85.

the civic opposition continued to display its disruptive capabilities. Finally released from the Gatehouse, Francis Jenks joined Sir Thomas Player in promoting an address to the crown in October 1676. In response to a request that came from "diverse citizens," common council agreed with "scarce ten opposing" to petition the crown about "the French potency at sea . . . [and] the importing of many commodities to the obstructing of trade." The Anglican magistrates apparently blocked this move, however; and disputes between the court of common council and the court of aldermen about magisterial privileges continued to plague the city. By March 1677, the civic opposition was objecting not only to the aldermanic veto and to the mayoral nomination of sheriffs but also to any interference by the court of aldermen in the naming of aldermen to sit on common council committees.[67]

By then, another session of parliament had begun; but it had begun badly for Shaftesbury and Buckingham, whose speeches on behalf of dissolution earned them lodging in the Tower. Chastened by the loss of these leaders, disoriented by Danby's manipulative strategies, and unable to agree upon their own agenda, Country MPs and lords proved no match for the Court in 1677. In the meantime, the ministry acted to check the growth of opposition in the Corporation. Government efforts to contain dangerous developments in the city had been evident as early as the winter of 1675–6, when the coffeehouses were briefly closed. The government's repeated orders for the suppression of urban conventicles revealed Danby's belief that religion was at the root of faction in London. Persecution on the scale of 1670 did not recur, but mayoral precepts against the election of unqualified common councilmen and aldermanic enforcement of the oaths did lead to a diminishment in the number of dissenters among the common councilmen in 1678.[68] (Table 3.1)

The civic opposition also suffered leadership losses similar to those of the parliamentary Country. Sir Robert Peyton, one of Jenks's associates, and Peyton's "gang" (including Sir Edmund Berry Godfrey) were removed from the Middlesex commission of peace as early as March 1676. Edward Nelthorpe and Richard Thompson were forced to retire from civic affairs when their bank failed. In 1677, Player and like-minded colleagues were purged from the London lieutenancy commission, and the government attempted to remove Player as chamberlain. Prior to the 1677 Midsummer's Day common hall meeting, Danby authored a proposal for the lord mayor to "resume" an allegedly ancient practice of nominating persons for chamberlain in a manner similar to the disputed mayoral nominations for sheriff.

---

[67] Journal 48, fols. 213, 218; Repertory 82, fols. 28–33; Repertory 83, fols. 87, 117–123; Morrice, P, 53, 57; *CSPD 1676–77*, pp. 375, 377, 388–9.

[68] Repertory 81, fols. 108, 118; Repertory 82, fols. 74, 90, 95; Repertory 83, fol. 45; *CSPD 1676–77*, pp. 449–50; *CSPD 1677–78*, pp. 34, 507; Haley, *Shaftesbury*, p. 403, S. Pincus, "'Coffee Politicians Does Create': Coffeehouses and Restoration Political Culture," *JMH* 67 (1995), 807–34.

The lord treasurer hoped that the Anglican lord mayor "and his party" might, by presenting alternatives to Player, replace him as chamberlain and thereby prevent the "malecontented party" from taking "heart and head again among the cittizens." A suitable Anglican candidate for the office was soon found to do battle with the "presbiterians" who supported Player.

Since 24 June fell on a Sunday in 1677, the election would ordinarily have been moved to Monday. But the lord mayor summoned the liverymen on the 24th anyway, in the hope that "the Fanaticks might be absent upon scruple of profaning the Sabbath." Danby's ruse failed, however, when "soe many thousands appeared, as few men living can remember," and only a few hands were raised against Player. When the government subsequently learned, in 1678, of the impending resignation of Sir William Dolben, the city's recorder, it responded similarly, developing a case for a right of royal nomination to that office. But Danby settled in the end for a recommendation to the aldermen that they select Sir George Jeffreys, once intimate with the opposition, but now a Court convert. Efforts to police the press and to suppress pamphlets critical of the government also continued in 1677–8.[69]

Despite these efforts, Danby was not as successful in managing London in 1677–8 as he was in managing parliament. His repudiation of Protestant religious accommodation for the sake of a coercive Anglican church-state aggravated the most enduring source of political conflict within the Restoration city. At the same time, fears that his policies opened the door for arbitrary government and Catholic conspiracy went unrelieved and were encouraged by the visibility of the Catholic heir to the throne. The renewal of the coercion of Protestants, while popery seemed to thrive with impunity, suggested to articulate London dissenters that the English Reformation was threatened internally by the leaders of church and state. Simultaneously, Charles's diplomatic entanglement in the designs of Louis XIV suggested to many English Protestants that reformation was threatened externally as well. Despite the apparent triumphs of the Court, then, the potential remained that a broad body of Protestants – ranging from sectarians to partial and full conformists – would unite in the defense of reformation and parliament against popery and a misguided prince.

PROTESTANTISM IN PERIL: THE COUNTRY'S CASE AGAINST THE BISHOPS

The pressure for a reconsideration of the Restoration settlement grew in 1675–8 in response to Country writing against the bishops and against the

[69] SP 29/396/185–6; BL M/863/11, Coventry MS (Bath Papers), XVI, fol. 109; Morrice, P, 53, 57, 91; *CSPD 1676–77*, pp. 11–12, 22, 527, 564; *CSPD 1677–78*, pp. 226, 411, 691–2; *CSPD 1678*, p. 473; Marvell, *Poems and Letters*, II, 345, 352; Henning, *House of Commons*, III, 233; Wall, "Marvell's Friends," p. 206; HMC *Ninth Report*, Part II, 69–79; Montaño, *Courting*, pp. 219–23.

Anglican church order. Even before the furore of the Popish Plot suggested that the Protestant Church of England was endangered by an international Catholic conspiracy, the Country had already made the "popish" practices of persecuting Protestant bishops a central issue of public debate. Country writers claimed that the bishops had driven the most ardent contemporary reformers out of the church; and in response, they revived the Protestant case against the bishops that had swept the prelates from the church in the early 1640s.

The Country's case against the bishops incorporated discourse already circulating within the urban dissenting community from which the civic opposition had emerged. The attack upon the bishops is, therefore, further evidence of the convergence of civic and parliamentary oppositions. Building upon the pleas for religious accommodation previously made by dissenting writers, Country spokesmen like the Earl of Shaftesbury and Andrew Marvell now furthered the cause of Reformed Protestantism by attacking what they saw as the principal obstacle to Protestant unity, namely, the powers and pretensions of the Restoration episcopate. Even before the public revelations about alleged Catholic plotting in 1678, then, the Country had challenged Danby's revival of sectarian alarms with its own revival of alarms about popery within the church.[70]

The occasion for the revival of the case against the bishops was the provision of Danby's test bill of 1675 that required an oath of all office-holders and members of both houses of parliament against altering the government of the church, as well as of the state. Reviving the Anglican confessional state upon these grounds – grounds even more exclusive than those of 1662–5 – was the means least likely to resettle church and state, according to Country writers. Instead, they championed the formula of comprehension and toleration that had been discussed in 1660–61, 1667–8, and 1672–3. "Persecution & English episcopacy is too narrow a foundation" to secure "peace & plenty," observed one writer, who reported that many, both "ye highest Cavaliers & best Protestants," had come to the conclusion that liberty for conscience was "ten times [more] likely to succeed as to ye settlement of this kingdom."[71]

The Country's case against the bishops was also encoded in the language of conspiracy that had conventionally been reserved for use against the Catholic

[70] Also see Goldie, "Danby, the Bishops and the Whigs" and M. Goldie, "Priestcraft and the Birth of Whiggism" in *Political Discourse in Early Modern Britain*, ed. N. Phillipson and Q. Skinner (Cambridge, 1993), pp. 209–31.

[71] Shaftesbury, *Letter from a Person of Quality*, p. 6; [Andrew Marvell], *An Account of the Growth of Popery and Arbitrary Government in England* (Amsterdam, 1677, and Westmead, Farnborough, Hants, 1971), p. 45; HMC *Ninth Report*, Part II, 68; Marvell, *Poems and Letters*, II, 343; *Bulstrode Papers*, I, 286, 301; Ashcraft, *Revolutionary Politics*, pp. 116–20; J. Marshall, *John Locke*, pp. 85–7.

and sectarian minorities. The thesis of Shaftesbury's printed attack upon the test bill, for instance, was that this "STATE MASTER-PIECE" had been "first hatch'd (as almost all the Mischiefs of the World have hitherto been) amongst the *Great Church Men*." The design of the prelates to safeguard Church structures from being "bounded, or limited by any humane Laws" was not, according to this argument, a new departure at all, but rather "a project of several years standing." Shaftesbury wrote that "Archbishop *Laud* was the first Founder of this Device"; and he maintained that the churchmen had renewed their campaign to make "*the Government of the Church Sworn to as Unalterable*" ever since their restoration. The earl found additional evidence for this argument in the Corporation Act, which had required a similar oath for office-holding in the boroughs, and which had thereby "kept out of the Magistracy" many "of the Wealthyest, Worthyest, and Soberest Men." The churchmen had similarly promoted restrictive oaths in the Militia Act, the Five-Mile Act, and the Uniformity Act, the last of which "was fatal to our Church and Religion," because it led to a "throwing out a great number of ... *Learned, Pious, and Orthodox Divines*."[72]

Country and city audiences were also encouraged to believe that the churchmen had played a counterfeit game against the Catholics. Even before the recent Declaration of Indulgence, Roman Catholics had enjoyed a *de facto* toleration "by the favour of all the bishops." Although the prelates "gave the Alarum of *Popery* through the whole Nation" in 1672–3, their true intent, according to Shaftesbury and Marvell, was to employ fears about the security of the church against their Protestant dissenting co-religionists. Since the failure of Protestant accommodation in 1673, "the Bishops [had] wholly laid aside their Zeal against *Popery*," claiming instead "that the Nation was running again into *Fourty One*." Eschewing the good Protestant bills advanced by the Country, the churchmen insisted that "the *Phanatique* ... is again become the *only dangerous Enemy*"; and they refused to "*live peaceably with the dissenting and differing* Protestants," either at home or abroad. The result was a church that fell dangerously short of encompassing all those loyal to the English Reformation and that was estranged from foreign Protestants as well.[73]

---

[72] Shaftesbury, *Letter from a Person of Quality*, pp. 1–3, 20, 34; Anthony Ashley Cooper, Earl of Shaftesbury, "The Earl of Shaftesbury's Speech in the House of Lords the 20th. of October. 1675," in Shaftesbury, *Two Speeches*, pp. 10–11; Marvell, *Account of the Growth of Popery*, pp. 58–9; *Bulstrode Papers*, I, 322.

[73] Shaftesbury, *Letter from a Person of Quality*, pp. 5–8, 23; Shaftesbury, *Letter from a Parliament man to his Friend*, p. 5; Marvell, *Account*, pp. 56 (misnumbered as 65), 63–4; [Andrew Marvell], *Mr. Smirke; or, the Divine in Mode* (1676) unnumbered, between pp. 40–1; [Andrew Marvell], "A Short Historical Essay, touching General Councils, Creeds, and Imposition in Religion," in *Mr. Smirke*, pp. 70, 72–3; W. Lamont, "The Religion of Andrew Marvell: Locating the 'Bloody Horse,'" in *The Political Identity of Andrew Marvell*, ed. C. Condren and A. D. Cousins (Aldershot, Hants, 1990), pp. 135–56.

Country spokesmen were employing language about the church that few had dared to speak openly since 1660. Their case against the bishops continued the puritan case for reformation of the church that had borne fruit in the 1640s; and the Country's arguments for resettlement of the church borrowed from the Presbyterian agenda of 1660–61. The Country leadership even included such veterans of the 1641–2 attack on the bishops as Baron Holles and Sir Harbottle Grimstone. But Country spokesmen did not merely suggest that the bishops had failed to preserve the heritage of reformation or were hostile to it. The Country also reversed Danby's claim that the crown required defense, as found in the test bill of 1675, against sectarians of "Dangerous and *Anti-Monarchical* Principles." Instead, claimed Shaftesbury, "the most dangerous sort of Men alive to our *English* Government," were not the sects at all, but rather the bishops themselves. The bishops were conspiring, according to Country argument, as much against the king's ecclesiastical supremacy as they were to weaken the country's Protestant traditions. They promoted divine right conceptions of their own authority and that of the monarch that were contrary to the "ancient constitution."[74]

The Country of 1675–8 was as obsessed as the Country of 1641–2 with the fear that the bishops sought to undermine the royal supremacy, a chief cornerstone of English Protestantism. Shaftesbury claimed that Danby's oath *"was the greatest attempt that had been made against the King's Supremacy since the Reformation."* According to him, an oath against any alterations of the government of the church would deprive the king of his freedom, as head of the Church of England, to promote Protestant reconciliation through indulgence. Indeed, the oath would "directly . . . set the *Mitre above the Crown*," in which case "the king's supremacy is overthrown." More outspoken, Andrew Marvell regarded attempts upon the king's supremacy as inherent in the very nature of episcopacy. His 1676 "Historical Essay, touching General Councils" was, in part, a political allegory about Charles II and the Restoration episcopate. According to him, ambitious bishops had, ever since the era of Constantine, "backed and ridden" civil governors and encroached upon the authority of the state, just as the churchmen had attempted in the 1675 test.[75]

Seeking to convert their *"Pontificate* into a Caiaphat," the Restoration bishops had also, according to Country interpretation, offered Charles II the

---

[74] Shaftesbury, *Letter from a Person of Quality*, pp. 9, 34; Goldie, "Danby, the Bishops and the Whigs," pp. 92, 95–6; C. Condren, "Andrew Marvell as Polemicist: His Account of the Growth of Popery, and Arbitrary Government," in *The Political Identity of Andrew Marvell*, pp. 157–87.

[75] Shaftesbury, *Letter from a Person of Quality*, p. 24; Marvell, "Historical Essay," esp. pp. 51, 67, 70, 72; J. Morrill, "The Attack on the Church of England in the Long Parliament," in J. Morrill, *The Nature of the English Revolution* (1993), pp. 81–2.

significant compensation of "absolute" authority over civil affairs in return for the loss of his ecclesiastical supremacy. The bishops, said the Country, maintained that the king held his civil authority by divine right rather than by legal grant; and they claimed the same divine foundation for their own jurisdiction within the church. When Shaftesbury rose in the House of Lords in October 1675 to declare that, "our all is at stake," his ultimate point was the contradiction between these divine right notions of monarchy, as revived by the bishops, and the Country principle "*That the King is King by Law.*"[76]

In attacking divine right government, while promoting the royal supremacy, Country writers demonstrated that they advanced the supremacy to preserve the Reformation rather than to advance the prerogative *per se*. Indeed, they perceived in the bishops' design to safeguard the Anglican order against any civil alterations an attempt also to "*overthr[o]w all Parliaments.*" The proper legislative business of parliaments was, after all, "the alteration, either by adding, or taking away, some part of the Government, either in Church or State." In seeking to deprive parliament of any legislative competence over the church, the bishops had intended as much to undermine parliament in 1675 as they had in the reign of Charles I: "Here the Mask was plainly pluckt off and *Arbitrary Government* appear'd barefaced," claimed Shaftesbury. Or, as Marvell put it, the test bill represented a "Dissettlement of the whole Birth-right of *England*" and presaged an entire "Alteration of Religion . . . [and] Government." Moreover, parliamentary government could scarcely be preserved against enemies in high places if JPs and MPs throughout the kingdom were required to forswear any resort to arms against the monarch or those acting in his name. "How . . . can [there] be a distinction then left," inquired Shaftesbury, "between Absolute, and Bounded Monarchys, if *Monarchs* have only the fear of *God*, and no humane Resistance to restrain them?"[77]

The Country's case against the bishops points back to 1659–60 as well as to 1641–2. The Restoration had originated in fears about the security of parliament and of Protestantism under a republican regime. But by 1675–8, many Reformed Protestants who had once worked for or accepted a Stuart restoration, for the sake of a secure church order, had come to believe that the restored bishops threatened to undo Protestantism, parliament, and the monarchy. The Country's case against the bishops both rehabilitated much language from the 1640s and challenged the nation to rethink the church settlement. Nonconformists in London and elsewhere had witnessed against Anglican exclusivity and parliamentary coercion, with increasing conviction,

[76] Haley, *Shaftesbury*, pp. 394–5; Marvell, "Historical Essay," p. 72; Shaftesbury, *Two Speeches*, p. 10; Shaftesbury, *Letter from a Person of Quality*, p. 34.
[77] Shaftesbury, *Letter from a Person of Quality*, pp. 16, 18–19, 25, 34; Shaftesbury, *Two Speeches*, p. 11; Marvell, *Account*, pp. 57–8, 60.

ever since 1662. In 1675–8, powerful parliamentary figures joined dissenting spokesmen in arguing that only Protestant accommodation could rescue the kingdom from the designs of the bishops.

In the city, the Country's case against the bishops confirmed dissenters and opposition electors in their rejection of coercion and in their insistence that authority should develop from consent. This result was clearly one intended by Shaftesbury and Marvell. They were well acquainted with the city and with leading dissenting citizens; and they each knew how important the city had been in 1641–2 and in 1659–60. They were also each able to combine legal, parliamentary, and Protestant language in rhetorical appeals well suited to an urban audience. And Shaftesbury's explicit endorsement of resistance, under some circumstances, pointed to a convergence of the Country and of London dissenters in the employment of additional language that contradicted the officially prescribed doctrines of passive obedience and non-resistance.

"Holy Church goes to Wrack on all Sides," Marvell sneered in the midst of this polemical campaign, which he found "infinitely pleasant." But many urban Anglicans were appalled by it and confirmed in their suspiciousness of dissent and opposition. Richard Baxter thought that those who distrusted nonconformists were left "as hot for Prelacy and their Violence as ever" in the wake of the Country attack upon the bishops.[78] Indeed, the political and religious polarization that would be expressed in the Whig and Tory parties was already present in London, in parliament, and in the press in 1675–8. The importance of this religious and political polarization of opinion on the eve of the Popish Plot cannot be over-stressed. Anglican Protestants and Reformed Protestants were about to experience, together, a cultural eruption of the xenophobic anti-Catholicism that had been building since the early 1670s. Nothing had more potential for uniting Englishmen of different perspectives than the national aversion to popery. However, the political nation was already so divided upon the eve of the Popish Plot that, neither in parliament nor in many localities, could leaders and articulate subjects agree upon solutions to the kingdom's peril.

In London, there stood, on the one hand, an urban community of dissenting and Reformed Protestants of different persuasions, many without the church, but some within it. They defined orthodoxy by reference to the scriptures, to the historic Reformation and its spokesmen, and to the doctrine of the priesthood of all believers. They professed a confidence in Christian liberty and condemned coercive practices that killed the spirit, dulled the mind, and trespassed upon God's sovereignty over conscience. On the other hand stood an Anglican establishment that defined orthodoxy by reference

---

[78] Marvell, *Poems and Letters*, II, 343; Baxter, *Reliquiae*, III, 141, 167.

to patristic tradition, by obedience to clerical authority, and by participation in parish communities. The clerical establishment condemned the assertion of individual belief that led to resistance in the state and schism in the church, and they regarded the coercion of the individual as a legitimate policy for the preservation of the body of Christ and the unity of the kingdom.[79]

CONCLUSION: LONDON AND THE POPISH PLOT, 1678–1679

The Popish Plot was a natural conclusion to the parliamentary and civic politics of the 1670s, just as it was the beginning of a Restoration Crisis that seriously unsettled the kingdom. The tales about Catholic assassination schemes and intrigue that were told by Titus Oates and others were credible because they confirmed fears that had already become increasingly widespread in London and the kingdom. Parliamentary affairs after 1675–6 confirmed Country spokesmen and London dissenters in their suspicions about a developing conspiracy against parliament and Protestantism. They took alarm again in 1677, for instance, about Danby's bill to limit any Catholic monarch's exercise of the royal supremacy by transferring episcopal appointments from the crown to the sitting bishops. They no more wanted the succession of divine right bishops than they wanted the succession of a Catholic prince. Neither were the civic and Country advocates of parliamentary government reassured by the crown's frequent adjournment of sessions in 1677–8. As proponents of international Protestantism, they were further disturbed when the ministry secured parliamentary agreement to fund an "actual War" against Louis XIV in Flanders but failed to ready newly raised troops for such a conflict. What else was necessary for the establishment of popery and arbitrary government than a coercive church, a Catholic successor, and a standing army?[80]

Fear rather than fabrication must remain at the center of historical interpretation of the Popish Plot and the ensuing Restoration Crisis. The fears that many English Protestants had developed about the sects had arguably been the most critical variable in shaping the punitive Anglican settlement that followed the Restoration. But, in 1678–9 and the years immediately thereafter, the fears that Reformed Protestants and Anglicans alike had developed about Catholics were the more critical and unsettling to many. The crisis that began with the Popish Plot differed from previous seventeenth-century outbursts of anti-Catholicism in one critical respect, however. The

---

[79] J. Spurr, "Schism and the Restoration Church," *JEcH* 41 (1990), 408–24; Spurr, *Restoration Church*, pp. 105ff.; M. Goldie, "The Theory of Religious Intolerance in Restoration England," in Grell, *et al.*, eds., *From Persecution to Toleration*, pp. 331–68.

[80] Grey, *Debates*, IV, 296, and V, 179; Marvell, *Account*, pp. 86–100; Goldie, "Danby, the Bishops and the Whigs," pp. 84–7; Haley, *Shaftesbury*, pp. 422–3.

word "party" was already being applied, and with good reason, to the "interests" and "factions" that competed in the parliamentary and civic arenas. From the beginning of the Popish Plot, Anglican magistrates suspected that the "fanatic party," or the "anti-Court party," was again driving the kingdom to the brink of civil war.[81]

The reciprocal suspicions between Danby's ministry and his London opponents were sustained by the confusing parliamentary sessions of 1677–8 that preceded the Plot revelations. At the time of the brief May 1677 session, the lord treasurer turned to the Corporation for a loan upon the credit of the excise. But he encountered reluctance to lend to a monarch who was seemingly unconcerned about French encroachments in Flanders. A year later, in April 1678, Danby was more successful, securing a loan of £100,000 from common council. The citizens' more favorable response reflected the mood of parliament, which had just supplied the crown for a projected war against France. But, as the citizens subscribed to the loan, public and parliamentary confidence that Charles intended to intervene against Louis waned. When Danby returned to the city in May 1678, to request more money, he exchanged angry words with Chamberlain Player, who had deliberately closed his books after the initial amount had been subscribed. The Corporation agreed to another loan of £200,000 in July, but lending was not enthusiastic.[82]

As anxiety about the ministry's purposes mounted in London, Secretary Williamson became equally anxious about opposition in the city. Extensive urban surveillance was carried out during the session of May and June 1678. From one informant, who visited numerous dissenting meetings, Williamson learned that the city's nonconformist clergy frequently "spoke against the bishops." A search of Francis Jenks's house turned up illicit pamphlets, including a defense of Shaftesbury's "cousin" John Harrington, who had been tried for publicly defending resistance under some circumstances. Williamson also learned that many citizens feared Charles's new troops would be used on behalf of what "they call arbitrary government." And he was informed that merchant Slingsby Bethel, who had written on behalf of conscience, had openly declared that the royal brothers were illegitimate.[83]

Many Londoners were already openly apprehensive about the security of the realm, then, when the first Plot revelations exploded in October 1678,

---

[81] *CSPD 1679–80*, p. 23; HMC *Ormonde*, NS, IV, 495–6; *Memoirs of Sir John Reresby*, ed. A. Browning (Glasgow, 1936), p. 183.

[82] Journal 48, fols. 374, 380, 406; Morrice, P, 82; Marvell, *Account*, [p. 127] (misnumbered as 108); Grey, *Debates*, IV, 372; *CSPD 1677–78*, p. 140; HMC *Seventh Report*, p. 470; Haley, *Shaftesbury*, pp. 447–8; Lacey, *Dissent*, p. 85; Henning, *House of Commons*, III, 251.

[83] Morrice, P, 91; HMC *Seventh Report*, pp. 469–70; *CSPD 1677–78*, p. 22; *CSPD 1678*, pp. 189, 202, 226–7, 246, 255–6, 260, 262, 313; Haley, *Shaftesbury*, p. 425–6.

and when the body of Sir Edmund Berry Godfrey was found on Primrose Hill. The fear that the largest Protestant trading city in Europe was imperiled by French and papal conspirators resembled similar great fears or alarums that had swept London in 1641 and in 1659–60. "Every inhabitant has brought in a store of arms for...his family," wrote one observer. The wave of fear that spread through the city was no doubt heightened by the familiarity of some citizens with Godfrey and his family or with Dr Israel Tonge, Oates's colleague in making revelations, who was rector of St Michael Wood Street. The popular belief that London had been fired by the papists in 1666 further fed anxiety. Prominent London churchmen initially showed as much concern as dissenters and opposition common councilmen. Thinking about the Paris massacre of 1572 and the Irish massacres of 1641, East India Governor Sir Nathaniel Herne, for instance, was ready to move his family out of London.[84]

As parliament began to investigate the Plot, the London magistracy acted to safeguard the city. Precautions were taken to prevent disturbances upon the lord mayor's day and upon 5 November. A royal order that recusants remove themselves by ten miles from London and Westminster was accompanied by a flurry of mayoral precepts. Ward returns were made of all resident foreign Catholics. The weekend watch was doubled. Posts and chains were placed in the major streets, and orders were issued to improve illumination at night. When a series of inexplicable blazes broke out early in 1679, they were attributed to the papists.[85]

Divergences between Anglican and opposition responses to the Plot were also apparent as early as November 1678. The spirited popular rejoicing in the wake of the king's speech to parliament of 9 November, for instance, revealed a wide gulf between royal intention and the expectations of some citizens. Celebrated in the city with bells, bonfires, and toasts, Charles's defense of the "true line" of succession was seen by some as promising a Protestant succession through the Duke of Monmouth. But a few days later, the mood of many citizens altered: false rumors about an arrest of the Earl of Shaftesbury, who had been fêted in the recent celebrations, threatened

---

[84] A member of a prominent merchant and gentry family, Godfrey had political connections to Sir Robert Peyton and other London opposition figures with Country affiliations. Newdigate Newsletters L.c. 689, 695 (3, 19 Oct. 1678); William Bedlow, *A Narrative and Impartial Discovery of the Horrid Popish Plot* (1679); HMC *Ormonde*, NS, IV, 473; Henning, *House of Commons*, III, 233; M. Knights, "London Petitions and Parliamentary Politics in 1679," *Parliamentary History* 12 (1993), 30; A. Marshall, "To Make a Martyr: The Popish Plot and Protestant Propaganda," *HT* 47 (1997), 39–45; A. Marshall, "The Westminster Magistrate and the Irish Stroker: Sir Edmund Godfrey and Valentine Greatrakes, Some Unpublished Correspondence," *HJ* 40 (1997), 499–505; De Krey, *Fractured Society*, p. 145; J. Kenyon, *The Popish Plot* (New York, 1972), pp. 45, 77.

[85] Journal 48, fols. 421–422; Journal 49, fols. 1–2; Newdigate L.c. 699–700 (1, 2 Nov. 1678); *CSPD 1678*, pp. 448, 491; HMC *House of Lords 1678–88*, pp. 59, 170–1; HMC *Ormonde*, NS, IV, 261, 469; Luttrell, I, 7–8; Haley, *Shaftesbury*, p. 495; Harris, *London Crowds*, p. 111.

to throw the city into an "uproar." And when the Lords hesitated to endorse the Commons' new test bill against Catholics, Sir Robert Southwell, clerk to the Privy Council, worried that the government might soon "hear of addresses from another place." Anglican aldermen in the Corporation had similar concerns about popular petitioning. When an effort was made in common council in November to thank parliament for its care of the Protestant religion and the king, they acted to block any such address.[86]

At the end of December, when Charles unexpectedly prorogued parliament until February, he clearly worried about the possibility of trouble in London; and he summoned the lord mayor and alderman to attend him in council. But the king's reassurances that he intended to disband the army, and not "to rule that way," did not calm citizens surprised and fearful about the unexpected prorogation. Rumors circulated in the city that troops returning from Flanders were to be quartered near London. Other citizens worried about the security of their trade and property in the absence of a parliament: "Some talked high of their tents &c., of shutting up their shops and much more." Some apprentices were reportedly ready to pull down Newgate prison and to see justice executed upon condemned Jesuits. The members of the Green Ribbon club were active in the neighborhood clubs to which many of them also belonged, spreading the word that "whatever is pretended, Popery and arbitrary government is intended, that a Parliament is not to come again." With good reason the government took measures, shortly after the prorogation, to suppress the printing of unlicensed books.[87]

By the middle of January 1679, Sir Thomas Player, Francis Jenks, and Sir Robert Peyton were circulating a city petition that advised Charles to take parliamentary counsel again as soon as possible. Probably working with Shaftesbury, these experienced advocates of popular addresses hoped not only to aid their friends in parliament but also to encourage the submission of petitions from other boroughs throughout the kingdom. Twenty thousand people, including many common councilmen, reportedly signed the London petition. When it was presented for Corporation endorsement, however, loyalist aldermen again employed their controversial veto. This action revived the ongoing quarrel between the aldermanic bench and opposition common councilmen and provoked popular indignation as well.

---

86 Repertory 84, fol. 7; Morrice, P, 95; LC MS 18,124, VI, fol. 138 (12 Nov. 1678); Newdigate L.c. 705 (14 Nov. 1678); HMC *Ormonde*, NS, IV, 277, 281, 285–6, 470, 473–4, 487; Grey, *Debates*, VI, 335–7; Luttrell, I, 3; Haley, *Shaftesbury*, 480, 499.

87 Morrice, P, 104; Newdigate L.c. 728, 730 (4, 11 Jan. 1679); LC MS 18,124, VI, fol. 166 (2 Jan. 1679); HMC *Ormonde*, NS, IV, 293, 495; *CSPD 1678*, p. 595; *CSPD 1679–80*, pp. 14, 19, 21, 22.

Papers weighted with bullets were thrown into the lord mayor's court, and they threatened reprisals if the magistrates failed to "satisfye the peopell."[88]

Disappointed in their petitioning, London dissenters and opposition common councilmen were equally dismayed when the king at last dissolved the Cavalier Parliament, in late January 1679, calling for the election of a new parliament, to meet in six weeks' time. Civic opposition spokesmen like Francis Jenks had long desired a dissolution. But their suspicions about the future of parliaments at the hands of the Court were actually increased when a dissolution finally came. The king's action was said to have "terrified most people," and a further "Great Allarme" spread about new fires in the West End and rumored French naval preparations.[89]

Given the opportunity to choose new members for the Corporation, many citizens opposed the election of any sitting aldermen, preferring instead prominent civic opponents of the ministry. These included Sir Thomas Player, Thomas Pilkington, Francis Jenks ("amongst a few"), and William Love, the outspoken dissenter who had sat for the city in the Cavalier Parliament. When common hall met to choose members, the liverymen returned Player, Pilkington, and Love. Alderman Sir Robert Clayton became the city's fourth MP. Yet this important triumph of the ministry's civic enemies did not rest upon a collapse of Anglican loyalism in London: Francis Jenks's provocative past and modest estate clearly made him unacceptable to some liverymen. Others expressed their loyalty in the nomination for parliament of Alderman Sir Joseph Sheldon, the nephew of an archbishop. Nevertheless, after almost a decade of frustration, the London advocates of conscience and consent had regained the political initiative in the Corporation. Loyalist hegemony had been broken, despite Anglican predominance amongst the aldermen.[90]

The goals of the London opposition in the interval between the last session of the Cavalier Parliament and the meeting of the new parliament were threefold. First, London dissenters and opposition common councilmen wanted a full parliamentary investigation of the Popish Plot, as their petition suggested. For them, the security of the realm required an independent parliament under the leadership of individuals devoted to Country principles and to the Protestant interest. But their militancy in pursuing this objective was already alarming London and Westminster loyalists. Sir Nathaniel Herne, for instance, was mindful of the parallels between 1679 and a former "dangerous time." Another loyalist worried that the "fanatic party" would

---

[88] LC 18,124, VI, fol. 174 (23 Jan. 1679); Newdigate L.c. 732 (16 Jan. 1679); *CSPD 1679–80*, pp. 19–20, 24; Haley, *Shaftesbury*, p. 499; Knights, "London Petitions," pp. 30–1; M. Knights, *Politics and Opinion in Crisis, 1678–81* (Cambridge, 1994), pp. 194–5.

[89] Newdigate L.c. 737–8 (27, 30 Jan. 1679); Luttrell, I, 6; *CSPD 1679–80*, pp. 67–8.

[90] Newdigate L.c. 748 (20 Feb. 1679); *CSPD 1679–80*, p. 63; HMC *Fitzherbert*, p. 13; Henning, *House of Commons*, I, 313; Jones, *First Whigs*, p. 42.

now "tread the whole path of their predecessors, and make things as fatal to the crown as formerly."

Secondly, London petitioners and many London electors were also acting in early 1679 on behalf of Protestant accommodation and liberty for conscience. Two of the newly chosen MPs were nonconformists: William Love had served on the Council of State under the restored Rump, and Thomas Pilkington had emerged as a spokesman for London dissenters in 1669–70. Sir Thomas Player and Sir Robert Clayton were conformists; but each was associated with the Country program for a resettled church in which episcopal authority would be subordinated to Protestant unity. The city's choice of MPs was, therefore, a clear repudiation, by the electoral majority, of Danby's initiatives on behalf of the exclusivist church of the Restoration episcopate.[91]

Thirdly, the London advocates of parliament and Protestant accommodation sought also to reanchor civic government in electoral consent. Three of the new city members – Player, Pilkington, and Clayton – had actively favored the recent claims of common council against the magistracy. In the attempted common council address of November 1678, these and other civic spokesmen had assumed that common council represented the citizens and spoke for them. When loyalist aldermen blocked that address, some opposition leaders had then turned to the electorate of the Corporation, to the freemen themselves, and had mounted a popular petition to the crown. This mobilization of the people on behalf of parliament and Protestantism was what led the lord mayor to condemn the January 1679 petition as rank "Lilburnisme." Civic opposition leaders clearly assumed, as Francis Jenks had in 1676, that the freemen had every right to speak for themselves and that the civic magistrates were as much the agents of the electorate as their governors.[92]

What the London opposition wanted on the eve of the new session was, then, parliamentary government, Protestant accommodation, and a reestablishment of the rights and liberties of electors and the common council. London dissenters and opposition leaders soon had much more to consider as well: by May 1679, when the new parliamentary session ended, the Restoration Settlement was beginning to unravel. The enforced departure of the Duke of York into a Flemish exile before the opening of parliament failed entirely to satisfy the concerns of a House of Commons that was determined to preserve the kingdom against Roman Catholicism. Neither were Country members satisfied by the forced retirement and imprisonment of Danby or

---

[91] In Middlesex, where Sir Robert Peyton was selected as a member, some electors addressed their new MPs about the need for Protestant union. Newdigate L.c. 752 (27 Feb. 1679); HMC *Ormonde*, NS, IV, 495–6; *CSPD 1679–80*, p. 77; Henning, *House of Commons*, I, 309, and III, 233; Knights, "London Petitions," p. 31.

[92] Newdigate L.c. 732 (16 Jan. 1679); *CSPD 1679–80*, pp. 19–20, 21.

by the opening of the Privy Council to such former Court opponents as Shaftesbury, the Earl of Halifax, and Henry Powle. Many MPs were similarly hostile to the proposals for limitations upon a popish successor that now came from some privy councilors. Instead, by the time of parliament's prorogation on 27 May, the House of Commons had foisted a bill of attainder against Danby upon the House of Lords; and they had disputed the validity of Danby's royal pardon. The Commons had also challenged the right of the bishops to sit in the Lords in capital cases; and most importantly, the House had voted overwhelmingly in favor of a bill to exclude the Duke of York from the succession.

Several leading members of the London opposition were also notable members of the 1679 House of Commons. The four city members held 100 Commons' committee appointments amongst them. Sitting for other constituencies, London merchants John Dubois and Thomas Papillon, London attorney George Treby, and Sir Robert Peyton held over 100 additional committee appointments. City merchants Sir Samuel Barnardiston and Sir Patience Ward were also members of the House. Barnardiston, Papillon, Thomas Pilkington, and Peyton served on the committee for providing security against popery. Treby chaired the important secret committee to investigate the Plot, on which Sir Thomas Player also sat. In debate, Pilkington urged the impeachment of the Duke of York for treason. Player actually argued on behalf of resistance, suggesting that "poor Protestants" would probably need to "take ... up arms" rather than "die like dogs" at the hands of "Popish Guards" under a Catholic prince. Not surprisingly, he moved the exclusion bill and served, with Peyton, on the committee to draft it. On 21 May, each of these London members voted with the Commons' majority for the exclusion bill. As their concerns and committee assignments suggests, however, they saw exclusion not as an end it itself but rather as a critical means in a broader attempt to "secure ... the King and Kingdom."[93]

A popular petition to parliament that was circulated in London in May 1679 also suggests that changing the succession was widely perceived by the civic opposition as a necessary but not exclusive means for securing Protestantism and parliament. Acting on behalf of the "commonality," James Hayes presented the petition to the common council for civic endorsement on 20 May. It encouraged parliament to persist with the "divers Methods, Means, and Ways" it had already initiated for the preservation of the king and "the Protestant Religion." Although the petition's text did not refer specifically to exclusion, it was said to have been promoted by City MP Sir Thomas Player, who had proposed the exclusion bill in the Commons.

---

[93] Grey, *Debates*, VII, 151–2, 238, 240; Henning, *House of Commons*, I, 597; II, 85, 237–8, 762–3; III, 203, 233, 245, 251, 581, 668.

Moreover, the London petition was clearly timed to encourage MPs in their consideration of the exclusion bill, which had been read for the first time on 15 May, and which received its second reading on the 21st.[94]

Both for its promoters and for Anglican loyalists, the May 1679 petition was also another skirmish in the debate about consent in the civic constitution that had been carried on, with interruptions, since the 1640s. Indeed, petition sponsor James Hayes had defended popular procedures in the Corporation since his initial common council service in 1650–51. The petitioners claimed to act "in the Behalfe of many Thousands more Loyall Protestant Subjects," and they presumed to instruct the London magistrates on how the city should respond to the critical state of the kingdom's affairs. In doing so, the subscribers acted upon Francis Jenks's argument that civic magistrates were agents of the freemen. And when the city's Anglican loyalist lord mayor objected to the petition's language, its backers apparently considered presenting the petition directly from the citizenry to the House of Commons. They would have done so as an example to the freemen of other localities in a manner consistent with their popular assumptions.

Was the city, then, re-embarking upon the courses of 1641? That question was on the minds of many by May 1679. In the Tower, the Earl of Danby needed no historical instruction about the meaning of city petitioning on this scale. He pointedly warned Charles of the danger such petitions had presaged in the past. In the Corporation itself, however, the fear of repeating past mistakes led both sides toward compromise. No aldermanic veto was employed against the petition, despite loyalist unhappiness that it lacked any reference to the "Lds Spirituall," in its salutation to the Houses of Parliament, or any reference to the Anglican order, in its defense of the "Protestant Religion." A committee of aldermen and common councilmen remedied these textual omissions and added language more acceptable to churchmen. But by then, the combination of a Commons' vote on behalf of exclusion and what appeared to be the beginning of a popular petitioning campaign had propelled the king into action.

Charles's prorogation of the 1679 parliament on 27 May was as unexpected and shocking to many citizens as the prorogation and dissolution of the previous parliament. The announcement "wrought as greate a consternation" in the city "as hath been known a long time." The reaction indicated the extent to which many citizens had regarded this parliament as their chief bulwark against Roman Catholicism. "The citty of London, wher[e] the

---

[94] CLRO Alchin B/33/15; Repertory 84, fol. 123; Journal 49, fol. 41; Newdigate L.c. 789 (26 May 1679); Haley, *Shaftesbury*, pp. 520–5; Knights, "London Petitions," esp. pp. 32–5; Knights, *Politics and Opinion*, pp. 202–3. Danby learned, from the Tower, that Pilkington and Player had actually sought to include an explicit reference to the bill against the Duke of York in the petition: Browning, *Danby*, II, 82.

anti-Court party had a great interest, seemed soe angry," wrote Sir John Reresby, "that some thought they would have risen; but all, with much adoe, kept quiet." The "much ado" included the king's instructions to the lord mayor and aldermen for enforcing laws against those dissenters "who went about to disturb the government."[95]

Charles's conviction that dissenters in the city were seizing upon the Plot to "disturb" the Restoration Settlement was not amiss. The historian who first analyzed the 1,500 names on the May 1679 petition's surviving signature roll has cautiously suggested that one in six were definite or probable dissenters. But the document's original wording, with its studied lack of reference to the established parochial order, suggests that this petition was a dissenting and Reformed Protestant vehicle from the start. About one-fifth of the subscribers to the 1670 London dissenting loan to the crown signed the petition roll, and its first two pages are awash with the names of other leading London dissenters.[96]

The commitment of dissenting Protestants to the city petition suggests that, in London, the developing crisis was as much about the church as it was about the succession. Indeed, the rhetorical effectiveness of the Country's recent case against the bishops ensured that the 1679 parliament met in an intellectual climate as marked by demands for ecclesiastical change and Protestant renewal as the heady early months of the Long Parliament. The pamphlet literature of the spring of 1679 revived much language from the earlier dissenting cases for conscience. *A Proposal of Union amongst Protestants*, for instance, drew upon the memory of "our first *Renowned Reformers*" to advocate eliminating divisive ceremonies that stood in the way of Protestant union. The *Proposal* supported Shaftesbury's 1675 program for comprehension, while William Penn revived interest in arguments for the toleration of those who could not be comprehended in his *One Project for the Good of England*. Both the *Proposal* and Penn insisted that the only true basis for religious accommodation was liberty for conscience. Had "this Freedom been granted Eighteen Years ago," Penn asserted, "*Protestancy* had been too Potent for the Enemies of it."[97]

[95] CLRO Alchin B/33/15; Journal 49, fol. 41; Repertory 84, fol. 123; Newdigate L.c. 789, 791–2 (26, 31 May and 2 June 1679); LC MS 18,124, VI, 227 (29 May 1679); Reresby, *Memoirs*, 183; Grey, *Debates*, VII, 345–6; HMC *Ormonde*, NS, IV, 516, 520; Knights, "London Petitions," pp. 32–3; Knights, *Politics and Opinion*, pp. 203–4; Browning, *Danby*, II, 82–3; Sharpe, *London*, II, 459; Haley, *Shaftesbury*, p. 525.

[96] CLRO Alchin MS 33/15; Knights, "London Petitions," pp. 39–43.

[97] HMC *Ormonde*, NS, IV, xviii, 510; *A Proposal of Union amongst Protestants* (1679), pp. 2–4; [William Penn], *One Project for the Good of England; that is, Our Civil Union is our Civil Safety* [1679], pp. 3, 6, 8; Knights, "London Petitions," p. 36; Knights, *Politics and Opinion*, pp. 200–2; H. Horwitz, "Protestant Reconciliation in the Exclusion Crisis," *JEcH* 15 (1964), 202–3; Goldie, "Danby, the Bishops, and the Whigs," pp. 80–1, 90–100.

But the case for a new church settlement was not to be won in this parliament. Under attack, the bishops became increasingly intransigent, and their message to Anglican loyalists throughout the kingdom was to stand fast in defense of the church established by law. When the 1679 parliament considered legislation to discourage the residence of Catholics in London, the bishops sought to impose the same oaths upon London dissenters as upon Roman Catholics. And when Shaftesbury and Country MPs sought to exclude the bishops from parliamentary deliberations about the fate of Danby and the Catholic lords in the Tower, as "capital cases," churchmen in both houses maintained the right of the bishops to be present.[98]

At Westminster, as well as in London, then, the divisions among those seeking the best means to preserve Protestantism and constitutional government were already obvious and deep-seated in 1679. In the Corporation, the civic opposition had deep roots and resources in the Reformed Protestant language and traditions of a strong dissenting community. In parliament, the leaders of the Country found some of their principal lieutenants among London MPs who had emerged from that community. Both Country leaders and the London opposition saw exclusion and Protestant accommodation as critical elements of a new settlement to replace one that had failed. For them, exclusion was a necessary device to preserve Protestant beliefs and a Protestant monarchy from a popish conspiracy that sprang as much from the Anglican leadership as from Rome.

For their part, Anglican loyalists in London and at Westminster had little doubt about the identity and heritage of those with whom they contended. As Sir Robert Southwell suggested, the true threat to Protestantism and monarchy came from a "malicious fanatic party" that sought "to thrive by all disquiets" in London and the kingdom.[99] For Anglican loyalists, the design of the fanatics to undo the Restoration Settlement and to return the kingdom to the chaos of 1649 or 1659 was the most dangerous conspiracy revealed in the unraveling of the Popish Plot. The outcome of this conflict between the advocates of two competing visions of settlement remained open in 1679, as both Reformed Protestants and Anglican loyalists considered all possible means for resolving it according to their own preferences.

---

[98] Goldie, "Danby, the Bishops and the Whigs," pp. 90–6; Spurr, *Restoration Church*, pp. 77–8.
[99] HMC *Ormonde*, NS, IV, 496.

III

Crisis, 1679–1682

Introduction: London and the Restoration Crisis, 1679–1682

The Restoration began in one great crisis about parliamentary government and Protestantism, and it concluded in another. In 1659–60, most Reformed Protestants had come to agree with their Anglican counterparts that the restoration of monarchy was the best means to secure parliament and the Protestant establishment. But by 1679–82, many of those same Reformed Protestants had come to agree with their onetime sectarian adversaries that the episcopal leadership of the church and the prospect of a Catholic successor endangered both Protestantism and parliament again. The greatest beneficiary of the first crisis, Charles II survived the crisis of 1679–82 through a combination of good luck and good wit.

Recent scholars have followed contemporaries and Whig historians in dwelling upon the importance of London to the crisis that overtook the kingdom in 1679. But the traditional account of the crisis has been pulled apart as historians have engaged in an extensive process of demythologizing directed at the conventions of Whig historiography. Scholarly fragmentation has replaced the comfortable consensus that prevailed into the 1980s. Almost every feature of the Whig interpretation of the "Exclusion Crisis" has been challenged by one historian or another.

Tim Harris has demonstrated the fallacy of the whiggish assumption that ordinary people in London naturally identified with opposition to the Court: instead, according to him, the variety of perspectives that flourished amongst the *menu peuple* inclined them to both sides of the divide between Charles II and his critics. Jonathan Scott and Mark Knights have reduced the political role of the Earl of Shaftesbury, who was long seen as the commanding figure of the opposition and of the entire crisis. Instead, according to Scott, Algernon Sidney and his republican associates were as visible as Shaftesbury in the culminating episodes of "England's troubles." According to Knights, the opposition lacked a unified leadership, as a variety of parliamentary politicians and factions contested with each other and with Charles for a resolution to the crisis. Both Scott and Knights also deny that the exclusion of the Catholic Duke of York from the succession was the central issue of the crisis. Exclusion was merely one solution to the problem of the succession, which in turn was merely one issue – the most important, for Knights, but not for Scott – in a broader crisis about Protestantism and parliament.[1]

The political ideas and the political structures of the crisis have also been rethought. Recent historians have paid much attention to the ideological aspects of a crisis that saw the composition of major political treatises by John Locke, Algernon Sidney, and several others, as well as the publication of Sir Robert Filmer's royalist manifesto of the early seventeenth century. Tim Harris has portrayed loyalist ideas as less absolutist and more legalistic than Whig historians allowed; and Mark Goldie has seen anti-episcopal discourse as an important element of the crisis.[2] Richard Ashcraft and Richard Greaves have portrayed opposition ideas as far more radical than was once thought, and Jonathan Scott has reconceived the history of seventeenth-century radicalism.[3] Scott maintains that the crisis saw a remarkable revival in the influence of republican ideas, especially in London. And Mark Knights argues that the contest in public opinion was of equal importance to that in parliament. For him, the key to understanding the crisis is recognition that the public became divided between contradictory networks of political belief.[4]

Finally, recent scholars have asked whether the crisis of 1679–82 was really a crisis about party. Was it the beginning of "the first age of party," one in which Whigs and Tories organized rival political movements to contest with each other in parliament and in the localities? Despite the appearance of such labels as Whig and Tory by 1681, Scott argues that historians have inappropriately read eighteenth-century political structures into the political experiences of the crisis. For him, the essential political characteristic of the crisis was its fluidity: changing fears about the primary source of the threat

---

[1] Harris, *London Crowds*; J. Scott, *Algernon Sidney and the Restoration Crisis, 1677–1683* (Cambridge, 1991), pp. 17–21, 24–5, 165, 179–97, for instance; Scott, *England's Troubles*, esp. chs. 8, 16, 19; Knights, *Politics and Opinion*, pp. 3–5, 78–106, 227, for instance.

[2] T. Harris, "Tories and the Rule of Law in the Reign of Charles II," *The Seventeenth Century* 8 (1993), 9–27; Goldie, "Danby, the Bishops and the Whigs."

[3] Ashcraft, *Revolutionary Politics*; R. L. Greaves, *Secrets of the Kingdom: British Radicals from the Popish Plot to the Revolution of 1688–89* (1992); Scott, *England's Troubles*, esp. Part II. Also see De Krey, "London Radicals and Revolutionary Politics"; G. S. De Krey, "Radicals, Reformers, and Republicans: Academic Language and Political Discourse in Restoration London," in *A Nation Transformed: England after the Restoration*, ed. A. Houston and S. Pincus (Cambridge, 2001), pp. 71–99. For rejections of "radicalism," see J. C. D. Clark, *Revolution and Rebellion: State and Society in England in the Seventeenth and Eighteenth Centuries* (Cambridge, 1986), especially pp. 6–9, 97–111; C. Condren, "Radicals, Conservatives and Moderates in Early Modern Political Thought: A Case of Sandwich Islands Syndrome?," *History of Political Thought* 10 (1989), 525–42.

[4] Scott, *Restoration Crisis*, pp. 61–2, 105–6, 125, 162–9, for instance; Knights, *Politics and Opinion*, pp. 153–5, 226, for instance. For republicanism, also see A. Houston, "Republicanism, the Politics of Necessity and the Rule of Law," in *A Nation Transformed*, pp. 241–71.

to parliament and Protestantism panicked the public first in one direction and then in another. Less iconoclastic, Knights sees the religious divide between Anglicans and dissenters as one source of continuity that eventually shaped political fluidity into two recognizable sides: parties were a result of the crisis rather than one of its causes. But nothing has proved more controversial than this rejection or revision of party; and other scholars, like Harris, have maintained party as the organizing principle for studying Restoration politics.[5]

The importance of London to the crisis of 1679–82 is, thus, one of the few matters upon which all its recent historians have agreed. For that very reason, a full narrative account about politics and opinion in London is essential to understanding the crisis, and study of London also provides an essential empirical proving ground for the new interpretive frameworks that have been suggested. At the same time, however, the city was an exceptional locality in England and in Europe as a whole. The size of its population and the influence of the Corporation of London on lesser corporations and localities made it unique. So did its large and fiercely independent electorate, its cadres of articulate political and religious activists of different perspectives, and its relatively high male literacy rate. The city's sophisticated facilities for the social exchange of ideas were virtually unrivaled in Europe, and it possessed most of the national press from which a new journalistic culture, recently examined by Lois Schwoerer, was born.[6] Yet these very exceptions made London as important in the crisis that challenged Restoration Stuart monarchy as were Boston, Paris, and St Petersburg in the revolutionary crises that shook subsequent royal and imperial regimes. Indeed, these features of metropolitan culture require a full integration of London's political history in 1679–82 with that of the crisis itself.

The task of integrating the history of London and the kingdom in the culminating crisis of Charles II's reign is divided among the chapters of Part III. Chapter 4 focuses upon the development of party during the long interval between parliaments in 1679–80 and during the two short parliaments of 1680–81. Chapter 5 reconstructs the contest between the London Whigs and Charles II for control of the city in 1681–2. Chapter 6 examines the language and ideas of party conflict in London and the communities that expressed them.

The analysis of London in 1679–82 that is offered here is consistent with some recent interpretations, but it contradicts others. Jonathan Scott's proposal that the crisis be understood as *the* Restoration Crisis is accepted,

---

[5] Scott, *Restoration Crisis*, pp. 21–5, 44–9; Knights, *Politics and Opinion*, ch. 5; Harris, *Politics under the Later Stuarts*.

[6] L. G. Schwoerer, *The Ingenious Mr. Henry Care, Restoration Publicist* (Baltimore, 2001).

although the narrative will follow contemporaries in referring to the crisis in a variety of ways rather than with a single name. The "Exclusion Crisis" of the textbooks and of historical convention is too narrow a construction for a crisis that was as much about religion as about the constitution and that had as much to do with the future of parliament as with the future of the crown. The opposition proposed nothing less than a new settlement of church and state, reopening the whole troublesome pack of issues that had vexed the kingdom since the reign of Charles I and that had already led to civil war and revolution. Lawrence Stone once referred to the crisis of 1679–82 as the first of a series of aftershocks of the great mid-century English political earthquake; but many contemporaries thought of it as more.[7] For them, it was an earthquake of similar proportions to that of the 1640s: it threatened to cause the same amount of damage, and the earth seemed to stop moving only in 1688–9.

Unlike some recent accounts, however, this narrative retains party as an essential element of the urban crisis and of the relationship between civic and parliamentary politics. The critics of party as a conceptual category have corrected some previous historians who read too much organization and central direction into the first Whigs and the first Tories. But even if they lacked the extensive local and national organization and the central directorates of modern political parties, the Whigs and Tories of the Restoration Crisis still have a strong claim to the status of parties.

Parties did not precede the crisis, nor were parties a result of the crisis. Rather, in London, in parliament, and elsewhere, parties developed with the crisis – and to a varying extent – as politicians and pamphleteers struggled to devise acceptable solutions to the precipitating issues. Party development, moreover, reflected varying degrees of initiative from below and above. That neither side ever achieved complete unity in its objectives is a quite understandable expression of how fundamental the issues were. Yet the diffusion of approaches and the confusion of the times cannot obscure the existence of a clear-cut division of the nation. Some political actors demanded a resettlement of church and state on the basis of a Protestant succession and Protestant accommodation, while others insisted that only hereditary succession and an exclusively episcopal establishment were acceptable. Some few who trimmed between these positions were suspected on both sides.

In London, the word "party" was employed to characterize both the civic opposition and civic loyalists well before the Whig and Tory labels were attached. Organization, especially on the part of Anglican loyalists, was episodic; but the political contest in which the opposition and loyalists were

---

[7] L. Stone, "The Results of the English Revolutions of the Seventeenth Century," in *Three British Revolutions: 1641, 1688, 1776*, ed. J. G. A. Pocock (Princeton, 1980), p. 24.

involved was one that encouraged organization. As episode followed episode in a cascading torrent of political clashes, party organization became more continuous. The recruitment of signatures for petitions, the orchestration of common hall votes, efforts to secure places on the aldermanic bench and common council, the distribution of effective electoral propaganda, and even experiments in negative campaigning all point to unusual efforts at organization. Several leaders of the London civic opposition were also catapulted into parliament, where they gave expression to party perspectives and shared in the direction of opposition strategies.

Moreover, the Whig and Tory parties in London drew upon two generations of debate about how best to secure king-in-parliament and a Protestant church establishment. Whig language tapped the histories of the civic opposition and the parliamentary Country and incorporated discourse about conscience that flourished in London's extensive Reformed Protestant community. Tory thought drew upon historic Anglican rationales and apologies for monarchy and episcopacy. The Whig and Tory positions were "polarities of belief," as Jonathan Scott maintains;[8] but each also developed from previous political movements, traditions, and postures; and each further defined ongoing arguments about what was most desirable in the settlement of the nation. As parties, the London Whigs and Tories were well rooted in the past from which they evolved. The Tory party was a vehicle for all those who had triumphed in the confessional, coercive state of the Restoration. The Whig party was a vehicle for many who were excluded from that confessional state and for all who wished to replace it with a broader Protestant political order. For the most part, however, the London opposition to Charles II was not a "republican community," as Scott has suggested: the Whigs were not exclusively the heirs of the ousted sectarians and commonwealthmen of 1659–60. Instead, and ironically, they were mostly the very Reformed Protestants who had, in their fear of the sects, contributed so much to the restoration of Charles II.

[8] Scott, *Restoration Crisis*, p. 14.

4

Parliament and Protestantism in crisis: the emergence of parties in London, 1679–1681

PARTY AND THE SUCCESSION, 1679–1680

The polarization of opinion, September–October 1679

The nearly two-year period between the prorogation of the 1679 parliament and the dissolution of the Oxford Parliament, in March 1681, saw two general elections, two sessions, and a renewal of Charles II's determination to maintain both his independence from parliament and a strict hereditary succession. It also saw a progressive polarization of public opinion, as the issues of the succession and of the church were debated in the press, in the streets, at the polls, and in parliament. In London, this period also included two controversial shrieval elections, one of which drove both the civic opposition and civic loyalists toward new forms of political organization. Historians have understandably focused their attention in these months upon the parliamentary confrontations between Charles and his adversaries. But the two sessions actually occupied less than twelve weeks in the autumn and winter of 1680–81 and another week in March 1681. The politics of the period were shaped less by the meeting of parliaments than by waiting for parliaments.

The dissolution of the 1679 parliament in July prompted little outward complaint from the civic opposition, probably because Charles also issued writs for the election of a new body, the meeting of which was announced for October 1679. But no session would actually occur between May 1679 and October 1680, as Charles repeatedly put off meeting with his newly elected parliament. The result was a sixteen-month political interval similar to the long prorogation of the Cavalier Parliament in 1675–7 in which the status of parliament had first become an issue. The parliamentary interval of 1679–80 was distinctive, however, because it saw unusual efforts at extra-parliamentary political organization, especially by those who sought to force Charles to meet parliament, but also by Anglican loyalists. In London, the long interval between parliaments in 1679–80 produced urban political parties that developed from the long-standing division of the city between Reformed Protestants and Anglican Protestants. When parliament finally met

174

in October 1680, it met in an atmosphere made even more critical by the preceding emergence of party and by the interconnections between debate at Westminster and party contests for power in the city. Indeed, as Roger North remembered, the unprecedented "Transactions . . . within . . . the City," much encouraged by the parliamentary enemies of York, produced "a grand Crisis of State, and hinged about the whole Machine of King *Charles* II's Government."[1]

This crisis was about the succession; and it was also about the settlement of both church and state. The succession was central to an opposition that desired to resecure the state on a firmer parliamentary foundation and to resettle the church upon a broader Protestant foundation. The opposition saw, in the succession of the Catholic York, the chief threat to each objective. But the succession was equally central to Charles and to Anglican loyalists for whom any tampering with hereditary monarchy was a violation of the existing settlement of church and state, which they labored to preserve. These issues went to the heart of the Restoration itself, and the confrontation between the party of a new settlement and the party of the old settlement reopened issues that had been forced rather than resolved in 1659–64.

The issue of York's succession and the related issues of parliamentary government and Protestant security were never far from the surface of London affairs after the dissolution of July 1679. The return of the Duke of Monmouth to Westminster in that month, after his military victory over Scottish rebels, for instance, was the occasion for popular rejoicing in London that also reflected widespread support for a Protestant succession.[2] The king's serious illness in late August 1679 raised the frightening prospect of an actual succession in the absence of any parliamentary preparation for one. Although Charles recovered, the Duke of York quickly returned from his Flemish exile to assert his right to the throne.

James's presence immediately revived political quarrels in the Corporation of London. Youthful crowds put out the Somerset House bonfires lit to mark his arrival. When the city's recorder, Sir George Jeffreys, appeared at Windsor in early September to congratulate James, opposition spokesman Sir Thomas Player appeared at the next court of aldermen with a printed paper of objections and with a hundred "considerable" and concerned citizens "of his party." Player's connections to Buckingham and to Monmouth suggest he acted in consultation with them, as do the coincident "conferences" between Monmouth's London friend, Sir Thomas Armstrong, and Buckingham's city

---

[1] Roger North, *Examen; or, an Enquiry into the Credit and Veracity of a pretended complete History* (1740), p. 595.
[2] Newdigate L.c. 809 (12 July 1679).

friend, Francis Jenks and his "gang." Assurances from the aldermen that Jeffreys had acted privately in congratulating James failed to satisfy Player and his delegation. They regarded York as "an enemy to [the] city," and they feared that loyalist Lord Mayor Sir James Edwards had intended to proclaim him as king in the event of Charles's death, despite the vote of the 1679 Commons against James's succession.

A week later, Player again appeared before the court of aldermen, this time with "several Hundreds" of his followers. In a lengthy speech, he stressed the seriousness of the Plot and attacked those "Protestants in Masquerade" who cooperated with the Catholics by denying its reality or by suggesting that the dissenters were the real danger to the kingdom. He claimed that the vote for exclusion in the 1679 House of Commons represented "the Voice of all the Commons of England," even if "it came not up quite to a Law." In these circumstances, the return of York represented a serious threat to public safety, and he called upon the lord mayor to double the city guards.[3]

Player's speech coincided with the climax of the ongoing shrieval election, which, to this point, had been a civic fund-raiser: fines had been collected, since June, from several nominees chosen by common hall for their wealth rather than for their willingness to serve. But Francis Jenks now presented himself as a candidate, injecting his advocacy of civic and parliamentary rights into the election. As a shopkeeper of modest means, Jenks promised that if he were chosen, he would "reduce the Charge [of the office] to such a moderation as might make it supportable by one of an indifferent estate." This effort to secure the shrievalty for the civic opposition failed, however, when the "moderate party" secured the election of loyalist sheriffs. And loyalists had further reason to celebrate upon the sudden and unexpected banishment of Monmouth, a measure exacted by the Duke of York in return for his own renewed retirement to Brussels. Monmouth's crime was, reportedly, his consultation with Country statesmen about the succession during his father's illness.[4]

Each of these events drove divisive political talk and divisive political print, and civic loyalists were as outspoken in talk and print as their opposition

[3] Newgate L.c. 831, 833, 835, 838, 844 (6, 9, 13, 20 Sept. and 4 Oct. 1679); LC MS 18,124, VI, 271, 273 (16, 20 Sept. 1679); *Domestick Intelligence* 7, 20, 22 (28 July and 12, 19 Sept. 1679); *An Account of the Proceedings at the Guild-Hall of the City of London on Saturday, September 13. 1679; Vindication of Sir Thomas Player, and those Loyal Citizens Concerned with Him* (1679); *The Vindicator Vindicated: or, a Sur-rejoynder on behalf of Sir Thomas Player* (1679); *CSPD 1679–80*, pp. 240, 243–4, 245; *Hatton Correspondence*, I, 194–5; HMC *Verney*, p. 475; Knights, *Politics and Opinion*, pp. 221–2.

[4] Newgate L.c. 804, 832, 834, 836–8 (28 June and 8, 11, 15, 18, 20 Sept. 1679); *Domestick Intelligence* 22 (19 Sept. 1679); HMC *Verney*, p. 475; *London's Choice of Citizens to Represent them in the Ensuing Parliament . . . October 7th. 1679*, p. 2; *CSPD 1679–80*, p. 244; Haley, *Shaftesbury*, pp. 545–6.

counterparts. Loyalist merchant John Verney observed that the city had become strongly "divided between the mad separatists, and the Church of England men." Other loyalist spokesmen were already developing the rhetorical comparisons between this crisis and that of 1641–2 that would become so pronounced in subsequent Tory discourse. They perceived, in Player's demand for a doubling of the guards, an opposition assumption that the city had, separately from the crown, a right to provide for its military protection. The chamberlain's proposal reminded loyalists of how the Corporation's employment of its trained bands in the 1640s had contributed to Charles I's loss of the city. "It's commendable in Sir T. P. to cloak the old grudge ... under a cloud of Publick Safety," sneered one of Player's critics, who suspected the civic opposition really wanted to force Charles II's hand about the succession.[5]

If Player's actions seemed contemptuous of the king's authority over the militia, Jenks's shrieval candidacy was judged by loyalists as hostile to the social hierarchy and to the church. Jenks's friends had apparently organized a subscription to support his shrieval expenses, but one loyalist writer shuddered at the social consequences of a "Puppet Sheriff" indebted to those who chose him. "During his Office he must have been Pensioner to the meanest Trades-man of his Party." And that party was also a party as hostile to the Anglican church order as to the crown: they are "of the Old Cutt," a "Club" of "stiff Protestants" that "care not a straw for Bishops." As far as loyalists were concerned, too many of "the Publique Offices" of the city were already in the hands of "Factious Persons" affected by the spirit of "Jenkism." Jenks himself was compared to John Venn, the radical City MP of 1641, whose armed followers had intimidated bishops and MPs.[6]

Suggestions that a spirit of Protestant unity and cooperation were apparent in the Corporation's autumn mayoral and MP elections are surprising, in light of such public wrangles. According to one report, Sir Robert Clayton was "unanimously" chosen Lord Mayor on 29 September. Similarly, according to another source, when common hall assembled on 7 October to elect the city's new members, the electors chose their old ones (Clayton, Player, Love, and Pilkington) with great "Concurrence" and "Unanimity." But these suggestions of unanimity merely expressed an opposition claim to speak for

[5] LC MS 18,124, VI, 274 (23 Sept. 1679); HMC *Verney*, p. 475; *An Answer to the Excellent and Elegant Speech Made by Sir Thomas Player ... On Friday the 12th of September, 1679*; *An Answer to a Pamphlet Intituled, A Vindication of Sir Thomas Player* (1679), p. 3; *Vindicator Vindicated*, p. 2.

[6] *Answer to Vindication of Player*, pp. 2–3; *A Hue and Cry after the Reasons which were to have been given on Thursday last, Sept. 18. 1679. to the Lieutenancy, by Sir T. P. and Others* (1679), p. 2; *A Letter from J. B. alias Oldcutt, to his Friend Mr. Jenks* (1679), pp. 1–2; *Venn and his Mermydons; or, the Linen-Draper Capotted* (1679), pp. 3, 7–8, 10–11; Manning, *English People and the English Revolution*, pp. 25, 106.

the broad body of citizens. So did the procured "endorsement" of the old MPs by unnamed "Eminent and Moderate Conforming Divines," despite the fact that two of them were nonconformists.[7]

In fact, polarization rather than any moderate anti-Catholic consensus was the dominant characteristic of political opinion in London at this time.[8] A show of electoral unanimity in the October 1679 common hall was orchestrated, but a "great opposition and contest" had, in fact, preceded the election. Presbyterian diarist Roger Morrice complained of "violent" tactics employed by the political enemies of the old members. On the other hand, Sir Robert Southwell, who was hostile to the old members, complained about the "industry, arts and anxiety" used to promote them. John Verney observed "great banding for Parliament men, many being minded to pass by Sir T. Player and Mr. Pilkington, who stick like glove and hand together." As the liverymen assembled in Guildhall on 7 October, one protagonist of the old members was apprehended for dispersing "Bills or Tickets." For their part, Anglican loyalist spokesmen in the hall sought to dissuade like-minded electors from approving the old members, insisting, "*It's* no longer Papists and Protestants, but Fanaticks and Church-of-*England*-Men." Verney attributed the choice of the old members to "the industry of the noncoms," and another observer suggested that dissenters made up half the opposition to the "Yorkist party." Despite some uncertainty and confusion, two political camps were clearly apparent in London: polarization was producing two parties.[9]

Choosing their MPs at the conclusion of six weeks of county and borough elections for the new parliament, London liverymen also had unusual opportunities to sample a "swarm" of electoral pamphlets, many of which were directed to them in part or in whole. Loyalist literature warned repeatedly that the Protestant establishment and the monarchy were endangered by dissenters seeking to exploit the crisis for their own ends. "The Papists, Quakers, Levellers, Brownists, and Fifth Monarchy-men are all...Confederated together" against the church and state, warned one writer, while another feared the opposition would return the kingdom to its former "wretched Distractions."[10]

---

[7] *Domestick Intelligence* 25–7 (30 Sept. and 3, 7 Oct. 1679); HMC *Verney*, p. 475. Also see *The Speech of Sir Robert Clayton Kt. Lord Mayor Elect...29th of September 1679.*

[8] Compare J. Scott, "Restoration Process," *Albion* 25 (1993), 628, and Scott, *Restoration Crisis*, pp. 47–8, with Knights, *Politics and Opinion*, pp. 215, 219–26.

[9] Morrice, P, 209; Newdigate L.c. 844 (4 Oct. 1679); LC MS 18,124, VI, 274 (23 Sept. 1674); *London's Choice of Citizens* (1679), pp. 1, 3; *Domestick Intelligence* 26, 28 (3, 10 Oct. 1679); HMC *Verney*, p. 475; HMC *Ormonde*, NS, IV, 541 and V, 219.

[10] *An Impartial Survey of such as are not, and such as are, fitly Qualified for Candidates for the approaching Parliament* [1679], p. 2; *A Letter on the Subject of the Succession* (1679), p. 6; HMC *Fitzherbert*, p. 21.

The literary defenders of the Restoration status quo had good reason to be alarmed as opposition pamphlets of autumn 1679 reiterated the anti-episcopal themes already proclaimed by Danby's foes. Reformed Protestant and opposition writers attributed the current unsettlement of the Protestant church and state to the arbitrary and coercive practices of the bishops as well as to the threat of a Catholic successor. *An Appeal from the Country to the City*, the opposition pamphlet that gained the greatest notoriety in 1679, for instance, singled out "over-hot church-men" as those persons most likely to lead the country toward arbitrary government. Similarly, the *Character of Popery and Arbitrary Government* condemned the "covetous and sycophant Clergy-men" who had pushed some "*Danbean* Senators" to "set up absolute Monarchy to be *Jure divino.*"[11] And *The Freeholders Choice* claimed that the "*Gothick* Model" of government – founded upon the great principle of "*Salus Populi*, the preservation of the people" – had already collapsed almost everywhere because of the influence of "*Knavish and Time-serving Priests.*" Advocacy of liberty for conscience was also frequently sounded in these electoral attacks upon the established clergy: "'Tis these Wolves in sheeps cloathing," thundered *The Freeholders Choice*, "who have eaten up the people of God like bread" in their promotion of "Persecuting and Sanguinary Laws." Or as another writer maintained, "the great Interest of *England* at this day is . . . to encourage the conscientious, and to restrain none but such as would restrain all besides themselves."[12]

Debate about the succession was as central to the division of civic opinion in the autumn of 1679 as debate about the church. Writing from London in September 1679, one churchman affirmed that the "great Subject of Discourse here" is "the Succession of the Duke of *York*." An opposition piece that appeared after the city's selection of MPs argued that the liverymen's "owning of their former Choice of Parliament-men" was an endorsement "in them of the Bill of Exclusion." The *Appeal from the Country to the City* was hostile to limitations and supportive of the Duke of Monmouth's claim to the throne. In fact, nothing could have been more contrary to the premises upon which the opposition built their cases for parliament and against the church

---

[11] [Charles Blount], *An Appeal from the Country to the City for the Preservation of His Majesties Person, Liberty, Property, and the Protestant Religion* (1679), p. 2; [Charles Blount?], *A Character of Popery and Arbitrary Government, with a Timely Caveat and Advice to all the Freeholders, Citizens and Burgesses* [1679]. For an alternate interpretation of this electoral literature, see Knights, *Politics and Opinion*, pp. 206–10, 214–16.

[12] *The Freeholders Choice: Or, a Letter of Advice concerning Elections* (1679), pp. 2–3; Blount, *Character of Popery and Arbitrary Government*, pp. 2–3; N.Y. and N.D., *The Protestant Conformist: Or, a Plea for Moderation, Contained in a Letter from One Conforming Minister to another: and His Answer to it* (1679), pp. 6–8; *A Seasonable Warning to the Commons of England; Discovering to them their Present Danger, and the only means of Escaping it* [1679], p. 4; Knights, *Politics and Opinion*, p. 244.

than the succession of the king's brother. How could parliament be secured, inquired one outspokenly exclusionist author, if Charles were succeeded by one "who hates our *Parliaments* with an implacable hatred?" Moreover, to accept a Roman Catholic as head of the Protestant establishment would be to "make our Church a great Monster."[13]

The electoral propaganda of the autumn of 1679 illustrates, then, how the concerns of the Popish Plot had developed into the broader issues of the Restoration Crisis. Reformed Protestants and Anglican loyalists beheld the problems of the kingdom through contrary discursive traditions: they came to terms with recent political and religious experiences using quite different vocabularies. The inability of the crown and of the 1679 parliament to agree upon solutions to the questions posed by the Plot fed a widening ideological division in the country. In London, rhetorical polarization intensified in the wake of that failure, as long-standing arguments for conscience were sharpened into arguments against the church leadership. Already by 1679 the future language of London whiggism could be detected in the opposition electoral literature, with its combination of anti-Court, anti-French, and anti-episcopal language with a defense of conscience and individual rights. If future Whigs demanded a resettlement of the kingdom, future Tories, for their part, were already entrenched in a defense of the Restoration status quo as the only preservative against a return to 1641. And if loyalists could rely upon the privileges of the Corporation magistracy to maintain their position, the civic opposition was already well versed in the organizational arts of mobilizing electors, promoting petitions, circulating their perspectives in print, and arousing public opinion.

Petitioning for parliament, November 1679–January 1680

These civic divisions widened after the election of London's MPs for the new parliament. A series of unexpected events in the autumn of 1679 further alarmed civic opponents of the succession of the Duke of York. York returned to the capital on 12 October *en route* from his continental exile to the more strategic location of Scotland. Two days later, Shaftesbury was dismissed as lord president of the council. On the 15th, the newly elected parliament was prorogued from 30 October to 26 January 1680. On the 20th, Charles knighted three loyalist civic leaders, including the new sheriffs, reportedly imploring them to "have a care of those who are enemies to the Church."

---

[13] *A Letter on the Subject of the Succession* (1679), p. 1; *A True Account of the Invitation and Entertainment of the D. of Y. at Merchant-Taylors-Hall, by the Artillery-Men, on Tuesday October 21st. 1679*, recto; *A Most Serious Expostulation with several of my Fellow Citizens in reference to their standing so high for the D.Y.'s Interest at this Juncture of time* [1679], pp. 2, 4; Blount, *Appeal from the Country*, p. 7; *Seasonable Warning*, p. 2.

Charles's language and his decisions suggest that, having already rejected exclusion, he was now also rejecting any broad parliamentary resettlement of the church in favor of Danby's confessional church-state.[14]

Citizens divided sharply in their response to these events. The Corporation extended an invitation to the king to attend the lord mayor's banquet for Sir Robert Clayton at the end of the month. But the city's invitation failed to include York, which was "taken badly" by Charles. This omission was made good when James was invited to attend the annual banquet of the Honourable Artillery Company. The company was dominated by leading loyalist citizens, and James was its captain general. James's visit to the city was too much for those who hoped for a Protestant succession, however. An anonymous note pinned on the gate of the banquet hall announced that any who attended would be accounted by "true Protestants" as enemies "of the King & Kingdome & betrayers of the Priviledges of the Parliament ... & the just Rights and Interests" of the city. At the banquet itself, some diners declined to join a loyalist health to James, and he was greeted in the streets by cries of "*No Pope, no Pope; No Papist, no Papist.*"[15]

The prorogation of parliament until January deprived Shaftesbury and other opposition leaders of their chief political forum; and James's departure for Scotland deprived them of their chief political weapon, namely, a visible Catholic successor. The "meal tub" plot revelations of October threatened the opposition with a further loss of momentum to the crown and Anglican loyalists. Thomas Dangerfield's tale of an alleged dissenting and republican conspiracy for a rising, which supposedly involved Shaftesbury and Monmouth, was quickly exposed as a fraud. It nevertheless sustained Anglican suspicions and anti-sectarian rhetoric, and it found a measure of confirmation in Sir Thomas Player's recent militia intrigues. The credibility of several Popish Plot witnesses had also been so damaged, by this time, as to support loyalist doubts about the entire Plot business. Under these circumstances, the massive London pope-burning procession of 17 November 1679 was orchestrated by York's enemies with the intent of refocusing public attention upon the popish threat.

The 1679 pope-burning was organized and paid for by the opposition club that met at the King's Head tavern, generally referred to by historians as the Green Ribbon club. It featured much popish paraphernalia and personnel: dozens of impersonated Catholic priests, friars, and dignitaries

---

[14] Newdigate L.c. 852 (23 Oct. 1679); HMC *Le Fleming*, p. 163; Haley, *Shaftesbury*, pp. 548–51; Hutton, *Charles II*, pp. 381–5; Knights, *Politics and Opinion*, pp. 59–62.

[15] Journal 49, fol. 68; Newdigate L.c. 851–3 (18, 23, 25 Oct. 1679); *A True Account of the Invitation and Entertainment of the D. of Y.*; *Hatton Correspondence*, I, 198; HMC *Le Fleming*, p. 163; Knights, *Politics and Opinion*, p. 224. Also see *CSPD 1679–80*, pp. 253, 272; HMC *Verney*, p. 476.

were accompanied by hundreds of torchbearers. In a grand conclusion to the procession, the pope was "sacrificed to the Fury of the People . . . [as] the Arch-Enemy of mankind." The route through the city, starting in Moorfields in the north and continuing to Chancery Lane in the west, was carefully chosen to draw the greatest crowds at the close of the workday. Perhaps 100,000 spectators lined the streets. The ritualized violence of destroying the pope in the Chancery Lane legal precincts symbolically appropriated English law on behalf of this Protestant *auto-da-fe*. The prominence of the "murdered" London JP, Sir Edmund Berry Godfrey, at the procession's head served to stress the city's danger, while the opposition's rebuttal of the Anglican case against dissent was also on show. Satan accompanied the pope as counselor, supposedly advising him that his best ruse was to disguise the Plot as "a Protestant Plot, and burn the City again."[16]

A spectacle of this scale and iconographic complexity obviously integrated a variety of cultural messages. Attacking the Duke of York in print and in speech was unwise, but this solemn attack upon popery provided an acceptable alternative. And, as a cultural rite of purgation, or a ritual cleansing of the kingdom and the city of papists, the event enabled Protestant citizens to reaffirm their loyalty to the Reformation and to the historic Protestant monarchy. Some Anglican loyalists were probably made uncomfortable, however, by the inclusion with the popish personages of eight bishops and archbishops, who were visibly identified by lawn sleeves, surplices, and embroidered copes – long time objects of puritan derision. If the dominant message of the day was anti-Catholic unity, the procession also reflected the specific political agenda of those who organized it.

As York's succession was challenged by burning the pope, the Duke of Monmouth was again heralded in the city as a Protestant alternative. Following the advice of Shaftesbury, Monmouth returned to the capital in late November. In doing so, he outraged his father, who correctly regarded his presence as an invitation to disorder: the duke's arrival precipitated a wild and spontaneous release of Protestant sentiment in London and Westminster. As these celebrations continued, Shaftesbury and a caucus of opposition lords meeting with him employed Major John Manley (once a Commonwealth office-holder and MP) to gather signatures in the city for a petition

---

[16] *Domestick Intelligence* 39 (18 Nov. 1679). Also see HMC *Verney*, p. 477. Previous accounts include J. R. Jones, "The Green Ribbon Club," *Durham University Journal* 49 (1956), 17–20; S. Williams, "The Pope-burning Processions of 1679, 1680, and 1681," *Journal of the Warburg and Courtauld Institutes* 21 (1958), 104–18; O. W. Furley, "The Pope-burning Processions of the Late Seventeenth Century," *History* 44 (1959), 16–23; Haley, *Shaftesbury*, p. 557; Harris, *London Crowds*, pp. 103–6; Scott, *Restoration Crisis*, pp. 57–8; A. Marshall, "To Make a Martyr."

demanding that parliament sit in January as currently scheduled.[17] This was
the first step in a petitioning campaign that dominated the kingdom's political discussion for the next two months. Tens of thousands of electors in
London and several counties would express their dissatisfaction with the
Court through the signing of petitions on behalf of an immediate session.
Many others refused to sign or expressed reservations about these proceedings. From the beginning of the petitioning process, both petitioners and
their opponents, the "abhorrers," recognized the centrality of London to
the endeavor. As an effort to force Charles's hand, the petitioning campaign
would obviously have greater force if it succeeded in the capital.

Historians have generally recognized the importance of the petitioning
campaign that gained momentum in London and the country in December
1679. But older arguments that the petitioning represented the concerted
actions of an organized and exclusionist Whig party have given way before
revisionist claims that the protection of Protestantism and parliament, rather
than exclusion, was the issue and that the petitioning occurred without party
organization. The evidence suggests, however, that the succession drove petitioning, and that petitioning further divided parties already emerging from
the long-standing division of English Protestantism.[18]

At first, the petitioning effort in London fared poorly. Lord Mayor Sir
Robert Clayton was indifferent to it and to efforts to promote a parallel address to the crown for a January session from the Corporation. Despite his
long association with the civic opposition, Clayton preferred Protestant accommodation to division; and after being personally harangued by Charles,
he also recognized that the king was more likely to listen to the voice of the
kingdom in parliament than in petitions. When Shaftesbury and sixteen peers
proceeded with their own address to the king on behalf of a session, Charles
rebuffed them in person. He also issued a proclamation against popular petitioning and another delaying the session promised for January. Parliament
was put off for ten months, until November 1680, although Charles kept the
possibility of an earlier session open by moving toward November in a series
of short prorogations. Those already concerned that Protestantism and parliamentary government were endangered by a popish succession found little
security in the postponement of the session. Many in the city also rejected
the proclamation against petitioning as infringing upon their "undoubted
right" to communicate their concerns to the government. Printed petition
forms were circulating widely in London within a few days of the address

---

[17] Newdigate L.c. 868 (1 Dec. 1679); LC MS 18,124, VI, 302 (29 Nov. 1679); *CSPD 1679–
80*, p. 295; *Hatton Correspondence*, I, 203–4; HMC *Verney*, p. 478; Knights, *Politics and
Opinion*, p. 230; *Hatton Correspondence*, I, 206; Henning, *House of Commons*, III, 13.
[18] Scott, *Restoration Crisis*, pp. 58–9; Knights, "London's 'Monster' Petition of 1680," *HJ* 36
(1993), 39–67; Knights, *Politics and Opinion*, ch. 8.

of the opposition lords, while "Caballs" on behalf of a petition from the Corporation continued.[19]

What did the petitioners want? Although the text of the London petition does not mention the succession or exclusion, attention to the context of the petition suggests that this omission reflected tactical considerations rather than opposition priorities. As had also been the case with the Corporation petition of May 1679, the language of this petition was seemingly chosen to encourage the broadest possible support, an objective incompatible with explicit attention to the divisive issue of the succession or to the divisive strategy of exclusion. Instead, the short text of the petition focused upon the "hellish popish plot," the danger to king and kingdom, the need to impeach or try suspected conspirators, and other grievances to be redressed by parliament. This language was likely to appeal to those who feared York or who preferred Monmouth, even though it was also intended not to alienate those who supported the parochial order and hereditary succession.[20]

Who, then, actually signed the London petition? The king's proclamation, the noisy royalist condemnations of petitioning, the increased surveillance of the press, and the general atmosphere of crisis all seem to have discouraged subscriptions from loyalists and churchmen. Much contemporary evidence, on the other hand, suggests that the London petition was strongly associated with the Reformed Protestant and dissenting community that had dominated opposition circles in the Corporation since the late 1660s. One news writer described the London "ringleaders of the sectaries" as going about in late December with "their pockets lined with petitions."[21]

That dissent was the predominant factor in the circulation of the London petition is suggested by the only modern analysis of its 16,000 surviving autographs. The petition was signed by some thirty-five dissenting London clerics, including John Owen, Robert Ferguson, Stephen Lobb, and Vincent Alsop. The lead taken by these respected and visible dissenting teachers encouraged subscription by lay advocates of conscience throughout London, Southwark, and Westminster. The leadership of nonconformists in promoting the subscription was further recognized in the choice of individuals to present

---

[19] Newdigate L.c. 869–73 (4, 6, 8, 11, 13 Dec. 1679); LC MS 18,124, VI, 306–8 (8, 9, 11 Dec. 1679); *Domestick Intelligence* 47 (16 Dec. 1679); *An Answer to a Letter written by a Member of Parliament . . . upon the occasion of his reading of the Gazette of the 11th of December, 1679*, p. 4; CSPD 1679–80, pp. 296, 307–9; *Hatton Correspondence*, I, 207–10; Luttrell, I, 29; Haley, *Shaftesbury*, pp. 560–1.

[20] *Domestick Intelligence* 52 (2 Jan. 1679/80); Knights, "London's 'Monster' Petition," p. 43. A broadside printed to encourage signatures to the petition was similarly directed, very broadly, against the Catholic threat: *A Speech made by a True Protestant English Gentleman, to incourage the City of London to Petition for the sitting of the Parliament* [1680].

[21] Newdigate L.c. 874–7, 879, 881–2 (15, 18, 20, 22, 27 Dec. 1679 and 1, 3 Jan. 1680); LC MS 18,124, VI, 313 (25 Dec. 1679); *Domestick Intelligence* 48–9 (19, 23 Dec. 1679); CSPD 1679–80, pp. 307, 364; HMC Ormonde, NS, V, 238; Haley, *Shaftesbury*, p. 561; Knights, "London's 'Monster' Petition," pp. 45–6.

Table 4.1 *Definite or probable dissenters on London common council, 1678–1683*

	Seats	1678	1679	1680	1681	1682	1683
Inner City	113	20	23	30	30	23	25
Middle City	88	14	14	22	26	21	18
City Without	33	4	5	6	6	8	4
Total seats	234	38	42	58	62	52	47

it to the king. Among the eight chosen for this task were Henry Ashurst (the younger), Anthony Selby, and Francis Charlton. Ashurst was from one of the city's foremost Presbyterian families, while Selby, a onetime common councilman and militia officer, had been described in 1660 as "a dangerous Sectary." Charlton was apparently both Shaftesbury's kinsman and Richard Baxter's brother-in-law. Clearly, London citizens who had long advocated conscience against religious coercion saw the sitting of parliament as an important means for relieving this grievance. Although it made no explicit reference to the succession or to the resettlement of the church, the petition was nevertheless an instrument of those who favored exclusion and reformation.[22]

The crown was in no doubt that dissent was the engine that drove the petitioning campaign in London. Hoping to discourage the adoption of a separate petition from the Corporation, Charles ordered the lord mayor and aldermen to enforce the religious qualifications for the selection of common councilmen at the wardmotes on 22 December. Fifty-eight known dissenters were nevertheless chosen for the 1680 common council, almost one-quarter of the total and the highest number since 1660. (Table 4.1) Sir Robert Southwell immediately noted, "upon the change of several members the petition is much promoted." Charles responded by admonishing the aldermen not to accept unqualified common councilmen and by seeking to dissuade Lord Mayor Clayton from convening common council before 26 January, when parliament would be formally prorogued. The king also refused to hear the London petition when it was presented to him on 13 January.[23]

---

[22] *Protestant (Domestick) Intelligence* 56 (16 Jan. 1680); HMC *Leyborne-Popham*, p. 168; Woodhead, *Rulers*, p. 146; Knights, "London's 'Monster' Petition," pp. 48–59; Knights, *Politics and Opinion*, p. 234n.; D. J. Milne, "The Rye House Plot with Special Reference to its place in the Exclusion Contest and its Consequences till 1685," Unpublished Ph.D. thesis, University of London, 1949, p. 189; Greaves, *Secrets*, pp. 117, 181, 383n.

[23] Repertory 85, fol. 49; *Domestick Intelligence* and *Protestant (Domestick) Intelligence* 49, 50, 56 (23, 26 Dec. 1679 and 16 Jan. 1680); *CSPD 1679–80*, pp. 312–13; [Sir Roger L'Estrange], *Citt and Bumpkin* (1680), pp. 1–5; HMC *Ormonde*, NS, IV, 569; *Hatton Correspondence*, I, 215–16.

When Clayton bowed to opposition pressure and summoned a common council for 20 January, the very week of the prorogation, dissent was as much an issue as the consideration of a petition. Attendance was heavy, with 183 of 234 common councilmen present. Some of the absentees apparently stayed away for fear of being disqualified on religious grounds, a fate that befell nine of those present. Sir Roger L'Estrange claimed that at least another twenty or thirty in attendance were similarly unqualified, while still other dissenting common councilmen probably had no difficulties about qualifying. Two questions were put to a vote. The first, which stressed the lawfulness of petitioning for parliament, was affirmed without a division. The second, for a Corporation petition to the crown at this time, was rejected. The common councilmen approved the question by a margin of eighty-eight to eighty-six; but only six of twenty-one aldermen (including Clayton) supported it. Recorder Sir George Jeffreys spoke for an hour against the question on the grounds that petitioning "might endanger the City Charter." In the wake of the vote, Charles continued to insist upon the removal of unqualified common councilmen, and new wardmotes were reported in some wards as late as March.[24]

The petitioning campaign also raises questions about the political organization of opposition and loyalist parties in the city in the winter of 1679–80. A London petition of this size, with more signatures than the famous "root and branch" petition of 1640, could not have emerged without considerable organization. Roger North remembered how "Agitators, being choice Party Men, and well instructed, went to every free Voter" with petitions, the results of their efforts then being assembled by "a select Assembly or Club, who had this Administration in Charge." North's hostile recollections were shaped by subsequent decades of party quarrelling, but his language about centralized and extensive party organization must nevertheless be taken seriously.[25]

Some evidence supports the revisionist dismissal of party as a factor in London petitioning. Sir Robert Clayton still clearly had reservations, and he was not alone among opposition leaders in the Corporation: they seem to have been generally divided about the merits of petitioning as a tactic. One news writer reported "a strange division . . . amongst the brethren of the Cabal, who . . . have divided themselves into parties." The City MPs and their friends among the magistrates apparently declined the opportunity to present the popular petition. And, although those who did eventually present it were not the "factious citizens of noe great note" of loyalist caricature,

---

[24] Journal 49, fol. 90; Newdigate L.c. 890 (22 Jan. 1680); LC MS 18,124, VII, 9 (22 Jan. 1680); Morrice, P, 248; L'Estrange, *Citt and Bumpkin*, p. 5; *Protestant (Domestick) Intelligence* 58, 70 (23 Jan. 1680, 5 March 1680); *CSPD 1679–80*, p. 376; Grey, *Debates*, VII, 465.

[25] North, *Examen*, p. 542; Knights, "London's 'Monster' Petition," pp. 42, 64.

none of them was currently serving as an alderman or even as a common councilman.[26]

On the other hand, a strong argument may be made that the petitioning campaign was a critical episode in the emergence of Whig and Tory parties in London. The petitioning campaign forced thousands in London and elsewhere to determine squarely where they stood in the emerging divide between loyalist supporters of the king and opposition supporters of parliament. Individual decisions to sign or to refrain from signing made in the politically charged atmosphere of December 1679 and January 1680 were not easily retreated from, for they must often have been reached in a high state of political passion. Many of the most visible London Whigs of the next three years were to be found among the petitioners. Their signatures were often offered in groups, suggesting that petitioning was a bonding event for men who signed together and who remained associated together in clubs, on juries, in their neighborhoods, and at wardmotes.[27]

This argument is not made to deny the presence of a political or a religious middle in London during the Restoration Crisis. The point is rather that those in the middle in December 1679 and January 1680 – those who may have preferred anti-Catholic unity to religious or constitutional conflict – had to choose, publicly, between two opposite courses of action. Clayton, who hoped that an emphasis upon Protestant unity might attract "moderates" toward broader opposition objectives, is a case in point. Although the lord mayor preferred accommodation, both before and after the common council of 20 January 1680, he also chose to petition, despite Charles's mutterings that a city petition could initiate a civil war. Furthermore, the common council vote of 20 January was really quite unlike anything in recent Corporation history. Preceded by signs of preparation, both on the part of urban dissenters and on the part of the crown and the loyalist magistracy, the common council vote split the Corporation down the middle. A clear majority of common councilmen willing to petition for a goal known to be loathsome to the king had been returned at the wardmotes. The situation had been salvaged for the crown only by its deliberate intervention and by the strength of loyalism among the city magistrates.[28]

---

[26] Newdigate L.c. 883, 885–6 (5, 10, 12 Jan. 1680); LC MS 18,124, VI, 315 (30 Dec. 1679); *Hatton Correspondence*, I, 216; *CSPD 1679–80*, p. 364. In addition to Ashurst, Charlton, and Selby, the petition's presenters included Ellis Crispe (recent sheriff of Surrey); Sir Gilbert Gerrard Bt., MP for Northallerton; John Ellis of St Paul's Churchyard (recent sheriff of Hertfordshire); Thomas Johnson of Stepney; and Thomas Smith, bencher of the Middle Temple: *Protestant (Domestick) Intelligence*, 56 (16 Jan. 1680).

[27] Knights, "London's 'Monster' Petition," pp. 53–8.

[28] Newdigate L.c. 891 (24 Jan. 1680); Haley, *Shaftesbury*, p. 564; Knights, "London's 'Monster' Petition," p. 65; Knights, *Politics and Opinion*, p. 256.

Moreover, the vote had been conducted in a fashion highly prejudicial to aldermanic authority: it was determined arithmetically, by adding the aldermanic votes on either side to those of the common councilmen. As L'Estrange pointed out, this procedure represented a "bringing down" of "the *Authority* of the *City* into the *Major part* of the *Commonalty*." No attention had been paid to the traditional rights of the aldermen to vote separately from common council or to veto any action approved by the common councilmen. Although the opposition had lost the vote, the vote nevertheless reflected its consensual understanding of Corporation politics and its elevation of the legislative authority of common council over magisterial privilege. Asserted in the civic revolution of 1648–9, and again in 1675–6, these ideas would soon by identified with urban whiggism.[29]

The discourse of Corporation politics by January 1680 was also increasingly full of language about "parties" and their activities, language that became even more noticeable after the petitioning campaign. Talk of "cabals" and of a "dissenting party" in the Corporation was not new, of course, but the range of activities engaged in by individuals associated with opposition in the Corporation had noticeably broadened. Public subscriptions on behalf of opposition candidates for civic office and attempts to mobilize the city's military resources for objectives not shared by all citizens suggest a more sophisticated kind of organization than the civic opposition had mounted in the past. So do the orchestration of anti-Catholic public opinion and the launching of the most widespread petitioning campaign in the city's history.

The party of opposition was not alone, however, in contemplating and implementing divisive political strategies on behalf of distinctive religious and constitutional objectives. The polemical vilification of Player and Jenks in the autumn of 1679, the circulation of literature hostile to dissent and to "republicanism," and the public expression of sympathy for the Duke of York each suggests that loyalism (or the "prevailing party against petitions") was also taking on new forms of association and political action.[30] So do the heavy attendance of those opposed to petitioning at the common council of 20 January and the aldermanic effort to remove dissenting common councilmen. The condemnation of popery in which most Londoners had joined since 1678 could no longer obscure the extent to which citizens had divided between contrary solutions to the issues of the Restoration Crisis.

Waiting for parliament, February–October 1680

Within a week of the loyalist victory in the Corporation, Charles prorogued parliament again, this time until 15 April; and he declared his intention to

---

[29] Journal 49, fol. 90; Newdigate L.c. 890 (22 Jan. 1680); LC MS 18,124, VII, 9 (22 Jan. 1679/80); *Protestant (Domestick) Intelligence* 58 (23 Jan. 1680).

[30] *CSPD 1679–80*, p. 376.

bring the Duke of York back from Scotland. In the coming months, as Charles moved toward a session in November through short prorogations, and as he sought to re-establish his brother's public role, he also unintentionally stimulated further attention to the issues of parliament and the succession. Indeed, the sequence of prorogations gave the opposition in London and the nation a series of dates around which to focus their demands. York's return to the capital in February also provided them with a visible Catholic successor whose presence sustained anti-Catholic sentiment. In London, the dominant characteristic of these months was not the alternation between political calm and political agitation, but rather the further embodiment of contrary approaches to settlement in opposite political parties.[31]

The crown's success in the Corporation in January was celebrated in early March when the king invited himself and the Duke of York to a city dinner with Sir Robert Clayton. The lord mayor's March feasting of the king and his brother demonstrated that both Clayton and Charles were willing to promote an accommodation between the Court and the city. Charles hoped to encourage civic loyalty through a display of favor; but he also needed a city loan of £100,000. As chief magistrate, Clayton recognized that, despite his own vote for a petition, the interests of the city were scarcely served by continuing political warfare with the crown in the absence of a parliament.[32]

But this civic show of loyalty and the public salutations of the king and York that marked their early morning return to Westminster were not evidence that "the factious" had been reduced to silence. Seeking to turn the political tables on the Court by launching another anti-Catholic initiative, the Earl of Shaftesbury now came forward with information he had been accumulating for some time about an Irish plot. Whether by coincidence or not, Sir William Waller discovered, at almost exactly the same moment, a conspiracy of loyalist Westminster apprentices to burn Cromwell, the Rump, and the Solemn League and Covenant in a public demonstration on 29 May, the king's birthday. The apprentices allegedly also intended to attack the bawdy houses and the nonconformist meeting places. Waller and other investigators believed that the Earl of Ossory, the imprisoned Catholic lords, and other "eminent" papists had encouraged the apprentices for their own purposes, but their intention to burn both the symbols and the premises of urban nonconformity may instead point to the effective revival of anti-sectarian motifs

---

[31] Knights, *Politics and Opinion*, pp. 264–5; Spurr, *1670s*, pp. 288–91.

[32] When Shaftesbury requested that Clayton also treat the Duke of Monmouth, the lord mayor first agreed and then thought better of his decision. Newdigate L.c. 906–7, 910–11 (28 Feb. 1, 8, 11 March 1680); LC MS 18,124, VII, 23, 28 (24 Feb., 9 March 1680); *CSPD 1679–80*, pp. 399–400; HMC *Le Fleming*, p. 166; HMC *Ormonde*, NS, IV, 580, and V, 293; *Hatton Correspondence*, I, 224; Luttrell, I, 37–8; Haley, *Shaftesbury*, p. 568; Knights, *Politics and Opinion*, p. 264.

by loyalist writers. Accounts of these new conspiracies and subsequent "discoveries" of plans to fire the city and to assassinate Shaftesbury, Sir Thomas Player, and others provided topics for newsletter and coffeehouse embellishment into April.[33]

Opposition figures worked to turn these discoveries to political advantage as the time for parliament (15 April) again approached. Their labors reveal additional elements of party organization. Waller and Player gathered a meeting of some eighty persons at a city tavern to consider ways and means of combating the new dangers. Shaftesbury, Monmouth, and others of quality joined a "Club of Gentlemen" in Queen Street who gathered monthly for the same purpose. Delegations of anxious citizens, including one headed by Player and possibly encouraged by Shaftesbury, twice visited Lord Mayor Clayton to express their concerns; but Clayton assured them that the magistracy could provide "for the peace and safety of the city" without a meeting of common council or a doubling of the guards. Although these efforts did succeed in re-creating an atmosphere of anti-Catholic insecurity, they failed completely to dissuade Charles from announcing a further prorogation of parliament, until 17 May, and from removing some who had opposed his decisions from positions of authority.[34]

Another strong indication of the divided state of political opinion in London was provided when Clayton invited Edward Stillingfleet, Dean of St Paul's Cathedral, to preach at the Guildhall chapel. Stillingfleet's sermon of 11 May 1680, *The Mischief of Separation*, would prove the most famous sermon of the Restoration Crisis. The dean claimed, both in his preface and in the treatise he authored in defense of the sermon, that his theme was the promotion of Protestant union, as Clayton had requested; but this apology was lost on the London nonconformists he singled out as designing "new revolutions" to "make our breaches wider." According to Stillingfleet, the dissenters' demand for resettlement of the Protestant order was intended to "overthrow the present *Constitution* of our *Church*." Moreover, the papists were using their demand for reformation to destroy the episcopal defenses of the Protestant establishment. The advancement of conscience was really a Catholic horse before the gates of a Protestant Troy: if ever a general liberty of conscience were established in England, Catholicism would be free to rage within the walls. The ecclesiastical debate of which Stillingfleet's sermon was

---

[33] Newdigate L.c. 916–18, 920, 922 (25, 27, 29 March; 3, 8 April 1680); LC MS 18,124, VII, 34–5 (23, 25 March 1680); Morrice, P, 255; *A Protestant Prentice's Loyal Advice to all his Fellow-Apprentices in and about London* (1680), p. 3; *The Plot Reviv'd; or a Memorial of the Late and Present Popish Plot* [1680]; *Protestant (Domestick) Intelligence* 76–81 (26, 30 March and 2, 6, 9, 13 April 1680); HMC *Ormonde*, NS, V, 293, 295–7; CSPD 1679–80, pp. 421–4, 432; Haley, *Shaftesbury*, pp. 569–73; Harris, *London Crowds*, pp. 166–8.
[34] LC MS 18,124, VII, 43 (20 April 1680); *Protestant (Domestick) Intelligence* 78 (2 April 1680); HMC *Le Fleming*, p. 166; HMC *Verney*, p. 478; CSPD 1679–80, p. 426; Haley, *Shaftesbury*, p. 573; Knights, *Politics and Opinion*, pp. 260–1, 269.

a part will be examined further in Chapter 6. The point to be made here is that the "latitudinarian" Stillingfleet had encouraged the loyalist reaction against dissent and had rejected any thought of accommodating conscience for the sake of Protestant unity.[35]

As the debate about the church intensified, so did debate about the succession. Even before the king's serious illness of 13 to 18 May 1680, the issue had come directly to the forefront of public discussion. The tensions occasioned by the presence of the Duke of York at Court and by the posturing of the Duke of Monmouth in public fed the circulation of rumors, beginning in April, that Charles and Monmouth's mother had been legally married. The king's ensuing illness and the revival of fears about an immediate succession also coincided with the presence in London, for the prorogation expected on 17 May, of leading nobles and gentry. Disappointed again in their hopes for a session, the civic and parliamentary opposition blamed all on York. According to one of the pro-Monmouth tracts printed at this time, the king's brother ought to have been tried during an immediate session for his "manifold treasons and conspiracies."[36]

Lord Grey of Wark subsequently suggested that an opposition conspiracy had occurred, at the time of the king's illness, to prevent a Catholic succession, should Charles die. He also remembered that "many of the eminent men in the city" had assured Shaftesbury of their willingness to rise at this time. The lack of corroborating evidence about such a conspiracy leaves Grey's tale little more than a fascinating curiosity. But that serious conversations about the succession occurred in London at this juncture cannot be doubted: opposition parliamentary figures, including Shaftesbury, Buckingham, and Monmouth, continued to meet in the city for well-noticed dinners. In late June, moreover, Shaftesbury and his associates again attempted to force a session: their new strategy was to procure a petition for a parliament, as well as an indictment of York as a popish recusant, from one of the Middlesex grand juries.[37]

---

[35] Edward Stillingfleet, *The Mischief of Separation* (1680), esp. unpaginated epistle and pp. 3, 22, 38–9, 58; Edward Stillingfleet, *The Unreasonableness of Separation* (1681), esp. pp. ii–vii, xiv, xix–xxii, xxxix. Also see G. S. De Krey, "Reformation in the Restoration Crisis, 1679–82," in *Religion, Literature, and Politics in Post-Reformation England, 1540–1688*, ed. D. B. Hamilton and R. Strier (Cambridge, 1996), pp. 231–52.

[36] LC MS 18,124, VII, 45 (27 April 1680); Newdigate L.c. 940 (29 May 1680); *A Letter to a Person of Honour concerning the King's disavowing the having been married to the Duke of Monmouth's Mother* [1680] in *Somers Tracts*, VIII, 195–208, esp. 198, 205, 206, 208; Robert Ferguson, *A Letter to a Person of Honour concerning the Black Box* [1680] in *Somers Tracts*, VIII, 187–95; *His Majesties Declaration to all his Loving Subjects, June the Second, 1680*; *CSPD 1679–80*, pp. 487, 491–2, 502, 504, 508, 509; Haley, *Shaftesbury*, pp. 574–7, 579–80; Knights, *Politics and Opinion*, pp. 268–9.

[37] *The Reasons for the Indictment of the Duke of York presented to the Grand Jury of Middlesex* [1680]; Ford Lord Grey, *The Secret History of the Rye House Plot* (1754), pp. 11–13; Haley, *Shaftesbury*, pp. 576–7, 580–1.

This new initiative coincided with the London shrieval election that began on 24 June 1680. This event was the first of three highly charged shrieval contests in 1680–82 that determined whether loyalists or the civic opposition would dominate the juries and legal processes of London and Middlesex for the ensuing year. One historian has interpreted the 1680 election as the pivotal event in a "republican capture of London" by the city friends of Algernon Sidney.[38] It is better understood, however, as a watershed in the development of urban parties. The election also stimulated assumptions about the London sheriffs as spokesmen for the liveried electorate and for the freemen upon whose behalf the liverymen acted in common hall. This understanding of the sheriffs as the premier spokesmen for the people expressed the consensual and participatory desires of many Reformed Protestant guildsmen.

The election of Slingsby Bethel and Henry Cornish as Sheriffs of London and Middlesex for 1680–81 was accompanied by intense political maneuvring in the Corporation. The outcome of the election remained in doubt for much of the time between the original common hall and the ultimate declaration of the election over a month later. Both the numbers and the commitments of the 3,000 or more liverymen who gathered in Guildhall on 24 June point to prior organization and premeditation. According to Roger Morrice, all but about 400 of the electors came committed to Bethel, who did have a republican past, and to Cornish, a leading civic nonconformist. They also came in support of the adoption by common hall of a petition encouraging the king to meet parliament a week later, on 1 July, the date to which it had most recently been prorogued.

That these electoral preparations in the city coincided with Shaftesbury's endeavors to employ the Westminster juries for political purposes was surely no coincidence. However, Lord Mayor Sir Robert Clayton sought still to avoid divisive political agendas in the Corporation, probably fearing that the election of Bethel might provoke Charles. As the electors gathered in the hall, they learned that Clayton had previously picked George Hockenhall (another wealthy dissenter) at the bridge-house feast as his choice for shrieval office, despite how controversial the mayoral prerogative of naming one sheriff had recently become.[39]

Clayton's promotion of Hockenhall proved unacceptable: many liverymen insisted that the lord mayor's preference was a mere "*Ceremony*" and not "a positive *Choice*." For over three hours, loyalist Recorder Sir George Jeffreys, the current loyalist sheriffs (who were presiding), the common sergeant, and the aldermen attempted to put up Hockenhall alone for election as one

[38] Scott, *Restoration Crisis*, pp. 115, 162–73; Scott, *England's Troubles*, pp. 192–3, 436–7.
[39] Morrice, P, 261–2; *A True Account of the Proceedings at the Common-Hall . . . 24th of June, 1680*; Scott, *Restoration Crisis*, p. 165.

sheriff before proceeding to an election between Bethel and Cornish for the remaining office. "This the Livery-men would by no means admit, but insisted it was their undoubted Right to chuse [both sheriffs]: the whole Hall standing as one man for their Priviledges, Rights and Liberties." In the end, Bethel and Cornish were chosen. Sir Thomas Player was re-elected chamberlain, and Thomas Shepherd was chosen one of the two bridgemasters. But the common hall concluded in disorder. The sheriffs adjourned the hall rather than read a petition presented to them for the sitting of parliament, despite an almost "unanimous" chorus of "*Petition, Petition, Parliament, Parliament.*"[40]

What lay behind these unusual city scenes? The petition presented on 24 June demanded that parliament sit "until Justice shall effectually take place upon all the . . . Popish Conspirators" and until it had provided for the security of the king's person and the liberties and religion of his Protestant subjects.[41] The petition made no mention of exclusion or even of the succession, but to argue that the succession was only a secondary concern of those who promoted it would be unwise. The agitation of the Court and of the London reading public about the issues of the succession, over the previous several weeks, confirms that York himself was perceived by his enemies as the greatest of the "Popish Conspirators." And Shaftesbury was concurrently seeking to capitalize upon this fear before the urban juries. Those who promoted the June 1680 petition had also hit upon a new strategy for expressing their sentiments within the Corporation. Having failed to get a petition through common council, they were now seeking the support of the parliamentary electorate itself.

Resettlement of the church was as important as an immediate parliamentary sitting to those who promoted Bethel and Cornish. "It must be an union of Protestants, both moderate sons of the church, and modest Dissenters, that must keep up the Ballance" against popery, claimed one tract printed in their support. Bethel and Cornish were themselves prominent dissenters interested in accommodation with the church and an end to religious coercion. An Independent, Bethel had been an articulate advocate of toleration since the 1671 publication of his *Present Interest of England*. Cornish, a dissenting cloth factor, was described in 1680 as closely associated with Sir Thomas Player. Neither Bethel nor Cornish had qualified for office by taking the sacrament prior to election.[42]

---

[40] Newdigate L.c. 952 (26 June 1680); *A True Account of the Proceedings*; Knights, *Politics and Opinion*, p. 270.

[41] *A True Account of the Proceedings*.

[42] Cornish was also related, through his daughter's marriage, to Henry Ashurst Sr, the city's foremost Presbyterian layman, and to his son of the same name, one of the presenters of the January 1680 "monster" petition. L.c. 955, 959 (1, 10 July 1680); *A True Account of the*

The crown took immediate notice of the election; but the Privy Council was at first more disturbed about the attempt to petition than about who was chosen Sheriffs of London and Middlesex. On the very day of the common hall, Charles also prorogued parliament for another three weeks. While the Council focused upon the threat to York from the Westminster grand jury, the court of aldermen was left to deal with the election of two unqualified sheriffs. Seeking still to observe all proprieties, Lord Mayor Clayton declared that, because neither man was qualified, another shrieval election was required.[43]

A second common hall on 14 July 1680 was preceded by even more obvious preparations that involved Charles II himself. The promoters of Bethel and Cornish announced their intention to re-elect them; and both men qualified for office by taking the Anglican sacrament. Cornish's candidacy was enhanced by his return on 13 July as one of two nominees for the vacant aldermanic place for Vintry, but loyalists on the court of aldermen refused to act on his nomination. The crown made extensive efforts to block the opposition candidates. The Privy Council sought the advice of the attorney general about disqualifying electors who could not demonstrate that they had taken the sacrament. Clayton was summoned to Court to hear the king's displeasure about the endeavors of "soe many restlesse & uneasy spiritts" in the city. Charles provided a list of acceptable loyalist candidates; and, using Recorder Jeffreys as a personal intermediary, he sought to discourage Cornish from standing. On the eve of the second common hall, the king dined in the city with serving Sheriff Sir Simon Lewis to encourage loyalist electors. And, as the liverymen assembled in Guildhall, they were offered a piece of negative campaigning: a loyalist broadside prominently displayed Bethel's name (together with Shaftesbury's) as a member of the Council of State appointed by the Rump in January 1660.[44]

The common hall of 14 July 1680 was both "exceeding full" and even more acrimonious than that of 24 June. According to Secretary of State Sir Leoline Jenkins, the "fanatic party" or the "restless party" showed far greater "diligence" than the "honest men." After a speech by Jeffreys, the common sergeant sought to put in nomination only those names on the list approved at Court. But when "the major part of the electors" or "the partie"

Proceedings; CSPD 1679–80, p. 620; Luttrell, I, 49; Woodhead, Rulers, pp. 19, 52. Bethel revised and enlarged The Present Interest of England as The Interest of the Princes and States of Europe (1680).

43 Repertory 85, fols. 183, 188; Newdigate L.c. 954–5; 959 (1, 10 July 1680); LC MS 18,124, VII, 67–8, 72 (26, 29 June; 10 July 1680); CSPD 1679–80, pp. 525, 528.

44 Repertory 85, fols. 186, 188; Newdigate L.c. 956, 959, 961 (3, 10, 15 July 1680); LC MS 18,124, VII, 73, 75 (12, 17 July 1680); CSPD 1679–80, p. 560; HMC Ormonde, NS, V, 342–3; A True List of the Names of those Persons appointed by the Rump Parliament to sit as a Council of State [1680]; Haley, Shaftesbury, p. 582.

learned that Bethel and Cornish were not on the list, they refused to allow
the election to continue until their names had first been put in nomination.
Three loyalists were also put up: mercer Sir William Russell, druggist Ralph
Box, and packer Humfrey Nicholson. After "much contest on both sides,"
a show of hands demonstrated that Bethel and Cornish had at least four
times as much support as any of the loyalists. The presiding sheriffs declared
them to have the majority; but they also accepted a demand for a poll by the
adherents of Box and Nicholson. The common hall concluded in confusion,
however, as the supporters of Bethel and Cornish surrounded Lord Mayor
Clayton and the sheriffs, insisting that the poll begin immediately. Recorder
Jeffreys brought news of these events to the king, who delayed his departure
for Windsor and summoned Clayton and the aldermen to the Privy Council.
Charles warned them of "the danger the charters of the City will be brought
to," should disorder continue.[45]

The shrieval poll, conducted between 15 and 22 July, was another sign
of how different this election was from previous electoral contests in the
Restoration city. Poll books were kept open continuously at Guildhall as
the friends of parliament and the friends of the king sought to maximize
polling on behalf of their respective candidates. One loyalist writer complained in the wake of the election about the "many little Citizens" who
have "become . . . States-men, and instead of minding their Shops and Business, are herded into little Parties." Responding to the common perception that the election was "of vast consequence" to the nation, Secretary
Jenkins worked hand-in-hand with Jeffreys and Alderman Sir Joseph Sheldon on behalf of "our side," that is for the "Conformist" candidates against
their "Nonconformist" rivals. Jenkins wrote to the Bishop of London encouraging him "to engage your clergy to do their utmost that the well-
wishers to the Church and the King come to the poll" and defeat candidates
known to favor a new church settlement. And, as the poll continued to
show a majority for Bethel and Cornish, he encouraged the current sheriffs to talk to the deputies and common councilmen whom they trusted
to "glean" the wards for "honest men" who had not yet polled. Charles
himself was also involved again, dining publicly with Sheriff Lewis, and
bringing with him many courtiers to encourage the polling of loyalist
citizens.[46]

---

[45] Newdigate L.c. 962 (17 July 1680); LC MS 18,124, VII, 74 (15 July 1680); Morrice, P, 264;
CSPD 1679–80, pp. 554, 558–9; HMC *Ormonde*, NS, V, 349–50; HMC *Verney*, p. 479;
HMC *Kenyon*, pp. 116–17; Knights, *Politics and Opinion*, p. 271.

[46] Newdigate L.c. 963–4 (20, 22 July 1680); LC MS 18,124, VII, 76 (20 July 1680); *A Seasonable Address to the Right Honourable, the Lord Mayor, Court of Aldermen, and Commoners
of the city of London, upon their Present Electing of Sheriffs* (1680), p. 2; Luttrell, I, 51;
CSPD 1679–80, pp. 557, 558–9, 565–6, 567.

After a week, the sheriffs closed the poll, not because they were happy with the results, but because the crowd of people in Guildhall demanded "No more" voting. Even then, Clayton and the aldermen waited another week before summoning the liverymen to a third common hall to hear an announcement of the outcome. In the meantime, loyalist deliberation about the situation continued. Secretary Jenkins considered proposals to declare one or both of the loyalist candidates elected, despite the poll. But he ruled out any ministerial intervention that could be construed as "illegal and arbitrary": such an action might produce an uproar in the city reminiscent of 1641, and it would surely invite parliamentary attention. In the end, concession appeared a wiser course than confrontation.[47]

The results of the poll were announced as 2,483 for Cornish, 2,276 for Bethel, 1,428 for Box, and 1,230 for Nicholson. The proclamation of Cornish and Bethel as the duly elected Sheriffs of London and Middlesex was loudly acclaimed. City MPs Sir Thomas Player and Thomas Pilkington and Dover MP Thomas Papillon also presented Lord Mayor Clayton with a new petition on behalf of the "Commons of London." Professing their loyalty to the king and to the Protestant religion, the petitioners requested a sitting of parliament, which had been prorogued once again, to 22 August.[48]

The shrieval election was now over, but the efforts it had provoked on both "sides" were unprecedented in the Corporation's electoral history. The opposition had sustained its majority through two common halls and a week-long poll. The poll figures suggest that 95 per cent of the 3,700 participating electors had probably voted, in party fashion, either for the two opposition candidates or for their two loyalist rivals. And although the opposition had secured its candidates in the end, the election had also prompted an extraordinary working alliance between the Secretary of State and leading civic loyalists. Jenkins complained that "the[ir] party had exerted its utmost vigour and diligence and ours has been slack as they use to be," but the loyalist magistrates and ministers were, in fact, beginning to learn the arts of political maneuvre from "the party" they opposed.[49] The increasing employment of party language to describe what was happening in the Corporation was a testimony to the further development of parties in reality, although that language confirms that one party still surpassed the other in zeal and strategic finesse.

The argument that the 1680 shrieval election provided Algernon Sidney in particular and republicanism in general with a London "power base,"

---

[47] *CSPD 1679–80*, pp. 558, 560–1, 567, 569, 573, 575.

[48] Journal 49, fols. 111–112; Newdigate L.c. 967, 969 (29 July; 5 Aug. 1680); LC MS 18,124, VII, 80, 82–4 (29 July; 3, 5, 7 Aug. 1680); *Proceedings at the Guild-Hall in London on Thursday July the 29th, 1680*; *To the Right Honourable Sir Robert Clayton Kt. Lord Mayor of the City* [1680]; *CSPD 1679–80*, pp. 579, 581.

[49] *CSPD 1679–80*, p. 573.

on the other hand, accords with little of its actual history. An examination of the principal supporters of Bethel and Cornish, for instance, points to the Whig future rather than to the republican past. The prominent citizens who acted as overseers of the poll for Bethel and Cornish included merchants John Dubois, Peter Houblon Jr, Lucy Knightly, Thomas Pilkington, Thomas Papillon, and Samuel Swynoke and Chamberlain Sir Thomas Player. These men, several of whom had been active in civic opposition since the mid-1670s, were part of an emerging party leadership rather than of any republican vanguard. Dubois, Pilkington, Papillon, and Player were exclusionist MPs in the parliaments of 1679–81. They and their colleagues were largely of dissenting or French Protestant backgrounds. Those overseers who returned to civic politics in 1689, after the political vicissitudes of the 1680s, did so as leaders of the London Whigs.

Only Slingsby Bethel's reputation as a commonwealthman supports the suggestion that the 1680 shrieval election marked a "republican capture of London."[50] Bethel's behavior as sheriff did reflect the commonwealth principles implemented in the Corporation in 1649–53. Rejecting the extravagant feasting and public display associated with the office, Bethel lived modestly as sheriff, entertaining few, praising frugality, and condemning ostentation. He championed this "reformation" of the shrievalty as the commencement of an overhaul of magistracy itself and suggested that the Corporation had previously given more "eye to Wealth... than Parts or Vertue" in the selection of sheriffs and aldermen. Like Francis Jenks, who sought the shrievalty in 1679, Bethel wished to open the London magistracy to men of virtue, "without any regard to... ranks and orders."[51]

But these goals were not widely supported among those who acted politically with Bethel in 1680, and Bethel's republicanism was less straightforward than that of Algernon Sidney.[52] If Bethel was tied to the republican

---

[50] Vilification of the London Whigs on the basis of Bethel's republican reputation became a convention of Tory propaganda, achieving poetic fame in John Dryden's caricature of Bethel as a myopic saint who believed "that kings were useless, and a clog to trade." *Seasonable Address*, p. 2; John Dryden, "Absalom and Achitophel" (1681) in *POAS*, II, 477–8 (lines 586, 615); *The Vindication of Slingsby Bethel Esq; One of the Sheriffs of London and Middlesex* (1681), p. 3; *Animadversions on the late Vindication of Slingsby Bethel Esq* (1681), p. 1; *A Seasonable Answer to a Late Pamphlet, entituled, The Vindication of Slingsby Bethel, Esq.* (1681), pp. 3–4; *The Last Words and Sayings of the True-Protestant Elm-Board* (1682); Scott, *Restoration Crisis*, pp. 162, 165–7; G. S. De Krey, "Slingsby Bethel," *Oxford DNB*.

[51] [Slingsby Bethel], *An Act of Common-Council... for Retrenching of the Expenses of the Lord Mayor, & Sheriffs, &c.* (1680), p. 6; Slingsby Bethel, *The Present Interest of England Stated*, revised text (1680), as found in Slingsby Bethel *The Interest of the Princes & States of Europe*, 3rd ed. (1689), pp. 16–17; *Vindication of Slingsby Bethel*, pp. 6–8.

[52] Henry Cornish, for instance, was offended by Bethel's failure to provide the customary shrieval feasting; and Cornish was suspicious about Bethel's choice of Richard Goodenough, another man with a republican reputation, as under-sheriff. Newdigate L.c. 969 (5 Aug. 1680); LC MS 18,124, VII, 83–4, 93, 103 (5, 7, 28 Aug.; 21 Sept. 1680); CSPD 1679–80, p. 620; CSPD 1680–1, p. 39.

past, his public principles in 1680 were more broadly those of Protestant accommodation rather than coercion, of king-in-parliament rather than the prerogative, and of the Country rather than the Court. His professed targets were oligarchy in the Corporation and a grasping hierarchy in the Church rather than monarchy *per se*. In 1680, Bethel appealed to Charles II, as the great "Protector of the whole Protestant Party" in Europe, to tackle the menace of France. He advanced his own reformation of the London magistracy as a safeguard in case Charles's successor was not as "vertuous" as he. His official behavior could also be understood as a civic application of the Country reaction against Court corruption and extravagance that had swept the opposition into control of the House of Commons in 1679. Bethel spoke the moral language of English republicanism, but he did so with an accent he shared with London Reformed Protestants and their parliamentary friends.[53]

As a critical event in the development of party in London, the 1680 shrieval election also pointed to conscience and to consent as fundamental priorities of the nascent Whig movement. The success of Cornish and Bethel was upheld in some prints, for instance, as an example to dissenters to be of service in "Corporations, throughout the Nation." When the new sheriffs took the oaths of the Corporation Act, their behavior was defended, in language derived from John Humfrey, as an encouragement to the accommodation of conscience. Indeed, according to one tract, conscience might enjoin dissenters to hold office for the sake of reform and the frustration of arbitrary government.[54]

The election of the new sheriffs by a determined electoral majority against the wishes of both the predominantly loyalist civic magistracy and the crown also pointed to the consensual premises of the first London Whigs. The 1680 London shrieval election saw the publication of many tracts that assigned ultimate political authority in the Corporation to the people rather than to the magistracy. One opposition writer accused the "*Great Ones*" in the City of concealing from the "*Little* ones" the benefits they were entitled to under the city's chartered grants. Another writer characterized the sheriffs as the "servants to the common Hall" and claimed that "the Citizens of *London*, by their Charter...may Make Sheriffs whom they will, and may Remove them when they will."[55]

---

[53] [Bethel], *Act of Common-Council*, p. 8; Bethel, *The Present Interest*, revised text (1680) in Bethel, *The Interest of the Princes* (1689), pp. 25–31, 74, where he expressed his hostility to the established clergy as a member of "our Church."

[54] *An Account of the New Sheriffs, holding their Office* (1680), pp. 2–4; [John Humfrey], *A Peaceable Resolution of Conscience touching our present Impositions* (1680). The argument of *An Account* was repeated and enlarged in *The Sheriffs Case. Whether, and How they may lawfully Qualifie themselves* (1681) and *The Case of the Sheriffs for the Year 1682*.

[55] *The Abridgement of the Charter of the City of London* (1680); *The Citizens of London, by their Charter* [1680]; CSPD 1679–80, p. 564.

If the election of the new sheriffs encouraged civic dissenters and the assertion of popular principles within the Corporation, it also had implications for the utilization of urban juries against the threat from popery. The freedom of jurors from judicial manipulation had been an important point for the opposition ever since the cases of Penn and Mead and of Bushell in 1670. This objective had acquired greater urgency in the wake of Lord Chief Justice Sir William Scroggs's dismissal, before the completion of its term, of the Middlesex grand jury that had been considering a presentment against the Duke of York for recusancy. But in early August, many in London were assuring "themselves by the meanes of the New Sherifes . . . they shall at Least have such Juryes . . . as will not let those who shall come to their Tryall upon the account of the Plot come off."[56]

As London citizens continued to wait for a parliament, with varying degrees of impatience and apprehension, political exchanges between the civic opposition and civic loyalists escalated. Printed papers critical of the Duke of York were again distributed in the city in August; but on 15 September, York was treated by the Artillery Company at Merchant Taylors' Hall, despite a ruckus amongst the merchant taylors about lending their hall for this purpose. Popular anti-popery was released again, a few days later, when a crowd subjected Mrs Elizabeth Cellier (the principal contriver of the "meal tub" plot) to a brutal pelting in the stocks. Political tension was thus quite apparent in the city as the annual common hall for the election of a new lord mayor (29 September) approached. The court of aldermen had finally accepted Sheriff-elect Henry Cornish as the new alderman for Vintry. But the prospect of the mayoral succession of Sir Patience Ward, the senior alderman below the chair, was clearly not a happy one for his loyalist colleagues or for the king. Ward had been an outspoken enemy of the Duke of York in the 1679 parliament; and his religious dissent was notorious.[57]

In the event, Sir Patience Ward was elected lord mayor on 29 September without serious opposition, but that Ward would preside over a deeply divided city was apparent from the outset. A dinner hosted by the lord mayor-elect, after his election, was spoiled when a health, proposed by some, to the Duke of York prompted the departure of "halfe the Company." When Clayton took the new sheriffs to Court to present them to the monarch, Charles not only refused to knight them, as was customary, but failed even to receive them. And when the common council, meeting on the eve of the opening of parliament in October, and for the last time under Clayton, invited Charles to Sir Patience Ward's mayoral feast, the king declined to attend. In the

[56] Newdigate L.c. 995 (16 Oct. 1680); LC MS 18,124, VII, 84, 111 (7 Aug.; 10 Oct. 1680); North, *Examen*, pp. 90, 94.
[57] Repertory 85, fols. 224–225; Newdigate L.c. 972 (12 Aug. 1680); LC MS 18,124, VII, 101–2 (16, 18 Sept. 1680); Luttrell, I, 55; *CSPD 1679–80*, p. 592; *CSPD 1680–1*, p. 33; HMC *Fitzherbert*, p. 23; Henning, *House of Commons*, III, 668; Haley, *Shaftesbury*, p. 588.

meantime, Monmouth had taken up residence in the city, as the Duke of York prepared for another departure to Scotland.[58]

Sir Patience Ward began his mayoralty, then, as the magisterial leader of a particular party in London. The shrieval election of 1680 had given London electors and magistrates, both opposition and loyalist, many reasons to consider and to use new forms of association. The circulation of outspoken political literature, the protraction of common hall proceedings, and the vigorous competition in procuring liverymen for a poll all suggest that polarization of opinion in London had generated rival efforts at organization. That the names of Whig and Tory – originally labels of abuse – had not yet established their currency over the long-standing names of "fanatic" and "church" parties (and their variations) is no argument against the reality of party development in London between September 1679 and October 1680. If language develops in response to the need to name, then not surprisingly, the naming of parties followed, rather than preceded, the emergence of these new expressions of political principle, practice, and discourse. Party names could only become current as church and state loyalists – on the one hand – and advocates of parliament, conscience, and electoral rights – on the other – came to recognize and oppose the organized political activities of each other.

Neither is the occasional and discontinuous nature of political organization in London in 1679–80 evidence against the emergence of party at this time. Even in England's ensuing "first age of party," between 1689 and 1714, party organization was episodic, imperfect, and geared to the rhythms of parliamentary, corporate, and festive political calendars. Indeed, as the histories of many modern political parties demonstrate, occasional and imperfect organzation – organization that tightens only when electoral or deliberative affairs demand it – is often the norm. Similarly, the obvious "moderation" of Sir Robert Clayton, as compared to the passionate language and precipitous actions of Sir Thomas Player or Francis Jenks, really provides no argument for substituting "factions" for parties in London in 1680. The divergence between Clayton and Player or Jenks is merely an example of the frequently encountered party tensions between pragmatic office-holders and zealous activists. Clayton agreed with Jenks, Player, and Bethel on the necessity of a Protestant succession, parliamentary government, and a reformed religious establishment. His caution, as an official civic intermediary between the Corporation and the crown, simply placed him at one end of

---

[58] Ward and Clayton both spoke at the 29 September common hall on behalf of Protestant union. Journal 49, fols. 144, 146; Newdigate L.c. 989, 994 (30 Sept.; 12 Oct. 1680); LC MS 18,124, VII, 107, 112, 114, 115 (29 Sept.; 12, 19, 23 Oct. 1680); Luttrell, I, 56; *Hatton Correspondence*, I, 238; *The Speech of the Right Honourable Sir Patience Ward* (1680); Haley, *Shaftesbury*, p. 591.

a spectrum of opposition opinion about what strategies were most likely to achieve these goals.[59]

The Westminster Parliament

No resolution of the Restoration Crisis was to be achieved during the two parliaments that met between October 1680 and March 1681. The polarization of opinion had hardened during the long wait for a parliament, through seven prorogations; and the polarization of opinion made compromise over constitutional issues even more difficult to achieve. In London, contrary opinions were now advanced by contrary parties; and the party of opposition had, through electoral means, captured much of the city government. When a parliament finally opened, on 21 October 1680, the mayoralty, the shrievalty, common council, and common hall were all in the hands of those who favored a Protestant succession and a resettlement of the church through Protestant accommodation. Feeling that circumstances now favored the accomplishment of their objectives, Reformed Protestants in London and their political leaders were nonetheless to be sorely disappointed.

Such parliamentary opposition figures as Shaftesbury, Buckingham, Monmouth, and Sidney fully appreciated the political resources that London provided them with. Indeed, the parliament of 1680–81 may be said to have opened in the city, on the eve of the first day of the session, when a massive gathering of Country MPs and lords dined at the Sun tavern near the Exchange.[60] In other ways as well, the parliamentary opposition had moved as much to the city as the city had moved to them. London had become an independent factor in the crisis, as essential an arena for political maneuvre as parliament itself. Just as much as his father before him, Charles II had lost political control of his capital, and that loss had momentous consequences for the nation.

Scholarly debate about which parliamentary figure had the greatest influence in London has obscured the creativity of the city's own opposition leaders in capturing the Corporation as a Reformed Protestant redoubt. Moreover, the leaders of London's opposition party were to play essential roles in the two parliaments of 1680–81. City MPs Sir Thomas Player, Sir Robert Clayton, Thomas Pilkington, and William Love provided leadership in the Commons through their speeches and committee work. They were

---

[59] For loyalist appreciations of Clayton, see *An Humble Address to the truly loyal Citizens of London* [1679 or 1680], p. 3; and *An Humble Address to all the truly loyal Commons of England* (1680), p. 3.

[60] Newdigate L.c. 997 (21 Oct. 1680); Haley, *Shaftesbury*, p. 593.

joined in these capacities by several London opposition leaders sitting for other constituencies – men like attorney George Treby, Lord Mayor Sir Patience Ward, and merchants John Dubois and Thomas Papillon. Treby, who was considered for Speaker, was a major source of members' information about the Popish Plot because he had chaired the committee of inquiry about Catholic conspiracy in the previous parliament. He was also chair of the committee of elections and privileges, where six other London members joined him.[61]

These civic spokesmen acted in parliament as independent associates of the Country grandees rather than as dependant subalterns in a disciplined or centralized party organization. Nevertheless, their leadership of an urban opposition party brought party experiences and party perspectives to bear in parliament. Party in parliament in 1680–81 may have lacked the structured forms and unity of conventional Whig historiography, but party nonetheless tied the civic and parliamentary oppositions together, cementing the "strict correspondency" between the city and the Commons. Charles sought to sever those ties when he abruptly terminated his Westminster parliament in January 1681 in favor of one in Oxford. Only by separating the Commons from "the rebellious city" could he hope to break the party that commanded each.[62]

At Westminster, the first three weeks of Commons' debate were dominated by discussion of the security of the king, the kingdom, and the Protestant religion. Many members believed that the Catholic threat had intensified during the repeated prorogations they had experienced. Their discussions led quickly to a consideration of the succession: the Commons resolved, as early as 26 October, and without objection, that the suppression of popery in England could not be effected without also acting "to prevent a Popish Successor." The strategy of exclusion was, as before, thoroughly imbedded in the consideration of a broader set of measures intended to remedy the nation's ills and to preserve its fundamental institutions against all threats.[63]

On 2 November, the Commons affirmed the resolution of the previous parliament that "the Duke of *York* being a Papist... hath given the greatest countenance and encouragement to the present Designs and Conspiracies" and appointed a committee to bring in a bill to disable York from the succession. After the adoption of this resolution, London merchant John Dubois was the first speaker to urge adoption of a bill to prevent a popish successor. The committee appointed to draft such a bill included George Treby and City MPs Thomas Pilkington and Sir Thomas Player. Player's early speech

[61] LC MS 18,124, VIII, 119, 124 (2, 11 Nov. 1680); *CJ*, IX, 637, 644–5, 649–50; Grey, *Debates*, VII, 395, 433–5, 464; Henning, *House of Commons*, I, 597; II, 85; and III, 581–2.

[62] HMC *Fitzherbert*, pp. 23–4.

[63] Grey, *Debates*, VII, 365; Knights, *Politics and Opinion*, pp. 78–80, 275.

on behalf of exclusion was among the most forceful given during the entire session, and it was also an indication of how strongly some citizens felt:

The City of *London* will not be left out in this matter. I know not where in the world to find an Expedient to save our Religion and Properties, but this Bill of Exclusion. . . . As for that one argument, of a Civil War that may come upon this Exclusion, I would let the World know, that we are not afraid of War upon that occasion. . . . Let us . . . be in a condition to fight for our Laws and Religion.

On 11 November a bill to exclude James was passed by the House of Commons.[64]

The succession was not the only critical matter that required the immediate attention of the Commons. By the time of the 11 November vote about exclusion, MPs had also acted to safeguard the right of petitioning; and they had begun to work on plans for Protestant union and for the relief of dissent. London experiences and London MPs were in the forefront of Commons debates about the right of petitioning. Indeed, the efforts of London Recorder Sir George Jeffreys, who had sought to discourage petitioning in the city, became central to the discussion. On 27 October, the Commons condemned actions against petitioning for parliament as subversive to "the ancient legal Constitution of this Kingdom" after receiving a petition from "divers Citizens" of London complaining about Jeffreys. Treby, London merchant Thomas Papillon, and the four City MPs were appointed to a committee to inquire into the obstruction and "abhorring" of petitions.[65]

Two days after adopting the exclusion bill, the Commons proceeded to condemn Jeffreys for his interference with petitioning in the city. In debate, Pilkington said Jeffreys was "a common enemy to mankind, and I hope you will use him accordingly." Lord Mayor Sir Patience Ward, Sir Robert Clayton, and Sir Thomas Player also spoke against Jeffreys. The recorder was excoriated for his part in convincing the king that the behavior of "so good a People as those of *London*" was seditious. Sir William Jones argued that political behavior like that of Jeffreys was perfectly calculated "to bring a Civil War into the Nation"; and Sir Henry Capel recommended the condemnation of Jeffreys as the best means for maintaining a good rapport between parliament and "that brave and Protestant City." The Commons placed all four City MPs, as well as Dubois, Treby, and Ward on a committee to address the king for the removal of Jeffreys from all his offices.[66]

---

[64] Grey, *Debates*, VII, 150–1, 395–6, 406, 413, 459; *CJ*, IX, 644–5, 651; Henning, *House of Commons*, III, 251; Knights, *Policy and Opinion*, pp. 80–2; Scott, *Restoration Crisis*, pp. 64–72.

[65] Grey, *Debates*, VII, 371–2, 386–8, 390–1, 470–1; *CJ*, IX, 640–1; Knights, *Politics and Opinion*, pp. 276–7; Henning, *House of Commons*, II, 85, 763, and III, 203–4, 251, 581–2.

[66] Grey, *Debates*, VII, 372, 461, 463–5, 470–1; *CJ*, IX, 653, 657; *State Tracts* (1689–92), II, 103; HMC *Le Fleming*, p. 176; Henning, *House of Commons*, II, 85, 238, 763, and III, 245, 251, 581–2, 668.

Significant Commons' discussion about how to achieve Protestant union and how to end persecution also preceded the passage of the exclusion bill on 11 November. Dissenting London MP William Love, who frequently drew upon his experiences in the Cavalier Parliament, was the first to speak on this subject. He located the root of the country's political troubles in the adoption of the Corporation Act, which "set us all together by the ears," rejoicing that the country now had a "Protestant Parliament" in which those of "this or that persuasion will spend their blood for the Protestant Religion." On 3 November, the day after its resolution against York, the Commons also resolved to prepare a bill for "the better uniting of all his Majesty's Protestant Subjects." John Dubois spoke on its behalf; and he was joined by Love and Sir Samuel Barnardiston on the committee to prepare it. On 6 November, before turning to its second reading of the exclusion bill, the Commons further resolved that the Elizabethan and Jacobean penal laws ought not to be extended to Protestant dissenters and that the draconian law of 35 Elizabeth against sectaries ought to be repealed.[67]

As the House of Commons pursued the issues of the succession, of petitioning, and of the church, MPs found support and encouragement from the party of opposition in London. Lord Mayor Ward had conferred with Lord Grey, Thomas Thynne, and other parliamentary exclusionists when they attended his mayoral banquet with the Duke of Monmouth on 29 October. Indeed, the commencement of Ward's mayoralty had been turned by some citizens into a street celebration of Monmouth's claim to the throne. Even before the Commons' vote of 11 November, rumors were circulating that the Corporation would petition for exclusion. On the day after the Commons' action, Ward summoned a common council, which adopted a Corporation address to the king. It was drafted by City MPs Clayton, Pilkington, and Player. They had the assistance of MP John Dubois, who was also a common councilman for Cripplegate Within, and Walbrook common councilman Michael Godfrey, a younger brother of the city's Protestant martyr.

The petition admonished Charles "to hearken & incline to the humble Advice" of his parliament for the preservation of himself and the "true Protestant religion." As Roger Morrice reported, this address "meant more" than it actually said: it was designed to increase the pressure on both the Lords and on Charles to accept exclusion. The address said quite enough for the king, however. Upon his receipt of it, Charles rejected the address as a "way of petitioning [that] shall not do with me." He directed the common council

---

[67] Grey, *Debates*, VII, 374, 414, 422–5; *CJ*, IX, 645, 647; Henning, *House of Commons*, I, 597, and II, 238, 763; Horwitz, "Protestant Reconciliation," p. 205; Scott, *Restoration Crisis*, p. 68.

to keep to its own business, and he cautioned the lord mayor to "have a care of those men that would Inflame things."[68]

The city's efforts on behalf of exclusion, as well as those of the Commons, came to naught on 15 November, when the House of Lords threw out the exclusion bill on its first reading. The city's response to this rejection came in the pope-burning of 17 November. This affair was less extravagant than that of the previous year, perhaps because many of the organizers of the 1679 pope-burning were now focused upon parliament or were sitting in it. Charles was understandably alarmed, however, when he learned about another concourse at the Sun tavern, in the wake of the Lords' vote, and about the apparent intention of some to burn York in effigy as a "Ninny." The "mock procession" of 17 November 1680 did include effigies of loyalist propagandist Sir Roger L'Estrange, depicted as playing upon a fiddle, and of Sir George Jeffreys, as well as of the usual Catholic dignitaries, all of which were consigned to Protestant flames. "Thousands of people crowded the street & all cryed out no popery no D of Y," according to one observer.[69]

Exclusionists in both houses of parliament were understandably angry and disappointed at the demise of their bill. London MPs were amongst those who expressed their frustration on 17 November, when the Commons considered the king's request that they provide funds for his garrison at Tangier. "I was sent hither to mind the Public," said William Love: "and now [that] the Ship is sinking," he would not support expensive dynastic policies that might only "impoverish the Nation." City MP Sir Thomas Player was even more impassioned. Claiming to speak "in the name of the greatest part of the Commonalty of the City of *London*," Player reaffirmed their support for "excluding the duke of *York*." And agreeing with such Country spokesmen as Sir William Jones, Colonel John Birch, and Colonel Silius Titus, Player insisted the city would "not give a penny for *Tangier*, nor any thing else, till all be secured."[70]

To suggest, however, that a fixation upon the single unobtainable goal of exclusion now left the House of Commons at an "impasse" or that the session was now "certain to be barren" seriously misreads the enthusiasm MPs had

---

[68] Journal 49, fols. 156–157; Morrice, P, 276; Newdigate L.c. 1008 (16 Nov. 1680); Luttrell, I, 60; HMC *Ormonde*, NS, V, 487; Grey, *Debates*, VII, 433; HMC *Verney*, p. 479; *To the Kings Most Excellent Majesty. The Humble Petition and Address...of the City of London* (1680); Henry Sidney, Earl of Romney, *Diary of the Times of Charles the Second*, ed. R. W. Blencowe, 2 vols. (1843), II, 123; Haley, *Shaftesbury*, pp. 597, 599–600.

[69] Newdigate L.c. 1009 (18 Oct. 1680); *The Solemn Mock Procession: Or the Trial and Execution of the Pope and His Minister, on the 17. of Nov. at Temple Bar* (1680); CSPD 1680–1, pp. 86–7; Haley, *Shaftesbury*, p. 602; Knights, *Politics and Opinion*, p. 279.

[70] Grey, *Debates*, VIII, 10, 14–15; *His Majesties Message to the Commons in Parliament Relating to Tangier. And the Humble Address of the Commons to His Majesty in Answer... 29 Nov. 1680.*

already shown for other projects. As they continued to investigate the Popish Plot, the Commons also considered other expedients for securing the Protestant religion, parliamentary government, and the rights of subjects. These endeavors they shared with the Lords, who proceeded from their rejection of exclusion to the consideration of such other succession strategies as limitations, a five-year banishment of York, and the divorce and remarriage of the king.[71]

The number of bills about religion considered in the parliament of 1680–81 is noteworthy. Indeed, attention to the church issue demonstrates the desire of MPs of different perspectives to resettle the nation's religious establishment in the interest of Protestant union. The deliberations about religion in this parliament provided the most significant parliamentary discussions of the church between 1673 and 1689. Dissenting spokesmen like John Humfrey and Richard Baxter, who were widely respected in the city, joined with Anglican parliamentarians like Daniel Finch and Sir Edward Dering in trying to work out a new religious settlement. Had the session not prematurely concluded in another confrontation about exclusion, the Commons would likely have adopted both comprehension and toleration bills, although their success in the Lords was less certain. Great hopes were raised that the policy of coercion on behalf of a "narrow" establishment was about to give way to a broader church that would also recognize the rights of conscience. Nothing could have been more satisfying to the Reformed Protestant community in London that had provided so much of the language and leadership of the civic opposition for a decade. But these hopes were to be frustrated not only by the early conclusion to the session, but also by distrust and by disagreement, even amongst dissenters.[72]

The only bill about religion to pass both houses of parliament was that for repealing the Elizabethan anti-sectarian act of 1593. Additionally, the House of Lords adopted bills to safeguard Protestant dissenters from the penal legislation against Catholicism and to remove Catholics from London; and the Lords also considered various other bills for securing Protestantism, including a measure to encourage foreign Protestant immigrants. The Commons considered measures to ban papists from London, to remove pluralities, and to remedy abuses in the ecclesiastical courts; and they passed a bill to provide for the easier naturalization of alien Protestants. All four City MPs were named to a committee to bring in a bill to repeal the Corporation

---

[71] Haley, *Shaftesbury*, p. 603; J. R. Jones, *The First Whigs: The Politics of the Exclusion Crisis, 1678–1683* (1961), p. 141; Scott, *Restoration Crisis*, pp. 64–72; Knights, *Politics and Opinion*, pp. 82–91.

[72] Horwitz, "Protestant Reconciliation," pp. 204–17; Haley, *Shaftesbury*, p. 619; Lacey, *Dissent and Parliamentary Politics*, p. 145; Spurr, "Comprehension, and the Toleration Act," pp. 936–7.

Act, a measure that would have weakened the statutory discouragement of dissenting office-holding in the boroughs.[73]

But by far the most significant religious bills considered in the Commons were the measures for comprehension and toleration that were discussed on 21 and 24 December. The brevity of the recorded debates about these measures is no measure of the interest they aroused in parliament or in the nation. The authors of the subsequent *Just and Modest Vindication of . . . the Two last Parliaments* (1681), for instance, turned to the issue of toleration before all others, reminding Charles about his Declaration of Breda, pressing again for Protestant union, and condemning the policy of persecution. The formula of comprehension and indulgence considered in 1680–81 was the very formula that Presbyterian John Humfrey and others had advocated for a decade, and the bills also showed the influence of their 1673 predecessors. The first bill permitted dissenters to enter the church despite their reservations about some of the Thirty-nine Articles and accepted the Presbyterian ordination of clergy before 1660. The second bill permitted Protestants who remained outside the church to worship behind open doors. Each bill represented a significant accommodation for the sake of conscience: together they offered a new formula for religious peace among Anglicans, Reformed Protestants, and sectarians. William Love argued that the comprehension bill would overcome the division that so encouraged Rome: "I hope we shall now take all Dissenters in, to save the Nation, with heart, hand, and shoulder, to unite against Popery."[74]

Despite the Commons consensus that developed in favor of these bills, they were apparently not formulated, before the prorogation, in terms that all dissenters could support. Roger Morrice reported that "all I have heard of who desire Comprehension, desire Indulgence also for others, tho: multitudes desire an Indulgence that most fervently oppose comprehension." Perhaps this was, in part, because the comprehension bill failed to embrace the reformation of episcopacy or of the parochial churches, and would thereby

[73] Newdigate L.c. 1020, 1026–7 (16, 30–31 Dec. 1680); LC MS 18,124, VII, 128, 131, 140–1, 143 (22, 30 Nov.; 21, 23 Dec. 1680; 4 Jan. 1681); Grey, *Debates*, VIII, 133, 164; *CJ*, IX, 664, 677, 681–2, 687, 692, 695–7; Henning, *House of Commons*, II, 85, 238, 763, and III, 203–4, 245, 251; Haley, *Shaftesbury*, pp. 618–19; Horwitz, "Protestant Reconciliation," p. 204.

[74] Grey, *Debates*, VIII, 271; [Algernon Sidney and Sir William Jones], *A just and modest Vindication of the Proceedings of the two last Parliaments* (1681), pp. 6–8, 22–5; Knights, *Politics and Opinion*, p. 289. For this authorship of the *Vindication*, see Scott, *Restoration Crisis*, pp. 184ff. For pamphlet discussion of comprehension and toleration, see [Edmund Hickeringill], *The Naked Truth. The Second Part* (1680); [Herbert Croft], *The Naked Truth*, 2nd ed. (1680); [William Chillingworth], *Mr. Chillingworth's Judgment of the Religion of Protestants* (1680); *A Proposal Humbly offered to the Parliament, for suppressing Popery* (1680); *Vox Regni: or, The Voice of the Kingdom* [1680]; *A Collection of the Substance of several Speeches and Debates made in the Honourable House of Commons* (1681).

have left some Reformed Protestants with a difficult choice between comprehension and separation. In any case, twenty years of London discourse about conscience seemed finally to be bearing some parliamentary fruit.[75]

By December 1680, the Commons' animus against those who had frustrated the parliament's sitting by advising prorogations or by discouraging petitions had also found an outlet in several impeachment resolutions. Amongst these were the impeachment of Sir William Scroggs, Lord Chief Justice of King's Bench, whose June 1680 discharge of the Middlesex grand jury, before the conclusion of its term, had foiled an indictment of York as a recusant. Not surprisingly, London MPs took a strong interest in the issue of judicial conduct, which had disturbed many in the city in 1670 as well as in 1680. Thomas Pilkington and Sir Thomas Player joined William Love and Sir Samuel Barnardiston on a committee to examine the behavior of judges. Love also brought witnesses to report about Baron Richard Weston's inflammatory speeches at the Kingston assizes. Barnardiston seconded the motion for the impeachment of Sir Francis North, Lord Chief Justice of Common Pleas. Sir Robert Clayton and Sir Patience Ward reflected on the behavior of Scroggs. And not coincidentally, on the last day of its term, on 29 November 1680, a Middlesex grand jury empaneled under the new sheriffs presented York to King's Bench as a recusant.[76]

If Charles took a dim view of these attacks upon his ministers and judges, he was equally alarmed by the reappearance of exclusion in new guises by mid-December. On 15 December the king spoke to both the Commons and the Lords to request supply for Tangier and to assure them of his willingness to consider methods to secure Protestantism that also preserved the succession. But the Commons instead resolved both that York's succession was inconsistent with the preservation of the "Lives, Liberties, and Properties" of English subjects and that a Protestant association should be established by statute to protect the king against "any Popish Successor." In its reply to the king's speech, the Commons reasserted the case against James and declined to consider supply until the Commons' agenda had been accepted. In the House of Lords, Shaftesbury suggested that supply could not be voted while James was busy raising forces in Scotland.[77]

[75] Morrice, P, 288; Horwitz, "Protestant Reconciliation," pp. 209–11.

[76] Newdigate L.c. 1023 (23 Dec. 1680); LC MS 18,124, VII, 139 (18 Dec. 1680); Grey, *Debates*, VII, 407, and VIII, 35, 52–60, 67, 71–97, 207–8, 226–9, 237–50; *CJ*, IX, 688, 691–2, 697–700; *CSPD 1680–1*, p. 94; L. G. Schwoerer, "The Attempted Impeachment of Sir William Scroggs, Lord Chief Justice of the Court of King's Bench, November 1680–March 1681," *HJ* 38 (1995), 857–8, 867, 869–73; Haley, *Shaftesbury*, p. 618; Henning, *House of Commons*, III, 417–18.

[77] Grey, *Debates*, VIII, 132, 147, 162–3, 168, 171, 186–98; *CJ*, IX, 679–80, 684–5; [Anthony Ashley Cooper, Earl of Shaftesbury], *A Speech lately made by a Noble Peer of the Realm* (1681); HMC *Le Fleming*, p. 177; Haley, *Shaftesbury*, pp. 606–10, 613, 615. This hardening

As the session headed toward its dramatic conclusion, the opposition strengthened its position in the Corporation. The Commons' vote against Sir George Jeffreys led to his resignation as Recorder of London, and common council elected Commons leader George Treby as his replacement. The Duke of Monmouth dined in the city on the eve of the 15 December confrontation between Charles and the Commons about the succession. Monmouth's return to Westminster was marked by popular salutations. On the same day, City MP Thomas Pilkington joined the court of aldermen for Farringdon Without, significantly enhancing the opposition presence within the London magistracy. To no avail, Secretary Jenkins sought to discourage the return of nonconformists to the 1681 common council at the 21 December wardmotes. Instead, a "great alteration of persons" took place, "they generally decrying all persons as were abhorrers or hinderers of petitioning." Over one-quarter of those chosen for common council can be identified as nonconformists. (Table 4.1)

At about this time, Slingsby Bethel also sought to exercise his shrieval prerogative of naming a new city freeman, selecting the Duke of Buckingham for the honor. Loyalist aldermen blocked Bethel's move, however, suspecting that Buckingham intended, as a freeman, to secure magisterial office in the Corporation and to enhance the London–Westminster opposition alliance. Indeed, rumors spread that, should another prorogation now occur, many members would continue sitting, perhaps in the city, with the assistance of the lord mayor. In Scotland, York feared that some in the city intended "to sett up a republike," and he hoped that "those violent gentilmen [in the Commons] will be sent home."[78]

The final confrontation between Charles and opposition MPs came after the king's unbending response on 4 January 1681 to the most recent Commons' address. In an extended debate on the king's message on 7 January, those MPs still present reaffirmed their resolutions and demands of December, stating even more explicitly that "untill a Bill be passed for excluding the Duke of *York*, this House cannot give any Supply to his Majesty." On 10 January, when members learned that the king was about to summon them to the Lords for a prorogation, they considered a series of defiant resolutions. They condemned those who had advised the prorogation as betrayers of the kingdom. They requested the reinstatement of the Duke of Monmouth in those

of the exclusionist line produced divisions among those who had led the fight for exclusion in the Commons. Some MPs took the occasion of the Christmas holidays to absent themselves from a parliament that had embarked upon precipitous courses, further thinning numbers at a poorly attended session. Also see Knights, *Politics and Opinion*, pp. 78–91; Haley, *Shaftesbury*, pp. 615–16; Jones, *First Whigs*, pp. 153–4.

[78] Morrice, P, 279; Newdigate L.c. 1013, 1019, 1022 (27 Nov.; 14, 21 Dec. 1680); LC MS 18,124, VII, 132, 154 (2 Dec. 1680; 3 Feb. 1681); *CSPD 1680–1*, pp. 106–7; HMC *Dartmouth*, I, 42 (letter of 25 Dec. 1680 is misdated); *Seasonable Answer*, pp. 2, 6.

offices of which he had been deprived by York's influence. They repudiated "the Prosecution of Protestant Dissenters upon the Penal Laws" as "grievous to the Subject, a weakening of the Protestant Interest, an Encouragement to Popery, and dangerous to the Peace of the Kingdom." They resolved "that the Thanks of this House be given to the City of *London* for their manifest Loyalty to the King [and] their Care . . . of the Protestant Religion." Indeed, a motion was introduced that the Commons should retire to the city and continue the session in defiance of the prorogation.[79]

The Commons resolutions about religion and about the city again emphasized the political intimacy that had developed between the civic and parliamentary proponents of a Protestant succession and Protestant accommodation. Just as had been the case in 1640–42, London MPs and their followers had contributed their votes and their voices to the reformation of church and state. And just as the five members of 1642 had fled to the city, so some Westminster exclusionists in 1680–81 were apparently prepared to pursue their objectives from the refuge of the city. In the event, the session did not continue in the city, although the liaison between militant MPs and citizens certainly did. Opposition citizens and MPs alike remained committed to exclusion and to Protestant accommodation: they were outraged when the act for repealing the Elizabethan statute against sectaries was lost, apparently because Charles refused to have it presented to him for signature. Unfortunately for these advocates of conscience, their increasingly provocative behavior was now further stimulating an Anglican-loyalist reaction that would aid Charles in his actions against parliament and the city during the next two years.

The Oxford Parliament

The Restoration Crisis reached its ultimate but inconclusive parliamentary stage during the three months from the Westminster Parliament of 1680–81 through the Oxford session of March 1681. Both the crown and the opposition recognized that their struggle had reached a decisive point. Many feared that the crisis might lead to civil war, as a similar struggle had in 1642. Each side appears to have taken defensive precautions in case the other side resorted to arms. But some historians have been too quick to perceive Charles's success at Oxford as the end of the matter. With or without a parliament, the opposition was reconciled neither to the succession of the

79 *CJ*, IX, 702–4; *Votes of the House of Commons* 58 (10 Jan. 1681); LC MS 18,124, VII, 145 (10 Jan. 1681); Grey, *Debates*, VIII, 234–7, 284–5, 289–90; HMC *Finch*, II, 101–2; Knights, *Politics and Opinion*, p. 279.

Duke of York nor to the coercion of Protestants. And, although Charles prevailed in parliament at Oxford, he had yet to prevail in the Corporation of London, which quickly took the place of parliament.

The Corporation responded so rapidly to the prorogation of parliament on 10 January as to suggest that civic and Commons leaders had already discussed how best to deal with a royal curtailment of the session. On the very day of Charles's action, Lord Mayor Sir Patience Ward received a petition from "several Eminent Citizens" about the Corporation's security against "the horrid and devilish design of the Papists" now "heightned by the Surprising Prorogation of this present Parliament." The petition requested a doubling of the watch and a prohibition of the presence of any soldiers other than the city's own trained bands. Reminiscent of similar requests in September 1679 and April 1680, the petition suggested that the Corporation should see to its military security independently from the crown, foreshadowing the anxiety about arms that would soon contribute to the political division of the nation. The citizens' petition also requested Ward to summon a common council, which he did for 13 January. One news writer suggested that, "the whole House of Commons will be invited to dinner and also many of the Lords at the public charge of the Chamber."[80]

When the court of common council met, apparently without any extraordinary parliamentary contingent, the City MPs communicated the Commons' vote of thanks to the Corporation. An attempt by loyalist aldermen to read a new letter from the king against seating dissenting common councilmen was narrowly defeated. Instead, another petition was introduced by James Hayes, no stranger to petitions or to protest, which demanded that "this present Parliament" should assemble on 20 January, the date to which it had been prorogued, "and continue to sit until they have effectually secured us against Popery, and arbitrary Power, and redressed the manifold Grievances which at present we groan under." A committee that included such leading MPs as Recorder Treby, Sir Robert Clayton, Sir Thomas Player, and John Dubois was appointed to revise the document for submission to the king.[81]

Unlike the Commons' resolutions of 10 January, the city petition did not mention exclusion, the succession, or the Duke of York; but it was still designed to support the Commons. The four MPs who assisted in drafting it

[80] *Protestant (Domestick) Intelligence* 87 (11 Jan. 1681); *CSPD 1680–1*, p. 131; Luttrell, I, 63. The petition may also be found in *Vox Patriae* (1681), in *State Tracts*, II, 125.
[81] Journal 49, fols. 170–171; Morrice, P, 293; LC MS 18,124, VII, 147–8 (13, 14 Jan. 1681); *Protestant (Domestick) Intelligence* 88 (14 Jan. 1681); *True Protestant Mercury* 6 (11–15 Jan. 1681); *The Humble Petition of the Lord Mayor, Aldermen, and Commons of the City of London ... 13th of January, 1680* (1681), pp. 8, 10–11, and in *State Tracts*, II, 123–4; *CSPD 1680–1*, 132; HMC *Kenyon*, p. 125. The petition introduced by Hayes is also found in *Vox Patriae* in *State Tracts*, II, 126.

were outspoken advocates of exclusion, and Charles perfectly well understood what the petition meant. He gave it short shrift, warning Lord Mayor
Ward to check "men that desire you to medle with those things that doe not
Concern you." On 18 January he announced the dissolution of parliament,
and he issued writs for the election of another parliament to meet in Oxford
in late March. This news was greeted with anger in the city. "But I believe
there is none so foolhardy as to offer to rise," reported an observer, who
added that, although many citizens might "wish well to a rebellion" at this
juncture, "they dare not speak their thoughts."[82]

Such rumors about rebellious thoughts point to the gravity of the situation in the kingdom and its capital by January 1681. Parliament had
been prorogued and dissolved amidst irregular and angry proceedings in
the Commons; and demands had been made in London that the Corporation provide for its own military security, even by banishing royal troops
from its midst. No wonder Charles sought to meet a parliament away from
the alarming atmosphere of London. For their part, leaders of the opposition party in London divided over how best to secure a Protestant and
parliamentary resolution of the succession question. As one historian has re-
marked, this period was as much a crisis for the exclusionists as it was a crisis
about exclusion. Clayton and Treby, who were close to Shaftesbury, sought
to avoid any confrontation with the crown before the meeting of the new
parliament. But other opposition spokesmen like Chamberlain Player and
Sheriff Bethel were actively preparing for confrontation. They took considerable satisfaction when the court of aldermen agreed to Bethel's request to
grant a civic freedom to the Duke of Buckingham. Enrolling in the prestigious
Merchant Taylors' Company, the mercurial duke-turned-citizen appears to
have encouraged these more outspoken opposition leaders.[83]

Charles's announcement that parliament would meet in Oxford scarcely
settled the city. The juries of London and Westminster resumed their political
courses amidst reports of conclaves of opposition grandees meeting in the city
and of performances of Shakespeare's *Richard II*. The Duchess of Cleveland
and other persons of quality were indicted for recusancy on 18 January. An
indictment of the publisher of Shaftesbury's December speech in the Lords
was returned *ignoramus*. On the last day of their session, the Old Bailey grand
jury indicated that they intended a presentment against the royal troops who
had recently and "contrary to the Charter . . . marched through with their

---

[82] Those delegated to present the petition to Charles included a few leading civic loyalists who
had opposed it. LC MS 18,124, VII, 148 (15 Jan. 1681); *Humble Petition of the Lord Mayor*,
p. 8; HMC *Kenyon*, p. 125; *True Protestant Mercury* 7 (15–18 Jan. 1681); *CSPD 1680–1*,
pp. 137, 139; Knights, *Politics and Opinion*, pp. 280–1.

[83] LC MS 18,124, VII, 154 (3 Feb. 1681); Haley, *Shaftesbury*, p. 641; Knights, *Politics and
Opinion*, p. 79.

drums beating and coullers flying"; but they were discouraged in this course by Recorder Treby.[84]

These actions were undoubtedly related in some way to the efforts of Essex, Shaftesbury, and other opposition peers to persuade Charles to meet the next parliament in Westminster after all. The king's cool response to their petition of 25 January, which complained also of the loss of bills for Protestant accommodation, was followed by a move to procure a similar petition from common council. But Sir Patience Ward's sudden grave illness undermined this scheme: the lord mayor's presence was required for a meeting of the Corporation in common council; and Sir Robert Clayton declined to act as mayor *pro tempore*.[85]

The London members for the Oxford Parliament were chosen in common hall on 4 February 1681, the old City MPs being returned "without oppositione." The sources reveal relatively little about the election itself, but it was followed by the presentation to the City MPs of a common hall address. The first in a number of such constituency addresses in the 1681 parliamentary election, the London address was one of the most assertive. Indeed, such instruction of MPs about their future parliamentary behavior reflected the participatory understanding of the Corporation's constitution advocated by the party of civic opposition. The London address assumed that the City MPs were as much the agents and representatives of the electors in common hall as the sheriffs. It must be seen as yet another innovative step in the development of party purposes and strategies. It called specifically for the exclusion of the Duke of York, but the demand for exclusion was also part of a broader program. The City MPs were encouraged "to secure the meeting and sitting of frequent *Parliaments*; to assert our undoubted Rights of *petitioning* . . . to promote the happy and long-wished for Union amongst all his Majesties Protestant Subjects; [and] to repeal the 35th of *Elizabeth*, and the *Corporation Act*." The address could not more effectively have reflected the program of resettlement pursued by opposition MPs in the last parliament.[86]

[84] Newdigate L.c. 1032 (20 Jan. 1681); *CSPD 1680–1*, p. 138; *Protestant (Domestick) Intelligence* 87 (11 Jan. 1681); Luttrell, I, 64; Haley, *Shaftesbury*, p. 623.

[85] LC MS 18,124, VII, 151, 153 (22, 25 Jan. 1681); Newdigate L.c. 1039 (8 Feb. 1681); *The Earl of Essex His Speech at the Delivery of the Petition* (1681); *CSPD 1680–1*, p. 151; Haley, *Shaftesbury*, p. 623; Knights, *Politics and Opinion*, pp. 293–4. The peers' petition and Essex's speech are also in *Vox Patraie* in *State Tracts*, II, 129–30.

[86] LC MS 18,124, VII, 155 (5 Feb. 1681); *A True Narrative of the Proceedings at Guild-Hall, London, the Fourth of this Instant February* (1681); *Protestant (Domestick) Intelligence* 95 (8 Feb. 1681); Luttrell, I, 66; Haley, *Shaftesbury*, p. 627; Henning, *House of Commons*, I, 313; Jones, *First Whigs*, pp. 162, 167–73; Knights, *Politics and Opinion*, p. 295. The London address is also in *Vox Patriae* in *State Tracts*, II, 132. These city happenings were not without effect on neighboring constituencies. Sir William Waller was one of those returned at

The interval between the two parliaments of 1680–81 was also noticeable for the circulation of "libels" reflective of the opposite perspectives of the two sides to the controversy. The issue of the succession and the remedy of exclusion figured in this public discussion; but as in the recent past, they were part of a broader debate. Opposition claims about episcopal mismanagement of the church and opposition demands for Protestant accommodation were much to the fore in this literature. The *Address to the Honourable City of London* (1681), for instance, blamed the threat to the country's "ancient Apostolick Religion" as much upon the clergy as upon popery. Another piece, *The Certain Way to Save England*, dwelt upon the need to choose as MPs "Persons of as large Principles as the Gospel will warrant," persons opposed to persecution and pledged to the maintenance of "Civil Rights."[87] John Humfrey chose this moment to republish his arguments for a broadened Protestant establishment that would include both parochial and separate churches:

> It should be declared [by Parliament]...that the Church...consists of the KING as the Head, and all the several Assemblies of the Protestants as the Body....I would have all our Assemblies *that are* Tolerable, *to be made* Legal *by such an Act*, and thereby parts of the *National* Church, as well as the *Parochial* Congregations.[88]

But loyalists were little moved by these appeals, claiming that "commonwealth Protestants," who had been "in actual Arms against his Majesty" once before, were preparing again to "invade" the government of church and state.[89]

Westminster, where an address was presented that also called for exclusion and further investigation of the Plot. In Southwark, Sheriff Bethel was one of two opposition challengers to the loyalists who had sat in the 1680–81 parliament. Despite the appearance of Buckingham and Monmouth on behalf of Bethel and his colleague, the election was lost to the loyalists. In Middlesex, opposition candidates were returned, despite an improved loyalist poll; and an address was presented with instructions almost identical to those voted by the city electors. Newdigate L.c. 1040 (10 Feb. 1681); LC MS 18,124, VII, 158, 165 (12 Feb. 5 March 1681); *The Address of the Freeholders of the County of Middlesex* (1681); *How and Rich: An Impartial Account of the Proceedings at the late Election of Burgesses for the Borough of Southwark* (1681); *Vox Patriae* in *State Tracts*, II, 127, 133; Henning, *House of Commons*, I, 309, 316–17, 416.

87 Newdigate L.c. 1046 (24 Feb. 1681); C. B., *An Address to the Honourable City of London* (1681), pp. 2, 6; *The Certain Way to Save England* (1681), pp. 9–10; Knights, *Politics and Opinion*, p. 290. Hostility to the bishops was also evident in an action commenced in the London sessions against the Bishop of London by Edward Whitaker, Buckingham's attorney. E[dward] W[hitaker], *The Bishops Court Dissolved: or, the Law of England Touching Ecclesiastical Jurisdiction Stated* (1681).

88 [John Humfrey], *Materials for Union, Proposed to Publick Consideration* (1681), p. 5. Also see *From Aboard the Van-Herring* [1681], *England's Appeal to the Parliament at Oxford, March 21st. 1680/1, Votes of the Honourable, the House of Commons...in Favour of Protestant Dissenters* (1681).

89 *Vox Populi: or the Peoples Claim to their Parliaments Sitting* (1681), pp. 2, 4–6, 13; [John Nalson], *The True Protestants Appeal to the City and Countrey* (1681), pp. 2–3. Also see Newdigate L.c. 1053 (12 March 1681); Elkhanah Settle, *Character of a Popish Successor*

As the war of words escalated in the press, the government and the oppo-sition prepared to move from words to the defense of church and state by arms, should that prove necessary. Within days of the election of City MPs, a public dispute had broken out about an attempt by Sir Thomas Player to alter the leadership of the Honourable Artillery Company. At the Company's an-nual selection of assistants and officers on 9 February, Player spearheaded a move to replace individuals too closely associated with the Company's Captain General, the Duke of York. The intention of those who acted with Player was to elect him as leader of the Company in order to circumvent royal control of its military resources. Sir Joseph Sheldon, president of the Company, and other loyalist functionaries blocked this effort, however, by declining to proceed to a new election of officers.[90]

The Artillery Company episode is particularly revealing in light of the charge of a contemporary informer, subsequently echoed in Lord Grey's rec-ollections, that Shaftesbury and others were engaged in military preparations at this time. Yet another informer claimed that Player had solicited support from city militia officers for the attempted takeover of the Artillery Com-pany and for action against royal troops in the city, should that prove nec-essary. Player's explicit endorsement, in parliamentary debate, of resistance in defense of the constitution lends some credibility to this charge. Comple-menting these city scenes, the Westminster grand jury again presented York as a recusant and presented the king's foot and horse guards as a "grand nuisance."[91]

The most likely explanation of these events is not, however, that Shaftes-bury and Player (who had stronger ties to Buckingham) were planning to initiate resistance to the king. Rather, they were more likely attempting to secure what military resources they could in the event that the king mili-tarized the conflict. Charles I had tried to arrest the Commons' leaders in 1642, and Shaftesbury now apparently suspected that Charles II intended to arrest him and other exclusionists at Oxford. Player particularly feared a show of military force in the city by the Earl of Feversham, the colonel of York's troop of horse.[92] The opposition had long been concerned that royal forces commanded by a popish successor, or those acting under him, would act against Protestantism and parliament. Now they feared the same from Charles II himself.

(1681); *Address to the Honourable City of London* (1681), p. 6; [John Nalson], *An Essay upon the Change of Manners. Being a Second Part of the True Protestants Appeal to the City and Country* (1681); CSPD 1680–1, pp. 159, 213.

[90] *His Majesties Letter to the Artillery Company: With an Account of their Proceedings . . . the 9th. of this instant, February, 1680/1; True Protestant Mercury* 14 (8–12 Feb. 1681); CSPD 1680–1, pp. 157, 171.

[91] Grey, *Secret History*, pp. 14–15; HMC *Kenyon*, p. 126; CSPD 1680–1, pp. 178–9; Haley, *Shaftesbury*, pp. 624–5, 629.

[92] CSPD 1680–1, p. 178.

Charles was equally distrustful of the opposition leaders in London and parliament. He took steps to put down an urban rising, if one should come. The cannons on Tower Hill were relocated to the Tower itself and to Woolwich for better security. The names of the London lieutenancy were reviewed. The Earl of Craven, colonel of the king's guards, requested more precise directions about the disposition of his troops in the event of "opposition" in the city while the king was at Oxford. The Middlesex JPs were summoned to the Privy Council to hear the king's command that they take especial care, in his absence, about persons arming themselves beyond their station. The court of aldermen and Recorder Treby were invited to hear the king say that "he hoped the citizens designed nothing but obedience to him and the laws" during his absence. In order to prevent the election of Player as leader of the Artillery Company, Charles invited the loyalist officers to Court to inform them that he himself would become their leader. The lord mayor was ordered to undertake a search for arms at Moorgate; and as the king prepared to leave for Oxford, he ordered Craven, in his absence, to take all necessary measures to suppress any tumult or resistance "by killing, slaying or otherwise howsoever destroying" any offenders.[93]

These royal preparations, some of which were quite obvious, further agitated citizens who continued to hope for a parliamentary and Protestant resolution of the crisis. Ten days before the opening of parliament, it was reported that "most" of the common council and many other gentlemen would accompany the City MPs part of the way to Oxford. Monmouth, Shaftesbury, and other lords came to London to join this procession; and courtiers worried about the "design of the Mayor and his brethren to make too great compliments" to Monmouth. In imitation of these plans, but with "far other intentions," Southwark loyalists contemplated accompanying their MPs to Oxford *en masse*. After the Oxford debacle, the great "Cavalcades of so many hundred Armed Men through the Streets of *London* to attend some persons towards *Oxon*" were condemned by loyalists as intended "to awe their Sovereign into Compliance" with exclusion. Indeed, opposition preparations for Oxford were given the very "Character of a Rebellion" in loyalist rhetoric. In fact, however, the crown held all the cards in this military drama. Those who rode armed to Oxford did so largely out of fear – and out of the need to give public expression to their fear – rather than in order to force the king's hand.[94]

---

[93] Newdigate L.c. 1032, 1045, 1048, 1050–1 (20 Jan.; 22 Feb.; and 1, 5, 8 March 1681); LC MS 18,124, VII, 165–6 (5, 8 March 1681); PRO PC 2/69 (Privy Council Register), pp. 244–5; *Protestant (Domestick) Intelligence* 104 (11 March 1681); *CSPD 1680–1*, pp. 166, 184, 199, 204, 208, 211, 213.

[94] Newdigate L.c. 1051–2 (8, 10 March 1681); *The Character of a Rebellion, and what England May Expect from one* (1681), pp. 3–4; [Robert Hearne], *Obsequium et Veritas: or*

The atmosphere in Oxford during the parliament's weeklong session, beginning on 21 March, was that of a political circus in which the king and the exclusionists postured on behalf of their different agendas. Charles had no need for a vote of supply after secretly securing money from Louis XIV. His purposes were, in a short session, to demonstrate his own respect for the law and for the church and to make his opponents look rash and unreasonable, so that he might subsequently act against them. For their part, parliamentary leaders like Shaftesbury and civic opposition leaders like Player came in hope of pursuing their investigation of the Popish Plot, of demonstrating the necessity of exclusion, and of securing Protestant accommodation. Unaware of Charles's new financial security, they hoped they could persuade the crown to accept their agenda in return for a vote of supply.[95]

But Oxford was not Westminster, and many parliamentary conventions did not hold. To the political excitement of a session was added the confusion of meeting in unfamiliar surroundings and with unusual accoutrements. Rumors reaching London indicated that most MPs were attended by twenty or thirty persons "well armed," while the king was reported to be sending for an additional regiment of horse and for the guns stored at Deptford. Thousands of people without lodging were said to be camping in the fields about the town. There they might purchase pamphlets and lampoons directed against the bishops and against James, such as those being circulated by London citizen Stephen College, the "Protestant joiner." Or they could reflect on the allegations about new plots against parliament and the city, intended for 25 March, that were officially communicated from London to the king by Lord Mayor Ward. In the city, rumors that the streets would shortly "run with blood" were rampant; but parliamentary debate was now isolated from the volatile state of public opinion in the capital. As one observer noted, "our Grandees . . . are out of their element, having noe Common Council nor Coffee Houses to support them." Scarcely had members and hangers-on accustomed themselves to their surroundings when Charles cleared the town by his surprise dissolution of 28 March.[96]

Three issues in which the London opposition MPs were deeply involved dominated the business of the Commons at Oxford. One of these was the search for Protestant accommodation, the first substantive issue to which the Commons turned. On 24 March, John Hampden moved an investigation into the loss, at the end of the last session, of the bill repealing the Elizabethan

---

A Dialogue Between London and Southwark (1681); *CSPD 1680–1*, pp. 202–3, 211–12, 215–16; Haley, *Shaftesbury*, p. 632.

[95] Haley, *Shaftesbury*, pp. 622, 632–3; Jones, *Charles* II, pp. 166–8.

[96] LC MS 18,124, VII, 171 (26 March 1681); HMC *Finch*, II, 106; *CSPD 1680–1*, pp. 218, 224–5, 379; *CSPD 1679–80*, p. 423 (miscalendared); *POAS*, II, 425–31; Haley, *Shaftesbury*, p. 632.

statute against sectaries, in circumstances that he regarded as "a breach of the Constitution." When the Commons voted to request a conference with the Lords about those circumstances, a committee that included the four City MPs, John Dubois, and Thomas Papillon was voted to draw up the Commons' reasons.[97]

The London MPs were also involved in the case of Edward Fitzharris, the latest Plot witness. An Irish Catholic on the fringes of the Court, Fitzharris had been apprehended in London in February in the midst of preparing a seditious pamphlet that he intended to attribute to the opposition to discredit its leaders. Originally interviewed by the Privy Council, Fitzharris then sought to protect himself from the Court with a spectacular Plot deposition, given to Sir Robert Clayton and Sir George Treby, that reflected strongly upon York and the queen. Indeed, Fitzharris offered to reveal yet further details to civic and parliamentary opposition spokesmen in hope of saving himself from a treason prosecution. At this point, Charles silenced Fitzharris by moving him to the Tower; but when parliament assembled in Oxford, the opposition impeached Fitzharris in the House of Commons as a means of gaining access to him. Clayton and Treby were sources of information about Fitzharris for the Commons; and the committee charged with the management of his impeachment included Clayton, Sir Thomas Player, Thomas Papillon, and John Dubois. When the House of Lords voted that Fitzharris should be tried according to the ordinary course of law rather than through an impeachment, Player was a principal speaker during protests in the Commons. Implying that Charles was attempting to stifle the awful truth about the Plot, Player moved a resolution, adopted by the Commons, that any judge, JP, or jury who proceeded to a trial of Fitzharris was guilty of betraying the constitution.[98]

The London MPs were involved, thirdly, in bringing in another bill of exclusion, one for which the Fitzharris case simply provided a further rationale. Sir Robert Clayton initiated debate about the security of the realm and the Protestant religion on 26 March with his motion for bringing in a bill against York. Suggesting that he had considered all the arguments for expedients other than exclusion, Clayton insisted that only exclusion would prevent the country from falling "into confusion and disorder." Commenting both upon the nature of representation and upon how London electors understood their relationship with the City MPs, he cited his obligation to abide by the instructions of the London address: "we can discharge our trust

---

[97] Grey, *Debates*, VIII, 295, 300–2; *CJ*, IX, 708, 711; Henning, *House of Commons*, II, 85–6, 763, and III, 204, 245, 251–2.

[98] Newdigate L.c. 1057 (24 March 1681); Grey, *Debates*, VIII, 303–5; 332–8; *CJ*, IX, 709–10; Burnet, *History*, p. 180; Haley, *Shaftesbury*, pp. 629–31; Jones, *First Whigs*, pp. 174–6; Jones, *Charles II*, pp. 168–9; Henning, *House of Commons*, II, 85–6, 238, and III, 204.

no better, than to observe the directions of those that sent us hither." Sir Thomas Player had spoken earlier, in the city, about his support for another exclusion bill, supposedly maintaining that "the disposing of the Crown was in the Commons and as alterable as the changing of pipes between men." Clayton was the intended chair of the committee appointed at the conclusion of the debate to draft another exclusion bill, and Recorder Treby and John Dubois joined him on the committee. But by the time their bill was read the first time on 28 March, the opposition had already provided Charles with sufficient examples of their unreasonableness for him to take the high political road of dissolution in defense of the constitution.[99]

CONCLUSION

Ironically, the strategy of exclusion, upon which Shaftesbury and the Commons leaders had repeatedly fixed to resolve the crisis, was the greatest obstacle to a real parliamentary resettlement of the church and state – one that was also acceptable to the king, the Lords, and the bishops. Having exploded two parliaments already, exclusion exploded the Oxford Parliament as well. Throughout the period from the 1679 parliamentary election through the dissolution of the Oxford Parliament, the London opposition had contributed mightily to the political polarization of the nation that produced this result. Nowhere was hostility to York expressed so continuously between September 1679 and March 1681, or in so many different forms, as in London. Nowhere had opposition to York been integrated into a political movement so capable of expressing a broad program of reform in church and state. Nowhere had conscience and the succession become so intertwined in political reflections about the crisis. And nowhere could the disappointed supporters of a parliamentary and Protestant resolution to the crisis better turn, after Oxford, than to London.

Despite the menacing atmosphere that marked the Oxford Parliament, however, Charles need not yet have worried overly much about risings or tumults on behalf of exclusion. Exclusion was by definition a strategy that could be effected solely through parliament; and throughout the crisis, the supporters of exclusion had placed their hopes in parliament and in the electoral process rather than in arms. They could not have foreseen that Oxford was the last chance to achieve their preferred solution. The series of prorogations and dissolutions that followed the end of the Cavalier Parliament led them to expect that another parliament would follow. They feared the arbitrary government of no parliament under a popish successor, but what

[99] Grey, *Debates*, VIII, 309; *CJ*, IX, 711; *CSPD 1680–1*, p. 178; Henning, *House of Commons*, II, 85–6, 238, and III, 582.

they had so far experienced under this prince was the impeding of parliament rather than its abandonment. Only with time would it become clear that Charles had embarked upon a new course that threatened to undermine parliamentary government itself, as his opponents understood it.

From the beginning, the Restoration Crisis in London had been as much about who would control the city as about whether parliament could secure a new settlement. And for this reason, the crisis had produced political parties in the city some time before Charles met his last parliament. After Oxford, the city became the principal extra-parliamentary stronghold of those who continued to oppose a Catholic succession. The greatest asset of those who had fought York in parliament was now neither their strength in the Commons nor any show of arms, but rather a party in London opposed to popery and to arbitrary government. In control of the common council, the common hall, and the shrievalty, the London party of conscience, of the Protestant succession, and of electoral and parliamentary rights was the chief threat to Charles's reacquired ascendancy. The crisis about the settlement of church and state now became a crisis about the city of London, the outcome of which would determine the future of settlement in Restoration England.

5

The contest for the city, 1681–1682

INTRODUCTION: THE CITY WITHOUT PARLIAMENT, 1681–1682

The Oxford Parliament was over on 28 March 1681, but the Restoration Crisis was not. Too many historical accounts have depicted Oxford as a climax to the crisis in which the opposition was decisively out-maneuvred by the crown. Still other writers have moved quickly from Oxford to the Whig conspiracies of 1682–3, leaping over the evidence for a party confrontation in London and elsewhere in 1681–2.[1] In fact, however, the parliamentary opponents of a Catholic succession were even more determined after Oxford to ensure a Protestant succession and to promote a church resettlement for the benefit of Reformed Protestants. For their part, Charles II and Anglican royalists resolved, after Oxford, to resecure the existing settlement in church and state by all means necessary. The result of these political positions was an eighteen-month extra-parliamentary confrontation between the crown and loyalists, on the one hand, and the opposition, on the other. Contemporaries did not prejudge the outcome of this confrontation, and historians need to be more faithful in capturing the political uncertainty of 1681–2.

John Dryden and other loyalist authors drew attention to the king's new-found resolution when they proclaimed the beginning of a "second restoration" after Oxford. Rhetorical strategies employed by the crown and by loyalists in 1681–2 to redirect public opinion have been the subject of recent study.[2] But the resettlement of local institutions and the recovery of loyalist hegemony in boroughs and corporations throughout the country were as essential to this second restoration as the stroking of public opinion. Both processes required strong and concerted measures in the single locality in which disaffection to church and state had proved most damaging, namely the Corporation of London. The city remained as central to the crisis, after

---

[1] See, for instance, Scott, *Restoration Crisis*, pp. 270–4; Scott, *England's Troubles*, pp. 202–4, 380–2, 443–4.

[2] See especially P. Harth, *Pen for a Party: Dryden's Tory Propaganda in Its Contexts* (Princeton, 1993).

221

Oxford, as it had been before: Charles could not regain dominion over his kingdom without also regaining dominion in his capital.

This political struggle in the city was also a struggle between two parties. In 1679–81, the civic opposition had demonstrated greater political spirit and organization than civic loyalists. But in 1681–2, loyalists fashioned a more vigorous partisanship, employing religion and ideology, historical reflection, local organization, and ministerial support. The opposition had made party a reality in London by the time of the Oxford Parliament. In 1681–2, the urban opposition and urban loyalists together would make party even more apparent in the London guilds and wards and in the city's streets and press.

Gradually, during 1681, the political names of Whig and Tory gained greater currency. They served as alternates rather than substitutes for such other designations as "fanaticks, covenanteers, [and] bromingham protestants," on the one hand, and "tantivies, Yorkists, [and] high flown church men," on the other.[3] A variety of names for the party struggle in the Corporation will also be employed here. The Whig and Tory names were new, but the political phenomena they described were not new; or rather, new names were required for developing phenomena that found more frequent, more aggressive, and more critical expression in 1681–2 than before.

The political struggle in London resumed almost immediately after the Oxford Parliament, as Shaftesbury, Monmouth, and other grandees retired from a dissolved Commons to a dissatisfied city. Although one observer reported the city to be "wonderfully still," opposition tavern talk about what to do next was actually quite vigorous. So was that of urban loyalists; and within a fortnight of the Oxford dissolution, press skirmishes also resumed in earnest.[4] Four different but related contests were observable in the city over the next two years. Civic Whigs and civic Tories continued to contest about parliament. They also contested in the courts, and they contested about their different understandings of the best means to settle the national Protestant order. Finally, they contested for control of the Corporation itself. Each of these contests will be introduced here and treated in greater detail in the chronologically overlapping sections that follow.

The first of these contests was a continuation of the pre-existent division about parliament and the succession, a debate that was focused upon future remedy as well as upon past misdeeds. Within a week of Oxford, opposition figures in the city were considering the convening of a common council to petition the crown for another parliament. The inability of the ailing lord mayor, Sir Patience Ward, to preside at such a meeting foreclosed this option for the time being; but the issues of parliament and the succession were nevertheless well aired in the city. The king's April *Declaration* of reasons for

---

[3] Luttrell, I, 124.   [4] Newdigate L.c. 1060 (2 April 1681); HMC *Ormonde*, NS, VI, 32.

the Oxford dissolution and the answering *Vindication of the Proceedings of the two last Parliaments* were the opening salvos in an escalating paper war in which loyalist and parliamentary writers sought to influence public interpretation of recent events.[5] "Ever since the dissolution of the last parliament," Narcissus Luttrell commented in September 1681, "the press has abounded with pamphlets of all sorts, . . . some, branding the two late parliaments, and standing very highly for the church; the other side defending the parliament, and cryeing up . . . the true protestant religion, and opposing a popish successor."[6]

Especially noticeable in the early months of 1681 was the growing sophistication of loyalist efforts to influence the urban and country reading audiences. Sir Roger L'Estrange's *Observator*, which commenced publication in April, is the best known of a cluster of loyalist journals that combined the reporting of news with serious and satirical commentary. One early purpose of these journals was to encourage loyal addresses of thanks to the king for the Oxford dissolution and for his *Declaration*. The first such address came from the loyalist Middlesex JPs, as the party divide in London became a contest between those who favored petitioning for another parliament and those who preferred loyal addresses to the crown. In the Corporation, both the shrieval election of June 1681 and the mayoral election of September 1681 were contests between the party of petitions and the party of addresses.

A second, overlapping struggle in London was a contest for control of the law and the courts. In the past, the civic and parliamentary oppositions had cooperated in turning law and legal process against targets suggested by the Popish Plot. Not surprisingly, in the wake of Oxford, discussion of the indictment of York for violating the recusancy laws was revived in the Old Bailey sessions. Increasingly, however, the crown contested with the opposition for control of the courts, for control of juries, and for the appearance of legal propriety in its political strategies. The mid-April indictment of dissenting printer Francis Smith for republican language foreshadowed a series of trials that would climax with the November 1681 indictment of Shaftesbury for allegedly plotting against the crown.[7]

Indeed, as the crown developed its case against the parliamentary promoters of exclusion as conspirators or plotters, a battle of the plots was joined in the London courts and prints. Loyalists and Whigs advocated the mutually exclusive realities of a "Presbyterian plot" and of the Popish Plot. And,

---

[5] Newdigate L.c. 1060 (2 April 1681); HMC *Ormonde*, NS, VI, 27; *His Majesties Declaration to all His Loving Subjects touching the causes and reasons that moved him to dissolve the two last Parliaments* (1681); [Algernon Sidney and Sir William Jones], *A just and modest Vindication of the Proceedings of the two last Parliaments* [1681]. For the authorship of the *Vindication*, see Scott, *Restoration Crisis*, pp. 186–8; Haley, *Shaftesbury*, pp. 638–9. For loyalist propaganda and addresses, see Harth, *Pen*, pp. 78–86.
[6] Luttrell, I,124.   [7] LC MS 18,124, VII, 179 (16 April 1681); Luttrell, I, 73.

in the absence of a parliamentary session, the legal sessions of London, in which most evidence about plotting was aired, became the foremost political arena of the nation. But the crown was unable to gain control of the London shrievalty – and thereby of the selection of London jurors – until the autumn of 1682. By then, the succession of *ignoramus* verdicts by London juries empaneled by Whig sheriffs had probably done Charles more good than harm. These verdicts aided Tory journalists in depicting the Whigs as advancing their interests at the expense of law and justice.

A third struggle within the city pitted the advocates of religious coercion against the proponents of conscience, or the advocates of the episcopal church settlement against the proponents of a more inclusive Protestant order. The visibility of dissenters among the supporters of a Protestant succession had angered Charles, and the outspoken language heard in 1680–81 on behalf of Protestant union had outraged Anglicans. Speculation about the likelihood of a retaliatory prosecution of dissenters began immediately after Oxford. Moreover, the king's *Declaration* singled out the last-minute resolution of the 1680–81 parliament against the statutory coercion of dissenters as the best example of parliamentary contempt for constitutional propriety. In reply, the authors of the *Vindication . . . of the two last Parliaments* paid as much attention to the hazards of persecution, to the advantages of Protestant union, and to the malignancy of the established clergy as they did to the case for exclusion.[8]

This aggressive defense of nonconformity was perhaps not the wisest posture for the advocates of parliament and conscience to take. As the maturing loyalist press belabored the commonwealth pedigree of Restoration nonconformity, it effectively redirected popular anti-sectarianism toward Reformed Protestants and also redirected some popular anti-clericalism from the Anglican clergy to their dissenting counterparts. The loyalist reaction of 1681–3 was as much religious as constitutional, and it was also distinctly reminiscent of the fear of fanaticism that had undermined a broad church settlement in 1660–62. Anglican polemicists were almost as successful now as then in suggesting that the debate about the church settlement was really a question of maintaining the Anglican order or permitting the destruction of all Protestant order.

Fourthly, the struggle in the city was also a struggle about control of the institutions and offices of the Corporation. This contest was one in which very different interpretations of the civic constitution – and especially of the importance of electoral consent – were at work. The contest for the

---

[8] Newdigate L.c. 1060, 1062 (2, 7 April 1681); *CSPD 1680–1*, pp. 228–9; *His Majesties Declaration*, pp. 5–6; Sidney and Jones, *Vindication*, pp. 6–8, 24–6. Also see *A Letter from a Person of Quality to his Friend* (1681), pp. 6–7. For popular anti-nonconformity in the crisis, see Harris, *London Crowds*, pp. 133–44.

Corporation began within a few days of the Oxford dissolution when the ministry began work upon an alteration of the London lieutenancy. The government's intention was to remove "the officers of the party" from leadership over the London militia. Court fears about the military security of the city during the political build-up to Oxford made such an alteration of the militia predictable; but the alteration was also intended as a strong signal to civic electors about who should enjoy leadership within the Corporation. The crown's substitution of prominent loyalists in the London lieutenancy commission for "the angry party" anticipated the hand-in-glove cooperation between civic Tories and the ministry that would eventually deliver the city to Charles after a climactic shrieval election in 1682.[9] For their part, the London Whigs came to perceive the contest for the Corporation as being as much a contest with the ministry and the crown as it was a contest with civic loyalists.

The outcomes of these four contests in London were far from certain. Moreover, historical accounts that assume the inevitability of a Court triumph often overlook the hardening of partisanship in 1681–2 and fail to explain adequately why some Whigs were prepared to resist the regime in 1682–3. In fact, throughout the months from April 1681 to October 1682, London Whigs and dissenters employed party and pressure on behalf of parliament, the law, Protestant union, and civic right. As late as the summer of 1682, many of them expected to prevail. Only after the Whigs found themselves bettered in the political contests of 1681–2 did conspiracy become attractive to those who had lost confidence in ordinary political courses. Only after the most promising legal and political means of preserving rights, property, and Protestant conscience against "popery and arbitrary government" had been attempted, was resistance seriously considered. And even in the autumn and winter of 1682–3, as some Whigs turned to resistance, most London Whigs remained committed to securing their objectives through the legal and constitutional strategies they had pursued in 1681–2.

THE CONTEST ABOUT PARLIAMENT

The struggle about parliament and the succession embroiled the Corporation again within a month of the Oxford Parliament. In late April, the rival promoters of a petition to the crown for another parliament and of a loyalist address to the throne simultaneously appeared before the court of aldermen. The text of the proposed petition reiterated familiar Plot narratives and rejected a Catholic succession. Promoted by such opposition figures as

---

[9] Newdigate L.c. 1074 (10 May 1681); LC MS 18,124, VII, 177–8 (12, 14 April 1681); HMC *Ormonde* NS, VI, 31; *CSPD 1680–1*, pp. 228–9, 231, 260; Luttrell, I, 75–6, 83.

Sir Thomas Player, Sheriff Bethel, John Dubois, and Thomas Papillon, the petition was undoubtedly connected to Shaftesbury's latest political maneuvre. The earl became a citizen of London through admission to the Skinners' Company, a move, like that of Buckingham before him, intended better to enable him to employ the city as a political counterweight to the crown. But the circumspect aldermen endorsed neither the address nor the petition. Instead, they sent both groups home with an admonition "to live peaceably with your neighbours," a sentiment that was completely ignored.[10]

The opposition petitioners also requested the lord mayor to call a common council so that the Corporation might adopt their appeal. Suspecting that Sir Patience Ward would be only too happy to comply, Charles ordered him in writing not to do so and sent his principal secretary of state to visit Ward to reinforce the message. Intimidation failed Charles on this occasion, however, just as it had failed the Rump in August and September 1659. Ward summoned a common council for 13 May. He informed the secretary that the city was wronged by those who had encouraged the king so to interfere with its privileges as to interdict the meeting of common council. The crown's failed orchestration nevertheless represented a significant broadening of its role in the city and a considerable stimulus to loyalist efforts. Overcoming his dislike of "addresses and popular appeals," Charles approved Secretary Jenkins's intrigues with Alderman Sir Thomas Bludworth, father-in-law of Sir George Jeffreys. These discussions were designed to encourage loyalist common councilmen to reject any petition on behalf of a parliament. Similarly, Charles encouraged the procurement of loyal addresses from Middlesex, Southwark, the London lieutenancy, and the Tower Hamlets.[11]

The court of common council of 13 May 1681 was a highly charged affair preceded by much strategizing on each side. On the 12th, Secretary Jenkins reported having "been all this day in the City," where he consulted with ten aldermen and with "every man supposed to be a speaker at the Common Council." He was excited about the enthusiasm with which those "of our side" were prepared to "enter into a conflict." But common council nevertheless voted for a petition, thanked the City MPs for their service at Oxford, and refused to consider an address of thanks to the king for his *Declaration*. As in January 1680, the vote for a petition was determined arithmetically: eighty-four common councilmen and seven aldermen in favor of a petition, "in all ninety-one"; and sixty-six common councilmen and eleven aldermen opposed, "in all seventy-seven." The court's refusal to honor the aldermanic veto prompted "the king's friends" to withdraw. Those inclined to petition

[10] LC MS 18,124, VII, 185 (30 April 1681); *CSPD 1680–1*, p. 256; *The Protestant Petition and Addresse* (1681); *The Petition of Divers Eminent Citizens of London* (1681); Haley, *Shaftesbury*, pp. 640–2.

[11] Newdigate L.c. 1075–6 (12–14 May 1681); *CSPD 1680–1*, pp. 266–7, 268–9, 272–3.

proceeded with a draft that defended parliament against papist designs to "dissolve the Ancient Government" through the device of "a Popish Successor." In their retirement from common council, the loyalist aldermen adopted the rejected address of thanks and entered a protest in the aldermanic Repertory. But the common council majority found support in a parallel petition of a Middlesex grand jury on behalf of "Annual Parliaments, until the business of the Kingdom be done."[12]

This division of the city was also reflected when the petitioners and the addressers sought to communicate with the king. Sir Robert Clayton and others who presented the petition from common council were rebuffed when they appeared at Windsor. Charles complained "that persons of quallity used to have notice when Visitts was to be made to them." When rival city delegations appeared, with more notice, before the council at Hampton Court, the king expressed his gratitude to loyalist aldermen who communicated the supportive address from their colleagues as well as the loyal addresses from the outlying environs and the lieutenancy. But the presentation of the common council petition, in the name of the Corporation, elicited the king's condemnation of it as a "pretended" city petition that lacked aldermanic endorsement and was designed to encourage commotion throughout the kingdom. "You are not the Common-council of the Nation," he told the petitioners, charging them to mind the business of the city and to leave that of the nation to those whom it concerned.[13]

Charles's rejection of the Corporation petition for a parliamentary sitting certainly did not settle the matter in the city. The issue of parliament remained in the foreground as the supporters of parliament and loyalist addressers prepared for the mid-summer common hall at which new Sheriffs of London and Middlesex would be chosen. Preparations for this election had begun at the annual bridge-house feast, held shortly after common council's adoption of the petition, when Lord Mayor Ward offered a health to Alderman Pilkington, a nonconformist and a Commons' advocate of exclusion. This exercise of the customary mayoral "election" of one sheriff was an odd employment of privilege, coming from Ward.

After some public discussion of other possible opposition nominees for sheriff, including the Duke of Buckingham, a colleague for Pilkington was

[12] Journal 49, fols. 204–207; Repertory 86, fol. 128; HMC *Ormonde* NS, VI, 62–3; *CSPD 1680–1*, pp. 274, 276, 278, 279–80, 305; *A Brief Account of what Pass'd in the Common Council* (1681); *A True and Brief Relation of the Proceedings of the Common-Council* (1681); *The Humble Petition and Address of the Right Honourable the Lord Mayor* (1681); *The Presentment and Humble Petition of the Grand Jury for the County of Middlesex* (1681); *True Protestant Mercury* 37 (11–14 May 1681); J. Marshall, *John Locke*, pp. 227–8; Ashcraft, *Revolutionary Politics*, pp. 314–15.
[13] Newdigate L.c. 1076–78 (14–19 May 1681); Luttrell, I, 84; HMC *Ormonde* NS, VI, 66–7; *The Answers commanded by his Majesty to be given* (1681); *Savile Correspondence*, p. 203n.

found in Independent Samuel Shute. A personal friend of dissenting clerics John Owen and Robert Ferguson, Shute was also the son-in-law of Joseph Caryl and a member of a family identified with London congregationalism since its origins.[14] Rumors circulated that Charles was searching for a legal means to impose sheriffs of his own choosing, but such a provocative course was avoided, for this year at least; and the "King's friends" agreed to advance common councilman Ralph Box and loyalist Humfrey Nicholson in preference to Pilkington and Shute. Two weeks before the common hall, "greate striving" had developed between "One Party," which was as eager to petition for a parliament in common hall as it had been in common council, and civic loyalists, who assembled a week prior to the election at an Artillery Company feast. There they resolved to address Charles in support of "his prerogative to dissolve parliaments and to appoint what place he pleases for them to sit in," words that were welcomed by Secretary Jenkins.[15]

Electoral success was predicted for Pilkington, and also for Box. Indeed, the king's friends clearly decided to concede Pilkington's election, as resting upon a mayoral prerogative, in the hope of furthering the election of Box. The election of one sheriff from each party would neutralize the shrievalty. In the event, the majority of hands on 24 June was declared to fall upon Pilkington and Shute. A lopsided poll, declared three days later, gave Pilkington 3,144 votes and Shute 2,245 to Box's 1,266 and Nicholson's scant 84. Secretary Jenkins received a full report about this unpleasant result from an unidentified city correspondent. Shedding much light upon party organization and strategy at this juncture, Jenkins's correspondent also revealed that "the Tory party" could not yet match the electioneering finesse of the "dissenting partie."[16]

Ward's nomination of Pilkington at the bridge-house feast in May had, in fact, been a party ruse intended to draw to Pilkington's candidacy those loyalist supporters of magisterial privilege who were offended by the common council's recent overriding of the aldermanic veto. According to Jenkins's informant, the reason for Pilkington's strong support was "that as many gave their hands for his confirmation [as the mayor's nominee] as for his election." Only after Pilkington and Shute were declared to have a majority of the hands, did the former repudiate the lord mayor's bridge-house

---

[14] Shute was also, curiously, the king's draper, a sinecure that may have recommended him to some loyalist electors. LC MS 18,124, VII, 193, 196 (19, 26 May 1681); Newdigate L.c. 1092 (25 June 1681); *CSPD 1679–80*, pp. 274–5; De Krey, "Samuel Shute," *Oxford DNB*; Woodhead, *Rulers*, p. 149.

[15] Newdigate L.c. 1081–2, 1087, 1091 (28, 31 May and 14, 21 June 1681); LC MS 18,124, VII, 203, 205 (11, 16 June 1681); *CSPD 1680–1*, pp. 316–17. Addresses were also promoted at this time from the Inns of Court: Luttrell, I, 99–101; *POAS*, II, 440ff.

[16] Journal 49, fol. 226; LC MS 18,124, VII, 206–7 (18, 21 June 1681); Newdigate L.c. 1090, 1092 (21, 25 June 1681); Luttrell, I, 102–3; *CSPD 1680–1*, pp. 330, 333–5.

nomination and call for a poll, on the grounds that he could accept the shrievalty only "if he was chosen by the Commoners."[17]

Jenkins was also informed that the many "pains" taken for Box and the great presence of "persons of rank and quality" had initially yielded a strong show of hands for him. But Box's cause miscarried as "the faction" resorted to their "usual lying" customs. Rumors were spread that Box was "a most severe man against all private meetings" and that he "had married his daughter to a Papist." The sheriffs were said to have purposely set up so many polling tables that individuals could poll more than once without detection; and the poll was carried out not by the usual civic officers but rather by associates of Bethel, like the under-sheriff, Richard Goodenough. When the poll was declared before a second common hall on the 27th, Sheriff Cornish ensured a large attendance of "their party" by sending out messengers who warned that loyalists might attempt to launch an address. Instead, however, after the declaration of Pilkington and Shute, the common hall responded to the king's rebuff of the common council petition for a new parliament by endorsing it and instructing Charles to be guided "by his great council the parliament." But Charles was no more impressed by the common hall petition, at its presentation, than he had been by that from common council.[18]

The London shrieval election of 1681 was a signal victory for the civic supporters of parliament. However much Charles had taken the initiative, and however much loyalism had regained its political edge, the city of London was still a city of opposition. The adoption of a civic petition for a parliament in May and the election of Whig sheriffs in June were, in fact, the political high-points for the London opposition during the Restoration Crisis. But the leaders of the civic Whigs had little time to savor these successes. Within a matter of days, the entire debate about parliament had taken on a very different complexion. A series of arrests of important London opposition activists and parliamentary spokesmen climaxed with the 1 July 1681 warrant against the Earl of Shaftesbury. The charges against them of treasonable words and actions against the king – of words spoken and of actions considered in London, in Oxford, and in parliament – placed the proponents of parliament on the defensive.

In the wake of these arrests, the loyalist Anglican press loudly urged the case against Shaftesbury, the Whigs, and the opposition understanding of parliament's responsibilities. Tory writers enjoyed an ideological field day with their argument that the Commons had, in the late parliaments, sought

---

[17] *CSPD 1680–1*, p. 333; *Impartial Protestant Mercury* 19 (24–8 June 1681); *The Proceedings of the Common-Hall of London. The 24th of June, 1681.*

[18] Newdigate L.c. 1097 (7 July 1681); LC MS 18,124, VII, 210 (28 June 1681); *CSPD 1680–1*, pp. 333–5; *To the Right Honourable Patience Ward…The Humble Petition of the Commons…June 27. 1681*; Luttrell, I, 103.

"Dominion" over the king. They ascribed to the Whigs the political premise *"that the Authority of the king, being only Derivative, was inferior to the authority from whence it was derived, which was the Parliament."* Quickly, also, Anglicans turned the Popish Plot into a Presbyterian contrivance intended to destroy the church; and parallels between 1681 and 1641 were worked out in great detail. The fruits of an unchecked parliament, according to loyalist authors were the "Pillage, Plunder, Sequestrations, Decimation, Free Quarter, unheard of Monthly Taxes and Excises" associated with the Long Parliament.[19] The issue was no longer whether parliament should meet, according to the Tories, but whether having met repeatedly, the Commons had not also followed leaders who defied the crown and undermined both law and the constitution.

As much as any of those charged with treason, parliament was thus on trial in the legal proceedings that occupied London and the nation for the remainder of 1681. The contest in the London courts quickly became the talk of the town, but the contest about a parliamentary sitting was also renewed frequently in London from the spring of 1681 through the spring of 1682. It was always just beneath the surface of civic affairs, and it was easily brought to the fore.[20] Talk of a new session accompanied the London mayoral election in late September, for instance. One loyalist peer wrote then that "the coffee houses . . . are full of the discourses of a Parliament," and Sir Robert Clayton learned upon the Exchange that it would sit on 28 November. On his return to Westminster from Newmarket in early October, the king complained that "I came to town but last night & they are already sending me to Oxon to chuse a parliament, but I know nothing of the matter."[21] Expectations of a parliament nevertheless continued, prompted in part by the international tensions that followed Louis XIV's military occupation of Strasbourg and parts of Alsace. But domestic events, too, could feed hopes of a session. No sooner had Shaftesbury been released after the London *ignoramus* of 24 November, for instance, than he and his friends began preparing again

---

[19] *The Devonshire Ballad* (1681); *The Character of a Rebellion*, p. 10; *Advice to the Men of Shaftesbury* (1681); [John Northleigh], *The Parallel; or, the New Specious Association* (1682).

[20] Loyalist and opposition apprentices, as well as loyalist and opposition citizens, for instance, debated the settlement of church and state in rival petitions. Newdigate L.c. 1095, 1108, 1111 (2 July and 4, 11 August 1681); *To the Kings most Excellent Majesty. The Humble Address of the Loyal Apprentices* [1681]; *Vox Juvenilis* (1681); *Loyalty vindicated from the Calumnies* (1681); *A Vindication of the Loyal London Apprentices* [1681]; *A Vindication of the Protestant Petitioning Apprentices* (1681); *A Just and Modest Vindication of the many Thousand Loyal Apprentices* (1681); *A Friendly Dialogue between two London Apprentices* (1681); *A Letter of Advice to the Petitioning Apprentices* (1681); *CSPD 1680–1*, pp. 340, 435; Luttrell, I, 123; Harris, *London Crowds*, pp. 174–5.

[21] Newdigate L.c. 1133–5, 1137, 1142 (6, 8, 11, 15, 27 Oct. 1681); LC MS 18,124, VII, 252 (11 Oct. 1681); *CSPD 1680–1*, pp. 490–1; HMC *Ormonde*, NS, VI, 165.

for a parliament. In December, former Sheriffs Slingsby Bethel and Henry Cornish and former Lord Mayor Sir Patience Ward were said to be busy collecting depositions for Commons impeachments of the entire ministry for falsely procuring the evidence upon which the charges of Whig plotting had been based.[22]

Perhaps the most serious prospect of a parliament came from January to March 1682. The refusal of Louis XIV to withdraw from Luxembourg threatened to draw Charles into military measures against France in league with Spain and his nephew, William of Orange. War would make a parliament inevitable. And among Charles's ministers, Halifax both favored a parliament and reconciliation with Shaftesbury. Exploiting the crown's vulnerability, Whig civic and parliamentary leaders did all in their power, as will be seen, to revive the issue of the succession as a method of forcing a session. Indeed, the civic Whig leaders and the "protestant lords" reportedly agreed in March 1682 upon a five-point parliamentary agenda intended to prevent York's succession and to promote Protestant union. Louis's unexpected abandonment of Luxembourg in that month freed Charles from any immediate need for a parliament, but it did not end Whig excitement about one.[23]

In fact, however, no amount of Whig talk about the need for another parliament could procure writs from a king opposed to the parliamentary device of exclusion. Instead, the principal result of the petitions and addresses of 1681 and of the continuing public debate about the recent parliaments was an intensification of party division in many localities and at all social levels. And, the longer Charles avoided a parliament, the more he stimulated the growing Whig perception that the current king might be as hostile to the ancient constitution and Protestant "liberties" of England as his Catholic successor.

THE CONTEST IN THE COURTS

The issue of justice remained in the political forefront after Oxford as the London courts replaced parliament as the kingdom's principal tribunal. Since the beginning of the crisis, the opposition had turned parliamentary business into political theatre in the pursuit of justice against alleged Catholic plotters. Now the crown took the initiative in turning legal process into public drama, claiming that the opposition had resorted to treasonable conspiracies to force unacceptable measures upon the king. The November 1681 treason trial of

---

[22] Newdigate L.c. 1158 (8 Dec. 1681); *CSPD 1680–1*, pp. 615–16; HMC *Ormonde*, NS, VI, 257, 262–3.
[23] Newdigate L.c. 1175, 1177 (19, 26 Jan. 1682); LC MS 18,124, VIII, 30 (16 March 1682); Hutton, *Charles II*, pp. 409–11; Haley, *Shaftesbury*, pp. 685–6.

the Earl of Shaftesbury is the best-known episode in the crown's campaign to turn the legal tables on the opposition. But Shaftesbury's trial needs to be placed in the broader context of a multifaceted legal contest between the first Whigs and the first Tories in which the institutions of justice were thoroughly politicized. Convinced that their opposites were determined to undermine both law and the Protestant constitution, each side sought to legitimate its position in the courts.

This politicization of judicial processes was unprecedented in English practice, and it was also pursued in the press with an eye toward public opinion. Electors and readers were asked to consider the evidence about plotting and to come to their own conclusions. Was the real danger from a broadened Catholic campaign to undermine the constitution by discrediting parliament, as the Whigs claimed? Or was the real danger from opposition conspiracies to force the king's assent, out of parliament, to a policy he had refused to countenance, in parliament, as the loyalists argued?

The contest for the courts began as a contest for control of the Irish witnesses whom Shaftesbury had gathered for the prosecution of the Popish Plot. The dissolution of the Oxford Parliament left open the fate of Edward Fitzharris, whose allegations against York and the queen had given the opposition vital evidence on behalf of exclusion. After Oxford, Charles II was determined to destroy Fitzharris in the hope of driving the remaining Irish witnesses to the Court with stories of testimony purchased and prompted by the opposition. But when Fitzharris was indicted and tried for treason as the author of a seditious libel in the late spring, Shaftesbury's civic allies sought to preserve his life for their own purposes.

Sheriff Bethel chose reliable Middlesex grand jurors to consider the indictment. Foreman Michael Godfrey and attorney Sir George Treby challenged the legitimacy of an indictment against a defendant already impeached by the Commons. When Fitzharris was nevertheless found guilty by a Middlesex trial jury, Shaftesbury sought to preserve him by claiming that Fitzharris had knowledge about the origins of the Fire of London. But neither this claim nor Fitzharris's offer to the crown to make additional revelations saved his life. His final confessions were, however, of enormous significance in the party conflict in London and the nation. Fitzharris claimed that Lord Howard of Escrick was the author of the libel for which he was convicted, that Sheriffs Bethel and Cornish had forced his Plot testimony, and that Howard and other opposition grandees had intended to seize the king to ensure the exclusion of his brother.[24]

[24] Journal 49, fol. 224; Newdigate L.c. 1086, 1090 (11, 21 June 1681); LC MS 18,124, VII, 208 (23 June 1681); *CSPD 1680–1*, p. 334; *ST*, VIII, 243–426; Haley, *Shaftesbury*, pp. 643–51; Harth, *Pen*, pp. 86–9.

The crown held these explosive revelations in reserve until after the London shrieval election of June 1681. Then it proceeded with a series of arrests. Among those charged with plotting against Charles was Stephen College, "the protestant joiner," an outspoken plebeian poet who had recklessly satirized Charles himself. College was intimate with the Whig grandees, had built effigies for the London pope-burnings, and had agitated against the king at Oxford. London activist John Rouse was also arrested. He had served Sir Thomas Player in recruiting the Wapping crowd and in finding funds to maintain Plot witnesses. Finally, the arrest of Shaftesbury indicated whose head the government was really after.[25]

The indictment of College before a London grand jury, quickly after these arrests, became a trial run for the government's case against Shaftesbury. But College's London inquest also served as a painful reminder to the crown of what it had lost in the recent shrieval election. The jury empaneled by the London sheriffs was the first of the famous packed juries of 1681, and its *ignoramus* verdict of 8 July anticipated the result of the government's prosecution of the earl. A jury of nineteen citizens more sympathetic to the London joiner could scarcely have been imagined. Most of them were tradesmen, like College himself. Twelve of the nineteen can be identified as nonconformists. Merchant Caleb Hooke (the most substantial of these) was, like Sheriff-elect Shute, a member of the Independent meeting originally gathered by Joseph Caryl. No fewer than eleven, including foreman John Wilmore, resided near Shaftesbury in Aldersgate Without. In returning their *ignoramus*, these jurors were also affirming the reality of the Popish Plot and rejecting the government's case for a Presbyterian plot. But they also opened themselves to loyalist perceptions that their partisanship was inimical to the security of the realm.[26]

---

[25] Newdigate L.c. 1091 (23 June 1681); *CSPD 1682*, pp. 170, 391; North, *Examen*, p. 585; *POAS*, II, 12, 425–31; Haley, *Shaftesbury*, pp. 650–3; Harth, *Pen*, pp. 87–91; Harris, *London Crowds*, p. 101.

[26] BL Egerton MS 2543, fol. 251; *The Two Associations* (1681); HMC *Ormonde*, NS, VI, 98; PRO SP 29/421/160; Newdigate L.c. 1097 (7 July 1681); DWL Congregational Library MS 52.a.38; Ashcraft, *Revolutionary Politics*, pp. 412, 426; Haley, *Shaftesbury*, pp. 657–9; Harth, *Pen*, p. 91; B. J. Rahn, "A Ra-ree Show – A Rare Cartoon: Revolutionary Propaganda in the Treason Trial of Stephen College," in *Studies in Change and Revolution*, ed. P. J. Korshin (Menston, Yorkshire, 1972), pp. 77–98. Some of the College jurors were so deeply involved in opposition councils in London as to come under suspicion of plotting against the government in 1683. These included Samuel Mayne (the son of a trial judge of Charles I), John Wilmore, and shoemaker John Armiger, who was allegedly intimate with Richard Cromwell: *CSPD 1683 (July–Sept)*, pp. 98–9, 268–9, 349; *BDBR*, II, 231–3. Analysis of the juror lists for the College, Rouse, and Shaftesbury trials is based on numerous sources including CLRO Alchin B/33/15; *The Little London Directory*; Woodhead, *Rulers*; the appendices to Gary S. De Krey, "Trade, Religion, and Politics"; and Arthur G. Smith's reconstruction of the London livery of the 1680s, now in my possession.

Like the contest about parliament, the contest in the courts had thus become a contest about public perceptions of propriety and impropriety, of who was acting within the law and who without. Encouraged by the flood of recent loyalist addresses and by the fulsome rhetoric of the loyalist press, the government indicted College again, this time in Oxford, where he was found guilty of treason in August and executed. Although the Whigs quickly canonized him as "that Protestant Martyr St. Stephen College," the Court and its apologists also used College's conviction to vindicate their claims about opposition disloyalty. Indeed, even before College's Oxford trial, the government arrested John Wilmore, foreman of his London jury, claiming Wilmore's complicity in the same plot for which College, Rouse, and Shaftesbury had been charged.[27]

By late summer, the politicization of justice in London and Middlesex was complete. Loyalist Middlesex JPs responded to the College *ignoramus* by insisting upon a right, derived from an Henrician statute, to inspect all juries empaneled by the Sheriffs of London and Middlesex. As the crown considered the legal advisability of such a course, Justice George Jeffreys became chairman of the Middlesex JPs and Court manager of the Middlesex sessions. In late August, in simultaneous sessions in Middlesex and London, Jeffreys and the sheriffs contested for control of the urban courts. In Middlesex, Jeffreys inspired the JPs' objections to the many nonconformists among the grand jurors empaneled by Under-sheriff Richard Goodenough, a member of the Green Ribbon club. When Sheriff Bethel backed up his assistant, the JPs responded by fining him and his shrieval colleague. By contrast, at the city sessions at the Old Bailey, the Whig sheriffs had their way in the empanelment of grand jurors.[28]

This legal standoff continued into the autumn, as Shaftesbury's trial approached. When Under-sheriff Goodenough returned grand jurors for the Middlesex October sessions, Justice Jeffreys and the JPs objected to all but two of them (including Shaftesbury's onetime city agent Francis Charlton) as "desperate sectaries." And when the new sheriffs, Pilkington and Shute, declined the JPs' order for their immediate attendance at the Middlesex sessions, claiming the priority of pressing city business, they were fined £100 apiece for such contempt. But in this assertion of the city's autonomy from Middlesex, the sheriffs were supported by a vote of the "fanatic party" in common council, who agreed to pay their fines.[29]

[27] Newdigate L.c.1098, 1113, 1165 (12 July, 16 Aug., 24 Dec. 1681); LC MS 18,124, VII, 228 (20 Aug. 1681); *ST*, VIII, 549–724.

[28] Newdigate L.c.1120 (3 Sept. 1681); LC MS 18,124, VII, 232 (27 Aug. 1681); *CSPD 1680–1*, pp. 426–7; HMC *Ormonde*, NS, VI, 98, 144–5; Luttrell, I, 110, 119–20; White Kennett, *A Complete History of England*, 3 vols. (1706), III, 402; Harris, "Green Ribbon Club."

[29] Journal 49, fol. 263; Newdigate L.c. 1136–7 (13, 15 Oct. 1681); LC MS 18,124, VII, 251–3 (8, 11, 13 Oct. 1681); *Strange News from Hicks's-Hall* (1681); HMC *Ormonde*, NS, VI,

The issue in these events, according to Secretary Jenkins, was "having justice denied to the King in his own Courts." The Old Bailey sessions of 17–18 October, which began with arguments about the religious nonconformity of the grand jurors and ended with an *ignoramus* upon the government's indictment of Rouse, seemed to confirm the Secretary's fears. Loyalists were outraged by the "unsufferable... insolence" of the jury's *ignoramus*, claiming that most of the jurors were such "as go to church to salve appearances and to conventicles out of devotion." Many of them were said to have contributed to the very fund, ostensibly for the support of the Irish witnesses, the government claimed Rouse had instead collected for treasonable purposes. Both the composition of the Rouse jury and its verdict foreshadowed the outcome of the government's presentation of its case against Shaftesbury.[30]

As the ministry considered and rejected alternatives to the indictment of the earl before a jury empaneled in the city, the sheriffs and the London crowd made their own preparations for Shaftesbury's appearance at the Old Bailey on 24 November. The jury chosen by the Whig sheriffs was again distinctive: foreman Sir Samuel Barnardiston and jurors John Dubois and Thomas Papillon were well known to Shaftesbury as exclusionist MPs. Many of the twenty-one jurors were well-to-do merchants; nineteen were either nonconformists or French Reformed Protestants with ties to English dissent. Juror John Cox was himself a dissenting lay teacher, and Leonard Robinson was a member of John Owen's congregation.[31]

Most notable about Shaftesbury's jurors, however, is the strength of their previous commitment to opposition politics or their visibility as London Whigs for the remainder of the late Stuart period. Indeed, the composition of the Shaftesbury jury nicely illustrates the political continuity between the opposition that had emerged in London in the 1670s and the London Whig party of the Restoration Crisis and the Glorious Revolution. Fourteen of Shaftesbury's jurors had been associated with political opposition in London or in parliament since the May 1679 London petition or earlier. Others were equally prominent in urban Whig politics during the Augustan age. Dissenting juror Humphrey Edwin was the London lord mayor of 1697

154, 184, 188; Luttrell, I, 132–3, 134–5, 136, 139; *CSPD 1680–1*, pp. 496, 500, 509, 517, 520–1, 525; Haley, *Shaftesbury*, p. 669.

30 BL Egerton MS 2543, fol. 251; Newdigate L.c. 1138–9 (18, 20 Oct. 1681); LC MS 18,124, VII, 255 (18 Oct. 1681); *Impartial Protestant Mercury* 52 (18–21 Oct. 1681); *The Two Associations*, p. 8; HMC *Ormonde*, NS, VI, 193, 198–9; *Savile Correspondence*, pp. 231–2; Reresby, *Memoirs*, pp. 233–4; *CSPD 1680–1*, p. 500; Haley, *Shaftesbury*, p. 672. Ten of the nineteen jurors can be identified as nonconformists. Unlike College's London jury, the Rouse panel was made up of substantial citizens.

31 BL Egerton MS 2543, fol. 251; Newdigate L.c. 1150–1 (19, 22 Nov. 1681); *Impartial Protestant Mercury* 62 (22–5 Nov. 1681); HMC *Ormonde*, NS, VI, 209, 220, 226, 229; *Hatton Correspondence*, II, 9; *CSPD 1680–1*, p. 521; Woodhead, *Rulers*, pp. 53, 140; Haley, *Shaftesbury*, pp. 672–6; Jones, *First Whigs*, pp. 191–2.

whose election fed the occasional conformity controversy. The home of dissenting juror Edmund Harrison would be a target of the Sacheverell crowds in 1710. Not surprisingly, given this jury profile, foreman Barnardiston led assertive jurors who were not only committed to Shaftesbury but who were also determined to damage the government's case beyond repair in any other court.[32]

The Whigs had their way with the jury, but they were not quite as successful in their orchestration of public opinion in the pageants of 5 and 17 November that preceded the trial. These street expressions of Protestant patriotism and anti-popery in 1681 displayed both party division and rival understandings about the illegal conspiracies that threatened the kingdom. On 5 November, Jack Presbyter was burned by Westminster schoolboys; and in the city, effigies of the pope were "rescued" when Whig processions in Aldersgate and on Tower Hill were ambushed. The opposition took more care in commemorating the accession of the great Protestant queen. One loyalist bonfire was extinguished; and acclamations of Shaftesbury and of the Duke of Monmouth were much in the air, as were denunciations of the loyalist newssheets, *The Observator* and *Heraclitus Ridens*.[33]

These were the festive preliminaries to the release of Whig sentiment in the city that accompanied the last great *ignoramus* of 1681. The "very great shout" in the courtroom at the announcement of the jury's verdict for Shaftesbury initiated a night of disorder in the city that has been overly sanitized in some historical accounts. Neither the crown nor loyalist contemporaries had any difficulty in construing the eighty bonfires between Aldersgate and the Exchange, the bell ringing, the drinking, and the stopping of coaches in Shaftesbury's honor as a "tumultuous riot." And, although we have learned that the Whig crowds of the Restoration Crisis had their loyalist counterparts, the crown and Tory publicists nevertheless made the Whig crowds the issue. The behavior of Sheriffs Pilkington and Shute during the crowd celebrations became a principal Court complaint. Pilkington was charged with ignoring an order from the Lord Chief Justice to disperse the crowd outside the Old Bailey, while Shute reportedly encouraged a gang led by his nephew and declined to protect one loyalist who refused to drink Shaftesbury's health.[34]

[32] De Krey, *Fractured Society*, pp. 114–15; Haley, *Shaftesbury*, pp. 677–9; G. Holmes, "The Sacheverell Riots: The Crowd and the Church in Early Eighteenth-Century London," *PP* 72 (1976), 66; Jones, *First Whigs*, p. 193.

[33] Newdigate L.c. 1150 (19 Nov. 1681); *True Protestant Mercury* 88–9 (5–9, 9–12 Nov. 1681); *Observator*, I, 74 (23 Nov. 1681); Luttrell, I, 142; *CSPD 1680–1*, pp. 561, 571–2; North, *Examen*, pp. 576, 577–9; Harris, *London Crowds*, pp. 159, 168–9.

[34] Newdigate L.c. 1156 (3 Dec. 1681); Morrice, P, 318; *An Account at Large, of the proceedings at the Sessions-House . . . 24 of November 1681*; HMC *Ormonde*, NS, VI, 236–8, 242, 244;

A royal proclamation and safeguards taken by the court of aldermen prevented a recurrence of these scenes after the earl's release. But the "misgovernment of the City by the sheriffs" had nevertheless been fully displayed. The crown commenced its *quo warranto* proceedings against the Corporation's charter within a fortnight. From the outset, the crown's legal challenge to the charter was intended to provide it with the control of the Corporation that it had lacked throughout the crisis. Successful or not, the government hoped that its case against the abuse of civic liberties would frighten restless citizens into political obedience and restore law and justice to a disorderly city.

The packed juries of 1681 also quickly became the target of Tory satire, providing evidence for loyalists of the hypocrisy of those who undermined the law in the guise of preserving the nation. Beginning with John Dryden, loyalist polemicists found in Sheriff Bethel a useful personification of Whig manipulation of the law in order "to punish those who serve the King, and to protect his foes." And what, inquired loyalists, was to be made of sheriffs like Pilkington and Shute, who aided and abetted popular rioting rather than preserving law and deference? What most sustained loyalists after November 1681 was their absolute conviction that they were acting to preserve the king's law and the church established upon it from those whose mockery of law could not be tolerated.[35]

Largely innocent of the plotting with which they were charged, Whig grandees and activists also drew conclusions about the law from the contest in the courts in 1681. The government's cases against College, Rouse, Shaftesbury, and others demonstrated to them the lengths to which ministers would go in suppressing those who had advocated parliament and Protestantism. For the Whigs, the ideological result of the contest in the courts was a firmer conviction that laws and liberty, religion and property, and the constitution itself were endangered. In the courts, they had already experienced "swarms of spies, informers and false witnesses." Indeed, as Algernon Sidney suggested, they had found in the courts that "if crimes are wanting, the diligence of well-chosen officers and prosecutors, with the favor of the judges, supply all defects: the law is made a snare." A growing number of London and Country Whigs were also coming to see the king himself as the greatest threat to law. In the courts, they had experienced a prince who

Luttrell, I, 146; *CSPD 1680–1*, pp. 583–4, 588–9, 591, 592; *ST*, VIII, 759–836; Harris, *London Crowds*, pp. 180–2; Haley, *Shaftesbury*, pp. 681–2.

[35] *POAS*, II, 477–9, 490–3, with quotation from lines 610–11. Also see *Heraclitus Ridens* 42 (15 Nov. 1681); *A Letter written from the Tower by Mr. Stephen Colledge* (1681); *A Letter from Mr. Edward Whitaker to the protestant Joyner* (1681); *The Arraignment of Co-Ordinate Power* (1683), p. 4.

sought, in John Locke's words, "to terrifie or suppress [his] Opposers as Factious, Seditious, and Enemies to the Government."[36]

As the contest in the courts continued into 1682–3, most London Whigs would become obsessed with the law and determined to defend their understanding of the civic and national constitutions before the courts. But as the crown slowly gained the upper hand in the courts, other Whigs – including Shaftesbury and some Whig principals – would adopt the position that a king who governed contrary to law could by right be resisted with arms. The contest in the courts would thus leave the Whigs uncomfortably poised and exposed between law and resistance.

THE CONTEST ABOUT THE CHURCH

Protestant accommodation without a parliament?

By 1681–2, Charles II had followed a vacillating course about religion for over twenty years, and he had frequently sought to avoid the active coercion required by statute. In the "second restoration" of 1681, however, Charles would commit himself to a renewed policy of persecution on behalf of the Anglican church order against those who sought to resettle the church for the benefit of dissenters. Anglican voices informed by the ecclesiastical experiences of the previous reign again shaped Charles's response to the problem of dissent. Interestingly, the Whigs were accused of engaging in a Presbyterian plot in 1681 rather than in a republican plot. The conspiracy in which they had allegedly engaged was supposedly intended to force the king's consent to reducing the authority of bishops as well as his consent to exclusion. And the comparisons loyalists made between 1641 and 1681 were effective because 1641 was the year of a parliamentary reformation of the church.[37]

The beginnings of Anglican reaction did not, however, alter the militant mood of London nonconformists or weaken their desire to achieve Protestant accommodation through a resettlement of the church. Drawing upon more than a decade of political experience in the Corporation, dissenting common councilmen and jurors confidently stood up to loyalist magistrates and judges. In the summer of 1681, one London JP noted how the nonconformists were even busy "building several new meeting-houses."[38] By the time of Shaftesbury's trial, London dissenters and their Reformed

---

[36] Algernon Sidney, *Discourses Concerning Government*, ed. T. G. West (Indianapolis, 1990), p. 269 (Chapter II, Section 27); John Locke, *The Second Treatise of Government*, ed. P. Laslett, in *Two Treatises of Government*, 2nd ed. (Cambridge, 1967), p. 428 (Para. 218).

[37] Newdigate L.c. 1105, 1123 (26 July, 13 Sept. 1681); Morrice, P, 313; Haley, *Shaftesbury*, p. 674; J. Morrill, "The Attack on the Church of England."

[38] *CSPD 1680–1*, p. 352.

Protestant friends within the church had sought quite dramatically to advance Protestant union again, this time through the electoral politics of the city. Only when their commitment to Protestant accommodation is emphasized can the curious mayoral election of September 1681 be properly understood.

The election of Sir John Moore to the London mayoralty was not a straightforward party affair, despite the escalating party conflict of 1681, and despite the increasing political polarization of the city. Historians have generally characterized Moore as a Tory because, in the final months of his mayoralty, he acted with the king and the ministry to deprive the Whigs of the shrievalty and the mayoralty for 1682–3. For this reason, he was condemned as a betrayer of the liberties of the city in 1688–9. But at the time of his election, Moore, who had once been a dissenter, was strongly identified with the cause of Protestant comprehension and toleration. Indeed, when the crown returned to active persecution after the Shaftesbury *ignoramus*, Moore acted briefly as an intermediary between London dissenters and the Court, pleading for the liberties of all Protestants against the popish threat. The willingness of many London dissenters to trust Moore as lord mayor, despite his return to the church, demonstrates how the London Whigs were truly the party of both conscience and accommodation. But the story of Moore's mayoralty also demonstrates that Charles and the Anglican establishment were as hostile to reconsidering the church settlement as they were to exclusion.

Embarrassed by the failure of ministerial efforts in the June 1681 shrieval election, Charles carefully positioned himself for the mayoral election of 29 September 1681. Because Moore was the senior alderman beneath the chair, he was the Court candidate perforce: Court promotion of any other alderman for the mayoralty would have strengthened the opposition's rejection of this traditional understanding of the mayoral succession. In reality, Charles was no more excited about the prospect of a former dissenter as lord mayor than he had been about the election of an actual dissenter as lord mayor for 1680–81. But Moore had, at least, supported the Court throughout the previous decade, most recently by promoting loyal addresses in the city in preference to opposition petitions.

Whig attitudes toward Moore are even more problematic. As early as May 1681, talk was already circulating that "the faction" would oppose his election as lord mayor. But the problem for those who distrusted Moore was the lack of a viable candidate amongst the four Whig aldermen beneath the chair. Aldermen Henry Cornish and Thomas Pilkington were strong leaders, but Cornish was only now completing his shrievalty, and Pilkington had only just been elected to his. The remaining two Whig possibilities, Sir Thomas Gold and Sir John Shorter, lacked the political stature of their junior colleagues, despite their experience on the bench.[39] Such leading Whigs as Pilkington, Monmouth, and Lords Essex and Russell were nevertheless committed to the election of Gold or Shorter as lord mayor. They sought to turn the election into an affirmation of the reality of the Popish Plot and a repudiation of the government's line about Presbyterian plotting.[40]

But other leading civic Whigs, including former Lord Mayor Clayton, current Lord Mayor Ward, and Recorder Treby favored a less provocative strategy. Charles was known to be hostile to the election as lord mayor of any alderman out of the customary sequence; and the crown's allegations about Whig plotting made a show of Whig constitutional propriety highly desirable. The opposition already controlled the shrievalty, the juries, and common council; and neither Protestant union nor the case for another parliament could be advanced by needlessly offending the king. Indeed, the mayoral election coincided with the renewal of rumors that another parliament would meet, probably in November. The acceptance of a cross-grained lord mayor, one who retained numerous dissenting friendships despite his own conformity, did not therefore seem too risky, especially if it demonstrated Whig good faith. Still hoping for a parliament, these London Whigs prepared for one by advancing the cause of Protestant accommodation in the city through their support of Moore.[41]

Both Whig strategies were at work in the Michaelmas common hall that left Sir John Moore as the city's chief magistrate. Nevertheless, Whig advocates of church resettlement had as much right to claim victory as the Court. At the invitation of retiring Lord Mayor Ward, Dr Gilbert Burnet (who was next-door neighbor to the dissenting Ward) opened the election by preaching a remarkable sermon about the need for Protestant unity in England against the common Catholic enemy. Burnet acknowledged that the present "heats" compared in "violence" to those of the civil wars; and he pleaded that they be composed in a "united" and "Reformed Church" and state, each free of the evil policy of persecution.[42]

Burnet's message was one that obviously appealed to Reformed Protestant electors and that encouraged Protestant union. In reply, many dissenting liverymen demonstrated their commitment to Protestant accommodation

---

[39] Newdigate L.c. 1082, 1103 (31 May, 23 July 1681); Luttrell, I, 128, 130; Burnet, *History*, II, 335; *DNB*, XXXVIII, 358–9.

[40] LC MS 18,124, VII, 248 (1 Oct. 1681); *Observator*, I, 59–60 (5, 8 Oct. 1681); *CSPD 1680–1*, pp. 473–80; Luttrell, I, 129.

[41] Newdigate L.c. 1133 (6 Oct. 1681); HMC *Ormonde*, NS, VI, 165, 180; *CSPD 1680–1*, pp. 457, 469–70, 490–1. This Whig division should not be construed as a division between moderate and radical candidates, an interpretation made in Henning, *House of Commons*, I, 314.

[42] CLRO Ward Assessment Books for the six-months' tax of 1680: Dowgate East, 6th precinct, St Laurence Pountney Hill; Gilbert Burnet, *An Exhortation to Peace and Union* (1681), esp. pp. 11, 27–35.

by supporting Moore, even though other Whigs were promoting Aldermen Gold and Shorter. At the conclusion of a poll, Moore had more votes than either of his opponents. Presbyterian diarist Roger Morrice claimed that Moore "was chosen Lord Mayor by the Dissenters[,] not by the Strength of the other party." And writing decades later, Burnet remembered that some dissenting teachers had actually worked their congregations on Moore's behalf. Moreover, Moore's sympathy for dissenters over the next few months indicated his own commitment to Protestant unity.[43]

But Whigs and dissenters who had sought to accommodate the crown in Moore's election were quickly to discover how little intention the crown had of accommodating them. When the new sheriffs, both dissenters, appeared at Court to invite the privy councilors to accompany the king to the mayoral feast for Moore, their friendly overtures were rebuffed by Charles with references to the unfriendly contest in the courts. The king seized the occasion to posture as "the only man in England that had not justice done him." He failed to knight the sheriffs, as was customary on this occasion; and he expressed his regard for the "honest part of the City," as against the "factious."[44]

The Privy Council had, in fact, already decided to answer the call for Protestant union by encouraging enforcement of the statutes against nonconformist preaching and meetings. In the city, the loyalist lieutenancy commissioners purged the trained bands of dissenting officers in October; and in November, the ministry gathered evidence about the possession of arms by sectarians in the eastern wards and parishes without the walls. In Middlesex, Justice Jeffreys began disturbing dissenting meetings in order to set an example for other counties. As Charles's comments before the mayoral feast indicated, this return to persecution was as much a response to the contest in the courts as it was a response to the continuing call for Protestant union. Or, as the Earl of Longford wrote, "While such factious Grand Juries are returned... the King will have no expedient left to bring that party to reason, but to put the laws in execution against fanatics and confine their ministers."[45]

The Restoration Crisis had now come full circle. Initially fueled, in part, by a reaction against Danby's exclusive Anglican polity, it was now driven as much by Anglican revulsion about *de facto* toleration and Protestant

---

[43] Morrice, P, 314; LC MS 18,124, VII, 248 (1 Oct. 1681); *The Speech of the Right Honourable Sir Patience Ward Kt.* (1681); *The Speech of the Right Honourable Sir John Moore Kt.* (1681); *True Protestant Mercury* 77 (28 Sept.–1 Oct. 1681); *Observator*, I, 60 (8 Oct. 1681); *CSPD 1680–1*, pp. 476, 484–5; Burnet, *History*, II, 335.

[44] Newdigate L.c. 1140 (22 Oct. 1681); HMC *Ormonde*, NS, VI, 212; *CSPD 1680–1*, pp. 544–5.

[45] Newdigate L.c. 1144 (5 Nov. 1681); HMC *Ormonde*, NS, VI, 154 (Oct. 1681, but misdated for Sept.), 208; *CSPD 1680–1*, pp. 511, 524, 550, 560–2; Luttrell, I, 134, 140–1.

accommodation. Reformed Protestants in London and elsewhere were soon confronted with a re-establishment of the intolerant cavalier state that had been erected by law in the early 1660s and revived in the mid-1670s.

Conscience and coercion: reviving the sectarian alarums

Even before the *ignoramus* in the Shaftesbury trial ended any Court patience with dissent, the government had issued subpoenas against several leading London dissenting clergy. John Owen, Thomas Jacombe, Thomas Watson, Matthew Mead, and others were charged with failing to attend their parish churches and with residing within a corporation. The lord mayor and aldermen were summoned before the council to hear the king's personal command that they suppress all conventicles. The prosecution of dissenters in London and elsewhere and the *quo warranto* against the city charter were, in fact, parallel Court responses to the decisions of the London grand juries. Each initiative was intended to assist in recovering control of London for the crown. The legal harassment of dissenters would intimidate Whig electors; and the legal challenge to the charter would discourage Whig manipulation of civic institutions and electoral procedures.[46]

Reformed Protestants in London quickly recognized the import of these challenges and rose to the occasion. In the city, the released Shaftesbury, as well as all those "protestant lords" and Whig citizens who flocked to him again for "the management of the whole business," attempted to thwart the return to persecution. Their response was a vigorous renewal of the demand for reformation of the church. In December, conclaves attended by such leading Whigs as Clayton, Pilkington, Player, and Ward were directed as much toward the advancement of reformation as toward Shaftesbury's agenda about the succession. According to a well-informed apprentice news writer, the earl believed the time was again ripe to "regulat[e] some errors [in the church] that have too longe been used & spaired amongst us."[47]

Shaftesbury's first public appearance after his release from the Tower became a popular celebration of Protestant unity and reformation in defiance of Anglican monopoly. When he worshipped at St Lawrence Jewry, the parish

---

[46] *CSPD 1680–1*, pp. 592, 607, 609, 630, 660; HMC *Ormonde*, NS, VI, 242, 244; Luttrell, I, 148; Kennet, *Complete History*, III, 403.

[47] LC MS 18,124, VII, 299 (13 Dec. 1681). This is the first in a series of valuable letters in this collection that continue through December 1682. They were written by an apprentice, whose name cannot be determined, to Sir William Scott, fifth laird of Harden. The news writer's narration of words and speeches in private Whig gatherings is so detailed as to be somewhat problematic. But as he once revealed to Scott, the writer had all his news "from my Mr who is a chiefe member of ym [the civic Whig leaders] & who keeps a Jornall of all yr proceedings," which explains the quality of his information. For these details, see *ibid.*, VIII, 30, 46–7 (16 March and 22 April 1682). For the outspoken political views and actions of Scott, the recipient of the letters, see *CSPD 1682*, p. 430; *CSPD 1684–5*, p. 303; Greaves, *Secrets*, p. 406.

church most intimately associated with the Corporation, the people were said to have spontaneously risen with a shout of "Lord Bless all Protestants in the world." At the same time, London dissenters flocked to conventicles in greater numbers than ever "so that every meeting house was so throng[ed] ... not a foot could be stirred ... every man having a Lusty kane in his hand." Loyalist aldermen demanded that Lord Mayor Moore enforce the king's orders against meetings, but he reportedly responded that only "mischief & ruine" would follow any attempt to interfere with the "free exercise" of Protestant faith. When the loyalist lieutenancy commissioners prepared to employ the trained bands against meetings, observers anticipated street confrontations similar to those of 1670. But fearing violence, Charles pulled back from confrontation and countermanded the lieutenancy preparations.[48]

As in the earlier crisis about conscience, London dissenters were at no loss for words in defending conscience against coercion. They pointed out the contradiction between welcoming Reformed Protestant refugees from Catholic persecution in France while persecuting English Protestants who agreed with them in doctrine and discipline. They argued that the last-minute resolution of the 1680–81 parliament against persecution constituted a rescission of some of the acts being applied against them. The conformist lord mayor was actually one of their most effective spokesmen. When Charles sent urgently for Moore on Christmas Eve, the lord mayor warned the king that those who advocated the return to coercion did not "understand the manners & natures of the Cittizens" of London. A fortnight later, Moore was again at Whitehall after Aldermen Clayton and Ward presented a petition against coercion that failed to alter royal policy, despite being signed "by severall Thousand Cittizens." Arguing that the division of the Protestant interest would only encourage the Catholics "to fall a playeing their old game againe," Moore reportedly offered himself as security for dissenting loyalty.[49]

That the renewal of religious coercion coincided with the election of common councilmen on 21 December was no accident. The ministry and its allies sought to turn the choice of common councilmen for 1682 into an electoral inquest about the loyalty of the dissenters and petitioners who had enjoyed an effective majority on that court for the preceding two years. Targeted for removal, in particular, were those who had acted against the crown on recent

---

[48] Newdigate L.c. 1161–3 (15, 17, 20 Dec. 1681); LC MS 18,124, VII, 279, 280, 282, 299, 304 (13, 15, 17, 20, 27 Dec. 1681); *Domestick Intelligence* 64–5 (29 Dec. 1681–2 Jan. 1682; 2–5 Jan. 1682); *CSPD 1680–1*, pp. 613, 630, 635; *CSPD 1682*, pp. 8, 20, 24, 27, 29 HMC *Ormonde*, NS, VI, 271.

[49] Newdigate L.c. 1161 (15 Dec. 1681); LC MS 18,124, VII, 307–9, and VIII, 2–3, 15 (24, 27 Dec. 1681; 5, 7 Jan. and 7 Feb. 1682); *The Ignoramus Justices* [1682]; *CSPD 1680–1*, pp. 613, 626, 631.

grand juries. A contest about the choice of common councilmen began in the parish vestry meetings that made nominations to the St Thomas's Day wardmotes. It continued into the early days of 1682, as electoral disputes in some wards required additional assemblies. Tory publications like *Heraclitus Ridens* labored to make dissent the issue, warning against the election of "men . . . [of] limber Consciences who can conform to the Rites of the church from S. *Thomas* day to *Twelfth*-day, and yet be *Dissenters* all the year after." The results of the election, which will be examined in further detail below, were interpreted among loyalists as a defeat for "the fanatic party" and as a triumph for the "churchmen" or the "honest party." John Wilmore and seven other common councilmen who had served on the grand juries for College, Rouse, and Shaftesbury were removed.[50] (See Table 4.1)

These attacks upon the London dissenters were the cutting edge of the continuing effort by loyalist polemicists to taint the causes of parliament and of Reformed Protestantism with the stigma of disloyalty and treason. The "sectarian alarums" of 1659–60 had worked one royalist miracle, and the loyalist press now revived those alarums in hope of achieving another. Over the winter of 1681–2, the Tories refocused the paper war about alleged Presbyterian plotting upon the draft association discovered among Shaftesbury's papers when he was arrested. This new association was the old Solemn League and Covenant revived, according to Anglican writers; and they pointed to the political ideas and practices of the London dissenters as evidence.

Where had the Whigs learned such rebelliousness? According to L'Estrange, the city meetings were schools of sedition, where the dissenting clergy, "have a *Bloudy Flag* set up in every *Pulpit*." Too many of the nonconformist teachers – the "bellowing renegado priests" of Dryden's strictures – had once signed the Solemn League and Covenant and supported still its goals of reformation in church and state. The "sacrilegious sects" of London were said to be preparing to "smite the idol [of monarchy] in Guild Hall," and they dared to claim "God's cause" was the same as "their own." The association was said to have been "first hatch't" during the 1680–81 parliament "when the Licentiousness of the *City* was such, as nothing but the Tumults in the late times could exceed it." According to churchmen, the Whig goal of repealing coercive religious legislation was intended again to pull down the bishops, to release the sects, and to return "the whole Kingdom" to the "*Levellers* and *Libertines*."[51]

---

[50] Newdigate L.c. 1164 (22 Dec. 1681); LC MS 18,124, VII, 281–2 (18, 20 Dec. 1681); *Heraclitus Ridens* 47 (20 Dec. 1681); HMC *Ormonde*, NS, VI, 273–4; *CSPD 1680–1*, pp. 637–8.

[51] LC MS 18,124, VIII, 1 (3 Jan. 1682); *Observator*, I, 106 (2 March 1682); John Dryden, "The Medal" (1682) in *POAS*, III, 46–59, with quoted phrases from lines 268, 203, 199–200; [Thomas Durfey], "The Whigs' Exaltation" (1682) in POAS, III, 10–14, with quoted phrase from line 49; [Northleigh], *The Parallel*, pp. 8, 22; *The Character of a Rebellion*, p. 6;

As Gilbert Burnet remembered, this surging flood of loyalist argument in 1682 was inspired by Anglican and clerical revenge against the London dissenters, against the juries they dominated, and against the ideals of reformation and Protestant accommodation they championed.[52] Indeed, the very visibility that London dissenters had achieved now became the chief liability of the Reformed Protestant cause. Tory writers worked the fear of the "fanatics" to great effect, as public alarm about the "sects" rose to the same level as public alarm about the "papists." The anti-sectarianism of 1659–60 had been a prelude to the restoration of Stuart monarchy, and the anti-sectarianism of 1681–2 became a prelude to the relaunching of that monarchy on the foundations of religious coercion and a strengthened prerogative.

At first, the assault against conscience was more effective on paper than in practice, as Charles's December 1681 retreat from the brink suggests. Until the loyalist recovery of the shrievalty in autumn 1682, the London dissenters held their own. Efforts by Tory justices, constables, and informers were often blocked by Whig and dissenting magistrates, by recalcitrant grand jurors still empaneled by Whig sheriffs, and by the ingenuity of those who attended conventicles. In Middlesex, grand jurors looked the other way at the presentation of alleged conventiclers, but they accepted bills against the secretary of state for irregularities in the committal of the same people! The London dissenters were, nevertheless, gradually being forced on the defensive; and their clergy recognized that the rhetorical ground was beginning to shift under them. As Southwark loyalist MP Peter Rich reported to Secretary Jenkins, in February 1682, "the teachers are afraid."[53]

Active coercion was renewed in earnest in late May and June 1682, this time to be driven more systematically by an Anglican establishment determined to break the back of Reformed Protestantism. In an effort at intimidation prior to the mid-summer election of sheriffs, the ministry and loyalist magistrates mounted weekly efforts to suppress urban conventicles. John Hilton and his gang of informers began to play a critical role in this effort. Those livery companies that offered their halls to dissenting meetings were threatened with *quo warrantos*. The Sabbath preceding the common hall of 24 June 1682 turned tumultuous when Thomas Jacombe and Vincent Alsop, as well as a Quaker speaker, were rescued from the constables who had apprehended them by a crowd armed with sticks and

---

Remarques upon the New Project of an Association (1682), p. 5; Harris, *London Crowds*, pp. 133–44; Harth, *Pen*, ch. 4.

[52] Burnet, *History*, II, 301–2.

[53] Newdigate L.c. 1171, 1179, 1181, 1192, 1196, 1205 (9 Jan.; 2, 7 Feb.; 9, 21 March; 13 April 1682); LC MS 18,124, VIII, 7, 15–16 (19 Jan.; 7, 9 Feb. 1682); Morrice, P, 322; *True Protestant Mercury* 133 (12–15 Apr. 1682); *CSPD 1682*, pp. 59, 75–6, 78–9, 82–3, 86–7, 93, 104–6; Luttrell, I, 165, 171–2; Haley, *Shaftesbury*, p. 688.

stones. As the noise of this confrontation in the Stocks Market mounted, nearby parish churches were reportedly deserted by the sympathetic and the curious. Other dissenting teachers had shown more prudence, however, sending "notice to their congregations that they will not preach during this persecution."[54]

The outcome of the shrieval election of 1682 – the climax of the contest for the Corporation and of the Restoration Crisis itself – would leave conscience exposed to coercion for the next three years. By autumn 1682, the ministry had discovered that the active persecution of a religious minority was itself the best evidence for the political crimes they had allegedly committed. In the insecure religious world of Restoration England, the coercion of Roman Catholics had fed the political frenzy of the Popish Plot. Now the coercion of Protestant dissenters would feed the Tory reaction. Anglican loyalists had one signal advantage in elevating anti-sectarianism over anti-Catholicism. They could argue that the sects had, in recent memory, overrun the kingdom with disastrous consequences for the Protestant order.

In the city, the revival of coercion and the strong ideological defense of uniformity would soon deprive nonconformists of the initiative they had taken in politics since 1670, and especially since 1675. But neither the loss of political initiative nor the experience of coercion would weaken the insistence of dissenters that the kingdom would find Protestant security only through accommodation, union, and indulgence. They saw that "hag Persecution" as the greatest enemy of the Reformed Protestant regime for which they contested.[55]

THE CONTEST FOR THE CORPORATION

Feeding party: the issue of the succession sustained

From the beginnings of the Restoration Crisis, the civic opposition had troubled the crown only slightly less than the parliamentary opposition. Whatever the technical and legal grounds of the *quo warranto* against the London charter, the crown's real case against the Corporation was its animus against the Whigs for their successful employment of corporate institutions

---

[54] Newdigate L.c. 1221, 1223–5, 1228 (25, 30 May; 1, 3, 10 June 1682); LC MS 18,124, VIII, 72 (22 June 1682); Morrice, P, 336–7; *Moderate Intelligencer* 1 (14 June 1682); *True Protestant Mercury* 15 (14–17 June 1682); Luttrell, I, 190, 193, 196; *CSPD 1682*, p. 255; M. Goldie, "The Hilton Gang and the Purge of London in the 1680s," in *Politics and the Political Imagination in later Stuart Britain*, ed. H. Nenner (Rochester, NY, 1997), esp. pp. 49–50.
[55] "The Medal Revers'd" (1682) in *POAS*, III, 61–95, esp. the subtitle and line 69.

and elections on behalf of exclusion and reformation.[56] Nevertheless, in the wake of the Oxford Parliament, the civic Whigs reaffirmed their commitments to the independence of common council and to the authority of common hall. In June 1681 they secured the appointment of a Corporation committee dominated by opposition aldermen and common councilmen to review the city by-laws. Their intention, apparently, was to repeal civic acts that reflected the more authoritarian understanding of the London constitution favored by the crown and loyalists. In its first meeting under Sir John Moore, common council also responded to the altercations between Tory justices and Whig sheriffs by choosing a committee, one again dominated by the Whigs, to defend the "Interest and right of this City to the Sheriffwick."[57] Nothing was more central to civic whiggism than this understanding of the sheriffs as the agents of the common hall electorate who chose them.

The acquittal and release of Shaftesbury in November 1681 was also a critical event in the continuing contest for the Corporation, for it redirected and re-energized both Whigs and loyalists in the city. A cabal of leading parliamentary and civic Whigs relaunched their party efforts at a December 1681 London meeting in which "deputies" were chosen to prosecute the Whig agenda in the country and in the city. In addition to Shaftesbury, these deputies included Monmouth, Howard, Colchester, Herbert, Clare, Sir Patience Ward, Sir Robert Clayton, Sir Thomas Player, Sheriff Pilkington, and merchant Palatia Barnardiston. They reportedly agreed to divide their labors. A group that included Shaftesbury was to remain in town in order to maintain Whig strength in the city. A second group that included Monmouth was to disperse into the country, apparently in order to prepare the counties for another parliamentary election. Both groups were to encourage Protestant dissenters to remain stalwart.

These decisions were not the acts of a dispirited and defeated Whig leadership. They instead reflected a continuing Whig determination to pursue the goals of a Protestant succession and a resettlement of the church order. These efforts were also clearly accompanied by new efforts at organization. Sheriff Pilkington's public dinner for Shaftesbury at Skinners' Hall on 14 December, for instance, was a party dinner; and the medal that was struck in Shaftesbury's honor at that time, the medal that provoked Dryden's poetic comment, was an additional sign of the renewal of Whig political vigor. Over twenty political meetings of the Whig lords and magistrates occurred

---

[56] LC MS 18,124, VIII, 137 (14 Jan. 1682); *CSPD 1680–1*, pp. 682–3; *CSPD 1682*, pp. 26–7.
[57] Journal 49, fols. 225, 254, 268; LC MS 18,124, VII, 268 (17 Nov. 1681); *CSPD 1680–1*, pp. 305, 632, 662.

between mid-December 1681 and mid-April 1682, another sign of the Whigs' aggressive relaunch of their endeavors.[58]

Just as interesting as these opposition activities in the city was the banquet Lord Mayor Moore provided for London loyalists and courtiers on the same day as Pilkington's fête for Shaftesbury. The initiative for the loyalist gathering came from the Court, where Moore's sympathy for dissenters had raised concerns. Perhaps Lords Conway, Grafton, and Hyde and their ministerial friends sought better to anchor the lord mayor to the Court by descending upon him for dinner and prevailing upon him to invite the loyalist aldermen. Their talk focused upon means for improving the king's interest in the Corporation – means that reportedly included the possibility of electing York, who was then in Scotland, captain of the Honourable Artillery Company. That the king's interest in the city required improvement was obvious. Although Charles had so far withstood the demand for a parliament, the contest in the courts had not gone well; and the demand for Protestant union was being expressed as strongly as ever.[59]

These ministerial and civic loyalists were certainly no strangers to one another. Nevertheless, the spirit of loyalist conversation now seemed more determined, and discussion between civic and Court figures was to become more constant in 1682–3. Although Tory organization often failed to match that of the Whigs, it was becoming tighter and better focused. Before the end of December, another notable loyalist dinner, one for which the king contributed the venison, brought together civic loyalists like Aldermen Bludworth and Raymond and Court spokesmen like Sir George Jeffreys. Perhaps referring to such dinners, both Sir John Reresby and the Earl of Ailesbury subsequently remembered the organization of a loyalist club that met within Ludgate at about this time. According to Ailesbury, the club's members grew quickly to a few hundred; and they labored in "their several wards" to achieve loyalist purposes.[60]

Among those purposes was a recovery of the Tory voice on common council. The selection of common councilmen in December 1681 was hotly contested, as has already been indicated; but Tory claims of sweeping victories were more a reflection of determined efforts than of convincing results. Despite loyalist pressure upon him, Lord Mayor Moore seems again to have promoted Protestant unity at the expense of Anglican recovery. The most significant loyalist gains came in wards like Tower and Castle Baynard, where

[58] LC MS 18,124, VII, 299, 304 and VIII, 1–46 (13 Dec. 1681–23 April 1682); Newdigate L.c. 1160 (13 Dec. 1681); Luttrell, I, 151; Dryden, "Medal," *POAS*, III, 38–9; Harth, *Pen*, p. 171.

[59] LC MS 18,124, VII, 299 (13 Dec. 1681); Newdigate L.c. 1161 (15 Dec. 1681).

[60] Newdigate L.c. 1164 (22 Dec. 1681); Thomas Bruce, 2nd Earl of Ailesbury, *The Memoirs of Thomas, Earl of Ailesbury*, 2 vols. (1890), I, 64–5; Reresby, *Memoirs*, p. 244.

the crown had an interest through the presence of the Customs House and the ecclesiastical courts, and where loyalist aldermen could influence the wardmotes. And in Cheap, Alderman Sir Robert Clayton was embarrassed by the elimination of five Whig common councilmen in a Tory sweep. But in Farringdon Without, Alderman Pilkington defeated an effort to reverse the election of some Whigs; and the Whigs made scattered gains elsewhere.[61] The result was a council in which known Tories may have outnumbered known Whigs on paper by as many as 125 to 107. (See Table 6.1) In fact, however, the election produced a hung common council, because Whig common councilmen, especially those who were dissenters, had always been more assiduous in their attendance.[62]

If this result represented a Tory achievement and a Whig disappointment, the Tories had, therefore, not found their voice by depriving the Whigs of theirs. The first common council of 1682 revealed this balance between the parties in the Corporation. Loyalist preparation was made with "all diligence imaginable"; and Sergeant Goodfellow, a churchman, was chosen to fill a vacant judge's position in the sheriffs' courts.[63] But the selection of common council committeemen for the next year required six hours of debate. It concluded with the Whigs gaining control of a new committee for the defense of the charter against the *quo warranto* and retaining control of the committee to review the by-laws.[64]

The charter defense committee included exclusionist MPs Clayton, Ward, Pilkington, Player, and Dubois.[65] They retained the services of a distinguished battery of Whig lawyers, headed by Sir William Jones and Commons'

---

[61] *Impartial Protestant Mercury* 75, 98 (6–10 Jan. and 28–31 March 1682); *Domestick Intelligence*, 87, 99 (20–23 March and 1–4 May 1682); Newdigate L.c. 1177 (26 Jan. 1682); *CSPD 1682*, pp. 141–2; Luttrell, I, 174; Henning, *House of Commons*, III, 246.

[62] Journal 49, fol. 293; Repertory 87, fols. 48, 53, 59–60, 78–79; Newdigate L.c. 1164, 1169, 1175 (22 Dec. 1681 and 5, 19 Jan. 1682); LC 18,124, VII, 281–2, 306 (18, 20, 22 Dec. 1681); Morrice, P, 322; *Domestick Intelligence* 65, 68 (2–5, 12–16 Jan. 1682); *Impartial Protestant Mercury* 70, 75, 77, 84, 88 (20–23 Dec. 1681; 6–10, 13–17 Jan. 1682; 7–10, 21–4 Feb. 1682); D. N., *A Letter from an Old Common-Council-Man to one of the new Common-Council* [1682], pp. 1–3; *The Case stated concerning the ... Doctors Commons, as to the Election of Ward-Officers* (1682); *The Case of the Ward of Castle-Baynard* (1682); *CSPD 1680–1*, pp. 633–4, 636–8; *Savile Correspondence*, 262; *Ormonde*, NS, VI, 273–4, 282; A. G. Smith, "London and the Crown, 1681–1685," Unpublished Ph.D. thesis, University of Wisconsin, 1967, pp. 209–10; Haley, *Shaftesbury*, p. 689.

[63] Repertory 87, fols. 64, 77; Newdigate L.c. 1175, 1177 (19, 26 Jan. 1682); LC MS 18,124, VIII, 139 (19 Jan. 1682); *Impartial Protestant Mercury* 78, 93 (17–20 Jan. and 10–14 March 1682); D. N., *Letter from an Old Common-Council-Man*, pp. 3–4.

[64] Journal 49, fols. 282–283, 293; Newdigate L.c. 1175, 1191 (19 Jan. and 4 March 1682); LC MS 18,124, VII, 280 and VIII, 7 (17 Dec. 1681, 19 Jan. 1682); Morrice, P, 329; *Impartial Protestant Mercury* 69 (15–20 Dec. 1681); *Domestick Intelligence* 69 (16–19 Jan. 1682); *CSPD 1682*, pp. 31, 34–5; HMC *Ormonde*, NS, VI, 298; Luttrell, I, 151, 159.

[65] Some historians have wondered whether the launching of the *quo warranto* against the charter was a first step in turning some Whigs toward the possibility of resistance. Evidence for plotting at this juncture is slim; however, and it is overshadowed by evidence pointing instead

Speaker William Williams. The web of connections between the civic and parliamentary oppositions was revealed once again in this convergence of the city *quo warranto* committee and Whig legal talent. The membership of the city committee also overlapped significantly with the opposition circles around Shaftesbury and Monmouth. As these and other "protestant lords" considered issuing a declaration in defense of the "Protestant Religion" and the "Rights & Liberties of ye peopell," the city committee began its defense of the charter. The first King's Bench arguments in the *quo warranto* case were made at the end of January. Crowds flocked to Westminster in support of the civic committee and the charter; and, at Guildhall, York's portrait was slashed "thro the shins" by an unknown hand.[66]

The organizational efforts of both parties were on display again in early March when Charles decided, before his departure for Newmarket, to test the political waters by announcing that York would return to the capital. As civic loyalists prepared to welcome the heir to the throne, the Whig magistrates fed party, literally, when they organized an extensive series of political banquets in the wards. These feasts were intended to maintain the issue of the succession and to "make their pairty as strong as they can" by giving citizens the opportunity to mingle with Shaftesbury, Monmouth, Clare, and other parliamentary grandees. They also demonstrated public support for the petition for a parliament that the Whigs brought to common council on 10 March in opposition to Lord Mayor Moore's recommendation of an address welcoming York. Just as much as the French opposition banquets of 1847–8, these London Whig banquets of 1682 were intended to arouse public opinion on behalf of changes to the regime.

The lord mayor's effort at political bridge-building provoked nothing but disdain from the Whigs. Chamberlain Sir Thomas Player reportedly urged that "Cezer should have his own, but no more." In a "full-house," loyalist common councilmen and aldermen succeeded in throwing out the Whig petition by a scant two votes. They hesitated to follow up this victory, however, declining to put their own address to the throne to a vote. An attempt to secure a "Congratulary addresse" to York in the loyalist-dominated court of aldermen was similarly derailed a fortnight later. Sheriff Pilkington and former Sheriff Bethel reportedly then condemned York as "that Cancerworme amongst us" and as "that Terantula." Opposition magistrates ignored repeated summons thereafter in order to deprive the court of aldermen of the

to the confidence with which the Whigs undertook the defense of the Corporation. LC MS 18,124, VIII, 12–13 (31 Jan., 2 Feb. 1682); Newdigate L.c. 1172 (11 Jan. 1682); James Ferguson, *Robert Ferguson the Plotter; or, the Secret History of the Rye-House Conspiracy* (Edinburgh, 1887), pp. 414–16; Ashcraft, *Revolutionary Politics*, pp. 350–1; Greaves, *Secrets*, pp. 101–2; Marshall, *John Locke*, pp. 229, 232–3, 240–3.

[66] LC MS 18,124, VIII, 5, 7–8, 10–12, 14 (14, 19, 21, 26, 28, 31 Jan. and 7 Feb. 1682); Newdigate L.c. 1177–8 (26, 28 Jan. 1682).

quorum it would need for an address. Secretary Lord Conway lamented to Secretary Jenkins that the loyalist "management of affairs" lagged still behind that of "the contrary party, who act by concert, [and] seldom fail."[67]

Indeed, as the city Whigs continued their campaign of feeding public opinion against York, they frustrated loyalist endeavors to make dissent and the association the more pressing issues. According to one observer, nightly opposition cabals to the number of fifteen or sixteen became commonplace during the king's absence. Shaftesbury treated Clayton, Ward, Player, Sir John Lawrence, the two sheriffs, and numerous other citizens in Cheapside before inviting some of them to a strategy session at Thanet House. Reportedly keeping a journal of their proceedings at this point, a Whig steering committee drafted and signed a statement of purpose in the hope that an anticipated French attack upon the Netherlands would require a parliament. Their program was one of implacable hostility to a Catholic successor and dedication to the "true Protestant religion," defined in the language of Protestant union.

The arousal of Whig political appetites in public dinners and ward treats continued unabated for a month, from mid-March through mid-April. Hundreds of Country gentry traveled to London to show their support for a parliament and for a Protestant succession. Even Lord Mayor Sir John Moore dined with the Whig aldermen and "the protestant lords" in early April, reportedly at his own invitation, and despite a royal command not to countenance in the city those out of countenance at Court. The lord mayor was now "in a dreadful pickell," according to one observer, caught between the Court and "ye peopell." Moore's public commitment to Protestantism and to the liberty of the meeting houses failed to secure the respectful Corporation response to the impending visit of York for which he had apparently still hoped. When the aldermen finally traveled to Westminster to greet the king upon York's return, their division was very apparent; and the Whigs among them refused to attend the king's brother.[68]

Unable to secure a gracious welcome for York from the Corporation, the Tories nevertheless celebrated his return with ritual burnings of Jack Presbyter, the association, and Shaftesbury in the West End, in Ludgate (where the Tory club met), and in Cornhill. And, copying a page from the political cookbook of their adversaries, they began preparing a banquet of their own in York's honor with the Honourable Artillery Company for 20 April. The Whig "Hedge Lane Lords" and their civic allies had no

---

[67] LC MS 18,124, VIII, 26–8, 32–3 (7, 9, 11, 21, 25 March 1682); Newdigate L.c. 1192–3, 1197 (9, 11, 23 March 1682); *CSPD 1682*, pp. 132, 136–7; HMC *Ormonde*, NS, VI, 335–6, 341–2, 347, 353, 356; Luttrell, I, 173; Haley, *Shaftesbury*, p. 689.

[68] LC MS 18,124, VIII, 29–30, 34, 37, 39–41, 51, 173 (15, 16, 28 March; 4, 6, 11 April; and 2 May 1682 [*bis*]); Newdigate L.c. 1196, 1204 (21 March, 11 April 1682); *CSPD 1682*, 147; Luttrell, I, 176–7; Haley, *Shaftesbury*, p. 693.

intention of permitting such an occasion to pass without challenge: they promoted an "antidiner" in honor of Monmouth to be held at Haberdashers' Hall the following day.[69] It was advertised as a commemoration of the providential deliverances of the king, "the Protestant Religion and English Liberties... from the Hellish and frequent Attempts of their enemies." It was also clearly intended to promote the Protestant rival to the Catholic successor. The chief organizers of the Whig feast were Aldermen Clayton and Ward, former Sheriff Bethel, and John Wilmore (the foreman of Stephen College's London jury). In the meantime, the Whig aldermen and lords continued to generate anti-Catholic enthusiasm through anticipatory banquets; and Whig apprentices prepared the pope and other effigies for an accompanying street show. So many tickets were purchased that the organizers of the "Anti-Feast" required a second hall for all their guests, who were said to include forty "dissenting" or exclusionist lords.[70]

Historians have paid insufficient attention to these rival banquets as evidence of party organization in the spring of 1682.[71] The "Protestant treat" was also a direct affront to the crown. It was a provocative political gesture in which the citizens of London were invited to demonstrate their distaste for York, while honoring Monmouth and the parliamentary leaders who sought to advance Monmouth's claim to the throne. The Whig leaders also went out of their way to appropriate for their dinner all the customary elements of a civic show of respect for the king or for his successor. Like the Artillery Company banquet for James, the Whig dinner was to be preceded by a sermon, reportedly an address upon the text "fear God, honour the King, and meddle not with those that are given to change." Charles responded to this affront on 19 April by forbidding the Whig festival.[72]

The king's order, made to the lord mayor and court of aldermen, accused the Whigs of a seditious challenge to his authority to proclaim public feasts and thanksgivings. According to one Whig source, a crowd of 300 citizens chanting anti-Catholic slogans accompanied Aldermen Clayton

---

69 LC MS 18,124, VIII, 37 (4 April 1682); Newdigate L.c. 1193 (11 March 1682). The phrase "Hedge Lane Lords" was frequently used by the apprentice news writer to refer to the Whig grandees associated with Monmouth, who resided in Hedge Lane, Charing Cross. The name is yet another indication of the extent to which civic and parliamentary Whigs had adopted Monmouth as the alternate Protestant successor.

70 *Domestick Intelligence* 92–3, 95 (6–10, 10–13, 17–20 April 1682); LC MS 18,124, VIII, 38, 40, 42–5 (6, 11, 13, 18, 20 April 1682); Newdigate L.c. 1205, 1207–9 (13, 18, 20, 22 April 1682); Luttrell, I, 179–80; Harris, *London Crowds*, p. 179.

71 But see N. Key, "Partisan Fraternity: the Political Culture of London's Public Feasts in the 1680s," paper delivered at "The World Of Roger Morrice," a conference at Clare College, Cambridge, 10–12 July 2003.

72 Newdigate L.c. 1209 (22 April 1682). Also see [John Dryden and Nahum Tate], "The Second Part of Absalom and Achitophel" (1682) in *POAS*, III, 326 (line 913) and 327 (notes for lines 914–15, 917).

and Ward to the lord mayor's residence to receive Charles's order. Despite their frustration, the aldermen calmed the crowd, which must have relieved some of the anxiety at Westminster. One account of the Privy Council discussion of the rival feasts suggests that the ministers were more panic-stricken than resolute. Believing their own rhetoric about Whig plotting, some of them had concluded that the Whig banquets were being driven to a tumultuous and perhaps even to a rebellious climax.[73]

This dinner duel ended in a draw rather than in the embarrassment of the opposition, as some writers have suggested. Accounts of the loyalist feast emphasize the lavishness of the cuisine and the quality of the 200 citizens and courtiers in attendance. Gathering first for a sermon at St Mary le Bow, the company then conducted York through the city to Merchant Taylors' Hall for the largest feast the Artillery Company had ever hosted.[74] Reports that dispirited Whigs met quietly in smaller tavern companies, sending most of their provisions to the prisons, would appear not to be the whole story, however. According to a sympathetic apprentice news writer, Monmouth traveled through the city to Sir Patience Ward's house as York processed to Merchant Taylors' Hall. Four companies of the trained bands, who had silently lined York's route, reportedly defied their officers and joined the crowds in cheering Monmouth. At an evening gathering of the Whig lords, Monmouth insisted, apparently over Shaftesbury's objections, that they obey the king's order against their feast and find "some other way . . . to solemnize ye day."

Accordingly, on the 21st, Lord Colchester invited the exclusionist peers, the Whig civic leaders, and some 500 citizens to a sermon and dinner at his London residence. These formalities were accompanied by a festive procession through crowded streets of several hundred Whig apprentices, apparently armed, who conducted a pope-burning that matched "that of 79" in its "splendor." After being addressed by their spokesman, Monmouth invited a delegation of the apprentices to dinner. The evening concluded with additional anti-papal bonfires and crowd acclamations of the Whig leaders. Several further Whig banquets, including a treat for Monmouth at Gray's Inn, were held during the next fortnight.[75]

[73] Repertory 87, fols. 147–148; LC MS 18,124, VIII, 45 (20 April 1682); *POAS*, III, 174–5; Haley, *Shaftesbury*, pp. 694–5; Greaves, *Secrets*, pp. 95–6.

[74] The response of the crowds in the streets is more difficult to determine, with partisan sources suggesting opposite conclusions. Newgate L.c. 1208–9 (20, 22 April 1682); LC MS 18,124, VIII, 177 (20 April 1682); HMC *Rutland*, II, 69; *Impartial Protestant Mercury* 104–5 (18–21, 21–5 April 1682); *Observator*, I, 133 (6 May 1682); *Domestick Intelligence* 95 (17–20 April 1682); *True Protestant Mercury* 135 (19–22 April 1682); CSPD 1682, pp. 173–4; Harris, *London Crowds*, p. 171.

[75] LC MS 18,124, VIII, 45–52 (20, 22, 25, 27, 29 April and 2, 6 May 1682); Newdigate L.c. 1209 (22 April 1682); *Domestick Intelligence* 96 (20–24 April 1682); Luttrell, I, 179–80; HMC *Rutland*, II, 69; *The Loyal Feast* (1682); Harris, *London Crowds*, pp. 177–8.

Charles was understandably outraged that something like the intended "Protestant treat" had come off, despite his orders; and he cautioned the lord mayor as he departed for Windsor. York retaliated before his return to Scotland in early May by launching a *scandalum magnatum* against Sheriff Pilkington, who had been so heavily involved in Whig efforts against him. The Catholic duke charged the dissenting sheriff with having said that he had fired the city in 1666 and had returned to cut the citizens' throats. As the Court's irate response indicated, the London and parliamentary Whigs had successfully sustained the issue of the succession through their banqueting campaign of early 1682. But the Court was now persuaded more than ever that treason and rebellion lurked in the London Whig gatherings organized in honor of Monmouth. "To dine in the City, that mark of the beast, is all o'er Geneva and treason at least," was the comment of one poetic observer.[76] Despite such loyalist hyperbole, however, the efforts of Whig leaders to advance their causes in public suggest that few of them had yet given serious consideration to the alternate, treasonable course of resistance.

Contesting the shrievalty

The London shrieval election of 1682 was a turning-point in all the London contests that followed the Oxford Parliament. The capture of the shrievalty by the ministry and civic loyalists enabled them to gain the upper hand in the contests in the Corporation and in the courts.[77] It also denied urban dissenters any shrieval protection, and it deprived the causes of parliament and Protestant union of important London spokesmen. Finally, and most importantly, the election resolved the ongoing crisis of church and state on the Court's terms. The London shrieval election of 1682 rather than the Oxford Parliament of 1681 was the climax of the Restoration Crisis, but this historical reality has too often been obscured by scholarly preoccupation with parliament and with parliamentary figures.

Contemporaries had no difficulty in recognizing the importance of the election in the crown's recovery of the kingdom. The Earl of Ailesbury wrote that the crown's capture of the London shrievalty was "like the axe laid to the root of the tree, which soon after fell to the ground." For their part,

---

[76] LC MS 18,124, VIII, 49–51, 178 (25, 27, 29 April and 2 May 1682); Newdigate L.c. 1213 (29 April 1682); *CSPD 1682*, pp. 188, 194; "A Game at Cards" [1682] in *POAS*, III, 233 (lines 55–6).

[77] The volume of political business in the courts had mushroomed since the release of Shaftesbury, as political antagonists on both sides of the party divide harassed each other with numerous suits. The government indicted several Whig publishers and printers; and one loyalist publisher was the target of reprisals by Whig magistrates. Newdigate L.c. 1179–81, 1192, 1214, 1217, 1219–20, 1228–30, 1232 (2, 7, 14 Feb.; 9 March; 4, 16, 20, 23 May; and 10, 15, 17, 20 June 1682); Repertory 87, fol. 128; *CSPD 1682*, pp. 199, 209–11.

London Whigs and dissenters refused to accept the outcome of the election as legitimate. Many of them were prepared to contest its validity in the courts; and others, including grandees like Shaftesbury, Monmouth, and Russell, considered or planned resistance in its wake. The election was similarly important in the resistance thinking of John Locke and Robert Ferguson, and of Algernon Sidney, who was indicted for riot for his part in it. The affair also spawned literature that influenced political debate throughout the late Stuart period and kept its memory alive for a generation.[78]

Recent historians have recognized the significance of this election better than its character, predating its conclusion and projecting its outcome in ways that oversimplify its complicated chronology.[79] The London shrieval election of 1682 was not an event that can be confined for narrative convenience to a single date or even to a single month. It was not an electoral episode but rather a traumatic electoral process that extended from May through September 1682 and that was contested in the courts for an additional six months thereafter. The eventual triumph of the Court in installing Tory sheriffs and a Tory lord mayor, as well, was spectacular; but these results were obtained only after a protracted and tumultuous party stand-off in which the city displayed its full potential for producing political disorder. The outcome was also in doubt throughout the whole process: many Whigs expected to prevail until the last minute.

Charles's ministers were determined in 1682 not to repeat their mistakes of the previous shrieval election. Reacting to the Whigs' successes in common council and to the advancement of Monmouth in ward treats, the two secretaries of state began conversations with civic loyalists about fixing the shrievalty by late March. The ministry's plan was for the lord mayor to employ the disputed prerogative of naming one sheriff on behalf of an individual recommended by the crown. The electors would then be instructed to endorse this choice in common hall, but they would be left free to elect the other sheriff. By late April, city gossip pointed to Dudley North as the king's designee for the honor of nomination, and Sir John Moore was instructed to cooperate as the ministry embarked upon an unprecedented course of intervention in the Corporation. A Turkey merchant recently returned from the Levant, North was also the brother of the Lord Chief Justice of Common Pleas. In mid-May, Moore drank to North at the bridge-house feast as his choice. Moore's inability to continue his moderating course between the

---

[78] North, *Examen*, p. 595; Ailesbury, *Memoirs*, p. 71; Locke, *Second Treatise*, p. 427 (Para. 216); J. Ferguson, pp. 414, 416–17; POAS, III, 207–77; J. Marshall, *John Locke*, ch. 6; Scott, *Restoration Crisis*, p. 273.

[79] Scott, *Restoration Crisis*, pp. 272–3; J. Marshall, *John Locke*, pp. 242, 243–4; Ashcraft, *Revolutionary Politics*, pp. 351–2;

Court and the Whigs was a dramatic demonstration of how the rise of party feeling forced moderate men to choose one side or the other.[80]

As the election approached, both parties made extensive preparations. The "protesting Lords" continued to meet in London, but they "kept yr Caballs close." James's second return from Scotland in late May and the king's simultaneous brief illness served to keep attention focused upon the succession. While Monmouth dined with Shaftesbury – rather presumptuously during a royal illness[81] – Whig and Tory crowds celebrated the king's birthday in different ways and often in conflict with one another: "There [was] not . . . a Tavern but some mischeife or an other happened in it." After some discussion of possible shrieval candidates, the Whigs settled upon Thomas Papillon and John Dubois, clearly rejecting the possibility of splitting the two shrieval offices by electing a single Whig colleague for North. The Whig choice of candidates was a provocative one. Papillon and Dubois had each been exclusionist MPs. Each had been a prime mover of the Corporation petition for a parliament in May 1681. Each had served on Shaftesbury's jury, and Papillon had been outspoken in dismissing the crown's case. Dubois was a member of the city committee for defending the charter; and, according to a report of December 1681, he had called the king a papist.[82]

The Whigs continued to hope that the prospect of a general war against Louis XIV would require a parliament. In the meantime, they were determined to maintain their power in the Corporation as an alternate political theatre to parliament. A week before the election, Shaftesbury led the Whig lords and "a vast body" of followers in an elaborately staged night entrance into the city. Whig spokesmen prepared the liverymen for the election with the publication of arguments against the lord mayor's proposed "imposition" of one sheriff. With the contest in the courts much in mind, one author informed electors that the "design of wresting from you the priviledge of chusing the *Sheriffs* . . . [is] in order to hang as many of you" as loyalist magistrates and ministers should see fit. Electors were also encouraged, individually, to take out actions against the lord mayor for breach of their "Rights and Priviledges," should he attempt to declare North elected against the will of the common hall. For their part, loyalist propagandists

---

[80] Newdigate L.c. 1218 (18 May 1682); LC MS 18,124, VIII, 58 (18 May 1682); A. F. W. Papillon, *Memoirs of Thomas Papillon, of London, Merchant. (1623–1702)* (Reading, 1887), pp. 207–10; North, *Examen*, pp. 600–1; Haley, *Shaftesbury*, p. 697.

[81] Lord Grey remembered a discussion among Shaftesbury, Monmouth, and other Whig grandees for a rising against York's succession during Charles's "second sickness." One recent historian has dated this discussion to May 1682: Greaves, *Secrets*, p. 103; Grey, *Secret History*, pp. 11–13.

[82] Newdigate L.c. 1213, 1223, 1271 (29 April, 30 May, 7 Sept. 1682); LC MS 18,124, VII, 295, and VIII, 61, 63, 191 (25, 30 May [*bis*] and 1 June 1682); *CSPD 1680–1*, p. 603; *CSPD 1682*, pp. 190, 220, 244.

took on Whig arguments in the press, and Tory aldermen promoted the candidacies of North and of druggist Ralph Box, who was invited to Whitehall for strategy conferences.[83]

Capturing the unusual atmosphere of the election that began on 24 June and that concluded only in late September is as important as reconstructing the details. It was accompanied by episodes of physical and rhetorical violence unparalleled since the collapse of the republican regime in 1659–60. Arms were present from the beginning. The lord mayor opened the election on 24 June with the trained bands in Guildhall and in the streets. A few days later he was reported as keeping guards "every night at his Gate," while speculation thrived in July and September about the disposition of the king's forces outside the city and about preparations in the Tower. Whig liverymen were described as flocking to one hall "armed as if they had been goeing to a Battall." By September, the government was clearly very anxious, recognizing that Monmouth's well-attended progress through the western counties and the activities of the London Whigs were coordinated, and fearing that they signaled a resort to arms. When Tory sheriffs were sworn on the hustings at the end of the month, Whig aldermen were forcibly removed from Guildhall by the trained bands and threatened with "military discipline" if they did not keep silent. Whig citizens understandably complained then "that they had a military power set over them."[84]

Many meetings of the Privy Council were devoted to the affair, and the chief ministers of state entered the fray as regular participants. The principal secretary of state's presence in Guildhall was decisive at critical junctures. The king himself was closeted with the lord mayor at Whitehall frequently, and he once met with Moore in the city. Personal insults and political slogans were hurled through the air: Secretary Jenkins learned what Sheriff Shute thought of him, for instance. Two electors were suffocated in one crowded hall in July when temperatures became as hot as tempers. The lord mayor claimed

---

[83] LC MS 18,124, VIII, 60, 66, 71, 202 (23 May and 11, 20, 22 June 1682); Newdigate L.c. 1236 (1 July 1682); *The Right of Electing Sheriffs of London and Middlesex*, p. 4; *A Modest Enquiry concerning the Election of the sheriffs of London* (1682); *The Prerogative of the Right Honourable the Lord Mayor of London, Asserted* (1682); *The Case of the Sheriffs for the Year 1682*, preface; *Speech of the Right Honourable Sir John Moore*, p. 1; *Moderate Intelligencer* 1 (14 June 1682); *Observator*, I, 160 (24 June 1682); CSPD 1682, pp. 243, 259, 262, 263, 277; Luttrell, I, 198. A few days before Midsummer, Aldersgate loyalists succeeded in electing Southwark MP Richard How(e) as their alderman, in succession to the recently deceased Sir Thomas Bludworth, against Whig candidates John Dubois and Sheriff Shute. Repertory 87, fol. 190; Morrice, P, 337; LC MS 18,124, VIII, 70–1, 199 (15, 17, 20 June 1682); *Moderate Intelligencer* 2 (14–17 June 1682); CSPD 1682, p. 245.

[84] LC MS 18,124, VIII, 74–6, 79–80 (27, 29 June and 6 July 1682); Newdigate L.c. 1275 (16 Sept. 1682); *The Rights of the City Farther Unfolded* (1682), p. 4; *An Impartial Account of the Proceedings of the Common-Hall...June the 24th, 1682*; *True Account of the Irregular Proceedings at Guild-hall...September 28. 1682*, pp. 1–2; CSPD 1682, pp. 386–90ff.; HMC *House of Lords 1690–91*, p. 49; Luttrell, I, 224.

he was nearly "trampled under" after being assaulted in a scuffle, and his dislodged hat was "kickt up & down ye hall" by electors who ridiculed him as a "Rogue Papist Torie." London election news and prints inflamed local political discussion as far away as Chester. The entire kingdom held its breath by the end of the election as many wondered whether civic tumults might again presage the commencement of rebellion.

Arguments extended from Guildhall into the streets and into the churches and dissenting assemblies: "Pulpits rattle too like kettle drums," complained one loyalist. The lord mayor fussed, in the midst of the election, that the dissenting teachers "daily preach against him & upon the priviledges of the City." All thirty youthful scholars from a Newington dissenting academy were present at one common hall, because "though they were no livery-men nor freemen, their lives liberties and fortunes lay at stake."[85] Some forty leading parliamentary and civic Whigs, half of them dissenters, were indicted for riot after the first common hall; and others were charged with riot in September. Some Whig citizens came to believe that they were already experiencing the arbitrary government they associated with Catholicism. In 1683, during the disclosures about Whig plotting, conspirator after conspirator would point to the London shrieval election as prompting their resort to rebellion and assassination.[86]

The initial election of sheriffs on 24 June was a decisive defeat for Charles and his ministers, despite their well-laid plans. Encouraged by the presence of numerous "Protestant Lords," the Whig liverymen resisted Moore's demand that they confirm Dudley North; and the lord mayor was unable to stop the sheriffs from proceeding with a poll for all four candidates. Indeed, Pilkington and Shute persisted after Moore's adjournment of the hall and departure, claiming that they were the proper presiding officers and *"the Kings Ministers."* Objecting to the poll, some loyalists went home; and some who sought to poll for the confirmation of North, as the lord mayor's choice, were turned away. But other electors of opposite sentiments rushed to participate: "There was not a *Livery-Gown*... to be had... for any money," jeered L'Estrange. As the poll continued, Papillon and Dubois began to acquire an overwhelming majority.

The hall filled again during the evening of the 24th as thousands of citizens gathered in expectation of a declaration of Papillon and Dubois. Lord Mayor Moore returned to the hustings to insist that, since he had already adjourned the hall, any polling was irregular. Slingsby Bethel reportedly urged electors

---

[85] LC MS 18,124, VIII, 74, 84, 100, 116 (27 June, 15 July, 22 Aug., 21 Sept. 1682); Newdigate L.c. 1242–3 (15, 18 July 1682); *Matters of Fact in the Present Election of Sheriffs* (1682), p. 3; *ST*, IX, 252–3, 257; *CSPD 1682*, pp. 264–5, 280, 286, 382; "An Ironical Encomium" [1682] in *POAS*, III, 223 (line 66); Luttrell, I, 207.

[86] GHL MS 507/21 Sir John Moore Papers; *CSPD 1682*, p. 270; HMC *Lords 1690–91*, p. 49.

to "Resist him," and Moore was greeted with shouts of "no Pensioner, no Bribed magistrate." The lord mayor was hissed when he attempted to clear the hall in the king's name; and, according to loyalist observers, some Whig electors then took up a chant of "Down with the sword, No lord-mayor, no king." Moore was pushed outside, and the sheriffs continued the poll. Although Pilkington and Shute considered declaring the election of Papillon and Dubois in defiance of the lord mayor's adjournment, they followed the advice of the "Protestant Lords" and adjourned the poll themselves until the next week. Nearby church bells were rung in anticipation of Whig success, and bonfires brightened the city at night.[87]

Whig "joy and gladness" were premature, however, as loyalists reacted strongly to these exertions on behalf of Papillon and Dubois. Secretary Jenkins saw the election as new evidence of the "same spirit of sedition in the City, that has laboured all this while ... to overturn the monarchy"; and he was determined to reverse it. Ardent Anglicans also perceived the possible election of two "Whiggish Walloons" known to favor a resettlement of the church as threatening. At the bridge-house sessions, the lord mayor now encouraged retaliatory indictments of Southwark dissenting preachers and of Alderman Sir John Shorter, the senior Whig alderman beneath the chair, for harboring them.[88]

The lord mayor, the sheriffs, and several aldermen were summoned before the king-in-council on the 26th. The atmosphere there was as heated as it had been in common hall. The sheriffs were charged with abetting tumults within and without Guildhall. When Sheriff Shute claimed the free election of two sheriffs by the liverymen was lawful, the king "in huff replied, that since they were such strict observers of the law, they should have the law." The king ordered the sheriffs driven to the Tower "through the city to see who durst medle with them." The sheriffs assured the king of the city's loyalty and calmed the enormous crowd that followed their coaches through the streets from Temple Bar to the Tower. This surprising turn of events nevertheless perplexed and angered the Whig citizenry: "66 never made a greater fire in yr howses than is now in yr hearts," commented one observer; and many Country gentlemen were said to be coming to town to encourage the declaration of Papillon and Dubois.[89]

---

[87] LC MS 18,124, VIII, 73–4, 203 (24 [*bis*], 27 June 1682); *Domestick Intelligence* 114 (22–6 June 1682); *Observator*, I, 161 (28 June 1682); *Impartial Account*; *CSPD 1682*, pp. 263–5, 270, 272; *ST*, IX, 252–64; Luttrell, I, 196–8.

[88] LC 18,124, VIII, 74–6 (27, 29 June 1682); Morrice, P, 337; Newdigate L.c. 1235 (29 June 1682); *CSPD 1682*, pp. 265, 272, 275; *POAS*, III, 217; Luttrell, I, 202; Henning, *House of Commons*, II, 237, and III, 202.

[89] LC MS 18,124, VIII, 74–6, 204 (27 [*bis*], 29 June 1682); Newdigate L.c. 1234 (27 June 1682); *CSPD 1682*, p. 272.

The outcome of the poll, still undeclared, remained in doubt, while rumors, charges, and recriminations mounted. When the liverymen met again in early July, the result was no more satisfactory to Charles or to Secretary Jenkins, with each of whom the lord mayor had again consulted. The Whig aldermen organized a general meeting of the Whig liverymen in the interval, and leading Whig citizens bailed the sheriffs from their confinement. On 5 July, the sheriffs summoned a common hall in which the assembled electors called for "no delay" in the proceedings, despite a written adjournment from the lord mayor. Completing their poll, Pilkington and Shute declared the election of Papillon and Dubois. The Whig candidates had some 2,700 votes each, 1,100 more than Box and North, who were hissed on their appearance. On the 7th, the lord mayor opened his own poll in Guildhall in the presence of Tory electors; but the hall quickly filled with "well Armed" Whigs responding to "expresses" sent out by Clayton, Cornish, Bethel, and Player. The possibility of armed confrontation gave way to legal battle instead, as attorneys for the lord mayor and the sheriffs appeared to debate their respective authority in common hall. These arguments continued before the king-in-council, with Sir George Jeffreys and Attorney General Sir Robert Sawyer speaking for the lord mayor and Commons' Speaker Williams and Henry Pollexfen defending the authority of the sheriffs. In exasperation, the king ordered that the election begin *de novo* on 14 July.[90]

Party preparations for the second election were even more intense than those for the first. Each side now understood the determination of the other, and each better understood how all the major legal, religious, and constitutional issues of the day were involved. The lord mayor was said to have spent £200 on loyalist treats to make his "party as strong as possible." For their part, the Whig leaders talked about introducing a petition for a parliament at the new common hall. The sheriffs tangled with the lord chancellor when they were summoned before the council, together with the lord mayor and court of aldermen, two days before the new election. Lord Nottingham argued on behalf of the lord mayor's privilege of choosing Dudley North, but Sheriff Pilkington reportedly responded that "it is a free Common hall," and the people would "not be so easily shuffled from" their right of electing sheriffs. In the meantime, the Whig press churned out inflammatory tracts that universalized the issues before the electorate: "Your priviledges and rights... are not only all at stake," suggested one of these,

---

[90] LC MS 18,124, VIII, 77–82, 208 (1, 4, 6 [*bis*], 8, 11 July 1682); Newdigate L.c. 1236, 1238–40 (1, 6, 8, 11 July 1682); *Domestick Intelligence* 117–18 (3–6, 6–10 July 1682); *Observator*, I, 166, 168 (7, 10 July 1682); *CSPD 1682*, pp. 278, 280–1, 284, *Hatton Correspondence*, II, 16; Papillon, *Memoirs*, pp. 218–19; Luttrell, I, 200, 204.

"but . . . the eyes of the World are upon you how you will maintain and defend them."[91]

Whig electors contended even more directly with ministers on 14 July after much "muttering and Caballing" the previous night. A "hot day at Guildhall" opened with the trained bands in the streets and with two hours of "hurly burly." Secretary Jenkins, Chief Justice North, Sir George Jeffreys, and Lords Ormonde, Hyde, Halifax, and Ailesbury worked the electoral crowed in competition with the "discontented Lords." Reacting to ministerial intervention, Francis Jenks sought to read portions of the 1642 parliamentary regulation of the Privy Council, printed copies of which were also circulating in the hall. The lord mayor attempted to limit the electors' choices to confirming Dudley North and to electing one other sheriff. He faltered when the sheriffs demanded a poll among all four candidates; but he recovered his nerve after meeting with Secretary Jenkins during a brief adjournment. Moore then proceeded to one end of the hall to open a poll with the approved format, while Sheriffs Pilkington and Shute proceeded to the other end to conduct a poll among all four candidates. Loyalists favored one poll; Whigs favored the other.

The next evening, the lord mayor and Tory aldermen appeared and declared the election of North and Box in their poll; but the sheriffs also came onto the hustings to declare the election of Papillon and Dubois, by a two-to-one margin, in a poll of some 3,000 electors. The night concluded with scuffles in the streets and with the lord mayor's retreat to Whitehall for further conferences. In the following days, Alderman Cornish and Chamberlain Player gave banquets in honor of the new Whig sheriffs, while the lord mayor treated North and Box, assuring them that the king would stand by their election.[92]

Challenging the ministry and the crown

Each party now claimed to have elected the sheriffs for 1682–3. The London Whigs and their Country allies were determined to make good the election of their sheriffs, but their strategies were heavily shaped by Whig legal

---

[91] Loyalist apprentices, who claimed to number in the "thousands," chose this moment to address the king against the Whig association; and another address from some loyalist citizens pleaded for the suppression of all conventicles and for the "close confinement" of Shaftesbury and Monmouth. LC MS 18,124, VIII, 82–3, 210 (11, 13 [*bis*] July 1682); Newdigate L.c. 1240–1 (11, 13 July 1682); *The Priviledg and Right of the Free-men of London, to chuse their own Sheriffs* (1682) p. 8.

[92] LC MS 18,124, VIII, 83–6 (13, 15, 18 July 1682); Newdigate L.c. 1242 (15 July 1682); *Moderate Intelligencer* 10 (14 July 1682); *CSPD 1682*, pp. 286, 289–90, 292, 293, 294–5, 305; *The Right of Electing Sheriffs of London and Middlesex, briefly stated and declared* (1682) p. 4; Luttrell, I, 206–7; *Matters of Fact*, pp. 3–4.

vulnerability. Because the current sheriffs and several Whig citizens were indicted for riot after the initial common hall, and because the charter was
also legally imperiled, the Whigs chose to maintain their cause through legal
courses rather than through tumultuous behavior or rebellious threats. This
resort to law was entirely consistent with the defense of juries and of legal
process that had been an element of Whig thinking since the party emerged
from the civic opposition of the 1670s. Yet loyalists were also right to imag-
ine that some Whigs were assaying the prospects of a resort to force by the
conclusion of the shrieval election on 28 September.

The challenge to the lord mayor's declaration of Tory sheriffs on 14 July
was immediate. Rumors spread that Moore's action would be repudiated
at the Michaelmas common hall, at the end of September, when the liverymen would assemble to choose his successor. In the meantime, a "great
club of ye Liverymen," presided over by such Whig leaders as Sir Robert
Clayton and Sir Patience Ward, discussed other options. Many of these electors appeared at successive July aldermanic courts to petition that the "duely
elected sheriffs" be summoned to seal their bonds to serve. Before the last of
these meetings, the lord mayor again conferred with the king; and Ormonde,
Halifax, Clarendon, Hyde, and both secretaries visited him in the city. Three
thousand liverymen, expecting and demanding confirmation of Papillon and
Dubois, were said to be in Guildhall when the lord mayor confronted their
spokesmen in the council chamber on the 27th. When Moore rebuffed the
petitioners, Alderman Clayton and Sheriff Shute defused the situation, assuring the crowd that Papillon and Dubois would, in the end, be declared.[93]

Hundreds of citizens also took another course against the lord mayor.
Shaftesbury and the Whig magistrates promoted a subscription, reportedly
of £20,000, to defray the legal expenses of liverymen willing to sue the
lord mayor for violating their electoral rights. As the contest in the courts
took this new direction, the King's Bench judges were swamped with writs
"Impeaching . . . [the lord mayor] of the highest Crimes Imaginable & even
so farr as . . . Treasone." Moore was required to raise bail; and Charles was
outraged at "how men durst affront even Justice it self" in attacking his
principal magistrate for the Corporation. The government assumed "the
trouble and charge" of answering these citizens' suits, a course that even
more obviously placed the crown on the wrong side of the law, as far as
Whig citizens were concerned. These new Whig strategies terrified Ralph

---

[93] Repertory 87, fols. 209–210, 216; SP 29/419/165, 168; LC MS 18,124, VIII, 86–92, 212,
216 (17, 18, 20, 22, 25, 27 [*bis*] July 1682); Newdigate L.c. 1243, 1246, 1248–9 (18, 25, 27
July 1682); *Moderate Intelligencer* 12, 14 (19–22, 26–9 July 1682); *Observator*, I, 177 (25
July 1682); *Domestick Intelligence* 122, 128 (20–24 July and 10–14 Aug. 1682); *Matters of
Fact*, p. 4; *A Paper subscribed and delivered . . . July the 20th 1682*, CSPD 1682, pp. 304–5,
315–16; Luttrell, I, 207–10.

Box. He feared his estate and reputation would suffer if he accepted an illegal election, and his well-known doubts left the resolution of the shrieval election open during the customary August recess of Corporation business.[94]

Did the strategies considered by the civic and parliamentary Whigs in August 1682 also include the organization of a rebellion? In his subsequent confession to complicity in Whig plotting, Lord Grey suggested that the opposition grandees had seriously discussed "having recourse to arms" in late summer 1682. Grey remembered attending "many meetings" at that time and listening to "innumerable proposals." He suggested that both Shaftesbury and Monmouth were directly involved in such plotting and that Monmouth's September visit to Cheshire was part of a broader plan to determine whether sufficient support for a rising could be found in the western counties.

Important elements of Grey's story are paralleled in Robert Ferguson's recollections; and London evidence also points to secretive Whig consultations in August, when an unusual number of "discontented Lords" and gentry remained in town. By the end of the month, the often well-informed Whig apprentice news writer reported that "nothing is to be seen but caballs of all sorts," noting particularly that "M[onmouth's] and Sh[aftesbury's] Courts are as throng[ed] as possible, looking more Like the Palaces of Kings than Subjects."[95] Grey subsequently dated to this time a report from Shaftesbury, that "the most considerable men" in the city "had promised him they would rise," if Monmouth initiated a revolt in the West. Gathering London intelligence more assiduously than ever, Secretary Jenkins learned that some citizens were indeed employing rebellious language. Violent words and violent behavior, possible indications of desperate intentions, had in fact become commonplace in the capital as the shrieval election remained unresolved.[96]

But Whig magistrates like Clayton, Shute, and Sir John Lawrence (each tied to Shaftesbury and to Monmouth) also made public efforts to maintain order in the ranks. Their endeavors suggest that sober heads continued to prefer customary legal and political processes to any form of organized violence. Monmouth and his noble friends seemed more interested in overt opposition

---

[94] LC MS 18,124, VIII, 93–8 (17, 29 July and 1, 3, 8 Aug. 1682); Newdigate L.c. 1243–7, 1250–1, 1271, 1275 (18, 20, 22, 25, 29 July and 7, 16 Sept. 1682); *True Protestant Mercury* 161 (19–22 July 1682); *CSPD 1682*, pp. 304, 369; Luttrell, I, 208.

[95] LC MS 18,124, VIII, 100–2 (22, 24, 26 Aug. 1682); *CSPD 1682*, pp. 302, 313–14, 326–8, 356–8; Grey, *Secret History*, pp. 23–33; J. Ferguson, *Ferguson*, pp. 417–18, 420; Haley, *Shaftesbury*, pp. 710–12; Ashcraft, *Revolutionary Politics*, pp. 353–6; Greaves, *Secrets*, pp. 107–12.

[96] LC MS 18,124, VIII, 108 (5 Sept. 1682): see note 47 for further details about this apprentice news writer. *Moderate Intelligencer* 13, 15, 17, 26 (22–6 July; 29 July–2 Aug.; 5–9 Aug.; 7–11 Sept. 1682); *True Protestant Mercury* 162, 173 (22–26 July and 30 Aug.–2 Sept. 1682); Grey, *Secret History*, p. 29; Goldie, "Hilton Gang," 50–2, 59–60.

to Charles's policies than in covert resistance. Some of the duke's Country supporters were openly circulating associations of support for the Protestant religion and for the Protestant successor. And some of them also reportedly signed a "League" to stand by Monmouth and his cause. When Monmouth departed London for his western tour, he did so publicly, again, with "a verry numerous Traine" that included the Earls of Essex, Kent, and Clare and Lords Herbert and Russell.

The most likely interpretation of Monmouth's tour is that the Whig grandees intended it as a further public demonstration to the government of popular hostility to the returned York. Their political futures and that of the cause they defended had come to rest too precariously upon the future of London juries and of the London shrievalty. Still without a parliament, and with local Whig office-holders jeopardized by pressure on borough charters throughout the country, the Whigs needed to demonstrate to the Court that they were not politically inert outside the capital. Monmouth's visit to Cheshire and adjacent counties was a natural extension of the effort to sustain the succession issue from London to the kingdom, and it was also timed for maximum effect. A show of strength elsewhere would assist Whig liverymen in a critical election that had momentous implications for both church and state.

But that a serious, concerted effort to raise a rebellion was already underway seems doubtful. The Whigs had recently survived a damaging series of treason trials, and they had to contend daily with charges of plotting in the loyalist press. With the outcome of the election still open, the wiser course would have been to avoid indiscreet talk. Unfortunately, the West Country crowds who shouted "A Monmouth, a Monmouth," did talk indiscreetly. The result was a panicky government even more determined to stay its course against "traitorous" opponents in the city.[97]

Whig determination was obvious when Corporation business resumed at an aldermanic court on 5 September. Thomas Papillon carried a poll that day against Dudley North to become master of the Mercers' Company, of which both were members; and John Dubois was chosen master of the Weavers' Company. Ralph Box appeared to offer his fine; and numerous Whig liverymen appeared to demand that the aldermen accept Papillon and Dubois as sheriffs-elect. Whig delegations appeared at the court of aldermen again on 12 and 14 September, when they were seconded by Middlesex freeholders

---

[97] This interpretation does not rule out the possibility that Monmouth's tour was intended to test the waters for the possibility of resistance, should that course become necessary. Indeed, the fact that leading Whig magistrates were cautioning their followers against more extreme courses may suggest that talk of resistance and violence was actually becoming more frequent. *CSPD 1682*, pp. 386–93; Grey, *Secret History*, pp. 29–33; J. Ferguson, *Ferguson*, pp. 418, 420; Ashcraft, *Revolutionary Politics*, pp. 354–5.

who claimed to be as concerned in the choice of sheriffs for London and Middlesex as the liverymen. What was now required, they argued, was not another election to find a successor to Box, as the lord mayor had indicated, but rather the acceptance of the sheriffs who had already been chosen.[98]

The Whig liverymen and freemen who attended the court of aldermen reminded the lord mayor that "the Law accounts such persons capital offenders" who would "presume to dispose of our lives and estates" by imposing pretended sheriffs. As rumors circulated that Moore would at last concede the shrievalty to the electorate, the Whigs began "gathering heart...[and] promising themselves successe." In fact, however, the crown remained adamant. When Charles and York returned to Whitehall on 13 September, the lord mayor was summoned and advised not to call a common hall for the election of a replacement for Box until 19 September, in order to give the government time to prepare. Charles postponed his planned trip to Newmarket; and the trained bands were again readied, as were the royal foot and horse guards.[99]

By this time, almost three months after the Midsummer common hall, the news writers agreed that "the discourse of this town" was "of nothing else" but the shrieval election. One writer suggested that the "heats and animosities of...[the] parties are so great that the consequences may be fatal." The apprentice news writer wished "from my heart the day may terminate peacefully," but he expected that it would not. The Whig leaders consulted with counsel. Some London Baptists were apparently approaching the election with the language of Armageddon on their minds. Whig activist John Rouse believed that soldiers would be employed against electors, but he boasted "it's present death for hundreds of them, for we shall have thousands to stand by us here and elsewhere."[100]

In the event, the common hall of 19 September produced as inconclusive a result as that of 14 July. Secretary Jenkins was again present, and Algernon Sidney saw the election from an adjacent balcony. Ironically, most of the "extraordinary" number of liverymen present in the hall came to protest the lord mayor's conduct of another election at all. To a deafening chorus

---

[98] Repertory 87, fol. 230; LC MS 18,124, VIII, 101–3, 108, 110–12, 230 (24, 26, 29 Aug. and 5 [*bis*], 9, 12[*bis*], 14[*bis*] Sept. 1682); Newdigate L.c. 1267, 1270–4 (29 Aug. and 5, 7, 9, 12, 14 Sept. 1682); *Moderate Intelligencer* 23 (28–31 Aug. 1682); *True Protestant Mercury* 174–5 (2–6, 6–9 Sept. 1682); *CSPD 1682*, pp. 311–12; Luttrell, I, 217–20.

[99] LC MS 18,124, VIII, 112–15, 235–6 (14, 16[*bis*], 19[*bis*] Sept. 1682); Newdigate L.c. 1272–5 (9, 12, 14, 16 Sept. 1682); *To the Lord Mayor and Court of Aldermen of the City of London* (1682); *A Paper presented by divers Citizens of the City of London, Sept. 5. 1682*; *A Fourth Paper presented by divers Citizens* (1682); *True Protestant Mercury* 176 (9–13 Sept. 1682); *CSPD 1682*, pp. 392, 394, 401, 403; Luttrell, I, 217, 219.

[100] LC MS 18,124, VIII, 113 (16 Sept. 1682); Newdigate L.c. 1272–3, 1275 (9, 12, 16 Sept. 1682); *CSPD 1682*, pp. 401, 403–5; Luttrell, I, 217.

of "noe Election noe Election," the common sergeant put up as a colleague for North the names of two civic Tories handed to him by the lord mayor. One of these was Southwark MP and JP Peter Rich. At a pre-arranged signal, loyalists waved their handkerchiefs and shouted for Rich. In response, Sheriffs Pilkington and Shute put the question of whether the electors wished to stand by their former choice, which touched off further shouting on behalf of Papillon and Dubois. In the confusion, the lord mayor declared the election of Rich and dissolved the hall "before...anybody...knew what was adoeing."

As the lord mayor departed, the sheriffs announced a poll on behalf of Papillon and Dubois; and pursuing a course that had previously landed them in the Tower, they persisted over the lord mayor's note forbidding a poll. Moore appeared again late in the afternoon to clear the hall, but Pilkington then leapt on the hustings to declare the election of Papillon and Dubois with over 2,000 votes each to a handful for electing Rich and confirming North.[101] The next morning, when Moore appeared at Guildhall, he was forced to flee into the council chamber when a Whig crowd rushed upon him "& certainly wold have pulled him to pieces." Only after several hours behind barricaded doors, and after the arrival of guards, did he go to Whitehall to inform the Council about the election.[102]

When Sheriffs Pilkington and Shute were summoned before the king-in-council on the evening of the 20th to answer for their behavior, they brought with them four leading Whig lawyers. Questioned about his authority to conduct a poll, Pilkington repeated his previous public statement that he acted on behalf of the "supreme authority in London," namely the liverymen assembled in common hall. According to one Whig account, Pilkington also informed the king-in-council that, since the lord mayor had jeopardized "our Lives, Religion & Liberty," the "peopell should fortify ymselvs against yr own Ruine." The sheriffs were again bailed, and the lord mayor returned to the city with an escort of the king's guards. The apprentice writer concluded that "this will end with ye sword," and the Whig leaders plotted further strategy at a dinner Pilkington offered his bail the following day.[103]

What that strategy would be became clear on 26 September when the court of aldermen met again, three days before the customary Michaelmas

---

[101] LC MS 18,124, VIII, 115, 236 (19[*bis*] Sept. 1682); Newdigate L.c. 1276 (19 Sept. 1682); *Domestick Intelligence* 139 (18–21 Sept. 1682); *True Protestant Mercury* 178 (16–20 Sept. 1682); *Account of the proceedings on the 19th. Instant*, 1682; "The Apology of A. Sidney" from Algernon Sidney, *The Works of Algernon Sidney* (1772), reprinted in *ST*, IX, 918; *CSPD 1682*, pp. 410, 412, 417; Burnet, *History*, II, 337; Papillon, *Memoirs*, pp. 221–2; Luttrell, I, 220.

[102] LC MS 18,124, VIII, 116, 237 (21 [*bis*] Sept. 1682); *CSPD 1682*, p. 417.

[103] LC MS 18,124, VIII, 116, 237 (21 [*bis*] Sept. 1682); Newdigate L.c. 1277 (21 Sept. 1682); *CSPD 1682*, pp. 415, 417–18; Luttrell, I, 221.

mayoral election, and two days before the customary swearing of the new sheriffs. The Whigs had determined to adhere to their election of Papillon and Dubois by attempting to have them sworn. And, if North and Rich were imposed upon the city instead, the Whigs anticipated that the liverymen could then be counted upon to elect a new lord mayor who would repudiate the "pretended" sheriffs. The aldermen were also informed by a Whig petition that any acceptance of North and Rich would not only constitute a "breach of their trusts" but also would "be the most notorious violation of the ancient and known rights and privileges of this city that has ever been committed."[104]

In the meantime, the issues of the succession and of electoral rights had been joined in the city upon Monmouth's return from Cheshire. Arrested at Stafford for fomenting popular tumults, Monmouth was bailed in London by several Whig lords, treated by Shaftesbury and Essex, and welcomed by such Whig activists as Sir Thomas Player and Michael Godfrey. If the arrest and interrogation of the duke were intended to deflate Whig hopes, however, these actions were complete failures.[105]

On 28 September, Papillon and Dubois appeared at Guildhall an hour or two before the expected swearing of the sheriffs on the hustings, as did "some thousands" of civic electors. Accompanied by the Whig aldermen and by the assistants of the Mercers' Company, they found Guildhall locked and patrolled by several companies of trained bands and some of the king's guards, "a thing expressly contrary to the *English* Constitution, which hath been jealous of nothing more than the preserving Elections free from force." The Whig aldermen nevertheless managed to get inside the hall through the hustings door. But a lieutenancy officer confronted them immediately, drawing up his soldiers on all sides, and physically removing them from the hustings. When the lord mayor appeared outside the hall, he was accosted by the still excluded liverymen, who found "fault with the Souldiers being there," and called Moore "perjured, betrayer of yr Rights and Priveledges, Papist &c." Although Moore commanded them to depart, "as having no business there," when he entered the hall, "about a thousand or more forced (through the Guards) in after him, before the Souldiers could make a stop." Inside the hall, the trained bands now confronted angry liverymen. Sheriff Pilkington worked the crowd, arguing "yt it wold not be wisdome in them to comitt any Ryot or outrage," since "ye Law" was available for remedy.

The lord mayor encountered the Whig magistrates, accompanied by Papillon and Dubois in the council chamber, where he accused them of

[104] LC MS 18,124, VIII, 119, 239 (26 [*bis*], 28 Sept. 1682); Newdigate L.c. 1279 (26 Sept. 1682); *Domestick Intelligence* 141 (25–8 Sept. 1682); *True Protestant Mercury* 180 (23–7 Sept. 1682); *CSPD 1682*, pp. 430–1, 433; Luttrell, I, 221–3.

[105] LC MS 18,124, VIII, 117, 119, 240 (23, 26, 28 Sept. 1682); Newdigate L.c. 1278–9 (23, 26 Sept. 1682); *CSPD 1682*, pp. 429–30, 432.

attempting to swear false sheriffs in his absence. Papillon and Dubois presented the aldermen with a paper indicating their willingness to undertake the office to which they had been elected, and the Whig aldermen demanded a debate. When Moore refused, the Whigs indicated their intention to proceed according to law, an intention that, under the circumstances, permitted them to stage a political tableau in which electoral rights were sacrificed to military power in the sight of thousands. Moore and the loyalist aldermen proceeded to the hustings for the swearing, with Dudley North and Peter Rich in train. The Whig aldermen also proceeded to the hustings with Papillon and Dubois. When the crowd moved forward, "the *Military Guards* ... closed again, so that the Liveries attending could not come near." The common sergeant began to administer the oaths to North and Rich, and then "Mr. Papillon and Mr. Dubois laid their hands also on the book, but the lord mayor commanded them in the kings name to depart and keep the peace: so they departed, and severall of the aldermen who were of their side went out of the court also." The ceremony continued "notwithstanding the great Noise of the people all the tyme cryeing No North No Riche a Papillione & Duboise." The new sheriffs departed the hall and were greeted by "a very great Number of Loyall men," who accompanied them through the streets to a celebratory dinner at Drapers' Hall.[106]

CONCLUSION: THE CURTAILMENT OF ELECTORAL CHOICE

Historical reference to the London shrieval election of 1682 ordinarily concludes with the suggestion that the crown and the civic loyalists had gained the prize from their opponents.[107] But the shrieval election actually concluded not with an undisputed Tory victory, but rather with a contest for legitimacy between pairs of Tory and Whig sheriffs. Just as Monmouth had been advanced as a Protestant alternative to York, so now Papillon and Dubois would be advanced as the true sheriffs in opposition to the "creatures" imposed by the ministry and the lord mayor. The Whigs claimed that the regime had prevented office-holders chosen by the electorate from assuming the offices to which they had been chosen: the king, his agents, and the trained bands had violated electoral consent. Indeed, the city had "come under a military government," according to retiring Sheriffs Pilkington and Shute.[108]

---

[106] GHL MS 3504; LC MS 18,124, VIII, 121, 240 (28 [*bis*] Sept. 1682); Newdigate L.c. 1280 (28 Sept. 1682); *Moderate Intelligencer* 32 (28 Sept.-2 Oct. 1682); *True Account of the Irregular Proceedings*; Papillon, *Memoirs*, pp. 223–7; Luttrell, I, 224–5.

[107] Haley, *Shaftesbury*, p. 704, Jones, *First Whigs*, p. 206; Harth, *Pen*, p. 207; Greaves, *Secrets*, p. 96; Henning, *House of Commons*, I, 314 (which misdates the mayoral election). But see a more reliable short account in Miller, *Charles II*, pp. 368–72.

[108] *Case between the Ld. Mayor & Commons*, p. 6; Luttrell, I, 225.

The Whigs nevertheless remained convinced that they could still elect a Whig lord mayor who would advance their case against shrieval usurpers. The mayoralty had frequently been on the minds of those contesting about the shrievalty. As early as July, Secretary Jenkins had prepared a memorandum defending the royal continuation of Lord Mayor Moore, if an unacceptable Whig were chosen, claiming a clause of the charter in support of such a royal prerogative. For their part, the Whigs had both promoted Sir John Shorter, the Whig alderman beneath the chair with the most seniority, and had also considered alternatives to Shorter because of his "simplicity" and "facill humor." In the event, the government and the loyalist magistrates hesitated to employ a supposed prerogative about which the lord chancellor was said to have doubts. But they did determine to contest the election on behalf of loyalist Sir William Pritchard, the senior alderman beneath the chair, with all other devices at their disposal.[109]

The government had, however, become overconfident. The ministers were unprepared for Whig tactics on Michaelmas. Not about "to suffer an Arbitrary unjust one to Rule" over them, the Whigs began preparing for Michaelmas at the conclusion of the common hall on the 28th. After the loyalist aldermen had departed the hall, the Whig aldermen had actually sworn Papillon and Dubois as sheriffs and then planned further steps with the Whig grandees at a great feast offered by the Earl of Kent.[110] On the 29th, Guildhall was patrolled by the trained bands, as on the previous day; but when Lords Halifax and Hyde and Secretary Jenkins sought to enter Guildhall for the election, "the peopell wold not suffer ym to enter." As the election proceeded, all the aldermen beneath the chair were put up for lord mayor. Dudley North, officiating as sheriff, claimed a majority of voices for Alderman Pritchard, and he communicated this result to the lord mayor and aldermen in the council chamber. But Papillon and Dubois, also acting as sheriffs, immediately appeared to charge electoral abuse in North's denial of a poll on behalf of the strongest Whig candidates, Aldermen Henry Cornish and Sir Thomas Gold. Sir Robert Clayton and the Whig aldermen then "rose up in a flash" in support of Papillon and Dubois, demanding a "fair poll." All the magistrates now entered Guildhall; and a poll was begun between Aldermen Pritchard and Sir Henry Tulse, on the loyalist side, and Aldermen Cornish and Sir Thomas Gold, for the Whigs. After two hours of polling, Cornish led, with Gold second; and the Whig aldermen demanded that "ye 4 Sheriffes" declare this result. Instead, Moore adjourned the poll until the following week.

[109] LC MS 18,124, VIII, 90, 100, 111, 122 (25 July, 22 Aug., 12 and 30 Sept. 1682); Newdigate L.c. 1274 (16 Sept. 1682); HMC *Ormonde*, NS, VI, 451–2; *CSPD 1682*, p. 302.
[110] LC MS 18,124, VIII, 121, 123 (28, 30 Sept. 1682); Newdigate L.c. 1281 (30 Sept. 1682).

Although irritated at the adjournment, the Whig citizens who accompanied Cornish home believed they had carried the election for him. Some courtiers also interpreted the common hall of 29 September as a Whig victory. Lord Arlington was astonished that the city would choose so "disaffected and seditious" a lord mayor as Henry Cornish. He and Ormonde thought the king should require a new election. On the other side, some Whig stalwarts suspected foul play was in the offing from a regime that had already curtailed electoral choice over the shrievalty. And, in the meantime, the government had learned about several secretive meetings that were reportedly intended to secure the king's agreement to exclusion by seizing him.[111]

But Whig sobriety again prevailed over reckless talk. On the 30th, the day when the Tory sheriffs were presented to the Exchequer barons at Westminster for royal confirmation, the Amsterdam coffeehouse was the site of a "great consult" of leading Whig magistrates and lawyers. At issue was how they could respond to the display of "Arbitrary power" they had experienced in recent common halls. Sir John Frederick, alderman since 1653 and an anti-cavalier lord mayor in 1661, carried the day with a speech on behalf of prudence. He well understood the temptation that many apparently felt to resort to desperate courses, but he argued that part of the loyalists' design was "to provock us to maintaine our priveledg by ye sword, & . . . set us forth to ye world with ye Character of Rebellious disloyall London." Frederick feared that any violence or "menaces & Thrates" would sink the Whig ship in charges "yt we brock ye Law." Instead, he argued, the Whigs' continuing adherence to law was the only means to "show to ye world how we have been abused." He was confident that the law would fairly decide between the imposed Tory sheriffs and those who had been rightfully chosen. In the meantime, he urged, "let us neither own ye one as Sheriffes nor pairt wt ye other as not Sheriffs."[112]

Both the hope of having Cornish's election as lord mayor confirmed and the priority of preserving the charter against the crown's *quo warranto* supported this line of reasoning. But loyalist observations that "the great business of the sheriffs" was now "completely settled" were unfounded.[113] In reality, the city was divided between those who regarded its current government as legitimate and those who regarded loyalists like North, Rich, and Pritchard as illegitimate vehicles for arbitrary practices. Moreover, and dangerously for the crown, the extent of ministerial intervention in London had

---

[111] LC MS 18,124, VIII, 122 (30 Sept. 1682); Newdigate L.c. 1281 (30 Sept. 1682); *Domestick Intelligence* 142 (28 Sept.–2 Oct. 1682); *Observator*, I, 217 (4 Oct. 1682); HMC *Ormonde*, NS, VI, 455; *CSPD 1682*, pp. 441–2, 448.

[112] LC MS 18,124, VIII, 14 (5 Oct. 1682); Henning, *House of Commons*, II, 363.

[113] LC MS 18,124, VIII, 124 (5 Oct. 1682); Newdigate L.c. 1281 (30 Sept. 1682); *CSPD 1682*, p. 441.

also destroyed the respect of many civic Whigs for the king and his chief officers. Although most leading Whigs were prepared to stand with Alderman Frederick against overt resistance, their stand rested, in part, on an assumption that Henry Cornish would be declared the lawful lord mayor-elect. But what if Frederick's confidence in the law proved unfounded? Indeed, many believed that the shrieval election had already curtailed electoral choice and replaced ancient civic practice and the law with a "military government." Like John Locke, some London Whigs were on the verge of asking whether actions already undertaken by the regime constituted a dissolution of the government itself or whether they so imperiled the law as to justify far more drastic responses.

6

Party matters: communities, ideas, and leaders in a divided city, 1679–1682

INTRODUCTION: PARTY AND POLARIZATION

The civic elections of 1682 revealed the extent of party feeling and party organization in London. Party confrontations were a natural expression of the different hopes and fears of divergent Protestant communities. This chapter examines both the Whig and Tory discourse that dominated the public sphere of London in the Restoration Crisis and the different communities in which these opposite political and religious languages flourished. It begins with a topographic analysis of urban politics that anchors the expression of partisanship in contrasting socio-geographic spaces in the Corporation of London. Party in London in 1679–82 was a neighborhood affair, an expression of the local networks of friendship and affinity that have already been seen, especially in the civic Whigs' political petitioning and feasting. The chapter also examines how urban debate about the succession and parliament was shaped by the different discursive traditions maintained in these party-inclined spaces. Finally, Chapter 6 examines the leaderships and the electoral followings of the two parties: they were captained by contrasting political elites and favored by contrasting collections of guild electors. The different communities, ideas, leaders, and electoral followings that sustained partisanship in London all suggest that party is no misplaced historical construction in analysis of the Restoration Crisis.

Historians have become wary of employing binary divisions in the analysis of early modern English political life, but a polarization of opinion nevertheless accompanied the expression of partisanship in London and the kingdom during the crisis. Long-standing disagreements between Anglicans, on the one hand, and dissenters and Reformed Protestants, on the other hand, intensified between 1679 and 1682, as parliament followed parliament, as electoral contest followed electoral contest, and as the printed production of opposition and loyalist pens mushroomed after the lapse of press licensing. A highly literate center of popular Protestant reading and reflection that was rivaled only by Amsterdam, London provided arenas for debate and disagreement that extended from its coffeehouses and taverns – and from its Exchange and crowded commercial courtyards – into parish meetings, wardmotes, and common hall assemblies. Moreover, the city's remarkable concentration of facilities for the social exchange of ideas was matched by its unsurpassed concentration of opinion-makers prepared to contribute to such exchanges. A hundred or more dissenting clergy challenged the efforts of their parish counterparts, while the loyalist polemics of press guardian Sir Roger L'Estrange and Court poet John Dryden were answered by the production of Whig journalists and lawyers like Henry Care and Edward Whitaker. The result, in 1679–82, was a tempest of disagreement about politics and religion in Europe's most vigorous public sphere that was as bitter, as contentious, and as polarized as the "rage of party" that followed the Revolution of 1688–9.[1]

Moderation is hard to find in the Restoration Crisis, although some historians have persisted in looking for it.[2] The "moderate" Presbyterian Richard Baxter, for instance, was as outspoken as any sectarian in maligning the bishops as "*dividing . . . silencing,* and *persecuting* Prelates" employed by the "Prince of pride and darkness . . . to smite the true Shepherds, and scatter the Flocks." Scholars must strain as hard to find any real moderation in the public language of Edward Stillingfleet, Dean of St Paul's, a "latitudinarian" previously admired by many dissenters and Reformed Protestants. Stillingfleet's famous sermon to a civic audience of May 1680 was one of the most outspoken condemnations of dissenting ideas and practices published since 1660. He held the dissenters entirely responsible for the division of English Protestantism, and he dismissed conscience as fanciful and prone to error. As demands for parliamentary resettlement of the church mounted, Stillingfleet rejected such a course as a truckling to the "insolence" of the sects, who were "filling the people with greater prejudices against our Communion" than ever before. He was prepared to accept only a very restricted indulgence of dissenters, with penalties, and without hope of comprehension except through acceptance of the existing order.[3] Exchanges between

[1] J. Habermas, *The Structural Transformation of the Public Sphere*, tr. T. Burger with F. Lawrence (Cambridge, Mass., 1989), pp. 27, 52, 57–67; Pincus, "'Coffee Politicians does Create'"; T. Crist, "Government Control of the Press after the Expiration of the Printing Act in 1679," *Publishing History* 5 (1979), 49–77; W. G. Mason, "The Annual Output of Wing-Listed Titles 1649–1684," *The Library*, 5th ser. 29 (1974), 219–20; Schwoerer, *Ingenious Mr. Henry Care*. For the number of dissenting clergy, see Newdigate L.c. 1477 (10 Jan. 1684). Whitaker, who was solicitor to Buckingham, produced several pamphlets in 1681–2.

[2] Scott, "Restoration Process," p. 628; Scott, *England's Troubles*, p. 442.

[3] Richard Baxter, *Church History of the Government of Bishops and their Councils Abbreviated* (1680), p. 458; Stillingfleet, *Mischief of Separation*, pp. 3, 17, 22, 54; Stillingfleet, *Unreasonableness of Separation*, Preface and pp. x, liv, xlvii, lxx, lxxix–lxxxvi; J. H. Fishman, "Edward Stillingfleet, Bishop of Worcester (1635–99): Anglican Bishop and Controversialist," Unpublished Ph.D. thesis, University of Wisconsin, 1977.

dissenting spokesmen like Baxter and Anglicans like Stillingfleet split the public sphere in 1679–82, filling the prints and coloring discourse with hostile language and invective.[4] The dean himself complained that serious matters had become the "Sport and Entertainment of the Coffee-Houses," as the hubbub spread from print to talk and back again: "At one Club they cry ... *Baxter* has it, *Baxter* has it," while "at another House they cry nothing but, O brave Dr. *Stillingfleet!*"[5]

Nuance did exist in civic debate and political confrontation, as the examples of Sir Robert Clayton and Sir John Moore suggest. But in the polarized state of opinion in 1679–82, nuance was driven to the extremes, as both these examples also illustrate. Whigs and dissenters could no more compromise their demands for a resettlement of church and state, through Protestant accommodation and a Protestant succession, than Anglican loyalists could compromise their attachment to the existing settlement. "It is ridiculous," wrote L'Estrange, "to talk of moderation in a case that admits of no excess." While some in church and state might seek to "trim" between opposite stances, they were suspected all around. Few, other than the Marquis of Halifax, ever self-identified with the name of trimmer or sought to turn it to credit. The point about trimming is rather that it was a label of Anglican abuse in an increasingly polarized political culture: it was a loyalist rhetorical tool for stressing that Anglican identity and Whig politics were mutually exclusive. Hence, the whiggish divine Gilbert Burnet was savaged by fellow Anglicans as a "Church-Trimmer," a "profest Enemy to all Ceremony," who had sought, with his Reformed Protestant associates, "to set up a new Church within the old." Trimming in the state was equally condemned. Those who "flatter the popular power as well as regal" were, according to Dryden "Damn'd Neuters" and "true to neither Cause."[6]

---

[4] Accounts of the literature of this controversy may be found in W. Orme, *Memoirs of the Life, Writings, and Religious Connexions, of John Owen, D. D.* (1820), pp. 414–17; G. R. Cragg, *Puritanism in the Period of the Great Persecution, 1660–1688* (New York, 1971), pp. 233–6; R. A. Beddard, "Vincent Alsop and the Emancipation of Restoration Dissent," *JEcH* 24 (1973), 163–7; Ashcraft, *Revolutionary Politics*, pp. 490–3. Although Stillingfleet is sometimes portrayed as provoking a dissenting response, he had in fact been provoked by the writings of the dissenting spokesmen for conscience, who in turn, replied to him. For discussion of Locke's response to Stillingfleet, see esp. J. Marshall, "John Locke and Latitudinarianism," in *Philosophy, Science, and Religion in England, 1640–1700,* ed. R. Kroll, R. Ashcraft, and P. Zagorin (Cambridge, 1992), pp. 255–6, 277 n.17; Marshall, *John Locke,* pp. 94–110.

[5] Stillingfleet, *Unreasonableness of Separation,* p. lv; *A Dialogue between Two Jesuits, Father Antony and Father Ignatius, at Amsterdam* [1681]. This polarization was not a simple division between dissent and the established church, for the dissenters were divided among themselves on a variety of issues, and Reformed Protestantism extended into the Church of England.

[6] *Observator,* I, 240–9 (13–29 Nov. 1682) with quote from 247 (25 Nov. 1682); *Last Words and Sayings; The Character of a Church-Trimmer* (1683); *POAS,* III, 451; John Dryden, Epilogue, lines 39, 41 to *The Duke of Guise* (1683) in *The Works of John Dryden,* ed. E. N. Hooker

The ideas that contributed to the polarization of opinion in London in 1679–82 were not entirely new ideas, even though they were often articulated in novel fashion. The issues of parliament and popery provoked the rearticulation of rhetorical traditions – especially traditions about consent and authority and about reformation – that had led to confrontation and civil war once before. This past weighed heavily on Anglican writers who regarded the teeming discourse of 1679–82 as signifying a breakdown in respect for authority in church and state that required reversal. Indeed, loyalist intellectuals like L'Estrange engaged in public debate not only to answer their opponents but also to close down the volatile public sphere itself. That "every Tap-house and Coffee-house" was "full of Wrangling and Dispute" was not a sign, for them, of intellectual vitality. Instead, in publishing their "*Malicious Libels*" in "one Book after another," the dissenters and Whigs were playing the sectarian fool in the Roman design to destroy the Protestant establishment of England. What was needed was an end to "*Writing* on *Both* sides" that did little but "*Enflame Differences* and beget *Heats.*"[7]

But the Tory endeavor to restrain the expression of different ideas about church and state was unrealistic. The polarization of opinion in London's vigorous public sphere was neither a stage in the crisis, nor a result of the crisis, but rather an enduring feature of the crisis and of the Restoration. Polarization was driven by incompatible Protestant agendas for church and state. In London, those agendas reflected the aspirations, histories, and memories of quite different Protestant communities. And those communities were, in turn, concentrated in the particular social and cultural locales in which party was bred, nurtured, and sustained.

DIFFERENT COMMUNITIES: THE TOPOGRAPHY OF PARTY

When the public sphere of Restoration London is mapped topographically, it proves to be a somewhat artificial construct, for the city was geographically divided between contrasting spaces in which different political and religious languages and ideas flourished. Freemen and householders of all social groups could be found on either side of the political and religious division of London. But the opposite partisan perspectives of the crisis were nevertheless embodied in enduring spatial communities with distinctive characteristics. The identification of these communities permits the establishment

---

and H. T. Swedenberg, Jr., 19 vols. (Berkeley, 1956–), XIV, 213, 330–2; *The Reformation, A Satire* [1683]. For a different view of trimming, see esp. S. Pincus, "Shadwell's Dramatic Trimming," in Hamilton and Strier, eds., *Religion, Literature, and Politics*, pp. 253–74.

7 *Observator*, I, 1, 240 (13 April 1681, 13 Nov. 1682); *Dialogue between Two Jesuits*; Stillingfleet, *Unreasonableness of Separation*, pp. x, xxxv.

Table 6.1 *Corporation of London: common council composition, 1680–1683*[9]

	1680	1681	1682	1683
Whig/opposition common councilmen				
Whig space (70 places)	44	51	51	50
Tory space (104 places)	34	35	24	12
Contested space (60 places)	27	27	32	31
Total Whig/opposition	105	113	107	93
Tory/loyalist common councilmen				
Tory space (104 places)	55	67	79	89
Whig space (70 places)	19	17	18	21
Contested space (60 places)	28	28	28	28
Total Tory/loyalist	102	112	125	138
Unknown/uncertain common councilmen				
All wards	31	11	3	5
Total common councilmen	238	236	235	236

of important continuities between the urban parties of the Restoration Crisis and the earlier civic conflicts of the civil wars and the Interregnum, just as it reveals similar continuities between 1679–82 and the subsequent conflicts of the Augustan age.

Elections to the London common council are the best guide to the topography of civic division. Table 6.1 and Figures 6.1–6.3 map the political landscape of the Corporation in the Restoration Crisis, as judged by elections to common council. They reveal a tripartite spatial division of the Corporation into a Whig-inclined space, a Tory-inclined space, and a space that was divided between the parties.[8] The topography of civic division in

[8] Wards have been included in the Whig-inclined space if more than 55 per cent of their common councilmen elected for 1680–83 were Whig or opposition. Wards have been included in the Tory-inclined space if more than 60 per cent of their common councilmen elected for 1680–83 were loyalist or Tory. Wards have been included in the contested space if between 40 per cent and 55 per cent of their common councilmen elected for 1680–83 were Whig or opposition. For another reading of electoral topography in 1680–83, see Smith, "London and the Crown," pp. 404–7.

[9] All common councilmen are listed alphabetically in Woodhead, *Rulers*. The party identifications of individual common councilmen have been derived from numerous sources including the appendices to De Krey, "Trade, Religion, and Politics" (III, 455–674) and the computer punch cards of London liverymen and common councilmen created by A. G. Smith. Inaccuracy, confusion, and incompleteness in the data sometimes lead to more or fewer common councilmen elected in particular wards for particular years than should be the case. Overall, the data lead to slightly more common councilmen per year than should have been elected. Sometimes the replacement of a deceased common councilman during a year has contributed to these results.

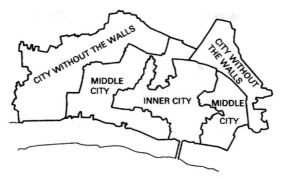

Figure 6.1 Corporation of London: Inner City, Middle City, and City
without the Walls

London during the Restoration Crisis is messy rather than clear-cut: the
Whig-inclined, Tory-inclined, and divided wards that made up these three
spaces did not constitute three perfectly contiguous geographic blocs. They
were nevertheless coherent spaces that exhibit significant historical and cultural differences.

Whig space

Whig space in the Corporation of London stands out most clearly in Figure 6.3. It included three different contiguous ward clusters:

1. Aldersgate Without and Cripplegate Without were both beyond the me-
   dieval wall to the north-west.
2. Portsoken and Aldgate straddled either side of the wall on the east.
3. Six smaller wards were located in the center of the city, two of them
   adjacent to the river.

These ten wards and parts of wards included about 30 per cent of all rate-
paying households in the Restoration city; and they also elected seventy
common councilmen, or about 30 per cent of the entire membership of
the common council.[10] As Table 6.1 suggests, these wards were relatively
impervious to the church-Tory campaign to resecure political control of
common council in the wardmote elections for 1682–3. They continued

---

[10] The number of rate-paying households in each ward has been based upon the ward assess-
ment books for the six-months' tax of 1680 at the CLRO. Also see M. J. Power, "Social
Topography," in *London 1500–1700: The Making of the Metropolis*, ed. A. L. Beier and R.
Finlay (1986), pp. 199–223.

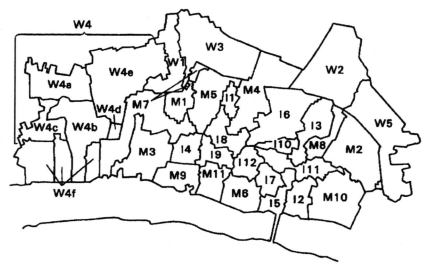

Figure 6.2 Corporation of London by ward

Inner City
I 1 Bassishaw
I 2 Billingsgate
I 3 Bishopsgate Within
I 4 Bread Street
I 5 Bridge
I 6 Broad Street
I 7 Candlewick

I 8 Cheap

I 9 Cordwainer
I 10 Cornhill

I 11 Langbourn
I 12 Walbrook

Middle City
M 1 Aldersgate Within
M 2 Aldgate
M 3 Castle Baynard
M 4 Coleman Street
M 5 Cripplegate Within
M 6 Dowgate
M 7 Farringdon Within

M 8 Lime Street

M 9 Queenhithe
M 10 Tower

M 11 Vintry

City without the walls
W 1 Aldersgate Without
W 2 Bishopsgate Without
W 3 Cripplegate Without
W 4 Farringdon Without
  W 4a St Andrew Holborn
  W 4b St Bride
  W 4c St Dunstan in the
     West
  W 4d St Martin Ludgate
     (part)
  W 4e St Sepulchre
  W 4f Extra-parochial
     liberties (Bridewell
     Precinct, The Temple,
     White Friars)
W 5 Portsoken

to return about five Whigs for every two Tories, as loyalists obtained a commanding common council majority from elsewhere in the city. These wards were the bedrock of political whiggism in London, providing over half the remaining Whigs on common council in 1683, when the London Tories resecured loyalist control of the Corporation. What was distinctive about

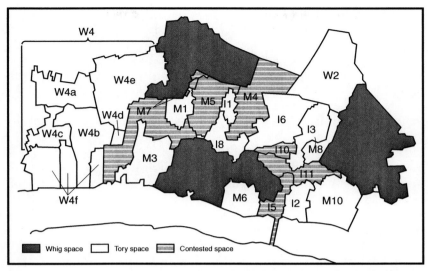

Figure 6.3 Corporation of London: Whig space, Tory space, and contested space

these wards, and why were they so strongly Whig? The four Whig wards on the periphery of the city and the six wards in its heart will be considered separately.

Aldersgate Without, Cripplegate Without, Aldgate, and Portsoken were among the wards with the largest populations in London: they included about 20 per cent of all rate-paying households in the Corporation. They were also relatively poor wards, judged by the average rates paid by their householders.[11] A significant proportion of the lodgers and meaner householders in these wards were new to the city and on the margins of its economic life and civic institutions. Aldgate, the only one of these wards within the walls, differed from the others in some respects. Despite its relative overall poverty, it contained several major commercial streets dominated by the households of some 100 wealthy merchants. Aldgate also included Africa House, on Leadenhall Street, the home establishment of the Royal African Company; and its cosmopolitan character was further enhanced by the presence of the city's only sizable Jewish population.

Again with the exception of Aldgate, which included several parish churches, this Whig area was characterized by weak parochial organization.

---

[11] Cripplegate Without and Portosken were, in fact, the poorest wards in the city. As a group, these four wards were also quite underrepresented on common council, choosing only nineteen common councilmen altogether, or about one for every 200 ratepayers.

Aldersgate Without and Cripplegate Without, with their sprawling populations, were each contained within the bounds of a single parish, while the parish of St Botolph Aldgate included Portsoken and an extensive urban area of Middlesex to the east of the city proper. The paucity of parish clergy and pulpits left these wards relatively unsusceptible to the political influence of Anglicanism; and where Anglicanism faltered, dissent flourished.

The strength of nonconformity in these wards was especially notable in Cripplegate Without, which was coterminous with the parish of St Giles Cripplegate. The ward's large population and its inadequate parochial presence attracted the residence of numerous dissenting clergy. At different times during the Restoration decades, such dissenting clerics as Edmund Calamy (the elder), George Cockayne, Thomas Goodwin, Philip Nye, and John Owen lived, ministered, or died in Cripplegate. John Milton lived in the ward until his death. Baptist civic leader and merchant William Kiffin had his residence there, not far from the meeting place of his church. The notorious dissenter, Sir John Shorter, was the ward's alderman during the Restoration Crisis. A 1683 survey of conventicles in London, Westminster, and the urban environs reveals that Cripplegate Without included more of them than any other ward: four Presbyterian and three Independent meetings, in addition to Kiffin's Baptist congregation. (See Table 6.2 for the geographic distribution of London dissenting meetings in 1683.) If Cripplegate Without was a center of dissenting worship and conversation, the frequent absence of the Anglican vicar of St Giles, who also happened in the 1670s to be the Bishop of Gloucester, further eroded the church's local ability to interfere with the circulation of unwelcome views. Indeed, leading parish dissenters like tallow-chandler Randolph Watson served as churchwardens. The parish received a resident vicar again in 1681, but the place was then filled by the Reformed Protestant Edward Fowler, who had as many friends outside the church as within.[12]

The social character of the adjacent ward of Aldersgate Without, coterminous with the parish of St Botolph Aldersgate, which had been strongly puritan in the 1640s and 1650s, was similar. Here a sprinkling of landed and middling residents also stimulated Whig and dissenting views. The Earl of Shaftesbury was the ward's most famous resident and an active patron of opposition artisans and agitators. The Countess of Exeter lived nearby and maintained the ministry of Presbyterian Thomas Jacombe. And Quakers

---

[12] PRO PROB 11: 380 Cann, qu. 69 (Edmund Calamy, the younger); *A List of the Conventicles or unlawful meetings within the City of London and Bills of Mortality* (1683); Matthews, *Calamy*, 124, 228, 370, 376; M. Goldie and J. Spurr, "Politics and the Restoration Parish: Edward Fowler and the Struggle for St Giles Cripplegate," *EHR* 109 (1994), 576–87.

Table 6.2[13] *Distribution of dissenting meetings in London and environs, 1683*

Urban area	Presbyterian	Independent	Sectarian	Area total
City within the Walls	12	5	5	22
City without the Walls	8	8	3	19
City of London sub-total	*20*	*13*	*8*	*41*
Middlesex: East and North	8	4	6	18
Westminster and West End	5		3	8
Southwark and Surrey	4	1	7	12
Sub-total for environs	*17*	*5*	*16*	*38*
Grand total	37	18	24	79

were a factor in the ward: the friends' meeting at the Bull and Mouth was in adjacent St Martin le Grand.[14]

As a group, then, these four Whig wards were a densely populated and impoverished area with a weak parochial structure – an area where articulate dissenting clergy and determined opposition leaders could make a real difference. The development of Restoration Anglicanism as a distinctive understanding of Protestantism, and as a clearly defined movement on behalf of the church and state established "by law," was slow here. Instead, these were wards in which Reformed Protestant and sectarian views, which had flourished among their populations before 1660, remained strong. Many urban newcomers who resided in these wards may have assimilated to urban life by following the lead of those who spoke the languages of conscience and of civic consent.

Four of the six Whig wards in the center of the city present a dramatic contrast with the Whig wards examined so far. The Inner City wards of Bread Street, Candlewick, Cordwainer, and Walbrook were among the most heavily represented on the court of common council and among the wealthiest in the city. The 1,200 householders of these wards constituted less than 7 per cent of the city's total.[15] As rated in any of the late Stuart assessments, half or more of their residents were middling or well to do. Walbrook and Candlewick, both near the Royal Exchange, had the highest proportions of overseas merchants among their householders of any wards in the city. Whig merchants Michael Godfrey and James Houblon were leading citizens

---

[13] Locations have been determined from *List of the Conventicles*. The sectarian category combines thirteen Baptist meetings, ten Quaker meetings, and one Fifth-Monarchist meeting.

[14] Liu, *Puritan London*, pp. 42, 72, 138, 174, 198; Matthews, *Calamy*, p. 293; De Krey, *Fractured Society*, p. 98.

[15] They nevertheless elected thirty-six common councilmen, some 15 per cent of the total court, or about one common councilman for every thirty-four households.

of Walbrook, for instance. Additional merchant members of the Houblon family resided in adjacent Cordwainer, as did members of such other leading French Reformed trading families as the Ducanes and the Jurins. The concentrations of prosperous retail shopkeepers and domestic merchants in these Inner City wards also contributed to their affluence. Bread Street, in particular, was a ward dominated by its middling sort.[16]

The residence of important French Protestant merchants in the Whig center hints at another distinguishing characteristic of these wards: they had long been at the heart of Reformed Protestant life and discourse in the metropolis. Ecclesiastically, their boundaries enclosed a honeycomb of small and often well-endowed parishes that offered a concentration of pulpits unmatched elsewhere in the city. A generation earlier, these parishes had been at the center of puritan London. Their citizens and clergy had been leading advocates of reformation in the Church. St Matthew Friday Street (in Bread Street), had, for instance, been the parish of the puritan divine Henry Burton, co-sufferer with William Prynne and John Bastwick, and one of the earliest clerical Independents. St Mary Abchurch (in Candlewick and Walbrook) had once provided haven for John Goodwin's gathered church. With Lazarus Seaman as its rector in 1643–62, Allhallows Bread Street had been a strongly Presbyterian parish, as had St Antholin Budge Row (in Cordwainer). Indeed, St Antholin boasted a puritan tradition reaching back to the beginnings of Elizabeth's reign, when the parish had embraced the Genevan pattern of summoning its inhabitants by bell for pre-dawn prayers and preaching.[17]

The Reformed Protestant culture of these Inner City wards had been fractured, by the late 1640s, by divisions among Presbyterians, Independents, and separatists. After 1662, however, the ejection of dissenting clergy, the emergence of conscience as a common ground in the struggle against religious coercion, and frequent intermarriage between families of different persuasions rekindled the local sense of Reformed Protestant community. Anglican ministry was re-established in the intricate network of parishes that made up these wards, but the population remained an incubator of Reformed Protestant perspectives. Many puritan families in these wards conformed after 1662, of course, whether fully, partially, or occasionally; but here conformity was as often a sign of continuing commitment to reformation in the national church as it was of the adoption of Anglican identity. Families who hoped for church resettlement often combined involvement

---

[16] Woodhead, *Rulers*, pp. 27, 54, 77, 93; De Krey, "Trade, Religion, and Politics," III, 545, 549–50, 564–5, 569, 625, 634, 636, 640, 645–6. For the number of merchants in each ward, as determined for 1692, with the poll tax returns, see *ibid.*, 612–22. My figures differ slightly from those in P. Gauci, *The Politics of Trade: The Overseas Merchant in State and Society, 1660–1720* (Oxford, 2001), pp. 25–6.

[17] Liu, *Puritan London*, pp. 37, 55–6, 86–7, 110, 112–13, 114–15, 126–7.

in parochial affairs with patronage of ejected clergy, and the presence of a French church in Candlewick was a further encouragement of Reformed Protestant identity. The boundary between dissent and conformity was a fluid one for many London Protestant laity in these wards, despite the efforts of the Anglican establishment to dichotomize religious practice into mutually exclusive camps. Far from driving the ambiguous into the church, persecution merely underscored the need for a broader church settlement to Inner City families who had long been committed to the Cromwellian ideal of Protestant accommodation.

Some citizens active before 1660 carried the case for Reformed Protestantism forward into the Restoration decades in these wealthy wards and parishes. Richard Baxter's Bread Street friend Henry Ashurst is the best-known example of such continuity, and the case of William Thompson of St Stephen Walbrook might also be offered. Brother of the famous civil war merchant Maurice Thompson, William Thompson had served his ward as alderman under Cromwell and remained a visible proponent of Reformed Protestant principles as City MP between 1659 and 1679. But with the passage of time, leadership in the wards of the Whig center was often taken by new men whose political and religious identities were shaped in the Reformed Protestant culture maintained by their fathers. Henry Ashurst's son William, for instance, was a Bread Street common councilman in 1678–83 and would become an alderman. William Thompson's son Samuel would serve as an alderman in the polity of toleration established by James II in 1687–8. In Candlewick and Cordwainer, the Reformed Protestant principles of Major Peter Houblon, John Jurin, and Harmon Sheafe (active in the 1640s) were passed to Captain Peter Houblon, Isaac Jurin, and Samuel Sheafe (active in the 1680s). The language and tradition of reform inherited by such younger men were often as important to them as their legacies of wealth and their trading stature.[18]

The remaining two Whig wards, Queenhithe and Vintry, were contiguous with these four wealthy wards but were rather different in social character. Dominated by its quays and warehouses, Queenhithe was a particularly poor ward with a population dominated by those who worked its wharves and the ships that docked at them. But if the social composition of Queenhithe was similar to Aldersgate Without and Cripplegate Without, Vintry shared a bit more of the prosperity evident in the Whig wards on which it bordered. It also shared in their puritan traditions. St James Garlickhithe, entirely within the ward, and St Thomas the Apostle, partially within it, had been parishes

---

[18] Liu, *Puritan London*, pp. 60, 85, 231, 234, 238; Woodhead, *Rulers*, pp. 19, 94, 100, 146, 162–3; De Krey, "Trade, Religion, and Politics," III, 565, 569, 591, 646; Henning, *House of Commons*, I, 558–9; III, 555–6; De Krey, *Fractured Society*, pp. 89–90.

in which Independents had flourished in the 1640s and 1650s. The most notable resident of Vintry, the Duke of Buckingham, also played a role similar to Shaftesbury's in Aldersgate Without in promoting local opposition. The aldermen and leading common councilmen of these wards further promoted conscience and consent: Sir John Lawrence, of Dutch Reformed background, for instance, had been Alderman of Queenhithe since the Interregnum; and the Presbyterian Henry Cornish became Alderman of Vintry in 1680.[19]

This topography of urban whiggism in the Restoration Crisis clearly points to the importance of dissent and Reformed Protestantism as the political bedrock of opposition. Rejection of religious coercion and the promotion of religious accommodation were critical common denominators for a political movement that attracted a diverse social following. Plebeian weavers on the city margins and merchant princes on the Exchange shared these objectives, as Whigs, with middling tradesmen and shopkeepers. Indeed, the Whigs reunited the powerful but disparate movement of rising merchants, prosperous artisans, and articulate mechanics who had stormed the church and state in 1640–42 with their demand for reformation. The social and religious building blocks of that movement had dissolved by 1649 as Presbyterian magnates, the gathered godly, plebeian sectarians, and the levelers of privilege pursued their diverging agendas. What gave the Whigs their power in London in the Restoration Crisis was their ability to knit these agendas together again in the language of conscience and consent.

Tory space

Twelve London wards or parts of wards were largely Tory or Anglican loyalist in the Restoration Crisis. With the exception of Dowgate, these wards were part of three Tory-inclined spatial clusters observable in Figure 6.3:

1. Adjacent Tower and Billingsgate faced the Thames, to the south-east, within the walls.
2. Three western wards – Castle Baynard, Farringdon Without, and Aldersgate Within – were not contiguous; but they were separated only by the elongated and politically divided ward of Farringdon Within.
3. A group of five contiguous and relatively wealthy wards in the north-central part of the city within the walls was also contiguous with Bishopsgate Without, on the city periphery.

Together, these wards included almost three-fifths of the city's rate-paying population, and they elected 104 common councilmen, or about 45 per cent of the total court. They differed considerably in size and representation. Tiny Bassishaw, with the fewest ratepayers of any ward, and some other small

---

[19] Liu, *Puritan London*, pp. 37, 87, 113, 162; Gauci, *Politics of Trade*, p. 27.

wards in the Tory center were as over-represented on common council as their Whig Inner City counterparts. Farringdon Without, on the other hand, with its 3,500 ratepayers (almost 20 per cent of the Corporation total), was the least well-represented ward in the city, despite having more common councilmen (sixteen) than any other.

As Table 6.1 makes clear, this space provided the crown with the edge it required for a more cooperative common council by 1683. Although one-third of the common councilmen chosen in these wards were opposition or Whig in 1680–81, only a dozen Whigs were returned from the entire area in 1683. The transfer of twenty or more common council places in these wards from the Whigs to the Tories gave the Anglican-loyalist party a commanding majority in 1683 that could not be compromised, even by the more assiduous attendance of Whig common councilmen. Moreover, if the selection of common councilmen for 1680 (in December 1679) is a reliable guide, these wards were predominantly loyalist from the beginning of the crisis. Their loyalism was neither primarily a reaction to Whig "excesses" in the parliaments of 1680–81, nor was it primarily attributable to direct action by the crown to contain whiggism. Instead, it was an enduring element of the political culture of these wards. What factors, then, made this city space so receptive to the language of Anglican loyalism, and why did Anglican identity take strongest root here?

The most significant common denominator of the Tory-inclined wards was the presence or influence of persons and facilities associated with the Restoration establishment. The ward of Tower, for instance, was adjacent to the military facilities and garrison that provided its name; and Tower also included the customs establishment that monitored the city's overseas trade. The Church dominated Castle Baynard, where the cathedral of the Bishop of London was located. As the site of Guildhall and other civic facilities, the ward of Cheap was the geographic center of a Corporation establishment in which loyalism had been a critical factor in appointments to office before 1680. Farringdon Without was a geographic and social borderland where the Court culture of Westminster was as evident as the commercial culture of the city. The residence of some gentry and courtiers and the proximity of the law courts and of the Whitehall royal establishment, further to the west, gave Anglican loyalism a strong voice here. A survey of the clusters of wards that composed the Tory space in London in the Restoration Crisis, beginning with the peripheral wards and moving to the center, will provide greater depth and evidence for these generalizations.

Tower and Billingsgate were wards dominated by the city's maritime commerce. Substantial numbers of overseas merchants resided in each ward. Some of them were Whigs and dissenters, but others like Sir Benjamin Newland were leading civic Tories. The Tory inclinations of many local electors and ward leaders were reinforced by the presence and the influence of numerous government office-holders. Indeed, the Court ordinarily exerted more influence in these wards than anywhere else in the city. For twenty years, Alderman Sir John Robinson was also Lieutenant of the Tower; and in that capacity, he and his officers had been especially vigilant in the early Restoration in monitoring and confronting dissent and opposition in the adjacent areas of the city and the eastern out-parishes. Robinson could also count upon support from the principal officers of the Customs House in Tower ward. In 1680, it was presided over by such influential courtiers and loyalist MPs as Sir George Downing and Sir Richard Temple (customs commissioners), Sir Nicholas Crispe and Sir John Shaw (customs collectors), and Edward Backwell (customs comptroller).[20]

Like the Lieutenant of the Tower, the chief customs officials exerted political influence through their powers of appointment to scores of places, both substantial and petty, and by their ability to provide work for local artisans and artificers. The middling sort of these wards, especially numerous in Billingsgate, looked to the Tower and to the customs establishment for business and opportunities. Similarly, the large laboring population of lightermen, watermen, and warehousemen who worked the docks and quays of the two wards, as well as others who worked Billingsgate market, were impressed by the local authority of the state, which was graphically displayed in executions on nearby Tower Hill. Interestingly, Thames-side watermen were prominent in the petitioning efforts of urban loyalists in 1681. Poorer laborers like these also sometimes had little political affection for the wealthy dissenting merchants and tradesmen so evident among the Whigs.[21]

Loyalism was thus the natural political language for Tower and Billingsgate. Of forty-one known dissenting meetings within the Corporation boundaries in 1683, none was located in these two wards. But the Anglicanism of the royal and clerical establishments was encouraged in the churches of Tower and Billingsgate. Notable for royalism in the early 1640s, Allhallows Barking was the largest parish in them. Its rector in 1680–83 was Dr George Hickes, who was made a royal chaplain in 1681 and was a future nonjuring bishop. In 1681, Hickes was charged by Slingsby Bethel and Edward Whitaker, legal associate of the Duke of Buckingham, with encouraging superstitious practices at Allhallows: he maintained an image of St Michael over the communion table. The dispute was a perfect example of how much difficulty exponents of the Reformed Protestant and Anglican loyalist positions had in appreciating each other's beliefs and practices.[22]

---

[20] De Krey, "Trade, Religion, and Politics," III, 613, 622; Henning, *House of Commons*, I, 578–9; II, 224–9, and III, 340–3, 429–30, 536–44; Gauci, *Politics of Trade*, pp. 25–6.

[21] *London Gazette* 1642 (11–15 Aug. 1681); *CSPD 1680–1*, p. 396; Harris, *London Crowds*, pp. 214–15, 221–2.

[22] [Jonathan Saunders], *The Sham-Indictment Quash'd* (1681); *List of the Conventicles*; Liu, *Puritan London*, p. 40; *DNB*, IX, 801–5; Goldie and Spurr, "Politics," 573; C. Haynes,

Some of the circumstances that supported the political language of Anglican loyalism in Tower and Billingsgate were also evident in the western cluster of Tory wards. But here, merchants, who were so visible in the eastern wards within the walls, were almost entirely absent; and the middling order was considerably weaker than in most Inner City wards. The two social factors most likely to sustain dissent and whiggism were simply lacking. A local elite drawn from the church and the gentry provided social leadership instead. In Castle Baynard, dominated by St Paul's Cathedral, churchmen naturally exerted much social influence. The ward was home to the cathedral dean and chapter, to other clerical officials, and to two church courts that provided business to the ecclesiastical lawyers, some of whom resided in Doctors' Commons. One of Castle Baynard's leading citizens in 1680 was Bishopsgate alderman Sir Joseph Sheldon, whose uncle had been Archbishop of Canterbury and whose brother-in-law would become Archbishop of York.[23]

Further to the west, in mammoth Farringdon Without, landed men brought the culture of the Court into the city, residing along the fashionable streets of St Bride and St Andrew Holborn. The adjacent Inns of Court also attracted many students from gentry families, and the manners and methods of the city were more mocked than mimicked at the Lincoln's Inn Fields playhouse. Such institutions as Bridewell, Fleet Prison, and the Sessions House at Old Bailey were local reminders of authority, and the state was visibly present in the nearby Courts of King's Bench and Chancery. None of these factors eliminated opposition or Whig views from the ward, of course. And dissenters were found here as elsewhere in London, with three Presbyterian and two Independent meetings located within the ward's parishes. The Green Ribbon club, which brought together landed and civic Whigs, met in a Chancery Lane tavern; and the Templars had been involved in the 1679 pope-burning procession. In December 1681, the better-organized Whigs actually captured over half the ward's common council places. Nevertheless, the ethos of Farringdon Without was quite different from that of wards with concentrations of dissenting commercial families; and plebeian householders more easily identified with the ward's numerous reminders of royal authority. Before a sustained Tory-loyalist effort, the Whigs failed in December 1682 to capture a single common council seat.[24]

The influence of the church was also as evident in Farringdon Without as in Castle Baynard. The ward's large parishes were dominated by churchmen

"Image Battles: The Politics of Religious Imagery, *c*.1680–*c*.1700," paper delivered at "The World Of Roger Morrice," a conference at Clare College, Cambridge, 10–12 July 2003.
[23] De Krey, "Trade, Religion, and Politics," III, 612, 616, 619–20; Woodhead, *Rulers*, p. 147.
[24] *List of the Conventicles*; D. Lemmings, *Gentlemen and Barristers: The Inns of Court and the English Bar 1680–1730* (Oxford, 1990), pp. 11–13; Harris, *London Crowds*, pp. 121, 214.

fully involved in the development of Anglican identity. Edward Stillingfleet, whose 1680 sermon was so critical in publicly confirming the separation of Reformed and Anglican Protestant cultures, was the popular preacher of St Andrew Holborn, as well as Dean of St Paul's. William Bell, vicar of St Sepulchre and archdeacon of St Albans, a onetime chaplain to Sir John Robinson, was described after his death, in 1683, as a "mighty loyalist." Henry Dove, vicar of St Bride, preached a sermon at the commencement of the 1682 mayoral election in which he rejected arguments for reformation, claiming instead "the government has the right to tye the consciences of men by the firmest bonds it can." Each of these clerics was a royal chaplain; and Stillingfleet and Dove also held pulpits at the Temple and the Rolls Chapel, further solidifying the connections between Anglicanism, loyalism, and the legal establishment.[25]

This confluence of church and Court interests in Farringdon Without gave the language of loyalism as much circulation here as in Castle Baynard. When loyalist courtiers and civic leaders organized their own club in 1681, they not surprisingly chose a meeting location in this area, near Ludgate. The site played off loyalist strengths in the two wards as well as in Aldersgate Within, the third of the Tory-inclined wards to the west. Moreover, the loyalist political culture of these wards was as important a factor in the Court's recovery of the London streets as in its recovery of the Corporation. Although the geography of the London crowd in the Restoration Crisis eludes simple generalizations, loyalist crowds from this Tory space – who were sometimes encouraged by students at the Inns – were quite visible in the loyalist reaction of 1681–3.[26]

The heart of the Tory space in the Restoration City was the north-central cluster of six wards that extended from the wealthy Inner City precincts of Bassishaw and Cheap through Broad Street to Bishopsgate (Within and Without) and Lime Street. Two of these wards (Bassishaw and Broad Street) included significant proportions of overseas traders among their household-ers, while the populations of Bishopsgate Within and Cheap included sizable middling elements. These population characteristics meant that the central Tory wards also included significant numbers of dissenting residents.[27] But

---

25 Henry Dove, *A sermon preached . . . at Bow-Church . . . the day for election of a Lord Mayor* (1682), p. 23; *DNB*, II, 175–6; V, 1282; XVIII, 1262–5; Turner, ed., 'Religious Condition," pp. 203–5.
26 Harris, *London Crowds*, pp. 121, 179–80, 214, 219–23; Ailesbury, *Memoirs*, I, 64–5; Reresby, *Memoirs*, p. 244; Henning, *House of Commons*, I, 670–1; Woodhead, *Rulers*, p. 33.
27 Indeed, the wards of the Tory center included far more dissenting congregations (three Pres-byterian, three Independent, and one Baptist) than the wards of the Whig center, with their single Presbyterian meeting. The parishes of the Tory center were larger and included more livery halls, warehouses, and other large commercial buildings suitable for meetings, whereas

these wards were predominantly loyalist, despite the Whigs' success in securing half the common council places in Bassishaw and Cheap in 1680–81.

Like other Tory-inclined areas, these wards were the site of numerous
offices and facilities connected to the Restoration establishments of both
the city and the state. The presence, work, influence, or residence of office-
holders connected to the restored order was a critical factor in sustaining
loyalism here. The citizens of Bassishaw and Cheap included officers of such
Corporation facilities as the sheriffs' courts, the Poultry Compter, and Black-
well Hall, the center of the domestic cloth trade. The strength of Anglican
loyalism among the Corporation aldermen, to whom these office-holders
were accountable, kept loyalism dominant among them and among those
they employed as well. In Broad Street, which extended to the Royal Exchange, major government office-holders promoted loyalty to the crown they
served. Both the Hearth Office and the Excise Office were located here, the
latter presided over by such establishment figures as Elias Ashmole, Charles
Davenant, and Sir Robert Southwell.[28] The meetings of the Royal Society at
Gresham College in Bishopsgate Within may have been a factor in the loyalism of that ward. The home facilities of the East India Company, the principal
joint-stock company of the Restoration, were located in Bishopsgate Within
and Lime Street, contributing to those wards' loyalist inclinations.

A complex of institutions and individuals tied to Guildhall and to the
Court, then, contributed to the dominance of loyalist conversation and perceptions in these central wards, despite the Reformed Protestant traditions
of many residents. Why either the adjacent external ward of Bishopsgate
Without or the Thames-side ward of Dowgate should also have been Tory-
inclined is not entirely clear. Whatever the case in these two wards, however,
the party of Anglican loyalism clearly attracted a diverse social and geographic following in the Restoration Crisis, just as did the London Whigs.
The middling element of urban society was generally not as numerous and
certainly not as assertive in the collection of wards that made up the Tory
space. But the loyalist language of obedience and order was clearly cultivated
at the top of the urban social landscape, just as the opposition language of
conscience and consent was sustained from the middle. The Tory creed was
one that was intended to protect those who derived power, profit, and pres-
tige from restored institutions in church and state, while plebeian elements in
loyalist crowds, often drawn from the Tory space, had their own social and
cultural reasons for disliking the cause of reformation. In these wards, the
crown, the church, and the Restoration legal and municipal establishments

the Whig wards were densely settled neighborhoods with few non-residential structures other
than their numerous parish churches. *List of the Conventicles*; *DNB*, XXI, 1–3.

[28] *DNB*, I, 644–6; V, 549–50, XVIII, 707–9; Henning, *House of Commons*, II, 196, and III,
459–60.

were successful in sustaining fears that dissenters and Whigs would again sink church and state in a sectarian and republican abyss.

Contested space and a divided city

The six remaining wards were divided between the parties, as judged by elections to common council for 1680–83. This politically contested space was composed of two contiguous geographical clusters:

1. Bridge, Cornhill, and Langbourn were in the east-central part of the city.
2. Coleman Street, Cripplegate Within, and Farringdon Within were mostly to the north-west of the city center, extending without the walls to the north.

Each of the divided wards bordered on both Whig and Tory wards, and each experienced contradictory political tendencies. Each had a sizable Whig-inclined middling element, but each also experienced the contradictory political influence of facilities and persons linked to various Restoration establishments. Each was a place where the divergent communities of Restoration London converged spatially; and the contradictory discourse of those communities circulated in each ward. Beyond these commonalities, the two clusters of divided wards were different in character; and their differences point to the more clear-cut topographical division in London politics that would emerge after 1689.

Of the divided central wards, Langbourn and Cornhill were among the three wealthiest wards in the city, judged by the total assessments of their residents in 1680. An overseas merchant headed one in every eight Langbourn households; and goldsmith-bankers were also prominent among the ward's social elite. The proximity of so many offices and institutions associated with the government, including part of the Royal Exchange in Cornhill, was a factor that encouraged Anglican loyalism.[29] On the other hand, both the social structures of these divided wards and their religious pasts pulled in the opposite direction. The middling sort made up at least one-third of the households in each; and when wealthier residents are also considered, over half (and in the case of Cornhill, about 70 per cent) of the ratepayers here were substantial ones. A generation earlier some of the parishes in these wards had been strongly puritan; and in 1683, five dissenting meetings here demonstrated the commitment of some substantial residents to further reformation of the Church of England. Both Bridge and Langbourn also included

---

[29] Smith, "London and the Crown," pp. 408–9; De Krey, "Trade, Religion, and Politics," III, 620.

sizable populations of Quaker merchants and shopkeepers clustered about the Grace-church Street meeting.[30]

Although these wards were divided between the parties when their common council elections for the entire period 1680–83 are considered, they had, as a group, become more whiggish by 1683, despite the exertions of their loyalist aldermen. After 1689, Bridge and Cornhill would become Whig-inclined, as the London Whigs increasingly became the party of the Inner City; but Langbourn would remain divided.[31]

The cluster of three divided wards to the north-west of the city center included prosperous parishes and precincts adjacent to Bread Street, Bassishaw, and Cheap, but overall they were less wealthy than the divided wards to the east. Overseas traders made up 5 per cent of the householders of Coleman Street, but few merchants resided in Cripplegate Within or in Farringdon Within. Several parishes in Cripplegate Within and Farringdon Within had been centers of Presbyterianism in the 1640s, and Farringdon Within was the site of two English and two Scots Presbyterian meetings in 1683. St Stephen Coleman Street had once been the parish of Independent John Goodwin, and it had provided, outside the walls, a breeding ground for sectarianism. In the 1680s, many middling and well-to-do residents of these parishes continued to speak the language of conscience and consent. That language also flourished in the Farringdon Within precincts near St Paul's Cathedral, where dissenting booksellers and stationers vied with their Anglican rivals in providing the printed materials that shaped political and religious discourse in the city.[32]

But the political culture of these wards was also heavily influenced by the presence of individuals and institutions tied to the restored order in church and state. Every part of Farringdon Within, for instance, was within sight of the adjacent cathedral complex. Moreover, the ward was home to two important professional monopolies with royal charters and royal connections, the Stationers' Company and the Royal College of Physicians. The royal printing house in Blackfriars was also located within the ward. Similarly, Cripplegate Within and the parts of Coleman Street within the walls were

---

[30] Thomas Goodwin's gathered church had worshipped at Allhallows Lombard Street (Langbourn), for instance; and Goodwin had lectured at St Benet Gracechurch (Bridge). At the height of the Puritan Revolution, Independents had also held the livings of Allhallows, St Leonard Eastcheap (Bridge), and St Margaret New Fish Street (Bridge). *List of the Conventicles*; *CSPD 1683–84*, p. 172; Liu, *Puritan London*, pp. 111–14, 183; De Krey, *Fractured Society*, p. 98.

[31] In 1680, thirteen opposition common councilmen served for these wards, compared to sixteen loyalists; but for 1683, the comparable numbers were nineteen Whigs and ten Tories. De Krey, "Trade, Religion, and Politics," III, 615, 617, 620; De Krey, *Fractured Society*, pp. 172–5.

[32] *List of the Conventicles*; De Krey, "Religion, Trade, and Politics," II, 347, and III, 616–18; Liu, *Puritan London*, pp. 70–1, 73, 75–7, 82–4, 115–16.

adjacent to the complex of civic institutions in Cheap and Bassishaw that was commanded by the Corporation's Anglican loyalist establishment. Indeed, that complex extended into Cripplegate Within, which included the Wood Street Compter and its officers, a civic market, and several company halls. Middling householders were largely absent from the parts of these wards adjacent to or external to the walls, and such poorer precincts were far more likely to follow the lead of civic Tories than that of an opposition so closely identified with the godly sort. Although these wards were divided politically for the entire period 1680–83, they were becoming somewhat more loyalist by 1682–3, as the civic Tories intensified their efforts. Both Farringdon Within and Coleman Street would become Tory-inclined after 1689, as the London Tories increasingly became the party of the Middle City.[33]

This topographical survey of political division in the Restoration city clearly demonstrates how the religious and cultural tensions of the English Revolution endured into the Restoration Crisis. The religious and political polarization of the crisis expressed the partisan inclinations of geographically distinct communities. The dissenting shopkeepers, retail merchants, and overseas traders who had become a community for conscience in the early Restoration (together with the more peripheral heirs of revolutionary sectarianism) were the electoral bedrock of Whig opposition to the Restoration establishment. Their presence defined a Whig space in the city, and they also carried their arguments about conscience and consent in the church into the Tory and contested spaces within the Corporation. But an Anglican loyalist community also flourished in the Restoration city, defining Tory space, drawing together courtly, civic, and clerical elites, and also uniting many of the rich and some of the poor against the godly middle. The new party names associated with the political exertions of these communities after 1680 were signs of an enduring division between Reformed Protestants and Anglican Protestants that was taking on more structured political forms. In London, parties were first generated in 1679–82, as these communities struggled to reform or to retain the institutions of the Restoration Settlement; and saying so is neither anachronistic nor whiggish.

DIFFERENT IDEAS

The Whig and Tory communities of London spoke different political and religious languages in the Restoration Crisis. Discourse within the Whig-inclined and Tory-inclined spaces of the Corporation reflected the different

---

[33] In 1680, twelve loyalist common councilmen served for these wards, compared to fourteen identified with the civic opposition; but for 1683, the comparable numbers were eighteen Tories and twelve Whigs. De Krey, "Trade, Religion, and Politics," III, 616–18, De Krey, *Fractured Society*, pp. 174–5.

identities they incubated: Reformed Protestant and dissenting identity in some neighborhoods of the city and Anglican identity in others. Language was at the heart of party and polarization in 1679–82, and the city's different socio-political communities were sustained by different ideas. In the Restoration Crisis, the Anglican royalist settlement in church, state, and city was especially challenged by particular traditions that had been maintained since 1660 in the Whig-inclined spaces of the Corporation. Chief among these were the Whig understanding of the role of electoral consent in the microcosm of the Corporation and dissenting understandings about reformation in the macrocosm of the Restoration church and state. In London, the crisis was as much about consent and reformation as it was about parliament and the succession; and the Tories were as vocal in rejecting Whig ideas about these matters as they were in rejecting Whig parliamentary agendas.

The microcosm: electoral consent and authority in the Corporation

Although the literature of the loyalist reaction of 1682–3, dominated by voices like those of Dryden and L'Estrange, is well known, historians have largely ignored the pamphlets, broadsides, and news-sheets of London's first Whigs as of local and transient importance only. But by 1682, the London Whigs had produced a distinctive civic literature that was intended to arouse and to instruct active citizens in the defense of rights and liberties threatened by the crown's designs against the electorate and the charter. Immediate rather than abstract, and ephemeral rather than abiding, this literature viewed the concerns of the Restoration Crisis from the bottom up, treating the Corporation of London as a local institutional nexus in which the great issues of the day were played out. These pieces are closer in their language to the discourse of ordinary Whig citizens and their leaders than the more sophisticated writings of the great Whig icons, Locke and Sidney, who were nevertheless influenced by civic Whig language.

Civic Whig literature also returned rhetorically to some of the issues faced by London citizens in the late 1640s and especially to the consensual understanding of the civic regime that had been institutionalized after 1649. That understanding had been replaced officially, in 1661–2, by the re-establishment of magisterial privilege and predominance. But neither Anglican royalist argument nor the passage of time had obscured many electors' memory of a more consensual civic order or weakened their attachment to it, as Corporation events in 1675–6 had demonstrated. By 1682, the civic Whigs' arguments about consent provided Tory writers with some of their most telling evidence that the Whig movement really was directed at undermining the settlement of church and state and returning the kingdom to the chaos of the 1640s.

Given the connections in the Restoration Crisis between the Whig leaderships in parliament and common council, one might expect civic Whig writing to focus upon the authority of the latter body as analogous to the House of Commons.[34] In fact, however, London opposition writers in the Restoration Crisis were far more restrained in defending the authority of common council against the magistracy than they had been in the mid-1670s. They knew that a common council might err, just as a parliament might; and they believed that the political and religious rights of London citizens were dependent neither upon the actions of parliament nor upon those of common council. Citizens might suffer at the very hands of the representatives they had chosen, as religious persecution authorized by statute had long demonstrated.

Sir John Moore's employment of mayoral prerogatives on behalf of the crown in the 1682 shrieval election brought these reservations about common council to the fore. Moore's claim of a right to name one of the sheriffs rested upon a by-law adopted and confirmed in common council, but the Whigs repudiated this act as an example of legislative error. "If an Act of Parliament may be null in itself . . . when it is against those rights which we enjoy by the Common Law of the Land," wrote one Whig author, then "surely an Act of Common Council may also be null, if it be against those Liberties which belong unto the Citizens by Charter and Prescription." Similarly, in 1683, when a Tory-dominated common council was confronted with a royal demand to surrender the charter, Thomas Hunt denied that the civic legislature had authority to surrender rights that did not derive from it or depend upon its acts.[35]

If civic Whig thought did not focus upon upholding the autonomy of common council against the civic magistracy, then what was its focus? Just as the shrieval election of 1682 reveals the limitations the civic Whigs placed upon the power of common council, so it points to their understanding of the real locus of authority within the Corporation. In championing the right of the electors to choose both sheriffs, the London Whigs treated the sheriffs – and, indeed, all magistrates – as the "Stewards" or "Servants" of the

---

[34] James Whiston wrote in 1681, for instance, that "the Common Council . . . are the *Representatives* of the People of the City," just as the House of Commons represented the people of the nation. James Whiston, *Serious Advice Presented to the Common Council of the City of London* (1681), p. 5; D. N., *Letter from an Old Common-Council-Man*, pp. 1, 3–4.

[35] The civic opposition also had less need to defend common council against the loyalist magistracy in 1679–81 because it controlled the mayoralty in those years. *Modest Enquiry*, p. 43; Thomas Hunt, *A Defence of the Charter, and Municipal Rights of the City of London* (1680), pp. 35–6; *The Lord Mayor of London's Vindication. Being an Answer* (1682), p. 2. Also see *Priviledg and Right*, pp. 4–5; *Right of Electing Sheriffs*, p. 3; *A Modest Enquiry*, pp. 38–40.

electors who chose them and to whom they were accountable.[36] The Whigs frequently suggested that electoral rights were grounded in the Corporation's charter, as granted by kings and confirmed by parliaments; but in reality they denied that the exercise of right and the exercise of power in the Corporation depended upon the charter, the king, or parliament. Instead, they believed that legitimate authority in the Corporation was derived from the consent of the freemen of the city; and this consensual understanding of the origins of authority was grounded in the "immemorial usage," the "uninterrupted Custom," and the "Common Law right" of the country's ancient constitution. The authority of the sheriffs, for instance, was not conferred by the crown but rather by the people who selected them. Historically, according to one Whig writer, "the Priviledge of chusing *Sheriffs* . . . belong[ed] to the *Free-holders* . . . and that Right they long enjoy'd without . . . any Act of Parliament [or the crown] . . . meerly by vertue of the Common-Law . . . upon the foundation of immemorial usage."[37]

Similarly, citing the commentaries of Sir Edward Coke and William Lambarde upon notable statutes of Edward I's reign, another author denied "the Citizens Right of chusing Officers, particularly *Sheriffs*, [is] founded originally upon their *Charters*, but it belonged unto them by the Common Law of *England*." In Saxon times, according to this argument, "the freemen, chose sheriffs by the name of portreeves, long before a mayor was in *London*." The sheriffs were, therefore, not just governors but governors whose power derived from the freemen, who consented to their election; and the common hall was really the ancient folkmoot in modern form:

The Election of these officers [the sheriffs] was anciently at a Court called *Falkmout,* [*sic*] which assembled in a Field . . . and in that Court did the Supream Power of the Citizens of *London* . . . subsist. And as it was only by reason of the inconveniences of meeting . . . in the open Air, and upon the reduction of the Election . . . to the livery, that the said Court was removed and transplanted to *Guild-Hall.*[38]

The citizens of London – or rather those who had been called to the liveries of their companies – continued to enjoy all these ancient electoral rights, according to Whig argument; and they had possessed their "Supream Power" without any historical interruptions. What they derived as "an entail from our Ancestors," they continued to enjoy as a possession confirmed "by the patents and Charters of our most Renowned and Victorious Princes,"

[36] *Lord Mayor of London's Vindication,* p. 5; *The Citizens of London; True Narrative of the Proceedings; To the Right Honourable Patience Ward; Impartial Account of the Proceedings; Priviledg and Right,* pp. 2, 7.
[37] *Nature of a Common-Hall;* Hunt, *Defence,* pp. 6, 39, *Modest Enquiry,* p. 25; *Priviledg and Right,* pp. 1–2.
[38] *Right of Electing Sheriffs,* p. 1; *Lord Mayor of London's Vindication,* pp. 2, 5; *Priviledg and Right,* pp. 1–2, 8.

acting in and through parliament. Thus, William the Conqueror "in acknowledgment of . . . [the City's] ancient Rights, granted and confirmed . . . *to the Citizens of* London *the whole City and Sheriffwick thereof,*" expressly continuing them in their accustomed choice of "*what Sheriffs they pleased from among themselves.*" Or, as Thomas Hunt argued, William's charter not only confirmed the citizens in all their ancient rights but was also an act of self-denial on the part of the monarchy. The conqueror's charter expressed a promise "that he should not by his power break in upon the Rights of the County of the City of *London,* of making their Sheriffs or other the Rights of the City." The city had, therefore, not been conquered by the Norman monarchy at all, and the consent of electors in the choice of magistrates remained the source of authority in the Corporation.[39]

References to the electors as the "greatest" power or the "supreme authority in London" were neither rhetorical flourishes nor a convenient rationalization. In Whig theory, the liverymen were "the people" of the Corporation, and their consent was the ultimate source of political legitimacy in the city. In making their electoral choices, the liverymen stood as representatives of all the freemen, acting not only on their own behalf but also on behalf of all householders, some of whom would become liverymen in time. "All the Free-men do chuse" in them, wrote one Whig publicist, just as "the Nation in the Election of Parliament-men is said to chuse its own Representatives, and yet only the Free-holders . . . are admitted to Vote."[40] The Corporation's system of government was representative, therefore; and the common hall represented potential citizens as well as including active ones.

As the largest electoral assembly of the people, the court of common hall enjoyed an expansive field of action that put it at the center of Corporation governance, according to Whig writers. Without "their own consent," proclaimed one author, the citizens in common hall "cannot be adjourned nor dissolved by any," the sheriffs included, and certainly not by the lord mayor, "till they have finished the business about which they are assembled." Although the lord mayor was vested with the responsibility "of Summoning the Free-men together, yet in case he should fail in convocating them . . . for the necessary affairs and occasions of the Corporation, they may come together of their own accord." If the magistrates could not interfere in the proper business of the liverymen in common hall, neither could common council, a less ancient body, one "first erected" by common hall, and one that had "receive'd several alterations by constitutions made in the Common Hall." In this Whig understanding of the Corporation, the electoral assembly of the

---

[39] *Rights of the City,* p. 1; *Right of Electing Sheriffs,* p. 2; Hunt, *Defence,* p. 39; *The Citizens Loss, when the Charter of London is Forfeited* (1683), pp. 3–4.
[40] *CSPD 1682,* p. 417; *Priviledg and Right,* p. 6.

liverymen embodied the consent of the people to the exercise of legitimate authority.[41]

In the polarized political culture of the Restoration Crisis, London Tories found this entire sequence of political reasoning objectionable and incendiary. Where the London Whigs looked to consent as a prerequisite for the legitimate exercise of authority in the Corporation, London Tories instead looked to hierarchical structures and to obedience to office-holders as the prerequisites for government. Where the Whigs elevated common hall, the Tories denigrated common hall. For them, in times past, common hall had been an assemblage of the "*Sober* and *Substantial Citizens*" of the twelve great companies. But in recent times, as the hall had expanded to include the liveries of many other companies, and as the liveries of those companies had in turn been enlarged, its social character had deteriorated, rendering it unfit for a primary role in Corporation affairs. Roger North characterized common hall as "a routish Assembly of sorry Citizens, not unlike the Mob at an inferior Corporation Election." Another loyalist writer dismissed the body as full of "*Mean Artificers*" and others of "*Low Condition.*" If "the *People* [were] to have the *Approbation* of . . . *Officers*, and *Ministers*," wrote L'Estrange, then "an *Absolute, Arbitrary*, and *Unaccountable Power*" would be "Lodg'd in the *Multitude*." What else would be necessary for "the Introducing of a *Democracy*, and making *London* a Theatre of *Violence*, and *Disorder*; as much as ever *Rome*, or *Florence* was." Or, as John Dryden suggested, if the Whigs could successfully maintain the "supreme power" of the freemen, they could also "make London independent of the Crown: A realm apart, the Kingdom of the Town."[42]

Against the emphasis of the Whigs upon the consent of the people and the delegated authority of the sheriffs as popular tribunes, the Tories advanced the prerogatives of the lord mayor. For them, the particular issue of the shrieval election of 1682 was "whether or no, a *Popular Innovation* shall break in upon an *Indisputable Prescription*" of the lord mayor to name one sheriff. The insistence of the Whigs that common hall elect both sheriffs was contrary to the lord mayor's "*consent*, & *against* his *Prerogative*." For, as lord mayor, according to the Tories, Sir John Moore was "the Prime and Supreme part" of the Corporation, "not only an Integral Part; but the most Eminent and Principal, as the Head to the Body." As for the London sheriffs, Tory writers saw little difference between the Sheriffs of London and Middlesex and the sheriffs of other counties, and they certainly saw no

---

[41] *Matters of Fact*, p. 2; *Rights of the City*, p. 3; Hunt, *Defence*, p. 35; *Case of the Sheriffs*, p. 24; *Nature of a Common-Hall*; *Priviledg and Right*, p. 8.

[42] *The Lord Mayor's Right of Electing a Sheriff* (1682), pp. 1, 8; North, *Examen*, p. 93; *Observator*, I, 29, 176 (2 July 1681, 24 July 1682); *POAS*, III, 277.

accountability of the sheriffs to the London electorate: "The *Sheriffs* are only the *King's Officers*, and not the Officers of the *Corporation*."[43]

But the Whigs would have none of this, for in their understanding the city's chief magistrate was subordinate and accountable to the people he served. They treated the lord mayor's presence at common hall as a courtesy rather than as a right. His role in summoning the liverymen was "merely out of Civility and Complement," and the liverymen could "not only resume it when they please, . . . [but] place it elsewhere." As one author suggested, "my Lord *Mayor* hath no Jurisdiction over the Common-Hall, being there only as a *Concivis* or fellow Citizen." Or again, "What Power the Mayor has is but delegated from the Citizens." Indeed, the lord mayor was as accountable to the electors as the sheriffs: "The Lord Mayor is not a Judge here, but an Officer; he is not to Rule them in the Common-Hall; but to serve them. . . . And it is a wonderful Arrogance, that . . . a Creature made by the pleasure of the Citizens, should take upon him a Power to controll . . . them."[44]

The response of many Whig citizens to Sir John Moore's refusal to accept the sheriffs they had elected in 1682 was, then, a defense of a consensual and historical understanding of the civic constitution against what they perceived as "arbitrary" mayoral behavior that would destroy it. In the political language that expressed their anger, the Whigs were prepared to employ all remedies against Moore that the law provided.[45] As they badgered Moore with scores of King's Bench suits, they also reminded him of the 1680 parliamentary impeachment of Lord Chief Justice Sir William Scroggs.[46] But citizens seeking protection of their electoral rights against a lord mayor need not, according to civic Whig thinking, wait for a parliament or for the outcome of suits at law. Acting on behalf of the freemen, common hall could act as a court of law "*to punish the Mayor and Aldermen when they stand against the duty of their places.*" A sitting lord mayor could be removed from office by the citizens and replaced "if he commit a crime against his Duty and Trust." Those who misrepresented the citizens at Whitehall could be disfranchised by common hall, and magistrates who broke oath with them could be indicted "upon the Statute of *Westminster*." Finally, responding to the rumored royal intent of continuing Moore as mayor for a second year, one author recalled the fate of Lord Mayor Sir Nicholas Brember. Beheaded in 1388, Brember had been condemned "for undertaking at the pleasure

[43] *Observator*, I, 154, 166 (14 June, 7 July 1682); *Lord Mayor's Right*, p. 6; *The City of Londons Loyal Plea* (1682), p. 1.

[44] *Priviledg and Right*, p. 8; *Rights of the City*, pp. 2–3; *Case between the Ld. Mayor & Commons*, pp. 6–7; *The Sheriffs of London for the Time Being, are the Proper Managers and legal judges of the election of Sheriffs* (1682).

[45] *Case between the Ld. Mayor & Commons*, p. 5; *Nature of a Common-Hall*; *Priviledg and Right*, p. 7; Papillon, *Memoirs*, pp. 217–18.

[46] *Rights of the City*, p. 3; Schwoerer, "Impeachment of Sir William Scroggs."

of the King, to be Mayor, without the consent, and against the will of the Citizens."[47]

The shrieval election of 1682 thus drove Whig writers to make more explicit the discursive assumptions about government that had long circulated within the civic opposition and within the city's Whig-inclined spaces. The authority of common hall was superior to that of a lord mayor – even a lord mayor backed by the crown – because common hall gave effect to the will of the people. Just as Whigs throughout the kingdom believed the future of Protestantism was at stake in the Restoration Crisis, so civic Whigs believed the future of electoral consent throughout the kingdom was at stake in the crown's effort to rein in the Corporation. They believed they were experiencing an "invasion and usurpation" upon their civic freedoms through the employment of "direct violence" by those determined to "rob us of our Birthrights." In Sir John Moore, the Tory shrieval "intruders" of 1682, and the loyalist aldermen, the London Whigs found incarnate the much-discussed hypothetical figures of inferior magistrates who trampled upon right and claimed the king's authority for their actions. But for the civic Whigs, a claim of royal sanction could not legitimize the exercise of power in violation of the rights of the citizenry and of the common law: "If the *King*...shall Commissionate any to do that which is against Law, that Commission is void," one writer asserted, for "the authority which the *King* hath, can be no other but what the Law does grant him."[48]

Tory responses to such language were often hyperbolic, but the hyperbole was an indication of the unbridgeable divide between the discursive conventions of Restoration loyalism and those of London's dissenters and Whigs. Sir Roger L'Estrange took the lead in rejecting the Whigs' submission of magisterial authority to the people's inspection: "The *Lord-Mayor* has as much Power...as the *King* can give him." If the Whigs were to prevail in "setting up the *Electors*" as "judges," then "a *Totall Dissolution* of the City-*Government*" would follow. L'Estrange did not hesitate to put the dispute about consent and authority in the Corporation into even broader contexts. The Whigs challenged the fundamental order of the land, turning "the course of *Providence*, and the *Nature of Things, Topsy Turvy*." Their principles would "set *Servants* above their *Masters; Subjects* above their *Sovereigns*; those that are *Governed*, above those that *Govern*." For L'Estrange, Whig arguments about consent in the city were an affront to monarchy itself. "He that strikes at the chair, strikes at the Crown," thundered the king's apologist: "If ye can but *once Top the Lord-Mayor and*

---

[47] *Rights of the City*, pp. 2, 4; *Matters of Fact*, pp. 1, 4; *Priviledg and Right*, p. 7.
[48] *Priviledg and Right*, p. 4; *Rights of the City*, p. 1; *Right of Electing Sheriffs*, p. 1; *Case of the Sheriffs*, p. 13.

Court of Aldermen with a *Common Hall*, 'tis but one step more . . . to the *Binding of your Kings in Chains and your Nobles in Links of Iron.*"[49]

L'Estrange was not mistaken in believing that the arguments of the London Whigs were as easily applied to Charles II as to those commissioned by him. Whig authors practiced circumspection in their consideration of the king's role in their contested affairs; but by 1682, many of them no more trusted Charles than they did his servants and ministers. One author who believed that Thomas Papillon and John Dubois had been deprived of their rightful shrieval election in 1682 explicitly compared Charles II to Richard II: "The imposing the Sheriffs upon the Cities and Counties contrary to Right and Custom . . . was made one of the Articles against *Richard* the 2d., for which he was deposed." And, as fears about the security of the city's charter mounted, Whig authors found it even more difficult to restrain their political language. Within months of the 1682 shrieval election, they were drawing out the implications of the crown's challenge to the charter. One writer was "full of Horror" as he confronted the "Disorders, Losses, Distractions, Mischiefs and Confusions" that would follow the "Destruction and the Death of so great a Body Politick." Thomas Hunt condemned the broader campaign of remodeling the boroughs by means of new charters as a dissolution of the government of the kingdom. "This new Mode of incorporating Citys and Towns, doth *ipso facto*, change the Government," he wrote, because it eliminated "the Peoples choice" in the election of MPs. Consent was the heart of the matter for these writers. It was "criminal" on the part of Charles's advisers to pursue courses that destroyed the "antient Government." And those courses also turned Charles into "a very mean" king, or "a Wicked and Miserable Tyrant," who disregarded the people's will in his manner of government.[50]

Civic Whig language about electoral consent and authority is critical in understanding what so aroused London Whig electors by 1682. It is also critical in establishing continuity between the restless citizenry of the 1640s and the aroused citizens of the Restoration Crisis. Arguments about consent, like cases for conscience, had first circulated extensively among London commonwealthmen, Levellers, and sectarians during the civil war and interregnum years. But between 1649–52 and 1679–82, a consensual understanding of the Corporation had been mainstreamed within the dissenting community from which the Whigs emerged. The geographical spaces within the Corporation that were Whig-inclined during the Restoration Crisis were spaces in which discourse about consent had been embodied within a particular population. Historians searching for the post-1660 history of civil war

---

[49] *Observator*, I, 163, 166, 346, 373 (1, 7 July 1682; 28 May and 12 July 1683).
[50] *Rights of the City*, p. 2; *The Citizens Loss*, p. 4; Hunt, *Defence*, pp. 6, 8–9.

"radicalism" would do well to focus on the social landscape represented by those urban spaces.

Anglican loyalist writers had no difficulty in perceiving this continuity between the political discourse of London Whigs and the discourse of those who had formerly sought to remodel church, state, city, and society. In the 1640s and now once again, according to loyalist argument, "the *Lord Mayor*, and *Aldermen* were to be *Levell'd* with the *Commons* [and] his Lordship's Authority of *Summoning* and *Dissolving...taken away*." And the civic Whigs' objectives within the Corporation revealed the implications of a broader Whig agenda for the kingdom, according to their opponents. Encroachments upon authority in the microcosm of the city would again bring "on by Degrees, the ruin of *King, Church*, and *People*." If not checked, the "Licentiousness of the *City*" would endanger social order throughout the realm, for the Whigs would also "teach the nobles how to bow, and keep the...gentry down." For civic loyalists, the king's assertion of royal authority, after Oxford, was the beginning of a recovery of the restored church and state from "Hydra, the many-headed monster," which had been released by "Rebellions Charter."[51] Such discourse was firmly rooted in the environs and neighborhoods of the city's Tory-inclined spaces. In Restoration London, different urban communities were the carriers of different ideas; and in the crisis of 1679–82, a polarized city fed polarization in the kingdom as well.

The macrocosm: the reformation of church and state

"There is now spread an *universal* demand of reformation," observed Sir Robert Southwell, early in 1679.[52] This demand came especially from London pulpits and from the London press. The chief intellectual advocates of reformation – men like Vincent Alsop, Richard Baxter, John Humfrey, John Owen, and William Penn – were London writers, London preachers, and spokesmen for London dissenters of different persuasions. Moreover, like the civic Whigs' language about consent and authority in the Corporation, the language of reformation had retained its attraction especially among the citizens in the particular urban neighborhoods that made up the Whig-inclined space within the Corporation. Contrary to Southwell, however, the demand for reformation was divisive, rather than unifying, from the beginning of the Restoration Crisis. Reformation was a discursive symbol for

---

[51] *Lord Mayor's Right*, p. 8; Northleigh, *Parallel*, p. 8; *The Charter; A Comical Satyr* (1682), in *POAS*, III, 439; *POAS*, III, 11; *The Last Will and Testament of the Charter of London* (1683); *An Act of Common Council for Regulating the Election of Sheriffs, and for Repealing the Treasonable and Disloyal Acts and Proceedings of that Court* (1683), p. 15.

[52] HMC, *Ormonde*, NS, IV, xviii .

the whole range of religious and political issues that separated dissenters and many Reformed Protestants from the leadership of the Anglican order. It was also a reminder that the religious issues that had convulsed the kingdom, parliament, and the city in the 1640s and again in 1659–60 and 1669–70 had not been satisfactorily resolved, in the minds of many, through the perpetuation of a coercive church settlement. Finally, the demand for reformation, which built upon previous dissenting arguments for liberty of conscience, also paralleled civic arguments about consent and authority in several important respects.

What, then, did dissenting and Reformed Protestant authors and citizens intend by their demand for reformation? What was their vision of a reformed and resettled church and a truly Protestant state? Why did the language of reformation persuade Anglicans that they again confronted the swarming sects of 1649 and 1659 rather than fellow Protestants seeking a strengthened church order? Focused upon parliament and the constitution, historians have largely neglected the literature about reformation in the Restoration Crisis. But like writings about consent and authority in the Corporation, this body of writing tells us much about how ordinary dissenting and loyalist citizens, to whom it was directed and whose discourse it reflected, comprehended the crisis that engulfed them and their institutions.

The dissenting authors of the Restoration Crisis followed their puritan predecessors in perceiving reformation as the ongoing work of the church rather than as an era of national or ecclesiastical history. The Presbyterian Vincent Alsop wrote that reformation should "be made *in what is necessary* ... as *often as is necessary*." All the dissenting authors of the crisis rooted their arguments for reformation in the purposes of "our first *Renowned Reformers*," the perfection of whose work lay neither in its completeness, nor in its array of ecclesiastical forms and practices, but rather in its goal of conformity to the "*Word of God*."[53]

According to these authors, however, the episcopal leadership of the parochial church order had turned its back upon the English Reformation. Like the Country spokesmen of the 1670s, they perceived the Restoration church settlement as a triumph of a "corrupted party" of clergy who had sought to reverse the Reformation with their brand of "popery" ever since the days of Archbishop William Laud. This "Retreat in Reformation" was unacceptable to true Protestant believers, who owed their allegiance to the author of conscience rather than to the "Prelatical party." For these writers,

---

[53] [Vincent Alsop], *Melius Inquirendum. Or, A Sober Inquiry into the Reasonings of the Serious Inquiry*, 3rd ed. (1681), pp. 31, 37, 67; [Vincent Alsop], *The Mischief of Impositions: or, an Antidote against a Late Discourse ... called the Mischief of Separation* (1680), unpaginated Epistle Dedicatory, B[1–2] and p. 80; *Proposal of Union*, p. 3.

reformation trumped clerical authority, and the voluntary assemblies created by people of conscience had a divine sanction that outweighed the secular sanction of the kingdom's parochial order. Alsop wrote, for instance, that both "Scripture" and "all Antiquity" would justify that believer, who "petitioning for Reformation" in his parish church, "humbly desiring he may have Christs ordinances upon Christs terms, and yet being denied his Right," turns "to some other particular Church of Christ." And Presbyterian John Humfrey was as explicit as any Independent when he claimed, "*Particular Assemblies* [like those of the dissenters] are of *Divine* [Institution]," whereas "*Parochial Churches* are of *Human* Institution."[54]

An end to the coercion of Protestants was, according to these authors, essential for a resettlement of the Church of England in accordance with its historic Reformation principles. Employing a particularly redolent metaphor of the 1640s and the 1650s, Richard Baxter castigated persecutors as "the seed of *Cain*." Alsop rejected "*persecution* for Religion" as "an impiety...abhorrent to the common light of Mankind." The coercion of the English prelates was the true popery of the crisis that needed to be eliminated for the sake of a Protestant future. The prelates' elevation of liturgy and ceremonial dictates over Protestant conscience was, in fact, the pattern upon which Rome had introduced "the whole Lirry of her superstitious Observances." As William Penn put it: "Conformity is *Coercive*, which is *Popish*."[55]

Moreover, as John Owen and John Howe argued, the continuing coercion of Protestant dissenters violated English law as well as Protestant tradition. According to Owen, the church settlement of 1662–5 was not "agreeable unto the laws of the land and liberty of the subjects." John Howe challenged the legality of persecution on the basis of legislative intent, for parliament had clearly sought accommodation in 1673, despite its failure to achieve it: "We may account the thing was in substance done...though it were not done *with that formality* as uses...to be stood upon." According to this argument, an explicit parliamentary abandonment of coercion in a new church settlement would restore the English church to its true

---

[54] Louis Du Moulin, *A Short and True Account of the Several Advances the Church of England hath made towards Rome* (1680), pp. 9, 22, 25; Alsop, *Mischief of Impositions*, pp. 4–5; Alsop, *Melius Inquirendum*, pp. 9–10, 37, 39, 203; [John Humfrey], *An Answer to Dr. Stillingfleet's Sermon, by the Peaceable Design Renewed* (1680), p. 6; *Proposal of Union*, p. 4; N. Y. and D. N., *Protestant Conformist*, pp. 6, 8.

[55] Richard Baxter, *Catholick Communion defended against both Extreams* (1684), p. 33; Alsop, *Melius Inquirendum*, p. [8]; Alsop, *Mischief of Impositions*, unpaginated Epistle Dedicatory, [A6]; Penn, *One Project*, p. 8. Also see [William Chillingworth], *Mr. Chillingworth's Judgment of the Religion of Protestants*, pp. 6–7; [William Penn], *Englands Great Interest in the Choice of this New Parliament* [1679], p. 4.

principles, provide the *"top-stone* to the *Reformation,"* and accomplish the "uniting [of] all Protestants." As John Humfrey reminded MPs in 1681, "Parliament is the Representative of the whole People of *England,* and . . . by Consent and Agreement, they might *Make* a New Constitution of the CHURCH."[56]

But what would a new church settlement, one closer to the spirit of reformation, look like? As he had in 1673, John Humfrey advocated a formula for Protestant union that combined the comprehension of Reformed Protestants with the toleration of sectarians under the "External Regiment" of the prince. The terms of comprehension should be sufficiently inclusive to embrace all who could "own" a reformed "public Liturgy," while toleration would loosely associate separate assemblies with a reformed national church, since they too would "own the King" as head of the Protestant order. Indeed, Baxter believed that the *"Auditories* or *Chappels"* gathered by "silenced Ministers and people" to supplement parochial worship were already auxiliary *"parts* of the *Parish Churches"*: church resettlement would merely facilitate the movement of these dissenters back into the parish order they had long sought to reform. And those assemblies that chose toleration rather than comprehension would nevertheless find succor in a broadened and reformed church structure. Humfrey maintained that bishops could, as "External Ecclesiastical Officer[s]," provide separate assembles with useful services and that separatists should be represented in Convocation together with the parochial churches.[57]

Such an ecclesiastical polity would clearly resemble the Cromwellian church that the restored Anglican ecclesia had replaced, with a broad parochial establishment at the center of a multiform Protestant order extending into the separate churches. Presbyterian spokesmen had become as comfortable with such Protestant diversity by 1679–82 as Independents and separatists had been in the 1640s. Once a champion of uniformity, Richard Baxter, for instance, now suggested that "a diversity of . . . circumstances . . . in divers Churches or Parishes, and sometimes in the same Church, is no . . . dreadful mischief." Alsop maintained "it's none of Christ's design to reduce all sincere believers to *an uniformity* in every Punctilio." And the author of a Protestant utopia of 1681 wrote that, "as long

56 [John Owen], *Some Considerations about Union among Protestants* (1680) in *Works,* XIV, 523; John Howe, *A Letter Written out of the Countrey to a Person of Quality in the City* (1680), p. 22; *Proposal for Union,* p. 3; Humfrey, *Materials for Union,* p. 4. Also see Sidney and Jones, *Vindication,* pp. 24–5.
57 Humfrey, *Materials for Union,* pp. 4–6; [John Humfrey], *An Answer to Dr. Stillingfleet's Book of the Unreasonableness of Separation* (1682), pp. 29–34; Humfrey, *Answer to Dr. Stillingfleet's Sermon,* pp. 27, 31; [John Humfrey], *The Healing Attempt* (1689), pp. 82–4; Richard Baxter, *Nonconformists Plea,* p. 117; Richard Baxter, *Second Part of the Nonconformists Plea for Peace* (1680), Preface A2[4–6] and pp. 184–7.

as there is any variety to be found in nature, it will be discernable in the difference of thoughts and opinions of men."[58]

A new parliamentary settlement along these lines would also banish the popish practice of coercion from the English church in favor of the Protestant practices of choice and consent. Nothing was more central to a truly reformed church settlement, according to the dissenting spokesmen of the Restoration Crisis, than "Consent and Agreement." Choice was at the heart of true Protestant church polity, according to dissenters of all persuasions. In a reformed church, just as in the apostolic church, believers must have freedom to choose their churches, and churches must have freedom to choose their pastors. Interference from clerical or social superiors in the choice of churches by believers and in the choice of pastors by churches must be abandoned. As Alsop wrote, *"every particular church ... has an inherent right to chuse its own Pastor, and every particular Christian the same power to chuse his own Church."*[59]

Moreover, in language that bears a striking resemblance to that employed by London Whigs about their magistrates, Presbyterian authors sought to redefine the office of bishop in a resettled Church of England according to the principle of consent they found in early Christianity. Baxter argued that "no man can be the *Bishop* ... of a Church ... against the ... Peoples will, or without their consent." According to Alsop, "particular assemblies" had, in the primitive church, acknowledged bishops as "prudential Creatures, erected meerly by their own consent." Baxter and Humphrey maintained, in the ancient church, "no Bishop had more than one worshiping assembly at once." They argued for a reduction of episcopacy through the multiplication of bishops: "I am for *more Bishops*, and not for fewer," wrote Baxter in an ingenious passage. Or, as Humfrey subsequently suggested, "Let there be as many Bishopricks as there are considerable Parsonages, or Parishes indowed."[60]

---

[58] Baxter, *Second Part of Nonconformists Plea*, p. 158; Alsop, *Melius Inquirendum*, pp. 19–20; *A Conference between a Bensalian Bishop and an English Doctor, concerning Church-Government* (1681), p. 5; Chillingworth, *Judgment*, pp. 6–7.

[59] Alsop, *Mischief of Impositions*, Epistle Dedicatory, [B2]; [John Owen], *A Brief Vindication of the Non-conformists* (1680) in *Works*, XIII, 313; Howe, *Letter*, pp. 24–5; Baxter, *Nonconformists Plea*, pp. 31, 71; Baxter, *Church History*, p. 7; Orme, *Memoirs*, p. 423. Compare this dissenting language to John Locke's 1681 suggestion that "Part of my liberty as a Christian and as a man" is "to choose of what church or religious society I will be of, as most conducing to the salvation of my soul." Locke, "Critical Notes" [Bodl. Lib. MS Locke c.34], fol. 74, as quoted by Ashcraft, *Revolutionary Politics*, p. 493; John Spurr, "Schism and the Restoration Church," esp. pp. 420–2.

[60] Baxter, *Nonconformists Plea*, Epistle, pp. 15, 25–6; Alsop, *Mischief of Impositions*, pp. 27–8; Humfrey, *Healing Attempt*, p. 44; Humfrey, *Materials for Union*, p. 5. Also see Baxter, *Nonconformists Plea*, pp. 10–17; Richard Baxter, *Church History*, Preface; Humfrey, *Answer to Dr. Stillingfleet's Sermon*, p. 8; Humfrey, *Answer to Dr. Stillingfleet's Book*, p. 28; Humfrey, *Healing Attempt*, pp. 57–81.

Their reclamation of a reduced episcopacy for a Reformed Protestant church order also directed these dissenting authors of 1679–82 to a consideration of Protestant statecraft, for they feared that the popery of the prelates was as inimical to the state as it was to the church. The English Reformation, which rested upon parliamentary statute, placed the bishops under secular authority; but diocesan bishops were, according to Reformed Protestant thought, always keen to re-establish their independence from king-in-parliament. "Coming into their Bishopricks and great Estates," observed London lawyer Edward Whitaker of the Restoration bishops, "they thought it hard that they must have their Spiritual Swords tied" by the state. Claiming that the practice of diocesan episcopacy in the parochial order had produced a "Church-Tyranny," Baxter suggested that this result was implicit in the nature of the unreformed episcopal office, for prelates "are commonly for . . . ruling by constraint."[61]

And, desiring to exercise unrestrained power in the church, the prelates collaterally encouraged "arbitrary power" in the state. The Laudians had corrupted Charles I, according to these authors. Would their successors also corrupt Charles II? Alsop maintained that the "roaring Ecclesiastical *Canons*" of the restored Anglican order supported an "unaccountable power in those that are [at] the Top" to require those "at the Bottom" to "do and say anything." More broadly, the dissenting argument became that "the Interest of [diocesan] Bishops, and their practice, is utterly destructive of, and repugnant to the establishment of Secular Powers," or at least to the preferred secular power of king-in-parliament.[62]

These arguments about consent and authority in the church point to important common rhetorical terms between dissenting discourse about the church and civic Whig discourse about the electorate. Moreover, the common criterion of consent, which was employed against civic magistrates and diocesan bishops, could just as easily be utilized to limit the authority of the prince in ecclesiastical affairs. Dissenting writers were at pains to emphasize their support for the royal supremacy. But they also stressed that the supremacy was to be exercised only "to secure and preserve the *great Charter* of *Christian Liberty*." No prince could "impose matters of *immediate Worship upon the Conscience*," for his responsibility for the church,

---

[61] Edward Whitaker, *Bishops Court Dissolved*, pp. 33, 35–6; Baxter, *Church-History*, p. 25; Baxter, *Nonconformists Plea*, p. 58. Also see [Henry Care], *A Perfect Guide for Protestant Dissenters* (1682), pp. 19–22; Bethel, *The Present Interest of England* (1681 version) in *The Interest of the Princes & States*, 3rd ed. (1689), pp. 21, 25–31; Humfrey, *Answer to Dr. Stillingfleet's Sermon*, p. 19. For the furious debate in the 1679 parliament and press about the voting of bishops in the House of Lords in capital cases, see Goldie, "Danby, the Bishops and the Whigs," pp. 90–6.

[62] Alsop, *Mischief of Impositions*, Epistle Dedicatory [A6]; Du Moulin, *Several Advances*, p. 10.

under God, was "to preserve, not to destroy, to propagate, not to alter, to encourage, not to innovate."[63]

But what if the prince should mistake his duty and, whether on his own initiative or at the urging of his prelates, constrain the free exercise of faith? How were believers to respond to a regime, Protestant or otherwise, in which secular or clerical authorities suppressed the expression of conscience? The answer offered by the dissenting advocates of reformation began again with the importance of consent and individual right, this time in the operations of the state. Although Richard Baxter insisted in conventional Protestant language that governors formally "receive their power" from God and "not from the people," he nevertheless maintained that no prince, in fact, ruled "antecedently to the peoples consent" or "choice" of who "should govern." The prince's power could also be "limited by *Contract with the people*," who, having "a right to their *lives, limbs, liberties and estates*" at the time of establishing their "Constitutive Laws," might secure these "*Liberties*," including that of conscience, from "the *absolute will* of the Soveraign." Robert Ferguson maintained that kings have "no . . . more power" than "what the Community have consented shall be so" under "the Rules of the Constitution." John Owen argued that the temporal establishment of Protestantism, by common agreement, in the Reformation made it thereafter a part of the people's "birth-right inheritance." And regarding liberty of conscience as among the "first Principles" of English government, William Penn warned that the continued violation of conscience would lead to the "decay" of the state, as the people withdrew their "Affections" from it.[64]

Did believers whose civil and religious liberties were violated by the state, or by clerics claiming the authority of the state, have a right, then, to resist such unjust exercises of authority? Not according to Baxter, who argued that believers must remain subject to duly constituted powers, even as they disobeyed civil and religious commands deemed, through the exercise of conscience, to be contrary to God's will. "When subjects may *not obey*, yet may they not by *arms resist* authority," Baxter wrote, also insisting that "inferior Magistrates are the subjects of the King . . . and have no power to depose him or to take up arms against him." Despite his endorsement of this classical Protestant premise, Baxter's own rejection of civil and ecclesiastical "Laws and Mandates" contrary to "*the Laws of Christ*, or *against the Common good*" as "*ipso facto* null" probably led some readers to a less guarded

---

[63] Alsop, *Melius Inquirendum*, pp. 323, 330, 360.

[64] Baxter, *Second Part of the Nonconformists Plea*, pp. 15, 36–8, 56; [Robert Ferguson], *An Impartial Enquiry into the Administration of Affair's in England* (1683), p. 27, Penn, *One Project*, pp. 2, 6.

position.[65] And they would have found explicit support for active resistance in the writings of Owen, Humfrey, and Ferguson.

According to Owen, the people were justified, when confronted by an effort to destroy their liberties and their religion, in "defending themselves in the Profession of the Protestant Religion by Arms." John Humfrey avowed that if agents acting in the king's name misused his authority, then "the People, or our inferior Magistrates" might raise "Arms or Force" to "withstand such violence." Ferguson, who ministered in London throughout the Restoration Crisis, was even more blunt. According to him, when "Princes violate the fundamental Contracts that are betwixt them and the people, the Community . . . are then absolved and freed from their Fealty." Chief amongst such violations for Ferguson was any design by the prince "to extirpate that Religion which the Lord hath revealed and appointed to be the Rule of our living." To resist such actions is not to oppose proper authority but rather to oppose the usurpation of God's sovereignty over conscience. Indeed, thundered Ferguson, "when Princes will be content with no less than the Scepter of Christ, they then deserve to have their own wrested out of their hands."[66]

Both the dissenting call for reformation and the political arguments that followed from reformation directly contradicted Anglican thought about obedience, clerical order, and non-resistance. Loyalist writers were, therefore, quick to condemn the demand for reformation as a threat to the Restoration Settlement as great as Roman Catholicism. Reformation was, for Anglicans, a "sham pretense," a cover for nonconformist defiance of "divine and human laws" and for the dissenters' disobedience "to their rightful prince." Conscience was not an inherent faculty for discerning divine will but rather a cloak for lawlessness. Anglicans perceived the critics of the church as again "brewing Sedition in a Sanctified Tub," or inciting the population to rebellion in the guise of reformation, just as they had in the 1640s. Dissenting abuse of the "sweet name" of reformation was "a Rank sign of [the] sickly and *distemper'd Times*" that had returned to ravage the kingdom. The idol of a "thorough Reformation" would now, as it had before, destroy deference and duty, replacing them with "*Rapine, Blood,* [and]

---

[65] Baxter, *Second Part of the Nonconformists Plea*, pp. 17, 48, 53, 57, 171; Baxter, *Nonconformists Plea*, p. 32. Baxter had been less restrained in his treatment of resistance in 1659: Baxter, *Holy Commonwealth*, ch. 12.

[66] [John Owen], *A Brief and Impartial Account of the Nature of the Protestant Religion* (1682) in *Works*, XIV, 537; Humfrey, *Answer to Dr. Stillingfleet's Sermon*, pp. 20–2; R. Ferguson, *Impartial Enquiry* (1683), pp. 3–4, 7, 26–8; Greaves, *Secrets*, p. 94. For Ferguson and resistance, see J. Marshall, *John Locke*, pp. 227ff.; Ashcraft, *Revolutionary Politics*, pp. 228–37; M. S. Zook, *Radical Whigs and conspiratorial politics in late Stuart England* (University Park, Penn., 1999), pp. 93–102.

Sacriledge," the "*Oblation*[s]" demanded of the dissenters by "their *Moloch Reformation*."[67]

Writing in 1683, Edmund Bohun claimed the dissenters had "engrossed the Title of Protestant" in their efforts to arouse the kingdom on behalf of reformation. But church apologists also countered the Reformed Protestant history of Anglican declension with a sacred history of their own. They anchored Restoration episcopacy in the history of ancient Christianity and in the practices of the "Martyr-Bishops" of the Edwardian Reformation. The dissenters had simply misappropriated the past for their argument that Anglican government was "unlawful and inconsistent with . . . our Reformation." Indeed, the dissenters' ritualistic cursing of the bishops was answered by an Anglican litany of condemnation of the leading dissenting clerics for substituting the tenets of Geneva, Amsterdam, and Edinburgh for those of Albion. Moreover, contrary to dissenting apologetic, liberty for conscience would lead not to Protestant unity but only to a "*breaking in pieces* of the *Constitution* of this *Church*" and a "Multitude of Sects." Talk of accommodation through comprehension and toleration was specious: ever since the Reformation the sects had devoured one another and established churches. The Presbyterians claimed seniority in a fraternity of dissenting persuasions; but, "They never *Did*, they never *Can* Unite in any *one Poynt*; but t' o'rethrow the *Right*." The disunity of their unsettlement of the English church would, in fact, provide the most "plausible argument to draw Men to the *Popish pretences* of *Unity*," permitting Rome to "hatch . . . Eggs in a Presbyters Nest."[68]

Anglicans rejected the idea that consent should be the basis for a resettlement of the church or the state as a return to the sectarian tenets of the Commonwealth. In the church, the principle of consent turned "*Union* into *Dissention*, and the Church into a *Conventicle*." Proposals for the multiplication and greater accountability of bishops would instead lead to a "total Extirpation of Episcopal Government." Applied to civil government, the idea of consent – or the "Democratical Principles" of the dissenters – would lead to even more disastrous consequences. As in the civil war and interregnum years, such ideas would leave "*Statute Laws insignificant, unless the very*

---

[67] *POAS*, III, 103; *The Loyal Subjects Litany* (1680); *A Dialogue between the Ghosts of the Two last Parliaments* (1681); [Sir Roger L'Estrange], *The Committee; or Popery in Masquerade* (1680).

[68] [Edmund Bohun], *Reflections on a Pamphlet, stiled a Just and Modest Vindication of the two last Parliaments* (1683), p. 78; Stillingfleet, *Unreasonableness of Separation*, pp. x, xxii, xxix, lxxx; L'Estrange, *The Committee; The Second Part of the Loyal Subject's Litany* (1680); *A Just Reproof to Mr Baxter, for His Pride and Insolence* (1680); *A Letter to Dr du Moulin, containing a Charitable Reproof for his Schismatical Book* (1680); *A Letter from Scotland, with Observations upon the Anti-Erastian, Anti-Prelatical, and Phanatical Presbyterian Party there* (1682); Northleigh, *The Parallel*, pp. 13, 33–4; *The Cavaliers Litany* (1682); *Dialogue between Two Jesuits; A True Description of the Bull Feast* (1683), p. 1; *POAS*, III, 224, 269, 367, 397.

Rabble [are] *set up for the sole Magistrates and Legislators.*" These notions would again lead the kingdom to the "destroying [of] the best of *Kings* to become Slaves to *five hundred Tyrants.*" What the dissenters really sought was not conscience and liberty but rather the same unrestrained dominion they had exercised in the days of the Rump. And that, according to Anglican writers, was an arbitrary rule indistinguishable from the political practices encouraged by Rome. Alternately, the dissenters' agenda would produce such a plethora of "Factions and Parties, and every Faction being in a State of hostility against the other, [that] the Prince for the Security of the publick Peace will be enforced to keep an Army."[69]

The Anglican response to dissenting arguments about reformation in the Restoration church and state demonstrates the depth of conviction that separated the hostile parties of the Restoration Crisis. And the debate about reformation also points to how fundamentally intertwined the issues of church and state were, both in the public sphere and in the opposite partisan spaces that made up the Corporation of London. Discourse about reformation and consent shared common terms, although the common terms of Whig and dissenting language were strikingly different from those of Tory and loyalist language.

The political discourse of the London Whigs looked to a normative "ancient constitution" in which the people had chosen governors who were accountable to them. Similarly, the religious discourse of London dissent looked to an ancient or primitive church in which religious assemblies had chosen pastors and bishops accountable to the faithful. For the Whigs and dissenters, if authority was derived ultimately from God, it nevertheless could be exercised only with the active consent of the people. A resettlement of the Restoration church and state required abandonment of the practice of coercion; and it could not be accomplished with a popish successor.

The political discourse of London Anglicans, on the other hand, treated the monarchy itself as the guardian of law and the epitome of the "ancient constitution." For civic loyalists, the magistrates were instruments of a king who exercised political privileges and powers in the interest of order. In the church, bishops and clergy held their authority immediately under the king, who presided over the parochial order, but ultimately under a God best served by uniformity in belief and practice. What was required to resolve the crisis of the day was not a new settlement enshrining reformation and electoral consent, but rather obedience to the settlement already in place, including the principle of hereditary succession.

---

[69] *True Description of the Bull Feast*, p. 2; Northleigh, *The Parallel*, pp. 29, 33–4; *A Parallel between Episcopacy & Presbytery* (1680), p. 1; *Matchiavel Junior; or the Secret Arts of the Jesuites* (1683), p. 4.

In London, these opposite political and religious languages arose from the historical experiences and memories of two different spatial communities. Charles II would regain control of the Corporation in alliance with a party shaped by the discourse of Restoration Anglicanism. But the triumph of the crown and the civic Tories could neither detach London dissenters and Reformed Protestants from the language that had shaped their community nor drive that language from public memory.

DIFFERENT LEADERS: A PROSOPOGRAPHY OF PARTY SPOKESMEN

Who were the London party leaders of the Restoration Crisis, the agents who organized and secured electoral participation on the scale revealed in 1682? As parties that spoke for diverging communities, the London Whigs and Tories of the Restoration Crisis differed significantly in their leaderships. Party leaders were community leaders; and the two different communities that converged and conflicted in the political culture of late Restoration London were led by spokesmen and office-holders with contrasting characteristics. Differing in religion, residential preferences, age profiles, occupations, and wealth and investments, the party leaders provide further evidence for both partisanship and polarization in London. Fifty leaders of each party will be analyzed here: all those who held or who were promoted for magisterial office in the Restoration Crisis or who were appointed to significant common council committees. (Selected biographical details about them are found in Appendices III–IV.)

Religion

Whig and Tory leaders differed in their religious commitments, as might be expected. As Table 6.3 indicates, forty-one of the fifty Whig leaders were dissenters or other Reformed Protestants outside the Church of England. The number of Whig leaders who were Independents is surprising because the occasional conformity required for office-holding was easier for Presbyterians. On the other hand, Independent meetings in London and its environs were concentrated in the city proper, as Table 6.2 indicates, giving Independents a significant presence within the Corporation. Independents among the civic Whig leaders of the Restoration Crisis included North European traders Sir Patience Ward, Sir John Shorter, and Thomas Shepherd. William Ashurst and his kinsmen John Lane and Henry Cornish were among the most notable Presbyterians.

The data in Table 6.3 also reveal the extent to which Reformed Protestantism rather than sectarianism was characteristic of the Whig leaders. Only Baptist Richard Bristow can be identified with sectarianism. Sectarianism

Table 6.3 *Probable religious persuasions of Whig party leaders*

Presbyterian	10
Independent	12
Dissenter, persuasion unknown	11
French Reformed	4
Dutch Reformed	3
Baptist	1
Anglican	6
No information	3
Total Whig leaders	**50**

survived in strength in London, as Table 6.2 indicates; but it survived in strength in the urban periphery rather than in the Corporation. Loyalist charges that the London Whigs' agenda in church and state represented a return to republican and sectarian dominance was, therefore, an exaggeration, although it was also clearly an effective exaggeration. The Whig leaders – and most of the congregations from which they came – were really the heirs of Cromwell's broad Protestant settlement rather than of the Rump and its sectarian allies. Presbyterian and Independent leaders had mended their political fences with the heirs of revolutionary sectarianism, but their political friendships with Reformed Protestants within the Church of England were just as important to them and to their purposes. Interestingly, civic Whig leaders drawn from Reformed Protestant ranks within the church included both the "moderate" Sir Robert Clayton and the more extreme Francis Jenks, as well as James Paul, son of a bishop and a treasurer of the Sons of the Clergy.[70]

Dissent was so widespread within the social ranks from which most party leaders sprang that even four Tory leaders, including Aldermen Sir John Moore and Sir William Turner, had once dissented from the coercive Restoration church. For the most part, however, the Anglican identity of the civic Tory leadership, like that of the Restoration church's clerical leadership, had developed in opposition to the Reformed Protestantism of the Whigs. Civic Anglicans were generally committed to the policies of persecution and non-resistance and hostile to the Whig agenda for resettling church and state. Tory aldermen and Southwark MPs Sir Peter Daniel, Sir Richard How(e), and Peter Rich, for instance, were vigorous in their enforcement of the Conventicle Act after the Oxford Parliament. Common Councilman William Withers (the elder) was zealous in his hostility to dissent, and he rejected

---

[70] PRO: SP29/418/199; Woodhead, *Rulers*, p. 127; Beaven, *Aldermen*, II, 114.

Table 6.4 *Residence of Whig and Tory city leaders: Whig space, Tory space, and contested space*

	Whigs	Tories
Whig space:	*16*	*3*
Aldersgate Without and Cripplegate Without	1	
Portsoken and Aldgate	4	2
Whig center (bloc of six wards)	10	
Queenhithe and Vintry	1	1
Tory space:	*20*	*29*
Tower and Billingsgate	3	6
Western wards	5	7
Tory center (bloc of five wards)	10	13
Dowgate	2	3
Contested space:	*11*	*14*
Divided center	5	5
Divided North-west	6	9
Outside the city or unknown:	*3*	*4*
Total party leaders	50	50

the 1689 oaths to the regime of William and Mary as inconsistent with the Anglican principle of passive obedience.[71]

Residence

Whig and Tory leaders were drawn from wards throughout the city, but the residences of the party leaders were nevertheless concentrated topographically in the communities for which they spoke. (Table 6.4) Party leaders who lived in the Whig space were overwhelmingly Whig, with only three Tory leaders resident there. No Tory leader resided in the wards of the Whig center, where such prominent civic Whigs as William Ashurst, Michael Godfrey, and Peter Houblon both lived and led.

Elsewhere in the city, resident Tory leaders were more numerous than their Whig counterparts. In the Tory space, resident Tory leaders outnumbered resident Whig leaders by almost three to two. Those wards were nevertheless home to a significant number of Whig leaders, including more than resided in the Whig space. In fact, as Table 6.5 suggests, Whig leaders were more numerous than Tory leaders as spokesmen for the prosperous Inner City wards considered as a whole. Similarly, Tory leaders were residentially concentrated in the Middle City wards that provided the sites, or were near to the sites,

[71] Henning, *House of Commons*, II, 188–9, 587–8, and III, 326–8; Luttrell, I, 410–11, 446; Morrice, Q, 163.

Table 6.5 *Residence of Whig and Tory leaders:*
Inner City, Middle City, and City without the Walls

	Whigs	Tories
Inner City wards	25	17
Middle City wards	17	27
City without the walls	5	2
Outside the city or unknown	3	4
Total party leaders	50	50

of so many institutional facilities associated with the Restoration regime in church and state. The two wards with the largest number of resident Tory leaders – five each – were Castle Baynard and Tower, both Tory-inclined and both in the Middle City. In Castle Baynard, in the shadow of St Paul's, the drapers and partners Alderman Sir Joseph Sheldon and Nicholas Charleton provided Tory leadership, as did Sir William Dodson, the king's woollen draper.[72] In Tower, many electors looked for leadership to such Tory merchants as Richard Alie, Sir Thomas Beckford, and Peter Paravicini, who lived near one another in Mincing Lane precinct.

Age

Table 6.6 reveals that the London Whig and Tory leaders differed significantly, as groups, in their life experiences of the kingdom's recent political and religious divisions. Both groups included men who ranged in age from their thirties to their seventies. Nevertheless, the Whig leaders included both greater numbers of older leaders and younger leaders than the Tories, while the Tories included significantly more men who had become active in the city in the first years of the Restoration.

More than half the Whig leaders had first come to prominence in London during the civil war and the interregnum years. As older men, they were open to loyalist charges of clinging to the religious and political agendas of the past. Whig Sir John Frederick, born in 1601, was the father of the city – its oldest active political leader; and as an MP, he was one of the fathers of parliament as well. His brother had fought for parliament in the early 1640s. Other Whig leaders first active in the 1640s and 1650s included Sheriff Bethel (*b.* 1617) and James Hayes (apprenticed in 1633), both common councilmen in the early 1650s, and City MP William Love (*b.* 1618),

---

[72] Woodhead, *Rulers*, pp. 60–1.

Table 6.6 *Age profiles of Whig and Tory leaders, considered by decades*[73]

		Whigs	Tories
Older leaders	(born in or before the 1620s)	27	19
Middle-aged leaders	(born in the 1630s)	10	22
Younger leaders	(born in the 1640s or the 1650s)	13	8
Unable to determine			1
Total party leaders		50	50

who had joined Bethel in 1660 on the Rump's Council of State. Some leading Whigs had been apprentices or young freemen during the era of civil war and carried forward attitudes shaped by their early political experiences. Indeed, Sir Samuel Barnardiston (*b.* 1620) had inadvertently provided a label for reformation in the 1640s, when his modest puritan locks suggested the roundhead epithet. Thomas Papillon (*b.* 1623) had fled to France in 1647 after taking a leading role in "Presbyterian" anti-army demonstrations. French Reformed merchant John Dubois (*b.* 1622) was a son-in-law of the prolocutor of the Westminster Assembly, and he was as committed to reformation of the English church in 1680–81 as his father-in-law had been a generation earlier.[74]

The Whig party of the 1680s was thus politically colored by the experiences and reflections of these older advocates of parliament and Reformed Protestantism. But the Whig leaders also included a greater number of younger men than the Tories, men who came to political maturity in the 1670s, as questions were again raised about the security of parliament and Protestantism. Most prominent among the younger Whig leaders were Recorder Sir George Treby (1643–1700) and merchant William Ashurst (1647–1720). A West Country lawyer and a leading member of all three exclusion parliaments, Treby played an instrumental role in parliamentary adoption of the Declaration of Rights in 1689 and resumed his office as Recorder of London before becoming Chief Justice of Common Pleas in 1692. Ashurst also remained a principal leader of the London Whigs after

---

[73] The birth years of fifty-six party leaders (twenty-eight Whigs and twenty-eight Tories) are known. The remaining birth years have been approximated and assigned to a decade by utilizing known data about the year of a leader's commencing his apprenticeship, obtaining the freedom, marrying, or first engaging in detectable occupational activity.

[74] Henning, *House of Commons*, I, 595–7; II, 237, 363–5; and III, 202–5; Woodhead, *Rulers*, p. 125; S. P. Anderson, *An English Consul in Turkey: Paul Rycaut at Smyrna, 1667–1678* (Oxford, 1989), pp. 88, 172, 249.

the Glorious Revolution, serving as alderman and MP, and as a national spokesman for English Presbyterians into the reign of George I.[75]

Broadly speaking, then, the Whig leaders represented a cross-generational alliance of older and younger advocates of reformation in church and state. Friendships and cooperation among the older and younger Whig leaders connected some who could remember the personal rule of Charles I to some who would guide the city through the turmoil of 1688–9. Both their opposition to a Catholic successor and their demand for reformation were influenced by previous episodes of anti-popery and Country zeal.

Despite loyalist rhetoric about the Whigs as men of 1641, the Tory leaders also included many older men who had experienced the civil war and political confusion of the 1640s and 1650s. Some of them had needed time to transition from their acceptance of interregnum regimes, suggesting again that Anglican loyalist identity was a Restoration creation. The oldest Tory leaders, Sir William Hooker (*b.* 1612) and Sir William Turner (*b.* 1615), for instance, had each doubted the wisdom of the coercive 1670 Conventicle Act. Other older Tory leaders included Alderman Sir Thomas Bludworth (*b.* 1620), who had been arrested by the Rump, and Edward Backwell (*b.* 1618), a banker to the crown who also had been a principal banker to the Commonwealth.[76]

The loyalism of the middle-aged leaders who were so much more evident among the London Tories naturally expressed their identification with the institutional settlement under which they flourished. Their commercial careers largely coincided with the Restoration itself. Sir William Pritchard (*c.* 1632–1705), the loyalist lord mayor of 1682–3, for instance, was a Southwark rope-maker whose profits as a supplier of naval stores to the Ordnance Office during Charles II's Dutch Wars enabled him to invest in a Buckinghamshire estate. Pritchard's success was mirrored by that of Peter Rich (*c.* 1630–92), the loyalist sheriff of 1682–3 and another Southwark supplier to the Ordnance, whose profits found their way into a Lincolnshire manor. Other Tory leaders who established their fortunes in Charles's reign and remained active into the 1690s included merchant Sir Benjamin Newland (*c.* 1633–99), a long-time Southampton MP, and goldsmith-banker John Johnson (1639–98): each provided Tory and joint-stock leadership after the Revolution.[77]

---

[75] Henning, *House of Commons*, I, 559–60, and III, 580–3; L. G. Schwoerer, *The Declaration of Rights, 1689* (Baltimore, 1981) pp. 43–7; De Krey, *Fractured Society*, pp. 89–90; Woodhead, *Rulers*, p. 19.

[76] BL Stowe MS 186, fols. 5–6; Henning, *House of Commons*, I, 578–9, 670–1; Woodhead, *Rulers*, pp. 21, 33, 92, 166.

[77] Henning, *House of Commons*, III, 135, 291–2, 326–8; Woodhead, *Rulers*, p. 99.

Table 6.7[78] *Occupations of Whig and Tory leaders*

	Whigs	Tories	Percent of all party leaders
Active or retired overseas merchants	32	21	53
Domestic merchants and traders	10	12	22
Industrial employers	3	6	9
Money-lenders: goldsmiths and scriveners	2	5	7
Apothecaries and druggists		3	3
Lawyers	2	1	3
Others and unknown	1	2	3
Total party leaders	**50**	**50**	

Broadly speaking, then, the London Tory leaders of the Restoration Crisis represented a convergence of older men, who developed a loyalist identity as they found security in the Restoration settlement, with middle-aged men, whose Anglicanism complemented their profitable participation in the Restoration establishment. These middle-aged Tory leaders had once been the urban complement to the youthful cavaliers who took up places in the Commons and Lords in 1660–61. As restored institutions came into crisis in the late 1670s, Tory leaders of both age cohorts remained committed to crown and miter as safeguards for a strong state and church establishment.

Occupations

Analysis of the London Whigs and Tories as spatially separated communities has also suggested some connections between partisanship and particular occupational groups. One of the anchors of the London Whigs was their reservoir of support within the central wards dominated by heavy concentrations of overseas merchants and domestic traders. Although these social groups were present in some Tory-inclined wards, the Tories also did well in some wards that lacked many merchants and in other wards that lacked a strong middling population. The stronger association between overseas commerce and the dissenting community from which the Whigs emerged is also apparent in the occupational profiles of party leaders, as found in Table 6.7.

---

[78] Occupations have been determined from a variety of sources, but chiefly from Woodhead, *Rulers*, and the appendices to De Krey, "Trade, Religion, and Politics," vol. III. Some merchants have been identified from the 1680s' port books, for which see note 80 below. Domestic merchants and traders include cheese-mongers, drapers, factors, grocers, haberdashers, lace-men, mercers, packers, pewterers, and salters. Industrial employers include brewers, ironmongers, soap-makers, sugar refiners, suppliers of naval stores, and tobacconists.

Table 6.8[80] *Trading specializations of merchant party leaders*

	Whigs	Tories	Percent of merchant party leaders
Northern Europe/Baltic	12	5	32
Spain and Portugal	11	5	30
Levant	8	6	26
Colonies	7	6	25
France	6	4	19
Italy	3	4	13
Specialization(s) unknown	4	5	17

Overseas traders made up over half the London party leaders of the Restoration Crisis, but overseas merchants were significantly more noticeable among the leaders of the London Whigs than of the London Tories. Almost two-thirds of the entire Whig leadership group were overseas merchants; but only two-fifths of the Tory leaders were. The merchant leaders of each party were drawn from the full range of London's trade with Europe, the Middle East, and the colonies of the West Indies and North America; and many merchant leaders pursued multiple trading specializations. (Table 6.8) Party leaders were especially drawn from the Northern European and Iberian trades. Almost a third of all party leaders who were merchants traded to the Low Countries, Germany, and the Baltic lands and/or to Spain and Portugal. Another quarter of the merchant party leaders traded to the Levant or to the colonies.[79]

The greater visibility of merchants as Whig party leaders and the striking predominance of Whig views amongst Northern European and Iberian merchants who were party leaders resulted from several factors. Concern about the crown's commitment to advancing overseas trade had been a formative element in the emergence of political opposition in London in the early 1670s,

---

[79] The number of Northern European traders among the party leaders is not surprising, because the northern cloth trades retained pre-eminence in volume over other branches of London's overseas commerce. The increasing importance of trade to Spain may have brought leading Iberian merchants into political leadership, while the greater wealth of merchants who traded to the Middle East undoubtedly contributed to the number of party leaders drawn from Levantine commerce. D. W. Jones, *War and Economy in the Age of William III and Marlborough* (Oxford, 1988), pp. 304–5; De Krey, *A Fractured Society*, p. 141; Priestley, "London Merchants," p. 214, n. 5.

[80] Trading specializations have been determined from a variety of sources, but especially from selected London port books for the 1680s, as transcribed by A. G. Smith: PRO E190/102/1, E190/114/4, E190/127/2, E190/128/2, E 190/131/1, E190/134/1, E190/141/1, E190/142/1, E190/144/1 & 4. The number of merchants actively trading to France in the period under consideration was reduced both by French tariffs and by the three-year embargo on the importation of certain French goods adopted by parliament in 1678.

particularly among traders who felt that English commercial prospects were dimmed by the rise of France. Suspiciousness about Charles II's attitude toward Louis XIV inclined many merchants to opposition and eventually to the Whig movement. Merchant leaders who specialized in Spanish commerce had been notable among those who subscribed to the 1674 anti-French *Scheme of the Trade*: they apparently feared, like Whig leader and commercial writer Slingsby Bethel, that English trade with Spain was imperiled by France. Northern European merchants who traded to the Low Countries had further grounds to suspect French intentions, while Reformed Protestant merchants of Dutch and French ancestry had their own reasons to doubt that a popish successor would advance the cause of Protestant trade.[81]

The character of the London Whigs' mercantile leadership is nicely illustrated by the activities of the five Whig party leaders of the Restoration Crisis who had signed the 1674 *Scheme of the Trade*: John Dubois, Michael Godfrey, James Houblon, Thomas Papillon, and Sir Patience Ward. All of them were onetime traders to France, but they saw the increasing commercial vitality of France as a threat rather than as an opportunity, as they drove their own expanding businesses. James Houblon and his brothers and relatives were leaders in the development of English trade with Spain. Michael Godfrey, also an Iberian merchant, was an associate of the Houblons whose business also extended to the North European trade in cloth. Godfrey was not only the brother of the man whose inexplicable death was at the center of the Popish Plot but also a cousin of Thomas Papillon, whose extensive commercial knowledge and investments made him a leading mercantile spokesman. Sir Patience Ward's concern about the development of English trade, apparent since the early 1660s, prompted his 1678 evidence before the Lords committee of trade, which contributed to parliamentary adoption of a three-year ban on many French imports.[82]

Religious identity, connections to Restoration institutions, and family circumstances tied other prominent merchants to Anglican loyalism. Tory leaders were almost as numerous as Whig leaders in several trading specializations, the Levant trade among them. Leading civic loyalists who traded to Turkey included Sir Samuel Dashwood, Thomas Vernon, and Sir Dudley North. Dashwood, the son of one of Charles II's excise farmers, became sheriff and an excise commissioner himself in 1683. Thomas Vernon, who

---

[81] Priestley, "London Merchants," esp. pp. 210–15; *A Scheme of the Trade* [1674]; Bethel *World's Mistake*, pp. 4, 8–9; P. Loughead, "The East India Company in English Domestic Politics, 1657–1688," Unpublished D.Phil. thesis, Oxford University, 1980, pp. 145–6.

[82] Morrice, P, 377; Priestley, "London Merchants," 209–17; Henning, *House of Commons*, II, 237–8; III, 202–5, 667–70; Woodhead, *Rulers*, pp. 62, 77, 93–4, 125, 170; De Krey, "John Dubois" and "Sir Patience Ward," *Oxford DNB*; C. E. Whiting, "Sir Patience Ward of Tanshelf," *Yorkshire Archaeological Journal* 34 (1939), 245–72; Luttrell, I, 200; De Krey, "Trade, Religion, and Politics," III, 486, 490, 564–5, 582; Papillon, *Memoirs*.

also traded to Italy, the colonies, and Northern Europe, was strongly associated with the Royal African Company. The scion of an aristocratic family, Sir Dudley North spent twenty years in the Levant before returning to England and coming to the attention of the Court through his brother Sir Francis, Chief Justice of Common Pleas. As the forces of Anglican loyalism regained control of the city in 1682–3, the political careers of these and other mercantile Tory leaders peaked. Dashwood and Vernon were knighted. Dashwood and North became aldermen, and North joined the customs commission.[83]

More than one-fifth of the London party leaders of the Restoration Crisis were domestic merchants or traders. Slightly more Tory leaders than Whig leaders were drawn from these occupational ranks, even though the Whigs found much electoral strength from the ranks of the middling sort. Prosperous drapers among the Tory political elite included the previously noted Castle Baynard leaders Alderman Sir Joseph Sheldon, his partner Nicholas Charleton, and Sir William Dodson. Among the Whig leaders from domestic commerce were Sheriff and cloth factor Henry Cornish, Sheriff and draper Samuel Shute, and haberdasher John Jekyll.[84]

Almost another one-fifth of the party leaders were drawn from three additional occupational groups: industrial employers (including naval contractors, ironmongers, brewers, and sugar refiners), goldsmiths and scriveners, and apothecaries and druggists. Although the most prominent moneylender in the city was Whig leader Sir Robert Clayton, party leaders drawn from these occupations were overwhelmingly Tory. Lacking as many mercantile spokesmen as the Whigs, Anglican loyalists seemingly sought out spokesmen from those occupational groups that could produce individuals of the same wealth and standing as overseas merchants. The most prominent of the Tory industrial employers was Sir William Pritchard, the loyalist lord mayor of 1682–3, whose works and warehouses in the Minories gave him influence in Portsoken and in the nearby ward of Tower. Similarly, Bishopsgate Alderman Sir Jonathan Raymond, who operated a brewery and owned tenements in Portsoken, enjoyed local influence there. Leading Tory industrial employers like sugar refiner John Genew and ironmonger and Alderman Sir George Waterman, each of whom resided in Dowgate, probably contributed to that ward's Tory inclination.[85]

---

[83] HMC *Lords 1690–91*, pp. 60–5; Henning, *House of Commons*, II, 195–6, and III, 149–51; Woodhead, *Rulers*, pp. 56–7, 122, 167; R. Grassby, *The English Gentleman in Trade: The Life and Works of Sir Dudley North, 1641–1691* (Oxford, 1994), esp. pp. 131–44; Anderson, *English Consul*, p. 92.

[84] Woodhead, *Rulers*, pp. 45, 52, 60–1, 98, 149; De Krey, "Henry Cornish" and "Samuel Shute," *Oxford DNB*; De Krey, "Trade, Religion, and Politics," III, 636.

[85] Henning, *House of Commons*, II, 84–7, and III, 291–2; De Krey, "Sir William Pritchard," *Oxford DNB*; Woodhead, *Rulers*, pp. 48, 76, 136, 172.

Table 6.9[86] *Wealth of Whig and Tory leaders: real property in 1680*

	Whig leaders	Tory leaders	All leaders
£81 p.a. or more	7	14	21
£61 p.a.–£80 p.a.	7	7	14
£41–£60 p.a.	14	10	24
£40 p.a. or less	17	11	28
Lodger	1	3	4
Not found/resident elsewhere	4	5	9
Total party leaders	**50**	**50**	**100**

Table 6.10 *Wealth of Whig and Tory leaders: personal property in 1680*

	Whig leaders	Tory leaders	All leaders
£81 p.a. or more	3	13	16
£61 p.a.–£80 p.a.	7	9	16
£41–£60 p.a.	18	8	26
£40 p.a. or less	17	15	32
Not found/resident elsewhere	5	5	10
Total party leaders	**50**	**50**	**100**

Wealth and investment

Despite the greater visibility of overseas merchants among the Whig party leaders, the commercial and investment establishment of Restoration London was Tory rather than Whig. The potential of London's Whig traders to become a civic establishment was obvious, but that development lay in the future. In 1679–82, the Whig leaders – as a group – trailed their Tory counterparts in the accumulation of wealth, as Tables 6.9 and 6.10 suggest.

Two-thirds of those party leaders who owned the most substantial London residences – real estate worth £81 p.a. or more in 1680 – were Tories. Those leaders whose personal property, including stock in trade, was assessed at a similar level were even more heavily loyalist. Despite the greater number of merchants among the Whig leaders, the Tory leaders apparently included more commercial magnates, as judged by their taxable property. Goldsmiths Edward Backwell and Sir Robert Vyner were among those party leaders with the most taxable wealth, despite their financial losses in the 1672 Stop of the Exchequer, as were Tory merchants Richard Alie, Sir Thomas Bludworth,

[86] Individual assessments taken from CLRO Ward Assessment Books for the six-months' tax of 1680.

and Sir John Moore.[87] Differences between the party leaders were minimal among the still very substantial property owners rated between £61 and £80 p.a. in each property category. But prosperous men of middling means were more frequently encountered within the Whig leadership than within the Tory elite: over two-thirds of the party leaders with personal property assessed at £41 to £60 p.a. were Whigs, as were three-fifths of those whose residences were rated at £40 p.a. or less. Prominent Whig merchants like William Ashurst, John Dubois, Michael Godfrey, James and Peter Houblon, William Love, and Samuel Swynoke were among the party leaders of middling wealth as judged by one or the other of these standards.

These data are consistent with some of the party leadership characteristics that have already been identified. As a party, the Whigs included a greater proportion of younger political leaders – and especially more trading men in the early stages of wealth formation – than the Tories. Moreover, as a party with geographical strengths in wards dominated by the middling sort, the Whigs included more spokesmen of middling rank whose ability to articulate political and religious goals made them leaders, despite their more modest circumstances. Obversely, the Tories were a party led by many men of middling age: merchants, traders, and employers whose commercial fortunes, begun in the 1650s or earlier in the Restoration, were peaking in the 1680s.

These generalizations find further support in Tables 6.11 and 6.12, which examine the stock subscriptions and trading company directorships of the party leaders. In the original 1672 subscription of the Royal African Company, and in the 1675 share-holdings of the East India Company, the investments of future Tory leaders were much greater than those of their Whig counterparts. The 1682 external East India subscription was supported by the Levant Company and by other merchants critical of the restricted capitalization of the East India Company,[88] but among London party leaders who participated in this subscription, the largest pledges came predominantly from Tories. Civic Tory leaders at the apex of their careers simply had more money for investment than older and younger Whig commercial men.

The heavy involvement of London Tory spokesmen in the direction of the Royal African Company, with its strong Court connections, is another example of the ties between civic loyalism and the Restoration order in church, state, and society. The Duke of York was the company's governor in 1680–85. Its sub-governors in those years included Tory Aldermen Sir Benjamin Newland and Sir Dudley North, and its directors included Tory

---

[87] The two most heavily taxed domiciles in the city were those of Whigs, however. The townhouses of Sir Robert Clayton (rated at £164) and of Sir John Frederick (rated at £140) must have matched those of the best landed families of the West End in their splendor.

[88] Many subscribers to the new 1682 East India fund hoped the government would establish a new company or broaden the existing one. Loughead, "East India Company," pp. 138–43.

Table 6.11[89] *Stock-holdings of Whig and Tory leaders*

	Royal African Company, 1672		East India Company, 1675		External India Subscription, 1682	
	Whigs	Tories	Whigs	Tories	Whigs	Tories
Over £2,000		1	1	2	3	12
£1,000–£2,000	1	3	2	2	3	2
Less than £1,000	6	8	6	8	3	
Total stock owned	£4,200	£12,200	£7,875	£19,200	£17,500	£59,000

Table 6.12[90] *Trading company directorships held by Whig and Tory leaders, 1660–1685*

	Royal African Company		East India Company		Levant Company	
	Whigs	Tories	Whigs	Tories	Whigs	Tories
10 years or more		1	3	2	2	1
5–9 years	1	6	2		2	3
1–5 years	2	5	3	4	2	
Total years	10	68	69	39	52	40

Aldermen Sir Samuel Dashwood, Peter Paravacini, Sir Henry Tulse, and Sir William Turner.

Whig party leaders of 1680–83 were significantly more visible among the Restoration directors of the Levant Company and of the East India Company, despite their smaller stock investments in the latter. The Levant Company, which was not a joint stock, clearly looked for leadership to active and enterprising Near Eastern merchants, among whom there were slightly more Whig leaders, like Sir Samuel Barnardiston and James Houblon, than Tory leaders. The same preference for leadership from active overseas merchants explains why the East India Company shareholders selected London Whig leaders for greater service on their governing court of committees.

[89] PRO T70/100, Royal African Company, General Court Minute Book, 1672–78, fols. 8–22; British Library, Oriental and India Office, H/1 (2) Home Miscellaneous Series, I (List of Adventurers, 1675); William Salt Library, Stafford, D(W)1778/Ii/703, 1682 external East India subscription list.

[90] Directors and years of service have been taken from BL Oriental and India Office B/26–B/38, East India Company Minute Books, 1657–88; PRO SP 105/152–54 Levant Company, General Court Minute Books, 1660–85; and the index to K. G. Davies, *The Royal African Company* (1957, 1975) pp. 377–90.

Barnardiston and Houblon were also long-time East India directors; and in the years of the Restoration Crisis, they were joined by such additional Whig merchants as John Dubois and Thomas Papillon, who was deputy governor in 1680–81. As an older foundation than the African Company, the East India stock also included numerous voting shareholders whose political and religious perspectives were formed in the 1640s and the 1650s rather than during the Restoration.

The East India Company was nevertheless subject to the same Court pressures as other trading companies, and the Restoration Crisis left the government unhappy with some of the company's leaders. In April 1683, as the standoff in London between the civic Whigs and the civic Tories concluded, the East India shareholders altered their governing court of committees, making more changes in leadership than in any other year of the Restoration. Several directors disliked by the Court, including Whig leaders Barnardiston, Papillon, and Alderman Sir John Lawrence, were removed in favor of loyalists. Barnardiston and Papillon promptly sold their shares, as did Whig leaders James Houblon and Michael Godfrey; but John Dubois and other Reformed Protestants continued as directors and investors.[91]

These contrasting occupational and wealth profiles of the party leaders of the Restoration Crisis point again to differences between the Whig-dissenting and Anglican loyalist urban communities from which the parties emerged. Even before the great multi-national wars for empire began in 1689, the London Whigs were a party led by merchants with international interests, contacts, and perspectives. They were clearly the party of London trade, with over four-fifths of their leaders in the early 1680s drawn from overseas and domestic commerce. The assertiveness of some Whig leaders was probably stimulated not only by their widespread participation in dissenting worship in violation of the coercive Anglican code but also by the risks and hazards that so many of them were accustomed to in their overseas business. Their advocacy of reformation in England was, moreover, stimulated by their personal awareness of the perilous situation of Reformed Protestantism abroad. And as men of modest wealth confronting an Anglican establishment, they were politically sensitive to the interests of electors of modest means who sought to preserve their participation in Corporation affairs through consensual practices.

The leadership of the London Tories, on the other hand, was drawn from a broader range of occupational groups within the city. Despite the leadership of numerous important overseas merchants, the party was more insular

---

[91] BL Oriental and India Office, East India Company, Minutes of the Court of Committees, 1682–3, B/37, fol. 134 (20 April 1683); Newdigate L.c. 1366 (21 April 1683); Loughead, "East India Company," pp. 164–5; W. R. Scott, *The Constitution and Finance of English, Scottish and Irish Joint-Stock Companies to 1720*, 3 vols. (1912, 1968), II, 146.

in perspective than the Whigs, more focused upon and more protective of the national and local institutions in which Restoration Londoners pursued domestic trade and found stability. Prospering under the hierarchical institutions that had been re-established in 1660, the London Tory leaders rejected the consensual principles and the Reformed Protestant objectives of their political adversaries as the primary causes for the collapse of governing structures in the 1640s. The greater insistence of the civic Tories on maintaining social privilege may also have reflected the natural occupational interests of preponderant elements in their leadership. Moneylenders like Sir Robert Vyner and John Johnson were heavily invested in the finances of the Court, the aristocracy, and the gentry. Manufacturers like Sir William Pritchard and domestic merchants like Sir Thomas Beckford, who supplied clothing to the navy, depended upon government contracts.[92] And retail traders were more dependent upon domestic markets, many of them dominated by county Anglican elites, than upon the foreign markets of Whig merchants. The broader occupational spectrum of the Tory leaders enabled them, therefore, despite their insistence upon magisterial prerogatives, to speak for Londoners of diverse interests and incomes who preferred stability to reformation and change.

DIFFERENT FOLLOWERS: THE ELECTORATE AND THE PARTIES

Although the London Whigs represented themselves as the party of the people – as the defenders of electoral consent – the electors of London were, in fact, divided between the parties by 1682. The division of the city was not just a division between communities and parties who spoke contrasting languages and who were led by spokesmen of contrasting character. It was also a division between blocs of livery companies that preferred different candidates for office. The results of only one common hall poll of the Restoration Crisis survive in sufficient detail for analysis: the poll for the London mayoral election of September and October 1682 between Tory candidate Sir William Pritchard and Whig candidates Henry Cornish and Sir Thomas Gold. But this poll, upon which Table 6.13 is based, probably reflects the division among the livery companies in the hotly disputed shrieval election of 1682 as well.

The development of party preferences within companies was obviously widespread in the mayoral election of 1682, despite the closeness of the poll: only a quarter of the livery companies did not provide a strong majority of their votes to the Tory candidate or to the two Whig candidates. Most of the guilds that actually divided between the rival candidates, rather

---

[92] Woodhead, *Rulers*, p. 28.

Table 6.13[93] *Party inclinations of livery companies, 1682*

Predominantly Whig	Predominantly Tory	Divided
	Substantial companies	
1) Dyers	1) Grocers	1) Clothworkers
2) Haberdashers	2) Vintners	2) Drapers
3) Skinners		3) Fishmongers
		4) Goldsmiths
		5) Ironmongers
		6) Mercers
		7) Merchant Taylors
		8) Salters
	Other major companies	
4) Coopers	3) Apothecaries	9) Distillers
5) Cordwainers	4) Brewers	10) Pewterers
6) Founders	5) Innholders	
7) Glovers	6) Scriveners	
8) Leathersellers	7) Stationers	
9) Upholsterers		
10) Weavers		
	Artisan companies	
11) Bakers	8) Barber surgeons	11) Armourers
12) Broderers	9) Bowyers	12) Blacksmiths
13) Carpenters	10) Bricklayers	13) Cutlers
14) Curriers	11) Butchers	14) Fruiterers
15) Farriers	12) Cooks	
16) Fletchers	13) Masons	
17) Girdlers	14) Musicians	
18) Glaziers	15) Painterstainers	
19) Joiners	16) Plumbers	
20) Plaisterers	17) Poulters	
21) Tallowchandlers	18) Saddlers	
22) Turners		
23) Waxchandlers		

than favoring one side over the other, were among the substantial companies whose liveries were top-heavy with overseas merchants and other wealthy

---

[93] Poll numbers by guild have been derived from *A List of the Poll of the several companies of London for a Lord Mayor* (1682). Companies have been considered predominantly Whig or predominantly Tory if 55 per cent or more of their liverymen favored either the Tory candidate or the two Whig candidates. The thirteen substantial companies include the twelve "great" livery companies and the Dyers' Company, which had the highest proportion of overseas merchants among their liverymen. (De Krey, "Trade, Religion, and Politics," III, 467; Gauci, *Politics of Trade*, p. 139.) The fourteen other major companies include those whose liveries also included a considerable number of citizens of middling or substantial means.

Table 6.14 *Party electoral strength from livery company categories, 1682*

	Whig Vote		Tory Vote	
	Electors	Percentage of party vote	Electors	Percentage of party vote
Substantial companies	963	*43*	959	*43*
Other major companies	566	*25*	548	*25*
Artisan companies	736	*32*	717	*32*
Total vote	2,265		2,224	

electors. The liverymen of the other major companies and of the artisan companies generally polled in a strongly partisan fashion; and generally the Whig candidates prevailed in slightly more companies in each of the three categories than their Tory rival. Why particular companies favored the candidate(s) of one party over the other is generally unclear, although religious and residential factors were probably important. Loyalist suggestions that the Whigs were overly dependent upon electors from the less substantial companies were clearly misleading, however: over half the companies that supported each party were artisan companies. Indeed, as Table 6.14 suggests, the broad social composition of Whig and Tory electorates probably did not differ significantly. Whig and Tory candidates actually attracted the support of exactly the same proportion of liverymen from each of the three categories.[94]

Generally, the identification of London electors with the political parties of the Restoration Crisis was quite high, as Table 6.15 suggests. About 69 per cent of those liverymen eligible to participate in the poll for lord mayor in 1682 did so, a proportion that tells against the argument that parties are post-1689 political structures.[95] If the ability to arouse electors is a critical party characteristic, then the London parties of the Restoration Crisis developed in response to an electorate that took their opposite agendas in church and state quite seriously.

Table 6.15 also demonstrates that the London Tory leaders had overcome their earlier difficulty in concentrating loyalist electors for important

---

[94] Translating these results into party preferences for different occupational groups is hazardous, given the discrepancies between the nominal and the actual trades of citizens in particular companies.

[95] Differences in the rate of participation in different kinds of companies are also evident. Participation is lowest in the artisan companies, in which many liverymen had little hope of playing a significant role in Corporation affairs. It is highest in the intermediate major companies: those companies included many middling domestic merchants and tradesmen who saw the vitality of the Corporation as critical to their own economic success.

Table 6.15[96] *Electoral participation by party from livery company categories, 1682*

	Whigs	Tories	All on livery	Participation in 1682	
Whig-inclined companies					
Substantial	312	189	761	66%	
Other major	368	208	809	71%	**Breakdown**
Artisan	428	240	1,011	66%	43% Whig
Total vote	1,108	637	2,581	68%	25% Tory
					32% Abstained
Tory-inclined companies					
Substantial	111	219	427	69%	
Other major	134	279	523	79%	**Breakdown**
Artisan	173	368	797	63%	49.5% Tory
Total vote	418	866	1,747	73.5%	24% Whig
					26.5% Abstained
Divided companies					
Substantial	504	551	1,567	70%	
Other major	64	61	175	71%	**Breakdown**
Artisan	100	101	335	60%	34% Whig
Total vote	668	713	2,077	68%	34% Tory
					32% Abstained

contests. In 1682, the rate of electoral participation in the Tory-inclined companies noticeably exceeded that for the Whig-inclined companies and the divided companies. Indeed, the higher rate of participation in the Tory-inclined companies assisted Sir William Pritchard in overcoming the advantage the Whig mayoral candidates enjoyed from the greater number of electors in the Whig-inclined companies. By 1682, the communities in conflict in London were, thus, equally well organized for their political competition.

Some evidence also suggests that the patterns of partisan identification in the livery companies, as revealed in the 1682 mayoral poll, were also enduring characteristics. The government had little doubt about the partisan

[96] The numbers of liverymen who polled in 1682 in the different company categories have been taken from *A List of the Poll*. The total numbers of liverymen for companies in each category have been taken from the computer punch cards prepared by A. G. Smith in the early 1970s. These cards, which are based upon company records and upon a variety of sources about the livery removals and additions under Charles II and James II, provide a reconstruction of the London liveried electorate between 1680 and 1688. The electors of five artisan companies (the Bowyers, Farriers, Fletchers, Masons, and Musicians), with a total poll of eighty-five in 1682, have been excluded from this table because Smith was unable to determine the size of their liveries in that year.

Table 6.16[97] *Most heavily purged livery companies, 1684–1687*

Predominantly Whig, 1682	Predominantly Tory, 1682	Divided, 1682
	Substantial companies	
1) Dyers		
2) Haberdashers		
	Other major companies	
3) Coopers		1) Distillers
4) Cordwainers		
5) Founders		
6) Glovers		
7) Upholsterers		
	Artisan companies	
8) Bakers	1) Barber surgeons	2) Armourers
9) Carpenters	2) Butchers	
10) Curriers		
11) Glaziers		
12) Joiners		
13) Plaisterers		
14) Tallowchandlers		

preferences of the electors of different guilds in its civic remodeling of 1684–7. Tables 6.16 and 6.17 list those companies that were most heavily purged (55 per cent or more of their total livery) and those that were least heavily purged (45 per cent or less) in the last years of Charles II's reign and in the first years of James II's reign. The tables also compare the extent of purging with the party inclinations of those companies' liveries in the 1682 mayoral poll.

Two-thirds of the twenty-three guilds that had been predominantly Whig in 1682 (Table 6.13) were targeted for the most severe remodeling by the crown. On the other hand, two-thirds of the eighteen companies that had been predominantly Tory in 1682 were among the least severely purged after 1684. The purge of civic electors in the guilds was intended to incapacitate the civic opposition and to place the city in the hands of reliable Anglican

---

[97] Liverymen have been identified by party according to their history on the livery as found in A. G. Smith's computer punch cards. Those known to have been liverymen only in 1680–84, those known to have been on the livery in 1680–84 and again in 1687–8, and those definitely discharged from the livery in 1684 have been regarded as purged Whig liverymen. The percentage of purged Whig liverymen in each company has then been compared to the total of all known liverymen in each company for 1684–7. Four companies have been disregarded: data for the Fletchers and Masons appear incomplete, and the Farriers and Musicians were removed from ranks of the livery companies. The Bowyers, Carpenters, Distillers, Glovers, and Plaisterers have been included, despite some issues with the data.

Table 6.17 *Least heavily purged livery companies, 1684–1687*

Predominantly Whig, 1682	Predominantly Tory, 1682	Divided, 1682
	Substantial companies	
1) Skinners	1) Grocers	1) Clothworkers
	2) Vintners	2) Drapers
		3) Salters
	Other major companies	
	3) Apothecaries	
	4) Brewers	
	5) Innholders	
	6) Scriveners	
	7) Stationers	
	Artisan companies	
2) Turners	8) Bowyers	
	9) Bricklayers	
	10) Cooks	
	11) Plumbers	
	12) Poulters	
	13) Saddlers	

loyalists, and the crown clearly thought it knew where both its friends and adversaries were concentrated within the London guilds.[98]

CONCLUSION

Party mattered in London in the Restoration Crisis: the civic Whigs and civic Tories expressed the opposite ideals, aspirations, and discourse of spatially differentiated neighborhoods and communities. One of those was a dissenting community with deep roots in the city's political and religious culture of Reformed Protestantism. Once a puritan community united on behalf of reformation, it had fragmented in the midst of revolution in the 1640s and 1650s, but it had grown together again politically in the early Restoration in response to the coercive Anglican state. The opposite community of Anglican loyalism was made up of all those who identified with the structures of the Restoration church, state, and Corporation. It was a community of people who feared that demands for conscience and consent would return all to the chaos of 1659 and before.

These differences in London are suggestive for the kingdom as well, for the discursive traditions and attachments that divided Londoners divided the

---

[98] For a somewhat different view, see M. Knights, "A City Revolution: The Remodelling of the London Livery companies in the 1680s," *EHR* 112 (1997), especially p. 1176.

kingdom's social and clerical leaders as well as many borough and county communities. Moreover, the division of London was itself a critical element in the politics of the kingdom, since the division of opinion in the city was quickly conveyed throughout the realm. The Restoration Crisis gave London Whigs and dissenters their best opportunity to advance conscience and consent – and reformation and a Protestant succession – in church, state, and city. But by 1682, their primary accomplishment had not been to realize any of these goals but rather to stimulate a determined and organized Anglican loyalist party in the city and elsewhere. In 1682–3, Anglican loyalism would triumph again in London and the kingdom: the capture of the London shrievalty and mayoralty by civic Tories were important steps in the crown's recovery of the city as well as in its discouragement of opposition throughout the realm. But this recovery was not easily accomplished: the civic Whigs were not prepared to accept it, even though their continuing efforts against the crown and Anglican loyalism were divided and, in the end, self-defeating.

IV

Crisis and conspiracy, 1682–1683

Introduction: Whig conspiracy and historical memory

In June 1683, about a year after the commencement of the London shrieval election of 1682, subjects throughout the kingdom were startled by the government's disclosure of a "horrid conspiracy" of the "fanaticks" to assassinate the king and his brother and to mount an insurrection. After years of loyalist charges about Whig disloyalty, the news concerning this Whig plot was an immediate and lasting sensation that dominated the prints and public conversation for months. Tory writers like Sir Roger L'Estrange and Thomas Sprat were quick to argue that the Rye House Plot, as historians would dub the affair, was a natural conclusion to Whig opposition in parliament and the city. The fanatics had at last been detected in their efforts to return the nation to the circumstances of 1649 or 1659.[1] The fact that most of those apprehended, tried, or executed for their part in plotting were London dissenters or national figures, like Lord Russell and Algernon Sidney, who had kept company with leading civic Whigs, did not escape loyalist notice.

The government's propaganda campaign and its successful plot prosecutions of Russell, Sidney, and many lesser figures enabled it, at last, to gain the upper hand against its opponents. Few were prepared to continue to oppose Charles II, his Catholic successor, or the church leadership, when opposition talk or behavior invited questions about loyalty or provoked suspicions about plotting. The treason trials that began in 1683 permitted a resolution of the Restoration Crisis on uncompromising loyalist terms. The coercive confessional state erected in the 1660s and again promoted by Danby in the 1670s was re-established, while loyalist prints excoriated Whig and dissenting leaders as the conspiratorial heirs of revolutionary sectarianism.

Yet many contemporaries found the Rye House Plot somewhat too politically convenient for Charles and the ministry. From the beginning, the loyalist interpretation of the Whig leaders as inveterate plotters who had

---

[1] See, for instance, *Observator*, I, 373, 379, 387 (12, 23 July and 15 Aug. 1683); *ST*, IX, 577–653, 817–903, and XI, 381–466; [Thomas Sprat], *A True Account and Declaration of the Horrid Conspiracy against the Late King* (1685); [Thomas Sprat], *Copies of the Informations and Original Papers relating to the Proof of the Horrid Conspiracy* (1685).

finally been caught in their conspiratorial machinations did not enjoy full public credibility. Even when the reaction against the discovery of plotting was at its peak, many were unconvinced. In London, the commitments and the traditions of the dissenting population who dominated the Whig-inclined spaces of the city discouraged ready acceptance of the government's claims. To many Whig citizens, the plot charges were largely government fabrications calculated to achieve strategic political results.

The government betrayed its anxiety about the credibility of its plot evidence by the number of printed answers it sponsored to Lord Russell's July 1683 scaffold denial of any treasonable actions. Moreover, the mysterious death in the Tower of the Earl of Essex, waiting his turn in court, on the morning of Russell's trial, was a public relations disaster for the government. The official claim of suicide carried little weight with those convinced that Essex had been done in by popish enemies or by the government itself. After the first round of executions, a paper was tacked up at Guildhall that suggested the citizens had been "betrayed into the hands of the papists" and that many would lose their lives for their Protestant loyalties. One London tradesman was hauled before the city sessions for contending that "there was noe such thing as the Conspiracy and that it was only a contrivance to render the Protestants as guilty as the Papists." Sir Samuel Barnardiston, foreman of Shaftesbury's *ignoramus* jury, was convicted of libel for referring privately to the evidence of treason as nothing but a "Sham Protestant Plot" invented by the ministry. As rumors of government deceit spread, L'Estrange took alarm: "It is almost incredible what impressions they have made on the people already," he wrote in August 1683. By summer's end, the apotheosis of men like Russell and Essex as Whig martyrs, a process that achieved state sanction after 1689, had already begun.[2]

Two interpretations of Whig behavior in London in 1682–3 were already current, then, in the last years of the reign of Charles II. Not surprisingly, loyalists preferred a conspiratorial interpretation of the behavior of their leading political adversaries. But dissenters and Whigs saw the treason trials as yet another Roman Catholic conspiracy against the rights and religion of Protestants.

---

[2] Newdigate L.c. 1405–06, 1454 (21, 24 July and 18 Oct. 1683); *The Tryal and Conviction of Sir Sam. Barnardiston, Bart.* (1684); *The Whig-Intelligencer: or, Sir Samuel in the Pound* (1684); *CSPD 1683 (July–Sept.)*, pp. 197, 222–3, 335; *ST*, IX, 709–94, 1333–57; Burnet, *History*, II, 403; Henning, *House of Commons*, I, 597; L. G. Schwoerer, "William, Lord Russell: The Making of a Martyr, 1683–1983," *JBS* 24 (1985), 41–71; L. G. Schwoerer, *Lady Rachel Russell: "One of the Best of Women"* (Baltimore, 1988), pp. 132–42; M. MacDonald, "The Strange Death of the Earl of Essex, 1683," *HT* 41 (1991), 13–18; Scott, *Restoration Crisis*, pp. 297–301, 340–1; Greaves, *Secrets*, pp. 210, 212–29.

From its beginnings, in the early eighteenth-century writings of Gilbert Burnet and White Kennet, Whig historiography emphasized variations of the contemporary Whig view of conspiracy. Whig historians did not deny that some Whig principals had considered resistance; but martyrs like Russell and Sidney clearly did so only for significant reasons and without resort to the sordid tactics ascribed to them by their enemies. In this heroic Whig interpretation, assassination schemes could only have been of interest to Oliverian relics, not to high-minded political idealists.[3] Lord Macaulay distinguished between the few "desperate men" who were lost in regicidal fantasies and the noble Whig design to undertake resistance to Charles II and James II for legitimate constitutional reasons. The real story of 1682–3 was not private Whig plotting but rather public Whig devotion to parliament, to Protestantism, and to personal liberties. The government's utilization of the manuscript of Sidney's *Discourses Concerning Government* as the second required witness to his alleged treason was but the most vivid example of how an increasingly arbitrary government had politically exploited a manufactured plot, or had exaggerated the evidence about plotting, for political advantage.[4]

After the demythologizing of Whig history began in the 1970s, the grounds for skeptical treatment of the evidence about plotting shifted from heroic to pragmatic grounds. Academic historians were reluctant to credit contradictory stories about plotting provided by men struggling to escape the gallows. The story of a plot to ambush the king at the Rye House in Hertfordshire, in particular, seemed best interpreted as a fiction developed by some of the conspirators to save their necks at the expense of others. According to this way of thinking, the true significance of conspiracy in 1682–3 was the way in which the government "crushed" the Whigs through its manipulation of "exaggerated and often fabricated evidence" in a series of show trials.[5]

An emphasis upon insurrection and assassination as the ultimate Whig strategies has, nevertheless, never been lacking in the historical literature.[6] Initially developed in the language of Tory reaction, this interpretation was advanced most strongly in the late twentieth century by those historians

---

[3] Burnet, *History*, II, 349–86, 398–405; White Kennett, *Complete History of England*, 3 vols. (1706), III, 408–12.

[4] Macaulay, *History*, I, 255–6. Also see G. N. Clark, *The Later Stuarts 1660–1714* (Oxford, 1934), pp. 99–101; Haley, *Shaftesbury*, pp. 707–24.

[5] Harris, *London Crowds*, pp. 150, 208, 223, 225; Alan Marshall, *Intelligence and Espionage in the Reign of Charles II, 1660–1685* (Cambridge, 1994), pp. 75–6; Scott, *Restoration Crisis*, p. 267.

[6] See, for instance, D. J. Milne, "The Rye House Plot with Special Reference to its Place in the Exclusion Contest and its Consequences till 1685," Unpublished Ph.D. thesis, University of London, 1949; J. H. M. Salmon, "Algernon Sidney and the Rye House Plot," *HT* 4 (1954), 698–705; I. Morley, *A Thousand Lives: An Account of the English Revolutionary Movement, 1660–1685* (1954).

seeking to reconstruct the "radical" actions and ideas of many Whigs and dissenters. In his provocative 1986 study of John Locke and "revolutionary politics," for instance, Richard Ashcraft construed Whig conspiracy in 1682–3 as "an organized attempt" to mount a rebellion against the government. As one of Shaftesbury's closest associates, John Locke was – in this view – fully involved in conspiracy. Moreover, according to Ashcraft, Locke composed the *Second Treatise of Government* in the hope of appealing to Shaftesbury's followers among the lower social orders of shopkeepers, traders, and skilled craftsmen – the same sorts of people who had once made up the Leveller movement.[7] Although Ashcraft's interpretation of Locke prompted a spate of criticism, other scholars endorsed his effort to put conspiracy at the center of Whig activities in 1682–3. Even the most systematic of Ashcraft's critics accepted much of his case for the political context of the writing of the *Second Treatise*.[8] And Locke was clearly not alone in endorsing resistance by 1682–3, as the language of London dissenters and Whigs demonstrates.

Yet neither those recent historians who have focused upon the public Whig commitment to parliamentary government and a Protestant succession nor those historians who have instead focused upon conspiracy have related the evidence about plotting to events in London. Assuming that the declaration of the Tory sheriffs in September 1682 constituted a loyalist capture of the city, historians have concluded that the political contest for the Corporation was over by autumn 1682. If some Whigs turned to conspiracy thereafter, they did so because the parliamentary and the civic arenas, in which they had hitherto engaged in opposition, were shut down after September 1682.[9]

This approach actually leaves out the dominant story of London politics in 1682–3, a story that bears significantly upon the resolution of the Restoration Crisis, upon the Revolution of 1688–9, and upon the composition of both Sidney's *Discourses* and Locke's *Second Treatise*. The London Whig leaders did not, in the autumn of 1682, surrender the Corporation to the crown or to Tory magistrates whose authority they rejected. Instead, they challenged the election of the Tory sheriffs before the Court of King's Bench for the next eight months; and they also pursued their claim to have elected the lord mayor for 1682–3. The civic Whigs' insistence that the sheriffs had

[7] Ashcraft, *Revolutionary Politics*, ch. 8, esp. pp. 344, 392.
[8] For interpretations supportive of or similar to Ashcraft's, see esp. Greaves, *Secrets*; Schwoerer, *Lady Russell*, pp. 106–9, 111–12, 124; De Krey, "London Radicals"; Zook, *Radical Whigs*. For John Marshall's critical response to Ashcraft, see *John Locke*, ch. 6, esp. pp. 226–32, 238–9, 242, 252–60, 262–5. Even more so than Ashcraft, Marshall sees the London shrieval election of 1682 as the critical event in persuading Shaftesbury and Locke that the government had dissolved the state through its arbitrary behavior.
[9] See, for instance, Haley, *Shaftesbury*, p. 724; Jones, *First Whigs*, p. 206.

no right to the offices they held was the centrepiece of continuing Whig legal maneuvres, including the defense of the charter, that kept the London courts busy as a fulcrum of the kingdom's politics. Indeed, London was as critical to the politics of the Restoration in 1682–3 as it had been during the parliaments of 1679–81.

These legal endeavors involved many Whig citizens who believed their rights had been abridged in 1682, and they involved important parliamentary leaders as well. After Shaftesbury's retreat into hiding and eventually into exile, the London Whigs found a new parliamentary spokesman in William Williams, a leading Whig lawyer and the Commons Speaker in the last two sessions. Williams's presence at the head of an urban Whig movement now dedicated to the preservation of rights through the law further emphasized the way in which the Corporation continued to function, for the opposition, as a parliamentary substitute, until the government's seizure of the charter in October 1683.

The collapse of London Whig legal efforts in May and June 1683 coincided with the climax of London plotting. But how exactly do the largely untold story of the London Whigs' public commitment to law in 1682–3 and the story of clandestine extra-legal Whig conspiracy bear upon each other? The narrative of the following chapter is an attempt to integrate these two different histories in order to explain their significance for the Restoration and for the Revolution of 1688–9. The chapter also attempts to bring together the two interpretations of Whig actions in 1682–3 that have been separated from the beginning of Restoration historiography. Some London Whigs did plot against the government, just as surely as the government exploited the evidence about plotting to undermine the Whigs. The government sought to bury the record of Whig commitment to the law by promoting its story of a Whig attempt to undermine law and the constitution. Whig historians and their successors, on the other hand, sought to marginalize the evidence about Whig plotting in order to advance their story of Whig commitment to the law and the constitution. And Sidney and Locke, both caught up in these events at the time, endorsed a resort to resistance after experiencing a critical failure of the Whigs' resort to law.

The predominant initiative of the London Whigs and their parliamentary friends in 1682–3 was, then, their sustained legal effort to preserve the civic charter, civic rights, and the causes of parliament and Protestantism. Plotting, on the other hand, was episodic, involved relatively few citizens, and retained its appeal primarily for those at the lower end of the Whig social spectrum. But the voices of London's plebeian Whig conspirators do need to be heard, for their own sake, as the rarely recorded voices of *menu peuple* acting upon their commitments to Reformation, to a Protestant succession, and to a consensual city. Whig grandees, lawyers, and merchants had again promoted ideas with the power to incite ordinary people to extraordinary actions, as loyalists claimed; and some humble London citizens, as well as a few more substantial ones, were prepared to act decisively.

The public hysteria released and encouraged by the government in its disclosures about plotting in June 1683 and in the trials it conducted thereafter also marked a conclusion to the Restoration itself. The story of Whig plotting was employed to drive the "second restoration" desired by loyalists to even more coercive and exclusive results than the first. The renewal of religious coercion was accompanied by a remodeling of local institutions in 1684–7 that was designed to eliminate dissenters and the opposition from the state and from local authority. The structures and politics of these years were fundamentally different from what had preceded them. The "Rye House Plot" of 1682–3 and the alarums of 1659–60 therefore frame the Restoration like a pair of matched bookends. A great fear of the sects and of the republicans had advanced Charles and the Anglican cause in 1660. A similar fear in 1683 seemed to resecure the cavalier church and state, to destroy the Whig movement and its goals, and to promote unequivocal loyalist hegemony. Both of these fears were driven from London and by London events; but whether the "second restoration" would succeed better than the first in the kingdom's unruly premier city remained to be seen.

7

The London Whigs between law and resistance: conscience, consent, and conspiracy, 1682–1683

THE LOSS OF THE INITIATIVE

The London shrieval election of 1682 had brought the king and the Whigs to the brink of a confrontation unlike anything seen in the city since 1641–2, except the standoff between the Rump and the Corporation in 1659–60. Although the government believed it had begun the political reconstruction of the Corporation with the declaration of Tory sheriffs on 28 September, the London Whigs were reconciled neither to this result nor to the process that had achieved it. Moreover, the boundary dividing legal action and maneuvre from the outright defiance of authority had begun to dissolve as Whig anger mounted through the summer months of 1682. Whig citizens had accused Lord Mayor Moore of seeking to impose his "will" upon them, contrary to law. They claimed that unjust and unlawful force had been utilized in an electoral process and that a "military government" had been established over them. They accused loyalist magistrates of violating their oaths and their "trusts" to preserve the rights of citizens. Most ominously, Sheriff Pilkington had defended the people's right to "fortify" themselves in defense of their "Lives, Religion, and Liberty." This was not the language of political acquiescence, and the London Whigs would have been surprised to learn that their contest with the crown was over.[1]

City and Country Whigs were, nevertheless, not entirely agreed about how best to proceed in response to the "imposition" of magistrates upon the city. The "great consult" of London Whig leaders at the Amsterdam coffeehouse on 30 September revealed a preference for challenging the shrieval election in the courts. But the careful rejection, in that discussion, of any resort to force suggested that some Whigs had considered resistance. In fact, Shaftesbury and other Whig grandees were now essaying the option of armed insurrection to prevent a Catholic succession and any further "invasion" of liberties. Secretive meetings of the Whig lords, including Shaftesbury, Monmouth,

---

[1] LC MS 18,124, VIII, 110, 116, 121 (9, 21, 28 Sept. 1682); *Modest Enquiry*, p. 27; Luttrell, I, 223, 225.

Grey, and Russell, had been underway since the beginning of the shrieval election. Their primary objective until September had been to prevent the imposition of Tory sheriffs on the city, although some sources indicate that discussion of resistance had actually preceded Monmouth's western progress in September.[2]

As the struggle over the shrievalty reached its September climax, so apparently did interest in rebellion within Shaftesbury's circle. Much evidence points to the initiation of talk about rebellion as the shrieval election concluded. Lord Grey claimed that the installation of Tory sheriffs in London had revived earlier discussions, among Whig peers, about the "necessity of having recourse to arms." Shaftesbury believed, according to Lord Howard, that "Pseudo-Sheriffs" had been "forcibly obtruded" on the city by the government; and the earl concluded, again according to Howard, that the Court would now proceed to manipulate the "administration of justice" throughout the kingdom. "From the Time of chusing Sheriffs," reflected Lord Russell, "I concluded the Heat in that Matter would produce something of this kind." Robert Ferguson, who acted as intermediary between Shaftesbury and Monmouth, maintained "there were no endeavours used towards the disturbing the Government till the Court fell upon plund'ring the City." Reflecting upon these events some years later, Bishop Burnet thought Shaftesbury had deliberately sought to make "use of the heat the city was in during the contest about the sheriffs" in order to create "a great disturbance" that would force "the king to yield every thing."[3]

A reconstruction of Whig endeavors in London between the declaration of the shrieval election, in late September, and Shaftesbury's departure for the Netherlands, in late November, nevertheless suggests that legal and extra-legal strategies were pursued simultaneously. Moreover, the public Whig strategy of pursuing remedy for the shrieval election in the courts, as agreed on 30 September, remained the dominant response. Now at the end of his mayoral tenure, Sir John Moore became the object of Whig legal reprisals intended to overturn his declaration of Dudley North and Peter Rich as sheriffs.

---

[2] LC MS 18,124, VIII, 100, [123] (22 Aug., 30 Sept. 1682); Sprat, *Copies*, pp. 33, 67–8; Grey, *Secret History*, pp. 23–33; J. Ferguson, *Ferguson*, pp. 414–18; Burnet, *History*, II, 349–50; *ST*, IX, 395–6, 431–2; Haley, *Shaftesbury*, pp. 710–12; Ashcraft, *Revolutionary Politics*, pp. 350–6; Greaves, *Secrets*, pp. 99–113.

[3] *The Speeches of Captain Walcot, Jo. Rouse, and Will. Hone* (1683), pp. 9–10; William, Lord Russell, *The Last Speech & Behaviour of William, late Lord Russel* (1683), p. 4; *The Tryall and Conviction of John Hambden, Esq.* (1684), p. 11; Grey, *Secret History*, p. 23; J. Ferguson, *Ferguson*, pp. 414, 420; R. Ferguson, *Impartial Enquiry*, pp. 59, 79; *CSPD 1683 (July–Sept.)*, pp. 154, 164; *ST*, IX, 431, 438; Sprat, *Copies*, pp. 67, 75; Sprat, *True Account*, pp. 8, 29, 33; Burnet, *History*, II, 350; Ashcraft, *Revolutionary Politics*, p. 352; J. Marshall, *John Locke*, ch. 6.

He was charged in several Whig suits with "injuriously and maliciously" employing a "strong hand and armed force" to prevent the election of Thomas Papillon and John Dubois in accordance with the will of the electors.[4] The civic Whigs were also determined to retain the mayoralty for one of their two candidates, Sir Thomas Gold and Henry Cornish. The poll for lord mayor on 29 September indicated that the Whig candidates had an electoral majority, but Moore had nevertheless continued the poll for another week, rather than immediately declaring it, leaving the Whigs suspicious about possible manipulation of the result. They still hoped that a new Whig lord mayor would oust the "pretended" sheriffs in favor of Papillon and Dubois.

Management of the Whig cause in London at this time remained in the hands of the directorate of parliamentary leaders, civic tribunes, and legal counsel who had been active in the city since the Oxford Parliament. Shaftesbury dined with the Whig aldermen on 30 September; but his exchange, thereafter, of his Aldersgate townhouse for clandestine residence has fed the supposition that he had already abandoned ordinary politics for plotting. Through his concealment, the earl sought protection against possible government reprisals under the new Tory sheriffs, but he had not abandoned customary courses. On 6–7 October he attended strategy meetings with leading civic Whigs, Speaker Williams, Henry Pollexfen, and other legal counsel retained by the city's *quo warranto* committee. And despite tensions that may have developed between Shaftesbury and Monmouth, the two men appeared together for worship at St Giles in the Fields on 8 October. This public appearance was intended to disprove rumors that the earl had fled the country for Amsterdam or Venice. A week later, as such rumors persisted, Shaftesbury processed, in response, through the city to a Covent Garden feast; and his "lodgings" were the site of another reported gathering of civic Whigs and legal men on the 19th. Whatever else he may have been considering, Shaftesbury had not yet abandoned electoral strategies in favor of arms.[5]

But the crown was equally determined to prevail in the London mayoral contest. Ministers saw the Corporation as a critical test in their developing plans to remodel the borough electorates throughout the country. If loyalist candidates could prevail in civic elections, then perhaps a voluntary surrender of the London charter could obviate the messier course of securing

---

[4] *CSPD 1682*, pp. 512–13.
[5] LC MS 18,124, VIII, [123], 125–6, 128–[30] (30 Sept. and 7, 10, 14, 17, 19 Oct. 1682); Newdigate L.c. 1284 (7 Oct. 1682); Luttrell, I, 227–8. Shaftesbury stayed briefly with Cripplegate common councilman Randolph Watson, then with Robert Ferguson, and eventually in Wapping. This account differs substantially from Haley, *Shaftesbury*, pp. 713–15, and Greaves, *Secrets*, p. 115.

a judgment against it in the courts. Secretary Jenkins was, therefore, particularly active in the city during the week between the commencement of the mayoral poll on 29 September and the announcement of its results on 4 October; and rumors circulated that if Sir William Pritchard failed to obtain an electoral majority, Charles would continue Moore as lord mayor for another year. Charles was sufficiently reassured about the outcome of the poll to leave for Newmarket, but when a "great Number" of liverymen assembled in Guildhall on 4 October for a declaration of the poll, the Court and the Tories were surprised. Sir Thomas Gold led the poll with 2,289 votes, while fellow Whig Henry Cornish had 2,258. Pritchard, upon whom loyalist electors had concentrated their vote, had a poll of 2,233, while only 236 had polled for Sir Henry Tulse, the second Tory candidate. Refusing to declare this result, Sir John Moore instead announced a scrutiny of those who had polled against lists of the eligible livery from each company.[6]

For the next three weeks, all civic and Court eyes followed the progress of the scrutiny. Loyalist scrutineers proceeded systematically through the livery lists, insisting that any liveryman who had not taken the company oaths or the oaths of allegiance and supremacy be disqualified.[7] The Whig scrutineers responded that Sir William Pritchard's poll included many Catholics or sham Protestants who had converted at the beginning of the Popish Plot. But the Whigs objected most strenuously to the removal from the poll of otherwise qualified Quaker and sectarian electors who had not taken the oaths, but who were nevertheless, "his Maties freeborne Prot: Liege People, and therefore by virtue of the Magna Charta have their voice and vote." They also rejected the authority of the loyalist magistrates to adjudicate between the conflicting claims of Whig and Tory scrutineers: Francis Jenks denied that the aldermen "had anything to do to meddle" in a common hall poll. On 19 October, Sir Robert Clayton demanded at a court of aldermen that Lord Mayor Moore declare the election on behalf of Gold. When Moore refused, the Whig aldermen formally asserted, in the presence of several Whig livery company masters, that the election had "Legally fallen upon Sir Thomas Gold." Having made their own declaration of the election, Clayton and the aldermanic Whigs retired to consult with Shaftesbury and with leading Whig lawyers.[8]

[6] Bulstrode Newsletters (6 Oct. 1682); LC MS 18,124, VIII, 124, 242–3 (3, 5 Oct. 1682); Newdigate L.c. 1282–3 (3, 5 Oct. 1682); Morrice, P, 342; HMC *Ormonde*, NS, VI, 465; HMC *Graham*, pp. 262, 358; Luttrell, I, 226–7; *CSPD 1682*, pp. 448–9, 451, 453, 462.

[7] Sir Roger L'Estrange claimed that at least 1,300 liverymen admitted, "to serve a *Turn*," since the mayoralty of Sir Patience Ward had failed to take these oaths. Repertory 87, fols. 248, 258; Newdigate L.c. 1288 (17 Oct. 1682); *List of the Poll*; *Observator*, I, 218, 236 (7 Oct., 6 Nov. 1682); *Domestick Intelligence* 144 (5–9 Oct. 1682); *CSPD 1682* pp. 475–6, 486–7.

[8] Jenks recognized only the authority of the Whig sheriffs as presiding officers in common hall. LC MS 18,124, VIII, 127, 129, [130], 246, 249 (12 [bis], 17, 19 Oct. 1682); Newdigate L.c.

Moore assembled common hall again only after Charles's return to Westminster from Newmarket and after further Whitehall consultations. A thunderous Whig din greeted his declaration to the liverymen on the 25th that Pritchard had prevailed by fourteen votes, after the poll had been trimmed of disqualified Whig votes. Francis Jenks leaped "upon the hustings and told the Ld mayor that hee made a false Report," and he was seconded by Alderman Sir John Frederick. The Whig leaders indicated both that they would bring further legal actions against Moore and that they would present Gold to the king as lord mayor-elect. But in the event, Pritchard appeared before the king and the lord chancellor for their approbation without his rival, as the Whigs retired to consider "particular wayes and methods . . . for the management" of their candidates' cases for the mayoral and shrieval offices. Among these, apparently, was a civic association, as many "entered in a bond not to pairt from the due and Legall chosen sheriffs and mayor."[9]

The mayoral installation of Sir William Pritchard on 28 October provided further evidence of the dangerous political impasse that had been reached. Whig leaders and electors would not honor a lord mayor imposed upon them against their consent. Pritchard's water-borne procession to Westminster for his swearing before the Exchequer barons was missing the barges of half the livery companies. The Whig aldermen declined to attend. As loyalist aldermen began preparations for a royal entertainment, Charles announced that he would not accompany the aldermen and judges back to the mayoral feast in the city. When the mayoral party, which did include several nobles, judges, and privy councilors, formally returned to dine at Grocers Hall, they found but a half-hearted welcome. The show in the Corporation was "not great, [there] being no Pageants and other ornaments for the day." Some companies, like the Skinners, had voted not to attend the mayoral procession at all; and other liverymen were there to jeer rather than to cheer.[10]

In the meantime, Shaftesbury and his current intimates turned to the active organization of an insurrection as the best means to retain the civic magistracy and to preserve the Whig cause. Meeting at various times in

---

1288 (17 Oct. 1682); *A Paper Delivered to the Lord Major and Court of Aldermen . . . Octob. 24, 1682; An Exact Account of the Proceedings at Guild-hall upon the Election of . . . Sir William Pritchard* [1682]; *Observator*, I, 237 (8 Nov. 1682); *CSPD 1682*, p. 485.

[9] The loyalist aldermen accepted a final poll of 2,138 for Pritchard, 2,124 for Gold, 2,093 for Cornish, and 236 for Tulse. They had eliminated 95 of Pritchard's votes in the poll and 165 of those who had voted for Gold and Cornish. Repertory 87, fol. 258; LC MS 18,124, VIII, 132, 252 (26 Oct. 1682 [bis]); Newdigate L.c. 1291–2 (14, 26 Oct. 1682); Bulstrode Newsletters (27 Oct. 1682); *Domestick Intelligence* 149 (23–6 Oct. 1682); HMC *Verney*, p. 480; *CSPD 1682*, p. 512.

[10] Repertory 88, fols. 13–14; Newdigate L.c. 1292–4 (26, 28, 31 Oct. 1682); LC MS 18,124, VIII, 254 (31 Oct. 1682); HMC *Verney*, pp. 480, 497; HMC *Ormonde*, VI, 470; HMC *Egmont*, II, 120; Luttrell, I, 231–3; *CSPD 1682*, p. 512; *Domestick Intelligence* 150 (26–30 Oct. 1682); *Observator*, I, 235 (4 Nov. 1682).

October with Monmouth, Russell, Howard, Grey, Robert Ferguson, and others, the earl claimed an ability to raise thousands of men, in short order, from Wapping. However, according to the subsequent accounts of both Lord Howard and Ferguson, with whom Shaftesbury stayed at one point, Shaftesbury also entertained the more easily arranged option of an assassination of Charles and/or of his brother. Ferguson subsequently suggested that some thought had been given to assassinating the king at the Rye House in Hertfordshire as he returned along the road from Newmarket to London before the last common hall. (The house belonged to Captain Richard Rumbold, a maltster and New Model Army veteran whose Whig and dissenting connections had apparently brought him into Shaftesbury's conspiratorial circle.) Another informant remembered a discussion about assassinating the royal brothers on their expected visit to the city during the mayoral installation of Pritchard. Regicide was unacceptable to Monmouth, however, who was both a king's son and a would-be-king.

A critical meeting of Monmouth, Lord Russell, Lord Grey, Colonel John Rumsey, and Robert Ferguson occurred in early November at the Abchurch Lane residence of Whig financier and wine merchant Thomas Shepherd.[11] Despite Monmouth's concerns about Shaftesbury's ability to stage an urban insurrection, those present at Shepherd's nevertheless agreed to support one, according to Grey and Ferguson. They assumed both that Shaftesbury's confidants among the civic Whigs would raise men and that thousands of dissenters and Whigs would join an insurrection, once it had begun. They also counted upon the organization of resistance in Taunton and Bristol. Again according to Grey and Ferguson, the conspirators developed detailed plans for overpowering the trained bands, for taking key positions in the city, and for moving toward Westminster. They fixed the date for the rising as 19 November, the Sunday following the traditional anti-popery outbursts on the anniversary of Elizabeth's accession. They also agreed to meet again a few days before that date to conclude their organization. At some point before this meeting ended, Alderman Henry Cornish, one of the disappointed Whig mayoral candidates, and a leader of efforts to overturn the shrieval election, joined the company.[12]

Historians who have been skeptical about this meeting have pointed to the denials about particular details made by some alleged participants and to the unlikely success of the plans. Why would Shaftesbury and Monmouth,

---

[11] Rumsey was a onetime Oliverian soldier now associated with Shaftesbury, and Ferguson represented the earl at this gathering. Newdigate L.c. 1396 (30 June 1683); Russell, *Last Speech*, p. 3; *CSPD 1683 (July–Sept.)*, p. 327; J. Ferguson, *Ferguson*, pp. 427–8; Woodhead, *Rulers*, p. 147; Haley, *Shaftesbury*, p. 716.

[12] Grey, *Secret History*, pp. 33–50; J. Ferguson, *Ferguson*, pp. 418–28; *CSPD 1683 (July–Sept.)*, pp. 70, 80; Sprat, *Copies*, pp. 27, 29, 68–70; Burnet, *History*, II, 350–1; *ST*, IX, 432–4, 450, 579; Haley, *Shaftesbury*, pp. 712–21; Ashcraft, *Revolutionary Politics*, pp. 356–62; Greaves, *Secrets*, pp. 113–23.

each of whom well knew the unpredictability of military skirmishing, have committed themselves to so risky a venture? In 1682, unlike 1642, the military resources of the nation were entirely in loyal hands, no parliament was in session, the kingdoms of Scotland and Ireland were relatively quiet, and there had been no collapse of local government.

Shaftesbury and his confederates would, of course, have been aware of the hazards of resistance themselves. However, in view of what had happened in London since June, they had reason to offer resistance; and they may also have believed that a narrow window for the success of an armed revolt was at hand. The mayoral election had demonstrated how committed the civic Whigs were to maintaining the principle of consent in the Corporation against a coercive regime. Surely, Shaftesbury and the other conspirators must have reasoned, the time to strike was now, before the crown and the loyalists had tightened their grip on the civic magistracy, and before the government employed all its resources against the Whig leaders and their dissenting followers. Thousands of determined citizens had just been mustered for a poll. Could not thousands also be summoned to strike a quick and decisive blow against an increasingly arbitrary regime?

The reported willingness of many London Whigs to enter into a civic association on behalf of the legitimate magistrates would have buoyed the Whig grandees in such thoughts, as would the rebellious language that other citizens were now apparently expressing, both in public and in private. The Baptist political club that met at the Salutation tavern in Lombard Street, for instance, was talking about a rising on 5 November to force Charles to agree to a Protestant succession and to Whig sheriffs, according to one loyalist informant. John Rouse, who was executed in 1683 for his part in subsequent Whig conspiracies, was a leading light among these Baptist clubmen. The same informant also learned, later in October, that members of Matthew Mead's Stepney Independent meeting were ready to "fight as resolute[ly] as . . . in the late wars."[13]

These preparations for rebellion on the part of Whig grandees and some plebs are, however, not the entire story of Whig responses to the London shrieval and mayoral elections. When the new legal term began on 23 October, just a few days before the declaration of the mayoral election, the city Whig leaders and their counsel appeared before the Court of King's Bench in full force. The delegation was headed by Sir Robert Clayton, the civic Whig with the greatest reputation outside London, and by Speaker Williams, who was already taking Shaftesbury's place as the principal Country ally of the London Whigs. These spokesmen entered a motion for a mandamus to require the lord mayor and aldermen to swear Papillon and Dubois as the "true

---

[13] One informant claimed that the new Whig association was intended specifically for "securing the King." LC MS 18,124, VIII, 124 (5 Oct. 1682); *CSPD 1682*, pp. 357, 403–5, 448, 495–6; North, *Examen*, p. 311; *CSPD 1683 (July–Sept.)*, pp. 216–18; Greaves, *Secrets*, pp. 156–7.

and legal" sheriffs. They also entered an action against Moore for accepting "an unjust Election and [for] Infringing . . . the priviledges of the Cittizens of London."

The Whigs clearly hoped that their mandamus on behalf of Papillon and Dubois would restrain Moore and the loyalist magistrates from overturning the Whig majority in the pending declaration of the mayoral election. Disappointed in this hope, they were not deterred from proceeding at law. Instead, they introduced a second King's Bench motion for a mandamus, this one to require the lord mayor and court of aldermen to recognize either Gold or Cornish as the legitimate lord mayor for 1682–3.

Even as Shaftesbury turned to the extra-legal strategy of resistance, then, some of his civic associates turned to the entirely legal strategy of trying their cause in the courts. But perhaps the distance between these two strategies was not as great as it might appear. The legal strategy of seeking to reclaim magisterial offices through the courts was actually rather problematic. The London Whigs refused to recognize the legitimacy of chief magistrates of the city who had the full confidence of Charles II. This left them rather precariously balanced between law and resistance, condemning the king's chief officers in the Corporation as usurpers, and seeking to impose upon him other officers whom he found abhorrent. In turning to law for remedy, the Whigs also ran the risk of merely finding that the law was as subject to royal manipulation as electoral processes had already proven. It was but one step further to argue that if the law itself was perverted by those in power, then government had dissolved, and individuals had a right to defend themselves and their property by offering armed resistance to those who ruled in an arbitrary manner. The resorts to law and resistance were, at this point, parallel strategies rather than opposites.

The hopes of Whig conspirators that they might turn outraged citizens into citizen soldiers were strengthened by the initially disappointing results of the new Whig lawsuits. The judges repeatedly delayed the issuance of the mandamus for Papillon and Dubois on technical grounds, before finally issuing it at the end of the term. They rejected the mandamus on behalf of the Whig mayoral candidates as unprecedented, probably because of the customary succession to the mayoralty of the senior alderman below the chair, the position that Pritchard had in fact occupied. The Whigs experienced further disappointment when the lord mayor and aldermen ignored the mandamus for Papillon and Dubois, regarding it as legally unenforceable before argumentation in the next term.[14]

---

[14] Repertory 88, fol. 13; LC MS 18,124, VIII, 131–2, 261 (25–6 Oct., 16 Nov. 1682); Newdigate L.c. 1291, 1297, 1305 (24 Oct. and 7, 28 Nov. 1682); Luttrell, I, 235, 237, 239–40, 247; *CSPD 1682*, p. 544.

In the meantime, as Whig grandees formulated plans for a civic insurrection, some urban plebs actually engaged in a significant civil disturbance. Streets that had been empty for the lord mayor's show were filled a week later in an unruly commemoration of the Gunpowder Treason, which occurred on Monday, 6 November, following the Sabbath. Hundreds of "robustick rude fellows," butchers' men, and apprentices roamed the city. Some of them were from Shaftesbury's ward of Aldersgate, some from Newgate, and others from as far away as Rotherhithe and Limehouse. Different bands converged at bonfires in Cornhill, near the Stocks Market. Encountering loyalists who cried "a York a York," they responded with "A Monmouth, a Monmouth" and "Stand to it, we'll make him king." Treason was clearly in the air, as the crowd turned riotous, defaced the signs of the Duke of York in Cheapside and of the Mitre tavern in the Poultry, and attacked the home of Sir Roger L'Estrange. The crowd verbally proclaimed the shrievalties of Papillon and Dubois; and when the new loyalist lord mayor arrived to disperse them with the trained bands, his commands were "answered with blowes." Several men and youths were eventually apprehended.[15]

The government was genuinely frightened. Whether Whig conspirators had played any part in encouraging these disturbances is impossible to say, but the crowds expressed public sympathy with the goals of Shaftesbury and other plotters. The Privy Council acted quickly to prevent anything similar from occurring on 17 November, not knowing, of course, that the conspirators had fixed on the 19th for their insurrection. The lord mayor and aldermen were summoned to Court to hear an order against any bonfires or assemblies on the anniversary of Elizabeth's succession. When the night in question arrived, it proved outwardly quiet, perhaps because of obvious preparations for trouble. The trained bands were present in significant numbers throughout the city and in Westminster. New sentry houses were placed near popular gathering points. Regular troops were deliberately kept outside the city; but the king's own regiment of horse was drawn up outside Temple Bar, and the rest of the royal guards were placed in readiness.[16]

Still, contemporary accounts of a peaceful 17 November were not the entire story. According to Roger North, the loyalist sheriff's brother, when the lord mayor and aldermen attended Court to hear the king's injunction against popular celebrations, one of the Whig magistrates pleaded with Charles not to prevent anti-papal pageants. Writing from hindsight, North regarded this

[15] LC MS 18,124, VIII, 257 (7 Nov. 1682); Newdigate L.c. 1297–8 (7, 9 Nov. 1682); Morrice, P, 343; *Domestick Intelligence* 153 (6–9 Nov. 1682); *Observator*, I, 239 (11 Nov. 1682); Luttrell, I, 236; *CSPD 1682*, pp. 528–30; Harris, *Crowds*, pp. 186–7.
[16] LC MS 18,124, VIII, 259–60, 262 (11, 14, 18 Nov. 1682); Newdigate L.c. 1299, 1301 (11, 18 Nov. 1682); Morrice, P, 345; Luttrell, I, 237; *Domestick Intelligence* 155 (13–16 Nov. 1682); *CSPD 1682*, p. 545, 547.

as a disingenuous effort to forestall military preparations and to leave the city open for the planned insurrection. Moreover, according to him, the sheriffs found numerous Catholic effigies on the 17th in a warehouse outside Bishopsgate, after the flight of those constructing these "equivocal Monsters."[17] But the rebellious Whig grandees had, in fact, lost their nerve, apparently abandoning any intention to initiate an insurrection under cover of anti-Catholic demonstrations. Since the early November planning meeting at Thomas Shepherd's house, Lords Grey and Monmouth had inspected the state of the king's guards at various locations. They had reportedly met again at Shepherd's with Lord Russell and Ferguson about 15 or 16 November. At that time, they concluded that a postponement of their rebellion for at least ten days was necessary: they had heard too little from Bristol and Taunton to feel comfortable about staging a London insurrection.

Shaftesbury was not at this meeting, but he had apparently come to even more sober conclusions. A rebellion could not be mounted without adequate preparations, but the time needed for such preparations would also provide the government with the time to launch new accusations against him and other Whig leaders. Within days, he left for Holland, "much broke in his thoughts," according to Bishop Burnet; and his associates in conspiracy shelved their plans for rebellion.[18]

The immediate prospect for resistance had collapsed, then; but who in the city might have been aware of what the Whig lords were planning? If, as has been suggested here, Shaftesbury continued to meet with civic Whig leaders throughout October, who among them was ready to pass from law to resistance, given the circumstances that now prevailed in the city? Thomas Shepherd, who hosted several of the conspiratorial discussions, clearly had made this move. He was described by one conspirator as "a man of the greatest interest in the City" and by another as the best man in the city "to be entrusted with a bank of money." He was probably brought into the plans of the Whig peers because of his political connections and financial resources. An Independent, and a friend of Robert Ferguson, who was an outspoken clerical advocate of resistance, Shepherd had also been considered for the shrievalty in 1681.[19]

The most prominent civic Whig leader likely to have known something about the plans of the peers was Henry Cornish. But the evidence for his involvement in conspiracy is circumstantial at best. When Cornish was tried

---

[17] North, *Examen*, pp. 576, 580.

[18] LC MS 18,124, VII, 297 (12 Dec. 1682); Grey, *Secret History*, pp. 43–7; J. Ferguson, *Ferguson*, pp. 428–9; Haley, *Shaftesbury*, pp. 721–2, 728–30; Greaves, *Secrets*, pp. 123–8.

[19] London Newsletters, VII, 196 (26 May 1681); *CSPD 1683 (July–Sept.)*, p. 327; *CSPD 1683–84*, p. 227; Grey, *Secret History*, pp. 28–9, 34, 37, 74–5; Sprat, *True Account*, p. 23; De Krey "Thomas Shepherd," *Oxford DNB*.

and executed for treason in 1685, part of the case against him was his alleged participation in the early November discussions at Shepherd's house. Grey claimed that Cornish "was to have been of our cabal"; and Howard remembered that Cornish had been "named to him as ready for action." But Cornish's denial, at his trial, that he had been present during any treasonable conversation was backed by the testimony of Shepherd himself, despite the obvious ill will between the two men. Still, Cornish's defense seems somewhat meretricious; and he did not deny attending the early November meeting at Shepherd's.[20]

Among other city Whigs likely to have known something were Francis Shute and his father, former Sheriff Samuel Shute, another friend of Robert Ferguson's. Samuel Shute was remembered by Lord Howard to have been "ready for action."[21] Some sources indicate that Cornish's onetime under-sheriff, Richard Goodenough, was also already involved in assassination plans by November 1682. But Goodenough was not well regarded by some civic Whig leaders, and his Westminster connections had so far been with Buckingham rather than with Shaftesbury.[22] What about Chamberlain Sir Thomas Player, who had long been among the most outspoken of the city Whig leaders? John Rouse, who was involved in the heated Baptist conversations at the Salutation tavern, had once been politically intimate with Player. But Rouse exonerated the chamberlain, from the scaffold, of any knowledge about his plotting; and he denied to an informer that he had communicated with Shaftesbury or with Monmouth at this time. If the government had evidence that implicated Player, it surely would have pursued it.[23]

Beyond these possibilities, there remain the names of a few of Shaftesbury's operatives among the Whig *artisanat*. Perhaps Randolph Watson, the Cripplegate tallow chandler and common councilman, with whom Shaftesbury lodged briefly in October, knew something. Lord Howard fingered John Cantrell, a Spitalfields weaver, as the likely recruiter of Shaftesbury's rebel army of "brisk boys" from the eastern out-parishes. Cantrell had been active previously in orchestrating pope-burnings and petitions. Charles Bateman, a Barbican surgeon, whose close ties to Shaftesbury eventually earned him

---

[20] Ferguson also insisted that, even though Cornish attended part of the meeting, he was not there during the critical discussion of insurrection. Grey, *Secret History*, p. 47; J. Ferguson, *Ferguson*, p. 427; *ST*, XI, 422, 443–4; *CSPD 1683 (July–Sept.)*, pp. 92, 191; Greaves, *Secrets*, p. 249; De Krey, "Henry Cornish," *Oxford DNB*. Ashcraft comes to a different conclusion, *Revolutionary Politics*, p. 357n.

[21] BL Harleian MS 6845, fol. 267; Sprat, *Copies*, pp. 30, 32; *CSPD 1683 (July–Sept.)*, p. 92; *ST*, IX, 392, 394.

[22] Sprat, *Copies*, pp. 12, 59, 70; *ST*, IX, 375, 424; Greaves, *Secrets*, pp. 131–2.

[23] *Speeches of Walcot, Rouse, and Hone*, p. 7; *CSPD 1682*, p. 495. But Rouse may also have promised to implicate Player, as well as Sir Patience Ward and Thomas Pilkington, in return for a reprieve: *CSPD 1683 (July–Sept.)*, p. 159.

a traitor's death, may also have been intimate with the earl during his last weeks in England.[24]

Little more can be said about the "considerable men" with whom Lord Grey thought Shaftesbury had discoursed. In any case, the coded and cryptic language that was characteristic of Whig conspiracy for the remainder of the 1680s suggests that few outside the inner circle of plotting peers had been told anything for certain. Discretion was as necessary for effective conspiracy as for recruitment. If Shaftesbury and other Whig peers were simultaneously planning a rebellion while supporting the civic Whigs in their legal and electoral strategies, the latter looked to the former for leadership, without fully knowing, apparently, where some grandees hoped to lead them. Actively pursuing relief at law, the London Whig leaders were largely unaware of plans for relief through resistance.

The London Whigs were nevertheless well aware by November that they had lost the political initiative and been thrown on the defensive. For some time, the Whigs had employed the courts as an alternate political venue to parliament; but within a few days of their installation, Tory Sheriffs Dudley North and Peter Rich were assisting the crown and the ministry in turning the legal tables on their opponents. Chamberlain Sir Thomas Player and Alderman Thomas Pilkington were among the earliest victims of loyalist revenge. The Privy Council took the lead in harassing Player. They first demanded an accounting of charitable funds entrusted to him, as chamberlain, for the redemption of English captives in North Africa. When no irregularities were found in these accounts, the Council questioned his prior disbursements of Treasury funds for the disbandment of the army. Although Player remained active in Corporation affairs after these challenges to his official conduct, he clearly had good reason for political circumspection.[25]

His friend Alderman Pilkington fared much worse. In November, the Duke of York's suit of *scandalum magnatum* against Pilkington was heard before a Hertfordshire jury. Pilkington had supposedly suggested the previous April that York had fired the city in 1666 and had returned from Scotland "to cut our throats." He now denied having spoken these words; and Whig Alderman Sir Patience Ward testified, in Pilkington's defense. But the jury found for York and awarded the duke £100,000 in damages. Pilkington had taken precautions to secure his estate from confiscation, but he himself was imprisoned. His resignation as alderman opened the Farringdon Without

---

[24] Sprat, *Copies*, p. 68; *ST*, IX, 432; *CSPD 1683 (July–Sept.)*, pp. 79, 428, 433.

[25] Repertory 88, fol. 8; LC MS 18,124, VIII, 256–7 (4, 7 Nov. 1682); Newdigate L.c. 1296, 1298 (4, 9 Nov. 1682); HMC *Verney*, p. 480; HMC *Egmont*, II, 121; Luttrell, I, 233; *Domestick Intelligence* 153 (6–9 Nov. 1682); *CSPD 1682*, pp. 523, 533; *CTB, 1681–85*, pp. 658, 703; Henning, *House of Commons*, III, 252.

seat to Tory recapture. Sir Patience Ward was also compromised in the wake of the judgment against Pilkington: suit was brought against him for offering perjured testimony.[26]

These were but the most spectacular episodes in a wide-ranging campaign against the persons and principles that had made the Corporation of London the most important extra-parliamentary opposition stronghold since 1675. Early in October, Sheriffs North and Rich replaced the grand juries chosen by their Whig predecessors. The stalwart loyalist jurors empaneled by the sheriffs quickly became partners for Anglican JPs in efforts to harry the Whigs and dissenters and to cleanse the public sphere of their political and religious language.[27] Individuals who had been outspoken in their defense of Thomas Papillon and John Dubois, the Whig shrieval candidates, were among those targeted for reprisals; and Dubois himself may have been the object of an attempted legal entrapment when a government informer offered him seditious writings. Vigorous ministerial efforts were made to silence Whig presses and to suppress the public fora that had sustained Whig conversation. Some printers and authors were presented; others quickly suspended their publications. The Stationers' Company adopted new by-laws to discourage scandalous imprints. The granting of new alehouse licenses was restricted to those able to demonstrate their conformity; and some coffeehouses were presented for permitting the reading of seditious pamphlets. Aldermen Cornish and Ward were presented before the Exchequer Court for allegedly mishandling funds for the rebuilding of city churches.

Advocates of liberty for conscience were treated with special severity. Prominent dissenting clergy like Richard Baxter and Stephen Lobb were apprehended. Attempts were made to distrain the goods of wealthy dissenters who had permitted conventicles to meet on their property. Alderman Sir John Shorter was indicted for attending a meeting. The Elizabethan conventicle act was applied against hundreds. The gang of informers headed by John and George Hilton successfully suppressed some conventicles, but others flourished despite harassment. The attorney general advised the Council that the livery companies of London might be purged of dissenting electors by a systematic administration of the oaths of allegiance and supremacy.[28]

---

[26] Repertory 88, fol. 22; LC MS 18,124, VIII, 265–6 (25, 28 Nov. 1682); Newdigate L.c. 1296, 1299, 1304–06 (4, 11, 25, 28 Nov. 1682); R. Ferguson, *Impartial Enquiry*, p. 52; CSPD 1682, p. 616; Burnet, *History*, II, 348; Henning, *House of Commons*, II, 246, 660.

[27] *Presentments of the Grand Jury for the County of Middlesex...the Eleventh day of October...1682*; *The Presentments of the Grand-Juries of the City of Westminster and County of Middx, Jan. 1682 [1683]*; *Presentments of the Grand-Jury for the Town and Borough of Southwark,...12th day of January...1682 [1683]*.

[28] Repertory 88, fol. 16; CLRO Waiting Book, XIII, 117; Newdigate L.c. 1286–91, 1294–5, 1298–1301, 1305, 1308–09, 1313 (12, 14, 17 19, 21, 24, 31 Oct.; 2, 9, 11, 14, 18 Nov.; 5,

The parish clergy were encouraged to forward the names of all who were deficient in their attendance at church or sacrament to Doctors' Commons. Rumors spread that thousands would be excommunicated in the London archdeacon's court, prior to the ward selections of common councilmen, to prevent their participation. Although only a few hundred were subject to church censure before St Thomas's Day, the process nevertheless aroused "a strange and hideous noise" among freemen concerned about their civic rights.[29]

Whig spirits were nevertheless sustained by two minor triumphs in the midst of this systematic campaign of intimidation. John Hilton, whose actions against London dissenting meetings enjoyed Court sponsorship, was discredited. When Hilton brought suit against Sir Robert Clayton in the Court of Common Pleas for failing to provide him with warrants against conventiclers, Clayton produced evidence of Hilton's prior conviction for forgery. And when several apprentices convicted for their riotous behavior in the Gunpowder Treason celebrations were pilloried on 9 December, they were acclaimed in the streets as Protestant heroes by throngs of "sturdy fellows." Nothing was hurled at them, as would have been customary. Instead, they were treated with gifts of money, wine, cakes, and fruit. Those in the stocks and their friends in the streets also drank healths to Monmouth, to the king, and to the Earl of Shaftesbury.[30]

Yet neither the disgrace of Hilton nor the resilience of anti-Catholic crowds could obscure the political losses of the London Whigs. The crown and the civic Tories had regained the initiative in the city, while the Whigs were ambiguously stuck between law and resistance. Still, important political questions remained open to contemporaries who could not foresee the subsequent failure of Whig strategies. London loyalists had reacquired the dominant magisterial positions; but would they also succeed in recapturing the Corporation, as a whole, or in recapturing common council, in particular? Whether Charles would actually sacrifice the Corporation and its historic charter for the sake of a firmer resettlement of church and state was also unclear.

7, 16 Dec. 1682); LC MS 18,124, VII, 302 (16 Dec. 1682) and VIII, 128, 249 (14, 19 Oct. 1682); Morrice, P, 340–1, 344, 348; *Domestick Intelligence* 145, 148, 152 (9–12, 19–23 Oct., 2–6 Nov. 1682); *Moderate Intelligencer* 37 (16–23 Oct. 1682); Luttrell, I, 228–30, 232, 237, 241; HMC *Graham*, p. 359; HMC *Verney*, p. 480; *CSPD 1682*, pp. 461–2, 467–8, 471, 474, 485, 522, 564; Goldie, "Hilton Gang."

29 LC MS 18,124, VII, [302–3] (16, 19 Dec. 1682) and VIII, 270 (19 Dec. 1682); Newdigate L.c. 1308–9, 1311, 1313–15 (5, 7, 12, 16, 19, 21 Dec. 1682); Morrice, P, 347; HMC *Verney*, p. 497; Luttrell, I, 242, 245–6; *CSPD 1682*, p. 557; Burnet, *History*, II, 339; A. G. Smith, "London and the Crown," pp. 268–9.

30 LC MS 18,124, VII, 297 (12 Dec. 1682); Newdigate L.c. 1304, 1310 (25 Nov., 9 Dec. 1682); Morrice, P, 346, Luttrell, I, 241, 243–4; HMC *Graham*, p. 406; HMC *Verney*, pp. 480–1; *CSPD 1682*, pp. 553, 572–3; Kennett, *History*, III, 407–8; Harris, *London Crowds*, pp. 187–8; Goldie, "Hilton Gang," p. 53.

The capture of the political initiative in London by the crown and the civic loyalists was clearly evident in the series of Corporation elections that followed Shaftesbury's departure for Holland. Far from accepting any loss of the city to the crown, however, the London Whigs and dissenters contested these elections with a determination borne of the conviction that critical Corporation offices were already possessed by "usurpers." Every office they lost, they believed, was a blow to the Corporation's charter, which they continued to defend against the crown's *quo warranto*. They were further buoyed by rumors about an impending parliament, the meeting of which, they hoped, would provide them with another opportunity for redress.[31] Yet, within weeks, the civic Whigs had suffered additional reverses in their electoral and legal pursuits. They were even more convinced that the laws of the land, the liberties of London citizens, and the customs of the city were being trampled upon by the architects of arbitrary government. And desperate times again produced desperate courses: some Whig grandees and some London Whig legal men renewed preparations for active resistance by January 1683.

December aldermanic contests in Bridge and in Farringdon Without, the latter following Thomas Pilkington's enforced resignation, gave the civic Whigs another opportunity to advance the cause of the sheriffs they claimed to have elected in 1682. For Alderman of Bridge, the Whigs put forward the names of Thomas Papillon and former Sheriff Samuel Shute, while in Farringdon Without, they promoted John Dubois and Monmouth's civic banker, Richard Hawkins. The churchmen responded with Sheriff Dudley North, as their principal candidate for Farringdon Without, while promoting Sheriff Peter Rich for Bridge, together with the ward's deputy alderman, Peter Daniel, who was also Sheriff of Surrey. Lord Mayor Pritchard presided over both wardmotes; and in each ward, after much local organization and disputed polls, the lord mayor declared for a mixed return to the court of aldermen of one Whig nominee and one Tory nominee. This strategy enabled the Tory-dominated magisterial bench to choose two new loyalist aldermen, Dudley North and Peter Daniel, without excluding Whig names from the ward returns.[32]

The political organization driven by these aldermanic contests was quickly redirected toward the election of new common councilmen throughout the

---

[31] Newdigate L.c. 1307 (2 Dec. 1682); HMC *Downshire*, I, 16; *CSPD 1682*, p. 572.

[32] Repertory 88, fols. 38, 42; LC MS 18,124, VII, 300–1, [302] (14, 16 Dec. 1682) and VIII, 269, 271 (5, 21 Dec. 1682); Newdigate L.c. 1301, 1308, 1310, 1312–15 (18 Nov. and 5, 9, 14, 16, 19, 21 Dec. 1682); Morrice, P, 348; Luttrell, I, 242–4, 245; *CSPD 1682*, pp. 557, 561, 573; HMC *Lords 1690–91*, pp. 53–4; Smith, "London and the Crown," pp. 216–17; Woodhead, *Rulers*, p. 86; Henning, *House of Commons*, II, 188–9.

city on 21 December. In co-opting North and Daniel to the aldermanic bench, the Tories ensured loyalist presiding officers in two-thirds of the city's wards. Crown commissioners were also appointed in each ward to administer the oaths of allegiance and supremacy to freemen who wished to participate, and the last Sunday before St Thomas's Day saw a politically inspired trained band sweep of major conventicles. For their part, the Whigs reminded electors that the civic oaths required freemen to elect common councilmen who would defend the charter. Captained by William Williams, they also prepared for St Thomas's Day with a furious renewal of their attempt to ensnare the loyalist magistrates at law.[33]

In mid-December, Williams appeared before the court of aldermen to warn Lord Mayor Pritchard about his failure to comply with the mandamus to invest Papillon and Dubois with the shrieval offices to which they had been elected. Reminding Pritchard that he had assumed the mayoralty "as a minister of Justice," Williams informed the lord mayor that, by failing to comply with the mandamus, he "stood obnoxious to the utmost Rigor of Law." Williams also threatened to impeach him before King's Bench at the beginning of Hillary term. And Sir Thomas Player informed Pritchard that the many electors of London and Middlesex to whom he had "denyed Justice" would "spend their Estates," in the legal defence of their rights, "rather then . . . [be] wronged."[34]

Williams and leading members of the Corporation's *quo warranto* committee, including Sir Robert Clayton and Sir Patience Ward, also attempted to take their cases against the lord mayor and on behalf of their sheriffs before Charles himself. They traveled first to Windsor, where they were unable to see the king. But on 20 December, Williams succeeded in entering the council chamber at Whitehall, where Charles and his councilors were forced to listen to the voice of the last two Commons in the person of their Speaker. Williams reportedly informed Charles that the citizens of London were "lyeing under the ponderous bonds of injustice." Requesting the king to "remove oppressione from their Streets," Williams asked that "Mr Papillon and Dubois may be put into the places they were Legally chosen to." But before commanding Williams's departure, Charles also took his stand on law, claiming that, since Rich and North had been returned to the Exchequer as "Legally chosen," he could not act without consulting the judges.[35]

Charles had been given a vivid personal experience of the continuing ability of "the faction" to disrupt the Corporation and the kingdom alike. Williams

---

[33] When Charles ordered the suspension of Alderman Sir John Shorter, for his presentment as a conventicler, he sought to remove Whig aldermanic influence from yet another wardmote. Repertory 88, fols. 43–4; LC MS 18,124, VII, [303] (19 Dec. 1682) and VIII, 270–1 (19, 21 Dec. 1682); Newdigate L.c. 1314–15 (19, 21 Dec. 1682); HMC *Downshire*, I, 16; *CSPD 1682*, pp. 572, 580, 583.

[34] LC MS 18,124, VII, 297, [303] (12, 19 Dec. 1682).

[35] *Ibid.*, fols. [303], [305] (19, 21 Dec. 1682).

had confronted majesty in the face: the king was charged with maintaining magistrates whose actions left the people "oppressed." Charles seemed almost aware that the Speaker and his civic Whig associates now occupied a political place between law and resistance. He therefore decided both to proceed with his *quo warranto* against the Corporation and to abandon the increasingly problematic defense of Tangier, the expense of which could entail a meeting of parliament for the sake of supply. In council, the king was advised that "He must be K: of London... before it [a parliament] could be called." And, in order to become "king of London," Charles needed to proceed with the expulsion of his opponents from the London magistracy and common council.[36]

Loyalist efforts to regain control of the court of common council for 1683 were successful in the end, but the process was messy, and the outcome was uncertain for some time. About fifty common councilmen from both parties were not rechosen; but since four-fifths of the newcomers returned to the 1683 common council were Tories, loyalist predominance upon that court was re-established. Polls and scrutinies were held or demanded in several wards; and some results were delayed for days, weeks, and even months. Churchmen made strong gains in three wards, including Farringdon Without, where newly elected Alderman Dudley North superintended the replacement, in a Tory space, of ten Whig common councilmen. In Aldgate, Thomas Papillon was unseated; and in Cripplegate and Bassishaw, John Dubois and Sir Thomas Player were similarly expelled. Still, over ninety Whigs remained on common council for 1683, and Tories made no inroads in the Whig urban space. (See Table 6.1.) In some wards, Whig electors and common councilmen successfully countered loyalist efforts. Bridge Whigs, for instance, not only elected largely Whig common councilmen but, "in pure revenge," humiliated Sheriff Rich by electing him ward scavenger.[37]

The first meeting of the new common council on 16 January 1683 revealed a new balance of political forces in the Corporation. The extraordinary business of that day consumed five hours. The Whigs sought to regain the initiative by promoting a successful motion of thanks to the *quo warranto* committee elected by the previous common council. Thereafter, however, loyalists dominated the meeting. Sir William Pritchard overruled Sir Robert Clayton's attempt to read a petition, probably about the shrievalty. Pritchard instead encouraged a motion to thank Sir John Moore, whom some Whigs had threatened to impeach, for his "great service" to the city as lord mayor.

---

[36] *Ibid.*, fol. 294 (21 Dec. 1682); Hutton, *Charles II*, p. 426.

[37] Repertory 88, fols. 46, 49, 55–56, 90, 92; LC MS 18,124, VII, [305], 293–4 (21 [*bis*], 26 Dec. 1682) and VIII, 272, 274–5, 299–300 (22, 23, 27, 28, 30 Dec. 1682); Newdigate L.c. 1315–18, 1320–2 (21, 23, 28, 30 Dec. 1682 and 4, 6, 9 Jan. 1683); Morrice, P, 349; HMC Egmont, II, 126; *CSPD 1682*, pp. 584, 592, 597; *CSPD 1683 (Jan.–June)*, p. 5; Smith, "London and the Crown," pp. 212–14.

This motion was strongly opposed by the "Dissenting partie," but it was carried by 119 votes to 86, the aldermen not voting. Only in the selection of a new committee to defend the Corporation's charter did the Tories yield to the Whigs. Hoping to maintain their ability to negotiate independently with Charles, the Tory magistrates and common councilmen acquiesced in the election of the old Whig committee, accepting four new Whigs to take the place of those who had lost their common council seats.[38] Nevertheless, the Whigs had clearly lost the dominant position in the Corporation of London.

As they contemplated these reverses, the London Whigs were staggered by additional blows. News of Shaftesbury's death in Amsterdam on 21 January was but one of these. The Court-loyalist campaign against Whigs, dissenters, and opposition discourse escalated in a variety of ways. The court of aldermen implemented a royal order against meetings in the livery halls and devised new methods for ward watches every Sabbath. Sessions dockets were crowded into the spring with proceedings against dissenters of all social ranks. A rumor that regular army troops would replace the trained bands in suppressing meetings and apprehending attendees caused "more alarum and affect than any thing" Roger Morrice had "heard of [in] many years," for it suggested the French dragonnades had come to London. When Thomas Hunt, who had been assaulted after publishing his defense of the charter, fled to Holland, another opposition voice was silenced.[39] Declining Whig prospects were also reflected at the Theatre Royal, in Drury Lane, where the first performances of John Crowne's *City Politiques* coincided with the January meeting of common council. Audiences flocked to see "a Ld Major, Sheriffs, and some Aldermen," including especially Sir Robert Clayton, "buffooned and reviled" on the stage.[40]

Given the extent of Whig despair in the wake of these reverses, the revival of plotting in December 1682 and January 1683 is not surprising. According to Lord Howard, a group of six Whig grandees met twice in January 1683 to reconsider the need for resistance. They were encouraged, again according to Howard, by the "disposition to action" that they had observed,

[38] Journal 50, fols. 1, 21; LC MS 18,124, VIII, 266, 281–2 (28 Nov. 1682 and 16, 18 Jan. 1683); Newdigate L.c. 1325 (16 Jan. 1683); Morrice, P, 351; *CSPD 1682 (Jan.–June)*, pp. 16–17; Luttrell, I, 246.

[39] Repertory 88, fols. 47, 52, 64, 67–68; LC MS 18,124, VIII, 279–81, 284, 289, 321 (9, 11, 16, 23 Jan.; 3 Feb.; 24 April 1683); Newdigate L.c. 1322–5, 1331, 1340, 1343, 1349 1365, 1366 1367 (9, 11, 13, 16, 30 Jan.; 20, 27 Feb.; 13 March; and 19, 21, 24 April 1683); Morrice, P, 351–3, 355; *The Presentment of the Grand Jury for the City of London . . . the 19th of April, 1683*; Luttrell, I, 252; *CSPD 1683 (Jan.–June)*, pp. 3, 10–11, 17, 185, 196; HMC *Graham*, p. 406; HMC *Egmont*, II, 126–7.

[40] LC MS 18,124, VIII, 283 (21 Jan. 1683); Newdigate L.c. 1327 (20 Jan. 1683); Morrice, P, 352; Luttrell, I, 246–7; Hunt, *Defence of the Charter*; "Introduction," to John Crowne, *City Politiques*, ed. J. H. Wilson (Lincoln, Nebr., 1967), pp. ix–xix.

"both in city and country." In addition to himself, Howard reported that this cabal included Monmouth, Russell, Essex, Algernon Sidney, and John Hampden. Although those involved would subsequently deny that their conversations were treasonable, Russell acknowledged, in his trial, that they had met. Lord Grey was not a member of this inner circle, but he claimed to have learned from Monmouth that the Whig council hoped to bring about "an happy accommodation between the king and his people in parliament" by means of coordinated risings in favor of Monmouth's succession. The group also reportedly agreed upon a declaration of their purposes in which Sidney and Essex, whom some suspected of republican designs, agreed to support Monmouth's claim to the throne. These Country Whig leaders also cultivated ties with the circle of disaffected Scotsmen around the Earl of Argyll.

A separate group of London conspirators who met regularly, after about Christmas 1682, in the Middle Temple quarters of barrister Robert West, and in the city, was soon in communication with this "council of six" aristocrats. The West group would provide multiple connections between Whig conspiracy and civic politics for the next six months; and the coincidence in time between the loss of the Corporation to the Tories and the commencement of plotting by this group is quite obvious. A student of Machiavelli with republican sympathies, West gathered many of this cabal of intriguers from his professional and political associates in the Green Ribbon club. He was known to John Locke and others among Shaftesbury's entourage, for instance; and he apparently had become involved in the earl's autumn discussions about resistance. Indeed, Burnet referred to West's group as "a company of lord Shaftesbury's creatures."[41]

The company included Colonel John Rumsey and Captain Richard Rumbold, each of whom had also been involved in Shaftesbury's earlier designs, and a coterie of lawyers with connections to the civic and parliamentary oppositions. Chief among these was the onetime under-sheriff for the Corporation, Richard Goodenough, who had been active in civic opposition circles since the early 1670s, and who had assisted in empaneling the ignoramus juries of 1681. Like West, Goodenough was an acquaintance of Thomas Shepherd, who met with the group as their plans took shape; and he was one of the attorneys involved in advancing the suit of Thomas

---

[41] Grey, *Secret History*, pp. 50–5; Sprat, *Copies*, pp. 9, 27, 34–5, 70–1; *CSPD 1683 (July–Sept.)*, pp. 80, 90; *ST*, IX, 373, 392, 434–5; Burnet, *History*, II, 352–7; Ashcraft, *Revolutionary Politics*, pp. 346, 360–1, 376; M. Cranston, *John Locke: A Biography* (New York, 1957), p. 248; Scott, *Restoration Crisis*, pp. 275–6; Greaves, *Secrets*, pp. 29, 131–9, 173. Francis Shute, son of the former London sheriff, was apparently an intermediary between the group of peers and the West group: *ST*, IX, 394.

Papillon and John Dubois for the shrievalty.[42] Other lawyers involved in the West group, to different extents, were John Ayloffe and Richard Nelthorpe. Ayloffe's political poetry suggests that he shared West's republican sympathies, and Nelthorpe was a political associate of Algernon Sidney. Like Goodenough, Ayloffe and Nelthorpe were among those charged with riot in the London shrieval election on 24 June 1682.[43] Yet another lawyer present at some meetings of the West cabal was Robert Blaney of the Middle Temple. Blaney's father, described in 1664 as a former "confidant" of Cromwell, had once been Shaftesbury's secretary.[44] The principals of the West group were, then, legal men of some repute, though not of the first rank; and many of them had taken an active part in civic politics since 1679.

By late February, West's group had resolved upon a scheme to assassinate Charles II in Hertfordshire on his return to London from the Newmarket races, expected to be about 1 April. The attempt upon Charles's life would occur as he passed the Rye House, in Hoddesdon, the property of Captain Rumbold. Robert Ferguson joined these "Rye House" conspirators after his return to England, both assisting in the recruitment of others and perhaps also reporting to Monmouth, who remained opposed to assassination. As their plans developed, the West group also considered attempts upon the Tower and upon the London loyalist magistrates; and they pursued connections with militant Whigs in Bristol.[45]

Both the aristocratic "council of six" and the more obscure West cabal were made up of people well known to the London Whig leaders. Yet little evidence suggests that many of them were aware of these conspiracies. Despite recent disappointments, civic Whig energies were instead largely directed toward the public strategies of defending their rights and of restoring legitimate magistrates to office through legal means. Although the hopes of the civic Whigs for redress at law would prove illusory in the end, their reading of the political situation they confronted is understandable. They retained a strong political presence in common council and important aldermanic voices. In the Court of King's Bench they expected impartial treatment

---

[42] *DNB*, VIII, 124; *BDBR*, II, 12–14; De Krey, "Richard Goodenough," *Oxford DNB*; Haley, *Shaftesbury*, pp. 665, 717–18; Haley, *William of Orange*, p. 59; Greaves, *Secrets*, pp. 140, 144.

[43] Sprat, *True Account*, p. 24; *POAS*, I, 228–36; *BDBR*, I, 30–1, and II, 259–60; *DNB*, I, 756, and XIV, 217; G. de F. Lord, "Satire and Sedition: The Life and Work of John Ayloffe," *Huntington Library Quarterly* 29 (1966), 255–73; Haley, *William of Orange*, pp. 58–9; Scott, *Restoration Crisis*, pp. 159, 177–8; 285; Greaves, *Secrets*, pp. 133, 137, 150, 172–3; Henning, *House of Commons*, I, 247.

[44] SP 29/93/3; *CSPD 1667*, pp. 17, 48; Sprat, *Copies*, pp. 23–4; *ST*, IX, 385–7; Haley, *Shaftesbury*, p. 440; Ashcraft, *Revolutionary Politics*, p. 114. Blaney was also a kinsman by marriage of Thomas Jacombe, the Presbyterian divine: PRO PROB 11: 387 Foot, qu. 50.

[45] J. Ferguson, *Ferguson*, pp. 431–7; Sprat, *Copies*, pp. 28, 30, 45; Burnet, *History*, II, 358–60; Ashcraft, *Revolutionary Politics*, pp. 363–7; Greaves, *Secrets*, pp. 147–8.

by judges who had not yet been pressured by the crown for its own political gain. Moreover, the civic Whig leadership had been enlarged to include some of the most prominent legal minds in the kingdom: Henry Pollexfen, William Thompson, and Speaker Williams now worked with the city's own distinguished recorder, Sir George Treby. With their assistance, the civic Whigs prepared to preserve the charter, to defend themselves against the charge of riot during the Midsummer's common hall of 1682, and to pursue their mandamus against the Tory sheriffs.

The city's rejoinder to the attorney general's case against the charter had been offered somewhat earlier, in October 1682. Now as then, the crown's claim that the charter should be forfeited because of the seditious language in the January 1681 London petition about parliament aroused more concern from the Corporation's Whig-dominated *quo warranto* committee than the crown's complaints about civic tolls.[46] King's Bench argumentation in the case resumed on 7 February, with Recorder Treby speaking on behalf of the Corporation. As might have been expected, given Treby's importance in the last three parliaments, his arguments universalized the issues of the London case, emphasizing its implications for the kingdom and for the common law itself. The recorder denied that the London charter could be forfeited to the crown. According to him, corporations could be dissolved, as bodies politic, only through acts of parliament or through the deaths of all their members. Neither, for Treby, could corporations be held accountable at law for the behavior of their officers, against whom alone the crown might have a case for its allegations of misconduct. The crown condemned the London petition of January 1681 as infringing upon the prerogative; but Treby stressed that subjects had an undoubted right to petition the crown. Observers were impressed by the argumentation on both sides, and the Whigs remained hopeful, both about the case and about the charter. Final argumentation in the *quo warranto* was delayed until the following term.[47]

King's Bench next took up the case against those accused of riot at the common hall of 24 June 1682. For Whig defendants, this case provided an opportunity to defend their belief that electoral consent could not be abridged by rulings of the lord mayor. A successful prosecution, on the other hand, would vindicate "the Ld Majors adjourning of the Common hall," as chief magistrate of the Corporation, against the wishes of a majority of the electorate and of Whig sheriffs who claimed the presiding role. The government

---

[46] LC MS 18,124, VIII, 250, 282 (21 Oct. 1682, 18 Jan. 1683); Newdigate L.c. 1289, 1296 (19 Oct., 4 Nov. 1682); HMC *Graham*, p. 359; Luttrell, I, 230.

[47] *ST*, VIII, 1099–1147; LC MS 18,124, VIII, [292] (8 Feb. 1683); Newdigate L.c. 1335 (8 Feb. 1683); Burnet, *History*, II, 344–6; J. Levin, *The Charter Controversy in the City of London, 1660–1688, and its Consequences* (1969), pp. 29–47; P. D. Halliday, *Dismembering the Body Politic: Partisan Politics in England's Towns, 1650–1730* (Cambridge, 1998), pp. 204–6.

was embarrassed when the case came up on 17 February. According to Luttrell, the Tory sheriffs had empaneled a "good" jury, "being in their own cause." But William Williams and the other Whig counsel successfully challenged the jury array as defective, thereby derailing the government's case, which had to be put off until the following term.[48]

In the meantime, the lord mayor and aldermen finally replied to the Whig mandamus about the shrievalty, arguing that Papillon and Dubois could not be installed in offices to which they "were not Elected." When the King's Bench judges accepted this reply, the Whigs proceeded with their individual suits against Sir John Moore and Lord Mayor Pritchard for declaring and accepting false sheriffs. Moreover, on 1 February, attorney Richard Goodenough, who was already engaged in the West cabal's extra-legal plotting, appeared at the court of aldermen to demand they provide bail and appoint attorneys to respond to suits brought against them by Papillon and Dubois. When the loyalist aldermen declined to comply with this demand, Goodenough proceeded to take out writs against each of them. These were delivered for execution not to the sheriffs, who were parties to the whole dispute, but rather to John Brome, the city coroner and clerk of the whiggish Skinners' Company. Brome was instructed to arrest the lord mayor and aldermen, an action that would have incapacitated the Corporation's Tory leadership. But Lord Mayor Pritchard persuaded Brome to take further legal advice before proceeding so precipitously. Goodenough's writs expired before much else could be done; but like Shaftesbury before him, Goodenough apparently regarded law and resistance as complementary strategies, at this juncture, rather than as opposites.[49]

These dramatic legal maneuvrings in the city left public attention focused upon what would happen in the courts when the Easter legal term began on 25 April. By then, much else of interest had also occurred in London, both in private and in public. The Rye House plotters, of whom Goodenough was still a principal, had proceeded to recruit a party of men to assail the king in Hertfordshire on his return from Newmarket along the London road. The intended assassination at the Rye House miscarried, however, when the king returned ten days earlier than expected and before the conspirators had completed their arrangements. Ironically, the Rye House plan, from which historians have derived a name for the entire cluster of 1682–3 conspiracies, was completely abortive. This abject failure has no doubt fed the chorus of skepticism about it ever since Burnet dismissed much of the "story" as

[48] LC MS 18,124, VIII, 297 (17 Feb. 1683); Newdigate L.c. 1336, 1339 (10, 17 Feb. 1683); Luttrell, I, 250; *CSPD 1683 (Jan.–June)*, p. 53.

[49] LC MS 18,124, VIII, 286, [292], 295 (27 Jan. and 8, 13 Feb. 1683); Newdigate L.c. 1329, 1332–34, 1361 (25 Jan.; 1, 3, 6 Feb.; 10 April 1683); *CSPD 1683 (Jan.–June)*, pp. 38–9, 41, 49; Papillon, *Memoirs*, p. 228.

an "incredible" tale told by West and Rumsey.[50] Yet, although the initial plan had failed, those involved in it continued to conspire and to engage in more open political affairs until the government's discoveries of June 1683. And the identities and expectations of those recruited for the assassination scheme provide an intimate glimpse into the volatile mix of legal maneuvring and resistance language that was driving Whig actions in the troubled city.

Who, then, were the intended Rye House assassins; and what did they and their legal associates intend to accomplish by killing the king? The West cabal had recruited assassins from the ranks of "fierce bigotted men in Religion" rather than restricting the project to gentlemen like themselves. Among those chosen for the task by Goodenough were Josiah Keeling, William Hone, James Burton, Nathaniel Gale, and men surnamed Jeffreys and Manning. Josiah Keeling, who eventually "discovered" the plot to the government, also recruited Andrew Barber and William Thompson. These men were mostly sectarians hostile to the "priestcraft" of the established church, and they were drawn from East End neighborhoods beyond the Whig space in Aldgate and Portsoken. Keeling resided in East Smithfield in the out-parish of St Botolph Aldgate, where Gale was his neighbor. Barber, Burton, and Thompson lived nearby in Wapping, as did Hone, who had recently relocated there from Southwark. A Baptist, Keeling had been expelled from his congregation for unknown reasons; but as a constable, he had worked to obstruct the harassment of dissenters. Hone worshipped wherever he found Reformed ministry – among the Independents, Baptists, and Presbyterians, and also "sometimes" within the Church of England. Manning had connections to Independent divine George Griffith.

These were men of humble trades, precisely the sort of "brisk boys" Shaftesbury claimed to command a few months earlier. Keeling was a down-on-his-luck oilman and salter who had previously been concerned in a Warwickshire coal work. The potential assassins also included a cheesemonger, a brazier, a joiner, a crape-weaver (or box maker), an instrument maker, and a carver. Perhaps the discussions within the West cabal about eliminating the unpopular chimney tax after the assassination and about converting the endowments of most university colleges to "public uses" owed something to these "mechanick" conspirators. Such objectives had commanded support a generation earlier from articulate artisans and the working sort.[51]

As suggested by the social identities of these men and those who recruited them, the Rye House conspiracy did not include a cross-section of the Whig movement in the city. With the exception of Shepherd, it involved no Inner

[50] Burnet, *History*, II, 364.
[51] Add. MS 41,803, fol. 55ff.; *ST*, IX, 365–72, 420–1, 573, 604, and X, 342; Sprat, *Copies*, pp. 1–8; Sprat, *True Account*, pp. 24, 45; *CSPD 1683 (Jan.–June)*, pp. 104–5, 331, 382; *CSPD 1683 (July–Sept.)*, pp. 71–2, 235, 372; *CSPD 1683–4*, p. 3; *CSPD 1685*, p. 134; *DNB*, X, 1188; De Krey, "Josiah Keeling," *Oxford DNB*; Greaves, *Secrets*, pp. 145–6, 151.

City merchant or retail shopkeeper of note, although Goodenough, West, and the other lawyers certainly knew such men. Instead, the cabal was a curious combination of West End lawyers, East End plebs, and old Cromwellians. Still, West End legal men and East End "mechanicks" were both groups that had accounted for much within the urban Whig movement.

Why did these particular men turn to plotting? What inclined them to participate in an undertaking that cost several of them their lives? Religious nonconformity was an obvious common denominator that linked artisan Baptist conspirators to plotters learned in the law. And so, interestingly, was the law itself. Joiner William Hone had acquired the nickname "Magna Charta" in London Whig circles after he set up a copy of the great charter of English liberties at Temple Bar. Some of the plotters had also been involved, in one way or another, with Stephen College, whose execution had demonstrated to them how fragile the law could be as an instrument of defense. Plotter Robert West had provided College with legal advice before his trial; and Robert Blaney had been a promoter of College's ballad, *A Raree Show*. Similarly, William Hone may once have been College's apprentice or journeyman; and Josiah Keeling's brother resided near College. Like the lawyers with whom they conspired, then, these artisans were willing to turn to extra-legal remedy to preserve the law itself. Fierce men, to be sure, they were not unsophisticated; instead they were thoroughly familiar with the issues of the day. Their backgrounds and activities give the assassination scheme a coherence that historians have overlooked, just as their names and motives give it a plausibility that overrides skeptical dismissals.[52]

The principles of conscience and consent informed the plans of the West group for a post-regicidal resettlement of the nation. They prepared a manifesto of their intentions that focused upon broadening the authority of an annually elected parliament. They promised liberty of conscience to all Protestants. And, because they believed that the Tory civic magistrates had become the willing agents of popery and arbitrary government, the resettlement of the Corporation was as important to them as the resettlement of the kingdom. According to Robert West, Sir John Moore was to be killed in the course of the insurrection for his part in the suppression of civic rights and Protestant liberty. "If the people did not pull him in pieces," Moore's flayed and stuffed skin was to be hung up before Guildhall as an example to any who would think of betraying the people's rights and liberties. The same fate was reserved for Sir William Pritchard and for those who had presumed to act, without warrant, as sheriffs. Thomas Papillon and John Dubois were, at

---

[52] Morrice, P, 468, SP 29/425/138; CLRO 1680 six-months' tax assessments for St Anne Blackfriars (Farringdon Within); Newdigate L.c. 1395 (28 June 1683); *ST*, VIII, 550, and XI, 414; *CSPD 1682*, p. 245; *CSPD 1683 (Jan.–June)*, p. 382; Greaves, *Secrets*, pp. 29, 118.

last, to assume the shrieval offices to which they had been elected, and Henry Cornish was to become lord mayor. If these Whig magistrates hesitated to act, they were to be "knocked on the head." This apparent distrust of the very Whig candidates whose names had inspired so much commotion in the Corporation for the past six months may point to some impatience with the legal remedies pursued by the Whig leaders.[53]

The failure of the Rye House assassination scheme did not discourage further plotting, either on the part of the West cabal or on the part of the disaffected Whig grandees. For their part, the grandees apparently continued to pursue the prospects for coordinated insurrections in London, the country, and Scotland. Thomas Shepherd sought to raise city money for them; but the grandees remained handicapped by lack of funds. The West group also met frequently to consider new plans, finding some encouragement from Ferguson, who continued in his role as a go-between with Monmouth. Yet the two groups remained somewhat suspicious of each other; and each was also divided internally by personality clashes and differing objectives.[54]

Lord Grey subsequently claimed that the plotting of the Whig grandees came to a head again in late April.[55] Interestingly, at precisely that time, on 24–5 April, Richard Goodenough organized the arrest of the Lord Mayor of London. This episode – ignored in most discussions of Whig plotting – provides further insight into how the London Whigs were lodged between law and resistance. For, if on the surface, the affair involved public legal action against a magisterial "usurper" who had accepted "false" sheriffs, it was also driven by men already committed to assassination and resistance. Some in the West cabal apparently intended to appropriate the legal strategy of the civic Whigs in order to pursue it in a more extreme manner. The arrest of the lord mayor was, in the first instance, an attempt to reverse the loss of the Corporation to the crown and the loyalists. But Goodenough and his fellow conspirators may have hoped thereby to draw the whole Whig movement into their broader design of checking arbitrary rule through all necessary means.

Goodenough, his brother Francis, Richard Nelthorpe, Josiah Keeling, and James Burton – all involved in the assassination scheme – are known to have

---

[53] For this reason, Sir Robert Clayton and Sir Patience Ward also apparently came in for criticism for having failed, during their mayoralties, to ensure the repeal of city by-laws that had facilitated the election of Moore and the Tory recovery of the Corporation. Add. MS 38,847, fols. 103–104, 108, 115; Newdigate L.c. 1402 (14 July 1683); *CSPD 1683 (July–Sept.)*, p. 433; Sprat, *Copies*, pp. 42, 55–6; *ST*, IX, 405, 420–1; Sprat, *True Account*, p. 61; Greaves, *Secrets*, pp. 140–1, 148–9.

[54] Grey, *Secret History*, pp. 55–68; J. Ferguson, *Ferguson*, pp. 431–7; Sprat, *Copies*, pp. 9, 16–18, 28, 30–3, 35–8, 41; *ST*, IX, 373, 378–81, 390–3, 398–401, 404; Greaves, *Secrets*, pp. 161–78.

[55] Grey, *Secret History*, pp. 55–67.

attended a Whig consult of some forty persons in Ironmonger Lane that preceded the action against Sir William Pritchard on 24 April. In preparation for the approaching legal term, Goodenough now renewed the writs that he had previously taken out against the lord mayor and aldermen on behalf of the Whig shrieval candidates. He did so with the consent of Papillon and Dubois, who had, according to Papillon, also insisted that the writs be served "with all respect" on the loyalist magistrates, only requiring them to make a court appearance in response to the Whig suits.

As in February, Goodenough entrusted the execution of the writs to John Brome, coroner for the Corporation. This time Brome had an interesting assistant: Josiah Keeling, the chief of the Rye House assassination squad, acted with him as a special bailiff. William Hone and Jeffreys, two of the picked assassins, may also have assisted the coroner. Brome and Keeling subsequently claimed that Richard Goodenough was the mastermind behind the affair. But Brome and Keeling were also accustomed to acting together: Brome had once been Keeling's partner in his Warwickshire coal work.[56]

Pritchard refused to give an appearance to the writ presented to him by Brome and his party on the afternoon of 24 April or to provide bail. The coroner then arrested him and took him prisoner to Skinners' Hall, because the writ, contrary to the instructions of Papillon and Dubois, apparently required either bail or imprisonment. Several loyalist aldermen were also immediately arrested by Brome and his assistants, as were others who came to Skinners' Hall to rescue Pritchard. By early evening, Richard Goodenough and Gilbert Nelson, a Whig scrutineer in the autumn mayoral poll, were also at Skinners' Hall to advise the coroner.[57]

To this point, the instigators of Pritchard's arrest could claim that they were merely carrying out a customary legal process against recalcitrant defendants. However, after the June disclosures about Whig plotting, loyalists claimed that the arrests of the civic magistrates had been intended to provide the pretext for a rising. The attorney general suggested that the conspirators expected loyalists to interfere with Coroner Brome's attempt to serve his warrants. The conspirators hoped, according to the government, that Tory

---

[56] Add. MS 41,803, fol. 55ff.; Journal 50, fols. 83–84; Newdigate L.c. 1361, 1397 (10 April, 3 July 1683); *ST*, X, 324–6, 339, 341–4; Papillon, *Memoirs*, pp. 228–30; *CSPD 1683 (July–Sept.)*, p. 5; *CSPD 1684–5*, p. 200.

[57] Nelson is described as a merchant in his affidavit about the lord mayor's arrest. A dissenting resident of Walbrook of this name, described in the 1690s as a lawyer, eventually became a member of the Council of Bermuda. *CSPD 1683 (Jan.–June)*, p. 204; *Exact Account*; De Krey, "Trade, Religion, and Politics," III, 579.

obstruction of a legal process would throw the Corporation into confusion and provide both the rationale and the opportunity for a rising.[58]

The interpretation is plausible, given both the identity of those behind the arrests, and other events on the evening of 24 April. As news of the lord mayor's seizure spread, the lieutenancy commissioners learned about the gathering in Moorfields and Spitalfields of "a great number of disorderly people" who were thought likely "to make disturbance." What role the Rye House plotters played in this gathering, if any, is unclear, as are the actual size of the crowd and its intentions. Nevertheless, the mobile was gathering near the armoury of the city Artillery Company, the seizure of which had already been discussed within the West cabal. The lieutenancy took the threat to order seriously, raising an entire trained band regiment. One company took up stations outside Skinners' Hall. Coroner Brome subsequently complained that they were there to "terrify him in the execution of his office." Other citizens were reportedly in "an Affrightment" about news that the king's guards were standing by to intervene, if necessary.[59]

In the meantime, the Privy Council had been thrown into session by the paralysis of legal government in the city. The government sent a message to Pritchard at 11:00 p.m. that he should sign a bond for his court appearance in order to secure release. However, Pritchard refused the bond offered to him by Goodenough and Brome when he discovered its failure to designate him as lord mayor. At midnight, the tables were turned on Brome and Goodenough, however. One of the sergeants in the sheriffs' courts arrived to serve a warrant on the coroner for his failure to make an appearance at the Poultry Compter in a prior debt suit against him. When Gilbert Nelson sought to bail the coroner, the lord mayor ordered the sergeant to arrest both Brome and Nelson, who were taken prisoner. Pritchard then left Skinners' Hall, in full state, accompanied by the trained bands and a crowd of supporters who had gathered outside.[60]

But the wrangle about arresting the lord mayor was far from over. On the following day, Pritchard summoned Papillon and Dubois to appear before him and several loyalist aldermen. Bringing a number of other Whig leaders

---

[58] Newdigate L.c. 1368 (26 April 1683); Bulstrode Newsletters, 29 April 1683; Luttrell, I, 256; *Observator*, I, 329, 378 (28 April, 21 July 1683); *CSPD 1683 (Jan.–June)*, pp. 206, 214; *ST*, X, 323, 329–30, 352, 367–8; HMC *Lords 1690–91*, p. 52; North, *Examen*, p. 617.

[59] London Newsletters, VIII, 322 (26 April 1683); Newdigate L.c. 1368 (26 April 1683); Bulstrode Newsletters, 29 April 1683; Luttrell, I, 256; *CSPD 1683 (Jan.–June)*, pp. 206, 215; *ST*, IX, 403–4, and X, 329–30; Sprat, *True Account*, p. 45; Sprat, *Copies*, pp. 40–1; North, *Examen*, p. 617; Roger North, *The Life of the Lord Keeper North*, ed. M. Chen (Lewiston, NY, 1995), pp. 99–100; Greaves, *Secrets*, p. 175.

[60] LC MS 18,124, VIII, 322 (26 April 1683); Newdigate L.c. 1368 (26 April 1683); Bulstrode Newsletters, 29 April 1683; Luttrell, I, 256; *CSPD 1683 (Jan.–June)*, pp. 204, 206, 214–15.

with them, Papillon and Dubois claimed that they had only "given order for [a] process to bring the right of the citizens [to elect them as sheriffs] to a fair trial in a peaceable and quiet way." This answer failed to mollify the Tory magistrates. Some of them now claimed, according to Papillon, that the Whig spokesmen were in league with "prowling fellows" and had intended to "over throw the Government, and cut our throats."

No sooner had Papillon and Dubois been dismissed, than Coroner Brome, now bailed, arrived for a second time with "a rabble" and with an attorney for John Dubois. Intending again to require bail bonds of Pritchard, the coroner was intercepted by the city marshal and a rival loyalist crowd. The coroner and his party retreated at this point, but the matter was quickly before King's Bench, where none other than William Williams appeared to support Brome. Acting again as the legal champion of the civic Whigs, Williams entered actions for Brome against the city marshal and others for obstructing the coroner in his "Legal proceeding" of executing court writs.[61]

"This affair affords variety of talk," noted Luttrell with remarkable understatement.[62] What is to be made of an episode in which leading civic and parliamentary Whigs had become the political agents of other Whigs who were, in fact, seeking to "over throw the government" and to eliminate the king and his civic allies? Curiously, Papillon and Dubois were at the home of Alderman Henry Cornish when they were approached by Goodenough to authorize the new writs;[63] and Henry Cornish had been at the home of Thomas Shepherd, some months earlier, on the same evening that leading Whig grandees had apparently contrived plans for an urban insurrection. Were the Whig leaders merely covering their tracks when they claimed that Goodenough and the coroner had exceeded their instructions? Did they know anything about what Goodenough and his henchmen were already discussing? And what *were* the intentions of the plotters in arresting the lord mayor and his aldermanic brethren?

Unfortunately, these questions cannot be answered conclusively, although a few assertions can be made. All accounts point to Goodenough, rather than to any of the civic Whig leaders, as the prime mover in the lord mayor's arrest. The professed objective of Papillon and Dubois, namely, forcing a legal resolution of their claim to office, was entirely consistent with the public course the civic Whigs had taken since September. Nevertheless, the vigor with which the Whigs were prepared to pursue their legal strategy left them

---

61 Newdigate L.c. 1368 (26 April 1683); Bulstrode Newsletters, 29 April 1683; Papillon, *Memoirs*, pp. 230–1; CSPD 1683 (Jan.–June), pp. 204–6, 215; ST, X, 324; HMC Lords 1690–91, p. 51.
62 Luttrell, I, 256.
63 Papillon, *Memoirs*, p. 228, ST, X, 344. Keeling also claimed that Joseph Ashurst, a member of the prominent Presbyterian family and son-in-law of Henry Cornish, was acting with Goodenough in the arrest of the lord mayor. ST, X, 326; Woodhead, *Rulers*, p. 19.

vulnerable to angry charges about fomenting resistance. Any distinction between law and resistance was clearly lost upon Tory magistrates who perceived the arrest of the lord mayor, whether on legal writs or not, as an attempt to overthrow the government. Roger North subsequently claimed if "the faction had not been timidous the attempt had turned to a right on rebellion."[64] Yet when the government subsequently had reason to search out evidence to link civic Whig leaders like Papillon and Dubois to the Rye House plotters, it either failed to do so or found none. If the action against the lord mayor had brought together some conspirators with William Williams and the civic Whig leaders, only the conspirators were seemingly in on their secret.

But what was their secret? What did the conspirators intend by arresting a lord mayor who they had already determined should be executed for his political crimes? If the West cabal meant to incapacitate the civic regime in order to stage some kind of resistance, the attempt had been poorly managed. Whatever the mood of the crowd near the armoury, the conspirators apparently made no effort to promote rebellion amongst them. And with neither a detailed plan nor the cooperation of the public Whig leadership, they could probably not have staged an insurrection anyway.

Perhaps, however, the intent of these Whig conspirators was less precipitous than the government subsequently claimed. Surely Goodenough and his fellows pursued their writs with some hope that they could force a legal vindication of "the right of the citizens" to elect magistrates of their own choosing. Goodenough and his friends were deliberately publicizing again the most volatile political issue that the city had experienced in the past year. What was more likely to renew the passions of Whig and dissenting citizens than a provocative public reminder that they were governed by magistrates whose claim to office belied the principle of consent? As the city's loyalist common sergeant lamented, "the Whigs have got a great deal of life by this business;"[65] and perhaps that was what Goodenough and his company intended. Whatever their precise plans, they needed to keep Whig spirits alive, both for the sake of recovering the city and to sustain the broader Whig objectives in church and state, whether through rebellion or not.

For his part, Charles was determined that this indignity to his civic magistrates should be "avenged," and the loyalist momentum in the Corporation now accelerated. The common council majority deprived Coroner Brome of his place.[66] An edgy government increased its surveillance of those Londoners whom it regarded as disaffected. And within a few weeks of the furore about the lord mayor, the legal strategy of the Whig leaders collapsed

---

[64] North, *Life*, p. 100; *ST*, X, 334.   [65] *CSPD 1683 (Jan.–June)*, p. 210.
[66] Journal 50, fols. 31, 83–84; Repertory 88, fol. 128; LC MS 18,124, VIII, 322 (26 April 1683); Newdigate L.c. 1397 (3 July 1683); *CSPD 1683 (Jan.–June)*, p. 210; HMC *Lords 1690–91*, p. 51.

in the face of adverse and orchestrated judgments in the Court of King's Bench. Suddenly, Whig hopes for legal remedy in defense of conscience and consent were gone: many citizens confronted, in their minds at least, a stark choice between resistance and accepting "arbitrary rule."

BETWEEN LAW AND RESISTANCE

The attempt to arrest the lord mayor coincided with the ministry's most significant step yet to undermine the Whigs' legal strategy. As the Easter term began, the crown replaced a King's Bench judge thought to have doubts about its *quo warranto* case with a justice loyal to the king's interest.[67] This substitution foreshadowed a series of adverse legal judgments that would bring Whig anger in London to fever pitch once again, renew the rationale for conspiracy, and bring significantly more citizens into resistance schemes.

King's Bench argumentation in the *quo warranto* case resumed on 27 April when Attorney General Sir Robert Sawyer provided six hours of point-by-point, precedent-by-precedent rebuttal to Recorder Treby's previous defense of the charter. Sawyer argued that the liberties of the city rested upon royal donation and that, like any other liberties granted by the crown, they could be seized for abuse. The London petition of January 1681 was such an abuse. Replying for the Corporation, Henry Pollexfen repeated Treby's arguments about the indissolubility of corporations and drew a variety of alarmist conclusions from the *quo warranto*. He claimed that not even the "maddest of times," those of Edward II and Richard II, provided any precedent for the dissolution of a corporation by forfeiture. "The very frame of our government is concerned," he suggested: a judgment against the city could prepare the way for an assault upon corporation charters throughout the realm. In this way, observed one news writer, "the House of Commons might be invaded" through the manipulation of franchises and "the Government destroyed." But Pollexfen's defense failed to impress Lord Chief Justice Saunders who reportedly claimed that, if the arguments made by the Corporation attorneys stood, then "corporations must be immortal ... and be so many commonwealths by themselves independent of the Crown and in defiance to it, whenever they thought convenient."[68]

---

[67] Newdigate L.c. 1365 (19 April 1683); Luttrell, I, 255; Burnet, *History*, II, 347. Lord Chief Justice Sir Francis Pemberton had, a few months earlier, been transferred from King's Bench to Common Pleas to make way for Sir Edmund Saunders. Saunders was thought to be more likely to favor the *quo warranto*: *DNB*, XV, 725, and XVII, 811.

[68] LC MS 18,124, VIII, 333 (1 May 1683); Newdigate L.c. 1370, 1372 (1, 5 May 1683); *ST*, VIII, 1147–1267, esp. 1213, 1240, 1256–7, 1261, 1266; HMC *Egmont*, II, 130–1; *CSPD 1683 (Jan.–June)*, pp. 222–3, 227–8; Levin, *Charter Controversy*, pp. 29–47; Halliday, *Dismembering*, pp. 207–8.

Anxiety among the civic Whigs increased on 8 May when the case against the London "rioters" was heard in King's Bench. After five hours of argumentation, fourteen leading civic Whigs were found guilty, among them Chamberlain Player, Alderman Cornish, conspirator Richard Goodenough, activist Francis Jenks, and former Sheriffs Pilkington, Shute, and Bethel. The judgment was a crushing setback to the party of common hall and of consent. Naming the Whigs, rather than the Tories, as legally culpable in the shrieval election of 1682, the judgment undermined the suits against Sir John Moore and other Tory magistrates on behalf of Papillon and Dubois. Moreover, this result established, contrary to Whig belief, that "the Lord Mayor had power to summons and adjourne or dissolve the common hall and that the Sheriffs had noe right to it." Williams and the other Whig lawyers moved for a stay of judgment; but this appeal eventually failed, and the Whig defendants were fined amounts ranging from £100 to £1,000.[69]

In the meantime, other legal blows rained upon the Whigs. The King's Bench perjury trial of Sir Patience Ward was a rematch between the counsel involved in the *quo warranto* case. Williams, Treby, and Pollexfen were unable to prevail on Ward's behalf against the arguments of the attorney general, the solicitor general, and Sir George Jeffreys. As the king treated the jury, Ward disappeared, reportedly *en route* to a Dutch exile. Legal action against Chamberlain Player was rumored, and reports circulated that scrivener Sir Robert Clayton would be prosecuted for extortion. Hundreds of additional Whig electors were also said to be facing immanent indictments for their roles in the 1682 shrieval contest.

For their part, the loyalist common council majority acted to mollify Charles in the event of an adverse judgment in the *quo warranto*. They reaffirmed the abrogation of offensive by-laws adopted during the civil war and interregnum years, and they endorsed the aldermanic veto over common council proceedings. By a vote of 113 to 78, the common councilmen reacknowledged the mayoral prerogative of naming one of the two sheriffs prior to Midsummer's Day. They provided the lord mayor with the annual right of naming two candidates for chamberlain. In response to these common council initiatives, Lord Mayor Pritchard toasted Alderman Peter Daniel as his choice for sheriff at the annual bridge-house feast.[70]

---

[69] The Whig counsel claimed in a bill of exceptions that the trial was faulty for several reasons including the empaneling of the jury by sheriffs who were principals in the disputed election. LC MS 18,124, VIII, 335–6 (8, 10 May 1683); Newdigate L.c. 1373, 1374, 1387, 1389–90, 1394 (8, 10 May and 9, 16, 19, 26 June 1683); *Observator*, I, 338 (14 May 1683); Luttrell, I, 257, 263; *ST*, IX, 188–298; *The Tryal of . . . for the Riot at Guild-Hall on Midsummer-Day, 1682* (1683); *The Proceedings and Judgment Against the Rioters* (1683).

[70] Journal 50, fols. 31–40; LC MS 18,124, VIII, 337–42, 347 (15, 17, 19, 22, 24, 26 May and 7 June 1683); Newdigate L.c. 1374, 1376, 1378–81, 1384, 1386–7 (10, 15, 19, 22,

This string of reverses for the London Whigs and their lawyers concluded with the King's Bench judgment of 12 June about the *quo warranto*. The judges found for the king, doing so in the absence of the mortally ill chief justice and without a lengthy rationale.[71] But the crown unexpectedly moved to delay having the judgment entered in court: Charles hoped to secure drastic voluntary concessions from common council without revoking the charter. At the behest of the loyalist leaders, common council adopted, in return, an abject petition to the crown, proclaiming the remorse of the citizenry "for the misgovernment of this City." Ironically, the Whigs, who had so frequently resorted to petitioning, now opposed any such petition as acknowledging the legality of an invalid King's Bench judgment.

When Lord Mayor Pritchard and a delegation of Tory common council-men presented their petition to Charles, they learned that the king desired a series of regulations of the Corporation that would curtail its autonomy and limit the electoral freedoms of the citizenry. As Lord Keeper Sir Francis North reportedly informed them, "when an independent commonwealth was setting up it was high time for his majesty to look after himself." The king would, therefore, vet future mayoral choices and select a lord mayor, should the ordinary electoral process not result in a magistrate acceptable to him. Similarly, in the event that the city elected sheriffs not to his liking, the king would name more suitable men. Charles also claimed oversight of elections to the offices of recorder, common sergeant, town clerk, coroner, and steward for the borough of Southwark. The court of aldermen was to be given authority to co-opt a magistrate of their choice for any aldermanic vacancy, should two wardmotes in succession fail to return acceptable candidates. These provisions clearly elevated royal and magisterial prerogatives above the consensual practices of common hall and the wardmotes. Indeed, they envisaged a measure of royal control more extreme than anything considered in 1661 during debates about the Corporation Act. The city was given a few days to submit to these regulations in order to receive a "confirmation" of its revised charter. If the deadline were not met, the king would have the judgment against the charter entered in court.

24, 26 May and 2, 7, 9 June 1683); Bulstrode Newsletters (7 June 1683); Morrice, P, 369; *Observator*, I, 346, 353 (28 May, 9 June 1683); Luttrell, I, 258–9, 260; *Act of Common Council for Regulating the Election of Sheriffs*; *The Proceedings at the Tryal of Sr. Patience Ward Kt.* (1683); *The Alarum: or an Hue-and-Cry after Sir Pa–t W–d* (1683); *ST*, IX, 299–352; R. Ferguson, *Inquiry*, p. 52; HMC *Kenyon*, p. 160; *CSPD 1683 (Jan.–June)*, pp. 259–60; Burnet, *History*, II, 348–9; Henning, *House of Commons*, III, 669.

[71] Lord Chief Justice Saunders, who died shortly thereafter, was reported to have concurred with the judgment. *An Account of the Proceedings to Judgment against the Charter of the City of London...the 12th of this Instant June. Anno. Dom. 1683*; *ST*, VIII, 1264–72; Burnet, *History*, II, 347.

The civic Whigs objected to any agreement to these terms. They maintained that common council could not surrender civic privileges guaranteed by acts of parliament. They claimed that those who voted to surrender charter rights were violating their oaths as freemen; and they threatened legal reprisals. "If the Tories will be so mad-blind as to run out of freedom into slavery, which will bring in Popery, let all those men's names be set down in writing," urged a Whig broadside, so that they might "be branded as traitors." But these arguments did not prevail at the common council of 20 June where, by a vote of 104 commoners to 86, the Corporation agreed to the king's demands. Common council also postponed the customary Midsummer's common hall until mid-July to give the magistrates more time to prepare for civic elections under these new constraints.[72]

Even as the common council agreed to the king's terms, public attention was being redirected to news about the discovery of a conspiracy to raise the city and to kill the king and his brother. The lieutenancy commissioners took extraordinary precautions, and both the militia and regular troops were soon conducting searches for suspected conspirators and their arms. In the first days of excitement about the discovery of Whig plotting, the atmosphere in London seems to have resembled the most anxious times of 1641, 1659–60, and 1678: "The inhabitants... have had orders to be ready with musket, powder, bullet, and match, at half an hours warning," Luttrell recorded. Under these circumstances, the shrieval election was again postponed, this time until September.[73]

The government's slow accumulation of evidence about Whig plotting over the next three months revealed all the conspiratorial episodes that had occurred in London since the 1682 shrieval election. The evidence also suggested that the West cabal had revived serious preparations for an urban insurrection in the second half of May. Historians have paid more attention to the previous conspiratorial episodes of 1682–3 than to the last one, perhaps because the Whig grandees were more visible in the plotting of autumn and winter. Yet the spring 1683 attempt to organize an insurrection was the most detailed scheme of them all, and it greatly enlarged the boundaries of conspiracy in London. Some forty citizens whose names do not previously figure in the records of conspiracy appear to have become actively involved

[72] Journal 50, fols. 81–83; LC MS 18,124, VIII, 349–53 (12, 14, 16, 19, 21 June 1683); Newdigate L.c. 1388–91 (14, 16, 19, 21 June 1683); Morrice, P, 370; *Observator*, I, 362–3 (23, 27 June 1683); Luttrell, I, 261; *The Humble Petition of the Lord Mayor...18th of June 1683*; HMC *Ormonde*, NS, VII, 49–50; *CSPD 1683 (Jan.–June)*, pp. 258–9, 317, 322, 329–30; Evelyn, *Diary*, IV, 319–20; *ST*, VIII, 1273–83; North, *Examen*, 633–5; Levin, *Charter Controversy*, pp. 50–1.

[73] Journal 50, fols. 83–84; LC MS 18,124, VIII, 354, 360 (23 June, 17 July 1683); Newdigate L.c. 1392, 1394, 1397, 1403 (23, 26 June; 3, 17 July 1683); Luttrell, I, 263–4; *CSPD 1683 (July–Sept.)*, pp. 101–2, 164.

in May and June or to have been approached by members of the West circle. Obscure for the most part, their very obscurity gives their shared story additional interest: the insurrection that Josiah Keeling's revelations thwarted would have been an insurrection of the common man. But how would it have occurred?

The failure of the April attempt to arrest the lord mayor had demonstrated the necessity of careful planning for any serious extra-constitutional action. With this need in mind, the West group divided London into twenty districts for the raising of a rebel force. A leader was to be appointed for each district with the responsibility of selecting ten lieutenants, each of whom would recruit an additional fifteen men. Richard Goodenough, who had spearheaded the attempt upon the lord mayor, was assigned the principal responsibility for recruiting the district leaders. Zachary Bourne assisted him in this task. Bourne was a Cripplegate brewer who had provided lodging for Robert Ferguson and had delivered letters between Ferguson and Thomas Shepherd. Bourne and Goodenough's clerk also apparently approached members of some Independent and Baptist churches. Josiah Keeling and Thomas Lea, a Baptist dyer of Old Street, who were appointed district leaders, recruited additional men. As the command for a rebel army began to take shape, Goodenough and Bristol lawyer Nathaniel Wade prepared a new draft of their objectives. They also re-established contacts with disaffected dissenters in the West and hoped for leadership from Monmouth. But as the circle of conspiracy widened, so did the insecurity and exposure of those who knew the most. By mid-June, an anxious Josiah Keeling, fearing for his life, had offered his first disclosures to Secretary Jenkins in return for a pardon.[74]

Why so many Londoners had become susceptible to the arguments of committed conspirators at this point is quite clear. The law had proved to be a weak reed in the hands of judges who bent justice for the sake of royal policy. The judgments against the city "rioters" and against the charter frightened many citizens. The historic Corporation with all its liberties and privileges had, in the words of one conspirator, been reduced to "a large village."[75] The principle of consent in civic politics had been undermined. The judgment against Sir Patience Ward and the rumors that other civic figures would be prosecuted for various offenses suggested that Whig lives and properties were no longer secure. The continued harassment of dissenters suggested that the Reformation itself was in peril. If the London Whigs had been poised between law and resistance before the legal judgments of spring 1683, some of them now perceived a more clear-cut situation. The difference

[74] BL Harleian MS 6845, fol. 268; Sprat, *Copies*, pp. 38, 50–4; *ST*, IX, 401, 413–19; *CSPD 1683 (July–Sept.)*, pp. 40–1, 70, 235–6, 321, 333, 336, 345; Ashcraft, *Revolutionary Politics*, pp. 367–70; Greaves, *Secrets*, pp. 178–87.
[75] *CSPD 1683 (Jan.–June)*, p. 314.

between law and resistance, never as fine in practice as in theory, dissolved in the minds of some into an angry impetus for any action that defended law and liberty.

But what were the thoughts of those who became embroiled in conspiracy in the last weeks before its discovery? The language of conspiracy remained opaque and elliptical. Some of those who agreed to the "undertaking" were uncertain about exactly what that undertaking entailed, other than protecting Protestantism, property, and liberty. The plot-masters paid more attention, in recruiting new men, to the recent Whig disappointments than to the ultimate goals of insurrection and/or regicide.

Goodenough, for instance, drew in artisans and tradesmen by appealing to their civic concerns. He had previously told Josiah Keeling that the "citizens of London... were like to be in slavery" without their charter, and Keeling identified his own purpose as being to "save the charter and the nation." Responding to Goodenough's suggestion "that our rights and privileges were invaded," Thomas Lea discoursed with others whom he recruited "about the loss of the City Charter" and the threat to the liberties of the citizens. He told John Noyes, a Cheapside draper, that since "there was an invasion of their liberties and properties," it would be well if Londoners confronted the king "with their swords in their hands" and "demanded" their rights. Since such angry language had circulated among civic Whigs before, Noyes may not have understood that Lea's words signaled the actual organization of a rebellion. Similarly, Clerkenwell barber-surgeon Nathaniel Brown subsequently denied to the Privy Council that he knew of "any design against the King." Rather, Brown believed, he had joined "an undertaking to retrieve the rights and privileges," language that covered a multitude of actions without naming any of them. Likewise, brewer Edward Cole was told to be "ready with person or purse" to counter a "French invasion." He only gradually realized that coded discussion about "taking" the goldfinch and blackbird referred to the king and his brother.[76]

Detected in the process of its development, this last conspiracy of 1682–3 was, then, still forming in the minds of those who were drawn into it. The language that circulated within the expanding circle of plotters was often ambiguous, and those apprehended offered conflicting recollections of who said what to whom. Yet, some new men were clearly grasping hands with those committed to regicide, perhaps without fully comprehending where their actions on behalf of rights and privileges might lead them.

Captain Thomas Walcott later emphasized the "largeness of communicating the design" at this time, and Robert West confessed that "a great number

[76] Add. MS 38,847, fol. 117; Sprat, *Copies*, pp. 1, 3, 10, 25, 29; *ST*, IX, 365, 368, 374, 391; *CSPD 1683 (July–Sept.)*, pp. 4, 128, 146, 155, 163, 348, 359, 389; Sprat, *True Account*, p. 43; Ashcraft, *Revolutionary Politics*, pp. 394–5.

of people" knew something of it. But who were the people who stumbled, in reaction or anger, into conspiracy in May and June 1683? Most of those drawn into the conspiracy in its final weeks appear to have been ordinary Londoners, *menu peuple* on the margins of the historical record. "The King is betrayed by his little people," lamented L'Estrange, when news of the first revelations broke.[77] Still, as conspiratorial talk and violent rhetoric spread within the overlapping circles of friends, tavern acquaintances, and business partners of those within the West cabal, it began to expand socially as well. By the time of Keeling's revelations, knowledge of some design afoot had clearly spread – and probably for the first time – from West End legal activists and East End mechanics into the ranks of the middling sort and into all the Whig spaces within the city.

Individuals in the drinks and victualling trades – including five brewers, a distiller, and a maltster – were among those now approached by the West cabal. As large employers of both skilled and unskilled workers, these men had valuable contacts and influence within the London plebs. And the pubs they supplied were easily converted into chambers of intrigue. Several other new men were in the cloth and clothing trades. Some of these, like Spitalfields weaver James Wood, "who never had £5 of his own," were quite poor. But others contacted now were more substantial men, as might be expected from the strategy of recruiting district leaders with the capability of raising other men. Joseph Helby, who said "he would not meddle in it," when approached by Josiah Keeling, had until recently been carver to the king's ships. A former constable of Mile End Green, Helby was also considered to be "a very rich man." Crispe Grainge, a brewer of Millbank, Westminster, had reportedly agreed to "be free of his purse" and was said to be able to raise several hundred men. He put up his own bail of £2,000. Hounsditch goldsmith Peter Essington and Aldgate draper Samuel Mayne were instrumental, after the disclosure of the plot, in providing secret refuge to Ayloffe and Goodenough. Essington and Mayne were substantial citizens, if not prominent ones: Essington had been picked for John Rouse's 1681 jury, and Mayne had been empaneled for Stephen College's London trial.[78]

If the social status of some of those approached at this time was superior to that of the assassins chosen the previous winter, their residences were also less concentrated in the East End. One-third (twelve) of the new

[77] Add. MS 38,847, fols. 91–92; *Speeches of Walcot, Rouse, and Hone*, p. 1; *CSPD 1683 (Jan.–June)*, pp. 184–5, 336; *CSPD 1683 (July–Sept.)*, p. 155; Ashcraft, *Revolutionary Politics*, pp. 402–3.

[78] BL Egerton MS 2543, fol. 251; SP 29/431/68, 29/432/100; Newdigate L.c. 1367 (24 April 1683); Sprat, *Copies*, pp. 3, 52, 56; *ST*, IX, 368, 415–16, 423; *CSPD 1683 (Jan.–June)*, pp. 219–20; *CSPD 1683 (July–Sept.)*, pp. 4, 41–2, 268–9, 313, 339, 349, 421–2; *CSPD 1683–4*, p. 71.

men whose addresses are known were from Wapping, Whitechapel, Stepney, Spitalfields and adjacent eastern neighborhoods. But another third (eleven) were from the northern wards of Aldersgate Without and Cripplegate Without, one of the principal Whig spaces in the Corporation. Indeed, some from Aldersgate Without, like glazier John Atherton, were former neighbors of Lord Shaftesbury and were the sort of people to whom the earl might have turned for assistance in autumn 1682.[79] Eight new conspirators or potential conspirators were from within the walls, including six from the retail and commercial concentrations around Cheapside, Threadneedle Street, Cornhill, and the Exchange. The Whig center was still under-represented in the conspiracy in proportion to its importance within the broader Whig movement, but the conspiracy was clearly spreading more deeply into the variety of locales from which the civic opposition had long been drawn.

The most pronounced characteristic of those drawn toward or invited into conspiracy in May and June 1683, however, was religious dissent. These were men who had, in recent months, experienced the coercion of their religious practices. Zachary Bourne, for instance, was said recently to have exchanged conventicles for the West End preaching of Gilbert Burnet. But Bourne's closest clerical friendships were with the Independents Stephen Lobb and Matthew Mead, who probably knew something about the plotting. After Keeling's disclosures, Mead was apprehended in flight with Bourne. Similarly, Cripplegate suspects Charles Bateman and John Whitby were promoters of reformed ministry within St Giles's parish. But each man had also attended conventicles, and staunch Anglicans objected to their parish involvement.[80]

The conspiracy had, then, clearly reached into the fluid Reformed Protestant boundary between the church and dissent; and it also extended, in the other direction, through the urban gathered churches into the hard core of sectarian enthusiasts. Joseph Helby, who was Matthew Mead's son-in-law, was also a lay leader of Mead's gathered church and had lost his position as constable for claiming that the conventicle laws were "against the Lawes of Jesus Christ." Aldersgate suspects John Armiger, John Atherton, Captain Thomas Bourne (Zachary Bourne's father), and William Thomas had all been previously reported to the government as irreconcilable dissenters. Like Josiah Keeling, Crispe Grainge and tobacconist Joseph Hickes were Baptists. So was James Wood, who said he "own[ed] the Sabbath day" and was "of Dr [Peter] Chamberlaine's religion." The most extreme sectary approached

---

[79] SP 29/421/160, 29/425/138/48; *CSPD 1683 (Jan.–June)*, p. 383; *CSPD 1683 (July–Sept.)*, pp. 91, 374; Greaves, *Secrets*, p. 183.

[80] SP 44/60/11; CLRO Conventicles Box 2, MS 6 (9 May 1683); *CSPD 1683 (Jan.–June)*, p. 371; *CSPD 1683 (July–Sept.)*, pp. 14–15, 63, 348; *CSPD 1683–84*, p. 358; Sprat, *Copies*, pp. 50–4; *ST*, IX, 413–19; Goldie and Spurr, "Politics," pp. 589, 591.

at this point may have been John Patshall, a "decrepit" brewer's clerk of Southwark, a Fifth Monarchist, and reputedly a drummer in Thomas Venner's 1661 rising.[81]

As knowledge of a conspiracy of some kind spread, it may also have passed via Zachary Bourne, John Rouse, and other intermediaries into the Bishopsgate Baptist club of Major John Gladman and into the congregation of Stephen Lobb. Suggested by the sources rather than firmly established, these connections are nevertheless consistent with the observed pattern of conspiratorial enlargement within overlapping circles of militant separatists. John Gladman's Bishopsgate Baptist friends included many with records of opposition to religious coercion. Gladman himself had once been a New Model agitator. Stephen Lobb's Fetter Lane congregation, made up "of poor zealous men," was said to have been confident that "their day is coming" and that their persecutors, including the royal brothers, would "soon be cut down."[82]

For men such as these, liberty of conscience was as much a goal of the conspiracy as the recovery of civic and parliamentary rights. Zachary Bourne recalled that establishing liberty of conscience was one of five objectives outlined by West and Wade, at this point, for Monmouth's approval. Thomas Lea told others "it was madness to pull down a government" alone, for "more ease . . . and freedom in worship" was also required. Thomas Walcott was speaking for many when he indicated, from the scaffold, that he had acted because of the necessity of "standing for liberty of conscience."[83]

The vast majority of London dissenters knew nothing about the latest conspiracy before the disclosures of Josiah Keeling, of course. Many of them were as shocked by the violent objectives of the plotters as were their Anglican neighbors. And Presbyterians, the most prominent Reformed Protestants, were almost entirely absent from the expanding ranks of urban conspiracy in May 1683. Nevertheless, the political language of reformation that Reformed Protestants shared with sectarians had, under the right circumstances, lent itself to the popular justification of resistance. That this

[81] SP 29/421/160, 29/425/180; PRO PROB 11: 453 Pott, qu 192 (Mead); CLRO Sessions File 319, Recognizance 7 (30 June 1684); Newdigate L.c. 1367 (24 April 1683); Morrice, P, 394; *CSPD 1683 (Jan.–June)*, pp. 104, 184, 219–20; *CSPD 1683 (July–Sept.)*, p. 4; Sprat, *Copies*, pp. 26, 41; *ST*, IX, 389, 404; Greaves, *Secrets*, p. 183.

[82] Gladman, a kinsman of Richard Rumbold, and his partner were actually manufacturing armor that may have been destined for the disaffected Scotsmen with whom they were also in communication. Sprat, *Copies*, pp. 61–2; *ST*, IX, 426–7; *CSPD 1682*, p. 496; *CSPD 1683 (Jan.–June)*, pp. 103–4, 184–5, 360; *CSPD 1683 (July–Sept.)*, pp. 30, 39–40, 47, 57, 321, 324–5, 355–6, 368–9; *CSPD 1685*, p. 168; Sprat, *True Account*, p. 81; *BDBR*, II, 11; Ashcraft, *Revolutionary Politics*, p. 369 and n.; Greaves, *Secrets*, pp. 85, 180–2.

[83] Sprat, *Copies*, p. 53; *Speeches of Walcot, Rouse, and Hone*, pp. 2, 7; *ST*, IX, 416, *CSPD 1683 (Jan.–June)*, p. 383; *CSPD 1683 (July–Sept.)*, pp. 40, 42, 154, 164; Greaves, *Secrets*, pp. 184–5.

was so should not be surprising, given the circulation of resistance language within English Reformed Protestantism before 1660, and given the rearticulation of that language by some leading advocates of conscience in the kingdom's ongoing crisis. Presbyterian citizens may not have been prepared to act against the government, but their language prepared others for such action.

Some leading conspirators in the winter and spring of 1682–3 were also republicans. Indeed, Monmouth's misgivings about the West cabal were a reaction to the commonwealth commitments of its leaders. And for their part, men like West and Ayloffe worried about attacking the king and his brother unless they had Monmouth's agreement to an acceptable format for resettlement of the state.[84] Additional evidence connecting lesser London conspirators to republican ideas or to the republican past is also not hard to find. Dyer Thomas Lea reported that John Patshall and Francis Eades had insisted, in their tavern talk, "they would not fight to pull down a government and set up the same." Patshall also reportedly asserted, in reference to Monmouth, that "they would have no more of the blood, they had too much of them already." Instead, "they would have a government as they pleased when the sword was in their hand." Thomas Bourne had been a London common councilman in the commonwealth years, and Samuel Mayne's father had served as one of the judges in the trial of Charles I. A number of older individuals within the conspiracy or on its periphery had been New Model officers.[85]

Republicanism was, nevertheless, not what drew the conspirators together, and it was not a dominant principle of selection as the conspiracy expanded. Thomas Lea believed "two-thirds [of the plotters] are for the Duke of Monmouth, others for a commonwealth."[86] Actual and potential conspirators were drawn together less by any commonwealth commitments than by what they perceived as an arbitrary alteration of the government and a whole-scale violation of the law. When Sidney and West happened to meet in the autumn of 1682, for instance, their conversation was not about the republican perspectives they shared. Instead, according to West, they discussed the declaration of Pritchard as Lord Mayor of London, "though not duly chosen," as a sign of how the nation would be "inslaved" unless care was not taken.[87] Apparent republican utterances were also sometimes less explicitly republican than they may appear. John Patshall's reputed rejection of Stuart monarchy, for example, was more expressive of his Fifth Monarchist

---

[84] Greaves, *Secrets*, pp. 142, 144, 149, 184–5; Scott, *Restoration Crisis*, esp. pp. 169, 173. Monmouth also had to confront republicanism within the circle of peers and grandees who had conspired with him: Grey, *Secret History*, pp. 53, 62–5.

[85] *CSPD 1683–4*, p. 77; Woodhead, *Rulers*, p. 35; *BDBR*, II, 231–2; *DNB*, XIII, 166–7.

[86] *CSPD 1683 (July–Sept.)*, p. 48.   [87] Sprat, *Copies*, p. 56; *ST*, IX, 421.

heritage than of any republican principles that he shared with men like West and Sidney. Republicanism was a political language that was spoken by some London dissenters; but among these conspirators, it was less pronounced than the discourse of conscience and consent.

Finally, since the conspiracy enlarged in May and June 1683 along dissenting family, business, and congregational ties within the London Whig movement, connections between the chief plotters and the civic Whig leaders need to be considered. The government was certainly interested in detecting any such connections. Thomas Papillon's house was searched in the early days of the Rye House plot paranoia; and with good reason, given that Goodenough had been an attorney acting upon his behalf. Sir Thomas Player was disarmed; and the home of Baptist doyen William Kiffin was searched. Additional evidence against leading civic Whigs and grandees was expected from Lord William Howard, who received preferential treatment after his arrest.[88]

Suggestive acquaintances between Whig leaders and plot principals are not, in fact, hard to find. The absconded Sir Patience Ward, for instance, was discovered hiding, in late June, in the home of conspirator Charles Bateman. That Ward was hiding with a designated district leader of the London uprising is more than a bit curious. He could have been safely in exile in the Netherlands, where he soon found refuge. Three different conspirators also implicated Whig activist Francis Jenks. He was said to have long favored assassination and to have been involved with Goodenough, Ayloffe and others in drawing up a justification for it. Thomas Lea claimed that John Jekyll, active in civic opposition since 1670, had met with Goodenough during the hatching of the conspiracy. Former Sheriff Samuel Shute, a defendant in the city riot case – a status he shared with conspirators Lord Grey and Richard Goodenough – also may have known that something was afoot.[89]

Despite this evidence, and despite the enlargement of the plot, most leading London Whigs appear, however, to have adopted a circumspect posture after the collapse of their legal strategy. Accustomed to pursuing their cause through elections, petitions, the prints, the courts, and the institutions of Corporation government, they had not yet endorsed extra-legal actions. Only in the case of Francis Jenks did the government find evidence that invited immediate investigation. And among the Whig magistrates, only Alderman

[88] L'Estrange expected Howard to incriminate such Whig leaders as Aldermen Clayton and Cornish and Recorder Treby. SP 29/425/43; Newdigate L.c. 1401 (12 July 1683); *CSPD 1683 (July–Sept.)*, pp. 83, 117; Joseph Ivimey, *The Life of Mr. William Kiffin* (1833), p. 61.

[89] BL Harleian MS 6845, fol. 267; Newdigate L.c. 1395, 1398 (28 June, 5 July 1683); Sprat, *Copies*, pp. 26, 30, 32; *CSPD 1683 (July–Sept.)*, pp. 5, 11–12, 71, 98, 221–2, 237; *ST*, IX, 388–9, 392, 394, and XI, 471–2.

Cornish was prosecuted for alleged involvement in plotting; but this prosecution was not initiated until after Monmouth's failed rebellion of 1685.

Jenks, who had long displayed his potential as a political provocateur, admitted to a seven-year acquaintanceship with Goodenough. Questioned before the Privy Council, Jenks did not deny knowledge of the conspiracy; but he also claimed, "what he has done was concerning the rights of the city and that he shunned *everything else.*" Jenks seemed, in other words, to make a distinction between the public Whig legal course that he had pursued with other leaders and the private conspiratorial strategy. Additional evidence points to impatience and estrangement between those driving the conspiracy and old Whig hands like Jenks. One informer reported in April, before the conspiracy broke, that "fanaticks" like Patshall and Hone were suspicious of Jenks, in particular, as too much "a politician."[90]

Among the Whig aldermen, Cornish had rivaled Thomas Pilkington in his outspoken suspicions about James, Charles, and the Court. The government's 1685 case against him rested in part upon Cornish's alleged presence at the November 1682 Whig conclave at Thomas Shepherd's house. But Cornish's conviction was also secured through the testimony of Goodenough, who had been pardoned after Monmouth's Rebellion in return for his evidence. Goodenough claimed to have visited Cornish, in the privacy of the latter's home, in Easter term 1683, at the time when "every thing [was] going against us." Goodenough testified that he had proposed to Cornish, whom he had previously served as under-sheriff, that "*now the law will not defend us . . .* some other way is to be thought on." When Cornish showed interest, observing that "the city is so unready, and the country so ready," Goodenough told him about the plans of the conspirators to assault the Tower. To this, Cornish reportedly agreed, "I will do what I can, or what good I can."[91]

Whatever their accuracy, Goodenough's recollections actually suggest, however, that magisterial Whigs and conspiratorial Whigs were as much talking past each other in May and June 1683 as they were talking to each other. They were bound together by a common cause: Cornish was a Whig lord mayor presumptive, should the conspiracy succeed; and Goodenough was an attorney for the men whom the Whigs recognized as the legitimate sheriffs of London and Middlesex. Yet Goodenough revealed that Cornish and he had been committed to different strategies for preserving civic rights before the legal disasters of Easter term 1683. Even the language in which Goodenough reported his overture to Cornish and Cornish's replies suggest the two men's distrust for one another. Considered as a whole, the Whig

---

[90] *CSPD 1683 (Jan.–June)*, pp. 184–5; *CSPD 1683 (July–Sept.)*, p. 79. (My italics.)
[91] *ST*, XI, 426–8. (My italics.)

movement was divided still between law and resistance, between the courts and the streets, and between those who were "ready" for resistance and those who were not.

Conspirators like Goodenough were also wary of leaders like Cornish because the cautious Whig legal strategy had, from their perspective, made decisive action even more necessary now than before. The wariness that prevented an understanding between Cornish and Goodenough, on a personal level, may be indicative of an emerging distrust on the part of sectarian plotters for the civic Whig leaders. "Nothing was to be expected from the Rich Old Citizens," Robert Ferguson supposedly informed Zachary Bourne, "and therefore half-a-dozen of them must be... Hang'd on their Sign Posts, and their Houses given as Plunder to the Mobile."[92] The effectiveness of the London Whig movement had always rested upon the cooperation of men drawn from a social spectrum that extended from peers of the realm and merchant princes to assertive mechanics like Josiah Keeling and Stephen College. But confronted with a choice between law and resistance, most Whig merchants and traders do not appear to have been eager, contrary to the jibes of their opponents, to retrace the political courses of the 1640s. Instead, the division between prosperous Reformed Protestants, especially Presbyterians, and sectarian and republican enthusiasts of lesser rank, that had contributed to the collapse of the revived commonwealth in 1659–60, seems again apparent in the alternate Whig strategies of 1682–3.

THE LOSS OF THE CHARTER

The London Whigs were left politically paralyzed and on the defensive by their division between law and resistance after the summer of 1683. One strategy had collapsed in the courts. The other strategy was exposed in the government's unraveling of Whig conspiracy and in the first plot trials of July 1683. "The partymen... about the town were crestfallen," Roger North remembered. In fact, the breaking of the plot left London dissenters more exposed to Anglican loyalist reprisals than at any time since 1662. And just as the great 1659–60 fear of the fanatics had helped destroy the revived commonwealth in favor of the restoration of monarchy, so Anglican royalists now eagerly anticipated that a "second Restoration" of church and state would rise above the ruins of faction and enthusiasm. The loyalist London aldermen and urban JPs increased their actions against conventicles and the dissenting clergy. Luttrell noted in September 1683 that, for the previous two months, "the pulpits... have been busied with nothing but discourses against the dissenters." As the government massaged the evidence about

[92] Sprat, *Copies*, p. 52; *ST*, IX, 417; Sprat, *True Account*, p. 44.

treason for maximum public effect, a flood of loyal addresses accompanied vigorous local actions against dissenters in other localities as well.[93]

When common hall finally assembled on 5 September, for the first time in almost a year, for the twice-delayed mid-summer elections, loyalism easily prevailed. Sir Thomas Player was removed as chamberlain and replaced by a loyalist deputy alderman. Alderman Peter Daniel was confirmed as sheriff, having been previously picked by Lord Mayor Pritchard; and Samuel Dashwood, another loyalist, was chosen as Daniel's colleague. Secretary Jenkins was pleased that the "good order and gravity" of the occasion "equalled the examples of the best of times." Another observer, however, attributed the results to "the whigg party not appearing" at the hall.[94]

In fact, Jenkins and his fellow ministers were about to learn that the spirit of opposition in the city was still far from eradicated. The government and its loyalist allies had recovered control of the city and intimidated the opposition; but they had not eradicated the Whig-dissenting community that dominated particular spaces in London and that had sustained Reformed Protestant and opposition discourse for two generations. Moreover, the Whigs showed signs of renewed political life when the government required the Corporation's assent to a document incorporating the regulations that common council had agreed to in June. Even leading Tories now discovered that their consent to regulation of the Corporation was more complicated than they originally thought. The instrument to alter the Corporation's government drawn up by the attorney general actually required the city to surrender the charter in the expectation of its being regranted by the king with the necessary regulations.

Surrendering the charter to the king was widely perceived as a quite different matter from surrendering the ultimate choice for major offices. The attorney general's procedure seemed to confirm Whig warnings: the freemen would be betrayed by their own representatives if common council voted to give up "their Customes and Priviledges." Several loyalist aldermen, including Sir John Moore, were said to oppose the instrument of surrender. After an aldermanic delegation to Westminster failed to alter the crown's demands, common council appointed a committee of aldermen and commoners, including a few Whigs to consult with counsel. Charles was so concerned that he declined to attend a Lieutenancy feast and put off his departure for

---

[93] Newdigate L.c. 1415, 1419 (3, 17 July and 9, 16 Aug. 1683); Luttrell, I, 278; North, *Life*, p. 101; Harth, *Pen*, p. 213.

[94] Loyalists also took heart at the number of bonfires and at the popular rejoicing on 9 September, a day of public thanksgiving for the king's escape from the "fanatick conspiracy." Journal 50, fol. 84; Repertory 88, fol. 173; LC MS 18,124, VIII, 383–4 (6, 11 Sept. 1683); Newdigate L.c. 1429–30, 1433–4 (6 [*bis*], 13 [*bis*] Sept. 1683); *Observator*, I, 401 (10 Sept. 1683); Luttrell, I, 278–9; *An Impartial Account of the Proceedings at Guildhall ... 5th ... September, 1683*; *CSPD 1683 (July–Sept.)*, pp. 369, 373–4.

Newmarket. When the new sheriffs appeared at the Exchequer Court for the customary royal approbation on 1 October, the king refused, for the time being, to permit their installation. The common hall election of Sir William Pritchard's successor as lord mayor was also postponed, by the king's command, until the situation was clarified.[95]

A year after the supposed recovery of the city by the crown, then, the Corporation and the government remained at loggerheads. Recorder Treby, who had defended the charter before King's Bench, played an important role in creating this new impasse. Acceptance of the instrument for surrender constituted a voluntary dissolution of the Corporation, he maintained: such an action would leave all who had voted for it open to lawsuits from the dissolved Corporation's creditors. Although Treby was unsuccessful in persuading the new civic committee to consult with other Whig lawyers of note, including William Williams, he and Henry Pollexfen were among those who guided its work.

When the committee reported to common council on 2 October, Treby's views prevailed against the advice of the attorney general and the solicitor general. He maintained that in a voluntary surrender, the citizens would "lose all their customes" and electoral rights, through their own act. But if King's Bench declared the charter forfeit, as the government threatened to ensure, such a declaration could subsequently be reversed, according to Treby, through a writ of error. Moreover, the principle of consent, upon which the authority of the magistracy rested, would be destroyed along with the Corporation itself, if common council agreed to a voluntary dissolution. "The whole frame of the Government of London is Altered and Given from the City," was Treby's judgment about the crown's legal instrument: "Kings will . . . prefer one man before another to these Offices, and it will be vain and lost labour in the Citizens to Choose any other."[96]

Treby's arguments prevailed at a court of common council that continued from 4:00 in the afternoon until 11:00 at night. After much "high and sharp debate," common council declined, by a majority of 103 to 85, to seal the attorney general's instrument for a surrender of the charter. Some Tories claimed this meeting was a "surprize" that had left many of their fellows absent from their places. But the result could not have been achieved without some loyalist votes against the surrender. Still, the Duke of York and other courtiers blamed the result on Treby and his party. The Whigs were said to

[95] Journal 50, fol. 95; LC MS 18,124, VIII, 390 (27 Sept. 1683); Newdigate L.c. 1441, 1443–4 (27, 29 Sept. and 2 Oct. 1683); Morrice, P, 376; *The Proceedings upon the Debates, relating to the late Charter of the City of London* (1683); *CSPD 1683 (July–Sept.)*, pp. 424, 427.

[96] Journal 50, fol. 99.

have been present in "great numbers" and to have been as "insolent" as at "any time these three years."[97]

The 2 October 1683 meeting of common council proved to be its last before the collapse of James II's regime five years later. The crown responded to the common council vote by causing the judgment against the Corporation to be entered in King's Bench. The charter was thereby forfeited, and the government of the city was seized by the king. "The pomp and grandeur of the most august city in the world changed face in a moment," recorded Evelyn. According to another observer, some civic Whigs regarded Charles's actions as a sort of victory: they had forced the king and the London loyalists into another public display of their disregard for the historic rights of the citizenry. But all "prudent men," thought Evelyn, "were for the old foundations." The king's actions had sobered even his friends.

Charles proceeded to authorize commissioners to govern the city on his behalf. But showing some sensitivity, he also replicated, as much as possible, the institutions of the late Corporation. Commissions were issued to Lord Mayor Pritchard, to the sheriffs elected in September, and to all the loyalist aldermen to hold their places at the king's pleasure and to serve as city JPs. Treby's place as recorder was granted to a loyalist attorney. Eight new loyalists were commissioned to take the place of the Whig aldermen, whose authority lapsed with the forfeiture of the charter. On 29 October, Sir Henry Tulse, the senior alderman below the chair, assumed the mayoralty from Pritchard, again through a royal commission and without any meeting of common hall. Although neither pageants nor a royal visit to the city were part of Tulse's installation, an effort was made to observe other customary formalities. But a plan to honor the new lord mayor with a loyal skimmington was discarded. Effigies of the replaced Whig aldermen were to have been ridden upon "Asses, with their faces backward, through the City." Such public ridicule of the city's leading Reformed Protestants was abandoned, however: perhaps it was thought too provocative a gesture so close to the popular anti-Catholic holiday of 5 November.[98]

---

[97] Journal 50, fols. 96–100; LC MS 18,124, VIII, 391 (2 Oct. 1683); Newdigate L.c. 1443, 1445–6 (29 Sept.; 4 Oct. [*bis*] 1683); Morrice, P, 376–7; *Proceedings upon the Debates*; Luttrell, I, 282; HMC *Graham*, p. 366; HMC *Dartmouth*, III, 125; HMC *Lords 1690–91*, pp. 50, 52; *CSPD 1683–4*, p. 13; Burnet, *History*, II, 396; Levin, *Charter Controversy*, pp. 53–4.

[98] Lesser officers were generally confirmed in their places, but only after the records of recent polls were examined for their political behavior. Repertory 88, fols. 184–185, 188; LC MS 18,124, VIII, 396–7, 404 (16, 18, 30 Oct. 1683); Newdigate L.c. 1440, 1445, 1447–8, 1451, 1453, 1455, 1458 (25 Sept.; 4, 6, 9, 13, 20 Oct.; and 1 Nov. 1683); Morrice, P, 384; Luttrell, I, 283, 285–6; Evelyn, *Diary*, IV, 342–3; HMC *Graham*, pp. 366–7; HMC *Dartmouth*, I, 95–6; *CSPD 1683–4*, pp. 10, 13, 16, 34, 45, 54, 56–7.

The "second Restoration" upon which Charles and the Anglican loyalists now embarked was profoundly different from the settlement of the early 1660s. In 1659–60, the belligerent response of London citizens to what they perceived as a coercive regime that intruded upon their charter and their right freely to choose MPs had contributed significantly to the collapse of the revived commonwealth. Reformed Protestants as well as Anglicans had then worked in London to restore Stuart monarchy as a necessary preservative for parliament, for electoral rights, for the Corporation's charter, and for a comprehensive parochial religious order. But now, reacting to the same Corporation that had played such a critical role in restoring his throne, Charles II had embarked upon a new political course. Celebrated by Anglicans, this manner of government was one that could not appeal to Whigs and dissenters. Many of them or their predecessors had acted in 1659–60 to re-establish the rule of law; but the new settlement that Charles now pursued seemed to them to subordinate law, parliament, chartered and electoral rights, the courts, and Protestantism itself to arbitrary regimes in church and state. Ironically, many London citizens now experienced from Charles II what they had feared, in 1659, at the hands of the Rump; and no amount of loyalist rationalization could obscure that fact.

CONCLUSION
LONDON AND THE END
OF THE RESTORATION

HISTORY: SETTLEMENT AND UNSETTLEMENT

The history of the last eighteen months of Charles II's reign is better considered with that of James II, who shared his brother's new manner of government. After 1683, they together sustained the most comprehensive effort the crown had ever undertaken to manage the localities, and by managing the localities, to manage parliament as well. Charles's abridgement of London's historic autonomy was but the first dramatic step in this initiative. What was intended was a new settlement of church and state, one that would prevent any repetition of the crisis that had just been weathered.

The means to resettlement were a mix of the old and the new. The proscription from local office-holding of those outside the church had been an Anglican loyalist goal since 1661. But the regranting of borough and guild charters that strengthened royal and magisterial authority and that purged companies, corporations, and electorates of many Whigs and dissenters was more drastic than anything attempted in 1662–3. The active persecution of dissenters for the sake of a comprehensive church and of a confessional state also revived older initiatives. What was different was the determination of the episcopal establishment rigorously to apply the coercive policies of the 1660s to the quite different circumstances of the 1680s. Two decades earlier, Reformed Protestants were still reeling from the unexpected disasters of 1660–62 and were reluctant to separate from parish communities they had so recently dominated. By 1682–3, however, the church was seeking to apply the coercive strictures of the 1660s to dissenting communities that had developed their own structures, identities, and histories.

While recognizing that the regime of 1683–8 was fundamentally different from that of 1660–83, historians have shied away in recent years from defining the difference according to anything like the classic Whig construction of "arbitrary government." Instead, influenced by the contemporary example of Louis XIV, and conceptually determined to avoid whiggish assumptions about the inevitability of 1688–9, many scholars have emphasized the potential for success of the new manner of government that Charles initiated. According to this way of thinking, Charles's burgeoning customs revenues and his French subsidies freed him from the need for parliamentary supply. His remodeling of the boroughs occurred with the active support of local Anglican elites. Contrary to the Whigs, Charles's Anglican supporters and the courts understood his new manner of government to be within the law; and the Anglican principles of passive obedience and non-resistance reinforced his authority.[1] The dissenting minority was cowed; and the Whigs – whether they were a party or not – were "crushed" or drastically reduced in numbers, spirit, and the capacity to cause trouble. James II quietly succeeded in February 1685. Both the successful remodeling of the boroughs and Monmouth's disastrously ineffective rebellion produced a cooperative parliament for him later in the year. James's subsequent demise could not have been predicted from the circumstances of his succession. Instead, it was largely produced by his own mistakes, and especially by his abandonment of the Anglican loyalist majority for a toleration that appealed only to minorities on the religious extremes.

Yet one recent study of seventeenth-century English political instability has rejected this interpretation, insisting instead that the state remained "fragile" upon the death of Charles II.[2] And the history of Restoration London suggests that Charles's return to religious coercion and his centralized management of the localities had greater potential for unsettling the kingdom than for settling it. Like the republican regime of 1659–60, and like the cavalier regime of the early 1660s, the new settlement launched after 1683 was both too proscriptive and too narrow. The city of London had, from 1659 through 1682, contributed to unhinging efforts at settlement that shared these characteristics. Nothing had been more artificial, in the Corporation, than the erection in the 1660s of a civic regime from which some of the most substantial and enterprising citizens were excluded. From the perspective of Restoration London, Charles's new way of governing was actually a hazardous enterprise: proscription and coercion had led before to unsettlement in the city rather than to settlement. And speaking more broadly, could a regime that excluded or marginalized those who had dominated the last three Commons on behalf of a Protestant accommodation and succession really achieve an enduring settlement? Could settlement be achieved by imposing

---

[1] See, for instance, J. R. Western, *Monarchy and Revolution: The English State in the 1680s* (1972), pp. 69–81, 93–108; Miller, *Charles II*, pp. 373–4; Miller, "Crown and the Borough Charters"; J. Miller, "The Potential for 'Absolutism' in Later Stuart England," *History*, 69 (1984), esp. pp. 203–7. For the remodeling of the boroughs, see Halliday, *Dismembering*, chs. 6–7.

[2] Scott, *England's Troubles*, pp. 410–11, 451–2.

the agendas of one party upon those who had followed the ideas and the leaders of the other?

In London, the last months of Charles's reign were as much characterized by institutional malaise as by the emergence of a new loyalist order. The attachment of London citizens, Tories as well as Whigs, to the customary patterns and rhythms of civic life made the whole process of regulation appear irregular and contingent, despite its royal imprimatur. Many regarded royal rule as nothing more than an interruption of the ordinary courses of civic life, which surely would resume in time. Indeed, as one of its first matters of business, the new loyalist court of aldermen formed a committee, in November 1683, to petition the king for a restoration of the city's liberties. During the next year, the loyalist lord mayor and aldermen were occasionally at odds with the government, and especially with Lord Chief Justice Jeffreys: the city seemed, in fact, to have two governments, one at Guildhall and one at Whitehall, the first trying to govern according to customary practices, the other improvising in an unfamiliar situation. At one point, Charles informed the aldermen that he never intended to "alter soe much as one custome in the city unless...of absolute necessity," an odd statement coming from a monarch who had recently acted to put all those customs in legal abeyance.[3]

In fact, Charles's government was engaged in window-dressing in 1683–5: it sought to preserve the outward forms of civic government, while shifting much power from London magistrates and electors to itself. The same awkwardness attended the regulation of the livery companies. As Charles, and James after him, proceeded with the purging of guild electors, they deprived the guilds of experienced leaders, disrupted the conduct of company business, and diminished any sense of common ownership for guild affairs on the part of the remaining liverymen. The most recent historian of this process suggests that "single-party ideologically-biased company government was not good for business," and neither was it good for settlement.[4] A civic order that embraced only part of the civic population was handicapped in settling the people it excluded. A party regime in the city that excluded the party that had dominated electoral polls in 1680–82 was handicapped in speaking for those it governed. A civic regime that rested upon royal fiat rather than upon electoral participation could not even satisfy loyalists, many of whom believed that a reincorporation of the city, with as much of the old charter as possible, was the best means to local settlement.

---

[3] Repertory 89, fols. 4, 35, 63–64; Newdigate L.c. 1467, 1471, 1501, 1503, 1511, 1533, 1536, 1553, 1558, 1561–2, 1571–2 (22, 29 Dec. 1683; 23, 28 Feb.; 18 March; 8, 15 May; 24 June; 5, 12, 15 July; 5, 7 Aug. 1684); LC MS 18,124, IX, 43, 104 (10 April, 13 Sept. 1684); Morrice, P, 407; *CSPD 1683–4*, p. 382; *CSPD 1684–5*, pp. 22–3, 138, 142, 167, 177, 240, 245; Luttrell, I, 302–03; Reresby, *Memoirs*, p. 380.

[4] Knights, "A City Revolution," 1168–9.

None of this awkwardness would have mattered quite so much if the civic opposition had been intimidated into submission. Conventional historiography does suggest that the government's efforts at intimidation were as effective as they were extensive. The persecution of Protestant dissenters continued, in the city and elsewhere, throughout 1684. London news writers detailed Sabbath counts of meetings disturbed by soldiers and of preachers and hearers taken before the magistrates. The provisions of the 1670 Conventicle Act were supplemented with prosecutions for riot. Hundreds appeared before the various urban sessions in each legal term and were fined; others were summoned before the diocesan court. Some dissenting clergy gave up preaching, while others who had preached languished in prison or died there. Whig organization was disrupted, and Whig talk was driven from the public sphere. The trials of leading Whigs for serious offenses left others understandably "wary in managing their discourses," while the elimination of common council, the reduction of common hall, and the regulation of the press and coffeehouses deprived the Whigs of public opportunities for political discussion. One loyalist writer exulted, early in 1684, that finally the "animosityes in making partys are laid aside & an honest man may eat his minst pye with content & not be called to ye poll from his Dinner."[5]

Yet persecution and intimidation in London in 1683–5 were not successful. Dissenting congregations were disrupted and Whig organization was "crushed," but few minds were changed and few commitments were altered. In fact, the dissenting response to persecution was often as spirited as in 1669–70. Printed defenses of nonconformity continued to circulate; "full and frequent meetings persisted"; and some congregations found ingenious methods of outwitting the soldiers and magistrates sent against them. When meetings became too hazardous to hold, funeral processions provided suitable substitutes and shows of strength. And although much Whig conversation was forced "underground," it nevertheless continued. Prominent Whig prisoners in King's Bench prison kept "a kind of an office," and Slingsby Bethel moved about the city with the prison ordinary "as if he was keeping his Shrievalty." In July 1684, a merchant was prosecuted for arguing publicly that Sir John Moore "betray[ed] the rights & liberties of the citty & . . . deserved a halter." The fact that such language was still spoken is as significant as the fact of its prosecution. As the Earl of Sunderland was

[5] Newdigate L.c. 1474, 1500, 1512, 1528, 1563, 1569, 1573–4 (3 Jan., 21 Feb., 20 March, 26 April, 17 and 31 July, 9 and 12 Aug. 1684); LC MS 18,124, IX, 65 (10 June 1684); Morrice, P, 409; *CSPD 1683–4*, pp. 61, 321, 335; *CSPD 1684–5*, pp. 140, 223; Goldie, "Hilton Gang," 49–53.

informed a few months later, the London Whigs were far from "reconciled to the government . . . and as willing to see a change as ever."[6]

If this campaign of harassment was intended to discourage the expression of political opposition and religious dissent elsewhere, then, it was a failure, at least in London. Despite its interruption of the corporate life of the city, the crown could not alter the political and religious culture of those urban spaces that had sustained Reformed Protestant perspectives since the 1640s. The "fanaticks" against whom Anglicans directed their attack were not a dispirited remnant of the puritan godly but rather an equally determined religious community established in broad socio-geographic locales and enclaves within the urban environment. Discourse about liberty for conscience and the need for reformation could not easily be eradicated from communities in which it had long been embedded. Neither could language about consensual practices or the accountability of magistrates easily be banished from minds long accustomed to employing it. These ideas had demonstrated their staying power; the government's coercive practices, on the other hand, had been tried and abandoned before.

Moreover, despite its heavy hand, the government was as much on the defensive in 1683–5 as the Whigs and dissenters. The employment of legal institutions for propagandistic purposes, the harassment of large numbers of dissidents, and the rhetorical demonizing of critics are not often the signs of a self-confidant regime: this was, in fact, an insecure regime still reacting against its loss of control but a few years earlier. By the autumn of 1684, the government and urban loyalists were already showing some signs of fatigue and overextension in their efforts to cleanse the city of dissenting and whiggish perspectives.

The treason trials of the Presbyterian cleric Thomas Rosewell and of the dissenting merchant Joseph Hayes in late 1684, for instance, were as significant in challenging coercive practices as the London trials and legal processes that followed the 1670 Conventicle Act. The prominence of each man, neither of whom could be connected to the Whig conspiracies of 1682–3, made their trials test cases for the contrary resolves of the government and the Whig-dissenting community. Charles pardoned Rosewell after a contentious trial: his treason conviction for seditious preaching rested upon dubious interpretations of his words by unreliable witnesses and upon flaws in the indictment. Hayes, the son of James Hayes, a leader of the contest against coercion in London in 1669–70, had remitted funds, by bill of exchange, to an outlawed traitor, Sir Thomas Armstrong, who had already been captured

---

[6] Repertory 89, fol. 142; Newdigate L.c. 1466, 1528, 1530, 1553, 1560, 1566 (20 Dec. 1683; 26 April, 1 May, 24 June, 10 and 24 July 1684); LC MS 18,124, IX, 49–50, 152 (24 and 26 April 1684, 13 Jan. 1685); Morrice, P, 433, 452; HMC *Ormonde*, NS, VII, 164; *CSPD 1683–4*, pp. 261, 269, 396–7; *CSPD 1684–5*, pp. 189, 223, 280.

and executed. But a jury of loyalist merchants and tradesmen found Hayes innocent, fearing a precedent for the prosecution of businessmen whose extensive dealings might unintentionally involve those charged with political crimes. The government had overplayed its hand in each case, producing a reaction that favored the defendants.[7]

Both Charles's death in 1685 and James's movement in the direction of toleration in 1686–7 make unfruitful any further discussion of the potential for success of the 1680s' re-establishment of the confessional, coercive state. But neither the patterns of religious and political expression in Restoration London nor the urban history of the last eighteen months of Charles's reign support the idea that settlement could be achieved on this basis. Charles had hitched his regime to a popular current of anti-sectarianism that was as strong as the anti-Catholic current of the Popish Plot. But anti-Catholicism had not lost its force in popular opinion. Through much of the Restoration, these opposite phobias had alternated in wreaking havoc on efforts to settle the kingdom. In James II's reign, they would combine to destroy a polity of toleration and turn unsettlement to revolution.

HISTORY AND THEORY: WHIG LANGUAGE AND EXPERIENCE

The London events of the early 1680s were also a defining trauma in the origins of the Whig-liberal tradition in Anglo-American thought and practice. Political talk about an "invasion" of rights, about the imposition of "slavery," and about the "destruction" of civil government and "military" rule was regularly heard in London's Whig spaces and public sphere by 1682–3. Out of the events that produced this discourse and their aftermath in 1683–8, Whig writers would fashion an enduring political mythology about their initial victimization and subsequent victory in a critical confrontation with arbitrary rule and popery. After the "Glorious" Revolution, generations of historians and statesmen would follow the themes of the first Whig writers, developing a heroic constitutional narrative about the defense of liberty against an authoritarian Stuart regime, and Whig language would prove as useful across the Atlantic as in England.

Algernon Sidney and John Locke, the authors of the two most significant political treatises to emerge from the Restoration Crisis, also translated Whig

---

[7] *ST*, X, 147–308, 311–30; PRO PROB 11: 391 Exton qu 80 (James Hayes); Newdigate L.c. 1550, 1597, 1599, 1606, 1615–19 (17 June; 4, 9, 26 Oct.; 18, 20, 22, 25, 27 Nov. 1684); LC MS 18,124, IX, 115, 131, 133–5 (9 Oct.; 18, 22, 25, 27 Nov. 1684); Morrice, P, 440, 446–8; Luttrell, I, 317–18, 320–2; *CSPD 1684–5*, pp. 61–2, 171, 177, 183, 221–4, 226, 290; Burnet, *History*, II, 443–7; S. Seymour, "High Stakes, Low Lies," paper given at Royal Holloway College, University of London, June 2002; Goldie, "Hilton Gang," 57–8; Ashcraft, *Revolutionary Politics*, pp. 411–12, 422. Ashcraft, pp. 343n and 348n, confuses James Hayes, the London father of Joseph Hayes, with Sir James Hayes.

experience into enduring political theory that universalized the issues of the day. Political historians have, however, not fully understood the contemporary context for Sidney's *Discourses* and Locke's *Second Treatise* because of their traditional focus upon parliament and "high" constitutional issues. Understanding the local London events in which the Restoration Crisis climaxed is, in fact, necessary fully to appreciate crucial passages in these texts, each of which was substantially composed in 1682–3.[8] Sidney was a participant in the London events of those years,[9] and Locke was a close observer of them.[10] Despite the differences in their arguments, both Sidney and Locke quite naturally shared political perceptions and vocabulary with the Whig citizens with whom they had interacted, both personally and intellectually. They employed much language that was heard in the London streets, shops, and coffeehouses because it was the common currency of Whig discourse. Each work also reflects the tension between law and resistance within the Whig movement in 1682–3: indeed, placing Sidney's and Locke's arguments about law and resistance within the broader contemporary Whig debate about these different strategies for the protection of Protestant rights and liberties is helpful in identifying their immediate intended audiences.

Parallels between contemporary London Whig discourse and the arguments of Sidney and Locke abound. The London Whigs, for instance, argued that magistrates were not primarily representatives of the crown but rather "Creature(s) made by the pleasure of the Citizens"; and Sidney correspondingly maintained that any governor was the "creature" of the people from whom his power was derived. Locke wrote that "in all lawful Governments the designation of the Persons, who are to bear Rule, is . . . originally

[8] Evaluation of these texts in the contemporary political context of 1682–3 includes B. Worden, "The Commonwealth Kidney of Algernon Sidney," *JBS* 24(1985), 15–16, 38–9; Scott, *Restoration Crisis*, pp. 201, 206; D. Wootton, "Introduction" to John Locke, *Political Writings of John Locke*, ed. D. Wootton (New York, 1993), pp. 49ff.; J. Marshall, *John Locke*, pp. 229, 238–9, 242–3, 257–8; Ashcraft, *Revolutionary Politics*, chs. 7–8. Also see M. Knights, "Petitioning and the Political Theorists: John Locke, Algernon Sidney and London's 'Monster' Petition of 1680," *PP* 138 (1993), 94–111.

[9] Sidney was one of those indicted for the city riot of 24 June 1682. He was, moreover, involved in the subsequent plotting of the Whig grandees; and he knew Robert West and other members of West's London conspiracy. *ST*, IX, 918; Scott, *Restoration Crisis*, p. 273.

[10] Locke was in London, at Shaftesbury's Aldersgate townhouse, for the duration of the London shrieval election, from May through September 1682, when his patron was most intimately involved with the London Whig leadership. After Shaftesbury's departure, Locke was again at Thanet House from December 1682 through February 1683; and he resided in London yet again from April to June 1683. These intervals coincided with the height of London plotting and of London Whig legal endeavors after the failure of Shaftesbury's own designs. Cranston, *John Locke*, pp. 222–6; John Locke, *The Correspondence of John Locke*, ed. E. S. de Beer, 8 vols. (Oxford, 1976–89), II, 519–600. Locke also purchased news accounts of the 1682 London shrieval election and some civic Whig tracts of 1682–3, including Thomas Hunt's *Defence of the Charter of London* (1683). Ashcraft contended that Locke himself was a conspirator: *Revolutionary Politics*, pp. 352n., 376–7, and 378ff.

from the People"; and the London Whigs, in fact, claimed that the citizens –
and not the crown – were the ultimate authority within the Corporation of
London.[11] Insisting upon the accountability of magistrates to the electorate,
they claimed common hall could punish or remove a high civic office-holder,
should "he commit a crime against his...Trust"; and Sidney assured the
people a right "perpetually [to] judge of the behaviour of their deputies."[12]

These and other parallel arguments suggest an intellectual congruence,
borne of common experience that tied Sidney and Locke to many of their
London Whig contemporaries. But the congruence went beyond parallel
language: Sidney, Locke, and the London Whigs were wrestling with the same
problem in 1682–3, namely, the circumstances under which it was legitimate
to substitute resistance for political remedy through the law. Sidney and
Locke each drew upon the sequence of events in London from the dissolution
of the Oxford Parliament through the 1683 Whig legal reverses in laying the
groundwork for their defenses of resistance. As did the urban Whigs, Sidney
and Locke each first considered responses at law to magisterial error. When
Sidney suggested that "gentle ways" prescribed by "Good Laws" should first
be tried to check "the vices or infirmities of the Magistrate," he captured
the position adopted by the London Whig leaders at their September 1682
Amsterdam coffeehouse consult. Or, as Locke wrote, also expressing the
position of most Whig leaders, "there can be no pretense for force" against
a magistrate or government when an "injured Party may be relieved, and his
damages repaired by Appeal to Law."[13]

But as Sidney and Locke prepared their treatises, the Whig legal strategy
collapsed before what both authors and the London Whigs experienced as
arbitrary government. Many of the examples of the betrayal of "trust" or of
the "dissolution of government" offered in the two texts reflect that common
experience. Sidney considered the manipulation of juries, the subordination
of King's Bench to the king's interest, and royal designs upon borough charters as violations of the "trust" upon which royal government rested. Among
Locke's examples of tyranny was any situation in which "the People shall
find the Ministers, and subordinate Magistrates chosen suitable to [arbitrary]
ends, and favoured, or laid by proportionably, as they promote, or oppose
them." And Sidney's first example of a situation in which "the laws of God
and man" justify "sedition, tumults, and war" was when individuals "take
upon them the power and name of a magistracy, to which they are not justly

---

[11] *The Case between the Ld. Mayor & Commons*, p. 6; Sidney, *Discourses*, pp. 510–11
(Chapter III, Section 33); Locke, *Second Treatise*, p. 415 (Para 198).

[12] *Case between the Ld. Mayor & Commons*, p. 5; *Matters of Fact*, pp. 1, 4; Sidney, *Discourses*,
pp. 531–2, 542 (III: 38, 40).

[13] Sidney, *Discourses*, pp. 542, 545 (III: 40); Locke, *Second Treatise*, p. 421 (Para 207).

called."[14] In these passages, the two authors point to the very situation the London Whigs claimed to have experienced in 1682–3, when "subordinate Magistrates," including the lord mayor and two sheriffs not chosen by the electorate, were imposed upon the Corporation.

The *Discourses* and the *Second Treatise* also review other critical events in the London Whigs' multi-faceted defense of parliament and Protestantism after the Oxford Parliament. Sidney complained, for instance, that when a magistrate promotes his own interest above the good of the people, those who would act in defense of their rights are liable to "persecution" for behavior to which such a "magistrate gives the name of sedition or rebellion." Locke pointed out that a prince seeking to extend his power beyond "lawful Authority" would likely also act to "terrifie or suppress" any who oppose his will "as Factious, Seditious, and Enemies to the Government."[15] So the London Whigs had experienced the crown's turn to coercion and intimidation in 1682–3, and their defense of themselves at law had merely won them such unsavory epithets.

But, according to Locke, a "*supreame Executor*" advancing his own will may also bend the courts to his purposes and employ "all the Arts of perverted Law" in order "to take off and destroy all that stand in the way." Here Locke's language reflects the manipulation of the judiciary that the London Whigs believed had begun in the 1681 trials of Stephen College and the Earl of Shaftesbury. By 1683, Sidney and Russell were among the chief victims of the government's conversion of the judiciary to its own purposes. In this "*long Train of Actings*," Locke detected not only a quest for "Arbitrary Power" but also surreptitious favor for "that Religion ... which is readiest to introduce it." This was the very scenario that the political and religious opposition to Anglican loyalism had sought to forestall, since the mid-1670s, through actions in London, parliament, and the kingdom.[16]

After reviewing these experiences of 1681–3 and others that may subsequently have been added to the manuscript, Locke "cannot tell," he wrote, how "the People" can be "hindered from resisting illegal force." And for his part, Sidney argued that when "a magistrate ... overthrows the law by which he is a magistrate," he "must be constrained."[17] Moreover, in making their transition from legal redress to extra-legal redress, Sidney and Locke pointed to the seeming inertia of many Whig leaders in 1682–3 who clung to law

---

[14] Sidney, *Discourses*, pp. 220, 467–8, 470, 531 (II: 24; III: 26, 38); Locke, *Second Treatise*, p. 423 (Para 210).

[15] Sidney, *Discourses*, pp. 433–4 (III: 19); Locke, *Second Treatise*, p. 428 (Para 218).

[16] Locke, *Second Treatise*, pp. 423, 431 (Para 210, 222).

[17] *Ibid.*, p. 423 (Para 219); Sidney, *Discourses*, p. 545 (III: 40). P. Laslett suggests that the text of chapter XIX of the *Second Treatise* shows signs of "successive correction and addition," especially in passages likely to have been added in 1689 (pp. 424n., 431n.).

even as the grounds for resistance became more numerous. Sidney suggested that an "ill magistrate" often seeks, with the assistance of "those who are of his party," to divide and to enervate citizens so that "they may neither care nor dare to vindicate their rights." Indeed, according to him, "those who would do it may so far suspect each other, as not to confer upon, much less to join in any action tending to the publick deliverance." Here Sidney's language seemingly expresses the same impatience with the cautious posture of the London Whig leadership that was expressed within Robert West's circle of conspirators. And Locke, too, fingered that cautious Whig posture when he wrote, in a frequently cited passage, that most people are "more disposed to suffer, than right themselves by Resistance." They are not prepared "to stir" until "the mischief" of an arbitrary government "be grown general."[18]

These considerations of Sidney's and Locke's grounds for resistance in the context of London politics in 1682–3 suggest that their immediate intended audiences were far broader than the republican circles or lesser urban orders from which most conspirators were recruited.[19] In fact, Sidney and Locke probably wrote not to persuade those who were most likely to engage in conspiracy, or who were already engaged in it, but rather to persuade potential readers who actually needed to be persuaded about the case for resistance. Their intended contemporary audiences were arguably the very dissenters and Reformed Protestants throughout the kingdom – and especially the citizens of London's Whig spaces – who had sustained the cause of a Protestant resettlement of church and state after the Oxford Parliament.

As Sidney and Locke well knew, the Reformed Protestant citizens of London had taken the lead in stopping the Rump in 1659–60, having then experienced in its behavior the same threat to a parliamentary and Protestant order that they now detected in Charles II. Then they had acted; and they had acted repeatedly against Anglican coercion ever since. But in 1682–3, when they believed they were finally confronted by an arbitrary state as well as persecuting bishops, many of them remained stubbornly attached to the law, slow to realize that the law itself was in jeopardy, and again separated strategically from sectarians and old republicans who were quicker off the mark. Resistance was most likely to succeed with the active support of the Reformed Protestant citizens of London, as it had in the 1640s and again in 1659–60: Sidney and Locke wrote to persuade them, and their Country associates, of the legitimacy and necessity of such a course. Well versed in Reformed Protestant thought, which included cases for and against resistance, Sidney and Locke sought to resolve the Whigs' inner tension between

---

[18] Sidney, *Discourses*, p. 434 (III: 19); Locke, *Second Treatise*, pp. 435–6 (Para 230).
[19] Scott, *Restoration Crisis*, esp. pp. 125, 162, 169, 172–3; Ashcraft, *Revolutionary Politics*, esp. chs. 6, 8. Also see J. Marshall, *John Locke*, pp. 280–2.

law and resistance by drawing them forward toward the resolute action the times demanded.[20]

In doing so, Sidney and Locke also provided subsequent historians with intellectual formulations that would become imprinted upon the first Whigs. In fact, however, some of the differences in language between Sidney and Locke and the first Whigs are as important as the similarities: the ideas of the first Whigs cannot simply be interpreted in light of the classic texts that turned their experiences into political theory. Sidney and Locke each constructed their central arguments about the state upon secular foundations. Sidney, in particular, drew upon historical readings, classical sources, and republican traditions that were unfamiliar to most London Whigs and dissenters. Moreover, as they drew principles from Whig experience, Locke and Sidney also transformed Whig language, separating it especially from the Reformed Protestant tradition that had contributed so much to it. As their translations of Restoration Whig language into theory came to inform subsequent Whig thought and historiography, Locke and Sidney thereby contributed to the relative neglect of religious dissent, liberty of conscience, reformation, and Protestant resettlement in historical interpretation of the Restoration.[21] The first Whigs came to be seen too often in the image of Sidney and Locke – as the progenitors of eighteenth-century constitutional arguments – and not also as the heirs of the puritan case for reformation of church and state.

But the contest that re-erupted in the Corporation of London in 1689 was, in fact, the same contest between Reformed Protestants and Anglican loyalists that had gone on for two generations and that, contrary to some historians, had already taken on a party character in 1679–83. As they had before, the London Whigs of 1688–9 initially advanced the causes of electoral rights in the Corporation, of Protestant accommodation in the church, and of ease for tender consciences. They remained the party of dissenters and of Reformed Protestants within the church, just as the Tories remained the party of the Anglican establishment. Their party quarrel continued, reignited

---

[20] Locke's religion has been the subject of recent scholarly disagreement. Ashcraft associated Locke with dissenters: *Revolutionary Politics*, ch. 3. J. Marshall argues that Locke was instead a latitudinarian Anglican, but he also sees Locke as having "moved decisively away from his clerical Latitudinarian friends" in 1681–3: *John Locke*, pp. 77–81, 284. Like Shaftesbury, Locke had, for some time by 1682–3, been a political champion of the Reformed Protestantism that lay behind the Whig movement, despite his earlier attacks on puritan tradition.

[21] Both Locke and Sidney argued on behalf of liberty of conscience, of course; and Sidney's Protestantism owed much to mid-seventeenth-century providentialism. Yet both authors also approached liberty of conscience primarily from the perspective of the state, and their treatments lacked the distinctive language of dissenting cases for conscience. See for instance, Algernon Sidney, *Court Maxims*, ed. H. W. Blom, E. H. Mulier, and R. Janse (Cambridge, 1996), pp. 99ff.; John Locke, "Essay on Toleration" (1667–8), in H. R. Fox Bourne, *The Life of John Locke*, 2 vols. (1876), I, 176, 182, 184, 187, 189, 193.

in part by the Whigs' desire to settle scores with those who had sacrificed the charter, destroyed the Corporation, and turned the law against them. Disgraced in 1682–3, the dissenting Thomas Pilkington was elevated to the mayoralty in 1689, while Anglican magistrates like Sir William Pritchard and Sir Dudley North answered to parliament for their conduct. The House of Lords rehabilitated Whig martyrs like Lord Russell and the dissenting Henry Cornish, and leading dissenting aldermen and common councilmen returned to service. Loyalist leaders, on the other hand, were initially thrown on the defensive for having cooperated with the crown in London events that were condemned in the Heads of Grievances and the Declaration of Rights. Yet, the civic church party soon discovered that the Revolution had not diminished the force of anti-sectarianism, which they utilized to prevent a broad church resettlement and to limit the toleration of 1689.[22]

The London Whigs' revolutionary moment was also a brief one, pointing again to the care that needs to be taken in connecting them to the endorsement of resistance by Locke and Sidney. As the old civic opposition developed into a new political and mercantile establishment, most London Whigs parted company with the resistance they had offered in 1688, while their attachment to consent also lost much of its political edge. The revolution secured Protestantism and parliament, finally providing some, though not all, of the new settlement that had long been desired. The toleration of 1689, limited though it may have been, resolved the most unsettling issue of the Restoration by ending the coercion of Protestants. Mostly satisfied with this resettlement, the Whig merchants and traders who became the urban establishment of the post-1689 commercial revolution soon proved as interested in managing the Corporation as their loyalist predecessors had once been. Party tactics in the Restoration Crisis had reopened the political arena to articulate artisans and mechanics; but urban Whig magnates quietly shelved the agenda of consent after 1689, leaving the *menu peuple* on the fringes of civic politics once again. The social complexion of the parties began to change. As the Whigs became the party of government, capital, and the shopocracy, the Tories became the party of the displaced and the marginalized, still adept at employing anti-sectarianism to arouse the plebs against the fanatics, as the Sacheverell riots would demonstrate in 1710.[23]

In the meantime, the revolutionaries of 1688–9 largely adopted an interpretation of the revolution as more a triumph at law than an exercise in the right to resist. Whig ambiguity about resistance resurfaced; and the tension between law and resistance was resolved, officially at least, in favor of law. Resistance language remained a part of the Whig-liberal heritage,

[22] De Krey, *Fractured Society*, chs. 2–3.
[23] *Ibid.*, pp. 65–6, 71–2, 177–91; Holmes, "Sacheverell Riots."

especially among those who combined it with commonwealth thought. But many Whigs preferred a sanitized version of the "Glorious Revolution" as an affirmation of the rule of law rather than a refoundation of a state dissolved through the illegal practices of princes. And for most Whig leaders, the law quickly became a social instrument for protecting the new order of trading wealth and empire against any who would threaten it, whether genteel Jacobites or traditionalist plebs. Resistance may have been offered in the past to the arbitrary practices of Charles II and James II; but the establishment of law in the revolutionary settlement made resistance obsolete, or so the Whig proprietors of the new commercial and financial order maintained.

Appendices

APPENDIX I

1670 London Dissenting Subscription

Name	Amount	Persuasion	Occupation	Residence
ADAMS Thomas	£50	Presbyterian	Draper	Farringdon Within
ADAMS Valentine	£50		Hatter	Candlewick
ALDWORTH Thomas	£100		Plumbing Contractor; Shipping & Insurance	Bishopsgate Within
ALLEN William	£50	Independent	Merchant	Tower
ARCHER John	£100	Independent Presbyterian	Merchant	Langbourn
ASHE Elizabeth	£100	Independent Presbyterian	Widow	Farringdon Within
ASHURST [ASSHURST] Henry Esq	£500	Presbyterian	Merchant	Bread Street
ASHURST (Sir) Henry (Bt)	£300	Presbyterian	Merchant	Cordwainer
ASHURST (Sir) William	£250	Presbyterian	Merchant	Bread Street
AYRAY [ARRIS/ AYRES] George	£100			Portsoken
BAGNALL John	£50			Bridge
BARD Maximilian Esq	£200	Independent	Haberdasher	Bread Street
BARKER Matthew	£500	Independent	Cleric	Aldgate

(cont.)

Appendix I (*cont.*)

Name	Amount	Persuasion	Occupation	Residence
BARKER Thomas	£150			
BARNARD Henry	£50			
BARNARDISTON Nathaniel	£700	Presbyterian	Merchant	Hackney
BARNARDISTON Palatia	£100	Presbyterian	Merchant	Bishopsgate Within & Hackney
BASKERVILLE [BASKERFIELD] Laurence	£50	Independent	Haberdasher	Cripplegate Within
BASS Richard	£100		Merchant	Tower
BATES Dr William	£500	Presbyterian	Cleric	Hackney
BAWDEN [BOWDON/ BADOWIN] John	£200	Presbyterian	Merchant	Aldgate
BELL Thomas Sr	£100	Independent	Merchant	Tower
BELL Thomas Jr	£100	Independent	Merchant	Tower
BLAKE George	£100		Merchant	Tower
BLANEY Robert Jr	£150	Presbyterian	Lawyer; Office-holder: Prizes Commission paymaster	Farringdon Without: Middle Temple
BLATT James	£100	Independent	Draper	Cornhill
BOOTH John	£200			
BOOTH Robert	£150	Presbyterian	Merchant	Walbrook & Hackney
BOWLES John	£50	Independent	Merchant	Cordwainer
BRENT Maj Edward Esq	£500	Baptist	Chalk dealer	Bishopsgate Without & Southwark
BRETT Capt John	£50	Independent	Merchant	Bridge
BROMHALL Capt Thomas	£100	Baptist	Warden, Fleet prison & urban landlord	Farringdon Without: St Martin Ludgate
BROOKES Samuel	£300			
BROWNE James	£50	Presbyterian	Merchant	Walbrook

Name	Amount	Persuasion	Occupation	Residence
BROWNSMITH Benjamin	£100		Merchant	Billingsgate
BUCKNER Ralph	£100			
BURTON Moses	£200	Presbyterian	Gentleman	Cripplegate Without
CASSE John	£100		Office-holder: Clerk of Rolls	Farringdon Without: St Dunstan in West
CLARKE Dep John	£20		Timber merchant	Queenhithe
CLUTTERBUCK Jerome	£50		Haberdasher	Bread Street
COCKETT Thomas	£500	Independent	Gentleman	Great Woolton & Childwall, Lancaster
COLDHAM George	£50	Presbyterian		Mapledurham, Oxon.
COLDHAM John	£200	Independent		Aldersgate Without & Tooting Graveney, Surrey
COLLIER Nathaniel	£100	Independent	Merchant	Southwark & Hawkhurst, Kent
COMBER Philip	£50	Presbyterian		Cripplegate Without
CRAWLEY Andrew	£50			Clapham
DAFFORNE [DAFFERN] Thomas	£100	Baptist & 5th Monarchist		Aldersgate Without
DANDY Andrew	£50	Presbyterian		Vintry
DELIMA Robert	£100	French Reformed	Merchant	Bishopsgate Within & Theobalds, Cheshunt, Herts.
DOLINS [DOLIN/DOLING] Abraham	£200	Dutch Reformed	Merchant	Vintry & Hackney
DUBOIS John	£100	French Reformed	Merchant	Cripplegate Within & Mitcham, Surrey

(cont.)

Appendix I (*cont.*)

Name	Amount	Persuasion	Occupation	Residence
ELLIS Richard	£100	Independent		St. Leonard Shoreditch
ESSINGTON Thomas Esq	£200	Independent		Cripplegate Within
EVERARD Samuel	£100	Independent	Merchant	Candlewick
EYLES John	£200	Baptist	Merchant	Bishopsgate Within & Bishops Canning, Wilts.
FARRINGTON Daniel Esq	£300		Merchant Scrivener	Broad Street & Camberwell, Surrey
FORTESCUE Edmond	£200	Presbyterian	Lawyer	Castle Baynard & the Savoy
FORTH Dannet Esq	£2,500		Brewer	
FORTH John Esq	£2,500		Brewer	Cripplegate Within & Hackney
FORTH William Esq	£500		Lawyer & Office-holder: Excise Commissioner	Highgate
FOSTER Jacob Esq	£150	Independent	Merchant	Dowgate
FREDERICK Sir John	£250	Dutch Reformed	Merchant	Coleman Street
FRENCH Laurence	£100		Gold-weaver	Farringdon Within
GETHING Maurice	£50	Presbyterian	Woollen-draper	Islington
GIBBS William	£100	Presbyterian	Goldsmith	Suffolk
GLOVER Thomas	£200	Presbyterian	Merchant	
GOUGE Thomas	£350	Presbyterian	Cleric	Farringdon Without: St Sepulchre
GOULD John Jr	£100	Independent	Merchant	Bishopsgate Without & Clapham, Surrey

Name	Amount	Persuasion	Occupation	Residence
GREGSON [GRIGSON] Nicholas	£500	Presbyterian		Cordwainer
GUNSTON John	£100	Presbyterian	Merchant	Cordwainer & Stoke Newington
HACKSHAW Robert	£100	Independent		Portsoken
HAMS Stephen	£200	Presbyterian	Cloth factor	Aldersgate Within
HARBIN [HARBORNE] Morren	£100			Dowgate & Croydon, Surrey
HARTLEY Thomas	£50	Presbyterian	Merchant	Broad Street
HAYES James	£1,000	Independent	Linen-draper	Bridge & Greenwich
HEDGES William	£50		Merchant	Bassishaw
HEWLING Benjamin	£500	Baptist	Merchant	Coleman Street
HORTON Owen	£500			
HOULTON Nathaniel	£100	Presbyterian	Silkman	Bread Street & Newington Green
HOVENAR Henry	£100		Merchant	Walbrook
HOWARD Matthew	£100	Presbyterian	Merchant	Cordwainer
HULBERT John	£100	Presbyterian	Linen-draper	Bread Street
HUNLOCKE Francis	£100		Shopkeeper or Painter-stainer	Broad Street
INNES James	£250	Presbyterian	Cleric	Westminster
IRETON John	£200	Independent	Merchant	Finsbury, Middlesex
JACOMBE Dr Thomas	£900	Presbyterian	Cleric	Aldersgate Within
JASPERSON Thomas	£200			
JEKYLL John	£700	Presbyterian	Haberdasher	Cheap

(*cont.*)

Appendix I (*cont.*)

Name	Amount	Persuasion	Occupation	Residence
JEMMOTT [JEMMITT/ JENNETT] Philip	£2,000		Brewer	Portsoken & Kentbury, Berkshire
JENNINGS William	£100			
JOHNSON Dep Abraham Esq	£100	Presbyterian	Merchant	Langbourn & Hackney
JOHNSON Joshua	£500			
JOLLIFFE [JOLLEY/ JOLLY] John Esq	£500	Presbyterian	Merchant	Broad Street
JOLLIFFE William	£500	Presbyterian	Merchant	Westminster
JORDAN Thomas	£50			
KAY [KAYE] John	£50	Presbyterian		Castle Baynard
KIFFIN William	£3,600	Baptist	Merchant	Cripplegate Without
KNIGHTLY Lucy	£500	Presbyterian	Merchant	Cheap & Hackney
LANE John	£200	Presbyterian	Merchant	Cheap
LANGLEY John Esq	£200	Independent	Merchant	Broad Street & Shoreditch
LEVER James	£150		Mercer	Candlewick
LEWES [LEWIS] Edward	£50	Presbyterian	Merchant	Walbrook
LIGHT Anthony	£50	Independent	Dyer	Christ Church, Surrey
MARWOOD George	£100		Merchant	Candlewick
MASCALL Robert	£200	Independent	Merchant	Bassishaw
MEAD Matthew	£600	Independent	Cleric	Shadwell, Stepney
MERRITON John	£100	Independent		Aldersgate Without
MERRITON Matthew	£50	Independent		Cordwainer

Name	Amount	Persuasion	Occupation	Residence
MERRIWEATHER Edward	£100	Presbyterian		Farringdon Within
MICKLETHWAITE Sir John	£700		Physician	Aldersgate Without
MICO Walter	£100		Merchant	
MOORE Robert	£100			
OWEN Dr John	£1,000	Independent	Cleric	Cripplegate Without
PARKES Stephen	£250		Scrivener	Bread Street
PENDARVIS [PENDARVES] Sarah	£250		Merchant's widow	Tower
PENNOYER William Esq	£200	Independent	Merchant	Lime Street
PERRYER George	£250	Independent	Merchant	Broad Street
PICKARD Thomas	£200	Independent	Joiner	Aldgate
PLAMPIN [PLAMPION] Thomas Esq	£100	Independent	Scrivener	Bread Street & Highgate
POWELL Samuel	£100	Presbyterian	Merchant	Broad Street
PRESCOTT Lewis	£500			
RANDALL Edward	£100			
ROBINSON Thomas	£100			
ROLFE Thomas	£100	Independent	Apothecary	Aldgate
SEAMAN Dr Lazarus	£100	Presbyterian	Cleric	Hammersmith
SHAW George	£50			
SHEAFE Harmon	£100	Independent Presbyterian		Cheap
SHEPPARD Matthew	£200	Independent		Vintry & East Sheen
SHIPTON Richard	£50	Presbyterian		Bridge & St Mary Newington, Surrey

(*cont.*)

Appendix I (*cont.*)

Name	Amount	Persuasion	Occupation	Residence
SHUTE Benjamin	£100	Independent	Linen-draper & Office-holder: Comtroller, Ports of Cardiff & Swansea	Cornhill & Hackney
SLATER Thomas	£200	Presbyterian	Cloth factor	Cripplegate Within
SMITH James	£100			
SOMERS [SUMMERS] Samuel	£50	Presbyterian		Bread Street
SOMERS [SUMMERS] William	£200	Presbyterian		Vintry
SPURSTOWE Henry Esq	£200	Presbyterian	Merchant	Bishopsgate Within
STAINES [STEANES] Dr William	£200	Independent	Physician	
STARKEY John	£200	Independent	Bookseller	Farringdon Without: St Sepulchre
STOPFORTH Richard	£200	Presbyterian		
STREET William	£50			Cripplegate Within
STRUDWICK Thomas	£100	Presbyterian	Grocer & Gentleman	Farringdon Without: St Andrew Holborn & Hampstead
THOROLD Charles Esq	£300		Merchant	Aldgate
TRENCH Dr Edmund	£100	Presbyterian	Physician	Aldgate
UNDERHILL Edward	£100	Independent	Grocer	Farringdon Within & Kensington
VERNON John	£200		Merchant	Broad Street
VYNER [VINER] William	£50	Independent		Bridge & Spittle Yard, Middlesex

Name	Amount	Persuasion	Occupation	Residence
WARING Thomas	£50	Presbyterian	Merchant	Coleman Street and Bethnal Green, Stepney
WATSON [WATTSON] Thomas	£450	Presbyterian	Cleric	Dowgate
WAVELL William	£50	Independent	Linen-draper	Bridge & Stoke Newington
WEBB William Esq	£200	Presbyterian	Clothier	Broad Street & Totteridge, Herts.
WESTERN [WESTERNE] Robert	£50			Cheap
WHITE Sir Stephen	£300	Presbyterian	Merchant	Broad Street & Hackney
WHITTINGHAM Henry	£50	Presbyterian	Merchant	Bishopsgate Within
WILMORE [WILLMORE/ WILMER] John	£100		Merchant	Aldersgate Without
WINSTANLEY James	£100	Presbyterian	Merchant	Bassishaw
WOOLLEY William	£50	Presbyterian	Lace silkman	Cripplegate Within

London dissenting common councilmen, 1669–1671

Name	Persuasion	Occupation
BELL Randall		Metalworker, jeweller, pawnbroker
BERRY Daniel	Independent	Wood-monger
BILLERS Joseph	Independent	Silkman
BILLINGSLEY John		Vintner, Innkeeper
BOWYER William	Independent	Tallow-chandler
BUCKNER John	Presbyterian	
CARLETON Matthew	Presbyterian	Merchant
COX James	Independent	Merchant
CULLUM John	Presbyterian	Woollen-draper
DANIEL William	Independent	
DAVIES Robert	Sectarian or Independent	
DAWSON Joseph		Merchant
DUCANE Benjamin	French Reformed, Presbyterian	Merchant
DUDSON Edward		Woollen-draper
FINCH Joseph		Merchant
FLEWELLEN William	Presbyterian	Office-holder: Keeper of Guildhall
GOODAY George	Independent	Bookseller
HAMPSON Henry		Merchant
HARRINGTON William	Independent	Merchant
HATCH Anthony		Brazier
HOLGATE William	Presbyterian	Merchant
HOWLETT Thomas		Soap-maker
HYATT William		Confectioner
JELLY William	Sectarian	
JENNINGS Richard	Independent or Presbyterian	Hatter
LENTHALL Thomas	Presbyterian	Merchant
MASCALL John	Presbyterian	Merchant
MOORE John	Independent, but subsequently conformed	Merchant

Name	Persuasion	Occupation
MOSSE Henry	Presbyterian	Scrivener
MOULINS Robert		Pewterer
NELTHORPE Edward		Goldsmith-banker
PARKER William	Subsequently conformed	Woollen-draper
PENNER Richard		Innkeeper
PILKINGTON Thomas	Presbyterian	Merchant
POWELL Thomas	Presbyterian	Merchant
RICHARDSON Joseph		Confectioner
ROBERTS Capt Nicholas	Sectarian or Independent	Ironmonger
ROBERTS William	Independent or Presbyterian	Merchant
SAMBROOKE Jeremy	Presbyterian	Merchant
SELBY Anthony	Sectarian	Oilman
SIBLEY Joseph	Sectarian	
STACEY John		Merchant
STAMP Thomas		Merchant
SWYNOKE Samuel		Merchant
THOMPSON Richard		Goldsmith-banker
TUNMAN Thomas		
TURGIS Edward	Presbyterian	Woollen-draper
UNDERWOOD Edward	Presbyterian	Apothecary
WHEATLEY Gabriel	Presbyterian	Merchant
WICKENS Samuel		Draper
WILDGOSS John		Carpenter

APPENDIX III. *Whig party leaders*

Name	Birth	Religion	Residence	Occupation	1680 Real Property	Personal Property	Stock Ownership; Trading Company Offices[1]
ALLEYN Sir Thomas	Active 1639	Dissenter	Tower	Merchant: Colonies	£100 p.a.	£60 p.a.	
ASHURST William	1647	Presbyterian	Bread Street	Merchant: Levant	£56 p.a.	£56 p.a.	
BARNARDISTON Sir Samuel	1620	Presbyterian	Bishopsgate Within	Merchant: Levant	£90 p.a.	£120 p.a.	£2,550 East India Co. 1675 East India Co. Dir. (20) Levant Co. Dir. (9) Levant Co. Dep. Governor (2)
BETHEL Slingsby	1617	Independent	Not found	Merchant: N. Europe	Lodger	Not found	
BRISTOW Richard	1630	Baptist	Bread Street	Domestic trader: Grocer	£70 p.a.	£48 p.a.	
CLARKE Edward	1627	Presbyterian	Farringdon Within	Merchant: Italy	£60 p.a.	£48 p.a.	
CLAYTON Sir Robert	1629	Anglican	Coleman Street	Scrivener	£164 p.a.	£78 p.a.	£ 500 Royal African Co. 1672 Royal African Co. Dir. (1)

Name	Date	Religion	Ward	Occupation			Offices
COLLET James	Active 1681	Independent	Vintry	Merchant: Iberia	£36 p.a.	£24 p.a.	
CORNISH Henry	Active 1659	Presbyterian	Cheap	Domestic trader: Cloth factor	£42 p.a.	£24 p.a.	£4,000 External East India 1682
COX John	Active 1659	Dissenter	Bridge	Industrial employer: Soap-maker	£36 p.a.	£30 p.a.	
CRISP John	Active 1664	Anglican	Bread Street	Domestic trader: Salter	£72 p.a.	£54 p.a.	£500 Royal African Co. 1672 £500 External East India 1682
DENEW James	1630	Dutch Reformed	Tower	Merchant: Iberia, Levant	£60 p.a.	£66 p.a.	
DUBOIS John	1622	French Reformed	Cripplegate Within	Merchant: France	£36 p.a.	£30 p.a.	East India Co. Dir. (4)
DYER Dep. Lawrence	Active 1669	Presbyterian	Cripplegate Within	Domestic trader: Pewterer	£33 p.a.	£28 p.a.	
ELLIS John	Apprenticed 1628	Dissenter	Castle Baynard	Merchant: unknown specialization	£29 p.a.	£45 p.a.	
FLAVELL Dep. John	1648	Dissenter	Walbrook	Merchant: Iberia, Italy	£27 p.a.	£30 p.a.	

(cont.)

Appendix III. (cont.)

Name	Birth	Religion	Residence	Occupation	1680 Real Property	Personal Property	Stock Ownership; Trading Company Offices[1]
FREDERICK Sir John	1601	Dutch Reformed	Coleman Street	Merchant: Iberia, Colonies, Italy	£140 p.a.	£78 p.a.	East India Co. Dir. (2)
GODFREY Michael	1624	Presbyterian	Walbrook	Merchant: N. Europe, Iberia, France	£60 p.a.	£42 p.a.	£250 East India Co. 1675
GOLD Sir Thomas	Married 1659		Cripplegate Within	Merchant: unknown specialization	£66 p.a.	£66 p.a.	
GOODENOUGH Richard	Active 1671	Dissenter	Farringdon Without	Lawyer	£21 p.a.	£12 p.a.	
HACKSHAW John	Married 1676	Independent	Langbourn	Merchant: unknown specialization	£32 p.a.	£28 p.a.	
HAMMOND John	Active 1670	Dissenter	Aldgate	Merchant: N. Europe	£21 p.a.	£42 p.a.	
HAWKINS Richard	1633		Farringdon Without	Scrivener	£85 p.a.	£42 p.a.	£400 Royal African Co. 1672 £4,000 External East India 1682

Name	Date	Religion	Ward	Occupation			Company
HAYES James	Apprenticed 1633	Independent	Not found	Domestic trader: Linen draper	Not found	Not found	£1,000 External East India 1682
HOUBLON James	Married 1658	French Reformed	Broad Street	Merchant: Iberia, Levant, France	£80 p.a.	£60 p.a.	£600 East India Co. 1675 East India Co. Dir. (11) Levant Co. Dir. (1)
HOUBLON Peter Jr	Active 1649	French Reformed	Cordwainer	Merchant: N. Europe, Iberia, Levant	£72 p.a.	£60 p.a.	£4,000 External East India 1682 Levant Co. Dir. (1)
HUTCHINSON Richard	1647	Independent	Candlewick	Merchant: Colonies	£16 p.a.	£12 p.a.	£500 East India Co. 1675 £2,000 External East India 1682 East India Co. Dir. (8)
JEKYLL John	1611	Presbyterian	St. Lawrence Lane, Cheap	Domestic trader: Haberdasher	£37.5 p.a.	£18 p.a.	
JENKS Francis	1640	Anglican	Cornhill	Domestic trader: Linen draper	£27 p.a.	£24 p.a.	
KNIGHTLY Lucy	1623	Independent	Cheap & Hackney, Middlesex	Merchant: N. Europe	Not in City	Not in City	£500 External East India 1682

(cont.)

Appendix III. (*cont.*)

Name	Birth	Religion	Residence	Occupation	1680 Real Property	Personal Property	Stock Ownership; Trading Company Offices[1]
LANE John	*c.* 1621	Presbyterian	Cheap	Merchant: Iberia	£52.5 p.a.	£36	£ 500 East India Co. 1675
LAWRENCE Sir John	Married 1643	Dutch Reformed	Bishopsgate Within	Merchant: unknown specialization	£84 p.a.	£132 p.a.	£1,600 Royal African Co. 1672 £1,000 East India Co. 1675 Royal African Co. Dir. (1) East India Co. Dir. (6)
LOVE William	1618	Independent	Aldgate	Merchant: Levant	£60 p.a.	£ 54 p.a.	East India Co. Dir. (2) Levant Co. Dir. (9)
MOR/R/ICE Dep. John	1630s	Presbyterian	Broad Street	Merchant: N. Europe, Levant	£54 p.a.	£44 p.a.	£ 400 Royal African Co. 1672 Royal African Co. Dir. (8) Levant Co. Dir. (11)
PAPILLON Thomas	1623	French Reformed	Aldgate	Merchant: Colonies, France	£69 p.a.	£64 p.a.	£1,775 East India Co. 1675 East India Co. Dir. (14) East India Co. Deputy Gov. (2)

PAUL James	Free 1672	Anglican	Cornhill	Domestic trader: Linen draper	£41 p.a.	£41 p.a.	
PILKINGTON Thomas	1628	Presbyterian	Dowgate	Merchant: Levant	£56 p.a.	£72 p.a.	Levant Co. Dir. (21)
PLAYER Dep. Sir Thomas	Married 1641	Anglican	Bassishaw	Chamberlain of the Corporation	£30 p.a.	£60 p.a.	
ROBINSON Leonard	Active 1677	Independent	Candlewick	Merchant: N. Europe	£40 p.a.	£28 p.a.	
SHEPHERD Thomas	Active 1677	Independent	Candlewick	Merchant: N. Europe, Iberia	£77 p.a.	£40 p.a.	
SHORTER Sir John	1625	Independent	Southwark, Surrey	Merchant: N. Europe, Colonies	Not in City	Not in City	
SHUTE Samuel	Married 1658	Independent	Cornhill	Domestic trader: Linen draper	£42 p.a.	£45 p.a.	£ 250 East India Co. 1675
STAMP Sir Thomas	1628	Dissenter	Bassishaw	Merchant: N. Europe	£48 p.a.	£60 p.a.	
SWYNOKE Samuel	Active 1666	Dissenter	Aldgate	Merchant: Iberia, Colonies, France	£40 p.a.	£42 p.a.	£ 400 Royal African Co. 1672 £ 200 East India Co. 1675
TREBY Sir George	1643	Anglican	Farringdon Without	Lawyer	Not found	Not found	

(*cont.*)

Appendix III. (*cont.*)

Name	Birth	Religion	Residence	Occupation	1680 Real Property	Personal Property	Stock Ownership; Trading Company Offices[1]
TURGIS Dep. Edward	c. 1620	Dissenter	Cordwainer	Domestic trader: Woollen draper	£18 p.a.	£32 p.a.	
WALKER William	1635		Farringdon Without	Industrial employer: Ironmonger	£48 p.a.	£30 p.a.	£ 400 Royal African Co. 1672 £1,000 External East India 1682
WARD Sir Patience	1629	Independent	Dowgate	Merchant: N. Europe, Iberia, Colonies, France	£94 p.a.	£96 p.a.	
WESTERN Thomas	1623	Dissenter	Tower	Industrial employer: Ironmonger	£56 p.a.	£66 p.a.	
WILMORE John	Active 1670	Dissenter	Aldersgate Without	Merchant: N. Europe	£20 p.a.	£40 p.a.	£ 500 External East India 1682

[1] Years of service in trading company offices are indicated in parentheses.

APPENDIX IV. Tory party leaders

Name	Birth	Residence	Occupation	1680 Real Property	Personal Property	Stock Ownership; Trading Company Offices[1]
ALIE Richard	1637	Tower	Merchant: Colonial, France	£120 p.a.	£100 p.a.	£ 400 Royal African 1672
AYLEWORTH Peter	Apprenticed 1643	Broad Street	Domestic trader: Grocer and Salter	£40 p.a.	£30 p.a.	
BACKWELL Edward	c. 1618	Langbourn	Goldsmith	£132 p.a.	£132 p.a.	£1,000 Royal African 1672
BECKFORD Sir Thomas	Married 1651	Tower	Domestic trader: Clothing supplier to navy	£120 p.a.	£120 p.a.	
BLUDWORTH Sir Thomas	1620	Farringdon Within	Merchant: Iberia, Levant	Lodger	£192 p.a.	£ 500 Royal African 1672 £1,500 East India 1675 £4,000 East India 1682 Royal African Dir. (3) East India Dir. (4) Levant Dir. (6)

(cont.)

Appendix IV. (cont.)

Name	Birth	Residence	Occupation	1680 Real Property	Personal Property	Stock Ownership; Trading Company Offices[1]
BOX Ralph	1627	Cheap	Druggist, Apothecary	£66 p.a.	£48 p.a.	
CHAPMAN Sir John	1633	Broad Street	Merchant: N. Europe, Iberia	£40 p.a.	£60 p.a.	£5,500 East India 1682
CHARLETON Nicholas	Apprenticed 1639	Castle Baynard	Domestic trader: Woollen draper	£90 p.a.	£84 p.a.	£ 250 East India 1675
DANIEL Sir Peter	Free 1656	Bridge	Merchant: unknown specialization	£30 p.a.	£48 p.a.	East India Dir. (2)
DASHWOOD Sir Samuel	1643	Bishopsgate Without	Merchant: N. Europe, Levant, Colonial, Italy	Lodger	£72 p.a.	£ 500 Royal African 1672; £ 500 East India 1675; Royal African Dir. (9); East India Dir. (2); Levant Dir. (6)
DODSON Sir William	1639	Castle Baynard	Domestic trader: Woollen draper	£70 p.a.	£72 p.a.	
EDWARDS Sir James	Apprenticed 1637	Bassishaw	Merchant: unknown specialization	£54 p.a.	£66 p.a.	£3,250 East India 1675; Royal African Dir. 1676; East India Dir. (13); East India Dep. Gov. (2)

Name	Date	Location	Occupation			Investments
GEFFREY Sir Robert	1622	Lime Street	Merchant: Levant	£90 p.a.	£40 p.a.	£400 Royal African 1672 £4,000 East India 1682
GENEW John	Apprenticed 1651	Dowgate	Industrial employer: Sugar-baker	£28 p.a.	£18 p.a.	£2,500 East India 1682
GILBOURNE Percival	1616	Cheap	Druggist	£18 p.a.	£12 p.a.	
GOSTLYN Sir William	1638	Castle Baynard	Domestic trader: Lace-man	£40 p.a.	£48 p.a.	
GRIFFITH Capt. Francis	Apprenticed 1647	Farringdon Within	Scrivener	£20 p.a.	£20 p.a.	
HAWES Nathaniel	1622	Bridge	Domestic trader: Cheesemonger	£42 p.a.	£36 p.a.	
HEATLEY Thomas	1619	Aldgate	Merchant: Levant	Lodger	£42 p.a.	£400 Royal African 1672 Royal African Dir. (3)
HOOKER Sir William	1612	Aldgate	Merchant: Italy	£96 p.a.	£64 p.a.	
HOW[E] Sir Richard	c. 1638	Farringdon Within	Domestic trader: Fishmonger, Lighter-man	£100 p.a.	£18 p.a.	
JEFFREYS Sir George Bt	1648	Cripplegate Within	Lawyer	£46 p.a.	£66 p.a.	
JOHNSON John	1639	Farringdon Within	Goldsmith	£100 p.a.	£18 p.a.	£250 East India 1675

(cont.)

Appendix IV. (*cont.*)

Name	Birth	Residence	Occupation	1680 Real Property	Personal Property	Stock Ownership; Trading Company Offices[1]
LANGHAM Thomas	Apprenticed 1650	Bishopsgate Within	Apothecary	£30 p.a.	£36 p.a.	£100 East India 1675; £2,000 East India 1682
LEWIS Sir Simon	Married 1667	Cornhill	Unknown	£78 p.a.	£42 p.a.	£1,000 Royal African 1672
LOADES Henry	1622	Billingsgate	Merchant: Iberia, Colonies	£42 p.a.	£30 p.a.	£700 East India 1675; £1,000 East India 1682
MIDGLEY John	Apprenticed 1648	Queenhithe	Scrivener	£84 p.a.	£120 p.a.	
MOORE Sir John	1620	Tower	Merchant: N. Europe	£120 p.a.	£144 p.a.	£9,850 East India 1675; East India Dir. (15)
NEWLAND Sir Benjamin	c. 1633	Tower	Merchant: Iberia, Italy, Colonies, France	£80 p.a.	£108 p.a.	£4,000 East India 1682; Royal African Dir. (7); Royal African Dep. Gov (2); Gov. (2)
NICHOLL[S] John	Apprenticed 1649	Farringdon Without	Industrial employer: Soap boiler	£120 p.a.	£96 p.a.	
NICHOLSON Humfrey	Not found	Not found	Domestic trader: Packer	Not found	Not found	£500 East India 1675

Name	Date	Location	Occupation			Investments/Offices
NORTH Sir Dudley	1641	Bassishaw	Merchant: Levant	Not in City, 1680	Not in City, 1680	£5,000 East India 1682; Royal African Dir. (2); Royal African Dep. Gov. (2); Sub. Gov. (1); Levant Dir. (5); Royal African Dir. (3)
PARAVICINI Peter	1637	Tower	Merchant: France	£120 p.a.	£96 p.a.	
PEAKE Sir John	1637	Bridge	Merchant: unknown specialization	£60 p.a.	£84 p.a.	
PRI[T]CHARD Sir William	c. 1632	Heydon Yard, Minories; Highgate, Middlesex; Great Lynford, Bucks.	Industrial employer: Rope-maker; Supplier of cordage & match to the navy	Not in City	Not in City	£5,000 East India 1682
RAWSTORNE Sir William	Apprenticed 1656	Not found	Unknown	Not found	Not found	
RAYMOND Sir Jonathan	1637	Dowgate	Industrial employer: Brewer	£116 p.a.	£96 p.a.	£5,000 East India 1682
RICH Peter	1630	Bankside, Southwark; Mablethorpe, Lincs.	Merchant: N. Europe	Not in City	Not in City	£1,000 East India 1682
RUSSELL Sir William	1643	Bishopsgate Within	Domestic trader: Draper	£24 p.a.	£29 p.a.	

(cont.)

Appendix IV. (*cont.*)

Name	Birth	Residence	Occupation	1680 Real Property	Personal Property	Stock Ownership; Trading Company Offices[1]
SHELDON Sir Joseph	Apprenticed 1647	Castle Baynard	Domestic trader: Woollen draper	£80 p.a.	£108 p.a.	£ 250 East India 1675
SKUTT Benjamin	1638	Bishopsgate Within	Merchant: Iberia, Colonial	£36 p.a.	£30 p.a.	£1,000 Royal African 1672 Royal African Dir. (9)
SMYTH Sir James	1642	Coleman Street	Merchant: unknown specialization	£60 p.a.	£66 p.a.	£5,000 East India 1682
STEVENTON Dep. John	Apprenticed 1637	Broad Street	Industrial employer: Tobacconist	£50 p.a.	£36 p.a.	
TULSE Sir Henry	Apprenticed 1636	Coleman Street	Merchant: unknown specialization	£40 p.a.	£66 p.a.	£ 500 Royal African 1672 £ 800 East India 1675 Royal African Dir. (7)
TURNER Sir William	1615	Farringdon Within	Merchant: France	£80 p.a.	£48 p.a.	£1,250 East India 1675 Royal African Dir. (6) East India Dir. (1)

	Free/Date	Street	Occupation			Company offices/Investments[1]
VERNON Thomas	Free 1661	Coleman Street	Merchant: N. Europe, Levant, Colonial, Italy	£120 p.a.	£54 p.a.	£500 Royal African 1672; £6,000 East India 1682; Royal African Dir. (9); Levant Dir. (23); Husband (13)
VYNER Sir Robert Bt	1631	Coleman Street	Goldsmith	£120 p.a.	£66 p.a.	£5,500 Royal African 1672; Royal African Dir. (3)
WATERMAN Sir George	Apprenticed 1631	Dowgate	Industrial employer: Ironmonger	£57 p.a.	£96 p.a.	£500 Royal African 1672
WISEMAN Sir Edmund	1635	Castle Baynard	Domestic trader: Mercer	£40 p.a.	£36 p.a.	£9,000 East India 1682
WITHERS William Sr	1625	Cheap	Domestic trader: Linen-draper	£45 p.a.	£24 p.a.	

[1] Years of service in trading company offices are indicated in parentheses.

BIBLIOGRAPHY

MANUSCRIPT SOURCES

Bodleian Library, Oxford

Carte MS
30	Miscellaneous Papers
47	Ormonde Papers (Newsletters)
73	Montague Papers, 1656–61
213–14	Ormonde Papers, 1650–63

Clarendon MS
60, 62–75, 80	Clarendon Papers, 1659–63

British Library, London

Additional Manuscripts
4107	Transcripts of State Papers, II
10,116–17	Thomas Rugge, Mercurius Politicus Redivivus, I–II
34,362	Collection of Political, Satirical, and other Poems of the Reign of Charles II
36,916	Aston Papers, XVI
38,847	Hodgkin Papers, II
40,712	Oxenden Papers, XVII

Coventry Manuscript
M/863/11	Bath Papers, XVI

Egerton Manuscript
2543	Sir Edward Nicholas Papers

Harleian Manuscript
6845	Historical Papers of the Sixteenth and Seventeenth Centuries

Stowe Manuscript
186	Transcripts of State Papers; 1631–1727

British Library, Oriental and India Office

B/26-B/38	East India Company, Minutes of the Court of Committees, 1657–88
H/1 (2)	Home Miscellaneous Series: East India Company, 1675 List of Adventurers

Corporation of London Records Office

Alchin B/33/15   May 1679 London petition and signature roll
Card Index of lenders to certain loans, 1660–64, comp. T. F. Reddaway, *et al.*
Common Council Papers (1659)
Conventicles Boxes
Journals of the Court of Common Council
Remembrancia
Repertories of the Court of Aldermen
Sessions Files
Sessions Minute Books
Waiting Books
Ward Assessment Books for the six-months' tax of 1680
MS 40/30   Chamber Accounts of 1670 loan to crown

Dr Williams's Library

Lyon Turner MS 89.32   Notes about London Sessions Rolls 1664–84
MS 31.P-Q   Roger Morrice, "Ent'ring Book, Being an
                                  Historical Register of Occurrences from April,
                                  Anno 1677 to April 1691"
Congregational Library
MS 52.a.38   Register of Bury Street, Duke's Place Meeting

Folger Shakespeare Library

Newdigate Newsletters

Greater London Record Office

MJ/SR/1389–90   Sessions of the Peace and Oyer and Terminer
                                  Rolls, Middlesex, 1670

Guildhall Library

MS 186/1   Militia of London, Commissioners' Proceedings,
                                  copy, 1660 and Lieutenancy of London,
                                  Commissioners' Minutes, 1677–82
MS 507/21   Sir John Moore Papers
MS 3504/12   Additional Papers of Sir John Moore
MS 3589   Parliamentary Proceedings temp. Charles II,
                                  1676–8

Library of Congress

MS 18,124   London Newsletters Collection, 1665–85

Public Record Office

Exchequer: King's Remembrancer, Port Books, London (1680–88)
E190/102/1
E190/114/4

E190/127/2
E190/128/2
E 190/131/1
E190/134/1
E190/141/1
E190/142/1
E190/144/1 & 4

PC 2/69	Privy Council Register: Charles II, vol. 16 (1680–83)
PROB 11	Prerogative Court of Canterbury: Will Registers
SP 9/26	State Papers Domestic: Williamson Collection, Index or "Spy Book" [1663]
SP 29	State Papers Domestic, Reign of Charles II
SP 44/60/11	State Papers, Entry Books: Military, Earl of Sunderland, 1679–83
SP 105/152–54	Levant Company, General Court Minute Books 1660–85
T70/100	Royal African Company, General Court Minute Book, 1672–8

Harry Ransom Humanities Research Center, University of Texas, Austin

Newsletters of Richard Bulstrode, 1667–89

William Salt Library, Stafford

D(W)1778/Ii/703	External East India subscription (10 April 1682)

PRINTED PRIMARY SOURCES

The place of publication is London, unless otherwise noted.

Newspapers and serials

Domestick Intelligence (1679–80, 1681–2).
An Exact Accompt of the daily Proceedings in Parliament (1659–60).
Heraclitus Ridens (1681–2).
The Impartial Protestant Mercury (1681–2).
The Observator (1681–3).
Londons Diurnal (1660).
The London Gazette (1665–85).
Mercurius Politicus (1659–60).
The Moderate Intelligencer (1682).
The Phanatick Intelligencer (1660).
The Protestant (Domestick) Intelligence (1680–81).
The Publick Intelligencer (1659–60).
The True Protestant Mercury (1680–82).
Votes of the House of Commons (1680–81).

Contemporary books, pamphlets, broadsides, and sermons

The Abridgement of the Charter of the City of London (1680).
An Account of the New Sheriffs, holding their Office (1680).

An Account of the Proceedings at Guild-hall, London, at the tolke-moot [sic] [1676].

An Account of the Proceedings at the Guild-Hall of the City of London on Saturday, September 13. 1679.

An Account at Large, of the proceedings at the Sessions-House . . . 24 of November 1681.

An Account of the Proceedings to Judgment against the Charter of the City of London . . . the 12th of this Instant June. Anno. Dom. 1683.

An Act of Common Council for Regulating the Election of Sheriffs, and for Repealing the Treasonable and Disloyal Acts and Proceedings of that Court (1683).

The Address of the Freeholders of the County of Middlesex (1681).

Admonition of the greatest Concernment [1659].

Advice to the Men of Shaftesbury (1681).

The Alarum: or an Hue-and-Cry after Sir Pa–t W–d (1683).

[Alsop, Vincent]. *Melius Inquirendum. Or, A Sober Inquiry into the Reasonings of the Serious Inquiry*, 3rd ed. (1681).

[Alsop, Vincent]. *The Mischief of Impositions: or, an Antidote against a Late Discourse . . . called the Mischief of Separation* (1680).

An Alarum to the City and Souldiery [1659].

Alderman Bunce his Speech (1660).

The Ancient Bounds, or Liberty of Conscience, tenderly Stated, modestly Asserted, and mildly Vindicated (1645).

Animadversions on the late Vindication of Slingsby Bethel Esq (1681).

An Answer to a Letter written by a Member of Parliament . . . upon the occasion of his reading of the Gazette of the 11th of December, 1679.

An Answer to a Pamphlet Intituled, A Vindication of Sir Thomas Player (1679).

An Answer to the Excellent and Elegant Speech Made by Sir Thomas Player . . . On Friday the 12th of September, 1679.

The Answers commanded by his Majesty to be given (1681).

An Apologeticall Narration (1644).

The Apology of Robert Tichborne and John Ireton [1660].

The Arraignment of Co-Ordinate Power (1683).

Ashhurst, William. *Reasons against Agreement with a late printed Paper* (1648).

At a Common-Councel holden at the Guildhall . . . 23 day of November 1659.

At a Common Councel holden in the Guild-hall London . . . 14th of December, 1659.

At a Common Councel holden in the Guildhall London, . . . the 20th of December, 1659.

B., C. *An Address to the Honourable City of London* (1681).

[Bagshaw, Edward]. *The Second Part of the Great Question* [1661].

Baker, Sir Richard. *A Chronicle of the Kings of England* (1665).

Baxter, Richard. *Catholick Communion defended against both Extreams* (1684).

Baxter, Richard. *Church History of the Government of Bishops and their Councils Abbreviated* (1680).

Baxter, Richard. *The Grand Debate between . . . the Bishops and the Presbyterian Divines* (1661).

Baxter, Richard. *The Nonconformists Plea for Peace: or an Account of their Judgement* (1679).

Baxter, Richard. *Reliquiae Baxterianae*, ed. Matthew Sylvester (1696).

Baxter, Richard. *Second Part of the Nonconformists Plea for Peace* (1680).

Baxter, Richard. *Two Papers of Proposals concerning the Discipline and Ceremonies of the church of England* (1661).

Bedlow, William. *A Narrative and Impartial Discovery of the Horrid Popish Plot* (1679).

Behold a Cry! (1662).

[Bethel, Slingsby]. *An Act of Common-Council . . . for Retrenching of the Expenses of the Lord Mayor, & Sheriffs, &c.* (1680).

Bethel, Slingsby. *The Interest of the Princes and States of Europe* (1680).

Bethel, Slingsby. *The Interest of the Princes & States of Europe*, 3rd ed. (1689).

[Bethel, Slingsby]. *The Present Interest of England Stated* (1671, 1681).

Bethel, Slingsby. *The World's Mistake in Oliver Cromwell* (1668).

[Blount, Charles]. *An Appeal from the Country to the City for the Preservation of His Majesties Person, Liberty, Property, and the Protestant Religion* (1679).

[Blount, Charles?]. *A Character of Popery and Arbitrary Government, with a Timely Caveat and Advice to all the Freeholders, Citizens and Burgesses* [1679].

[Bohun, Edmund]. *Reflections on a Pamphlet, stiled a Just and Modest Vindication of the two last Parliaments* (1683).

[Booth, Sir George]. *The Declaration of the Lords, Gentlemen, Citizens, Freeholders* [1659].

A Brief Account of what Pass'd in the Common Council (1681).

A Brief Confession or Declaration of Faith; set forth by . . . Ana-Baptists (1660).

[Buckingham, George Villiers, 2nd Duke of]. "The D. of Buckinghams Speech in the House of Lords, the 16th. of November 1675," in [Anthony Ashley Cooper, Earl of Shaftesbury], *Two Speeches* (Amsterdam, 1675).

[Buckingham, George Villiers, 2nd Duke of]. *A Speech made by the Duke of Buckingham, the First Day of the Session of the Parliament* (1677).

Burgess, Cornelius. *Reasons shewing the Necessity of Reformation* (1660).

Burnet, Gilbert. *An Exhortation to Peace and Union* (1681).

By the Committee of Safety. A Proclamation (1659).

Calamy, Edmund. *Eli Trembling for Fear of the Ark* (1662).

[Care, Henry]. *A Perfect Guide for Protestant Dissenters* (1682).

Caryl, Joseph. *Englands Plus Ultra, both of hoped Mercies, and of Required Duties* (1646).

The Case between the Ld. Mayor and Commons of London (1682).

The Case of Edward Bushel, John Hammond, Charles Milson and John Baily [1671]. Lincoln's Inn Library.

The Case of the Sheriffs for the Year 1682.

The Case of the Ward of Castle-Baynard (1682).

The Case stated concerning the . . . Doctors Commons, as to the Election of Ward-Officers (1682).

The Cavaliers Litany (1682).

The Certain Way to Save England (1681).

The Character of a Church-Trimmer (1683).

The Character of a Rebellion, and what England May Expect from one (1681).

The Charter; A Comical Satyr (1682).

[Chillingworth, William]. *Mr. Chillingworth's Judgment of the Religion of Protestants* (1680).

The Citizens Loss, when the Charter of London is Forfeited (1683).

The Citizens of London, by their Charter [1680].

The City of Londons Loyal Plea (1682).

The City's Remonstrance and Addresse to the King's most excellent Majesty (1661).

A Collection of the Substance of several Speeches and Debates made in the Honourable House of Commons (1681).

[Collins, John]. *A Word in Season to all in Authority* (1660).

A Complete Collection of Farewel Sermons (1663).

A Conference between a Bensalian Bishop and an English Doctor, concerning Church-Government (1681).

[Corbet, John]. *A Discourse of the Religion of England* (1667).

[Corbet, John]. *The Interest of England in the Matter of Religion* (1660).

[Corbet, John]. *A Second Discourse of the Religion of England* (1668).

[Corbet, John]. *The Second Part of the Interest of England* (1660).

[Coven, Steven]. *The Militant Christian, or the Good Soldier of Jesus Christ* (1668).

[Croft, Herbert]. *The Naked Truth* (1675).

[Croft, Herbert]. *The Naked Truth*, 2nd ed. (1680).

[Crofton, Zachary]. *Berith Anti-Baal* (1661).

Crofton, Zachary. *Reformation not Separation* (1662).

D., C. *A Seasonable Letter of Advice delivered to the Lord Mayor of London* [1659].

D., M. *A Short Surveigh of the Grand Case of the Present Ministry* (1663).

Declaration and Vindication of the Lord Mayor, Aldermen and Commons of the City of London (1660).

Declaration of Many Thousand well-affected Persons [1660].

A Declaration of several of the People called Anabaptists, in and about the City of London (1659).

The Declaration of the County of Oxon to . . . Monck (1660).

Declaration of the Nobility and Gentry that adhered to the Late King (1660).

A Declaration of the Nobility, Gentry, Ministry . . . of Kent [1660].

A Declaration of the People of England for a Free-Parliament [1660].

The Devonshire Ballad (1681).

A Dialogue between the Ghosts of the Two last Parliaments (1681).

A Dialogue between the two Giants in Guildhall (1661).

A Dialogue between Two Jesuits, Father Antony and Father Ignatius, at Amsterdam [1681].

Dove, Henry. *A sermon preached . . . at Bow-Church . . . the day for election of a Lord Mayor* (1682).

[Dryden, John]. *Absalom and Achitophel. A Poem* (1681).

Dryden, John. *The Duke of Guise* (1683).

[Dryden, John]. *The Medall. A satyre* (1682).

[John Dryden and Nahum Tate]. *The Second Part of Absalom and Achitophel* (1682).

Du Moulin, Louis. *A Short and True Account of the Several Advances the Church of England hath made towards Rome* (1680).

[Du Moulin, Peter]. *England's Appeal from the Private Cabal to the Great Council of the Nation* (1673).

The Earl of Essex His Speech at the Delivery of the Petition (1681).

The Engagement and Remonstrance of the City of London [1659].

England's Appeal to the Parliament at Oxford, March 21st. 1680/1.

Englands Present Case Stated [1659].

The Englishman, or a Letter from a Universal Friend (1670).

An Exact Account of the Proceedings at Guild-hall upon the Election of . . . Sir William Pritchard [1682].

An Express from the Knights and Gentlemen now engaged with Sir George Booth; To the City and Citizens of London (1659).

[Fairfax, Thomas]. *Declaration of . . . and the rest of the Lords, . . . at York* [1660].

The Fanatique Powder-Plot [1660].

[Ferguson, Robert]. *An Impartial Enquiry into the Administration of Affair's in England* (1683).

Ferguson, Robert. *The Interest of Reason in Religion* (1675).

Ferguson, Robert. *A Letter to a Person of Honour concerning the Black Box* [1680].

The Final Protest and Sense of the City [1659].

A Fourth Paper presented by divers Citizens (1682).

The Freeholders Choice: Or, a Letter of Advice concerning Elections (1679).

The Free-Mens Petition: to the Right honourable, the Lord Mayor, Aldermen, and Commonalty of the City of London [1659].

A Free Parliament Proposed by the City to the Nation [1660].

A Friendly Dialogue between two London Apprentices (1681).

From Aboard the Van-Herring [1681].

Goodwin, John. *Prelatique Preachers None of Christ's Teachers* (1663).

Griffith, Matthew. *The Fear of God and the King* (1660).

Gumble, Thomas. *The Life of General Monck* (1671).

Harrington, James. *Aphorisms Political* (1659).

Harrington, James. *A Discourse Shewing, that the Spirit of Parliaments, with a Council in the Intervals, is not to be trusted for a Settlement* (1659).

[Hearne, Robert]. *Obsequium et Veritas: or A Dialogue Between London and Southwark* (1681).

[Hickeringill, Edmund]. *The Naked Truth. The Second Part* (1680).

His Majesties Declaration to all his Loving Subjects, June the Second, 1680.

His Majesties Declaration to all His Loving Subjects touching the causes and reasons that moved him to dissolve the two last Parliaments (1681).

His Majesties Letter to the Artillery Company: With an Account of their Proceedings . . . the 9th. of this instant, February, 1680/1.

His Majesties Message to the Commons in Parliament Relating to Tangier. And the Humble Address of the Commons to His Majesty in Answer . . . 29 Nov. 1680.

[Holles, Denzil, Baron Holles]. *The Long Parliament Dissolved* (1676).

How and Rich: An Impartial Account of the Proceedings at the late Election of Burgesses for the Borough of Southwark (1681).

Howe, John. *A Letter Written out of the Countrey to a Person of Quality in the City* (1680).

A Hue and Cry after the Reasons which were to have been given on Thursday last, Sept. 18. 1679. to the Lieutenancy, by Sir T. P. and Others (1679).

An Humble Address to all the Truly Loyal Commons of England (1680).

An Humble Address to the truly Loyal Citizens of London [1679 or 1680].

The Humble Address of the Lord Maior, Aldermen and Common-Council of the City . . . the 9th of August (1659).

The Humble Petition and Address of the Right Honourable the Lord Mayor (1681).

The Humble Petition of Many Inhabitants in and about the City of London (1659).

The Humble Petition of the Lord Maior, Aldermen, and Common-Council of the City of London (1659).

The Humble Petition of the Lord Mayor, Aldermen, and Commons of the City of London . . . 13th of January, 1680 (1681).

The Humble Petition of the Lord Mayor . . . 18th of June 1683.

[Humfrey, John]. *An Answer to Dr. Stillingfleet's Book of the Unreasonableness of Separation* (1682).

[Humfrey, John]. *An Answer to Dr. Stillingfleet's Sermon, by the Peaceable Design Renewed* (1680).

[Humfrey, John]. *The Authority of the Magistrate, about religion, discussed* (1672).

[Humfrey, John]. *A Case of Conscience* (1669).

[Humfrey, John]. *A Defence of the Proposition* (1668).

[Humfrey, John]. *The Healing Attempt* (1689).

[Humfrey, John]. *Materials for Union, Proposed to Publick Consideration* (1681).

[Humfrey, John]. *The Peaceable Design; being a Modest Account, of . . . the way of Accommodation in the matter of Religion* (1675).

[Humfrey, John]. *A Peaceable Resolution of Conscience touching our present Impositions* (1680).

Hunt, Thomas. *A Defence of the Charter, and Municipal Rights of the City of London* (1680).

The Ignoramus Justices [1682].

An Impartial Account of the Proceedings at Guildhall . . . 5th . . . September, 1683.

An Impartial Account of the Proceedings of the Common-Hall . . . June the 24th, 1682.

An Impartial Survey of such as are not, and such as are, fitly Qualified for Candidates for the approaching Parliament [1679].

Jenks, Francis. *Mr. Francis Jenk's Speech in a Common Hall, the 24th of June 1679.*

A Just and Modest Vindication of the many Thousand Loyal Apprentices (1681).

A Just Reproof to Mr Baxter, for His Pride and Insolence (1680).

The Last Will and Testament of the Charter of London (1683).

The Last Words and Sayings of the True-Protestant Elm-Board (1682).

[L'Estrange, Sir Roger]. *Citt and Bumpkin* (1680).

[L'Estrange, Sir Roger]. *The Committee; or Popery in Masquerade* (1680).

L'Estrange, Sir Roger. *Considerations and Proposals in Order to the Regulation of the Press* (1663).

L'Estrange, Sir Roger. *Interest Mistaken; or, the Holy Cheat* (1662).

[L'Estrange, Sir Roger]. *A Necessary and Seasonable Caution, concerning Elections* [1660].

A Letter agreed unto, and subscribed by, the Gentlemen, Ministers, Freeholders . . . of Suffolk. Presented to the Lord Mayor (1660).

A Letter and Declaration of the Nobility and Gentry of . . . York to . . . Monck [1660].

A Letter from a Person of Quality to his Friend (1681).

A Letter from divers of the Gentry of the County of Lincolne to . . . Monck [1660].

A Letter from J. B. alias Oldcutt, to his Friend Mr. Jenks (1679).

A Letter from Mr. Edward Whitaker to the protestant Joyner (1681).

A Letter from Scotland, with Observations upon the Anti-Erastian, Anti-Prelatical, and Phanatical Presbyterian Party there (1682).

A Letter from the Lord General Monck and the Officers under his Command to the Parliament (1660).

A Letter of Advice to the Petitioning Apprentices (1681).

A Letter of November 12. from General Monck (1659).

A Letter of his Excellencie the Lord General Monck, to the Speaker of the Parl. (1660).

A Letter of the Apprentices of the City of Bristoll, to the Apprentices of the Honourable City of London (1660).

A Letter on the Subject of the Succession (1679).

A Letter sent to the Right Honourable, the Lord Mayor ... by Lieutenant Colonel Kiffin [1660].

A Letter to a Person of Honour concerning the King's disavowing the having been married to the Duke of Monmouth's Mother [1680].

A Letter to Dr du Moulin, containing a Charitable Reproof for his Schismatical Book (1680).

A Letter to Sir Thomas Alyn (1659).

A Letter written from the Tower by Mr. Stephen Colledge (1681).

The Life and Approaching Death of William Kiffin [1660].

Lilburne, John. *The Charters of London: or the second Part of Londons Liberty* (1646).

Lilburne, John. *Londons Liberty in Chains Discovered* (1646).

A List of the Conventicles or unlawful meetings within the City of London and Bills of Mortality (1683).

A List of the Poll of the several companies of London for a Lord Mayor (1682).

London's Choice of Citizens to Represent them in the Ensuing Parliament ... October 7th. 1679.

London's Liberties; or a Learned Argument of Law & Reason (1651).

London's Out-Cry to her Sister-Cities [1659].

The Lord General Monck, his Speech delivered in Parliament (1660).

The Lord Mayor of London's Vindication. Being an Answer (1682).

The Lord Mayor's Right of Electing a Sheriff (1682).

The Loyal Feast (1682).

The Loyal Subjects Lamentation for Londons Perverseness (1661).

The Loyal Subjects Litany (1680).

Loyalty vindicated from the Calumnies (1681).

[Marvell, Andrew]. *An Account of the Growth of Popery and Arbitrary Government in England* (Amsterdam, 1677 and Westmead, Farnborough, Hants., 1971).

[Marvell, Andrew]. *Mr. Smirke; or, the Divine in Mode* (1676).

[Marvell, Andrew]. "A Short Historical Essay, touching General Councils, Creeds, and Imposition in Religion" in *Mr. Smirke*, 44–76.

Master Edmund Calamies Leading Case (1663).

Matchiavel Junior; or the Secret Arts of the Jesuites (1683).

Matters of Fact in the Present Election of Sheriffs (1682).

Milton, John. *Areopagitica* (1644).

Milton, John. *Brief Notes Upon a Late Sermon, Titl'd, The Fear of God* (1660).

Milton, John. *Considerations touching the Likeliest Means to Remove Hirelings* (1659).

Milton, John. *Samson Agonistes* (1671).

Milton, John. *Treatise of Civil Power in Ecclesiastical Causes* (1659).

[Mocket, Richard]. *God and the King* (1663).

A Modest Enquiry concerning the Election of the sheriffs of London (1682).

A Most Serious Expostulation with several of my Fellow Citizens in reference to their standing so high for the D. Y.'s Interest at this Juncture of time [1679].

N., D. *A Letter from an Old Common-Council-Man to one of the new Common-Council* [1682].

[Nalson, John]. *An Essay upon the Change of Manners. Being a Second Part of the True Protestants Appeal to the City and Country* (1681).

[Nalson, John]. *The True Protestants Appeal to the City and Countrey* (1681).

A Narrative of the Proceedings of the Committee of the Militia of London [1659].

The Nature of a Common-Hall Briefly Stated (1682).

The New Litany (1659).

No King but the Old King's Son (1660).

[Northleigh, John]. *The Parallel; or, the New Specious Association* (1682).

Nye, Philip. *The king's Authority in dispensing with ecclesiastical laws, asserted and Vindicated* (1687).

Nye, Philip. *The Lawfulness of the Oath of Supremacy, and power of the king in Ecclesiastical Affairs* (1683).

Orthodox State-Queries [1660].

[Owen, John]. *A Brief and Impartial Account of the Nature of the Protestant Religion* (1682).

[Owen, John]. *A Brief Vindication of the Non-conformists* (1680).

[Owen, John]. *Indulgence and Toleration considered* (1667).

[Owen, John]. *A Peace-offering in an Apology* (1667).

[Owen, John]. *A Sermon Preached to the Honourable House of Commons . . . with a Discourse about Toleration* (1649).

[Owen, John]. *Some Considerations about Union among Protestants* (1680).

[Owen, John]. *Truth and Innocence Vindicated* (1669).

The Out-Cry of the London Prentices (1659).

Πανα ρμονια. *Or, the Agreement of the People* (1659).

A Parallel between Episcopacy & Presbytery (1680).

A Paper Delivered to the Lord Major and Court of Aldermen . . . Octob. 24, 1682.

A Paper presented by divers Citizens of the City of London, Sept. 5. 1682.

A Paper subscribed and delivered . . . July the 20th 1682.

[Parker, Samuel]. *A Discourse of Ecclesiastical Politie*, 3rd ed (1671).

Peace to the Nation [1660].

Penn, William. *The Great Case of Liberty of Conscience* (1670).

[Penn, William]. *Englands Great Interest in the Choice of this New Parliament* [1679].

[Penn, William]. *One Project for the Good of England; that is, Our Civil Union is our Civil Safety* [1679].

The Petition of Divers Eminent Citizens of London (1681).

The Petition of Mr. Praise-God Barebone, and several others, to the Parliament (1660).

The Petition of the Rump . . . to London [1660].

The Plot Reviv'd; or a Memorial of the Late and Present Popish Plot [1680].

The Prerogative of the Right Honourable the Lord Mayor of London, Asserted (1682).

The Presentment and Humble Petition of the Grand Jury for the County of Middlesex (1681).

The Presentment of the Grand Jury for the City of London . . . the 19th of April, 1683.

The Presentments of the Grand-Juries of the City of Westminster and County of Middx, Jan 1682 [1683].

Presentments of the Grand Jury for the County of Middlesex . . . the Eleventh day of October . . . 1682.

Presentments of the Grand-Jury for the Town and Borough of Southwark,... 12th day of January... 1682 [1683].

The Priviledg and Right of the Free-men of London, to chuse their own Sheriffs (1682).

The Proceedings and Judgment Against the Rioters (1683).

Proceedings at the Guild-Hall in London on Thursday July the 29th, 1680.

The Proceedings at the Tryal of Sr. Patience Ward Kt. (1683).

The Proceedings of the Common-Hall of London. The 24th of June, 1681.

The Proceedings upon the Debates, relating to the late Charter of the City of London (1683).

A Proposal Humbly offered to the Parliament, for suppressing Popery (1680).

A Proposal of Union amongst Protestants (1679).

A Proposition in order to the Proposing of a Commonwealth or Democracie [1659].

The Protestant Petition and Addresse (1681).

A Protestant Prentice's Loyal Advice to all his Fellow-Apprentices in and about London (1680).

[Prynne, William]. *Seasonable and Healing Instructions, Humbly tendered* [1660].

[Prynne, William]. *Summary Reasons, humbly tendered... by some Citizens and members of London, and other Cities... against the new intended Bill for... Corporations* [1661].

[Prynne, William]. *To the Right Honourable, the Lord Mayor, Aldermen,... of London... the Humble Petition and Address of the Seamen, and Water-men* (1659).

A Psalme sung by the People, before the Bone-fires [1660].

A Pulpit to be Let (1665).

The Reasons for the Indictment of the Duke of York presented to the Grand Jury of Middlesex [1680].

The Reformation, A Satire [1683].

Remarques upon the New Project of an Association (1682).

Remonstrance and Protestation of the Well-affected People of the Cities of London and Westminster, and Other the Cities and Places within the Commonwealth (1659).

The Remonstrance of the Apprentices in and about London [1659].

Remonstrance of the Knights, Gentlemen, and Freeholders of the County of Gloucester [1660].

Remonstrance of the Noble-men, Knights, Gentlemen... of the late Eastern, Southern, and Western Associations [1660].

The Remonstrance of the Soldiery [1660].

The Resolve of the City [1659].

[Reynolds, Edward]. *A Seasonable Exhortation of sundry Ministers in London to the People* (1660).

The Right of Electing Sheriffs of London and Middlesex, briefly stated and declared (1682).

The Rights of the City Farther Unfolded (1682).

[Rudyard, Thomas]. *The Peoples Antient and just Liberties asserted, in the Tryal of William Penn, and William Mead* (1670).

The Rump serv'd in with a Grand Sallet (1660).

Russell, William, Lord. *The Last Speech & Behaviour of William, late Lord Russel* (1683).

The Saints Freedom from Tyranny Vindicated (1667).

[Saunders, Jonathan]. *The Sham-Indictment Quash'd* (1681).

A Scheme of the Trade [1674].

A Seasonable Address to the Right Honourable, the Lord Mayor, Court of Aldermen, and Commoners of the City of London, upon their present electing of Sheriffs (1680).

A Seasonable Answer to a late Pamphlet, entituled, the Vindication of Slingsby Bethel, Esq. (1681).

A Seasonable Warning to the Commons of England; Discovering to them their Present Danger, and the only means of Escaping it [1679].

The Second Part of the Loyal Subject's Litany (1680).

A Serious Manifesto of the Anabaptist and Other Congregational Churches (1660).

Settle, Elkhanah. *Character of a Popish Successor* (1681).

Shaftesbury, Anthony Ashley Cooper, Earl of. "The Earl of Shaftesbury's Speech in the House of Lords the 20th. of October. 1675," in Shaftesbury, *Two Speeches* (Amsterdam, 1675).

[Shaftesbury, Anthony Ashley Cooper, Earl of]. *A Letter from a Parliament man to his Friend* (1675).

[Shaftesbury, Anthony Ashley Cooper, Earl of]. *A Letter from a Person of Quality, to his Friend in the Country* (1675).

[Shaftesbury, Anthony Ashley Cooper, Earl of]. *A Speech lately made by a Noble Peer of the Realm* (1681).

[Shaftesbury, Anthony Ashley Cooper, Earl of]. *Two Seasonable Discourses* (Oxford, 1675).

The Sheriffs Case. Whether, and How they may lawfully Qualifie themselves (1681).

The Sheriffs of London for the time being, are the Proper Managers and legal judges of the election of Sheriffs (1682).

[Sidney, Algernon and Sir William Jones]. *A just and modest Vindication of the Proceedings of the two last Parliaments* (1681).

The Solemn Mock Procession: Or the Trial and Execution of the Pope and His Minister, on the 17. of Nov. at Temple Bar (1680).

A Speech made by a True Protestant English Gentleman, to incourage the City of London to Petition for the sitting of the Parliament [1680].

The Speeches of Captain Walcot, Jo. Rouse, and Will. Hone (1683).

The Speech and Declaration of his Excellency the lord General Monck delivered at Whitehall [1660].

The Speech of Sir Robert Clayton Kt. Lord Mayor Elect . . . 29th of September 1679.

The Speech of the Right Honourable Sir John Moore Kt. (1681).

The Speech of the Right Honourable Sir Patience Ward (1680).

The Speech of the Right Honourable Sir Patience Ward Kt. (1681).

[Sprat, Thomas]. *Copies of the Informations and Original Papers relating to the Proof of the Horrid Conspiracy* (1685).

[Sprat, Thomas]. *A True Account and Declaration of the Horrid Conspiracy against the Late King* (1685).

State Tracts: Being a Collection of Several Treatises Relating to the Government (1689).

[Sterling, Sir Samuel]. *An Answer to the Seditious and Scandalous Pamphlet* (1671).

Stillingfleet, Edward. *Irenicum* (1661).

Stillingfleet, Edward. *The Mischief of Separation* (1680).

Stillingfleet, Edward. *The Unreasonableness of Separation* (1681).

Strange News from Hicks's-Hall (1681).

Stubbe, Henry. *An Essay in Defence of the Good Old Cause* (1659).
Stubbe, Henry. *A Light Shining out of Darkness* (1659).
T., S. *Moderation: Or Arguments and Motives tending thereunto* (1660).
Three Speeches made to the Right Honorable the Lord Maior (1659).
To his Excellency the Lord General Monck. The Unanimous Representation of the Apprentices [1660].
To the General Council of Officers. The Representation of divers Citizens of London (1659).
To the Kings Majesty. The humble and grateful acknowledgement of many Ministers . . . in and about London (1660).
To the Kings most Excellent Majesty. The Humble Address of the Loyal Apprentices [1681].
To the Kings most Excellent Majesty. The Humble Petition and Address . . . of the City of London (1680).
To the Lord Mayor and Court of Aldermen of the City of London (1682).
To the Right Honourable, our right worthy and grave Senatours . . . The most humble Petition and Address of divers Young Men [1659].
To the Right Honourable our Worthy and Grave Senators. . . . The further humble Petition and Remonstrance of the Free-men and Prentices (1659).
To the Right Honourable Sir Robert Clayton Kt. Lord Mayor of the City [1680].
To the Right Honourable the Council of State. . . . The Humble Petition of many thousand Citizens and Freemen of London [1660].
To the Right Honourable the High Court of Parliament, . . . the . . . Petition of Praise-God Barebone (1660).
To the Right Honourable the Lord Maior, Aldermen, and Common Councel. . . . The Humble Petition and Remonstrance of Several Inhabitants and Citizens [1660].
To the Right Honourable the Lord Maior, Aldermen, and Commons of the City of London. . . . The Humble Petition of divers Well-Affected Householders and Freemen [1660].
To the Right Honourable, the Lord Mayor, Aldermen, . . . of London . . . the Humble Petition and Address of the Sea-men, and Water-men [1659].
To the Right Honourable Patience Ward . . . The Humble Petition of the Commons . . . June 27. 1681.
To the Supreme Authority of the Nation: An Humble Petition on the behalf of . . . Quakers (1660).
To the Supreme Authority of the Nation . . . The humble Petition of the Common-Council of the City of London (1659).
A True Account of the Invitation and Entertainment of the D. of Y. at Merchant-Taylors-Hall, by the Artillery-Men, on Tuesday October 21st. 1679.
True Account of the Irregular Proceedings at Guild-hall . . . September 28. 1682.
A True Account of the Proceedings at the Common-Hall . . . 24th of June, 1680.
A True and Brief Relation of the Proceedings of the Common-Council (1681).
A True Copy of the Letter sent from the Lord Mayor, Aldermen and Common-Council . . . on the 29th of December, 1659. Directed to . . . George Monck.
A True List of the Names of those Persons appointed by the Rump Parliament to sit as a Council of State [1680].
A True Narrative of the Proceedings at Guild-Hall, London, the Fourth of this Instant February (1681).
The True Protestants Appeal to the City and Countrey (1681).
The Tryal and Conviction of Sir Sam. Barnardiston, Bart. (1684).

The Tryal of... for the Riot at Guild-Hall on Midsummer-Day, 1682 (1683).

The Tryall and Conviction of John Hambden, Esq. (1684).

The Two Associations (1681).

Two Letters; the One, Sent by the Lord Mayor... to Gen. Monck [1660].

Vane, Sir Henry. *A Needful Corrective or Ballance in Popular Government* (1659).

Venn and his Mermydons; or, the Linen-Draper Capotted (1679).

A Vindication of Sir Thomas Player, and those Loyal Citizens Concerned with Him (1679).

The Vindication of Slingsby Bethel Esq; One of the Sheriffs of London and Middlesex (1681).

A Vindication of the Loyal London Apprentices [1681].

A Vindication of the Protestant Petitioning Apprentices (1681).

The Vindicator Vindicated: or, a Sur-rejoynder on behalf of Sir Thomas Player (1679).

Votes of the Honourable, the House of Commons... in Favour of Protestant Dissenters (1681).

Vox Juvenilis (1681).

Vox Patriae (1681).

Vox Populi: or the Peoples Claim to their Parliaments Sitting (1681).

Vox Regni: or, The Voice of the Kingdom [1680].

Watson, Thomas. *Heaven taken by Storm* (1670).

Wee the Knights, Gentlemen, Ministers, and Free-Holders of the County of Warwick (1660).

The Whig-Intelligencer: or, Sir Samuel in the Pound (1684).

Whiston, James. *Serious Advice Presented to the Common Council of the City of London* (1681).

W[hitaker], E[dward]. *The Bishops Court Dissolved: or, the Law of England Touching Ecclesiastical Jurisdiction Stated* (1681).

Williams, Roger. *The Bloody Tenent of Persecution* (1644).

[Wilson, Joseph]. *Nehushtan: or, a sober and peaceable Discourse* (1668).

[Wolseley, Sir Charles]. *Liberty of Conscience, the Magistrates Interest* (1668).

[Wolseley, Sir Charles]. *Liberty of Conscience upon its true and proper Grounds asserted and Vindicated* (1668).

Y., N. and N. D. *The Protestant Conformist: Or, a Plea for Moderation, Contained in a Letter from One Conforming Minister to another: and His Answer to it* (1679).

Other printed primary sources and editions

Acts and Ordinances of the Interregnum, ed. C. H. Firth and R. S. Rait, 3 vols. (1911).

Ailesbury, Thomas Bruce, 2nd Earl of. *The Memoirs of Thomas, Earl of Ailesbury*, 2 vols. (1890).

Baxter, Richard. *A Holy Commonwealth*, ed. W. Lamont (Cambridge, 1994).

Baxter, Richard. *Calendar of the Correspondence of Richard Baxter*, ed. N. H. Keeble and G. F. Nuttall, 2 vols. (Oxford, 1991).

Bulstrode, Sir Richard. *The Bulstrode Papers* (1897).

Burnet, Gilbert. *Burnet's History of My Own Time*, ed. O. Airy, 2 vols. (Oxford, 1897–1900).

Calendar of State Papers, Venetian, 1657–75.

Calendar of State Papers, Domestic, 1659–1685.

Capel, Arthur, Earl of Essex. *Selections from the Correspondence of Arthur Capel Earl of Essex 1675–1677*, ed. C. E. Pike (1913).

"The Character of the Lord Mayor of London, and the whole Court of Aldermen," *The Gentleman's Magazine* 39 (1769), 515–17.

Christie, W. D. *Letters addressed from London to Sir Joseph Williamson*, 2 vols. (1874).

Clarendon, Edward Hyde, Earl of. *Calendar of Clarendon State Papers preserved in the Bodleian Library*, ed. F. J. Routledge, 5 vols. (Oxford, 1872–1932).

Clarendon, Edward Hyde, Earl of. *State Papers collected by Edward, Earl of Clarendon*, 3 vols. (Oxford, 1767–86).

The Clarke Papers. Selections from the Papers of William Clarke, Secretary to the Council of the Army, 1647–1649, ed. C. H. Firth, 4 vols. (1891–1901).

A Collection of scarce and valuable tracts . . . of the Late Lord Somers, ed. Sir W. Scott, 13 vols. (1809–15).

A Complete Collection of State Trials, ed. T. B. Howell and T. J. Howell, 34 vols. (1811–28).

Crowne, John. *City Politiques*, ed. J. H. Wilson (Lincoln, Nebr., 1967).

Dering, Sir Edward Bt. *The Parliamentary Diary of Sir Edward Dering 1670–1673*, ed. B. D. Henning (New Haven, Conn., 1940).

Dryden, John. *The Works of John Dryden*, ed. E. N. Hooker and H. T. Swedenberg, Jr, 19 vols. (Berkeley, Cal., 1956–).

English Historical Documents, 12 vols. (Oxford, 1955–77), VIII, *1660–1714*, ed. A. Browning (1953).

Evelyn, John. *The Diary of John Evelyn*, ed. E. S. De Beer, 6 vols. (Oxford, 1955).

Grey, Anchitel. *Debates of the House of Commons from the year 1667 to the year 1694*, 10 vols. (1763).

Grey, Forde Tankerville, Earl of. *The Secret History of the Rye House Plot* (1754).

[Harrington, James]. *The Political Works of James Harrington*, ed. J. G. A. Pocock (Cambridge, 1977).

Historical Manuscripts Commission:
  Fifth Report, Part I
  Ninth Report, Part II
  Dartmouth, vols. I, III (11th Report, Appendix v; 15th Report, Appendix i)
  Downshire, vol. I (Series 75)
  Egmont (Series 63)
  Finch (Series 71)
  Fitzherbert (13th Report, Appendix vi)
  Graham (7th Report, Part I, Appendix)
  Kenyon (14th Report, Appendix iv)
  Le Fleming (12th Report, Appendix vii)
  Lords 1678–1688 (11th Report, Appendix ii)
  Lords 1690–91 (13th Report, Appendix v)
  Leyborne-Popham (Series 51)
  Ormonde, NS, vols. 4–7 (14th Report, Appendix vii)
  Rutland, vol. 2 (12th Report, Appendix v)
  Verney (7th Report, Part I, Appendix)
Journals of the House of Commons.

Kennett, White. *A Complete History of England*, 3 vols. (1706).

The Little London Directory of 1677 (1863).

Locke, John. *The Correspondence of John Locke*, ed. E. S. de Beer, 8 vols. (Oxford, 1976–89).

Locke, John. "Essay on Toleration" (1667–8) in H. R. Fox Bourne, *The Life of John Locke*, 2 vols. (1876), I, 174–94.

Locke, John. *The Second Treatise of Government*, ed. P. Laslett, in *Two Treatises of Government*, 2nd ed. (Cambridge, 1967).

Ludlow, Edmund. *The Memoirs of Edmund Ludlow*, ed. C. H. Firth, 2 vols. (Oxford, 1894).

Ludlow, Edmund. *A Voyce from the Watchtower; Part Five, 1660–1662*, ed. A. B. Worden (1978).

Marvell, Andrew. *Poems and Letters*, ed. H. M. Margoliouth, 3rd ed., 2 vols. (Oxford, 1971).

The Mather Papers, Collections of the Mass. Hist. Soc., 4th ser., 8 (Boston, Mass., 1868).

Middlesex County Records, ed. J. C. Jaeffreson, 4 vols. (1887–92).

Mordaunt, John. *The Letter-book of John Viscount Mordaunt, 1658–60* (1945).

Newcome, Henry. *The Diary of the Rev. Henry Newcome* (Manchester, 1849).

The Nicholas Papers: Correspondence of Sir Edward Nicholas Secretary of State, 4 vols. (1886–1920).

North, Roger. *Examen; or, an Enquiry into the Credit and Veracity of a pretended complete History* (1740).

North, Roger. *The Life of the Lord Keeper North*, ed. M. Chen (Lewiston, NY, 1995).

Ogilby, John. *The Entertainment of His Most Excellent Majestie Charles II* [1662], ed. R. Knowles (Binghamton, NY, 1988).

Owen, John. *The Works of John Owen*, ed. W. H. Goold, 16 vols. (1850–53).

Papillon, A. F. W. *Memoirs of Thomas Papillon, of London, Merchant. (1623–1702)* (Reading, 1887).

Parliamentary or Constitutional History of England, 24 vols. (1760–63).

Penn, William. *The Political Writings of William Penn*, ed. A. R. Murphy (Indianapolis, 2002).

Pepys, Samuel. *The Diary of Samuel Pepys*, ed. R. Latham and W. Matthews, 11 vols. (Berkeley and Los Angeles, Cal., 1970–83).

Reresby, John. *Memoirs of Sir John Reresby*, ed. A. Browning (Glasgow, 1936).

Rugg, Thomas. *The Diurnal of Thomas Rugg 1659–61*, ed. W. L. Sachse (1961).

St Bartholomew by the Exchange, London. *The Vestry Minute Books of the Parish of St Bartholomew Exchange in the City of London, 1567–1676*, ed. E. Freshfield (1890).

Sermons of the Great Ejection (1962).

Savile, Henry. *Letters to and from Henry Savile, Esq., . . . including letters from his brother George, Marquess of Halifax* (1858).

Sidney, Algernon. *Court Maxims*, ed. H. W. Blom, E. H. Mulier, and R. Janse (Cambridge, 1996).

Sidney, Algernon. *Discourses Concerning Government*, ed. T. G. West (Indianapolis, 1990).

Sidney, Henry, Earl of Romney. *Diary of the Times of Charles the Second*, ed. R. W. Blencowe, 2 vols. (1843).

State tracts: being a Collection of several treatises relating to the Government, 2 vols. (1689, 1692).

Thompson, E. M., ed. *Correspondence of the Family of Hatton*, 2 vols. (1878).

Turner, G. L., ed. "The Religious Condition of London in 1672 as reported to King and Court by an Impartial Outsider," *TCHS* 3 (1907–8), 192–205.

[Turner, G. L., ed.] "Williamson's Spy Book," *TCHS* 5 (1911–12), 242–58, 301–19, 345–56 (transcribed from SP 9/26).

Warriston, Sir Archibald. *Diary of Sir Archibald Johnston of Wariston*, 3 vols. (Edinburgh, 1911–40).

Whitelock, Bulstrode. *The Diary of Bulstrode Whitelocke*, ed. R. Spalding (Oxford, 1990).

Whitelock, Bulstrode. *Memorials of the English affairs from the Beginning of the Reign of Charles the First* (Oxford, 1853).

Wolseley, Sir Charles. *The Reasonableness of Scripture-Belief (1672)*, intro. R. W. McHenry, Jr (Delmar, NY, 1973).

SELECTED SECONDARY SOURCES

Abernathy, G. J., Jr. *The English Presbyterians and the Stuart Restoration, 1648–1663* (Philadelphia, 1965).

Anderson, S. P. *An English Consul in Turkey: Paul Rycaut at Smyrna, 1667–1678* (Oxford, 1989).

Ashcraft, Richard. *Revolutionary Politics & Locke's Two Treatises of Government* (Princeton, 1986).

Beaven, A. B. *The Aldermen of the City of London*, 2 vols. (1908–13).

Beddard, R. A. "Vincent Alsop and the Emancipation of Restoration Dissent," *JEcH* 24 (1973), 161–84.

    "Wren's Mausoleum for Charles I and the Cult of the Royal Martyr," *Architectural History* 27 (1984), 36–49.

Beier, A. L. and R. Finlay, eds. *The Making of the Metropolis: London 1500–1700* (1986).

Bosher, R. S. *The Making of the Restoration Settlement: The Influence of the Laudians 1649–1662* (1951).

Brenner, R. *Merchants and Revolution: Commercial Change, Political Conflict, and London's Overseas Traders, 1550–1653* (Princeton, 1993).

Browning, A. *Thomas Osborne Earl of Danby and Duke of Leeds, 1632–1712*, 3 vols. (Glasgow, 1944–51).

Burgess, G. *The Politics of the Ancient Constitution: An Introduction to English Political Thought* (University Park, Pa., 1992).

Christie, W. D. *A Life of Anthony Ashley Cooper, First Earl of Shaftesbury. 1621–1683*, 2 vols. (1871).

Clark, J. C. D. *Revolution and Rebellion: State and Society in England in the Seventeenth and Eighteenth Centuries* (Cambridge, 1986).

Condren, C. "Andrew Marvell as Polemicist: His Account of the Growth of Popery, and Arbitrary Government," in C. Condren and A. D. Cousins, eds., *The Political Identity of Andrew Marvell* (Aldershot, Hants., 1990), 157–87.

    "Radicals, Conservatives and Moderates in Early Modern Political Thought: A Case of Sandwich Islands Syndrome?," *History of Political Thought* 10 (1989), 525–42.

Davies, K. G. *The Royal African Company* (1957, 1975).

De Krey, G. S. *A Fractured Society: The Politics of London in the First Age of Party, 1688–1715* (Oxford, 1985).

"London Radicals and Revolutionary Politics," in Harris, *et al.*, eds., *The Politics of Religion*, 133–62.

"Radicals, Reformers, and Republicans: Academic Language and Political Discourse in Restoration London," in A. Houston and S. Pincus, eds., *A Nation Transformed* (Cambridge, 2001), 71–99.

"Reformation in the Restoration Crisis, 1679–82," in D. B. Hamilton and R. Strier, eds., *Religion, Literature, and Politics*, 231–52.

"Rethinking the Restoration: Dissenting Cases for Conscience, 1667–1672," *HJ* 38 (1995), 53–83.

Elliot, D. C. "Elections to the Common Council of the City of London, December 21, 1659," *Guildhall Studies in London History* 4 (1981), 151–201.

Farnell, J. E. "The Navigation Act of 1651, the First Dutch War, and the London Merchant Community," *EcHR*, 2nd Ser., 16 (1964), 439–54.

"The Usurpation of Honest London Householders: Barebone's Parliament," *EHR* 82 (1967), 24–46.

Ferguson, J. *Robert Ferguson the Plotter; or, the Secret History of the Rye-House Conspiracy* (Edinburgh, 1887).

Fletcher, A. "The Enforcement of the Conventicle Acts 1664–1679," in W. J. Sheils, ed., *Persecution and Toleration* (Oxford, 1984), 235–46.

Gauci, P. *Politics and Society in Great Yarmouth 1660–1722* (Oxford, 1996).

The Politics of Trade: The Overseas Merchant in State and Society, 1660–1720 (Oxford, 2001).

Gentles, I. "The Struggle for London in the Second Civil War," *HJ* 26 (1983), 277–305.

Grassby, R. *The English Gentleman in Trade: The Life and Works of Sir Dudley North, 1641–1691* (Oxford, 1994).

Goldie, M. "Danby, the Bishops and the Whigs," in Harris, *et al.*, eds., *The Politics of Religion*, 75–105.

"The Hilton Gang and the Purge of London in the 1680s," in H. Nenner, ed., *Politics and the Political Imagination in later Stuart Britain* (Rochester, NY, 1997), 43–73.

"Priestcraft and the Birth of Whiggism," in N. Phillipson and Q. Skinner, eds., *Political Discourse in Early Modern Britain* (Cambridge, 1993), 209–31.

"The Theory of Religious Intolerance in Restoration England," in O. P. Grell, *et al.*, eds., *From Persecution to Toleration*, 331–68.

Goldie, M. and J. Spurr. "Politics and the Restoration Parish: Edward Fowler and the Struggle for St Giles Cripplegate," *EHR* 109 (1994), 572–96.

Greaves, R. L. *Deliver Us from Evil: The Radical Underground in Britain, 1660–1663* (New York, 1986).

Enemies under his Feet: Radicals and Nonconformists in Britain, 1664–1677 (Stanford, 1990).

Secrets of the Kingdom: British Radicals from the Popish Plot to the Revolution of 1688–89 (1992).

Greaves, R. L. and R. Zaller, *Biographical Dictionary of British Radicals in the Seventeenth Century*, 3 vols. (Brighton, 1982–4).

Green, I. M. *The Re-Establishment of the Church of England 1660–1663* (Oxford, 1978).

Green, T. A. *Verdict according to Conscience* (Chicago, 1985).

Grell, O. P. "From Persecution to Integration," in O. P. Grell, J. I. Israel, and N. Tyacke, eds., *From Persecution to Toleration: The Glorious Revolution and Religion in England* (Oxford, 1991), 97–127.

Habermas, J. *The Structural Transformation of the Public Sphere*, tr. T. Burger with F. Lawrence (Cambridge, Mass., 1989).

Halliday, P. D. *Dismembering the Body Politic: Partisan Politics in England's Towns, 1650–1730* (Cambridge, 1998).

Haley, K. H. D. *The First Earl of Shaftesbury* (Oxford, 1968).

William of Orange and the English Opposition 1672–4 (Oxford, 1953).

Hamilton, D. B. and R. Strier, eds., *Religion, Literature, and Politics in Post-Reformation England, 1540–1688* (Cambridge, 1996).

Harris, T. "The Bawdy House Riots of 1668," *HJ* 29 (1986), 537–56.

London Crowds in the Reign of Charles II: Propaganda and Politics from the Restoration until the Exclusion Crisis (Cambridge, 1987).

Politics under the Later Stuarts: Party Conflict in a Divided Society 1660–1715 (1993).

"Tories and the Rule of Law in the Reign of Charles II," *The Seventeenth Century* 8 (1993), 9–27.

Harris, T., P. Seaward, and M. Goldie, eds. *The Politics of Religion in Restoration England* (Oxford, 1990).

Harth, P. *Pen for a Party: Dryden's Tory Propaganda in its Contexts* (Princeton, 1993).

Henning, B. D. *The House of Commons 1660–1690*, 3 vols. (1983).

Horle, C. W. *The Quakers and the English Legal System, 1660–1688* (Philadelphia, 1988).

Horwitz, H. "Protestant Reconciliation in the Exclusion Crisis," *JEcH* 15 (1964), 201–17.

Houston, A. "Republicanism, the Politics of Necessity and the Rule of Law," in A. Houston and S. Pincus, eds., *A Nation Transformed; England after the Restoration* (Cambridge, 2001), 241–71.

Hutton, R. *Charles the Second, King of England, Scotland, and Ireland* (Oxford, 1989).

The Restoration: A Political and Religious History of England and Wales, 1658–1667 (Oxford, 1985).

Jones, J. R. *Charles II: Royal Politician* (1987).

The First Whigs: The Politics of the Exclusion Crisis, 1678–1683 (1961).

"The Green Ribbon Club," *Durham University Journal* 49 (1956), 17–20.

Keeble, N. H. *The Literary Culture of Nonconformity in later Seventeenth-Century England* (Leicester, 1987).

Key, N. E. "Comprehension and the Breakdown of Consensus in Restoration Herefordshire," in Harris, *et al.*, eds., *The Politics of Religion*, 191–215.

Knights, M. "A City Revolution: The Remodelling of the London Livery Companies in the 1680s," *EHR* 112 (1997), 1141–78.

"London Petitions and Parliamentary Politics in 1679," *Parliamentary History* 12 (1993), 29–46.

"London's 'Monster' Petition of 1680," *HJ* 36 (1993), 39–67.

"Petitioning and the Political Theorists: John Locke, Algernon Sidney and London's 'Monster' Petition of 1680," *PP* 138 (1993), 94–111.

Politics and Opinion in Crisis, 1678–81 (Cambridge, 1994).

Lacey, D. R. *Dissent and Parliamentary Politics in England, 1661–1689* (New Brunswick, NJ, 1969).

Lamont, W. "The Religion of Andrew Marvell: Locating the 'Bloody Horse,'" in C. Condren and A. D. Cousins, eds., *The Political Identity of Andrew Marvell*, 135–56.

Levin, J. *The Charter Controversy in the City of London, 1660–1688, and its Consequences* (1969).

Liu, T. *Puritan London: A Study of Religion and Society in the City Parishes* (Newark, Del., 1986).

Lindley, K. *Popular Politics and Religion in Civil War London* (Aldershot, 1997).

Macaulay, T. B., Lord Macaulay. *The History of England from the Accession of James the Second*, 6 vols., ed. C. H. Firth (1913–15).

MacDonald, M. "The Strange Death of the Earl of Essex, 1683," *HT* 41 (1991), 13–18.

Marshall, A. *Intelligence and Espionage in the Reign of Charles II, 1660–1685* (Cambridge, 1994).

"To Make a Martyr: The Popish Plot and Protestant Propaganda," *HT* 47 (1997), 39–45.

Marshall, J. "The Ecclesiology of the Latitude-men 1660–1689: Stillingfleet, Tillotson and 'Hobbism'," *JEcH* 36 (1985), 407–27.

"John Locke and Latitudinarianism," in R. Kroll, R. Ashcraft, and P. Zagorin, eds., *Philosophy, Science, and Religion in England, 1640–1700* (Cambridge, 1992), 253–82.

Marshall, J. *John Locke: Resistance, Religion and Responsibility* (Cambridge, 1994).

Matthews, A. G. *Calamy Revised, being a revision of Edmund Calamy's account of the ministers and others ejected and silenced, 1660–2* (Oxford, 1934 and 1988).

Miller, J. *After the Civil Wars: English Politics and Government in the Reign of Charles II* (Harlow, 2000).

Charles II (1991).

"The Crown and the Borough Charters in the Reign of Charles II," *EHR* 100 (1985), 53–84.

"The Potential for 'Absolutism' in Later Stuart England," *History* 69 (1984), 187–207.

Montaño, J. P. *Courting the Moderates: Ideology, Propaganda, and the Emergence of Party, 1660–1678* (Newark, Del., 2002).

Morrill, J. "The Attack on the Church of England in the Long Parliament," in J. Morrill, *The Nature of the English Revolution* (1993), 69–90.

Orme, W. *Memoirs of the Life, Writings, and Religious Connexions, of John Owen, D.D.* (1820).

Pearl, V. *London and the Outbreak of the Puritan Revolution* (Oxford, 1961).

Pincus, S. [C. A.] "'Coffee Politicians Does Create': Coffeehouses and Restoration Political Culture," *JMH* 67 (1995), 807–34.

Protestantism and Patriotism: Ideologies and the Making of English Foreign Policy, 1650–1658 (Cambridge, 1996).

"Shadwell's Dramatic Trimming," in Hamilton and Strier, eds., *Religion, Literature, and Politics*, 253–74.

Pocock, J. G. A. *The Machiavellian Moment: Florentine Political Thought and the Atlantic Republican Tradition* (Princeton, 1975).

Porter, S., ed. *London and the Civil War* (1996).

"The Social Topography of Restoration London," in A. L. Beier and R. Finlay, eds., *London 1500–1700: The Making of the Metropolis* (1986), 199–223.

Priestley, M. "London Merchants and Opposition Politics in Charles II's Reign," *BIHR* (1956), 205–19.

Reay, B. *Quakers and the English Revolution* (1985).

Schochet, G. J. *Patriarchialism in Political Thought* (New York, 1975).

Schwoerer, L. G. "The Attempted Impeachment of Sir William Scroggs, Lord Chief Justice of the Court of King's Bench, November 1680–March 1681," *HJ* 38 (1995), 843–73.

The Declaration of Rights, 1689 (Baltimore, 1981).

The Ingenious Mr. Henry Care, Restoration Publicist (Baltimore, 2001).

Lady Rachel Russell: "One of the Best of Women" (Baltimore, 1988).

"No Standing Armies!" The Antiarmy Ideology in Seventeenth-century England (Baltimore, 1974).

"William, Lord Russell: The Making of a Martyr, 1683–1983," *JBS* 24 (1985), 41–71.

Scott, J. *Algernon Sidney and the English Republic, 1623–1677* (Cambridge, 1988).

Algernon Sidney and the Restoration Crisis, 1677–1683 (Cambridge, 1991).

England's Troubles: Seventeenth-Century English Political Instability in European Context (Cambridge, 2000).

"Restoration Process," *Albion* 25 (1993), 619–37.

Seaward, P. *The Cavalier Parliament and the Reconstruction of the Old Regime, 1661–1667* (Cambridge, 1988).

"Gilbert Sheldon, the London Vestries, and the Defence of the Church," in Harris, et al., eds., *The Politics of Religion*, 49–73.

The Restoration (New York, 1991).

Sharpe, R. R. *London and the Kingdom*, 3 vols. (1894–5).

Spurr, J. "The Church of England, Comprehension and the Toleration Act of 1689," *EHR* 104 (1989), 927–46.

England in the 1670s: "This Masquerading Age" (Oxford, 2000).

The Restoration Church of England, 1646–1689 (New Haven, 1991).

"Schism and the Restoration Church," *JEcH* 41 (1990), 408–24.

Stone, L. "The Results of the English Revolutions of the Seventeenth Century," in J. G. A. Pocock, ed., *Three British Revolutions: 1641, 1688, 1776* (Princeton, 1980), 23–108.

Swatland, A. *The House of Lords in the Reign of Charles II* (Cambridge, 1996).

Thomas, R. "Comprehension and Indulgence," in O. Chadwick and G. F. Nuttall, eds., *From Uniformity to Unity, 1662–1962* (1962), 189–253.

Tolmie, M. *The Triumph of the Saints: The Separate Churches of London, 1616–1649* (Cambridge, 1977).

Wall, L. N. "Marvell's Friends in the City," *Notes and Queries* 204 (1959), 204–7.

Western, J. R. *Monarchy and Revolution: The English State in the 1680s* (1972).

Weston, C. C. and J. R. Greenberg, *Subjects and Sovereigns: The Grand Controversy over Legal Sovereignty in Stuart England* (Cambridge, 1981).

Woodhead, J. R. *The Rulers of London 1660–85* (1965).

Woolrych, A. "Introduction" to *Complete Prose Works of John Milton*, gen. ed. D. M. Wolfe, 8 vols. (New Haven, 1958–82), VII, *1659–1660*, 1–228.

Wootton, D. "Introduction" to John Locke, *Political Writings of John Locke*, ed. D. Wootton (New York, 1993), 7–122.

Worden, B. "The Commonwealth Kidney of Algernon Sidney," *JBS* 24 (1985), 1–40.
"Toleration and the Cromwellian Protectorate," in W. J. Sheils, ed., *Persecution and Toleration: Studies in Church History*, 21 (Oxford, 1984), 199–233.
Zakai, A. "Religious Toleration and its Enemies: The Independent Divines and the Issue of Toleration during the English Civil War," *Albion* 21 (1989), 1–33.
Zook, M. S. *Radical Whigs and Conspiratorial Politics in late Stuart England* (University Park, Pa., 1999).

UNPUBLISHED SECONDARY SOURCES

Chivers, G. V. "The City of London and the State, 1658–1664," Unpublished Ph.D. thesis, Manchester University, 1961.
De Krey, G. S. "Trade, Religion, and Politics in London in the Reign of William III," Unpublished Ph.D. thesis, Princeton University, 1978.
Farnell, J. E. "The Politics of the City of London (1649–1657)," Unpublished Ph.D. thesis, University of Chicago, 1963.
Fishman, J. H. "Edward Stillingfleet, Bishop of Worcester (1635–99): Anglican Bishop and Controversialist," Unpublished Ph.D. thesis, University of Wisconsin, 1977.
Harris, T. "The Green Ribbon Club."
Key, N. "Partisan Fraternity: The Political Culture of London's Public Feasts in the 1680s," paper delivered at "The World Of Roger Morrice," a conference at Clare College, Cambridge, 10–12 July 2003.
Loughead, P. "The East India Company in English Domestic Politics, 1657–1688," Unpublished D.Phil. thesis, Oxford University, 1980.
Middlesex County Records. Calendar of Sessions Books, 1638–89, 1709–51, 21 vols. (typescript, 1911–23): Calendar for 1664–73 (Books 217–301). BL
Milne, D. J. "The Rye House Plot with Special Reference to its Place in the Exclusion Contest and its Consequences till 1685," Unpublished Ph.D. thesis, University of London, 1949.
Seymour, S. "High Stakes, Low Lies," paper delivered at Royal Holloway College, University of London, June 2002.
Smith, A. G. Computer punch cards with biographical data about London liverymen and common councilmen in the 1680s.
"London and the Crown, 1681–1685," Unpublished Ph.D. thesis, University of Wisconsin, 1967.

INDEX

Titles in the series